Medicine and Magnificence

Medicine and Magnificence

British Hospital and Asylum Architecture,
1660–1815

Christine Stevenson

Published for

The Paul Mellon Centre
for Studies in British Art

by

Yale University Press
New Haven and London

Set in FF Scala by Best-set Typesetter Ltd, Hong Kong
Printed in China through World Print Ltd

Library of Congress Cataloging-in-Publication Data

Stevenson, Christine.
   Medicine and magnificence: British hospital and asylum architecture, 1660–1815/
Christine Stevenson.
      p. cm.
   Includes bibliographical references and index.
   ISBN 0–300–08536–2 (cloth: alk. paper)
   1. Hospital architecture—Great Britain—History. 2. Asylums—Great Britain—Design
and construction—History. 3. Hospitals—Great Britain—Design and
construction—History. 4. Health facilities—Great Britain—Design and
construction—History. I. Title
RA967 .S725 2000
725'.51'0941—dc21   00-043489

A catalogue record for this book is available from the British Library.

10 9 8 7 6 5 4 3 2 1

Photograph credits. The Wellcome Library, London: figures 1, 3, 4, 10–14, 19, 20, 22, 27–29, 32–38, 43–48, 50, 51, 54, 59, 64, 65, 68, 69, 71–75, and 78–86. By permission of the British Library (shelfmark 522.l.39): figure 2. The Guildhall Library, Corporation of London: figures 5, 9, and 23. Royal College of Physicians of London: figures 6 and 7. The Walpole Society: figure 8. Author's photographs: figures 15–18, 30, 31, and 40. © Crown Copyright. National Monuments Record: figures 21, 56, 66, 67, and 70. Crown copyright material is reproduced by permission of English Heritage acting under licence from the Controller of Her Majesty's Stationery Office. Figure 70 is a detail of Adm 140/329, in the Public Record Office. The Warden and Fellows of All Souls College, Oxford: figures 24–26. By courtesy of the Trustees of Sir John Soane's Museum: figures 39, 60, 61, 76 and 77. Glasgow University Library, Department of Special Collections: figures 41 and 42. © The British Museum: figure 49. Hampshire Record Office and the Jervoise of Herriard Collection: figures 52, 53, and 57. Liverpool Record Office, Liverpool Libraries and Information Services: figure 55. © National Maritime Museum, London: figure 63.

Contents

Acknowledgements

Robert Bruegmann, Emmakate Buchanan, Helen Collins, Richard A. Hayward, and Rachel Kennedy have allowed me to cite, and to benefit a great deal from, their M.A. and Ph.D. dissertations. Otto Pelser gave me a copy of his dissertation about veterans' hospitals; Geoffrey Hudson and John Bold read my draft chapters about the same subject. The chapters must now be the better for their advice, as I certainly was for their encouragement. Christopher Lawrence, Richard Hewlings and Leonard Smith loaned me their typescripts before publication; Anne Digby and James Alsop passed to me useful information about the architecture of those important buildings, the York Asylum and the Norfolk and Norwich Hospital. When it comes to Bethlem Hospital and the Edinburgh Infirmary, I'm indebted to the expertise and generosity of Jonathan Andrews and Michael Barfoot, respectively, who let me read their work when it was still unpublished, and commented on mine. Robert Thorne read a draft chapter for me, and Roy Porter and David Trotter read a lot of them, more than once. In thanking them for their help with a book that (it perhaps occurred to them) was taking a strangely long time to complete, I must add the name of Jeremy Taylor, an example of the sort of friend one can make through a shared interest in hospital architecture. After all this help, and more, which I've received, the errors that remain are all mine.

My colleagues at the University of Reading, and not least my former colleague Alan Windsor, have given me a lot of moral and practical support. Robert Baldock has been a kind and patient editor; the two readers he found for the manuscript were fortunately a little less patient and I thank them too. The staff members of the libraries and archives visited during the course of this research, and others with whom I've corresponded, have been unfailingly helpful. That I'm particularly appreciative of the help I received at the Wellcome Library, Sir John Soane's Museum, and the Manuscripts Section of the Library of the National Maritime Museum will surprise no one who has also worked in these places.

Finally, I gratefully acknowledge the financial support this project has received. In 1994 I was awarded an Historical Award by the Scouloudi Foundation, and a Humanities Research Board Award under the British Academy's Research Leave

Scheme. Both the latter and, in 1998, a grant from the University of Reading's Research Endowment Trust Fund, allowed me to take invaluable research leave. In the spirit of true magnificence, some among my suppliers of illustrations have waived reproduction fees, and a Dorothy Stroud Bursary awarded by the Society of Architectural Historians of Great Britain has helped me with the remaining costs.

Introduction

*He said, 'How few of his friends' houses would a man choose to be at, when he is
sick!' He mentioned one or two, I recollect only Thrale's.*
— James Boswell's *Life of Samuel Johnson*[1]

As a study of the new hospital and asylum buildings of England and Scotland in
the 'long' eighteenth century between Restoration and Regency, the present book
complements others with a later or broader focus: Jeremy Taylor's *Hospital and
asylum architecture in England, 1840–1914* (1991) and *The architect and the
pavilion hospital* (1997); Grace Goldin's chapters in her and John Thompson's
The hospital: a social and architectural history (1975); and *English hospitals
1660–1948* (1998), by Harriet Richardson and her colleagues at the former Royal
Commission on the Historical Monuments of England.[2] *Medicine and magnificence* can afford to be more comprehensive than the last two about British hospital architecture in the period, but it is not definitively so. What were in their
day substantial buildings still need description, let alone analysis, and I hope that
this book will demonstrate, first, the intrinsic architectural interest of the hospitals, and indeed their excellence within contexts broader than the history of their
type, and secondly the relevance of this topic to other kinds of cultural and socio-
historical enquiry.

Still, this is the book that I once wanted to read about eighteenth-century hospitals, because I was curious to know how their contemporaries understood them
as buildings. This interest can be traced back to an accident-prone childhood,
when I began to like the Ottawa Civic Hospital just because it was complicated:
I had never seen any place like it. Complicatedness held charms (though also
terrors) for my protagonists too. Discovering what else this architecture meant
to them has required attention to how hospitals were built, as well as what was
built, and to how texts and images show them, as well as what they show. This
introduction explains the history of hospital architecture in general terms, and
the form that this history of it will take.

In 1678, Henry Savile wrote to his friend the Earl of Rochester from a house in Leather Lane, Holborn, long a resort of prostitutes and of surgeons treating venereal disease:

> this is a place from whence you cannot expect much newes . . . heer I have chosen a neate privacy to sweat in and soe finish the last act of a long teddious course of Physick which has entertained mee ever since December last . . .

In fact he had some news, for a couple of mutual acquaintances ('my most pocky friends, companions and mistresses', Rochester saluted them in his reply) were there too:

> I confesse I wonder att myselfe and that masse of Mercury that has gone downe my throate in seven monthes, but should wonder yet more were it not for Mrs Roberts, for behold a greater than I . . . what shee has endured would make a damd soule fall a laughing att his lesser paines.[3]

Savile sweated, heavily wrapped, in vapour baths, perhaps after being smeared with mercury ointment; the mercury he was swallowing would have caused his mouth to fill with saliva. The spit, and the sweat, were to expel the poison of the disease.[4] The treatment was terrible to endure, but at least the hot-house (so-called because of the baths) offered a privacy that St Bartholomew's and St Thomas' hospitals, which both maintained 'foul' or 'sweat' wards, could not.[5] It looked like other London houses.

The surgeons Barton and Ginman (the last name may be Rochester's joke) perhaps lived there too. The overwhelming majority of sick, including mentally ill, people in history who have not been nursed in their own home have stayed in someone else's.[6] This was the practice in antiquity, and much more recently, for example in Japan, where Western-style hospitals started as small apartment houses around a doctor's private clinic.[7] Even after hospitals became a familiar presence in European towns, they were not clearly preferable to the alternatives. America documented their status clearly as its frontiers and its immigrant communities moved west: in the late 1880s, for example, the Kansas Conference of the Lutheran Church explained that it was only the lack of a good Swedish boarding-house that was prompting it to open a hospital for its people travelling to Kansas City, Missouri to consult doctors.[8]

As charities, the new eighteenth-century hospitals, like earlier ones, extended to strangers the care, the love (*caritas*) indeed, that one might normally reserve for oneself and one's relations. Though many accepted payment, the vast majority of their patients were poor and in providing meals, beds, and shelter hospitals went a long way towards curing some of them: skin ulcers, for example, are and were understood as sometimes amenable to decent nutrition.[9] When, however, the Middlesex Hospital, London (opened 1745) ruled that those who needed food but not medicine were not the proper objects of its charity it was making an institutional distinction, not a therapeutic one.[10] Hospitals were also places that housed and educated children, like the Foundling Hospital in London and George Watson's Hospital in Edinburgh, or which were sanctuaries for those incapacitated by old age or chronic infirmity, like the Royal (naval) Hospital, and Trinity Hospital, both in Greenwich. An 'infirmary' is however always for the sick and injured, though from a defined community (Chelsea Hospital had one). Some of the new hospitals called themselves infirmaries and avoided ambiguity; 'physical hospital', for physic that is, never caught on.[11] The infirmaries may also have wished to signal that they served a defined community – the working poor – or simply convey a becoming and rational modesty. 'Hospital' evoked almshouses, but also London's big, wealthy, and more-or-less politicized 'royal' foundations, St Bartholomew's, St Thomas', and Bethlem, as well as Guy's Hospital, created by one man's extraordinary beneficence.[12]

Any residential institution, including a penal one, did what in different circumstances families could be expected to do, and recourse to one is likelier to have signified a temporary crisis than a permanent place on the social margins.[13] They were surrogate households, temporary for one kind of member, permanent for another (the staff) and borrowed their vocabularies and their hierarchies from real households. The model's potency, however, derived from something more than the kind of help that institutions offered, because 'family' meant more than it does today. In the 1720s, for example, Daniel Defoe described Wilton House, Wiltshire: the 'lord and proprietor, who is indeed a true patriarchal monarch, reigns here with an authority agreeable to all his subjects (family) . . .'. Defoe was praising a patriarchy including not just the Earl of Pembroke and his blood relations but more than one hundred servants and retainers, who together formed the family, an economic unit larger than most in England then.[14] What interests me is not so much the application of such an organization to a residential charity, but if and how the architecture of a Wilton House was applicable too.[15]

Until their usefulness was established and more funds were raised, many new eighteenth-century hospitals started off in houses that required little more refurbishment than a boarding-house would, but in 1768 the Irish physician Edward Foster firmly repudiated such casualness. 'In general, Houses have been rented for Hospitals, which are as fit for the Purposes, as Newgate for a Palace.'[16] In this way hospitals began to be differentiated from houses, or at least identified as presenting requirements that only very good houses could meet though not, yet, additional ones: the air of the Leeds Infirmary, its Dr Walker boasted in 1802, was 'not in general much less pure and healthy than in private houses', so high were its standards of cleanliness and ventilation.[17] John Aikin MD (1747–1822) however recommended Greenwich as a model for hospitals for the acutely ill, with the proviso that such patients would require a greater volume of circulating air and hence larger apartments than the aged and infirm.[18] Greenwich differed from the kinds of hospitals Aikin was contemplating (which would refuse anyone not likely to get well), but the same building might work for both. Architecture cannot be exhausted by a medical programme, any kind of programme.[19]

Only at the end of the 1850s did the difficulties of hospital design begin to be widely addressed in Britain, and drawn to specialist attention. Florence Nightingale (1820–1910), at the time often identified as the pre-eminent specialist, wrote to an officer of the Swansea Infirmary in 1864 that a hospital was as difficult to construct as a watch; no building 'requires more special knowledge'.[20] Medical men, then young, later recalled this era as one of widespread public confusion and concern about hospital architecture.[21] Epidemic 'hospital fevers' – gangrene and the others associated with wound sepsis – may have become more common because longer-lasting and more invasive surgery was undertaken after anaesthesia came into regular use at mid-century, or simply because surgical wards were becoming overcrowded. The infections throve, and one result was an intense and often disputatious search for their sources that included, among other suspects, the very forms of the buildings.

This search required another: for a historical framework, a place to position itself. In 1856 *The Builder*'s editor George Godwin praised Jean Bourguet's St André Hospital in Bordeaux (1825–29), whose planning 'principles' had been 'laid down seventy years ago, by a number of skilful medical men in France so as best to unite health and convenience in such an edifice'.[22] The principles were those of the pavilion-ward plan, first published in 1788 for the rebuilding of the Hôtel-Dieu in Paris. The histories of hospital architecture that began to appear twenty years after Godwin's editorial, and like it always with a view to current practice – and, for decades, with a view to the pavilion plan too – customarily saw the history as one of the increasing, though not steady, ingress of medical skill and with it health and convenience.[23] In 1976 this progressivism found support in a surprising quarter. *Machines for healing: the origins of the modern hospital*, by Michel Foucault and his students at the Collège de France, aims to show the precision with which those origins can be located and identified with both the pavilion and, more generally, with the triumph of medical science over architecture, understood as an academic art. 'Certain modern programmes, certain big mechanisms', they wrote, appeared in virtual silence: we cannot identify the precise origins of schools, collective dwellings, offices. There is one great exception. A big bang inaugurated hospitals' modernity, and it deafened Paris in 1788.[24]

If Foucault and his colleagues hoped that their frank teleology would provoke more general re-examination of how and where historians located modernity, their demonstration lost its edge because its historical conclusions seemed unexceptionable, though not its premises. Robert Bruegmann remarked in 1979 that reports of the death of architectural tradition are usually premature, and Adrian Forty, the next year, suggested that more attention should be paid to the motives of those who actually controlled hospitals than to scientific advances, because 'there is no reason why scientific knowledge should be applied to buildings, or to anything else, unless it is in someone's interest to do so'.[25] Historians have begun to emphasize that neither the needs of the poor, nor even the threat that they might have been understood as presenting, ever determined the form that any charity took during our period.[26] The old consensus that the science of the time explains only so much about hospital architecture, especially that dating from before or without reference to the Hôtel-Dieu debates, has taken its place as a corollary of this broader thesis. Though the forms of a number of hospitals and asylums built since the fifteenth century have been identified with hygienic desiderata, no one claims that medicine was anywhere of definitive significance.[27]

In the course of writing this book however I began, a little surprised, to attribute more and more authority to medicine, inasmuch as it could pertain to architecture. That pertinence did not include bone-setting or administering mercury, for example, because houses sufficed for these procedures in the period covered and some houses were preferable to hospitals. The medicine here comprises less localized measures attending to the problems presented by the hospital environment itself, its congregation of the sick. Peculiar and undesirable as it was, such congregation seemed inevitable given the real terms according to which civilization functioned, or failed. In Britain in the 1730s, the measures necessary for warming, airing, and segregating hospital patients were for the first time explicitly described as achievable with, as well as in spite of, hospital architecture. Three decades later, with the rate of construction accelerating, specific formal arrangements that might best manage these ends began to be described too, and thereafter with increasing precision. In this way, the presence or fact of new hospital buildings fed into new ways of showing them, of writing about them. These demonstrations were, however, more complex than the 'medicine' of my title suggests.

Hospital buildings were not the subjects of systematic appraisal in Britain before the 1780s; nor did architects fill the gap. But what of eighteenth-century France, which saw the publication of notable architectural treatises? There all discussion was coloured by the realities of a system in which institutions called hospitals were central to virtually every form of poor relief. Architectural analysis became mired in vast economic issues:

> Hospitals must be solidly but simply built. With absolutely no other kind of building is luxury more destructive of propriety. Houses lodging the poor should have something of poverty about them. . . . Magnificence announces too much money in the foundation, or too little economy in the administration; . . . Too much beauty in a house [of charity] . . . stifles charity. . . . The poor must be lodged like the poor. Great cleanliness and convenience but no ostentation at all.[28]

The passage is more interesting than it appears. Marc-Antoine Laugier (1713–69) was prescribing not a hospital but a bulwark against the physiocratic clichés that charitable foundations tie up potentially circulating and useful funds, hospitals turn workers into layabouts, and so forth. The original is also rich in substantives – *commodité*, *bienséance* on the one hand, *somptuosité*, *magnificence*, *faste* on the other – which are now hard to translate. 'Propriety' and 'convenience' are feeble shadows of the tremendous, all-embracing fitness that the first set invoked and as for the second, 'luxury' and 'ostentation' make us think of Gucci and gilt, not the thin edges of unreason and disorder.[29] But it must be admitted that the most radical architectural theorist of his day lacked a certain imaginative specificity in the face of hospitals, and such devotion to appearances would be seized upon as symptomatic of architects' incapacity to confront what was soon the *problem* of hospital design.

What about luxury? John Sekora has explained it as 'one of the oldest, most important, and most pervasive negative principles for organizing society Western history has known'.[30] The publication, in 1977, of his *Luxury* coincided with that of the first of William McClung's studies of how architecture may eschew it, of how a building may be virtuous, studies which have been important to the present book. A new interest in eighteenth-century England's 'consumer revolution', meanwhile, began to encourage re-examinations of other forms of visual and literary culture in the light of luxury's class-relativity.[31] However, one of luxury's most fundamental antitheses is function, or fitness, and unlike other art forms buildings are hard to divorce from their functional premises. Architecture accordingly had a distinctive power within the pervasive luxury critique, whose application to houses is now receiving attention from literary and architectural historians.[32] This book extends the attention to surrogate houses, hospitals, where old forms of attack were reinvigorated by their new targets.

I implied earlier that the house in Leather Lane (as opposed to St Bartholomew's or St Thomas' hospitals, which also treated the venereally diseased) was not something that I could write about. There is a story to be told about the conversion of town houses to hot-houses in the sixteenth and seventeenth centuries, or about the five 'pesthouses, sheds or huts' built for London's plague victims in the same period,[33] but this is a book about 'high' (though often only middling high) architecture, relatively big, expensive, and permanent buildings whose pictures were made, and whose architects' names are mostly known. It is also about the problem that high architecture presents for hospitals. In 1792 Hugh Williamson, an Edinburgh-trained physician of North Carolina, testified before a Congressional committee investigating provision for American sailors:

> I do not contemplate the building of two or three great houses in some of our principal cities; houses that might administer to the vanity of a nation, rather than to the general comfort of sick and infirm sailors.

Instead, Williamson argued, lodgings should be hired, or hospitals built, obviously in a minor key, at every American port of entry.[34] When he set vanity against comfort, and when the phrenologist J. G. Spurzheim claimed two decades later that the new Edinburgh asylum (see Figure 79, p. 208) had cost so much to build that it could not afford to admit pauper lunatics,[35] they were saying that high architecture precludes charity, that you can minister to vanity or to the sick poor, but not to both.

Attacks on architecture as the antagonist of charity go back to the Middle Ages, and suspicion of selfish display is even older.[36] In these discussions, which since the Renaissance have been about nothing less than the degree of individualism that can be permitted in a prosperous and secure commonwealth, architects could be made to stand for sterile luxury, as opposed to appropriate magnificence or hospitable expansiveness. Roger North (1653–1734), a gentleman and amateur architect, wrote entertainingly in the 1690s about the professional: if you try to thwart his expensive 'crotchets', 'he puffs and snuffs, grows weary of the work, and unless highly obliged, leaves you in the mortar'.[37] North recommended that his peers act as architects for their own houses and in this way get what they and their friends need for comfort and good cheer, without crotchets and without mortar-baths.

What is the 'end of riches?' asked North, who answered: 'plenty without excess, neatness and elegancy of living, charity to the poor, and liberality to inferiors'.[38] The end of riches is a collective, a vision of simple but comfortable hospitality. From there it is not such a long jump, etymologically[39] or practically speaking, to hospitals. North described the intensity of the intellectual and creative satisfaction to be derived from building for hospitality, and there are real echoes in the minute books of construction committees whose members discovered it for themselves, particularly because their guests arrived with such an intriguing variety of needs. One needed an 'Itchy Room' (a naval example) as well as a housekeeper's room.[40] North's suspicion of architects as children greedy for ornamental gratification and heedless of cost also re-emerges occasionally. It is customary to attribute the expressions of discontent that began to be published around 1770 to medical science's growing involvement with hospital design. But when the American surgeon John Jones (1729–91) described the charitable labour and expenditure showered on buildings that *killed* their patients,[41] he was also extending an old theme. Hospitals, maybe precocious in their differentiation as building types, were also heir to ancient anxieties about luxury and envy, individualism and display, and central to the articulation of these anxieties was the distinction between architectural luxury, or useless ostentation, and the noble liberality that is true magnificence. For the Austrian physician Johann Peter Frank (1745–1821), hospitals' 'best and only ornaments' are a healthy site, efficient planning, and painstaking administration. The French physicist Jean-Baptiste Le Roy (1720–1800) wrote that 'great, extreme cleanliness, as pure an air as possible – one cannot say it too often; this is the true, the only magnificence that one seeks in these buildings'.[42]

Searching the libraries of Paris after the fire of 1772 at the Hôtel-Dieu there, Le Roy found not one book on hospital design though plenty (he later claimed) about how to build a palace, or a theatre. 'People always prefer things that are flashy and frivolous to those that offer only miserable utility.' Since then, he explained, a glut of projects for rebuilding the Hôtel-Dieu had merely translated surface glitter to a new object: 'sacrificing, as is rather our habit, principle to props, the authors of these designs seem to have forgotten that decoration is the least part of such a building'.[43] In a fine summation, Foucault wrote of 'ceremonious but inept' architecture, a conscious echo of such texts as the hostile review, published in 1786, of another rebuilding proposal: 'only rarely is luxury allied with utility, and nothing would make the heart heavier than the sight of misery hidden behind Corinthian columns'.[44] The phrasing is odd (is misery hidden, or is it in sight?) and the sense familiar: hospitals are whited sepulchres, their façades handsome screens for rotting flesh. The publications that arose in the wake of the Hôtel-Dieu fire clarify, perhaps to a unique extent, the issues raised by what Rémy Saisselin has called the Enlightenment against the Baroque: that is, the demonstration of the 'discrepancy between the outward trappings of power, rank, and wealth, and true merit'.[45] For Le Roy this merit was the main thing, *le principal*; his denunciations of *accessoire* and *décoration* formed part of a much wider, and older, critique of architectural luxury.

When addressed to hospitals, the critique was eventually very destructive. At the simplest and most violent level, it was not clear that they needed to exist. Again, the issue was confused by the way in which the hospital was not yet entirely distinct from the poorhouse; either way, however, they were emblems of the failure of families, or of society, that might be put right directly. The redefinition of a hospital, as a place for relatively short-term medical care, offered no respite at a time when any procedure could be conducted in a house; Hugh Williamson knew that hired lodgings would do. John Jones wrote that hospitals killed people, a really flagrant rupture of utility. In English-speaking countries, military doctors, whose work encouraged them to think about the danger that the sick presented to one another, but which also forced them to consider the problem of caring when no houses were available (soldiers are by definition away from home), were notably nihilistic about architecture. They celebrated ephemerality; Richard Brocklesby (1722–97) advocated 'convenient hovels' and 'occasional hutts' of wattle and thatch for regimental hospitals, and his admirer, the American James Tilton (1745–1822), log cabins 'upon the plan of an Indian hut' (see Figures 3 and 4, p. 27).[46] It is in such ways that architecture has always been reconciled with nature: as its completion, or fulfilment, in the direct service of utility.[47]

The most aggressive attacks upon architecture came from psychiatry (the term is anachronistic but less distracting than, say, 'antimaniacal science'),[48] because it was bound up with architecture in ways more complex and specific than general medicine. For one thing, it *was* concerned with appearances. At least since Robert Burton's *Anatomy of melancholy* (1621) essayists had enjoyed imagining psychological states shaped and modified by physical surroundings. The idea of the asylum was bound up with that of the successful management of mental illness a century before the connection was made with somatic disorders; of all the ills that beset us, lunacy was the first to be defined as something that should be treated away from home. Acutely conscious of this rupture, psychiatric reformers then explicitly set out to recreate homes. For, if an asylum's 'outside appears heavy and prison-like it has a considerable effect upon the imagination',[49] wrote John Bevans, the architect of the (Friends') Retreat in York, which opened in 1796. With such statements the 'distinction, both ethical and phenomenological, between "being" and "seeming"'[50] that had underlain an ancient debate about architecture and luxury is on its way to dissolution.

Hospitals in these ways revivified an old antithesis between charitable hospitality and selfish luxury. Chapter 1 describes the hospitable ideal, after an account of the older Continental hospitals that seventeenth-century England admired, an admiration coloured by some anxiety about selfishness. The second part of the chapter turns to three more particular eighteenth-century preoccupations and their relations to the older and wider one: the doctrinal or at least social embarrassments presented by charitable architecture; settlement projects that, in reverting to the myth of the georgic community, also retreated from institutionalization; and finally the unhealthiness of hospitals. Just because Britain saw the complete reconstruction of the ancient London foundations Bethlem, St Thomas', and St Bartholomew's, and the purpose-building of more than fifty new hospitals and asylums in this period, it seems useful to begin the book by explaining how, over the same period, the type was being shown as undesirable and even, logically speaking, impossible.

Chapters 2 and 3 return to the seventeenth century and its great new constructions: for the insane, Bethlem ('Bedlam'), and for soldiers and sailors Chelsea and Greenwich. Though the latter were not hospitals in the modern sense, the distinction did not necessarily affect their interest for promoters of unambiguously medical hospitals (Aikin was not alone in recommending Greenwich as a model),[51] and their interest for us is anyway broader than that. Like Bethlem they were made up of galleries and cells, respectively emblematic of the palatial and monastic attributes with which contemporary praise regularly endowed them. This kind of planning, and praise, links them to older domestic architecture, but their construction also inaugurated and sometimes directly inspired new ways of evaluating architectural modernity against the standards set by the past. These hospitals helped make it possible to consider what constituted a public building and to investigate the limits of charitable display, topics taken up again in Chapter 4. Bethlem's influence on later asylum construction was enormous, and not just in terms of its planning. A developing distaste for its appearance may clearly be traced, and to trace the course of that reception is to trace the course of eighteenth-century thinking about how asylums should look, and be looked at, which is Chapter 4's major subject.

The next three chapters concern the relationships between funding, form, and air at general, civil hospitals. Chapter 5 explains their construction as a process, and examines the rhetorical uses to which the process was put in what was perceived as an increasingly competitive and demanding charitable milieu; not all were 'voluntary' hospitals but the ethos of free volition was general. In this chapter the Edinburgh Infirmary is the major example, because both its construction and its struggles in the market-place were described with exceptional verve. In surveying the new construction, including conversions, Chapter 6 turns more directly to medicine, beginning and ending with the question of how much we can allowably infer about medical intentions from what was built. We can at least conclude that volition, or voluntarism, which was supposed to have got the hospitals built in the first place, played a part in understandings of the freedom that both their patients, and air, were supposed to enjoy in them. Chapter 7's subjects are air as it was believed to engender disease in hospitals, and attempts to redeem the latter by quasi-organic means of ventilation. The analogies drawn between buildings and bodies feature in a chapter that has much to say about ships, too: there are conceptual as well as historical relations between them and hospitals.

Chapter 8 begins with the most obvious example of those relations, the hospital ship which, highly unsatisfactory in terms of air, was none the less a durable solution to the problem of caring for sick sailors simply because it kept them away from land. The new naval hospitals at Haslar and Plymouth were sited so as to let them share the ships' great advantage, and planned with a view to avoid-ing their disadvantages; both desiderata were met by isolation, which literally means island-ness. The biggest hospitals in England, they were also (after Bethlem) the most famous, in part because of the way they were used in French deliberations about the rebuilding of the Hôtel-Dieu in Paris. The last part of this chapter summarizes the later history of these deliberations because in them Haslar and Plymouth were identified as pavilion-ward hospitals, which they were not, but the identification encouraged and sharpened new, British ways of writing about the type.

Charity falls victim to luxurious superfluity, but it ornaments hospitable houses. It is an ornament used by Christian proprietors but not by architects, in the first instance because they are not proprietors. Chapter 9 discusses orna-ment's place in hospitals and concludes with a return to the asylum, but now in the context of the early nineteenth century. It shows how architects might be accused of spending money on façades at the expense of the poor behind them, and of neglecting true magnificence for the sake of the false kind. The final chapter centres on the Derby Infirmary – which, like Edinburgh's, received splendid explanations, as well as a splendid, though very different building – to show the radical changes in the understanding of medical charity, and hospital architecture, that manifested themselves in the early years of the new century. It also indicates what is, as far as this book is concerned, the future of hospital architecture.

Chapter 1

Hospitality, monuments, and patriarchal medicine

Leaving aside monastic infirmaries, which served comparably varied functions, when we speak of medieval English hospitals we mean leper houses (of which most had become redundant, and some derelict, by the mid-fifteenth century), almshouses, and shelters for pilgrims and other travellers and for the sick poor.[1] Most were almshouses, in the sense that the brethren and sisters who tended the visitors and formed the permanent community themselves became infirm in time, and relatively few of the 1,100 or so hospitals founded before the Reformation were ever for the sick poor alone. (The proportion seems to have been comparable in Scotland.)[2] What we would call a hospital was therefore more of a function than a place, and a function scarcely to be distinguished (at most places) from other forms of the pastoral care to which all hospitals were dedicated. Their most important work, which they shared with other kinds of religious house, was prayer, including prayer for the souls of the founders.[3]

From the late fourteenth century, new English foundations rarely provided for sick visitors, as opposed to long-term residents, and by 1535 (that is, before the dissolution of religious houses began) only thirty-nine of any size were still providing for the sick poor.[4] This work had become increasingly difficult, or unwelcome, for almost three centuries.[5] A vision of hospitals so good, therefore, that no one would prefer to 'lie sick at home' might seem to be less Utopian than entirely irrelevant.[6] But Thomas More was, in 1516, arguing for collective public action upon poverty and illness. He was echoed in Reformation polemics about hospital masters growing fat at the expense of the lean poor, of which at least one (from c.1542) also called for medically staffed houses for the infirm to be set up in every town.[7] Later Englishmen also proposed new hospitals for 'Rich as well as Poor, so instituted and fitted as to encourage all sick persons to resort unto them' (William Petty, in 1676); their aim was medical instruction and the perfection of therapeutics. But such counter-intuitive schemes (what did the rich, or the art of medicine, have to do with hospitals?) prompted no general action.[8]

These men did not plan hospitals, they planned for hospitals, but their recommendations formed part of a broader prescriptive genre that had sometimes attended to architecture too. The *Trattato d'architettura* (1465) by Antonio Averlino Filarete elaborates the ways in which particular buildings and institutions were to interact, aesthetically and functionally, with others and with his ideal town, Sforzinda, as a whole. He illustrated Sforzinda's hospital, and explained its dynamic functioning with great care. Though there are important differences, it is effectively Filarete's Ospedale Maggiore in Milan (begun 1456), a large rectangular cloister with a central church between two enormous crosses, one for each sex, each inscribed by additional wings to make four smaller courts. Each cross had its own altar, which all the 'sick people can see . . . because the altar is exactly in the middle of the cross'. Milan's hospital (now part of its university) was centuries in construction.[9] A few years earlier, Leon Battista Alberti prescribed more generally in his *De re aedificatoria* (1452, first printed 1486). Hospitals, he wrote,

> should be divided up and laid out as follows: the curable should be kept somewhere separate from those, such as the decrepit and the insane, who are admitted not so much to be cured as to be nursed until struck down by fate. In addition, the women, whether patients or nurses, should be kept apart from the men. And, as in a family home, it is best to have some apartments more private than others, depending on the nature of the treatment and the inmates' way of life . . .[10]

(Though Alberti conceived of something capable of separating different sorts of patients, this did not distinguish hospitals from houses: rather, normal domestic obligations merely acquired a mild urgency.) *De re aedificatoria*, in which a church is a *templum*, sometimes wishes to obscure the difference that Christianity had made to architecture and it consistently offers the ancients as a model: the design of *prisons* could in most ways follow theirs. Alberti's praise for hospitals 'built at vast expense' constitutes virtually his only reference to contemporary architecture,[11] which suggests that even champions of antiquity might bow to hospitals that were already the pride of Tuscany, and which for the next two hundred years set the standard for the rest of the world.

Through the gradual addition of wards terminating in a shared altar, Florence's S. Maria Nuova, founded in 1288 with twelve beds for the poor, had by the end of the fourteenth century assumed the shape of a cross, a configuration that had become standard for Italian hospitals over the course of the century, though its origins are unclear.[12] During the planning of the Ospedale Maggiore, Duke Francesco Sforza of Milan asked his ambassadors to obtain details of the staffing, financing, and layout of S. Maria Nuova (which he also sent Filarete to see) and of S. Maria della Scala in Siena, which again was cruciform, and the Venetians in turn sent Bramante to study the Ospedale Maggiore in 1484.[13] By then hospital architecture was clearly an identifiable subject for investigation, although one inseparable from hospital organization. English hospitals, by contrast, do not seem to have been considered as a distinct institutional, let alone building type. The most exceptional thing about Henry VII's Savoy Hospital in London (built 1505–17) was therefore not its great size, cross-shape, or provision for daily medical attendance, but the reason for all three: its planning, in the widest sense, after S. Maria Nuova, the most prestigious of foreign models.[14]

In 1645 John Evelyn (1620–1706) admired everything about the Ospedale di Sto Spirito in Rome (begun 1474): 'as much curiosity, sweetnesse and Conveniency as can be imagin'd'. Following his guidebook, he noted the 'stately Cupola' at the junction of the (then) two great wards, over an altar 'in sight of the sick, who may both see, & heare Masse as they lie in their beds'.[15] Writers not only credited the cruciform plan with hygienic advantages, including ventilation (for whose sake the chapel was sometimes moved from the crossing-point),[16] they invested it with the powers of separating different classes of inmate, or at least men and women, and facilitating surveillance. Hospitals not only protected the 'Country from beggers', as Evelyn put it,[17] their very spatial organization implicitly rectified the disorderly promiscuity of urban existence. In the sixteenth century, Catholic and Protestant countries had seen the emergence of a new and roughly speaking more critical attitude towards the urban poor, and in particular towards the discrimination of the deserving from the undeserving: the able-bodied, the sturdy beggars. This change manifested itself in a new interest in hospitals, and more generally in secularized and rationalized schemes and institutions for the relief of the deserving.[18]

Even Martin Luther referred to the 'fair' hospital buildings that he saw on his way to Rome in 1510;[19] not until the seventeenth century did Italy begin to lose its primacy in hospital architecture. Evelyn was, in the phrase just quoted, actually writing about Amsterdam, where in 1641 he visited workhouses and an insane asylum. 'But none did I so much admire as an Hospitall for their lame and decrepid souldiers, it being for state, order & accommodations one of the worthiest things that I think the world can shew of that nature'; this admiration would bear fruit when he assisted in the planning of Chelsea Hospital. A few years later he was deeply impressed by the Paris hospitals, especially the Hôtel-Dieu and the Charité, whose princeliness extended to the very care of the pauper sick, 'being sometymes (as I have seene them) served by noble Persons men and women';[20] such service was not uncommon from pietist French aristocrats. Most impressive of all in Paris was the Hôpital Saint-Louis (1607–12: Figure 1) for plague victims designed by Claude Vellefaux and founded by Henri IV, an ornament to the town of a piece with the king's other great urban projects, like the Place des Vosges. With its distinctive stone quoins and *chaînes* against brick, the hospital also looks like the Place des Vosges; it was a style, Hilary Ballon has argued, grand by virtue of its masonry, and one then equally appropriate for châteaux, which, like the plague hospital and the town square, were also inward-turning, with their display towards their open centres.[21] It was praised accordingly: 'more like the Palace of a king, than the King's Palace itself', said one English visitor in 1656, or so it seemed: 'it is not safe venturing nigh it'.[22] Saint-Louis's reputation was heightened by the closer kind of analysis that began to emerge a century later, unusually for a hospital so much older than the analysis: a 'very fine hospital . . . whose construction was intelligently dedicated to healthfulness and the comfort of the sick'.[23]

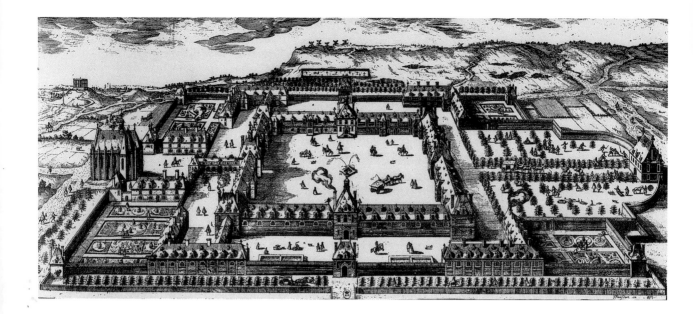

When new, the Hôpital Saint-Louis showed that monumentality and permanence could serve intermittent, epidemical emergency, and it prompted reflections on the desirability of comparable provision in London, comparable containment for the plague and the poor. The Privy Council sent a description of it in 1630 to the London justices, as a model for a workhouse as well as a hospital, and Charles I's physician Theodore Turquet de Mayerne, who had also served the king's father-in-law Henri IV, the next year proposed the construction of four or five plague hospitals, one to be named 'King Charles's Godshouse', that is an *hôtel-dieu* (and *hôtel-roi*), or 'the King's hospitall of health'.[24] The project came to nothing; much obscurer pesthouses and domestic quarantine continued to be London's defences against the plague. Nor, with one surprising exception, did it see any substantial civil-hospital construction that century. Besides the increasingly moribund Savoy, the general hospitals were St Thomas' and St Bartholomew's, medieval foundations reconstituted after the Reformation along with Christ's Hospital, a school; the workhouse, Bridewell; and Bethlem, the hospital for the insane. Together they were the 'royal' hospitals, administered by the City of London. It was Bethlem, the smallest and poorest, which first got splendid new accommodation, in 1676 (see Figure 5, p. 32); the general hospitals waited decades longer and meanwhile travellers wondered at those abroad.

The frets of luxury

English Protestants and Catholics alike praised the French and Italian hospitals, but the formers' enthusiasm was sometimes tempered by a little unease about the Reformation. It may have been God's judgement on a false religion, but where Paris, Tuscany, and Rome boasted clean, capacious, and bustling hospitals, England perhaps offered 'Remaynes enough left for a man to give a guesse what noble buildings, &c. were made by the Piety, Charity, and Magnanimity of our Forefathers'.[25] In 1598 John Stow described how, after the Dissolution and the enclosure of old common lands, London saw new 'summer-houses', banqueting houses

> like Midsummer pageants, with towers, turrets, and chimney tops . . . for show and pleasure, betraying the vanity of men's minds, much unlike to the disposition of the antient citizens, who delighted in the building of hospitals and alms-houses for the poor, and therein both employed their wits, and spent their wealths in preferment of the common commodity of this our city.[26]

Stow distinguished the modern pleasure arising out of gratified vanity from the ancient delight that was God's reward for building for the poor. That had arisen, not least, from the employment of one's wits, but it was not selfish.

In 1841 A. W. Pugin revived and sharpened Stow's contrast to show how true Christian selflessness, as manifested in hospitable houses for the poor, had been swept away by Henry VIII's avarice. The evil was also stylistic: Pugin explained how the hateful triumph of the 'luxurious styles of ancient Paganism' over 'self-denying Catholic principle' had taken comparably concrete form at Somerset House (1547–52), London, to whose sumptuousness, he wrote, St Paul's' cloisters, six churches, and three bishop's palaces were sacrificed for the sake of their brick and stone.[27] The Dissolution had indeed untied a great deal of ecclesiastical masonry, about whose quarrying and re-use secular builders may or may not have had misgivings;[28] the dissolving was, anyway, endlessly replayed in discussions about the right use of riches. What has been called the 'resentment topos', for example, became inescapable in country-house poetry: 'No widow's tenement was racked to gild / or fret thy ceiling'.[29] In praising Lewis Pemberton, Robert Herrick (1591–1674) was using Matthew 23:14 – 'Woe unto you, scribes and Pharisees, hypocrites! for ye devour widows' houses' – but the figure was fed by a habit of thinking whereby architectural devouring and transmutation – almshouses to summerhouses, St Paul's cloisters to Somerset House, the widow's house to the fretted ceiling – stood for luxurious vanity's supersession of wit's useful exercise. In Milan, explained Filarete, the foundations of the men's side of the great hospital were built with stone from noble houses demolished for the purpose;[30] that was the way to do it.

Herrick's selection of the gilded and fretted ceiling, as a synecdoche for all that Pemberton's house was not, had more specific antecedents. In the second Book of Horace's *Odes* (23 BC), ceilings stand for the men who play at country living and in so doing destroy country life: 'No gold or ivory gleams / On panelled ceilings in my house'.[31] Plutarch (AD *c*.50–*c*.120) used ceilings to illustrate how Lycurgus, the early Spartan lawgiver, had sought to preserve Sparta against the alien infection of craftsmanship. One of his enactments 'was directed against extravagance, to the effect that in every house the ceiling should be made with an axe, and the doors only with a saw, not with any other tools'.[32] Luxury, to use Bernard Mandeville's definition, admittedly a Spartan one, is whatever is 'not absolutely necessary to keep a Man alive'[33] and craftsmen were luxurious, superfluous, because they were not soldiers. (In Sparta, *fortifications* were luxuries.)

Plutarch added another anecdote: 'It was such conditioning which (according to the story) prompted the elder Leotychidas, when he was dining at Corinth and viewed the lavish, coffered design of the ceiling of the room, to ask his host if timber there grew square.' The point to the joke is, William McClung has explained, an extension or 'redefinition of luxury not as mere superfluity but as a violation of the essential nature of a being or thing'.[34]

Arguments about where necessity, and naturalness, end and luxury begins seem to be a necessary adjunct to civilization. It is a 'protean – not to say colossal' vice,[35] whose detection is a way of thinking about the entire world. Public detection, however, generally avoided specific cases: who wanted to annoy the (still) powerful? And who wanted to annoy God: criticism of over-elaborate hospitals was not frequently recorded before 1700, and the targets of such examples as do exist are those parts of the buildings readily representing founders' vanity (funerary chapels) or the diversion of funds to less-than-needy objects (masters' lodgings).[36] Philibert de l'Orme suggested in 1568 that the wealthy bourgeois might 'found hospitals or colleges serving the poor, and the public good, instead of building a heap of stately and magnificent homes that serve only anxiety and ill-will';[37] build a religious house, that is, if you have the urge to build. But De l'Orme emphasized hospitals' worldly service, and a century later William Petty used a fundamental opposition to entirely modern ends, in proposing the construction of hospitals for the rich as well as the poor: 'Every sort of such hospitalls to differ only in splendor, but not at all in the Sufficiency for the means and remedy for the Patients health'.[38] Hospitals might differ in splendour, though not sufficiency, depending on whether their inhabitants were rich or poor; they were no longer God's houses.

One of Alberti's arguments in *De re aedificatoria*, a kind of textbook for patrons, is that a fine building constitutes an exercise of civic and familial duty, as well as a manifestation of personal wealth and honour.[39] Because architects regularly defined themselves as the ones who could do it, the importance of distinguishing magnificence, that is, a contempt for meanness and moderation,[40] from extravagance provides a refrain in their writings. Luxury is self-regarding ostentation and magnificence the reverse, a noble largesse that scorns to calculate personal return. And in this distinction fine buildings provided more than an obvious example of needless and heedless expenditure, for luxury could, when applied to architecture, also marry extravagances and unnaturalnesses with a fundamental rupture of the Christian ethic: the failure of hospitality.

For the English, one of the most characteristic and attractive attributes of the past, the world which was lost but emotionally ever present, was the direct, unselective, and hearty hospitality offered in the great hall which had been the physical focus of older English houses, and was the spiritual focus of this nostalgia.[41] Hospitable houses were, almost by definition, big old houses. An entire poetic genre attests to this, as does Evelyn's diary: Wotton, his birthplace, was 'large & antient, suitable to those hospitable times'; another house is 'capacious, & in form of the buildings of the Age in Hen: 8 & Q. Eliz: time & proper for the old English hospitality'.[42] They were also rural houses: as North explained, the 'latter ages have bin more addicted to a citty life, after the French way', and the fashion had encouraged a tidier, thriftier sort of building that required less land, and resulted in something less capacious.[43] Hospitable houses were unstylish houses, which had grown up piecemeal, over the years as need dictated, but not by plan, not symmetrically. It was hard, North wrote, to 'project any elegance of disposition within or without' on a 'rambling foundation' with a high hall.[44]

Francis Bacon (1561–1626) summed up the great distinction when he wrote that 'Houses are built to live in, and not to look on'.[45] 'Thou art not, Penshurst, built to envious show': in Ben Jonson's poem (probably written in 1612), Penshurst Place is praised in opposition to some unspecified foil that is literally showy.[46] 'So great men's houses should be builded great, / And not so much for prospect, as receipt' as another poet had it, around 1665.[47] Greatness was not the problem; the key distinction was that between outward-turning hospitality ('receipt') and a selfish vanity ('prospect') that according to the poets could be discerned in polished pillars (Jonson) and other shiny variations on the gilt ceilings. These were not, finally, houses with which architects' names were associated. Age, rambling capacity, rusticity, the absence of stylishness (that is, of architecture or an architect with capital As) signified, not just the way the hospitable house functioned as the heart of the 'reciprocal interplay of work and nature in the creation of a good life' but its very equivalence, as a fabric, *with* nature – as equivalent, anyway, as fallen humanity can achieve.[48] It is a literary construction, but one drawing upon real changes that had taken place in the planning and appearance of gentry houses, and in the ways that these houses worked.

At the end of the century, Ned Ward (1667–1731) regretted 'that so noble a palace, which appears so magnificent and venerable, should not have the old hospitality continued withinside' as he passed Northumberland House, the London home of the Percys: that hospitality had ended with the male line, only a few decades previously. Ned's 'friend' (a rhetorical convenience) amplified. The quality were now so 'degenerate from their ancestors' that they spent their money on 'whoring, gaming, and foppery' rather than 'relieving the distress of their neighbours, supplying the wants of poor friends and relations, and (to the honour of themselves and [their] country) giving charitable entertainment to strangers and travellers'.[49] This entertainment had sustained a community of dependants and guests;[50] Ward's example neatly encapsulates hospitality's collateral relations with charity and with luxury. Though Northumberland House also showed that all this virtue might be found in houses that were neither rural nor modest, the conventional understanding of the hospitable house remained most relevant to hospitals. Most new eighteenth-century hospitals were built in stages, and expansively, and on sites which, if not quite rural, at least in London lent themselves to pointed contrasts with narrow and unwholesome urban confines. Though the final result was often symmetrical and even stylish, piecemeal construction then resumed its moral significance, just as construction without architects came to do.

'Whoever lives with him is taken care of in Sickness as well as in Health': in 1729 Bernard Mandeville (1670–1733) characterized the 'fine Gentleman' in his account of the extinction of the species.[51] The theme was conventional and so was his accusation that modern ladies and gentlemen preferred to offload ailing and ageing members of their households on to strangers' hands and charity. 'They are very void of Humanity' – Alexander Monro *primus* (1697–1767) was instructing his daughters on household management – 'who suffer their Servants to be in such a forlorn miserable State as a poor Creature in Sickness must be when turned out among Strangers'.[52] The principle was ancient, and some eighteenth-century hospitals tried to enforce it by prohibiting their governors from nominating their domestic employees for admission, but medical diagnosis could justify its breach. The Edinburgh Infirmary where Monro taught and practised admitted its contributors' servants, but some of them were understood to suffer from contagious illnesses that threatened the rest of their families.[53] The hospitable ideal however had more, and sharper, implications for the institutional care of the sick than the servant problem, and the new, medical situations for old ways of thinking about architecture mentioned above. The rest of this chapter examines three: distaste for a vanity supposed to be cloaking its selfishness with palaces for the poor; and the related dreams of a return to man's natural way of life on the rural estate or in the colony, and of the hospital without walls.

Golden names

In translating the Bible into English, William Tyndale (c.1495–1536) controversially rendered the Vulgate *caritas* as 'love', that is, what one feels, or should feel, when giving.[54] Mandeville did the same, defining charity in 1723 as

> that Virtue by which part of that sincere Love we have for our selves is transfer'd pure and unmix'd to others, not tyed to us by the Bonds of Friendship or Consanguinity, and even meer Strangers, whom we have no Obligation to, nor hope or expect anything from.

This is a rigorous definition, as Mandeville well knew; it precludes any kind of personal gain, even that of 'Honour and Reputation'.[55] But it is not far from the charitable entertainment that Ned Ward mourned. For charity in this sense directs a personal relationship that does not discriminate on grounds of need, or deservingness. In other words, we don't reward the virtuous: God does, and He will reward us. But by 1723, charity effectively meant help to the needy, and help in the form of money, as opposed to hospitable offers of food, drink, and lodging, and the word could already signify an institution. Schools, almshouses, and hospitals, which provide an additional layer of separation between charity and its objects, are a long way from love,[56] but the institutional had become the dominant mode of giving by the eighteenth century.

No matter how many poor they actually assisted in comparison to those getting forms of outdoor (domiciliary) relief, residential institutions became prominent on the British urban scene after 1700, and were founded in considerable number and variety. An outstanding example is presented by Edinburgh, where one decade, the 1730s, saw an orphanage, 'Charity Work-House', boys' school, and a hospital begin construction, at least three of them to the designs of Scotland's pre-eminent architect, William Adam (1689–1748), and all on a considerable scale. They joined a 300-year-old almshouse, the school Heriot's Hospital, and two turn-of-the-century foundations for poor girls: in Edinburgh, at least, there was a relatively sudden and thorough institutionalization of the poor.[57] But institutions did not dislodge the myths of hospitable charity; if anything the reverse. The extended family provided the obvious model for their government, and in them the poor did not receive the money of whose use they are 'very incompetent Judges' (an English sermon of 1736).[58] If, as the promoters of some new English hospitals suggested, parish relief for the sick poor had commonly consisted of cash handouts,[59] this was both ineffectual and probably unchristian, too. 'Advice and Medicines are to the Sick, what Food is to the Hungry, and Clothes to the Naked': an essay published in 1741 drew on both the Sermon on the Mount and a native ideal of charitable gifts in kind, lovingly and personally tendered.[60]

Around 1700, Ned Ward confidently speculated about the benefactors whose names were listed on St Bartholomew's walls. 'If it were not for seeing their names in great letters, to vainly beget amongst men an opinion of their piety', they would not have given a groat.[61] Great names would become interestingly problematic, certainly in Edinburgh, where in 1735 backers of the Orphan School made a fine distinction in assuming (they claimed) that its 'Charitable Contributors would 'tis like be offended to have all their Names *printed*, but due Care is taken to have them all *recorded*'.[62] Their townsman 'Philasthenes' wrote in 1739 that there could be no greater honour than to have one's name among the contributors to the new Infirmary building ('must not his Posterity be the better looked on for it'), but Philasthenes' *alter ego* Alexander Monro *primus* later claimed, magnificently, that he had not been persuaded to give more than £48. Two pounds more would have enforced the gilt application of his name, along with those of other contributors of £50 or more, on the wall of the managers' room.[63]

Monro was an avowed enemy of the 'too general Way of Life introduced by Luxury', in which connection he explained this renunciation. But why should a painted name be luxurious? An article published in a London periodical, *The World*, in 1756 makes this more comprehensible. In admiring a 'famous' hospital building and its 'decorations of more cost, perhaps, than utility', the unnamed writer 'discovered two or three long tablets, with several names inscribed in large golden characters, which in my simplicity I took for the votive histories of the poor'.[64] In investigating these golden names, he discovers that they, no less than the statues and portraits similarly commissioned by legators to be installed at hospitals, record only 'ridiculous . . . ostentatious charities', that is, bequests that left the donors' own families in beggary.[65] A monument is, literally, a reminder of something or someone; hence, possibly, a hospital, or a name on a tablet in a hospital. The luxury lay less in the gilt of the lettering, or the portraits and statues, than in the sheer uselessness of a charity which erects such monuments, and the public honour and reputation that they construct, in turn, over the lawful but private claims of kin.[66] The names stood for luxurious self-aggrandizement just as posthumous charity was standing in for impersonal charity, and impersonal love is no love at all.

Even the single-handed raising of a charity could attract this sort of conventional censure. A good example is the Devonshire Hospital (almshouse) in Derby, which Joseph Pickford rebuilt for the 5th Duke in 1777. The result had 'more the appearance of magnificence than charity', judged one visitor in 1782. The street front was indeed magnificent; narrow pavilions with giant Doric columns flanked a lower screen, also stylar, bearing a large carved escutcheon. 'Who dresses a pauper in lace, instead of that modest elegance that ought to have dignified the front?' asked another traveller in 1791; there 'we are treated to an ostentatious display of the Duke's Arms and Crest', a name in effect.[67]

Meanwhile, evocations of a direct, living, and private charity scarcely to be distinguished from hospitality, and which had prevailed in another, long-ago England, were printed in abundance and continued to be.

> He chased no Starv'ling from his Door,
> Nor pinch'd the Wages of the Poor;
> But at his House the Hungry's fed,
> The Hireling finds unmeasur'd Bread,
> The needy Trav'ler Board and Bed.[68]

Mandeville's thumping couplets in *The grumbling hive* (1705) satirize a nostalgic genre with a future. With its own irony, Alexander Pope's poetic 'Epistle' to Lord Bathurst ('Of the use of riches', 1733) celebrates the Man of Ross, whose charitable self-effacement was such that his real name had almost been lost ('And what? no monument, inscription, stone? / His race, his form, his name almost unknown?'), and whose only commemoration was '. . . yon Alms-house, neat, but void of state, / Where Age and Want sit smiling at the gate'. This was no Devonshire Hospital and the Man of Ross was no Duke of Devonshire, whose almshouses' tenants would for good measure be described as healthy young slackers allowed to rent their apartments and gardens to others.[69]

It is in this pervasive context – even the Man of Ross (John Kyrle) was accused of vain charity and ostentation by one disappointed relation[70] – that we have to read Mandeville's dissection of the fruitful vices that pass themselves off as virtues, in his 'Essay on Charity, and Charity-Schools' (1723). His example was Dr John Radcliffe (1650–1714), who bequeathed a fortune to Oxford University, which did not need it, at the expense of his relations, who did. It was Radcliffe's vanity, and not true charity or love of learning, which prompted his bequest, wrote Mandeville; in a famous formulation, 'Pride and Vanity have built more Hospitals than all the Virtues together'.[71] He elaborated on it in at least three other places in his writings, nowhere to better effect than in the *Free thoughts on religion* (1720) in his 'character' of Emilia who, like *The World*'s vain old ladies and gentlemen, excels in presenting the 'Outward Signs of Devotion', a phrase Mandeville liked well enough to make the title of the chapter.[72] Though her neighbours do not know it, Emilia is a retired prostitute, malicious and censorious; they do know that she is fond of theological dispute.

Half a Year ago she made her Will, and left every Farthing she has to rebuild the Front of a little Alms-House. . . . Over the Porch is to be her Effigy in Stone, with an Inscription of her own indicting underneath it. Since she had this Design, she often Visits the poor Inhabitants, to whom she gives what Charity she can spare, and who, in return, take her to be a Saint, and trumpet her Praise all over the Country.

Rebuilding the *front* of the almshouse is particularly nice. Here Mandeville was playing with the old theme of the house that delights the eye but not the stomach, whose gate is wider and fairer than its larder. Emilia alive gives only what she can spare, and her posthumous front will represent but not give relief to the poor.[73]

In demonstrating the public benefits of pride and vanity, though not Emilia's, Mandeville was also expanding on Ned Ward's sneer at the City tradesmen who sought to purchase a reputation at St Bartholomew's. The most famous of them was Thomas Guy (1645–1724), who built a hospital for the London poor that opened in 1728, and left more than £200,000 in his will towards its maintenance. The inscription on his funerary monument (from 1779) reasonably compared this to royal endowments, but at the time there were mutterings about the selfishness, the unchristianness, of denying rightful heirs.[74] Guy's was the last great bequest of its kind in London and in 1736 the Mortmain Act codified the superior claims of property rights over those of charity. The Act was (as one speaker in the House of Lords explained) to protect the heirs of anyone happening 'to fall into that delirious ambition of erecting a palace for beggars, and having his name engraved in gilded letters above a superb portico', or 'his statue set up in the area of any charitable palace'.[75] Guy was one (posthumous) target; others, broader, were pseudo-charitable deliriums and the social up-endings represented by beggars' palaces.

In so far as Britain had ever arrived at a consensus about the proper ways of going about charitable construction, that was questioned, occasionally sharply, in the eighteenth century, which identified the name and the monument, the outward signs of devotion, as the points where selfishness began. Best not to overstate the case, however. In 1731 and again in 1738 promoters of Bath's General Hospital announced that contributors' names would be published in the newspapers, not anticipating that this would deter the fastidious. Edward Bayly turned delicacy to unscrupulous advantage when preaching on behalf of the same hospital in 1749: donations will 'make thy memory revered far more, than gaudy escutcheons on thy hearse, or pompous titles on thy monument'.[76] Most decisively, of course, what people write, and read, need not bear any relation whatever to what they build: hundreds of almshouses and scores of other kinds of residential charities were founded or, like Devonshire's, rebuilt in England over the course of the century.[77] Their construction did, however, prompt complaints about useless monuments, as well as more extended analyses. Was not *any* sort of construction just Emilia's almshouse front, that is, pure appearance incapable of encompassing or relieving poverty, its essential causes and medical consequences?

In 1736 a 'Letter' reprinted in the *Gentleman's Magazine* referred to 'Hospitals, which very often are but so many Monuments of ill-gotten riches, attended with late Repentance'. We assume that this sweeping statement refers to the Mortmain Act (and used in this way, it did), but it is a quotation from the political economist Charles Davenant's *Essay upon . . . the ballance of trade* (1699). By 'hospitals' Davenant (1656–1714) had meant almshouses; readers in 1736 should have realized this once they understood that he had set them up in opposition to employment. But the letter then glosses over the distinction by remarking that William Penn (1644–1718), founder of Pennsylvania and hence a great employer, should be counted a greater benefactor to the nation than either the almshouse founder Thomas Sutton (1532–1611) or the hospital founder Thomas Guy.[78]

Employment dominated every aspect of social theory then, as part of the single desideratum on which a mass of pamphleteers agreed: a large, healthy, and industrious population and, concomitantly, the threat of the growing numbers of unhealthy or, more commonly, healthy but idle poor.[79] Where 'all work no body will want', wrote Davenant, who told his readers that of the 1,330,000 persons then living on the charity of others in England, only 330,000 were too young to work, and thousands were annually perishing 'by those Diseases contracted under a slothful Poverty'.[80] This was the familiar argument of such political arithmeticians as John Bellers (1654–1725), whose *Essay towards the improvement of physick* (1714) also explained that it was employment, not alms, that constituted true charity, and which calculated a £200 loss to the kingdom with the death of every 'Able Industrious Labourer, that is capable to have children'.[81] 'Political arithmetic', William Petty's phrase, seems appropriate to such crankily precise computations of value; it is not economics.[82]

Giving alms no charity is the title of a pamphlet Daniel Defoe (?1661–1731) published in 1704. But was it or was it not? Surely the Man of Ross's alms were charity, as opposed to the self-aggrandizement supposedly manifested by Devonshire's hospital. But Defoe's target was not alms in the sense of loving personal gifts, or even that of the statutory (Poor Law), parish-based system of relief. It was the misguided charity that turned 'strouling fellows' into beggars, and begging into a form of employment.[83] In failing to target its recipients properly, this kind of charity was luxurious, that is, otiose, unproductive, and interfering with an order that was certainly natural, and probably divine, too. 'He that will not work shall not eat', wrote Bellers, quoting St Paul.[84] Unemployed and undeserving recipients of charity might also include buildings. Bellers perhaps thought that only an ostentatious deployment of typefaces would do in condemning a Neapolitan hospital endowed, he wrote, with 400,000 crowns per annum:

> But the Building of *Gaudy Palaces*, instead of *convenient Hospitals* for the Poor, is more *Ostentation* than *Charity*; whilst the Ornaments, especially of *Paintings* and *Carvings* are EXTRAVAGANCES, THAT WOULD ELSE HAVE PROVIDED FOR MANY OTHER POOR.[85]

One eighteenth-century legator to St Bartholomew's specified that his £200 should be 'for the use of the Poor only and not for building', which nicely sums up the case.[86] Bellers's 'convenient Hospitals' in this instance does mean the institutions for the sick for which he called; the first of the voluntary hospitals, which loudly proclaimed their utility as restorers of workers,[87] would be founded five years later, in 1719. It was the Westminster Infirmary, in London. The use of 'infirmary' might have signalled the difference between it and a 'hospital', a word then vulnerable to the myths of the golden names and the million mostly slothful unemployed.

Native American architecture

In examining the ineffectuality of institutional care for the poor, and the vanity that institutions often represented, the *Gentleman's Magazine*'s wide-ranging 'Letter', mentioned above, quotes at length from the *Reasons for establishing the Colony of Georgia* (1733). The colony was a project, chartered in 1732, for coloniz-ing and Christianizing the wild frontier of South Carolina with persecuted Protestants from the Continent and 'unfortunate People in the Kingdom of reputable Families',[88] and the reasons for it came down to the preservation of lives. Georgia would be the salvation of those headed for death in the streets, on the gallows, by their own hand, in the 'Horrors of a Dungeon' (for begging) and, remarkably, because they had never been conceived (unborn to couples renounc-ing marriage for fear of poverty).[89] As envisaged by its founder James Oglethorpe (1696–1785), Georgia would stand as a community of white yeomen on terms of 'Agrarian Equality' and forbidden the assistance of slaves, or of professional lawyers, who would bring with them 'dependence', the luxurious vices of sloth and speculation. The colony was in such ways to recreate 'old times in England',[90] something Oglethorpe also found among the indigenous Yamacraw (Creek) people there, as he described to the elder Samuel Wesley in 1734:

> . . . having plenty of all things meerly necessary, and desiring nothing more, their Genius's, not being pressed by Poverty nor clogged by Luxury, exert themselves with great Lustre: . . . Their houses are Covered with barks of Trees, their Floors of Clay, their Windows are not glazed and their Doors have rarely any Iron Hinges. In these Mansions they live much more contented than our great men in Palaces. . . . They think the English very unwise who waste life in Care and Anxiety merely to heap up Wealth, for to raise Discord amongst their Heirs and to build lasting Houses for to make their Children incapable of bearing the Inclemency of their native Air.[91]

The town of Savannah began, in early 1733, as four large tents; by the end of the year it consisted of forty frame houses 'floored with rough Deals, the Sides with feather-edged Boards unplained', Spartan fashion, and Yamacraw fashion (Figure 2).[92]

A simple, active, rural existence was healthier and more natural than one 'pressed' by poverty, perhaps within an institution and even a dungeon, or alter-natively 'clogged' by the city's diversions and luxuries. This truism scarcely

2. The frontispiece to the *Reasons for establishing the Colony of Georgia* (1733) illustrates that, like the Yamacraw beside whom they build, the settlers will not be 'clogged' by architectural luxury.

needed the exotic witness of the native Americans, generally supposed to enjoy rude health.[93] Oglethorpe explained their healthfulness, which was both physical and psychological, in terms of a fundamental expansiveness, or freedom, epitomized by the unglazed windows.[94]

The interests of George Berkeley (1685–1753), who in 1734 became Bishop of Cloyne, Ireland, paralleled Oglethorpe's in some ways, not least in a respect for clay floors. In *The querist* (1735–37) Berkeley posed 595 rhetorical questions whose responses, cumulatively formulated, would direct the reader to a wide-ranging mental essay around the central theme (Query 1) of 'Whether there ever was, is, or will be, an industrious nation poor, or an idle rich?', the nation being Ireland. Query 373 was about Dutch workhouses, so well managed that in them a child four years old might earn its keep; others concerned the efficacy of penal slavery as an antidote to 'idleness and beggary'. Should workhouses not be built 'with clay floors, and walls of rough stone, without plastering, ceiling, or glazing?'[95] Berkeley, an intimate of Lord Burlington's, was like his friend an amateur architect and a knowledgeable and radical critic of the art; they seem to have met, around 1720, through their shared enthusiasm for public works (Chapter 4).[96] Public works are an antidote to private luxury and unemployment for the Querist, who extends his tolerance to fine houses, which might equally provide 'for the magnificence of the rich, and the necessities of the poor'.[97] Architectural magnificence was, unlike architectural luxury, the lawful and honest reflection of value. The necessities of the poor are not workhouses, however unceiled and unglazed; we are rather returning to the panacea of employment, this time on a building site.

Berkeley had also lived in America (Rhode Island) for a few years, pursuing his own project for Christianizing the wilderness. As the first, as some saw it, of England's Atlantic colonies, Ireland already identified with America, and Berkeley's real colony would be Cloyne.[98] There he 'set up a spinning school for the children, and a house of work for sturdy vagrants; . . . provided winter relief and employment . . . ; he sowed hemp; he sowed flax; he encouraged homespun; his sons might employ a Cork tailor, but he wore Cloyne-made clothes and Cloyne-made wigs' and experimented with Cloyne-made tar-water on his dependants. He got the idea for this panacea, he claimed, from a native American specific against smallpox.[99]

Luxury is not a simple obverse of primitivism, as John Sekora has been careful to show. The opposition cannot, at least, explain the monotony of the attacks upon the supposed luxury of the poor.[100] However, restoring the paupers to frugality, productivity, and health was an enterprise fuelled by primitivist myths that Oglethorpe and Berkeley found among the native Americans. Georgia and Cloyne manifested a natural form of poor relief, natural because it was rural and centred on communal labour.[101] Both men were determined, on behalf of their poor, upon an independent self-sufficiency that even extended to the tar-water, a simple medicine that needed no apothecaries or doctors for its dispensing. The independence was however not absolute. The tribe must be led by a wise father-figure, a patriarch indeed: 'In their manner of Living', wrote Oglethorpe about the Yamacraw, 'they resemble much the patriarchal age'. 'Mr. Oglethorpe' (a merchant of South Carolina meanwhile described him) 'is extremely well beloved by all his People; the general Title they give him is Father. If any of them is sick, he immediately visits them, and takes a great deal of Care of them.'[102]

In his *Natural history* Pliny the Elder (AD 23–79) described how, two centuries earlier, Cato had himself physicked his sons, his slaves, and his friends on his rural estate, hierarchically ordered as an extended family. We could call this natural, or primitive medicine. Pliny's point was that medicine had been admirable to the ancients, but not the medical profession, not taking a fee to save a life.[103] The principle remained honourable (and the practice common: the Man of Ross dispensed medicine to his poor, too),[104] but there were other ways of imagining the care of sick paupers that managed to insist upon professionalism while evading hospital buildings, whose uselessness might extend to deadliness.

In 1774 John Coakley Lettsom, who four years earlier had founded the General Dispensary in Aldersgate Street, wrote that

> Great cities are like painted sepulchres; their public avenues, and stately edifices seem to preclude the very possibility of distress and poverty; but if we pass beyond this superficial veil, the scene will be reversed.[105]

Promoters of the dispensaries that began to be founded in London in the 1770s, which offered medicines and medical advice but not beds, were quite specific about the uselessness of stately edifices, and the misery that they might be concealing. In the first instance, they asked for funds on the grounds that they did not have to divert any to construction. As the *Plan* of the Surrey Dispensary, 'for the Relief of the Poor . . . at their own habitations', argued in 1777,

> The immense sums expended on building and supporting great houses are more usefully employed in relieving a number of objects from the distresses of sickness. . . . A very great number of patients are accommodated at a small expence [including] those of the most useful part of the poor . . .

– that is, the 'industrious artizan'.[106] The minutes of the Westminster General Dispensary (1774) are specific on the support that great houses require: 'A large portion of the Subscription to Hospitals is exhausted by the Building, Servants, Coals and Provisions, so that the remainder for the real purpose of the institution is much reduced'. In other words, funds that should have gone directly to the object, and objects, of the charity were instead transmuted into masonry, and not into medicine, broth, and linen. The argument was not specious, inasmuch as the London and the Middlesex, both voluntary hospitals, began to suffer serious financial problems in the 1770s and they may indeed have been too eager to build new wards, which in the event stayed empty.[107]

There was another argument against buildings, too. Many of the inmates of London's 'noble hospitals',

> from the nature of their disorders, became worse, by being pent up in close wards and impure air; without mentioning the contagion incident to hospitals, which frequently infected most of those who were confined therein.[108]

In houses, however, the 'various disorders are treated apart, free from the noise, impurities, or confinement of a publick ward; and from every species of contagion'.[109] By 1777, the dispensaries' promoters could assume that philanthropic men and women in their turn understood how contagion's many species throve, in horrific interminglings, on hospital wards. All the 'pious labour and expence' that had gone into the hospitals, wrote the American military surgeon John Jones the year before, had been not only 'in a great measure useless, but even fatal and destructive to . . . the intended purpose, that of healing the diseases of the sick poor'.[110] It is to the military doctors that we turn for the final part of this chapter, because they offered the clearest and most dramatic accounts of architecture's economic and medical failures.

Jones's countryman James Tilton in 1813 published a small book called *Economical observations on military hospitals* ('economical' meaning 'organizational'). Tilton's immediate model was the *Oeconomical and medical observations . . . tending to the improvement of military hospitals* (1764) by Richard Brocklesby, which had similarly addressed itself to regimental officers and what Tilton called 'government' as well as to medical staff. Tilton also paid his respects to John Pringle's *Observations on the diseases of the army*, first published in 1752 and subsequently in many editions. However Tilton, a former 'Physician and Surgeon in the Revolutionary Army of the United States', was happy to point out that his predecessors were constrained by the clientage inevitable in a monarchy; his own recommendations arose out of republican conditions. It was Brocklesby, Tilton wrote, who had inspired his use of tents and, when these proved insufficient against the hard Revolutionary winter of 1779–80, his distinctively American

3. James Tilton's hospital for wounded and acutely ill American soldiers 'upon the plan of an Indian hut'.

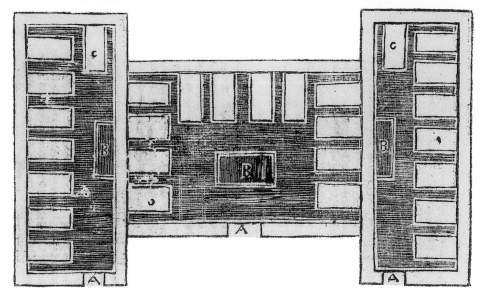

4. The plan of Tilton's hut (reversed here for legibility); the middle ward was for fever patients and the others for the wounded.

solution to the problem of accommodating sick and wounded soldiers. 'The best hospital I have ever contrived was upon the plan of an Indian hut.' This was a log cabin of three large rooms; smoke from open fires escaped through small openings in the roof ridges (Figures 3 and 4). The 'wards were thus completely ventilated' and the smoke combated 'infection'.[111]

Arguing that the general military hospitals must be made smaller, and must restrict the range of cases they accepted, Tilton wrote that it had become evident that the

> humane and benevolent design of large and extensive hospital accommodation must necessarily be defeated in the execution; that profusion and extravagance serve only to precipitate destruction and ruin, and that economy and frugality are necessary to the success of our hospitals.[112]

Neither of his British models had so clearly addressed the inherent luxury (profusion and extravagance) of large hospitals but, directed by a model of disease that saw air circulation and the destruction of diseased fabrics as the great prophylaxes, Pringle (1707–82) advocated the use of 'churches, barns, or ruinous houses' for the accommodation of sick and wounded soldiers in preference to insufficiently ventilated hospitals, and his ruins were inestimably influential. Brocklesby in 1764 similarly recommended 'convenient hovels' and 'occasional hutts' of wattle and thatch that could be raised and then razed in a trice. The same year, Donald Monro (1727–1802), son of the Edinburgh Infirmary's Alexander, published his *Essay on the means of preserving the health of soldiers*, about his experiences with the British camps in Germany. Monro conceded that 'public Buildings' with 'large dry airy Apartments' were well fitted for the soldiers, but in 'Summer, when the Moveable or Flying Hospital is ordered into Villages, large Barns, and the largest airy Houses, are the best'.[113] The emphasis on airiness was conventional, but nicely evocative in conjunction with the 'Flying Hospital'; the practical difficulties of army medicine, often conducted on the move, also predisposed the military physicians to ephemerality and with it Tilton's 'economy and frugality'. The Scottish army surgeon Alexander Small had studied, he wrote, Pringle and Monro with profit and in a paper written some time in the 1770s he extended the principle to the civil sphere with the help of his friend Benjamin Franklin (1706–90). German immigrants to Pennsylvania, obliged to live at first in a large barn, endured the winter very well; Swiss urban poor in large 'shattered houses', cold as ice, survived epidemic diseases better than their snug rural cousins.[114]

The military men were distinctive for the ardour with which they demolished architecture; the delight with which they reported how nature had guided their lucky experiments. For, in spite of their praise for their predecessors, the huts and ruined houses were always serendipitous. Pringle, Brocklesby, and Tilton did not (they implied) seek out such odd alternatives to hospitals, but were obliged to use them by the force of circumstance, after the windows were broken, and then discovered how well they worked.[115] Well into the nineteenth century, astonishment remained conventional in these narratives of health restored within, and by, apparent ugliness, transience, and ruin,[116] even as the paradox was itself applied to effect. Patients are safe from gangrene, wrote the Edinburgh surgeon John Bell (1763–1820), only outside the 'circle of the infected walls'. So let the surgeon

> hurry them out of this house of death; let him change the wards, let him take possession of some empty house and so carry his patients into good air; let him lay them in a schoolroom, a church, on a dung-hill, or in a stable; let him carry them anywhere but to their graves.

For those doctors who could, well into the twentieth century, remember the epidemical hospital gangrene, the call to the dung-heap retained singular force.[117]

Nature guided the forms of the military men's buildings, too. At a time when theoretical quests for architecture's origins formed part of programmes for its renewal,[118] they actually built the kind of primitive hut that Vitruvius had described and Laugier reconstructed and found, they wrote, that it worked.

The question was whether the architecture might be reconstructed on the basis of that new, primitive knowledge.[119] Could the artful disposition of wards and windows, even of heating and ventilation systems, achieve a reconciliation with nature and its good air? – or must hospitals, including civil hospitals, stay in the huts? Such questions remained current even longer than the astonishment.[120]

We would not expect the eighteenth-century military doctors to cite Laugier or Vitruvius, and their antiquarianism took a more precise form. While Pringle merely regretted the silence of the classical authors about camp diseases,[121] Brocklesby, following a hint from Richard Mead, noted that the Old Testament had prescribed for the filth produced by 'infirmaries, or hospitals, in all countries'. There the

> seeds of infection once sown, continue, in some instances, to spread infectious diseases, and to contaminate the house, as much as ever the walls of the Israelites were infected with the filthy leprosy, which is said to have germinated from the walls of their tents, or hutts, in their tedious per[e]grination towards the Land of Promise.

Dr Mead had noted how it was the priests, the men of learning, who adhering to Mosaic precept did the right thing: scraped the walls and if necessary pulled down the entire infected house and carried the materials right out of the city.[122] Tilton similarly found, in Deuteronomy 23:12–14, instruction that American soldiers had at first ignored to their cost:

> Thou shalt have a place also without the camp, whither thou shalt go forth abroad: And thou shalt have a paddle upon thy weapon; and it shall be, when thou wilt ease thyself abroad, thou shalt dig therewith, and shalt turn back and cover that which cometh from thee: For the Lord thy God walketh in the midst of thy camp . . . therefore shall thy camp be holy . . .

Human excrement had been everywhere at the 1776 encampment at King's Bridge, New York and a 'putrid diarrhoea was the consequence. . . . Many died, melting as it were and running off by the bowels'.[123]

Medicine that was literally patriarchal, that is of the line of Abraham, offered apposite illustrations for military physicians (and maybe literary models too). God's injunctions were issued during the Israelites' slow journey back to the Promised Land and eighteenth-century armies were on the move too. Brocklesby and Tilton's use of the Old Testament, like their advocacy of the most primitive kind of shelter for ailing soldiers, links them with those modern patriarchs Oglethorpe and Berkeley, who would protect the poor from luxury in the clay-floored hut. This is not to deny the modernity (as we might call it) of their ideas, or the worldliness (as they would have defined it) of their activities. Oglethorpe founded Georgia partly out of his experience as the chair of a parliamentary committee inspecting prisons with a view to their reform.[124] The military writers were as central to the eighteenth century's redefinitions of disease, and of the hospital, as Berkeley was to its epistemology. The architect Samuel Wyatt was inspired by Brocklesby's *Observations* to invent what he called the 'Moveable' military hospital, of which an example was in 1788 dismantled and re-erected in front of the king within an hour. Eighty-three feet long, it seems to have been the world's first substantial prefabricated building (one was shipped to New South Wales).[125] I do want to point out the intensity with which they sought providential or natural guidance for their work, and the strength of the consensus on the pressing need to detect luxury in guises which, if not all new, were all sharply relevant: the pauper's sloth, the charitable palace, the deadly hospital.

From sneers at the gilding of tradesmen's names and at the palaces they made for paupers, to warnings about the contagions that brewed in noble wards, a variety of preoccupations conspired to destabilize the idea of the hospital by demonstrating the gaps between vanity and charity, the spaces behind the masks and fronts. There were those who held, in the eighteenth and nineteenth centuries, that utility would never be found in architecture, as opposed to the tent and the hut. But as an institution and a type, the hospital not only survived, but embarked upon the career that (by any reasonable standard) remains splendid to this day. We might therefore decide, not just that rhetoric has one history and construction another, but also that they are interdependent. Accusations of ostentatious waste retained their edge and their relevance. New construction was in turn explained, not with direct reference to the general critique (to that extent the two histories *were* separate) but by praise for particular buildings that however shared the same powerful terms of reference. London's Foundling Hospital, wrote Sophie von la Roche (1730–1807) in 1786,

> has been reproached for its over-lavish expenditure on buildings, with the result that fewer children can be accommodated. I did not think it extravagant, but large and healthy for the poor creatures, who also had their recreation before meals.[126]

The antithesis of the buildings and the children was almost proverbial, but La Roche was making another distinction, between lavishness and lavishness that is only apparent: a less expensive orphanage would be a false economy, because it would be less healthy. Such demonstrations pointed to the cleanliness, space, light, and pure air and water that were expensive to procure and maintain, especially on city sites, and frankly admitted the extravagance of these provisions compared to those that civilization normally allocated to the urban poor.[127] Nature however offers these boons in abundance. One opposite of luxury is this natural, or positive luxury.[128]

The next two chapters develop themes just introduced: the old-fashioned house and nostalgia for the hospitality it extends, and the ordering power of institutions whose intervention had come to substitute for such direct social exchanges. In returning to the seventeenth century, and specifically to Bethlem, Chelsea and Greenwich, they also begin this book's examination of how hospitals were built in the century and a half after the Restoration and how the buildings' assumed meanings and functions changed.

Chapter 2
Palaces and hospitals

What is the opposite of luxury? Good husbandry, wrote Defoe, thinking of the 'extravagant' luxury of the poor, while Berkeley contrasted public works with the 'private' luxury of the rich.[1] We all know inappropriateness and superfluity when we see them, and since antiquity the Western world has seen a great deal of writing attacking them. Luxury found few defenders before the mid-eighteenth century, when attention began to be directed to the economic functionings of such conventional exemplars as the 'gilt Charriot'. The most notorious exception was the physician and author Bernard Mandeville, for whom gilded coaches were, like grand houses and fine linen, a reliable and encouraging index of 'Prodigality, That Noble Sin'.[2]

Mandeville defended the sin by naturalizing it, by showing that it was a pre-requisite for civilization itself.[3] Luxury is anyway (he wrote) so relative over time as to be meaningless; everything is a luxury, or rather was once. Meat, once the privilege of the affluent, was now eaten by the poor too, and thirty years previously, he impertinently supposed, not even in a palace would his reader have found anything as comfortable as the 'Easy Chair' in which he or she now sat.[4] In *The fable of the bees* (1714), he turned the new French and English military hospitals to similar account:

> If the ancient Britons and Gauls should come out of their Graves, with what Amazement wou'd they gaze on the mighty Structures every where rais'd for the Poor! Should they behold the Magnificence of a Chelsea College, a Greenwich Hospital, or what surpasses all [of] them, a Des Invalides at Paris, and see the Care, the Plenty, the Superfluities and Pomp which people that have no Possessions at all are treated with in those stately Palaces, those who were once the greatest and richest of the Land would have Reason to envy the most reduced of our Species now.[5]

Louis XIV ordered the construction of the Invalides, begun to the designs of Libéral Bruant (or Bruand, c.1635–97), in 1670. The king's own testament would declare that 'Among the various foundations we have made, none was nearly so useful to the State', and it was arguably the most influential of any sort in seventeenth-century Europe.[6] The eldest of its many children were built by the English: the Royal Hospital at Kilmainham, near Dublin, begun in 1680 to designs by William Robinson (1645–1712), and Christopher Wren's (1632–1723) Royal Hospital at Chelsea, also for soldiers (1682–89), and its naval counterpart at Greenwich (begun 1696). Ignoring, or ignorant of, handsome but obscure Kilmainham, Mandeville called them all palaces to make his point about luxury's relativity. To these examples he could have added Bethlem Hospital for lunatics as rebuilt in 1674–76 to the designs of Wren's friend Robert Hooke (1635–1703), 'for many years the only building which looked like a palace in London'[7] (Chelsea and Greenwich being too far from London to count) and the most domestic-looking of them all.

Stately lodgings for the poor

Sitting as it did at the top of the secular hierarchy, the palace – a great house, that is – was a convenient metaphor for praising lesser types, and one that was often used in applause for London's rebuilding after the Great Fire in 1666. George Elliot exhorted his readers to,

> Go view each street, and stand amaz'd to see,
> With what fair Fabricks they adorned bee;
> Each House a Palace, and may entertain
> A KING in State, with all his Noble Train . . .[8]

The further one strayed from private-domestic types, the better the palace worked. A friend of Jonathan Swift's wrote to him from France in 1735 that the

5. Bethlem Hospital. The governors presented Robert White's large engraving to themselves and to the king and the Duke of York in 1677.

Chantilly stables could be mistaken for a palace ('some hundreds of *Yahoos* are constantly employed in keeping it clean'); the 'fairest Pallace in *Milan* (I *may say in Italy*) is the great Hospitall, a square of Columnes and Porches six hundreds Rods about; fitter to be the Court of some Kings than to keep Almes men in' was how an English traveller described the Ospedale Maggiore a century earlier.[9] Benjamin Franklin boasted that the Pennsylvania Hospital (begun 1755) 'gave to the beggar in America a degree of comfort and chance for recovery equal to that of a European prince in his palace'.[10] Hospitals could illustrate, not just the relativism of past and present, but that of old worlds and new.

Bethlem (Figure 5) was a special case. For hardened seventeenth-century poets, trained in the art of paradox, a palace for lunatics was irresistible. The grandeur of Hooke's building was in the anonymous 'Bethlehems beauty' (1676) affectionately identified as a danger to public mental health: *everyone* would want to live there. 'So Brave, so Neat, so Sweet it does appear, / Makes one Half-Madd to be a Lodger there'. The danger was compounded for Bethlem's actual inhabitants, for the new building permitted a new spin on lunatics' proverbial inclination to give themselves great pedigrees:

> And those pour Souls, whose Crazed Brains advance
> Their roving Fancies to the Extravagance
> Of being Princes, needs must think it True,
> When they shall such a Towering Pallace view.[11]

In 1710 Richard Steele pretended to find 'Five Dutchesses, Three Earls, Two Heathen Gods, an Emperor, and a Prophet' in Bethlem, whose architectural delusions provided at least one more poet with a joke:

> Magnific to their wild, delighted Eyes
> Peruvian Roofs, and Parian Columns rise;
> Beneath their Thrones the Nile and Ganges meet,
> And waft unbounded Riches to their Feet . . .[12]

In Hildebrand Jacob's *Bedlam* (1723), the inmates are again over-stimulated by giant pilasters.

The story, which entered London legend, that Hooke had at Bethlem actually copied a palace, the Louvre (or alternately, the Tuileries) in Paris, started around 1700.[13] The Revd Thomas Bowen (1749–1800) permitted himself a mildly scatological twist: Hooke's borrowing of the design of the (meta-palatial) 'Chateau de Tuilleries, at Versailles' so much offended Louis XIV that he had St James's Palace used as a model for some 'very inferior' French offices.[14] In Hooke's day the Tuileries (begun 1564) stood as a long range of distinctly roofed pavilions facing west to its gardens, and it was in its length, its shallowness, its pavilions, and in this outlook that it resembled Bethlem. This is not quite enough for a model, but the resemblance worked and continues to work at other levels. It made a good joke, which turns on anticipation of the Sun King's reaction to the implied comparison between French courtiers and English pauper lunatics. For insiders like Bowen, whose *Historical account* of Bethlem was printed at its governors' order, it was a way of indicating what, indeed, we should apprehend in the face of Hooke's building: that it is big and handsome, but also domestic-looking (that 'friendly mansion', he called it). As such, and for all the jokes, the new hospital was the icon for a kind of charity explained as distinctively arduous quite simply because its objects would not thank and could not praise their benefactors, at least not until they recovered their senses.[15] Comparable selflessness resided in the very gulf between the magnificence of the building and the humbleness of the charitable objects. They did not accord, which was the point, and this is an understanding extensible to other palatial hospitals.

Peter the Great, staying near Greenwich at the end of the century, obligingly told his royal cousin that if he were William, he would hand Whitehall over to the sailors and keep the hospital for himself.[16] The joke continued to be nourished by the perverse pride Londoners took in the supposed grubbiness of their palaces compared to many of their hospitals, which was never entirely undermined by the developing preoccupation with the gaudy and viciously useless palace for beggars. In the early nineteenth century they were still reporting with delight that foreigners reckoned London's charitable institutions to be 'more fitted, by their grandeur and extent, for the residences of kings' while the palaces looked like pauper hospitals.[17] The foreigners were right, too, inasmuch as James Thornhill's paintings and the 'twenty-five pairs of columns, which are all very high, strong and elegant' which Zacharias Conrad von Uffenbach admired at Greenwich in 1710, for example, would (in 1728) be reckoned as costing £6,685 and £27,088 respectively:[18] princely sums. The congruence of palaces and hospitals was however also historical and functional.

As buildings for large, hierarchical households, palaces, whether royal or not, accommodated a wide range of administrative and juridical activities. Acknowledging this complexity, Roger North wrote in his treatise of a

> greater extent of building, such as Bedlam, Chelsea Colledge [Hospital], or Hampton Court [Palace], which speaks a provision to be made for various and numerous sorts of people; and is rather a compound than a simple fabrick. Whereas singleness doth not become it, as it doth a church or small house.

There are two distinctions here, between the compound and the simple building, and between the variety and 'singleness' of appearance respectively appropriate to them. The problem with compound fabrics was to find the variety. The 'pinking of walls with too many apertures', that is long rows of windows, produces something that 'looks more like a colledge, or inne; where a world of people come for mere accommodation, and it speaks littleness within'.[19] North cheerfully cited Christopher Wren's new part (1690–96) of Hampton Court as a case in point. His friend's Chelsea Hospital avoided the difficulty with its portico, frontispieces, and 'pavilions which terminate the wings', as did, by different means, his palace at Winchester (begun in 1683 but never finished). 'I have many examples of this sort of decoration by breaks; and the cheif [sic], and where it was most necessary' was Bethlem's, 'where so long a range could not well be better distributed to give the whole a grace, and take off the fastidiousness of its length'.[20] 'Fastidiousness' here has the old meaning of tedium.

In July 1674 the Bridewell and Bethlem Court of Governors decided that the new Bethlem at Moorfields, just north of London Wall, would be a 'single building and not double'.[21] Here the singleness is that of the range: a double building is a double-pile building, one divided by a spine wall or corridor to form two parallel rows of rooms.[22] This relative compactness offered practical advantages, and Hooke was about to embark on an ingenious exploration of double piles that began with Montagu House, Bloomsbury (1675–79).[23] Bethlem was however not compact, but an inordinately long (around 600 feet) and thin (40 feet) block, soon to be efficiently and definitively described as two rooms each hundreds of feet long (the 'galleries') superimposed between basement and attic, with rows of cells behind them, to the south.[24] The Bethlem minutes' 'single building' refers to the way in which each floor accommodated only one row of cells. The more economical alternative was two rows on each side of a spine wall, such as Wren planned for Chelsea and Greenwich, or on each side of a gallery-corridor, as at the wings added to Bethlem between 1725 and 1736 (see Figure 32, p. 89),[25] and at many later asylums.

North identified single piles with two old domestic types functionally, if not always literally, centred on their halls. The oldest was built 'court fashion', around courtyards; court fashion, too, in the sense that such enclosures were by then the prerogative of only the greatest households. But the type none the less remained 'fit for a colledge or hospital, to be devided into cells, and chambers independent of each other'.[26] Such houses had flourished when gentlefolk lived in large households, which might include other gentlefolk in their service; like them, colleges and (almshouse) hospitals required self-contained lodgings, each with its own or shared door. North also associated single-piling with another, newer kind of house, the hall-and-cross-wings type he called an 'H' or 'half H' after its shapes, the latter being most common.[27] The double pile was more economical than the half-H, as both North and Roger Pratt (1620–85) explained – one got the same space for less walling and roofing – and more convenient because distances were shorter and it offered its users a choice of routes through the building.[28]

Flexibility of circulation is not particularly important for institutions whose residents, except when in their own rooms, follow a communal routine, and the independent chambers permitted by single-piling were still appropriate for the institutional architecture of North's day. Certainly undesirable were what he identified as the disadvantages of a house that is too compact: noisiness, and the gloom and smells originating in a failure of light and air.[29] The single pile has the advantage here. North agreed with Pratt's earlier judgement that it lies 'open to all winds, and weather', and 'having through lights' (windows on both sides) 'looks too glaring',[30] but a certain amount of glare and wind was welcomed at later, and unambiguously medical, hospitals. In 1768 Edward Foster emphasized that hospitals must be 'single Houses, with numerous Windows on each side opposite to each other; by which means a Renovation of fresh Air is in our Power . . . were the Houses double, from the necessary Partitions running along their Middles, . . . this Circulation could not be procured'

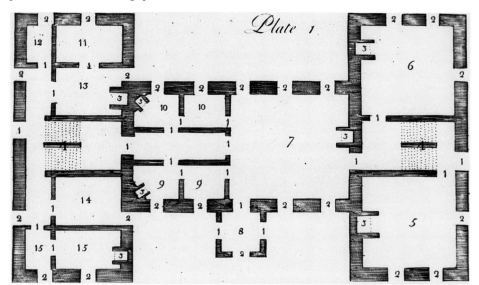

6. Foster's ground-plan for a small Irish hospital. This floor was to be reserved for domestic uses, as it would be the dampest and least airy.

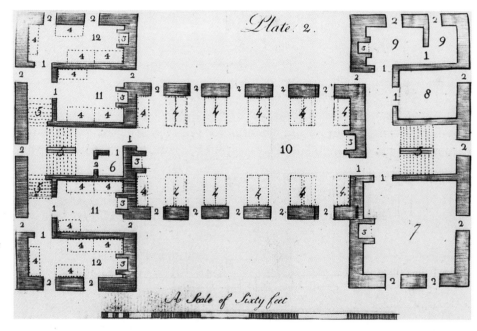

7. Foster's plan for the two upper floors of his hospital. Air circulation would, he admitted, have to be partly sacrificed for the sake of separating men and women in the big ward, but he did not explain how this would be done.

(Figures 6 and 7).[31] The Winchester Hospital, the earliest of the eighteenth-century English provincial foundations, at first occupied an old courtyard house, and we could call Edinburgh's purpose-built Infirmary a half-H (see Figures 52 and 41, pp. 136 and 112). North might have understood both as illustrating, again, the way in which old domestic types remain relevant to hospitals, though no longer on account of their chambers, or cells.

By 'hospitals' North however meant almshouses, whose modern form, 'consisting of cottages each with its own fireplace and offices, developed during the fifteenth century'.[32] Its ultimate origin was the monastic infirmary, a long hall with a chapel at one end. In such halls the beds, placed at right angles to the walls, were screened for the sake of privacy and warmth with curtains, and later often with wooden and even masonry partitions. Civil (non-monastic) hospitals afterwards saw the same development, which turned the halls themselves into narrower circulation spaces, sometimes called galleries. Though the arrangement, minus the chapels, was maintained until the eighteenth century at hospitals like St Thomas', by the fifteenth century new hospitals were increasingly for permanent residents and not short-term guests and they were built with much more marked attention to the separation of the dwellings, which had their own entrances.[33] At this point, the examples of university colleges and great houses built court-fashion seem to have become more important for new almshouses than their direct antecedents, the converted infirmary halls.[34]

English almshouses were presenting a variety of plans in North's day. Hooke's own Aske's Hospital in Hoxton (Figure 8; *c*.1690–93) offered little houses with rooms front and back, like terraced houses. Morden College, Blackheath was founded in 1695 and is traditionally attributed to Wren; at both Morden, arranged around a quadrangle, and Aske's, like Bethlem a long thin block, the first-floor rooms rested on open ground-floor loggias.[35] Single-room almshouses sharing stairs with others could open on to the closed equivalent of the loggia, an upper-storey corridor-gallery, but this arrangement, which is reminiscent of the sub-divided infirmary halls and approaches that of Bethlem and the military hospitals, was rare at seventeenth-century almshouses.[36]

Colleges and hospitals were, for North, related species; cousins, perhaps, whose grandmother was the courtyard house. These departures from the proto-type 'followed as branches, up to the originall stem, will be found to derive from natural singleness and simplicity'. He was here referring to domestic custom and

8. The Haberdashers' Aske's Hospital, an almshouse and school in Hoxton, north of London. Hooke's last documented building looked like Bethlem and its plan was in some ways comparable.

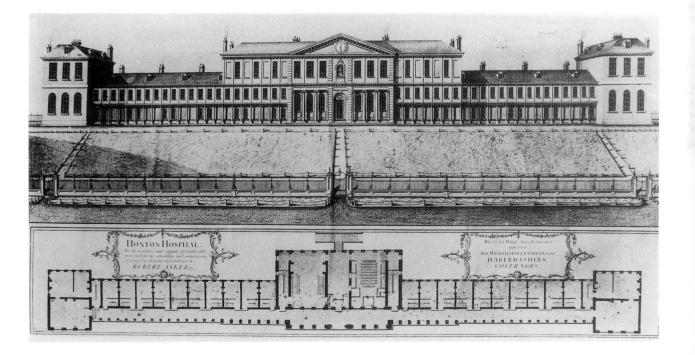

organization, but these were things he understood to be bound up with architectural form. With Bethlem and Chelsea we find a further link to palaces through 'compound' form, whose design presented a problem: how could the architect avoid monotony, the littleness of spirit that is the result of little rooms all in a row within? Such buildings were modern but archaic, for they represented the survival of the older sort of house offering rooms to inhabitants who, as members of the household but not of the family that owned the house, had a functional, and literal, place in that house analogous to that of Bethlem's or Chelsea's inmates.

Inhabitants and visitors

North's treatise suggests that Bethlem and the military hospitals, conventionally praised as palaces, were palatial, or at least quasi-palatial, in both their physical and domestic organization. The last embraced not just staff and inmates, but casual visitors: tourists, we can certainly call them. The distinction between 'inhabitants' and 'visitors' drawn by Bill Hillier and Julienne Hanson will be useful for understanding how these organizations worked together, but it will need to be complicated a little for the sake of the tourism.

The 'inhabitant' of a building is not necessarily inside it, but is rather the person 'with special access to and control of the category of space created by the boundary'.[37] The two categories of person properly admitted to any building are its inhabitants and 'visitors' who have a legitimate reason for being there: at a great house, for example, in the expectation of customary hospitality. A related distinction is that between a deep and a shallow space, measured by the number of intermediary spaces between it and the outside world. The inhabitant of a deep space meets the visitor in a shallow space, a place of reception. Through the gate and the front door, into the hall – still a shallow space, a circulation space – and even to a family bedroom, how far one entered a house was a fairly direct index of social status. Books of household ordinances (domestic regulations) from the early modern period are 'rich in advice about the application of this social geography to the reception of strangers' because miscalculations either way were embarrassing.[38]

Thomas Markus has shown the historical usefulness of this framework in relation to many kinds of institution. With its help we can understand the physical and domestic workings of Hooke's Bethlem, which happens to be a building dominated, in Western cultural memory, by visiting.

Bethlem was open to people with no personal or official relation to the lunatics, as it had been at its former site near Bishopsgate. Casual visiting also remained common at other residential charities in London during the eighteenth century, including Bethlem's sister institution Bridewell.[39] Bethlem at Moorfields was unique in the extent to which the visiting determined its regulation, though active exploitation of its distinctive asset, the sight of the insane, may have begun much earlier. In 1598 a visiting committee of governors complained about the filth there in terms suggesting that it was the casual visitor's reaction they were concerned about; the first recorded reference to the 'shew of Bethlem' came twelve years later.[40]

At Moorfields, by another old tradition, departing visitors were encouraged to make a donation at the 'poor's boxes' by the door – perhaps personally and pointedly encouraged, but the infamous entrance fee is, strictly speaking, a myth. The donations provided a tidy income but were perhaps less important as a direct source of revenue than as a ritual leading to more substantial support, for example a bequest yielding regular income. Testators were not, however, sought among the prostitutes and apprentices eagerly and influentially described around 1700 by the comic essayists Ned Ward and Tom Brown in their accounts of Bethlem's galleries. ''Tis an almshouse for madmen, a showing-room for whores, a sure market for lechers, and a dry walk for loiterers', wrote Ward.[41] Whatever his reliability – few were the places at which he was not, Ned claimed, importuned by 'commodities' in an early and influential example of the genre Mark Hallett calls the London 'topography of whoredom'[42] – the Bethlem governors were anxious to attract a genteel audience for their good work and sought through their officers to filter out the 'lewd and disorderly'.[43] Respectable callers to the 'hospital house', potential benefactors, would by contrast be encouraged to give through their self-identification as guarantors of good management. The charity's very accessibility suggested that it had nothing to hide. More specifically, the regulations, including a table showing the inmates' diet, were prominently displayed at Moorfields and otherwise publicized in a display that (we might think) constituted a kind of shallow space, as the institution turned its disciplinary inside, out.[44] One of the governors' motives for constructing Hooke's great new building, or at least one of the advantages they perceived in this magnificence after its creation, was its attractiveness as a place to visit and assume one's Christian responsibilities.

Visitors entered Bethlem's front yard by side doors flanking the gates (Figure 9). The most distinguished, like Charles II on his visit in August 1676, were doubtless received at and admitted through the gates, which were topped by celebrated depictions of Raving and Melancholy Madness, so-called (Figure 10); the royal lion and the unicorn stood on the piers to each side. The door beyond led into a narrow passage, flanked by the Steward's room and the 'Committee room' used to examine patients upon admission and discharge, and then to the hall.[45] Stairs at the back of the hall led up to the first-floor lobby, at the front of which was the Governors' room, which had the balcony visible above the door in Figure 9. In this way the hospital was organized around a central, vertical axis suitably distinguished by tables of benefactors' names in the entrance hall and, in the Governors' room, a portrait of Henry VIII (Bethlem's putative founder) and other objects of interest.[46] No part of this axis was open to patients (in 1708 Edward Hatton explained that the hall was rather dark, but it was the 'only proper place' in which the tables of names, with their carved cherubim on top, 'could be exposed to publick view . . . and at the same time secured from the distracted People'),[47] because on each side of the hall on the ground floor, and the lobby on the first floor, were iron grilles with gates in them. Beyond these grilles stretched the galleries, lit by the windows that gave this front a relatively high window-to-wall ratio. At the back of the galleries on both floors, on the south side against London Wall and the City beyond, were the cells for the lunatics, thirty-four on each side (see Figure 22, p. 63).[48]

9.   A detail of White's print of Bethlem (Figure 5).

(facing page) 10.   The life-sized statues always attributed to Caius Gabriel Cibber, erected on Bethlem's gate in or soon after 1677 (they look slightly different in Figure 9). The only part of the building to survive, the statues are now in the Bethlem Royal Archives and Museum.

Hooke's Bethlem was demolished in the early nineteenth century, and no plan survives, but other stairs surely ran down at the ends of the galleries on each side of the building, as they did at its successor, designed by James Lewis (*c.*1751–1820; Figure 11). These gave staff access to the galleries, attic, and basement, and permitted patients to be escorted down to the exercise yards on each side of the building, which was divided between men on the east side, and women on the west (on the left as we face the façade). To this extent the hospital maintained three distinct spatial systems: the shallowest set of rooms around the hall, stair, and first-floor landing, for the visitors and senior staff and officers; and the twinned sets for the male and female patients and junior servants, comprising the galleries, cells, and yards, made deeper, as spaces, by the simple presence of the iron grilles with their locked gates.

Bethlem was however regulated in such a way as to make its spatial organization more complicated than that. The grilles, whose installation was still uncontentious in December 1675, became the subject of dispute four months later.[49] 'Severall Governo.[rs]' present at a meeting on 20 April 1676 contended that the grilles 'will obscure the Grandeur and Prospect of the said Galleryes',[50] which were, or at least had become understood as, an integral part of the building's magnificence. A gallery could be almost any built space perceptibly longer than it was wide, but the word also held the prestigious connotations today still conveyed by 'long gallery'.[51] Some governors got carried away by those connotations, particularly after they themselves inspected the unfinished building to see if the grilles really would interfere with its visual impact. On site, too, they perhaps realized that they had built themselves the longest galleries, and indeed

one of the longest built spaces in England; Bethlem at Moorfields was, overall, about the length of Ely Cathedral, and the galleries ran virtually its full length. The effect must have been wonderful at a time when large, modern, *regular* construction was very rare, and to persons untroubled by the later associations of endless institutional corridors. (A. C. Pugin's view [Figure 38, p. 101] of a gallery at 'new' St Luke's Hospital, whose plan followed Bethlem's in important ways, gives something of the effect.) A meeting on 5 May decided to omit the grilles, which were not installed until 1689 and then justified as ensuring the separation of male and female patients (though at least two women had by then been impregnated by members of staff).[52] Thereafter some patients were allowed the freedom of the galleries when visitors were there; others could be viewed through the wickets on the cell doors.

The grilles did not after all hinder the prospect or the essential conception of the building. Until the 1780s, topographers simply described Bethlem as a shell around two enormous galleries superimposed, without reference to the iron grilles or the central stairwells. As 'Bethlehems beauty' had it in 1676:

Since, *Strangers* that Survey the *Galleries*,
Find the *Vast Length* wearies their Travelling eyes;
And some cry out, 'If such a Place befits
'*Madmen, Henceforth who'le Study to be Wits*?['] (ll. 41–44)

The poem's joke about the hospital's grand, psychologically destabilizing exterior was moved inside. At the same time, it became clear that Bethlem was to take

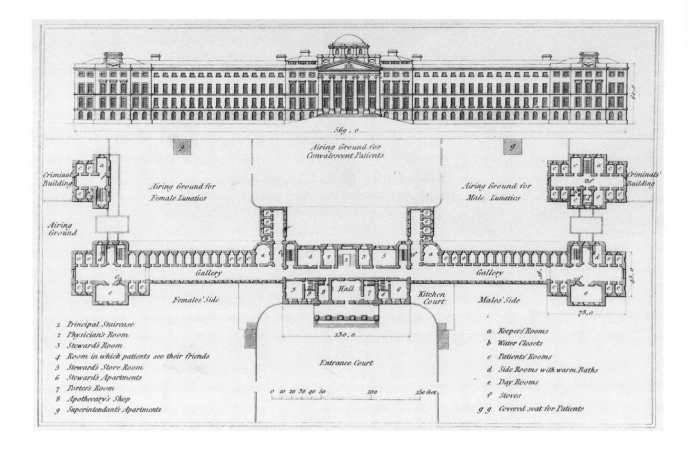

11. Bethlem Hospital as new-built in St George's Fields, Southwark. The plan signals an appeal to serious 'connoisseurs' of the *Illustrations of the public buildings of London* (1825–28) edited by John Britton and A. C. Pugin.

its place among the buildings – English great houses, great European hospitals – that strangers seek out.

A gallery's proportions were distinctive, and with them the word's root meaning of a space in which one walks, but not its form, or functions. 'Gallery' could also refer to what we would call a loggia, or a cloister or courtyard walk, as well as a corridor,[53] but its associations were often grander, as the Bethlem poem and its governors' actions suggest. In the sixteenth century, many English gallery-rooms were equipped with paintings and tapestries, something that eventually furnished the word's modern meaning; the diversion offered by the pictures, analogous to windows affording prospects, contributed to the healthfulness of strolling.[54] Some were very long indeed – that at Bridewell Palace was around 200 feet – but their connotations of reflection and (re)creation were strong enough for the poet Marvell to describe his own soul (furnished with portraits of his mistress) as 'The Gallery', without bathos.[55] North provided another shading by suggesting that galleries 'of the mid[d]le sort, not wholly decorated to parade, nor to private use' were useful when entertaining guests of the middle sort with a social status a little lower than one's own, as it pleased them and was convenient for you, the host.[56] Galleries' old-fashioned lack of functional specificity and, in spatial terms, their shallowness, remained useful in negotiating a relationship always susceptible to fine gradations, and increasingly those brought by the tourism which, as it became a business at many houses in the eighteenth century, was explicitly identified with the old hospitable rituals.[57]

When strangers (to return to Hillier and Hanson's usage, which is not much different from the seventeenth century's) visited Bethlem, or Chelsea, or one of London's other residential charities, they became visitors at a place of reception. This transformation was the specific responsibility of one or more hospital employees. Chelsea's Keeper of the Council Chamber (its job titles were suggestively archaic-sounding, even Gilbertian: this functionary was also the Wardrobe-keeper and the Comptroller of the Coal Yards) was to 'wait upon all Persons of Quality who wish to see the Hospital, and to show them the Halls, Wards, Chapel, Walks, etc.'. The Sexton's duties similarly included forbidding dogs, and women wearing pattens, entrance to the chapel (whose floor was paved in marble, which had cost £400).[58] The Greenwich Porter, gowned and staffed, was permitted to keep one-quarter of his tips for showing the hospital, and in particular the ceiling of the Painted Hall, which became one of the sights of London even before it was finished in 1712.[59] At Bethlem, whose domestic organization was inextricably bound up with customary hospitality, all the senior officers had responsibilities for the regulation of visiting, especially the Porter.[60] House rules prescribed how far – as well as when, and which – visitors could enter various spaces: Chelsea's Usher of the Hall was 'not to suffer strangers to come into the Hall when the Pensioners are at dinner, but if they desire to see them eat to admit them to the Gallery' ('gallery' here as in balcony).[61]

We might guess that many of the proverbially garrulous Chelsea pensioners would have preferred a little variety and sociability at meals, which were supposed to be conducted with cruel decorum, but they had no say in the matter.[62] Most lived in the hospital until they died, but they were not inhabitants in the particular sense described above. In what Hillier and Hanson call 'reversed' buildings, broadly speaking those of a public-institutional type, the 'visitors – those who do not control the knowledge embodied in the building and its purposes – come to occupy the deeper primary . . . cells': the pensioners are the visitors at Chelsea, the insane the visitors at Bethlem. It is the members of staff, the true inhabitants, who occupy and control the shallower circulation areas.[63] Bethlem, Chelsea, and Greenwich however had two kinds of visitor. First were those who lived there, perhaps until they died. Second were the daily visitors, admitted subject to rules very similar to the ordinances of more conventional households, and provided that they took their pattens off for the sake of the chapel floor. In relation to these temporary visitors, the military veterans *and* the lunatics – though not the old sailors – could however assume the role of inhabitant, in Hillier and Hanson's sense, as guides to the building and its occupants. This was a role that they valued: it made a break in the routine, and was rewarded with tips and a pleasurable sense of expertise.[64] It also gave them their own measure of control over shallow spaces, of which we can take the Bethlem galleries as an icon.

Recreational galleries were seldom built after the third quarter of the seventeenth century but open, external galleries remained useful at great houses – including the greatest, Blenheim Palace, Oxfordshire, begun in 1705 – as links to detached offices, and within office courts, that not incidentally augmented the grandeur of the whole. Piazzas, as they were often called in this context, also maintained their place within military- and general-hospital construction, providing as they did ward access sweeter-smelling than an enclosed corridor and hence also suitable for convalescent strolls. Though it was at hospitals for the mentally ill that it survived longest, well into the nineteenth century, Hooke's translation of the recreational gallery from the domestic to the institutional realm inspired Wren at Chelsea and Greenwich.

Discipline

Mandeville's paragraph about the hospitals, quoted at the beginning of this chapter, would have reminded many readers of the controversy about a permanent standing army, which had been inescapable around 1700.[65] Here and elsewhere he signalled his acceptance of a professional soldiery, something bound up with hospitals for veterans, and with luxury too. The professionalism, or not, of warriors was an issue reaching the very core of a 'perception of human personality . . . that to be a person one must be a political agent, and that to be a citizen one must be a bearer of arms'.[66] This is the ideal of classical, 'civic humanism', and by its terms the standing army was substituting mercenaries for the citizen militia, and for duty, money values of the kind promoted by City and court interests that reduced social relations to a pernicious, raw simplicity dictated by the terms of commerce.[67]

The seventeenth and eighteenth centuries 'discovered the body as object and target of power'.[68] Michel Foucault's analysis of the manufacture of *corps dociles* can be used to recast the ideal just described as a precognitive antipathy to the forms of discipline accompanying standing armies, as distinct from the gentlemanly militia and the 'vassalage' relation it exemplifies. Vassalage was a 'highly coded, but distant relation of submission, which bore less on the operations of the body than on the products of labour and the ritual marks of allegiance'. Civic humanists would have agreed with Foucault's definition, after suitable translation: their vassalage to higher authority did not touch the independence that was the essence of personal and civic virtue. Vassalage may in turn be distinguished from another older form of discipline, that of the conventual enclosure.[69] To understand the way in which the late seventeenth-century military hospitals served as emblems of the older disciplines, especially the monastic, while acting on behalf of the new, is to go a long way towards understanding them.

Foucault is clear on the ways in which earlier disciplinary relations and types differed from the new 'projects of docility' (*schémas de docilité*).[70] He is less interested in the part that money played in these new disciplines, the money to which distaste for mercenaries points us. The hospitals for veterans stood not only as Foucauldian enclosures, the 'protected place of disciplinary monotony', but as substitutes for the cash transactions that (any civic humanist could have told you) brought corruption in their wake. In this way they represented an ideal to which they were, after all, radically antithetical. As institutions each came to manage, not only buildings and their inmates, but an entire pension system embracing many more men than could be accommodated. At first, however, it seemed as if all the invalids qualified for admittance to Kilmainham and Chelsea (reckoned as 5 per cent of the armies' establishments) could enter the hospitals, which Charles II imagined serving in place of the pensions.[71] The buildings were reifications of a new administration, as if orderly bookkeeping had touched down and solidified into masonry. As replacements for money, they also affirmed an old kind of charitable hospitality, and the older kind of discipline that goes with it. These things, at least, were part of what the hospitals were, and were supposed to be. The cost of these affirmations would be high. The hospitals administered a system that was, at least in England, far more open to corruption than that which the county magistrates ran before, partly because in-pensioning, accommodating the men, was anyway so expensive.[72]

Historians used to exclaim at the way that the construction of the veterans' hospitals took priority over that of clinical hospitals for the military, but how useful would the latter then have seemed? A sick or wounded soldier or sailor is first treated in camp or on board ship, but this was impracticable if there were too many casualties; or undesirable, if the man suffered from a contagious illness. Then he was sent away, or put ashore (most seventeenth-century English naval warfare was conducted in coastal waters), to enter a temporary hospital fitted up, usually in houses but in barns if necessary, by a regimental or naval surgeon or by a private contractor, perhaps a local surgeon. They undertook to shelter, feed, bandage, and physic the sick in return for salaries and/or a contract payment per man.[73] Beds could be rented in suitable civil hospitals, if there were any (the south of England, aside from London itself, had none), but the London hospitals, St Thomas' and St Bartholomew's, considered the payments inadequate compensation for the nuisance: special regulations had to be drawn up at the former, for example, to enforce an eight o'clock bedtime and a ban on smoking in bed.[74] Easier in this respect were the Savoy Hospital and Ely House, which as a Commissioner for Sick and Wounded John Evelyn obtained for naval use, because they were simply buildings, not institutions: the Savoy was moribund and on its way to dissolution.[75]

Though used only during wartime, the Savoy and Ely House had a legacy as dedicated hospitals (which also held disabled pensioners) entirely under military control.[76] Evelyn wanted an 'Infirmarie' of 400 or 500 beds built at Chatham, Kent. Encouraged early in 1666 by the king, Evelyn went to the Navy Board, which was also enthusiastic,

> but I saw no mon[e]y, though a very moderate expense, would have saved thousands to his Majestie and be[e]n much more commodious for the cure and quartering [of] our sick & wounded, than the dispersing of them into private houses, where many more Chirurgeones, & tenders [attendants] were necessary, & the people tempted to debaucherie.[77]

This was already an old refrain, and it echoed in English naval records for the next century. Hospitals for the sick and wounded run by the Navy itself would save money both by economies of scale and by cutting out rapacious contractors; they would enable the care of greater numbers, prevent desertion or at least get it down to tolerable levels, and keep sailors from the drinking and gambling increasingly defined as problems for their health (they wagered their clothes) as well as for their discipline. For all the debauchery, however, care for the acutely ill and wounded was best organized on the spot. Evelyn himself envisaged the Savoy restored as a hospital for the poor and his new infirmary serving other uses when peace came.[78] The last he would have sited at Chatham, a major port, because transporting casualties was difficult. It took seven months, for example, for 300 men wounded in August 1704 at the battle of Blenheim (a village on the Danube) to reach Chelsea, where the Board admitted forty-one 'whose wounds are run[n]ing'.[79]

The difference between a hospital for veterans and one for the sick and wounded is exemplified by the order of November 1690, to establish a temporary hospital *at* the Kilmainham Royal Hospital, but even the 'fixed' hospital then set up was insufficient for a moving war, and a 'marching' (or 'flying') hospital was ordered a few months later. This was to consist of twenty-five tents, each 20 feet long and capable of holding eight men on four beds, 'to be made so that at the end they may be joined together and that there may be a tent pole to every tenth foot, so that in every tent may lie 200 men'.[80] Compared to this fleet 'architecture', Kilmainham was truly static but stasis, and with stasis monumentality, was arguably its most important attribute; like the other hospitals, it was to stand as a reminder of a new and permanent fiscal discipline. However, given the choice between the monument and the tents (for which read, any kind of temporary shelter) for the acutely ill and wounded, informed opinion preferred the tents. They spared the men the travel, and kept them close to the officers whose duty it was to keep an eye on them (and their guards), a job the surgeons did not want.[81] Temporary accommodation was, finally, uncommitted to any *place*, where the diseases brought by the acutely ill, or engendered by the wounds of others, might accumulate.[82]

Religious military camps and the Hôtel des Invalides

Seventeenth-century French political and religious authority worried incessantly about what it perceived as the new pauperism and the civil and moral threat this posed. One manifestation was the foundation in 1656 of the Paris Hôpital Général des pauvres, the emblem of Foucault's 'great confinement'.[83] The Hôpital Général, of which many more would be founded in France, was not a hospital for the sick. The 'generality' referred to the variety of *maisons* that joined the organization before 1781 and held the aged, the infirm, abandoned children, beggars, vagrants, and prostitutes – all of whom right-thinking people did not want on the streets. These men and women, the deserving and the undeserving poor, were put to work, and to prayer.[84]

Its backers envisaged something truly global in the Hôpital's powers of disposition, hopes well represented by an outline plan made in 1658 by the royal architect Antoine Duval, who was close to the aristocratic *milieu dévot* then so concerned for the spiritual welfare of the poor. This was for the rebuilding of St Denis de la Salpêtrière ('La Salpêtrière'), the *maison* on Paris's south-eastern fringe whose foundation accompanied that of the Hôpital Général itself. Duval was instructed to 'obviate the inconvenience of the irregular buildings' of the old saltpetre factory, then in use for the paupers; his plan shows a symmetrical grid of twenty-one courts formed by residential blocks and dividing walls, each named after the occupants of the surrounding buildings.[85] French was then rich in terms for the different species of sturdy beggars comprising the undeserving poor, though the *bons pauvres*, reduced by misfortune, did not require much further discrimination. The plan resembles those of French hospitals and Jesuit *collèges* built since the end of the previous century and the ultimate model for all of them was the Escorial, built in 1563–84 to the designs of Juan de Herrera for Philip II of Spain. In 1664 Ann Fanshawe described this 'unparalleled fabric of the world', 'with seventeen courts, and gardens therunto. Every court contains a different office. . . . It contains a very fine palace, a convent, and a college and hospital; all which are exactly well kept and royally furnished.'[86] The Escorial was not only magnificent, but notably multi-functional. Duval's orderly anatomy of poverty was never achieved: as replanned by Louis Le Vau and perhaps his successor Libéral Bruant, and finally completed in 1756, the Salpêtrière was an open arrangement of blocks and parterres.[87] The most spectacular French realization of the type was the Hôtel des Invalides, begun in 1671 to Bruant's designs.

Behind its moated ditch and the great stretch of its entrance front, the Invalides centres on its Royal Court lined at ground level by arcading (Figures 12 and 13). Behind the arcades were the once-celebrated refectories, which together could seat 1,500 men at a time.[88] Above these, behind the first floor's open 'gallery' – as *A pattern of a . . . well-governed hospital* (1695), the English translation of Le

12. An engraving (1831) after A. C. Pugin, of the entrance front at the Hôtel des Invalides. The print does well by the distinctive tympanum with its relief of Louis XIV on horseback.

13. The Royal Court at the Invalides, in an engraving (1830) after A. C. Pugin.

Jeune de Boulencourt's *Description générale* (1683) called it – were rows of rooms, each accommodating several pensioned soldiers. On the second and third floors of the wings flanking the Royal Court, and throughout those surrounding the subsidiary courts, these rooms run on both sides of central corridors. The keys to Le Jeune's plans identify each floor's corridors in the plural, but as sharing a common dedication (like a church) and comprising a single route around the entire building: the 'Corridors de St Charlemagne qui r[è]gnent partout', for example ('round about all the House', said the *Pattern*, which had no floor plans and got a bit confused without them, 'is called, the *Gallery* or *Ward* of Charlemaine').[89] The whiff of monarchy in *règnent* seems appropriate, but the awkwardness of the phrasing reminds us that corridors were then no more common in France than they were in England. The Invalides' miles of corridors were in their way as remarkable as Bethlem's galleries, built a couple of years later.

The Invalides did not yield much to the Escorial in functional complexity. It was a hospital for the sick and wounded (the infirmary, seen on the upper left of Figure 14, was itself the third biggest hospital in Paris and, it was long thought, one of the best),[90] *hospice* for pauper officers and soldiers, and barracks for old soldiers who could still perform guard and honour duties. Historians now emphasize its policing functions, looking at the Invalides as its neighbours might have done – neighbours loosely speaking, for, like the Salpêtrière's, the site was relatively remote, on the still-windswept plaine de Grenelle to the west of the Faubourg St Germain. (The *Pattern* described this isolation as 'surrounded by pleasant Fields and Pastures, which render the Situation of it no less Agreeable, than the Air that is breathed there makes it Healthful'.)[91] Drink and plunder may no longer, in 1670, have been the more or less accepted perquisites of French military service (pillage, Cardinal Richelieu had said, encourages the men) but former soldiers, including deserters, were a threat to civil order; they had after all been trained to fight. As an institution for keeping its inmates off the streets, the Invalides was analogous to the Hôpital Général.[92]

Like the Hôpital Général, too, the Invalides was supposed to be suffused with piety, and specifically conceived as a kind of monastery, where the invalids prepared for a better world by attending church daily and practising handicrafts. They were 'heaven's militia'.[93] Architecturally, monasticism was suggested by the arcading of the Royal Court, nobly and austerely formed by arches on piers with a continuous band at impost level, by the endless rows of '*Dormitories*, or Sleeping Rooms, as in Convents',[94] and most importantly by the hospital's enclosure, behind its moats and walls, and a self-sufficiency graphically confirmed by Le Jeune's six floor plans, from granaries in the attics down to what might be the world's vastest wine cellars. The arrangement of the double church, with its enormous basilican retrochoir (the 'Eglise des Soldats') accessible from the hospital

14. The ground-floor plan of the Hôtel Royal des Invalides, from Le Jeune de Boulencourt's sumptuous publication. The key has 121 items, beginning with the chapel's dome.

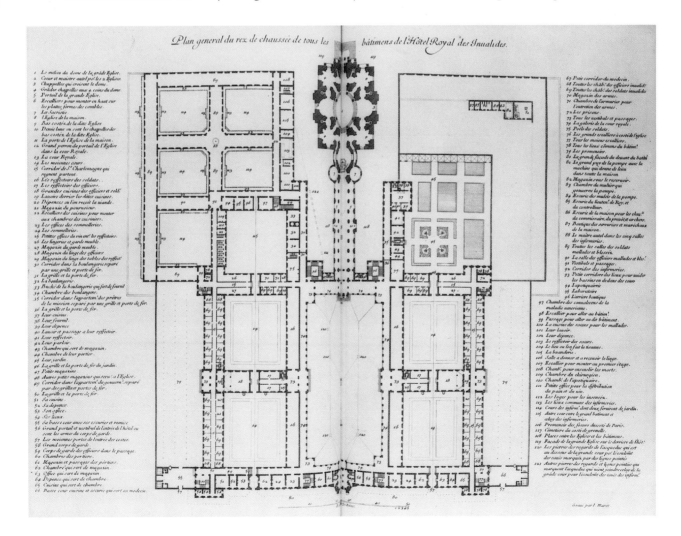

Plan general du rez de chaussée de tous les bâtimens de l'Hôtel Royal des Invalides.

and, on the other side of the altar, the centralized nave ('Dôme') with its door to the outer world is the most precisely conventual of all.[95]

The monastery, wrote Alberti, reversing the equation, is a 'form of religious military camp, where a number of men . . . may come together for a life of piety and virtue'.[96] The disciplines of the monastery, a word deriving from the ecclesiastical Greek for 'living alone', however differ from those exercised in the hospitals. Chelsea's government, borrowed from the Invalides, was that of a regiment of foot and its pensioners were, like Kilmainham's, to be 'disciplined and regulated as near to the Practice of War in Towns and Garrisons as properly may be'.[97] That regulation came to embrace the architectural differentiation of class. As first designed, Chelsea's accommodation was relatively uniform compared to that at the Invalides, whose plan always maintained the social distinctions, but that seems not to have anticipated the entry of troops whose rank was equivalent to that of a private of foot, but whose pay and status were not: the yeomen of the regiments of horse, and the gentlemen of the Life Guards.[98] With the hospital's enlargement under James II, Wren gave these men not only their own courts within the complex, but their own kinds of (shared) rooms, something further removing practice from the conventual ideal of equality under God. Proponents of the new institutions and of the projects of docility that they exemplified none the less required a metaphor with which to explain the hospitals, and the docility, to themselves. When Evelyn wrote of the men at Chelsea 'as in a Coledge or Monastrie' and subject to 'Laws & Orders . . . in every respect as strickt as in any religious Convent', he was perhaps recalling the derelict Chelsea College then still on the site (which James I had founded as a kind of Protestant order of 'able Divines for refuting Errors and Heresies'), but he was also applying the most forceful image of a cleanly bachelor life available to him.[99] For the French, the convent remained useful for indicating sweet orderliness. In the later eighteenth century Jean-Noël Hallé called Greenwich 'as clean and salubrious as a convent'; and Pierre-Jean Grosley described its 'neatness which may be compared to the cells of our nuns', as well as old sailors reading the folio bibles supplied to each of the galleries, while others waited their turn.[100] Queen Mary had reportedly wanted, without metaphor, to put them 'in a probable way of ending their days in the fear of God'.[101]

The second hospital for veterans was built in Ireland; Charles II approved the construction of the Royal Hospital at Kilmainham near Dublin in 1679. Begun the next year, by 1684 it was ready for the first of the 300 invalids who, in the king's words, 'by reason of Age, Wounds, or other Infirmities' incurred, 'are grown unfit to be any longer continued in Our Service'.[102] At Kilmainham four arcaded ranges surround a square court (Figure 15); one holds the dining hall and chapel. The rooms for the men (four to a room, two to a bed) had their own doors to the open gallery on the ground floor, or to the corridor above it. This arrangement is that of the Invalides, or at least of those of its floors without a central corridor. The resemblance extends to such details as the impost moulding on the arcade piers, and the semicircular tympana over Kilmainham's external doors (Figure 16), which echo that over the Invalides' entrance.

The hospital of the Invalides, as opposed to its church, has by way of classical orders only two pairs of Ionic pilasters flanking the entrance, and columns in the vestibule behind. Bruant seems to have rejected classical architectonic display in favour of a witty, old-fashioned use of figuration: the fans of trophies over the entrance-front dormer window and Louis XIV as a *cavalier* in profile on the tympanum of the great arch there; on the roofline of the Royal Court behind are rearing horses and dormers wearing suits of armour (Figure 17).[103] The carving, which did not come cheap, may have signalled a kind of austerity in its archaism; it was not conventionally stylish, or modern in the Paris of 1670. At Kilmainham, more lavish in one respect in using the orders for door surrounds, the tympana are filled by rich trophy piles of cannons, exploding grenades, pikes, torches, shields, and winged and plumed helmets.[104] Greenwich, abundantly stylar, also has a great deal of figurative carving (there would have been more, had funds permitted), and Bethlem boasted the most famous architectural sculpture in England: Raving and Melancholy Madness (Figure 10). In the next century, such decoration was explicitly identified as a central attribute of buildings whose publicness had as much to do with public instruction and exhortation as public access or function, and even – as the architect

15. The Royal Hospital, Kilmainham, now the Irish Museum of Modern Art.

James Gandon (1742–1823) suggested – with the dissemination of public wealth among the wide variety of crafts and professions that make the decoration.[105] Though Chelsea was built with (or at least planned to have) martial reliefs in the recessed rectangles above the hall and chapel windows,[106] by and large it eschews obvious statements about fighting valour and regal munificence. Perhaps, however, Wren's centrepieces to the ward blocks (Figure 18), which can be alternately read, visually, as a temple front interrupted by an

(above) 16. One of Kilmainham's semicircular tympana, carved in pine.

17. The roofline of the Invalides' Royal Court. The specifications for the hospital's masonry work fill 1,000 pages in large folio.

18. Chelsea Hospital,
the centre of one of the
ward wings.

institutional grid of windows or as a grid obscured by a temple front, comprise
an even wittier illustration of the ambiguous position of the old soldiers, at
once the king's dependants, or children, and his person's defenders.

Chelsea and the cell

The only single rooms, at least for the veterans, at the Invalides were the 'loges
pour les insenséz', for the mad, the tiniest of the spaces shown on Le Jeune's
ground-floor plan (Figure 14), in the wing beneath the infirmary crossing at top
left. 'Lodges' was how *A Pattern of a . . . well-governed hospital* translated Le
Jeune's *loges*.[107] The translator was not being delicate, just incompetent: in
English in 1695 such rooms were called cells, without prejudice. The word had
not acquired penal overtones, because prisoners did not yet live alone, unless
they were the subjects of exceptional punishment, or privilege.[108] Bethlem's
rooms were 'cells', but so were the readers' cubicles in Wren's near-
contemporary Trinity College Library, Cambridge (1676–84).[109]

Bethlem's cells were celebrated. 'A hundred Rooms in curious order Stand / Each with its Bed and Furniture at hand' ('Bethlehems beauty', ll. 45–46). Hatton emphasized the asylum's size, to demonstrate not so much its magnificence as the capacity and healthfulness of an institution whose governors provided every patient with his or her own 'Room in a good Air, proper Physick, and Diet gratis'.[110] John Strype's great new (1720) edition of John Stow's *Survey* of London also linked the cells with the regimen: 'As for the Care and Cure of the Patients, here is undoubtedly the greatest Provision made for them of any publick Charity in the World; each having a convenient Room and Apartment to themselves where they are locked up a[t] Nights'.[111] 'Apartment' conveys that in these spaces the mad were supposed to be apart from, safe from, one another.

Christopher Wren's old mentor Thomas Willis advised, in the ominously titled *De anima brutorum* (1672), that 'Furious Mad-men are sooner, and more certainly cured by punishments, and hard usage, in a strait room, than by Physick or Medicines'. Willis believed that frantic or chronic lunacy had to be left to cure itself, within disciplinary constraint. Such medical nihilism however also constitutes optimism, about the therapeutic possibilities of the physical form and domestic organization of hospitals with such strait – that is, narrow and/or secure – rooms:

> In inveterate and habitual Madness, the sick seldom submit to any Medical Cure; but such being placed in Bedlam, or an Hospital for Mad people, by the ordinary discipline of the place, either at length return to themselves, or else they are kept from doing hurt, either to themselves, or to others.[112]

Protesting Bethlem's 'very great impropriety and cruelty of allowing the poor unhappy sufferers to become spectacles for the brutal curiosity of the populace', John Aikin was unwilling to credit its building with an arrangement that in 1771 was self-evidently desirable (the 'absolute necessity of a separate room or cell for every patient is very apparent')[113] and perhaps older than he knew. At Bishopsgate too, Bethlem's charges seemingly inhabited long chambers partitioned into cubicles.[114]

The word 'cell' was originally purely architectural. The Latin *cella* means a small apartment, especially one flanked by several others; it had crossed into English by the fourteenth century, when 'cell' was used for conventual houses. It was Hooke who began using the word in its other modern sense. In *Micrographia* (1665), on his investigations with one of the first microscopes, we can trace Hooke's search for a word to describe, metaphorically, the tiny structures he saw in a thin slice of cork (Figure 19): pores? boxes? He happily hit upon 'cell', which evoked not just their uniformity and distinctness, but the evident strength of these structures' slender partition walls.[115] Not until the nineteenth century was the biological cell considered the fundamental unit in the physical structure of animals or plants; 'cell theory' may, oddly but understandably, have been encouraged by architectural applications at places like Bethlem, Chelsea, and Greenwich. In providing cells at the last two Wren departed, as Robinson at Kilmainham had not, from the example of the Invalides. In this way his hospitals

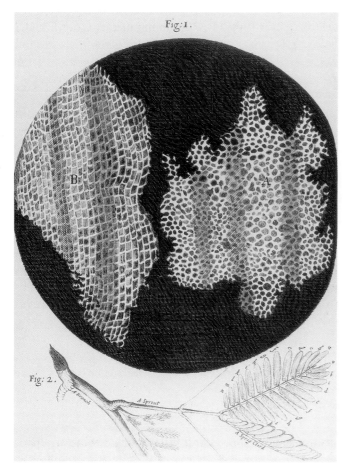

19. Slices of cork viewed under 'magnifying glasses', from Robert Hooke's *Micrographia* (1665).

not only lent themselves to monastic metaphors, they approached the old but still approved arrangement of clinical hospital wards.

In recognition of the scarcity of hospitals still accepting the sick on a temporary basis ('for lack of them, [an] infinite number of poor needy people miserably daily die'), Henry VII founded the Savoy Hospital, with one hundred 'beds garnished, to receive and lodge nightly one hundred poor folks'.[116] The royal foundation was magnificently equipped; 20 shillings was spent on the workmanship of each bedstead, which had a curtain 'on its outer side' and a 'seyling' over, as well as, evidently, a chest beside it.[117] The paupers were granted the modern comforts in what was in some ways a deliberately old-fashioned foundation. It would be interesting to know how many of the 108 bedsteads survived into the later seventeenth century, which saw the Savoy's takeover by the military, but it is not necessary to posit any precise source for a very old arrangement of beds that themselves formed a sort of cell, and which remained self-evidently sensible until its identification, in the second half of the eighteenth century, as a dangerous impediment to air circulation. (Or, alternatively, as a funnel for air: as ever, ventilation's students could have it all ways.)[118] When, in the mid-1660s, Hooke's future friend the naval surgeon James Yonge found himself a prisoner of war in a Rotterdam hospital, he counted himself lucky:

> It was a fair house with several long rooms, one apartment being for chirurgical concerns, two for physical for men and another apartment, remote from these, for women. . . . [Our room] was about 22 or 24 feet broad, and I believe near 100 feet long, of good height, with glass windows on each side. The beds were enclosed like cabins the whole length of the house, each having a window in it . . .[119]

The beds offered the privacy and warmth that the patients might require from time to time, and Yonge thought that his ward was airy and light, or so we can infer from his mentioning its height, relative slenderness, and the windows on both sides.

In 1680, exceptionally, the English Board of Ordnance at the king's prompting prepared to build a hospital in Portsmouth for the 'accommodation of ye sicke men of ye sd Garrison from time to time'. Its construction was financed by the sale of £1,500 worth of timber from 'dotard & decayed trees' from the royal New Forest.[120] The hospital was two-storey, with a total of four wards, each 40 by 30 feet. The contract specifications, and what remained of the hospital in 1947, suggest that ten beds were arranged back-to-back in two rows down the middle of each ward. Each bed would form its own enclosure,

> 4 foot wide by 6 foot 3 inches long, $1\frac{1}{2}$ foot high of deal board. In front of each curtain rods with two hooks and a corni[ce] at the top of each bedstead. From the ground floor to the top of each bedstead is eight foot high and the top covered with whole deal board close jointed for the full breadth of the bedstead. Partitions between each bedstead of deal board . . .[121]

The contract was signed in 1681 with the brothers Thomas and John Fitch, builders of great experience that in John's case included regular collaboration on Hooke's major projects of the previous decade, including Bethlem.[122] Thomas Fitch may have designed the Portsmouth garrison hospital, unique for its period and in which Charles II continued to take a particular interest; none the less it seems to have lasted only until 1694, when the building was turned into a barracks.[123] Measuring 120 by 35 feet overall,[124] its proportions resembled Bethlem's, though its arrangement of bedstead-cells did not. That did anticipate Chelsea's, where at 6 foot square the cabins were wider but slightly shorter than Portsmouth's.

John Evelyn first spoke about Chelsea Hospital with Sir Stephen Fox, the king's prime mover in the project, in September 1681, four months after the date on the Portsmouth contract; Charles laid the foundation stone in February 1682, not quite two years after Kilmainham's start. We imagine that Wren anticipated the work with the 'great Pleasure and chearfulness' with which (Nicholas Hawksmoor wrote) he later embarked on Greenwich.[125] We know that he undertook it with an eye to the Invalides; Kilmainham was the other antecedent within the new building type. The rejection of the prototypes' court enclosures for a three-sided arrangement open to the river was predictable, given Chelsea's site and John Webb's twenty-year-old projects for palaces similarly arrayed, at Whitehall and Greenwich.[126] Though Wren extended them to make smaller, though still open, side courts after 1685, as they were first planned Chelsea's ward blocks were effectively isolated, attached to the central block only at their north ends. We can, as Margaret Whinney suggested, infer Wren's 'practical humanity' from the light and air this admitted to the wards,[127] and in this respect, as well as in his creation of galleries serving as recreational as well as circulation spaces, Wren showed that it was Bethlem that had provided his most useful single model.

In fact, aside from the infirmary wing and some of the other accommodation undertaken after 1685, whose plans (four-bedded rooms opening off corridors) do recall the Invalides,[128] the latter's influence on Chelsea was more organizational than formal. This is not to say that it fell outside the architect's purview. Wren 'prescrib'd the Statutes and whole Oeconomy of the House', according to *Parentalia*, and until 1712 he sat on the small committees and commissions that successively managed the in-pensioners and (their main activity) the out-pensioners.[129] This is an extension of an architect's normal responsibilities, though Wren had predecessors within this short tradition. As it happened, he was notably trustworthier than they. William Robinson, who also served as Deputy Paymaster of the Irish forces among many other offices, held a succession of positions at Kilmainham, culminating in the acting governorship.

20. Chelsea Hospital in a view, first published in 1744, also showing the famous Rotunda in the Ranelagh pleasure gardens. One-sixth of the early expenditure on the Hospital, tens of thousands of pounds, went on the gardens and terraces.

Robinson's friend the gentleman-architect Richard Jones, Earl of Ranelagh was a commissioner for Kilmainham's construction and had much to do with Chelsea's; he was also the English Paymaster-General and therefore the Chelsea Hospital Treasurer.[130] Such varied responsibilities arose, not just out of military-architectural practice, but out of a more specific recognition that at the hospitals physical form was inseparable from disciplinary organization.

As designed for Charles II, Chelsea Hospital consisted of a single quadrangle (now called the Figure Court) open to the great terrace and causeway running down to the Thames. Beneath them were the 'water gardens' and orchards (Figure 20), destroyed when that part of the river was embanked in the nineteenth century.[131] The loss has perhaps distorted our impression of the hospital, whose dimensions determined the lines of these constructions and plantings. Chelsea's austerity would not have been softened by such a foreground, but it would have appeared more consciously elegant.[132] The Figure Court is flanked by the ward wings, whose river pavilions held the Governor's and the Lieutenant-Governor's houses. Behind is the north wing, containing the chapel and dining hall. Wren intended the infirmary to be housed in the three storeys above the vestry and chaplain's apartments, east of the chapel's apse, but the arrangement changed with the decision to enlarge the hospital.[133] The smaller Light Horse and Infirmary courts were added to each side during James II's reign, increasing the length of the north front to 800 feet; several detached buildings were put up under William and Mary.

The ward wings are longitudinally divided, internally, by a brick wall on each of four storeys, including the attic (Figure 21). Central passageways connect the paired 'Long Wards', the 200-foot galleries formed in this way, and give access to the lavatories in the projections on the wings' outer sides. The galleries, warmed by two chimney-stacks with fireplaces facing both ways, each contained twenty-four wooden 'cells' or cabins, lined up against the internal wall and separated by Doric pilasters. 'The space between the pilasters is filled with four fielded and moulded panels, two of which form the door, while the other two screen the bed, the upper one hung to open like a shutter, and give the inmate of the berth a view outside at will.'[134] In 1710 Von Uffenbach was unimpressed: these 'apartments are no more than closets boarded off from the long and none too broad passages'.[135] Beside the doors at each end of the galleries, at the end of the line of cells, were larger ones for sergeants, four to a floor. They projected a few feet clear of the rest, permitting a view down the ward; it was a true enfilade, appropriate to the institution. The sergeant's cabin held, besides his own halberd, the muskets for his mess of twelve men.[136] Each mess had its own fireplace; two messes formed a gallery, which had its own table in the Great Hall; two galleries, one floor, formed a company.[137]

'In the first instance', Foucault has written, 'discipline proceeds from the distribution of individuals in space' and the 'disciplinary space is always, basically, cellular'.[138] Architecture generates, or makes possible, the disciplinary *schémas* at least as much as they define the architecture. At Chelsea, under construction for a decade before any men were moved in, the physical structure does seem to have anticipated the organizational structure with which it dovetailed so

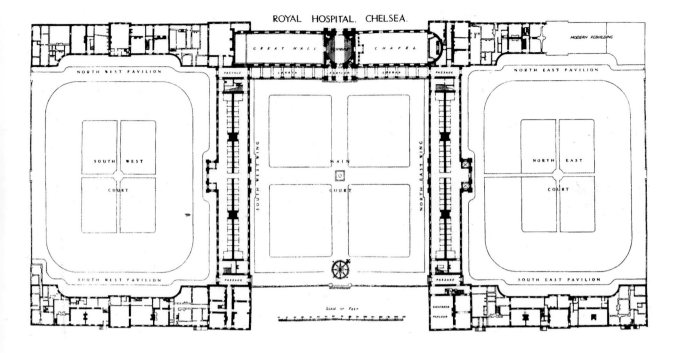

21. Chelsea's plan, as recorded in 1927.

closely.[139] Wren's design was ready to show to the Archbishop of Canterbury by May 1682 and an undated memorandum that Wren probably drafted at the same time describes the proposed hospital:

> The two sides of ye [Figure] Courte are double building in three stories and garrets . . . [together] containing 16 galleries, in each of which are 24 Cells divided off with partitions of wa[i]nscot, and two larger Cells for corporalls in each gallery, accommodating in all 416 single beds, & each gallery hath two large chimnies and cisternes and conveniencys for water. 4 great Staircases at both ends of each Wing convey to all the Galleries.[140]

The cells, by definition to be understood in replication along a gallery, were parts that stood for the whole. A specimen gallery in the west wing was completed in 1685 to show the king, and Ranelagh recalled how he had furnished, in 1688,

> forthwith two of the sixteen Galleries with beds and all other necessaries; . . . the King . . . came on purpose to Chelsea to see the said two Galleries when furnished, with which being well pleased he ordered that the rest be furnished in like manner; that before that could possibly be done the Revolution happened.[141]

The cell was also the space that would enclose, and as such could stand in for, each human recipient of the charity. It might thus also encourage potential donors, including monarchs. Money was a problem even early on at Greenwich, and just before Christmas 1698 the members of the Fabrick Committee decided to show the other Royal Commissioners (of whom there were a couple of hundred) and other potential subscribers the progress of the works by having the joiner finish 'one of the Middle Cabbins in one of the Wards'.[142] (Though it had already decided that the King Charles Block be 'finished with Wainscot and as near the manner, as may be, as Chelsea College is', in October 1698 it resolved to have 'curtains before the beds instead of wainscoat', probably to save money.)[143] But only ten men, all members of the Fabrick Committee anyway, plus the Astronomer Royal, came to look at the cabin.[144]

In 1786, the writer Sophie von la Roche visited Bethlem. There, perhaps confused by some account of the hospital's medieval origins, and undeterred by the idea of a Baroque monastery (commoner in her native Germany than in England), she thought that Hooke's building had been a monastery, something confirmed by the sight of the cells.[145] She made good use of her mistake. Where formerly an 'abundant piety . . . peopled the cells with voluntary entries; now the grief of unrequited love, the pangs of vanity, ambition, hate and affliction . . . bring – oh, how many – hither!' Foucault could have done a lot with that. The spaces once allocated to monastic discipline, the voluntary mastery of one's self, now held individuals who were in Bethlem only because of their failure to regulate their sins (vanity, hate) and their emotions (love, grief).

There was an old understanding that almshouse inmates needed what Defoe called a 'study, or large closet, for their retreat'.[146] The terms of late medieval hospital foundations had sometimes specified the 'need for seclusion as an aid to prayer, reading, and meditation'; this, and not warmth or privacy, was the ultimate functional justification for cells.[147] It was in this spirit Evelyn proposed, in an early conversation about Chelsea, the inclusion of a 'Librarie, & mentioned severall books &c. since some souldiers might possibly be studious, when they were at this leasure to reco[l]lect',[148] and that Grosley remarked the Greenwich Bible-reading a century later. The men's cubicles at Greenwich had glass windows, reported La Roche, who sincerely loved cells. In these little houses the men made their own worlds, with 'sea and land charts, with the voyages they have made marked out on them, or spots where storms have been overcome or battles fought, where they have lost an arm or a leg, or conquered an enemy ship'.[149] The old sailors however read their Bibles in the warmth of the galleries with their fireplaces, just as they ate their meals in the halls. Communal dining was still the rule at some almshouses, too: they, like the hospitals, maintained old forms of domestic organization. By then, however, most almshouses had sprouted the chimneys indicating that every person had his or her own fireplace.[150]

Bethlem's galleries were identified as autonomous subjects of celebration, graceful and ample spaces; Chelsea's and Greenwich's were not, though La Roche admired the panelling and the rugs in the latter's. At all three hospitals, however, the compression of the accommodation (too small for the individual chimneys that would not have been wise at Bethlem anyway) required the enclosed communal spaces that served for recreation, as well as circulation, which the almshouses did not need and did not have. Can the difference also be accounted for by the types of inmate? Were the soldiers and sailors, as well as the lunatics, thought to require the discipline, Foucault's *surveillance*, which is not just permitted but manifested by that extra spatial layer, the gallery?[151] The question seems important, but the disciplinary significance of the closed gallery was not felt in England at the time, or was anyway not articulated.

Though the palace was too limited for Bethlem and the military hospitals, which embodied forms of discipline that required a conventual metaphor too, the comparison was traditional, and as a way of affiliating the hospitals with older institutional and domestic types it made sense. The hospitals were old-fashioned buildings, cellular in the sense of additive as well as in the form of their accommodation, and their broad functions were not dissimilar to those of great houses. These functions included the hospitality offered to casual visitors who came, in part, to admire galleries and cells and we are struck by the keenness with which the Bethlem governors anticipated their public and considered how the grilles in the galleries might affect the view. The hospitals also encouraged the development of new ways of praising architecture, which is to say of thinking about it, that increasingly attended to its specific place in the public world.

Chapter 3
Publicity and public buildings

My Introduction quoted the correspondence between the Earl of Rochester and Henry Savile, when in 1678 Savile found himself in the house in Leather Lane, finishing the 'last act of a long teddious course of Physick' for venereal disease. To his news that their friend Mrs Roberts was among those 'met here from several corners as mad folks do in Bethlem', Rochester replied with a sketch for a masque, a 'small romance' on the theme of 'unfortunate lovers': 'I would . . . make the sun with his dishevelled rays gild the tops of the palaces in Leather Lane'.[1] The masque may have been prompted by Savile's theatrical metaphor (the 'last act') and the gilt-topped palaces by the reference to Bethlem, whose new building had then been open for two years. Underneath its heraldic, gilded vane, a dragon rampant on a sphere (see Figure 9, p. 40), Bethlem was full of unfortunate lovers too, supposedly.[2]

Bethlem's enormous stretch across Lower Moorfields was enabled by an unusually elongated plan, which was never published. To that extent it is like a backdrop for a masque, a 'pageant' as they were called;[3] it is sheer appearance. That appearance can exemplify, too, what Bruno Zevi has described as a 'Baroque' conception of urban space, by which the

> walls of a building, and especially its façades, no longer constitute the limit of the interior space of the building, but of the interior space of the street or square, and are thus to be characterized in terms of the urbanistic void they help create.[4]

The urban spaces that Bethlem and the military hospitals made were remarkable enough in themselves, and the space can be metaphorically extended. Printed books and pictures explained the hospitals' architecture, equipped them with anecdotes, and showed them to be serving the public, as well as their immediate charitable objects. They made the hospitals visible to distant audiences.

Restoration

After the preliminaries, which included the decision that the new Bethlem building should be a single pile, a committee of about twenty-two governors, which

22. Smith's unique view (1812) of Bethlem's south side, hard by London Wall, shows a building about to be demolished. A pathetic hand holding what seems to be a windmill-toy emerges from one of the cells, whose windows were unglazed.

met independently of the general Court, began taking care of construction. Its first three reports, read into the Court minutes in October 1674, are almost entirely about the wall that was to surround the hospital.[5]

Every eighteenth-century London topographer recited the measures of Bethlem's walls: 680 feet long, 70 deep.[6] They rivalled the stretch of the ancient London Wall that then ran 9 feet away from Bethlem's south front, and which 'in some measure, acts as a screen' to it, as the antiquarian John Thomas Smith wrote in 1815.[7] He made an etching of the screen (Figure 22), behind which we see a huge chimney-stack and grilled cell windows. On each side of the building began the new wall, which would be 14 feet high (the governors' committee decided), with a 'Coping ... intended to p'vent the Escape of Lunatikes', around the yards where they would 'walk and take the aire in order to [aid] their

23. A detail of White's
print of Bethlem (Figure 5).

Recovery'. At the front the wall would be only 8 feet high, so 'that the Grace &
Ornament of the said intended Building may better appeare towards Morefeilds'.
Eight feet would be high enough because the inmates would not be allowed to
walk in the front yard. For the benefit of spectators closer to Bethlem's 'Ornament & Beauty', six apertures would be introduced into the front wall in the form
of what the committee called 'open Iron Grates', each at least 10 feet broad
(Figure 23). Roger Pratt associated such 'transparent windows' with grand Continental houses, where they were admitted into courtyard walls to permit views
of 'beautiful objects' outside: 'gardens, woods, walks, fountains, statues, etc.'. At
Bethlem they were there to let people look in the other direction, a reversal that
can stand for the governors' intense concern for the visibility of their future
building's ornament and beauty.[8] The grates were precisely analogous to those
planned for the Bethlem galleries but not at first installed after the dispute,
eighteen months later, described in the last chapter.

By mid-1675 the building committee faced a decision important enough to be
referred to the general Court of Governors and in July the Court decided, after
argument, to face the hospital's middle and end pavilions with stone. The
cheaper option was to set stone dressings against brick, which is how the lower
wings between were treated. The pavilions were very prominently roofed, too,

and the cost of the cupolas similarly gave the governors pause a couple of months later.[9] Their construction was however soon approved, and the pavilions indeed became the 'Three ornamentall fronts', the 'Three highbuildings', the 'three high ornamentall buildings', as the minute book was describing them.[10] The stone and its carving into pediments, Corinthian pilasters, swags, festoons, lion skin, and coats of arms were manifestly magnificent, as was Bethlem's sheer stylishness. The pavilions' balustraded platforms and cupolas, in particular, were then a wonderful fashion at new houses; even if never used, as they perhaps were not at all the houses, or at Bethlem, they still evoked the privilege of surveying the world from one's rooftop.[11]

As its governors knew, the primary space (in Zevi's terms) Bethlem created was that north of the building, which defined Lower Moorfields. This primacy was and is reinforced by the north front's endless replication in eighteenth-century prints: though among London's hospitals only Chelsea and Greenwich were illustrated more often, we have almost no other views of Bethlem, no other standpoint now.[12] But architectural viewing was intended to be a pleasantly complex activity there, comprising the sight of the façade over the front wall and through its grates and, inside, the long galleries and rows of cells. The viewing *from* the building and its galleries, and particularly that over picturesquely disreputable Moorfields, was emblematized by the turrets on those prominent roofs, the governors' balcony, and (of most practical use) the galleries' windows, which took up a proportion of the wall that was large by the standards of the day. This was an urban-Baroque display in many ways, and one of the showpieces of a city starved of stylish new construction after civil war, plague, and fire.

Private suburban madhouses had already begun to advertise their 'excellent' air when in May 1674 the Bethlem governors agreed to rebuild on a new site 'for health and Aire'.[13] The complete appreciation of their architectural show demanded a complex understanding because Bethlem was also supposed to be regarded as healthy. The façade and its display towards Moorfields was made possible by an inordinately thin building that was thereby, in turn, available to the air of Moorfields, the space to which the display was directed. The interrelations are implicit in John Evelyn's passing reference to Bethlem, 'magnificently built, & most sweetely placed in Morefields, since the dreadfull fire',[14] and in later uses of its former site at Bishopsgate to contrast old unwholesomeness and ruin with new salubrity and beauty. Hatton described how, the hospital having grown 'Old and Ruinous, and too small', the City granted to the governors a new 'Situation much more commodious as to Air, &c.' for the 'present spacious Structure'. The new edition of Stow's *Survey*, whose account of Bethlem was composed with the help of its physician Edward Tyson (1650–1708), similarly compares the old hospital, cramped within an 'obscure [dark] and close Place, near unto many common Sewers' with the large, 'stately and magnificent Structure' and its ample provision 'for the Lunatick People, when they are a little well of their Distemper, to walk for their Refreshment'.[15] The most striking celebration is the earliest, as 'Bethlehems beauty' (1676) invokes the unmediated healing that air offered:

Th' Approaching Air, in every gentle Breeze,
Is *Fan'd* and *Winnow'd* through the neighbouring *Trees*,
And comes so *Pure*, the *Spirits* to Refine,
As if th' wise Governours had a Designe
That should alone, without *Physick* Restore
Those whom *Gross Vapours* discompos'd before . . .

The poet then catches up the 'Conceit', which is (appropriately) 'stifled' by the evident abundance of medical skill and remedies to hand in the building.[16] The governors claimed a high 'Cured and Discharged' rate[17] on behalf of that skill and for a while, more implicity, as a result of the building's spaciousness and airiness.

'Of necessity we are immersed in the surrounding air', wrote the second-century physician Galen to explain its importance to health and disease. Though earlier writers, including Vitruvius, had long assumed that importance, it was as one of Galen's six 'non-naturals' that air formed a category in later medical texts.[18] Its qualities and effects were manifold, but generally speaking sweet-smelling and moving air was healthy, while stinking and stagnant air was not, and might indeed actively produce disease, including mental disease. When Hooke's Bethlem was built it was still widely understood, after Galen, that air and with it smells – real, material substances ('Gross Vapours') – enter the brain through the nasal cavities.[19] To remove odour was therefore to remove more than a nuisance, and medieval and early modern concern for promoting good air in houses, hospitals, and towns seems to have centred on the smell that was practically and theoretically speaking inseparable from infection.[20] The difference between good and bad air formed part of a more general way of understanding the healthiness of environments that was not necessarily anti-urban (the country had its smells and swamps), but which was generally suspicious of urban congestion. Moorfields itself had been laid out with walks and trees early in the century for what James I called the 'recreation of our people', in an example for future London squares immediately credited with specific benefits to health too.[21] Andrew Wear has summarized the categories structuring a 'well-articulated body of knowledge about the health of the environment': on the one hand, motion, light, and airiness and on the other, stagnancy, gloom, and stench.[22]

If only because of that knowledge it is not surprising that the celebrations of Bethlem's reconstruction in many ways replicate those in the poetry written about that of the City itself after the Fire of 1666: the sunny and airy salubrity that replaces former obscurity is an unfailing theme in a sizeable genre. In 'Londons resurrection' (1669), a 'Salamander-Muse' (salamanders proverbially survive fire unscathed) inspired Simon Ford to eight lines encompassing the commercial, health, and safety benefits of London's new and wider streets:

And where *Commerce* in *crowded Throngs* was pent,
Or *Fires* coop'd up had rag'd for want of *vent*:
Where *obscure Lanes* obscurer Facts did hide:
And *Pests* by being straitned, spread more wide:

Traffique in spacious Streets shall now be free,
And *Flames* soon *spent*, or soon *supprest* shall be.
Days' Eye each where shall *skulking Sinners* trace,
And *transient Air* infectious steams shall chase.[23]

The proximity of the skulkers and the infections, in the last couplet, is not coincidental because praise for Bethlem's rebuilding and praise for London's shared political as well as hygienic premises. Bad air lurked in obscure close places, and the political and religious dissent of the Interregnum not only figured as a still infectious madness but was literally identified with the madness healed at Bethlem. Air's symbolism was inescapable in Restoration London, and not readily to be disentangled from projects for practical action.[24]

The 'Fire' poetry itself drew upon the complex rhetoric that had surrounded the restoration of the king himself in 1660, an event often described in architectural metaphors; it was helpful to think of the new society as having 'arrived like a grand completed edifice, for all time'.[25] Metaphorical reconstruction thus surrounded real building, after 1660 and especially after 1666, when certain projects lent themselves to metaphor in turn. These naturally included St Paul's Cathedral (begun 1675), but its praise was muted, or rendered more general, by the slowness of the work, by Wren's determined secrecy about its form, and, after its emergence from the scaffolding, by a sense in some quarters that the new St Paul's in no way equalled the old.[26] More satisfactory for poets were the Exchange, as rebuilt to the designs of Edward Jerman between 1667 and 1671, and Hooke's Bethlem; these three together inspired the bulk of the poetry published about new public buildings between 1666 and 1720 or thereabouts.[27] They were in their different ways made to stand for England's own regeneration by the return of its lawful king: St Paul's for the religious settlement and the supremacy of the Church, the Exchange for the commercial empire that peace would bring, and Bethlem for London's willing devotion to a charitable tolerance that would contain and cure the madness that the civil war had been. Other public buildings and rebuildings, among them the military hospitals, do not seem to have inspired poets. Chelsea and Greenwich perhaps came too late for the salamander muses' most active period, but there is no doubt that Charles would have liked Chelsea to have caught their attention.

Kilmainham was funded by sixpence in the pound deducted from the pay of the troops in Ireland.[28] An equivalent system, the 'poundage', was Chelsea's main source of revenue,[29] and Greenwich's was the sixpence deducted from the monthly wages of every registered seaman from 1696 on.[30] Some funds for the construction of the last two came from the monarchs, and from the public, but by and large it was their future inhabitants who built and maintained these hospitals. Put this way it seems nonsensical to call them charities, but that is what they were called. Stephen Fox described Chelsea as springing from the 'innate goodness of his Sacred Majesty, who seeing old land soldiers . . . beg for not being able (by age or infirmity) any longer to continue their duty' was so affected that he offered £2,000 out of his personal funds to begin the hospital.[31] Charles's own letter of October 1684 to William Sancroft, Archbishop of

Canterbury describes how in commencing 'so pious, & charitable a work we have of our own royal bounty already expended great sums of money', to such effect that the 'goodly fabric' and its 'purpose in great part erected is visible to all beholders'. But as the great work was more than his personal bounty could encompass, he would write to all the bishops earnestly inviting them to set an example for the clergy.[32]

How would the king have publicized Chelsea (for that is what the proposed letter-writing amounted to) had the Treasury in fact released the funds he had asked for in January 1682?[33] Probably in much the same way. The royal-charitable model made sense of the administrative innovation and made palatable, at least to Sancroft (who had been Charles's personal chaplain), the standing army for the safety of the royal person.[34] It might even encourage others to give, though few did so and they were Court men; not the least interesting thing about Chelsea is the unpopularity of what it stood for. (The House of Commons had declared the standing army illegal as recently as April 1679.)[35] The king's preamble to the Archbishop suggests that he and Stephen Fox were expecting a royalist constituency: he had

> often times with great grief observed that many of our loyal subjects, who formerly took up arms for us, or royal father of blessed memory, to resist that torrent of prosperous rebellion, which at last overturned this monarchy, & Church, or who afterwards followed us into foreign countries . . . are now . . . reduced to so extreme poverty, that some of them have been forced to beg bread . . .[36]

Chelsea stood as a very precise emblem of what Foucault called vassalage; Charles was explaining his obligation to the men who had defended his father and himself, monarchy and Church, against 'prosperous rebellion'. He had in any case an intriguing challenge, presented by Louis XIV.

Publication

In 1713 Thomas Wilson explained that the foundation of Kilmainham had been inspired by that of the Invalides, that 'stupendious Pile . . . of whose Splendor, Grandure and Decorum, the Publick Printed Description speaks at large'.[37] The splendour of the Invalides, integral grist to Louis XIV's mill of glorification, had been broadcast by Le Jeune de Boulencourt's *Description générale de l'Hôtel Royal des Invalides établi par Louis Le Grand . . . Avec les plans, profils & elevations de ses faces, coupes & appartemens* (1683), a large folio with eighteen even larger (since folded-in) engravings by Jean and Daniel Marot and Pierre Le Pautre, the best men in the world for such work. The book explains its own publication:

> That which has already been published about the Hospital has aroused curiosity abroad and prompted a great, neighbouring King and other foreign princes to wish for plans and an accurate description of it.[38]

To 'publish' something is to allow it to become generally known. As Captain-General of his father's forces, the Duke of Monmouth inspected the Invalides site in 1672 and again in 1677. A few months after the second visit he wrote to the marquis de Louvois requesting a plan 'taken from the model, with all the elevations, because the King would be very pleased to see it'.[39] Drawings were apparently sent in 1678; nine years later the Secretary-at-War William Blathwayt was reading Le Jeune's book for the sake of its information about the Invalides' government, which he wished to adapt for Chelsea's.[40] Wren, who had a lot to do with that government, also acquired a copy at some point.[41]

The *Description* also explains its illustrations (see Figure 14, p. 49) and in a pointed and interesting way. Le Jeune was careful to guide the reader's use of them, so that not just splendour but utility can be apprehended. The fifth chapter, for example, explains that while the hospital's beauties will be readily apparent (*connuës & sensibles*) to everyone from the elevations already offered, *plans geométraux* with their keys will now show the location of the bakeries and the infirmaries and so forth. Finally, for those readers wishing to reach another level of understanding that approaches – Le Jeune acknowledged – the purely technical (*ne regarde que les Sçavans en cét Art*), he was happy to help with the conventions. What is a ground plan? 'It is what allows us to see a building born on and rising from the ground.' What do we see on the ground plan?

> The black and the white distinguish what is enclosed by walls, like the churches and the apartments, from what is open to the air, like the courts and the gardens. The black indicates such masonry as the pilasters and the external and load-bearing walls. Some of the walls are uninterrupted – the four refectories, for example, are lit on one side only – but nearly all the rest have windows, whose sills are marked by two parallel lines.[42]

Le Jeune was educating his audience in the conventions of architectural representation. The occasion was a building whose novelty of type, as well as significance to France's martial goals and glory, demanded that his readers be given the opportunity to apprehend a magnificence extending to windows' placement on plans, as well as on elevations.

The *Description* does not neglect more conventional appeals to its readers' imaginative appreciation and begins with a poetic encomium to Louis XIV, the great spirit dwelling within the great building. Here, the river asks:

> 'What sudden miracle has given birth to this great palace and its extensive apartments in this delightful place?' With an astonished gaze, the Seine wonders if she isn't perhaps looking at another Louvre.

Miracles are generally sudden, and the suddenness was important; Le Jeune had already reminded his readers that its speed of construction was not the least part of the hospital's grandeur.[43]

The same claim had already been made for Hooke's Bethlem. In September 1674 four years were still privately being allowed for construction,[44] but the letterpress on White's engraving (see Figure 5, p. 32) explains that it was built in the fifteen months between April 1675 and July 1676. The boast, repeated by an inscription in the entrance hall, and by later London topographies and guide-books, was an exaggeration of a venerable type.[45] 'Great Application' had since antiquity constituted part of architectural magnificence ('I had so many masters and labourers', Filarete boasted about the Ospedale Maggiore, 'that we had all the main foundations dug in one day')[46] and was particularly impressive in a London still rebuilding a decade after the Fire. In this way, too, Bethlem epito-mized a general theme. Ford described the amazement of Royal Thames, just like that of his sister Seine in the Invalides poem. The river, still dazed and sur-prisingly singed by the 'late dismal Horrors', is astonished by the magnificent, and magnificently sudden, appearance of London's 'rising Structures'.[47]

Its governors' concern with how Bethlem should be viewed extended to its representations. In January 1677 they began arranging the production of White's engraving, which was big enough to need three plates. The gover-nors insisted on checking his first pulls for accuracy, and at the same time resolved to enter with Stationers' Hall their prohibition of unauthorized depictions of the building.[48] In March Hooke, who had long wanted to get Bethlem's picture printed, intervened, telling the governors that (as their minutes summarized),

> itt is very necessary that a ground plott of the said Hospitall should be made wth a large Scale in one of the Vacancyes of the said plott that so the whole contrivance of the said Building may be plainely seene.

On one of the 'vacancies' of Moorfields, as depicted in the print, Hooke would have a plan of the building – he assured the Court that engraving the plan would cost no more than engraving the field – and an 'Inscript[i]on ... w[ch] hee [Hooke] promises to make to show the severall Conveniences of the same Building'.[49]

Micrographia, which translated the cell to the living world, made a substantial contribution to the developing technology of integrating printed, explanatory texts and figures.[50] Hooke was also a cartographer, who had just seen the publi-cation of the large map of London that he designed together with John Ogilby. The map had been intended to feature 'draughts and prospects of all the famous buildings' but showed them only in outline, as footprints.[51] Now, in an attempt to put Bethlem on the map, one might say, as something more than a site outline, Hooke proposed 'that in th'other Vacancy of the said Plott a prospect of that parte of the Citty where the said hospitall is situated should be made'. Both the Court minutes and his diary[52] suggest that Hooke got his way about the building plan and the prospect (a district map, I think, perhaps in perspective) though he evi-dently did not. The governors may have decided that the insertions would detract from the effect of the north front, or indeed from Moorfields' expansive 'vacancy' which was no vacancy at all, but rather a powerful boon to 'health and Aire'. The opportunity to anticipate Le Jeune's explanation of contrivance and convenience, the depth behind the screen, was lost along with the floor plan and its key, just as the graphic demonstration of new Bethlem's literal and figurative place in new London was lost along with the map.

Britain got nothing to compare with Le Jeune's book before the publication (in 1789) of Cooke and Maule's *Historical account* of Greenwich. The dedication to *A Pattern of a . . . well-governed hospital*, published anonymously in 1695, explains that its intention is to bring the rare and expensive volume to English readers' attention because King William has just formed his 'Noble Resolution' to convert Greenwich to a hospital. The *Pattern* reduced the large French folio to a duodecimo with a single picture, a site plan folded several times into the binding, and it necessarily omitted the explanation of how to read a plan. Kilmainham, the first of the English military hospitals, was also the first to get its own book: Thomas Wilson's *Account of the foundation of the Royal Hospital of King Charles II near Dublin* (1713).[53] Wilson reprinted many useful data, including the hospital's accounts and its lengthy charter, but the unillustrated *Account* takes no particular interest in Kilmainham's architecture, aside from a bow to its handsomeness and utility. Only the 1728 *Remarks on the founding and carrying on the buildings of the Royal Hospital at Greenwich* by Nicholas Hawksmoor (1661–1736), who had begun assisting Wren at Greenwich in 1696 and had been Assistant Surveyor there since 1705, can compare with the *Description* in its insistence on its subject's centrality to the 'Protection and Defence' of the realm, to the 'Magnificence and Order' of the state and its monarchs, and to the 'Science' of architecture.[54] Hawksmoor had kind words too for Louis XIV's and his minister Colbert's promotion of their nation's 'Arts and Arms' through the Invalides. England's former arch-enemy 'had been truly a Royal Mecaenas had it stopt here'.[55]

Greenwich

The hospital for seamen at Greenwich, begun in 1696, was not finished until 1752 and its infirmary finally rose in 1763–64. It is a building in many parts, designed by several men mostly constrained by what had already been built on the site. Alone among the palatial hospitals of the later seventeenth century, it began with the conversion of a royal palace, the building begun to the designs of John Webb (1611–72) in 1664, and itself only the first part of his replacement for the old Greenwich palace, demolished at the same time. But Charles II apparently lost interest in the project. The new block was boarded up by early 1670, and its interior never decorated with Webb's metaphorical presentations of the wisdom and magnificence of the Stuarts. Money was one problem (even the shell cost the king £36,000) and politics was another. Charles murmured into happy architects' ears of rebuilding Whitehall as well as Greenwich but, as John Bold has pointed out, great palaces were the prerogative and the pleasure of absolute monarchs and the king could not comfortably appear to be assuming that role.[56] His 'habitual palatial musings' would be more safely directed towards Chelsea and perhaps, vicariously, Bethlem.

The Commissioners for Sick and Wounded Seamen were in June 1691 asked to estimate the cost of adapting what is now called the King Charles building to a hospital, and Queen Mary granted its use the next month. The conversion began in February 1692. The Commissioners' need for a hospital was underlined by the aftermath of the great naval battle of La Hogue three months later, but La Hogue was not followed by others, and the impetus slackened. Though the Admiralty, Navy Board, and Commissioners looked at Wren's plans in the autumn of 1692, fresh stimulus came only with Mary's death two years later and Wren was appointed to the Subcommittee for the Building (the 'Fabrick Committee') in late 1695, several months after William formally commissioned the hospital.[57]

Hawksmoor wrote that there was then talk of demolishing Webb's block for the sake of its stone, and hinted that this had arisen out of iconoclasm, not thrift, with the idea that Webb's giant Corinthian order was too good for the sailors. But what was the corollary? – that the Corinthian was too good for England. 'Why would you take down what is Good, and erect a beggarly Fabrick; is there no Distinction to be made between a private Alms-house, and an Hospital built by the State?'[58] Here he was, he wrote, paraphrasing the voices of reason that had prevailed.

It is worth halting for a moment for the sake of this threatened demolition, because in telling the story thirty years later, Hawksmoor was playing on current anxieties with a subtlety for which he has never received credit. Evidently conscious of a need to answer the prevailing suspicion of monumentalizing of the sort commonly supposed to be manifested by private palaces for beggars, he was trying to use the critique's own terms of reference. It is after all the palaces that should be supplying stone for godly charity, in the ideal reversal of the biblical devouring-and-translation trope: 'Woe unto you, scribes and Pharisees, hypocrites! for ye devour widows' houses.' Greenwich had, as Hawksmoor did not fail to report, been founded as much for their widows and orphans as for the seamen. To demolish the palace for the sake of the widows' houses (or rather, what those houses represented, architecturally) would, he was saying, not obviate the luxury but exacerbate it, by substituting useless beggarliness for useful magnificence.[59]

Frankly inspired by the opening of yet another commission for the building works the previous year, Hawksmoor was arguing for funds with which to complete the embodiment of the 'charitable provision', or what he more privately called the 'huge pile'.[60] The task was to make Greenwich's magnificence, and cost, palatable and he used the story of the King Charles building's rescue to make the point that the hospital would impress foreigners. Queen Mary, 'who had a great Passion for Building' had doubtless, he thought, also known that England 'ever made the most insignificant Figure when the Naval Power was either sunk, neglected, or broken' and that is why she asked Wren to build Greenwich 'with great Magnificence and Order'.[61] Even structures built for the sake of their 'Grandeur only' in antiquity, like the Pyramids, or Trajan's Column, had drawn 'Crowds of Strangers to see them, to the no small Advantage of the Country'. How much more 'worth the Observation of Strangers', asked Hawksmoor rhetorically, was this magnificent emblem of naval prowess, and how much more advantageous to Britain? The idea that expenditure on public works is an investment in national honour and reputation was an old one; Filarete used it too.[62] What this kind of public work – this kind of hospital, as opposed to Filarete's – allowed was Hawksmoor's next argument, which involved making the poor Briton himself a kind of stranger, also drawn by splendour, and to the advantage of the splendid. He quoted another monarch, the new King George II, who had just asked Parliament to attend to the 'Increase and Encouragement of our Seamen . . . , that they may be invited rather than compell'd by Force and Violence, to enter into the Service of their Country'.[63] Military hospitals, or at least assured care for the sick, had long been regarded as powerful aids to the recruitment of soldiers and sailors; the audience for Greenwich's apparent luxury included men who might enter the hospital two decades or so after first sighting it, two decades in which they would serve their country. Hawksmoor was trying to extend the definition of magnificence to embrace solutions to real national problems, right down to the violence of Navy recruiters. More riskily, he was also suggesting that magnificence might give the appearance of luxury, an appearance however serving noble ends.

Anyway, 'with as much Indignation as her excellent good Temper would suffer her', Queen Mary had ordered that the King Charles building 'should remain, and the other Side of the Royal Court [be] made answerable to it'.[64] Hawksmoor also credited her passion for building with the preservation of the view, and the access, between the Thames and Inigo Jones's Queen's House. The stipulation, confirmed by the grant of land made in October 1694, frustrated Wren's hope, evident in his first designs, of running the hospital around three sides of a square open to the river, Chelsea-fashion, and as Webb had once hoped for his palace.[65] In January 1696 the Grand Committee approved the Fabrick Committee's proposals to alter and fit up the old King Charles building that, together with the 'Base' block to be built behind it to the east, would be 'capable of entertaining and lodging 350 disabled Seamen' and their fifty 'necessary Attendants'. A royal warrant was issued to this effect in April, eighteen months after the granting of the charter, but no one committed themselves to an overall scheme at this point.

The 'warrant' designs for the conversion of the King Charles building and its enlargement are dated 28 October 1696;[66] the ground-floor plan mostly corresponds to that shown in the plan of the entire hospital (Figure 24) ordered to be printed three years later. A comparison with Webb's designs suggests that his long double pile lent itself nicely to its new use.[67] Though the fine entrance vestibule was preserved, the ground-floor state sequence on both sides could, by knocking out partition walls, be replaced by dining halls.[68] Behind the spine wall and on the first floor (where the royal long gallery suited as it was) wards, which is what these galleries were called, were formed the same way, and in the attic storey doubled cabins were simply installed along the entire front. Wren's 'dissection' drawing shows an entresol inserted in the original block's rear pile, between the ground and first floors.[69] The purpose-built base block was to be linked to Webb's block at ground and entresol level by 'Gallerys of communication', a covered corridor or pedestrian bridge on top of an arcade dividing the narrow court. Just under 350 cabins are drawn in these designs, those in the base block making it look like a Chelsea ward-wing.[70]

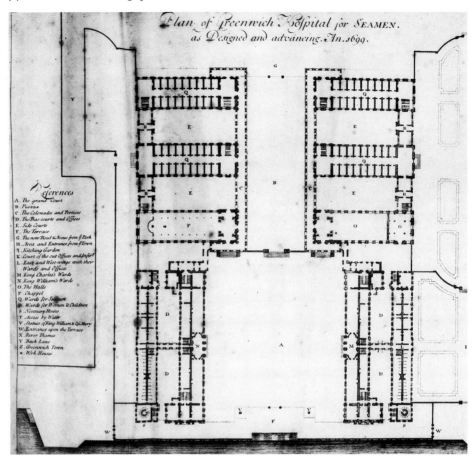

The other buildings would show the variety with which cells and galleries could be arranged. After its completion in 1728 and before that of the infirmary proper, the Queen Anne building contained the large infirmary wards, in parallel ranges arranged back to back on all floors, with bed-cabins.[71] Behind, in the King William and Queen Mary buildings, finished in 1708 and 1752 respectively, four-, six-, and eight-bedded rooms were ranged on each side of central corridors, approximately as shown in the 1699 plan, though the ward blocks themselves would be reoriented soon after. Grosley described them:

> The beds are enclosed and placed three on each side. Each chamber being open at the top, at a distance of three feet from the ceiling, has a door and a window, in a line parallel with those of the opposite chamber.
>
> In consequence of this disposition of the rooms, of the circulation of air which it occasions, and of the neatness which may be compared to that of the cells of our nuns, the whole inside of this hospital has quite a different appearance from that of the same kind of buildings in other countries.[72]

For John Aikin, the best plan for hospital wards comprised a 'range of cells or small rooms opening into a wide airy gallery, having a brisk circulation of air

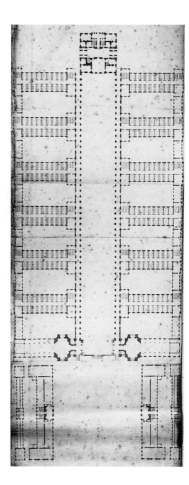

(*facing page*) 24. A detail of the plan of Greenwich ordered to be sent to subscribers in 1699. 'King Charles's Wards' (M on the key) are in Webb's block; to its right is the base block built for the hospital. These two are matched by what would be the Queen Anne building. Beds in the two ward blocks behind, and parallel to, the chapel and hall (o and p) were to be arranged in small wards, in the manner shown in the next illustration.

25. Wren's plan for Greenwich showing twelve ward blocks.

through it', and he suggested that Greenwich 'will give a good idea of this disposition'.[73]

As Kerry Downes has explained, designs survive of two other Wren projects that exceed the site as it was defined in October 1694. One would have side-stepped the Queen's House and abandoned the King Charles building, while the other, 'which was drawn out in some detail, proposed seven ranges (hall or chapel and six ward blocks) on either side of the vista, with arcades linking their inner ends and running up to the Queen's House to form a long closed court' (Figure 25).[74] Here, in simply listing the ward blocks in parallel rows, Wren departed radically from the models presented by the Invalides, Kilmainham, and Chelsea. Then, apparently, came another project, which shows the same cabin arrangement but reduces the numbers of ward blocks (now linked by a colonnade) to three each side, plus the hall and chapel, and which does fit the site.[75] Wren's plans for the hall, which can be dated to April 1698, seem to have accompanied this last project,[76] but the middle blocks were soon turned to make the three-sided courts of the present William and Mary buildings.

Greenwich is as well documented as any other building of the period, but the things thought worth writing down during its construction did not include the medical justifications, if any were offered or needed to be offered, for the various forms Wren proposed for it between 1694 and 1700. For it we have no 'Bethlehems beauty', a contemporary guide to how we should be looking. And this is a pity, especially because these designs constitute a 'bit of prophecy', as Grace Goldin called the twelve-ward-block project, essentially the pavilion-ward plan to be 'reconstructed . . . on logical principles' by Frenchmen who, in the 1780s, seized upon the Plymouth naval hospital (1756–61) as the almost accidental exemplar of the type (see Chapter 8).[77] The identification of Wren's drawings as a kind of buried treasure, which goes back to their first publication in 1929,[78] however needs qualification, just because of the pavilion plan's future importance. He did not, first, propose pavilion wards, long open rooms, but detached blocks filled with small wards flanking a central corridor, the arrangement followed at most of the purpose-built dormitory blocks. It was the small wards that aroused Aikin's admiration, which in turn encouraged the British, not French, consensus on their desirability evident by 1800 (Chapter 10). Finally, however, small wards are not evident in the bird's-eye perspectives (see Figures 27 and 29 showing a version with three parallel blocks, and available all over the place in the eighteenth century, as explained just below). In these prints the blocks' fenestration *does* make them look like pavilion wards, should anyone have cared: as to that, we just do not know. The treasure, anyway, was not so well buried after all. The very fact of the variants (fourteen, eight, and six blocks ranged) however suggests that Wren himself would have found scholarly fascination with his prophecy a little puzzling. The blocks' slenderness self-evidently permitted the admission of light and air, and their insulation meant they could be arranged in greater or lesser numbers at will, and as funds gradually permitted. The test for him was to link the blocks, both literally and visually, to make them a unity.

In December 1698 the Greenwich Fabrick Committee ordered a cabin fitted up for exhibition and at the same time and for the same reason – to reassure and encourage subscribers and through them perhaps find more – determined to have prints of the hospital made.[79] Pictures for such a purpose were almost unprecedented in England, and Greenwich's contributed to the St Paul's Commission's dawning realization that 'publicity was no bad thing' (it was then uncertain about the reliability of the coal-tax revenue).[80] After two decades of successful secrecy about the cathedral's form, its Commission paid Jan Kip in the late spring of 1701 for an engraved prospect and plan.

Publication carried risks. In 1710, John Vanbrugh (1664–1726) told the Duke of Marlborough that drawings of Blenheim and its bridge were on their way, and warned the Duke to keep them to himself:

> The drawings are true but in no measure prepared for an Engraver to work after. I therefore desire Your Grace will please not to let them go out of your hands so as any body can take a copy, lest they should be published (as so often happens) to great disadvantage.[81]

The disadvantage was threefold. One did not want to let piratical printmakers seize the profit and moreover do so with inferior productions that might, finally,

be taken from out-of-date designs. Such had long been Wren's experience at St Paul's and now, more embarrassingly (because no pirates were involved), at the cathedral and Greenwich too. Kip's pictures of St Paul's were never issued, evidently because they showed designs for the west towers and dome that Wren had already discarded, but two of the three Greenwich engravings were: Kip's bird's-eye 'prospect', of which 100 copies were ordered in June 1699,[82] and the plan that was ordered to be printed three months later. Only Simon Gribelin's 'large view', a human-eye perspective (Figure 26) was held back.[83] In April 1700 a 'printed draught' was presented to William III, and the Fabrick Committee resolved that 'sets of the Draughts of the Hospital be delivered to such of the Subscribers as have paid their Subscription'.[84] The problem was, they showed the wrong project, that with three parallel blocks (and two ward blocks) on each side, which was probably penultimate to the final one.[85] Once in circulation, however, pictures are hard to stop. A version (Figure 27) of Kip's view was published in 1707, long after the plan was fixed. A later print by Kip (Figure 28) that simply omits the middle ranges in the rear courts appears in the 1720 edition of Stow's *Survey*, which had been a long time in preparation. The Greenwich directors were meanwhile aggrieved by the appearance of yet another variant of Kip's first print (like Figure 27), and in November 1708 they agreed that an advertisement be put in the *London Gazette* disowning it:

Whereas a print of the Royal Hospitall for Seamen at Greenwich was lately published without the approbation or knowledge of the Commissioners and Governors which print is 'Notoriously false and much to the discredit of that noble Structure, notice is hereby given to the end that no persons may be

26. Gribelin's perspective (1699) of Greenwich. The ends of the ward blocks, as then planned, are seen behind the domed chapel (on the left) and hall.

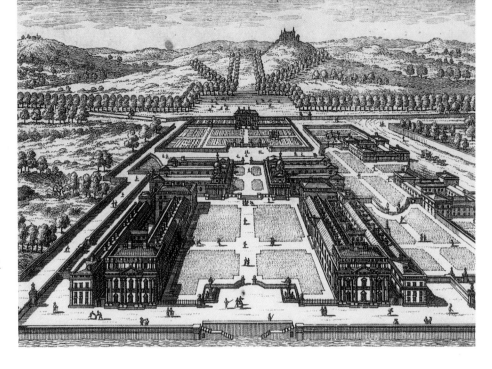

27. This view of Greenwich appeared in *Les Délices de la Grand' Bretagne* (1707), published by a Leiden book- and printseller. The book was dedicated to Queen Anne, whose officers were not pleased by such reappearances of the premature bird's-eye view of 1699.

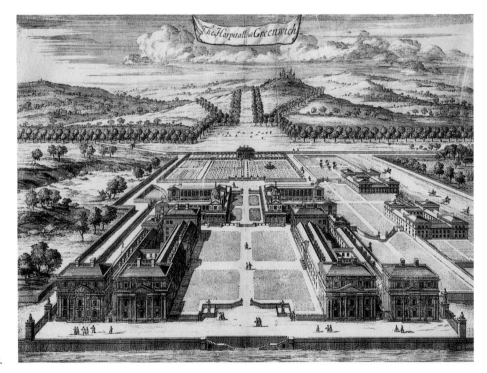

28. Greenwich in an engraving by Jan Kip, from Strype's 1720 edition of John Stow's *Survey of the Cities of London and Westminster.*

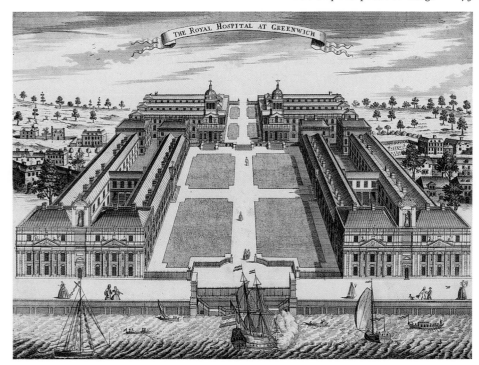

THE ROYAL HOSPITAL AT GREENWICH

29. Nicholls's large engraving of Greenwich (1728) shows the flag towers (of which only one was built, and later taken down) on the riverside pavilions.

imposed on thereby and to inform the publick that a true and perfect design is in preparation, and will be published by Order.'[86]

Yet a third print (Figure 29), by Sutton Nicholls, was in the printseller John Bowles's catalogue by 1728. Hawksmoor's book, at least, should have then made it evident that the parallel ranges were not going to be built but, undismayed, if he even noticed the problem, Bowles published it in his *London described* of 1731.

According to his son, Wren's secrecy about St Paul's began with the rejection of the Great Model back in 1674. This had determined him 'to make no more Models, or publickly expose his Designs, which (as he had found by past Experience) did but lose Time, and subjected his Business many Times, to incompetent Judges'[87] – a policy that also allows for changes undergone by big projects, years in construction. It was one that could not be maintained with buildings whose publicness was a product not just of their function, but also of their funding.

A 'Humour of Colonades'

Entering the Royal Court of the Invalides (as *A pattern of a . . . well-governed hospital* translated Le Jeune's *Description*),

> You are surprized with the Sight of Fourscore Portico's or Piazza's [simply *portiques*, in the original], which sustain Fourscore more, forming large Galleries [*grandes galleries*], which serve for agreeable Walks in all times.[88]

In front of the north range at Chelsea, as Hatton described it, is a 'Gallery elevated on Columns under which the Pensioners can sit and take the Air, and at the same time are secured from Rain and other Bad Weather'.[89] Definitions of porticoes, piazzas, and galleries had not yet settled down, and the covered walks merge with what makes them covered, and both with the spaces they frame.[90] Hawksmoor gave the best functional definition in describing Greenwich's equivalent 'Porticos', which

> are intended for Communication from the Hall and Chapel in the Wards and Dormitories; and to protect the Men from the Inclemency of the Weather, and give them Air, at any time, without incommoding them, very useful where a Number of People are to inhabit in One College.[91]

Communication and air were astonishingly expensive and a long time building: the colonnade on the hospital's west side, the only one finished when he wrote, cost £14,288 4s.11d.[92] The coupled Doric columns today start on the river side of the rear, Queen Mary and King William buildings, and then turn back towards the Queen's House to run for about 350 feet (Figure 30).[93]

At both of his hospitals Wren preferred colonnades to the Invalides' arcading, though for the twelve-ward-block design he did try arcades with attached Doric columns.[94] One of his fragmentary tracts, so-called (which he seems to have begun in the mid-1670s), however disparages half-columns 'stuck upon' or 'hung-on' walls, where they served no structural use. Architecture, according to Wren, was still in the grip of a millennia-old 'Humour of Colonades'.[95] The phrase is irresistible, though it makes the section title a little misleading because what we would call a colonnade, Wren called a portico. For him porticoes had a particular interest, for in them he found the origins of the classical orders themselves. Colonnades are as prominent in the tracts as they are at Greenwich, where they were much celebrated:[96] what the galleries' length was to Bethlem, the number of columns making galleries was here. Gribelin's perspective (see Figure 26) is really a perspective of them.

Wren's first tract refers to Vitruvius' *Ten books on architecture*, which proposes a wide-ranging system of equivalences between buildings and the human body to illustrate its central project of directing architecture towards the immutability, the fixed rules, of nature. Vitruvius' stories of the origins of the orders in different somatic types (the man, the maiden, the matron) in turn illustrate this system of equivalences. These stories powerfully irritated Wren, who wrote that Vitruvius had in fact led us to the '*true* Way to find out the Originals of the Orders',[97] presumably in his fifth book, about public buildings, and in particular its chapter on 'Colonnades and walks'. Everywhere, Wren wrote, when 'Men first cohabited in civil Commerce', they needed places in which to meet. In cold countries, these were enclosed and roofed, but in the Mediterranean, 'where Civility first began', 'they desired to exclude the Sun only, and admit all possible Air for Coolness and Health: this brought in naturally the Use of Porticoes, or Roofs for Shade, set upon Pillars'.[98] The pillars supporting these porticoes had an origin more likely than the human body which (Wren pointed out) is not often perfectly cylindrical:

'A Walk of Trees is more beautiful than the most artificial [artful] Portico', but walks of trees are not practicable for a busy forum or market-place. The porticoes were built instead, artful equivalents to lines of shady trees whose trunks in this way become columns (Figure 31).[99]

Around 1770, the Irish architect Michael Wills remarked that, in northern climates, the 'orders are used but for very little more than ornament'.[100] Opportunities for really *building* with columns were few, and for Wren a major charm of porticoes was that their beauty arose directly from their structural use. He would have been gratified by the way in which the Navy would use them in the Mediterranean, where 'civility' first began after all. In 1739 the engineer James Montresor made a design for a Gibraltar 'Hospital for 413 Men' and two more for 1,000 men, of which the first would have boasted a colonnade or 'Piazza in front 136 feet long'; the second two-storey 'Piazza[s] 70 feet square' around large courtyards surrounded in turn by ward blocks; and the third, similarly, a 'Colonade with a Gallery over it' around a single, very large central court.[101] Again, we are a little confused – is the 'piazza' the space surrounded by the colonnade, the space under it, or the colonnade itself? – and again, we realize that the distinctions did not much signify.

Tract II returns to the porticoes to develop Wren's thesis of the arboreal origins of the orders and the brief third tract explains how the Doric order perpetuates, in stone, the carpentry of the first, wooden porticoes.[102] And then Wren described how the columns had been used, in quantities permitted by production on a factory scale, to make porticoes that formed the spines of entire new cities: Alexandria, Palmyra, Tarsus. Dinocrates had drawn the principal streets of Alexandria and these were then set out by porticoes made of the 'hundreds of Pillars, of all sorts . . . to be bought at the Quarries ready made, where great Numbers of Artizans wrought for sale of what they raised'. The quarters between the streets and cross-streets, behind the porticoes, were then filled in with buildings: 'Thus were Cities suddenly raised', in another miracle.

On the 1699 plan of Greenwich (see Figure 24) the space between the colonnades is called the 'Piazza', but the space is itself the 'Colonade' ('*Columnatio*') on the plan Hawksmoor published in 1728. This colonnade, in the singular, he described as the first of the buildings the visitor reaches after King Charles and Queen Anne, though it consists of two parts, the porticoes ('*Porticus*'):

> The Colonade, having a Portico on the right and left Hands of Doric Pillars 20 Foot high, crowned with an Entablement and Ballustrade of Portland Stone, each of which Porticos is in Length 430 Foot, and both together sustain'd by 300 Pillars and Pillasters.[103]

The porticoes make a great building which is a space, closed at one end by the Queen's House, with which their perspective aligns so neatly, and at the other open to the river, from which the hospital is meant to be viewed. It would be reached through one of eight gates to the enclosure, whose names Hawksmoor's key again offers in loving translation: *Porta Thamesina*, *Porta Sabrinensis* (Severn), *Porta Tinocena* (Tyne). We should take his Latin at face value;[104] a new city would be made in the antique way, though not very quickly.[105]

Queen Mary had, Hawksmoor explained, rejected the idea of using the shell of Winchester Palace for the hospital, because the palace was 'out of the way, and not frequently seen'. Her uncle had chosen Winchester for its proximity to the coast; Portsmouth, then becoming the biggest naval port in Britain, is not far. It would have been a good site, but not one 'in the View of all the World'. For Greenwich, like Chelsea, the Thames provided transportation and water, but at least as important was its provision of a changing audience on its way to and from the metropolis, '(the Grand Emporium) London'.[106]

A few years before Hawksmoor published his *Remarks*, Daniel Defoe described the Thames. Everyone, he wrote, knows the river's wonders, the 'splendour of its shores, gilded with noble palaces, strong fortifications, large hospitals, and public buildings' but,

> I find none has spoken of what I call the distant glory of all these buildings. There is a beauty of these things at a distance, taking them *en passant*, and in perspective, which few people value, and fewer understand; and yet here they are more truly great, than in all their private beauties whatsoever. Here they reflect beauty, and magnificence upon the whole country, and give a kind of character to the island of Great Britain in general.

31. Greenwich, looking
north towards the river.

Defoe reassured us that he would sing 'no songs here of the river in the first person of a water nymph, a goddess, (and I know not what) according to the humour of the ancient poets'.[107] Not *that* ancient; Defoe was about nine years old when Simon Ford had the Thames sit up and take astounded notice of London's new buildings. Ford's stout assertion of collected wonders is, however, as far from Defoe's acute observation of a glory '*en passant*, and in perspective' as the static view encouraged by Bethlem's splendid north front is from that made by Greenwich's colonnades, which indeed ask for the long, and moving vantage-point.

'Architecture has its Political Use; publick Buildings being the Ornament of a Country', wrote Wren.[108] 'Political' here means something very broad indeed, for such architecture 'establishes a Nation, draws People and Commerce; makes the People love their Native Country, which Passion is the Original of all great Actions in a Common-wealth'. Bethlem and the military hospitals were made 'public' buildings, which does not simply mean that they were not private houses. The word had other, more morally engaged opposites: hidden or particular, as in Defoe's 'private beauties'; trivial and selfish.[109] Wren explained public buildings as those that can instil a productive passion, that speak to a people. The notion was not new, but it was now increasingly directed to an ever-widening analysis of utility embracing not just new functions (the care of veterans, or of lunatics), but the pride, prosperity, and (not least) tourism that would result. Calls for public works became deafening in the first four decades of the next century. In them, hospitals continued to provide a symbolic centre of gravity because, as public works for which antiquity provided no precedent, they were modernity's bench-mark. In those calls, however, finding the line between, as Berkeley put it, public works and private luxury, the magnificences of the rich and the necessities of the poor, was made problematic by two things: a near-obsessive concern to find forms of employment that would discipline the poor out of their own private luxury, and the unedifying architectural politics of the Age of Walpole.

'I once thought [Greenwich] wou'd have been a publick Building but it will sink into a deformed Barrac[k]', Hawksmoor wrote in disgust in 1734,[110] five years after Thomas Ripley, a protégé of Sir Robert Walpole, and therefore everyone's architectural dunce, got the Greenwich surveyorship that he had every right to expect. (In the event, Ripley did well by the hospital.)[111] Vanbrugh had already decided which way the wind was blowing, and mourned Hawksmoor's lost opportunities: what could Colbert not have done with him? 'I don't Speak as to his Architecture alone, but the Aids he cou'd have given him, in almost all his brave Designs for the Police.' By the last Vanbrugh meant what Hawksmoor himself called 'Polite Government'; 'police' was anyway a

> thing I never expect to hear talk'd of in England, Where the Parts of most of the Great men I have ever Seen or read of, have rarely turn'd to any farther Account, Than getting a Great Deal of Money, and turning it through their Guts into a House of Office[112]

– that is, a necessary-house or latrine. The passage needs some explanation, because its joke leaps three ways at the word 'into'. The money is, first, that which normally makes the journey from guts to house of office; it is also what *makes* houses of office, an undistinguished building type. Money also buys the offices, the government positions, which enable the building.[113] The complaint would find many, more priggish echoes, in which an anxiety that Britain engage in public works met others, about appropriate forms of charitable display.

Chapter 4
Looking at asylums

In 1708, Edward Hatton called Chelsea Hospital's a 'Situation and a Building that would be taken by Strangers . . . for the Palace of a Prince', and told the stranger directly that at Greenwich was being built 'one of the most sumptuous Hospitals in the World, much liker the Palace of a Prince than a Harbour for the Indigent'.[1] The comparison worked both ways, however, and some found no true magnificence at Greenwich. In 1733 Sir John Clerk of Penicuik visited the hospital, for him, too, 'one of the most sumptuous buildings of the whole world'. But,

> One cannot but with indignation observe that the old broken seamen of England are lodged like kings and the kings like seamen, for the King's palace at St James's is no ways comparable to this hospital . . .[2]

Sir Thomas Hewett had already written to a friend complaining of 'strange Bulky Buildings',

> Composed of Towers, Breaks, Rustick Key stone etc. out of all maner of proportion & reason; Our Great publick Buildings are neither Palaces Castles or Hospitalls, but of a strange Hodge podge mixture loaded with stone without any propriety relating to their Use; Foreigners are all of the same opinion.

'There will be a time', Hewett predicted, 'when men will wish there h[a]d been no such Empericks [quacks] in Building & curse Hawksmoor . . . the most illeterate magotty & dishonest Fellow lieving'. He was surely referring to Greenwich Hospital, where the quack Hawksmoor was Clerk of the Works; it certainly has some remarkable keystones and then sported a tower (see Figure 29, p. 79) that was not universally admired.[3] Simple personal loathing, bulkiness, and hodge-podge typologies together aroused Hewett's disgust.

St James's was one of the seven royal houses to which Charles II had returned; Henry VIII had more than twenty.[4] Among the rest, Whitehall burned, Charles was the last monarch to sleep in the Tower, and Greenwich was given to the sailors in the young Queen Mary's loving translation, so carefully explained by Hawksmoor. Palatial hospitals continued to be the stuff of self-congratulation, but the real palaces did not. And in some quarters Hewett, for example, surely represented the problem, not the solution. As Surveyor-General from 1719 to 1726 he was not, as Hawksmoor claimed, the 'most infamous that ever was made', but his was a political appointment, and he presided over little construction. As the Office of Works became more political (in the narrow sense), less work of political use (in Wren's sense) was conducted. Faction blamed faction for stalling architectural renewal; everyone earnestly wished that monarchy would set the example; and a new aesthetic of a 'practical antiquity'[5] informed all the reiterations of the desirability of public works.

Greenwich continued to attract sporadic accusations of indecorum, but Chelsea seems to have eluded criticism, at first because it was finished and paid for and always, one suspects, because it looked plainer.[6] Given its function, Bethlem's appearance practically courted comment, but the jokes could easily acknowledge the spiritual appropriateness of that magnificence. After 1700 they ceased to do so, and Bethlem's critical misfortunes as a building were sharpened by a growing distaste for spectatorship in the institution. Hooke's plan was also, however, the model for those of London's next great asylums, George Dance the Younger's St Luke's (1782–87), and James Lewis's Bethlem in Southwark (1812–15), the hospital's third home. They conclude this chapter and with it this book's account of hospitals made of cells and galleries.

False taste and Christian modernity

English Baroque architecture, that of Bethlem and the military hospitals, can be strikingly original, and some must have prized it for this quality.[7] We cannot be sure, in the absence of positive architectural criticism, but we can adduce the frenzied *anti*-individualism of Robert Morris (*c*.1702–54), the outstanding architectural writer of his generation.[8] Thus, the *Essay in defence of ancient architecture* (1728) would defend it, specifically, against the 'Infection' of 'Novelty and Singleness'. By 'ancient' Morris also meant modern architecture, at least modern architecture as it had begun to be practised and preserved against its enemies (as he wrote) by Richard Boyle, 3rd Earl of Burlington (1694–1753) and other aristocratic virtuosi in the Palladian circle.[9]

Though the subject was his obsessive concern, Morris avoided the word 'luxury'. The vice was 'ambitious Ostentation' and the architectural vice lay in the 'Deformity' of 'incoherent Parts, consisting of no Foundation, but the Emptiness and Shadow of Appearance'. While renouncing the old word, Morris rejuvenated the old critique with a metaphor of disease. Novelty and singularity 'spread and extend themselves'; the 'soft Infection' steals 'insensibly upon the soft and effeminate Breast' and tempts architecture's 'young Proficients' away from the 'Paths of Truth'.[10] This is lively. Christian iconography had once figured luxury as a woman, and susceptibility to it was still conventionally identified with effeminacy, in both men and women. But by 1728 luxury's sexuality (as opposed to its gender) had almost been forgotten, though not by Morris, who described something aggressively wayward, even masculinized, preying upon and infecting young proficients.[11]

The undesirability of 'capricious' ornament is a commoner refrain in Palladian-inflected writings. The complaint stemmed, Peter Borsay has suggested, from an anxiety about social ranking. Classicism had now 'permeated deep into the middling ranks', at least in its simpler manifestations, pedimented doorcases and so forth, and was losing value as a status indicator. Escalation into some kind of architectonic war was not the answer, if only because defeating the middling ranks in this way might become expensive as well as ridiculous, but restraint was:

> Palladianism thus helped to wrestle away cultural control from the mass market at a time when standards were at risk of becoming socially debased, and placed authority back into the hands of a narrow group of *cognoscenti* and patrons who could afford to employ their services.[12]

The anxiety, even the anger, apparent from the late 1720s and 1730s does seem acute enough to suggest that the stakes were high. 'There is surely nothing more absurd than to see, as one often does, a *Venetian* Window and a *Grecian* Portico stuck on to an old decaying Mansion': so an essay of 1739 from the journal *Common Sense*.[13] Its ostensible target was however not 'tawdry Gilding and Carving' but the corruption of public offices that paid for the tawdriness. To that extent, absurdity was also sinister, and corruption was also material, a crumbling fabric masked. But what exactly betrayed the 'false Taste of Magnificence', in Alexander Pope's phrase; what were the 'idle ornaments' that 'charm the vulgar, but disgust the judicious', as Isaac Ware (1704–66) described them?[14] That is seldom clear. Anxiety about architectural luxury is almost always of the free-floating sort, and architects such as Ware were best advised to keep it that way. As the *Common Sense* essay suggests, disgust was, in any case, prompted by the juxtaposition of modernity with decay, of social pretension with actual rank, and there was no sense in attacking particular devices. But Venetian windows would become a useful synecdoche for all that mortar, largely thanks to Pope.

Eighteenth-century Palladians sought to restore architecture to the path of truth, to the forms and principles of the ancients. The quest involved a general revision of magnificence, and more specific appeals for a considered emulation of the public works of antiquity, usually the Rome of Augustus and Vitruvius.[15] Pope (1688–1744) accordingly consoled his friend Burlington, who might at least pursue the magnificence proper to a great man's 'private works' until the public realm beckoned,

> Till Kings call forth th'Idea's of your mind,
> Proud to accomplish what such hands design'd,
> Bid Harbors open, public Ways extend,
> Bid Temples, worthier of the God, ascend . . .[16]

A few years later Burlington's protégé Richard Savage (c.1697–1743) published *Of public spirit in regard to public works*, a long poem with a publication history complicated by Savage's unwillingness to miss out on any *cause célèbre*. In 1737 that was the Georgia Colony and the version published that year concludes with Public Spirit showing England's emigrant poor how to enjoy nature's plenty in America.[17] Those who remain at home however require public works, to employ them and if necessary to shelter them:

> From peasant Hands imperial Works arise,
> And *British* hence with *Roman* Grandeur vies;
> . . .
> Tho' no vast Wall extend from Coast to Coast,
> No Pyramid aspires, sublimely lost;
> Yet the safe Road thro' Rocks shall, winding, tend,
> And the firm Cause-way o'er the Clays ascend;
> Lo! stately Streets, lo! ample Squares invite
> The salutary Gale, that breathes Delight.
> Lo! Structures mark the charitable Soil,
> For casual Ill; maim'd Valour; feeble Toil . . . (ll. 93–94, 105–12)

The works of British peasant hands are imperial in their prosaic, useful solidity as well as in their charity.[18] As such they amplify and refine the ancient models. The 'salutary Gale' implies a similar enhancement, but now to nature, who will be guided around England's new streets and squares and hospitals as she will be tamed in Georgia's forests.

Hospitals provided a useful confirmation that God's majesty had enabled the new Augustans to surpass the old. The author of 'Bethlehems beauty' (1676) may not sufficiently have credited ancient works ('vain ostentation'), but his opposition of modern virtues to antique squandering, 'Whilst we for Use and Charity do Build' (ll. 4, 5), would be wholeheartedly endorsed. Again, Bethlem's exceptionality encouraged the emergence of new forms of praise for architecture in England, as the Invalides did for France. Le Jeune's dedication (1683) to Louis XIV explains that the Invalides is *plus superbe* than the Colosseum. Strange comparison, we think, until we realize that it is not about architecture, but destinations for veterans! Soldiers had no civil skills or trades with which to support themselves after leaving the army, and this

> consideration was the Ground of all those Provisions made by the Romans for Disabled Soldiers; . . . altho' in those Times they did not Erect Buildings for their Co-habiting together when Disbanded. . . . But our Modern Princes having the Experience of former Times in View, *endeavour still to outdo the past*; and this entering into the thoughts of Lewis the 14th of France, produced that stupendious Pile by him named the Invalids . . .[19]

So Thomas Wilson explained, more calmly, in 1713.

'Greece had her exquisite statues; and Rome her public baths and edifices; but Christianity hath raised up monuments of compassion and beneficence unknown both to ancient Greece and Rome', wrote John Coakley Lettsom, a devout Quaker, in 1775. Voltaire noted robustly that modern Rome boasted nearly as many houses of charity as the ancient city had triumphal arches and other public monuments to bloody conquest. Such realizations kept the *philosophe* going. For Samuel Johnson, his own age, not on the whole a splendid one, at least built almshouses and hospitals. 'Those antient nations who have given us the wisest models of government, and the brightest examples of patriotism . . . have yet left behind them no mention of alms-houses or hospitals, of places where age might repose, or sickness be relieved.' This 'tenderness' was 'known only to those who enjoy . . . the light of Revelation'.[20]

Venetian windows

Pope's preface to his poetic 'Epistle' (1731) to Burlington explains that 'false Taste' and good sense are mutually exclusive. 'Heav'n visits with a Taste the wealthy fool' (l. 17), one of the 'Bad Imitators & Pretenders'[21] whom Burlington had unwittingly served. The fools, as Pope showed him in six lines ending with a brilliant compression,

> Reverse your Ornaments, and hang them all
> On some patch'd dog-hole ek'd with ends of wall,
> Then clap four slices of Pilaster on't,
> That, lac'd with bits of rustic, makes a Front.
> Or call the winds thro' long Arcades to roar,
> Proud to catch cold at a Venetian door . . .

Pope himself explained the Venetian door as 'A Door or Window, so called, from being much practised at Venice by Palladio and others'.[22] The three-light opening

32. Bethlem as it looked after the wings for 'incurables' were built into the exercise yards on each side of the original hospital.

with an arched centre had been practised by Burlington too, but Pope was under-lining the nonsense of its indiscriminate use under English skies. When he wrote the poem, Venetian windows had recently and very prominently been used at Bethlem's first new wing (built 1725–28 and seen in Figure 32) for what its gov-ernors called 'incurably mad mischievous and ungovernable lunatics'.[23] Was this a coincidence? The question is unanswerable, but it is worth asking in connec-tion with the building's continuing reception.

'Bethlem Hospital' (1717) is by one John Rutter, who ominously introduced it as 'this Firstling of my Muse'. But the poem is accomplished, and interesting on the architecture:

> The Building not inelegant or poor
> For such a use, the careful Architect
> Conveniency, and Strength, and wholesome Air
> Consider'd, more than what might please the Sight.

So far so good, but,

> The curious Eye observes Proportion just,
> And all the Rules of Art, cornice and fr[i]eze,
> Adorning Pilasters Entablature,
> With Festoons; Ornament enough or more,
> Than may seem fit for the ill-fated Plight
> Of those, who dwell therein, distracted Men.[24]

This, the last poem to praise Bethlem's airiness, is the first to suggest that there was something weird about the festiveness of Hooke's building. The logic of Bethlem's beauty was clearly explained in the 1676 poem of that title: 'BEDLAM! That shall a lasting *Witness* be / Of this great Cities generous *Piety*: / Magnificent Foundation! Such as shows / The greatness of their Souls by whom it Rose' (ll. 31–34). The building is here a great monument to great souls, but the identification was under attack by 1700.

For Ned Ward, consistently contemptuous of the City's government, its asylum ('this ostentatious piece of vanity') stood, like Wren and Hooke's Monument to the Fire itself, as a monument only to heartlessness and pride. Updating a ven-erable theme, Ward claimed that both had been built with money diverted from the City's Orphans' (and widows') Fund. Moreover, 'they were mad that built so costly a college for such a crack-brained society . . . it was [a] pity so fine a building should not be possessed by such as had a sense of their happiness'. For Thomas Brown (1663–1704),

> *Bedlam* is a pleasant Piece, that it is, and abounds with Amusements; the first of which is the building so stately a Fabrick for Persons wholly unsensible of the Beauty and Use of it: The Outside is a perfect Mockery to the Inside, and Admits of two Amusing Queries, Whether the Persons that ordered the

Building of it, or those that inhabit it, were the maddest? And whether the Name and Thing be not as disagreeable [i.e., different] as Harp and Harrow?[25]

The real madmen were those who had ordered the building of Bethlem, whose beauty was thrown away on its inhabitants. Insensible of the beauty, the mad were also insensible of its mockery (Brown's word), then as now meaning both derision and a sham, or counterfeit. A façade, what Morris would in a more general way call the 'Emptiness and Shadow of Appearance', might even be actively malevolent towards those sequestered behind it.

In 1734 James Ralph (1705–62) published his *Critical review of the publick buildings, statues and ornaments* in London, a book then unique in its attempt to assess specific buildings, new and old, by a more or less consistent standard of appropriate elegance and economy.[26] Bethlem, Ralph wrote, is 'very well situated in point of view', an important criterion for him, and 'laid out in a very elegant taste'. But the 'middle is not large, or magnificent enough for the whole, and, by being exactly the same, both in size and decoration, with the [original] wings, seems even less, and more inconsiderable than it really is'. This judgement accords with the Palladian preference for dominant centres. The new wings for incurables (the second was by now under construction) were made Palladian by their large Venetian windows but, Ralph continued, they did not compensate for the centre's inadequacy and moreover failed to 'appear of a piece with the rest'.[27] Bethlem thus took its place among the decaying mansions (as the *Common Sense* essay would call them) whose owners fondly imagined that a little vamping and stuccoing, a Venetian window stuck on, would make them stylish.[28]

The other side of one of these windows appears in a print published the next year, in 1735 (Figure 33). It is a pirate copy of the most famous picture of Hooke's Bethlem, which is the final destination of *The Rake's progress*; the eight paintings in Hogarth's series served as both advertisements and studies for his own prints. A consortium of printmakers reconstructed the scenes on the basis of verbal accounts provided by their agents, sent to look at the paintings – for the printmakers themselves would have been speedily shown the door. This ingenuity had interesting results for their pictures, which seemingly differ from Hogarth's according to what caught, or failed to catch, the spies' attention. It is odd, for example (as David Kunzle has pointed out) that the Bedlam scene omits the female visitors Hogarth showed in the gallery (Figure 34).[29] The pirates correctly understood the Rake to be doomed in his madness and hence in the new wing for incurables,[30] and either assumed that Hogarth had shown its Venetian window or put it in anyway just to make the narrative point. Either way, the window was distinctive.

Compilers of London's historical topographies liked to crib from their predecessors and they did not question Bethlem's appearance, which is invariably 'stately' or 'magnificent'. The description in *London and its environs described* (1761), attributed to its publisher Robert Dodsley (1703–64), hence follows a well-trodden path: the 'most magnificent edifice of this kind in Europe'. The text then however departs from convention; what kind of edifice was it, after all?

HE IS CHAINED RAVING MAD IN BEDLAM.

33. A pirated version of the last scene of *The Rake's progress*, published shortly before Hogarth's own. The plagiarists included the dog, but not the female visitors.

This building upon the whole shows more the good intentions, than the good taste of the founders of this charity, the style of architecture being very improper for an hospital for madmen.

The antithesis of good taste and good intentions now seems almost comic, but it suggests something of the power of 'taste' then: fittingness, selectiveness. In accordance with the time-honoured concept of decorum, here in the form of the simplest, most additive sort of equation of ornament with social function, which included social ranking, Dodsley went on to suggest that, if Bethlem's pilasters were really necessary, those of the Tuscan order (so plain that it was rarely used) would have been preferable to Corinthian (the most elaborate).[31] He was really writing about necessity, and not just the necessity for pilasters: we are back to Thomas Brown, and whether the 'Name and Thing be not as disagreeable as Harp and Harrow'.

Topographers were meanwhile developing a stock account of another asylum, to which Dodsley again added an interestingly architectural shading. St Luke's

Hospital in Windmill Street, Upper Moorfields was begun at the end of 1750 to the designs of George Dance the Elder (1695–1768) and admitted its first patients six months later.[32] Little is known about it, but a few prints allow us to understand Dodsley's description of a 'neat but very plain structure . . . Nothing is here expended on ornament, and we only see a building of considerable length, plaistered over and whitened, with ranges of small square windows, on which no decorations have been bestowed' (Figure 35).[33] Earlier accounts had not underlined St Luke's physical plainness but rather an organizational austerity exemplified by the regulations, much reprinted, that 'The Patients in this Hospital shall not be exposed to publick View'; 'No Moneys received for the Use of this Charity, shall be expended in entertaining the General Court or Committee at any of their Meetings.'[34] Bethlem's other operations – the school for charity, the arena for civic ceremony – were pointedly discarded in favour of dedication to the study and cure of insanity,[35] and within a decade or so of St Luke's' foundation this single-mindedness was explained as manifested in an absence of ornament. The final section of this chapter returns to St Luke's'

34. Hogarth's print (1735) after his painting of the Rake in Bedlam.

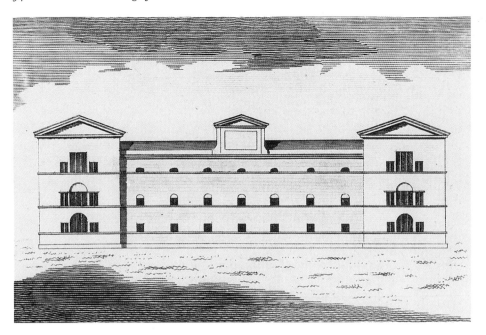

35. The first St Luke's Hospital, as illustrated in a *New and universal history* of London in (1775).

and in particular its windows (not all of which were small and square, we notice), but we can now look at another, final meaning attached to Bethlem's beauty.

Tom Brown had, in 1700, developed his theme in a very influential way; his is apparently the first printed reference to a story that Bethlem had been modelled on the Louvre. The resemblance permitted two jokes, of which one was evergreen, the implied insult and Louis XIV's reaction. The second died with Brown, at least in its explicit form:

> if we have been witty upon the *French* in giving *Bedlam* the Resemblance of the *Louvre*, they have been even with us to a Witness, by making a Present of a Disease to us, which may be bargain'd for with no more Difficulty than half a Turn in the *Long Gallery*.[36]

Bethlem's visitors might present you with the French, that is venereal, disease. Brown's wit was not careful, and I don't want to force it to carry too much weight. He was however playing with a powerful image, a 'cloacal trope' with strong connotations of sexual corruption later and most famously developed by Jonathan Swift in his 'excremental' or dressing-room poems: 'Such gaudy *tulips* raised from *dung*'.[37] In explaining it, Pat Rogers has suggested that

> at least one famous aphorism – 'A woman is a temple built on a sewer' – . . . carried the right overtones of slightly comic disgust. . . . A ditch could run beneath imposing buildings, as a fair countenance concealed the nastiness below[38]

– or behind. In Swift's dressing rooms, the axis of disgust, or revelation, is a distinctively vertical one, down into the chamber-pot: 'O! may she better learn to keep / "Those secrets of the hoary deep." '[39] This is a fundamental metaphor indeed, but the opposition of nature and artifice, essence and appearance, also works horizontally, as inside and outside.

Ornament or inappropriate dress, writes Ronald Paulson, summarizing the early Christian Tertullian, 'is the woman's attempt to make herself what she is not, by altering the exterior to suggest an equivalent inner change'. The application of cosmetics was even worse, strictly speaking blasphemous in the implied censure of what Tertullian called God's plastic skill.[40] For modern Christians, at a more mundane level cosmetics might also obscure the visible signs of venereal disease, the pox's emergence 'from its hiding places in the body', which would normally or naturally betray the 'difference between appearance and reality, between bravado and pretended distinction and the common rottenness inside'.[41] Hence the danger of the painted prostitutes who waited behind Bethlem's palatial façade, or front, with its Corinthian pilasters (recall its centrality in London's 'topography of whoredom'). 'No Doric, nor Corinthian pillars grace / With imagery this structure's naked face': Thomas Carew's 'To my Friend G. N. from Wrest' (1639) can usually be relied upon to supply a couplet apposite to yet another elaboration of the luxury critique, here that of the mask.[42]

Bethlem had already begun to attract criticism less ostensibly playful than Brown's. While acknowledging, in 1689, that 'Gallant Structure . . . to be one of the Prime Ornaments of the City of London, and a Noble Monument of Charity', Thomas Tryon was the first publicly to beg its governors not to expose the patients 'to the Idle Curiosity of every vain Boy, petulant Wench, or Drunken Companion', who 'seldom fail of asking more than an hundred impertinent Questions' of them. Thirty years later, the Revd Benjamin Ibbot described how these 'sad objects' show 'us to ourselves in the worst Disguise, by turning to us the weak and dark Side of Human Nature' and demonstrate the foolishness of pride in 'Wisdom, or in any intellectual Attainments'. This is a neat summary of lunacy's didactic function, its place in God's scheme. But, Ibbot continued, the sight of 'those unhappy Wretches . . . should never be made Matter of Sport, and Pastime, Recreation and Diversion. This is a barbarous and inhuman Abuse of such sad Spectacles'.[43] The contrast between the focused search for charitable meaning, on the one hand, and on the other impertinent, idle, and random viewing, finds parallels in Ralph's distinction between people who exercise their discriminatory taste when looking at buildings, and those who rely on 'vulgar reports or common fame, to excite their attention', and in Morris's contempt for inappropriate ornament, applied only to 'attract the Gazer's Eyes'.[44] To all of them, I think, Lucy Gent's history of a way of approaching architecture that is more interested in surfaces ('looking at') than spaces ('looking through') is relevant. Gent hypothesizes that, after a contested reception in England a century earlier, 'since 1700, the "looking through" implied by perspective has . . . been more highly valued than "looking at"' until challenged by early twentieth-century painters and, we could add, by critics who in the 1980s began to question architectural modernism's 'lack of interest in the face'.[45]

As Jonathan Andrews has shown, over the course of the eighteenth century the polite classes withdrew from Bethlem, speaking both figuratively and, as far as we can tell, literally; they anxiously distanced themselves from what was increasingly seen as a tasteless kind of diversion for the idly curious.[46] Though casual visiting was curtailed when, in 1770, the hospital began requiring visitors to obtain a ticket from a governor first, 'curiosity', unselective scanning for recreational purposes, remained the antithesis of more focused searches for meaning in the plight of the insane. 'For nineteenth-century reformers, as for twentieth-century historians', Andrew Scull has written, 'here was the quint-essence of the classical response to madness, and the occasion for the most lurid retrospective reconstructions of the defects of the *ancien régime*: within [Bethlem's] walls, the crazed were reduced to a spectacle'. And in this recon-struction, Hogarth's picture of the final destination of *The Rake's progress* remained definitive.[47]

With enormous skill, Hogarth translated into a picture the Bethlem list of a by then familiar sort: the mad king, the mad astronomer, the mad poet and so forth. But who are the visitors, the two women standing by the cell of the mad king? 'Curious spectators of this melancholy sight', is the first recorded answer, written at the widowed Jane Hogarth's invitation by John Trusler in 1768, when Bethlem was still entirely open to casual visitors. Trusler made the connection, suggesting that Hogarth had introduced the women to 'brighten this distressful scene, and, draw a smile from him, whose rigid reasoning might condemn the bringing into publick view, this blemish of humanity', that is, the king. Leering at his nakedness, while pretending to avert her gaze, the woman with the fan is comic, because she is a hypocritical prude.[48] Most subsequent commentators felt constrained to ignore the nakedness, and hence the comedy, but one excep-tion was the German physicist and belletrist Georg Christoph Lichtenberg (1742–99). Are the women 'perhaps ladies of the Court?', he asked: 'They are just being received in audience, and at the same time receive from a distance a benediction which they accept with much better grace than was intended.' One of the women holds a fan that ostensibly shields her from the sight of the king and in particular from that of his penis, which he holds behind his leg: in fact she is clearly looking at him through the struts of her fan. He is urinating, we assume: a stream is visible in the engraving, though not in the painting. This is the 'benediction', offered by a madman who is also a beautiful nude. 'What are the ladies doing here?' asked Lichtenberg again; is it possible that they just want 'to look at the naked and behave charmingly as if they did not see them?'[49] That they are voyeurs was evident to Lichtenberg, as was their importance within the picture, which Hogarth conveyed with colour in the painting[50] and light in the print. Their sexual interest in the king is impertinent and to that extent femi-nine; the identification of other people's curiosity was, I suspect, ultimately a gendered one in the eighteenth century.[51] Too easily satisfied by colourful inci-dent, it remained ignorant of higher theological or medical aims. The differ-ence in ways of looking reproduces, now in the form of feminine against masculine, the dialectic sketched above between surface and essence, Tom Brown's 'Name and Thing'. By their vivid presence inside the asylum, the two women dramatize a general anxiety about what might or might not be made of its exterior.

In the 1755 edition of his *Essai sur l'architecture*, Laugier wrote that 'too much beauty in a house [of charity] stifles charity, because curiosity becomes sated; the poor must be lodged like the poor'.[52] His pauper hospital would have looked very different from Hooke's, but the abbé Laugier was confirming its inhabitants' Christian function as the objects of charitable curiosity. The prescription is also noteworthy for its prescience. The image of the curious gaze getting snagged, distracted from charity, by madly inappropriate beauty would be a durable one. Laugier's French successors would develop a more general doctrine of architecture as a 'species of expressive language', which culminated at the end of the century in a full theory of character extolling its potential for shaping human psychology and society.[53] Something very like this development can be traced in English writing about Bethlem, and even more explicitly in that about the two St Luke's hospitals.

Lunette windows

In 1788 Jacques Tenon (1724–1816) named Bethlem and the brand new St Luke's as model asylum buildings; they and the naval hospital at Plymouth were the most perfect hospitals, for their distinct purposes, that he knew.[54] Given Bethlem's institutional reputation in some quarters, it perhaps needed a stranger to claim its excellence as a building, and St Luke's' essential resemblance to one begun more than a century earlier. As a voluntary hospital, St Luke's is generally credited with inspiring the foundation of the seven provincial asylums built between 1765 and 1799 (Leicester's is seen on the left in Figure 56, p. 140) and the debt probably extended to its planning, as far as that could be followed at smaller institutions.[55] The asylums that began to be built under the terms of the County Asylum Act of 1808 certainly used the range of cells (or later, sometimes, small wards) banked on to a gallery serving as both corridor and day room.[56] In various distributions, and sometimes on the radial plan whose first monumental example was the Glasgow Asylum (opened 1814; see Figure 80, p. 209), this remained the fundamental unit at larger nineteenth-century asylums.[57] Not until about 1860 was it questioned in the British medical press. Detached blocks were then proposed to replace the wings whose origins one writer found in the 'long galleries and gloomy cells of desecrated monasteries, which were the first asylums', and which the specialist architect G. T. Hine called the 'old' plan, for him modelled on prisons, 'which in time became known as the corridor type'.[58]

The first asylum building known to have copied Hooke's (and apparently the only one at which the debt was explicitly acknowledged) was Dublin's. Jonathan Swift was at least by 1731 determined to 'build a house for fools and mad', and St Patrick's Hospital, founded by the terms of his will, opened in 1757, twelve years after his death.[59]

In 1732 Sir William Fownes, who as a former Lord Mayor of Dublin had, he explained, first become concerned with the plight of its 'miserable Lunaticks', wrote to Swift about their possible accommodation. That for the peaceable insane ('such as are not so outrageous but melancholy &c') Fownes envisaged with a

piatsa for a stone Gallery for walking dry and out of that severall Lodging Cells
... – this may be of such a size as that it may be Enlarged in Length or by a
Return & over head the same sort of a Gallery & little Rooms or Cells opening
the Doores into the Gallery – For by Intervalls the objects Effected may be
permitted to walk at times in the Gallerys – this is according to the Custom
of London

– as everyone knew. (Swift had anyway been a Bethlem governor since 1714.) No
storey need be lofty, Fownes wrote, but each should be 'sufficiently airy and 20
Foot wide whereof 10 for a gallery and 10 for Lodges – each Lodge 8 or 10 feet
broad [and] as there is a Fund so many goe on' – that is, may be built.[60] The reference to airiness is interesting, as is Fownes's attention to the ways in which
form follows funding. From a self-sufficient core – the length of the lodging-
wing will depend on the size of the initial fund – expansion must be easy ('no
necessity for any Plans or Architects') and might be attractive ('Perhaps there
may appear some well disposed persons who will say they will make this
Enlargmnt & so others').[61] These considerations encouraged Fownes's proposal
for two storeys of cells fronted at ground level by an open, loggia-gallery and
above by a closed (he must have imagined it so) corridor-gallery. The scheme
illustrates the way in which galleries were still understood in terms more functional than physical. It also illustrates the continuing relevance, for lunacy, of the
military hospitals' small rooms and sheltered walks, for this was Kilmainham's
arrangement.

Michael Wills built the boundary wall and prepared a plan for St Patrick's in
collaboration with the two medical governors, but the project of another architect, George Semple (c.1700–80), was accepted in 1749. Notes made around that
time ('Semple's cells, agree exactly with the cells of Bedlam Hospital', for
example) suggest that his plan was chosen over Wills's for its greater conformity
to Hooke's. At St Patrick's the cell-gallery wings were folded back to fit the site,
making a U shape,[62] the first of the permutations in which such wings would be
arranged. It was not an ideal solution, because the view from St Patrick's' gallery
windows was of other gallery windows. This was duller than Moorfields, proverbially the haunt of wrestlers, hacks, whores, rioting apprentices, pie-sellers,
jugglers, and men doing something called playing at cudgels.[63] 'Gallery' started
to lose its meaning as a place in which, or from which, to view.

The old meaning however acquired a gloss in 1815, when an investigative
Parliamentary Committee of Madhouses in England became interested in gallery
views. Did convalescents at Hooke's building not 'take great pleasure in looking
out the window at the end of the gallery'? it asked the Bethlem Steward, George
Wallett. They did, and Wallett added that 'many of the patients said, they had
heard [the windows] were so constructed' at the new building in Southwark (see
Figures 11 and 78, pp. 42 and 207): 'they hoped it was so, they asked me whether
it was so or not; that it was a great pleasure and amusement for them to look
out'. The Revd John Becher, testifying about arrangements at the Nottingham
Asylum a few weeks later, was asked if the patients could ever look out of the
windows. 'Yes,' he replied, 'ours is a system of great tenderness and indulgence;

36. New St Luke's, a magazine illustration from 1785. Figures standing in a featureless plain point at the great front.

the patients have very cheerful prospects'. Patients' prospects at St Luke's were grimmer, according to Edward Wakefield, who reported that its galleries overlooked the large parish cemetery at St Luke's Church. Interments occurred there almost daily, 'under the very eyes of the unfortunate people who are confined' in the hospital.[64] (Perhaps they were all really glossing Samuel Johnson: 'You no more think of madness by having windows that look to Bedlam, than you think of death by having windows that look to a church-yard'.)[65]

Bethlem's relatively large gallery windows do not look as if they opened (see Figure 23, p. 64) and in 1787 Tenon described them as fixed, but those on the pavilions could have had hinged casements.[66] Both types appear conventionally domestic. St Patrick's' entrance façade was lined by offices with similarly ordinary windows, probably sashes; with its cells pushed around to the sides, it could look more domestic than most general hospitals would.[67] In contrast was the first St Luke's' display front, which was evidently not the entrance front (Figure 35). Plastered and 'whitened', looking south across Moorfields towards its rival, this was a distinctive sight in mid-century London, not least for the abstract, witty plays on the theme of the Venetian window on the fronts of its side wings (which like those at St Patrick's extended back at right angles to the centre). It was Bethlem's window, but if any homage were intended it was not to the institutional rival. The façade was not entirely distinctive, for St Luke's looked rather like St George's (and certainly St George's as shown in Figure 51, p. 134), the general hospital designed in the mid-1730s by Isaac Ware, the future scourge of idle ornament. Unlike Bethlem but like St Luke's, St George's was a voluntary hospital, and the only other in London to have got (more or less) purpose-built quarters by mid-century. St Luke's' governors at first intended to devote themselves to the relief of persons who, though poor enough to be proper charitable objects, were not paupers in the legal sense,[68] and in this respect too, they conceivably imagined their hospital as more like St George's than Bethlem, a substantial proportion of whose inmates were forwarded, and supported, by their home parishes.

Bethlem's public, north side presented its galleries' windows, but the small windows in St Luke's' central range were probably those of cells, which would also face south when the hospital was rebuilt in the 1780s. They make their own play, with the ground floor's squares acquiring crowns of blank lunettes in the middle storey, and becoming lunette windows at the top. The surviving sectional drawings entered in 1777 for the architectural competition for the new St Luke's all show barrel-vaulted cells lit by high lunettes tucked into the ceiling curves, which suggests that the arrangement was stipulated, and may suggest that it had been followed on the top floor, at least, of the old building.[69] It was certainly used throughout the new asylum as it was built (Figures 36 and 37), where the younger Dance (1741–1825) expended some care on the lunettes: his drawings explain ingenious semicircular shutters.[70] The masonry of the vaulting reduced the fire risk, and perhaps muffled noise,[71] while the windows' size and height – they began about 9 feet from the floor – were supposed to limit external stimuli that might, for example, exacerbate a frenzy. Patients in asylum cells might safely contemplate what they could of the sky. Comparable considerations directed the use of lunette windows at some new prisons in the mid-1780s.[72] The light and the sights permitted by asylums' gallery windows, by contrast, represented the beginning of the convalescent's reintroduction to the world, or a consolation for the tranquil but incurable.[73]

The elder Dance's building was 'so much decayed', it was reported in 1776, that a replacement would soon be erected.[74] St Luke's was to be rebuilt on a new site in Old Street, and on Bethlem's scale (540 feet long).[75] A competition for the design was advertised the next year; the younger Dance, who had succeeded his father as the hospital's Surveyor, seems not to have entered. James Gandon won the £100 premium but Dance got the commission, in 1778, though four years passed before he projected something cheap enough for construction to be approved.[76] A hundred or so patients were transferred to Old Street in early 1787, after some delay while the hospital was opened to public inspection.[77] This gratifyingly popular experiment served, among other things, to underline St Luke's' distance from what were rapidly becoming figured as the bad old days of asylums, for this Christmas open house was to be the general public's first and last chance to look.

37. An early nineteenth-century perspective of the new St Luke's, one of the *Beauties of England and Wales*; Dance varied the window patterns again on the sides of the hospital.

38. One of the women's galleries at St Luke's, an aquatint (1809) by A. C. Pugin and Thomas Rowlandson, who contributed the figures. 'Today . . . a madhouse which looked like a setting for the hallucinations of madmen would never do', John Summerson wrote about this picture in 1943.

Any detailed instructions given to the competitors have not survived, but Pierre du Prey has shown what we can deduce from the drawings. A window type seems to have been specified; cell and gallery wings were also standard. The young John Soane (1753–1837) entered two designs in which the cell wings curve more or less tightly around to the front; the project with the tighter curves can be considered the second entry.[78] In both, the wings make wedge-shaped exercise courts separated by a central spine formed by an entrance pavilion on the street and behind it an enclosed corridor (the 'Cover'd Way for the several Wards & Infirmary etc.') leading to the area between the cells for women on the left (west) and men on the right. Soane would have segregated the sexes with some ingenuity, considering that their numbers are not equal in his projects. (The first is for 138 women and 113 men, and the second for 144 women and 106 men.)[79] In this he was assisted by Bethlem's technology of gallery grilles; the second plan shows the 'iron gates', and the central zone between them simply displaced to the right, so more cells join the women's side. Grilles were certainly used at the new hospital.[80]

Dance's St Luke's was much more like Bethlem than any of the competition projects were, though it had two short rear wings at right angles to the central range; Pugin showed a junction (Figure 38).[81] On three floors, men and women were divided by the central stairhall, and from that hall by the grilles and gates. St Luke's' galleries were a fraction narrower than Bethlem's and at times became more corridor-like, as some cells were ranged at the back of the building; they lined virtually the full length of its front. On the rear (north) façade Dance matched window types to the greater variety of spaces behind them, and in the

39. The rear (north) elevation of St Luke's, half of Dance's drawing (too big to photograph in its entirety) which accompanied the contract of 1787. It does not show the short side wings to be added when funds permitted, but which were, in fact, built without delay.

process achieved a truly rational elegance (Figure 39). Large, arched windows (which could be opened at the top) illuminated the galleries and permitted that rather unsatisfactory view of the burial ground.[82] Huge windows lit the central stairwell, like Bethlem's closed to patients. The projections in the centre of each wing held the 'pump recesses' which, exceptionally, got a different shape of window on each floor, with lunettes on top, and lunettes folded open to make the portholes beneath. To the right is the projection made by the superimposed latrines. These and the cells had a very distinctive window type, a lunette set within an arch reveal otherwise 'blind', or filled in. *La croisée est en mur plein jusqu'au cintre*, wrote Tenon: the window is walled up as far as the arch.[83] This was a neutral, and natural reading – Tenon surely saw many such openings filled in, or never made, to avoid the window tax – but the St Luke's window would later be interpreted as a narrative device. The lunatics were walled up, or rather shielded, from the world.

On the rear elevation of Soane's second competition entry each cell lunette on the top floor and its partner on the floor beneath are set within a single and similarly blind arch reveal.[84] An inspiration for this device might have been Dance's prodigal All Hallows London Wall (1765–67; he was twenty-four when he designed it). The church's semicircular clerestory windows appear, externally, to be simply incised out of giant blind arches, at the points at which these begin to spring (Figure 40). Dance was a neo-classical architect, but he liked Baroque ambiguity, the visual puns, and All Hallows's wall could alternatively be read as an open arcade whose lower part has been walled up, in a process complete on the westernmost bay, which has no window. Soane's superimposed lunettes in their high blind arches have been credited with inspiring Dance at St Luke's,[85] but their composition is unambiguous. Dance's single lunette within an arch reveal is the psychologists' rabbit-and-duck, a pattern that can almost simultaneously be read two ways: the window cut into the arch, or the opening left by the wall's upward advance.

Walls did, curiously, advance this way at the reformed prisons that began to be built in the mid-1780s, whose cell and ward blocks were raised on arches that were then often filled in to impost level. The 'piazzas' thus formed could be used as work areas whose walls did not interfere overmuch with air circulation because the lunette shapes remained open.[86] Walling-up came to be the dominant reading of a window type used at new asylums until the 1810s (see Figure 79, p. 208). The Bedford Asylum, built 1809–12 to the designs of John Wing, was in 1831 called a handsome building, even beautiful, 'but for the upper segments of the blank and arched windows which alone are open; and which being furnished with iron bars, present the revolting idea of confinement'.[87] And in 1815 walled-up windows were, again, the subject of parliamentary inquiry, though it was gallery, not cell windows that were examined. The first report (11 July 1815) of the committee investigating English asylums concludes with a section on Bethlem at Southwark, just about to be occupied. In spite of the expert testimony (summarized above), establishing that the 'greatest advantage might be derived from the Patients having opportunities of seeing objects that might amuse them', the windows in the new Bethlem's galleries were 'so high that patients could not see out'. Richard Upton, the architect who superintended construction, had testified that these windows' lower parts had indeed been filled in,

40. Dance's All Hallows London Wall.

conformable with the opinion of some of the medical officers, for the purpose of avoiding the irritation to which [the patients] are said to have been subject at Moorfields, by the sport of boys and others from the road, and also as being out of the reach of *being broke*

– the 'road' implying that patients had been vulnerable on the old hospital's south side. But Upton assured the committee that the windows had been 'planked up' to a height of five feet, not ten as it had thought. Some of Bethlem's medical officers meanwhile disavowed any influence on, or indeed much knowledge of, the new building's form and siting, to which the committee had a number of objections.[88]

In his *Memoirs* (1835), Soane described dinner with some colleagues and an 'eminent physician'. St Luke's, said the doctor,

> always excited gloomy reflections in his mind, and gave him no other idea but that of a hospital for mad persons. Every member of the company observed that a greater compliment could not be paid to the powers of architecture.[89]

This dull company understood that architecture's powers may be measured by the strength of the sensations that it inspires and second by the appropriateness of those sensations' emotional tone to the building's function. This was 'character', and musings on this quality often have the circularity of Humphry Repton's 'we admire St Luke's Hospital as a mad-house and Newgate as a prison, because they both announce their purposes by their appropriate appearance, and no stranger has occasion to inquire for what uses they are intended'. They look like what they look like, in other words, and Repton's stranger-tourist, unlike Edward Hatton's a century earlier, will not be deceived or delighted by hospitals resembling palaces or 'palaces [that] may be mistaken for hospitals'.[90] Dance was in any case acknowledged as a master of character's production.

In writing about character, it would become possible to translate the 'train of thought', which a characterful building could start in the observer's imagination, into a narrative by 'characteristic architecture' itself, as Repton (1752–1818) defined it in 1803: every 'building ought to "tell its own tale," and not . . . look like anything else'.[91] As the century progressed, it also became possible to understand buildings as telling tales about themselves, their own function. James Elmes (1782–1862) explained in 1847 how St Luke's' external surfaces

> are divided into a series of semicircular recesses and piers. The semicircular part, which is near the ceiling of each story, gives light and air to the cells without exposing the unhappy inmates to the gaze, and often derision, of the multitude, as was the case in the old hospital in Moorfields.

The last refers either to the first St Luke's or to old Bethlem and I think the latter, because it had become emblematic of staring. Elmes continued that the hospital's 'whole aspect is commanding and is highly characteristic of the use to which it is designed . . . few buildings in our metropolis, or perhaps in Europe, surpass this for unity and appropriateness of style'. Its characteristic mounting made the St Luke's lunette both functional and an icon of functionality.[92]

Like a Venetian window stuck on to a crumbling house, cosmetics may conceal decay: for several reasons Bethlem became vulnerable to a close variant of this old theme. But cosmetics were (and are) also prophylaxes and social duties, protecting the skin against external damage and infection, and contributing to one's illustrative, but accurate, self-representation as a member of the social order.[93] The difference is that between the Venetian window and the lunette within the arch reveal. St Luke's' mask was, in other words, the good kind, and the self-representation of the building as a whole was as powerful as Elmes explained. In his analysis, however, illustration begins to take precedence over actuality, ' "seems" over "is" ', as Edward Kaufman describes the way in which Victorian debates about truth, or functionality in architecture inevitably turned to the representation of function.[94]

The name and the thing, as Tom Brown wrote, were as different as harp and harrow; he also showed the rotten sexuality behind Bethlem's fine mask, a sexuality and a disease that a quarter-century later Robert Morris found, more generally, in the deformations of 'Novelty and Singleness'. The harrowing thing about Bethlem anyway came to be the visiting, not the visited – ostensibly, at least. As Andrews has pointed out, repugnance at the custom cannot really be distinguished from repugnance at the sight of the mad.[95] The predatory implications of spectatorship at Bethlem anyway did nothing for its architecture's reputation. Casual visiting was from the outset prohibited at St Luke's, London's next asylum, twenty years before Bethlem's governors began restricting it there. James Elmes finally explained the distinctive cell windows of the younger Dance's characterful south front as both sheltering the insane from the gaze of the curious, and illustrating the shelter. Behind *that* mask, however, St Luke's was very similar to Hooke's building.

Though varied in appearance, none of the general hospitals prompted the criticism that they lacked character or were indecorous; nor was the tale they were telling, in Repton's words, ever made explicit. It was partly, however, a story about funding.

Chapter 5

Raising the hospital, each performing his part

In his *Adventures* (1753) by Tobias Smollett, MD (1721–71), Ferdinand, Count Fathom considers various stratagems for advancing his career as a London physician. Some are too popular to be much use ('ordering himself to be called from church, alarming the neighbourhood with knocking at his door in the night, receiving sudden messages in places of resort, and inserting his cures by way of news in the daily papers'), and the master plan is anyway to acquire

> interest enough to erect an hospital, lock, or infirmary, by the voluntary subscription of his friends; a scheme which had succeeded to a miracle, with many of the profession, who had raised themselves into notice, upon the carcases of the poor.[1]

Smollett was playing to a gallery that was cynical about physicians, and historians now emphasize the layman's part in the foundation of the eighteenth century's new 'voluntary' hospitals. The adjective signified their support out of free and personal volition and not, for example, by the iron-clad terms of some charitable trust in perpetuity.[2]

A voluntary hospital began with an appeal for gifts, not uncommonly after an initial bequest.[3] The living gifts came from individuals and corporate bodies, including townships,[4] who might also promise to make regular annual payments, the subscriptions. Either could give them the right to nominate in- and outpatients and to call themselves, variously, governors, donors, sponsors, or subscribers; the number of patients one might sponsor could be the product of fairly complex reckonings devised for the sake of a reliable income.[5] 'Though superficially an investment,' Peter Borsay has written about the theatres, assembly rooms, and libraries also being organized on this associational basis, 'the comparatively small size of many shareholdings, and the user-rights associated with them, suggest that many contributors thought primarily in terms of consumption.'[6] Unlike lending libraries, hospitals, whether new or old, did not in theory offer any direct service to the governors and tradesmen associated with them; the dividends were prestige, obligation, and, for voluntary hospitals' governors, some automatic rights to ensure and enjoy usefulness. It was these rights which made an important difference between, say, Bethlem and St Luke's. Even a big gift to the old, royal hospital carried with it no governorship, at least not in theory, and hence no right of 'Inspection', as St Luke's pointed out:[7] Bethlem was at once too available to the public, and too unavailable. 'By the Oeconomical Administration of Hospitals,' wrote Edward Foster in 1768,

> I mean that Superintendence which all their Donators should have over them. For Charity is mere Ostentation unless proper Attention is paid to the Application of the Sums destined to Purposes of public Utility.[8]

Superintendence could, predictably, be figured in terms of luxury and its antitheses.

Smollett's readership was perhaps cynical about the new hospitals, too. While these charities presented themselves as gatherings of different ranks and denominations devoting themselves to the sick poor, their activities were often more interestingly particular than that. Adrian Wilson has, for example, explained how the first voluntary hospital, the Public Infirmary at Petty Lane (1719, opened 1720, to become the Westminster Infirmary) arose out of the revival of the Westminster Charitable Society, itself founded by a group of Tories not only anxious to keep the working classes Christian, as they defined that state, but to get the two Westminster parliamentary seats for their party.[9] The second was the Edinburgh Infirmary, founded in 1729 in an atmosphere of Hanoverian zeal and of struggle, as Michael Barfoot has shown, between the city's medical- and surgical-professional interests. From the Westminster a group of governors in 1733 departed in a flurry of more or less libellous pamphlets to form St George's, to be followed by the London Infirmary (subsequently Hospital, 1740) and the Middlesex Hospital (1745). The Edinburgh Infirmary acquired its royal charter in 1736, the year that saw the foundation and opening of the Winchester Hospital, the first in the English provinces. By 1760 twelve more had opened their doors,[10] three more in Scotland,[11] and one in the colonies: Philadelphia's Pennsylvania Hospital, founded in 1751. London meanwhile saw the first specialist hospitals, one for venereal cases and three for women lying-in.[12] With charity schools they were the eighteenth century's 'most striking innovations in the welfare pattern',[13] and as buildings they constituted its first consciously 'reformed' type. The following chapter describes the buildings and this one, how they were built.

Useful expertise

Gubernatorial privileges could be granted to donors of expertise, like medical men, or clergy who raised funds.[14] The Foundling Hospital persuaded George Frederick Handel, performances of whose music netted it a fortune during his lifetime, to accept a governorship in 1750. The Foundling was extraordinary for its cultivation of 'Gentlemen Artists', of whom fifteen in 1746 'agreed to present Performances in their different Professions for Ornamenting the Hospital' and were promptly elected governors, but charity was not readily separated from fashionable culture.[15] The principle is personalized by William Hogarth, a founder-governor of the Foundling, whose later eagerness to use it (and St Bartholomew's) for showing his paintings does not obviate his and Jane Hogarth's interest in its primary aim. For the hospitals, the elections enacted an ideal of collaborative production, unconstrained by cash exchanges, among men of all ranks (all that counted, anyway).[16] At St Bartholomew's, in 1787, Jacques Tenon was told that every citizen who paid £50 might be elected a governor – the baker and the cloth merchant sat with 'les plus grands seigneurs' – provided he had a good character and useful expertise.[17] St Bartholomew's was not a voluntary hospital but Tenon correctly apprehended little difference in this respect: the ideal was not confined to the new foundations.

Another of the Foundling's founder-governors was Theodore Jacobsen (d. 1772), who designed the new building described in Chapter 8. A successful merchant, Jacobsen was a 'Gentleman well versed in the Science of Architecture', whose project was in 1742 chosen over others by professionals also versed, one might say, as gentlemen.[18] Amateur architects were not rare in eighteenth-century Britain, but those who gave themselves the 'trouble of building for others' (as Sarah Churchill put it) were rarer, and Jacobsen was exceptional for engaging with such large public buildings as the Foundling and soon the Royal Hospital, Haslar.[19] The Surveyor James Horne (d. 1756) however supervised the Foundling's construction, and he would do the same for the naval hospital though not, there, for free.[20] Professionals such as he were regularly elected governors, and an example of what that might entail is presented by Boulton Mainwaring's early career at the London Hospital.

In July 1747 Mainwaring (1702–78), the London's Surveyor, attended one of the weekly meetings of its 'house' committee. The hospital, then occupying four houses in Prescot Street and a couple in adjoining Chamber Street (they are just north-east of the Tower), was plagued by a cold bath overflowing into the apothecary's workshop and by its Chamber Street neighbours, who were threatening legal action over its thrifty habit of pumping the cesspool out into the street instead of cutting a drain to the sewer in the main road. Six months later, the committee decided to recommend to the next governors' Court that Mainwaring be appointed a governor in recognition of his regular attendance and assistance, with five guineas annually towards his expenses, as long as he retained the surveyorship which, if salaried before, was no longer.[21] A higher mark of distinction would have been the staff signifying a life governorship soon presented, for example, to Mr Theodore Janssen, who had managed to secure for the hospital £100 out of a surplus remaining from a City subscription fund.[22] In May 1751, the London's newly formed building committee resolved that 'Something ought to be done' about building, and began requesting designs. Mainwaring produced eight in greater or lesser variation before the end of the year, which must be some kind of record, and meanwhile convinced the Commissioners of the Land Tax to exempt the charity from paying duty on the three houses sitting on its future site at White Chapel Mount, land itself secured only after prolonged searches and negotiations in which he had been active.[23]

Mainwaring might have been encouraged, during these months, by the hope of building, as well as designing, a new hospital. Receiving relatively little for their designs, many architects made their living by construction and 5 per cent of completed cost was a common fee.[24] The plan finally settled, the London's committee asked him, in December 1751,

> to Acquaint them with the usuall Allowance given to Surveyors of Buildings. He Informed them that it was Usual to al[l]ow from Two & a half to Five P. Cent But if he should be thought proper to be Employed as such, he Submitted the Consideration of any Gratuity Intirely to This Committee . . .

James Gibbs (1682–1754) had however recently declared that he would accept no 'acknowledgement, or satisfaction' for his work at St Bartholomew's, whose Court thanked him for this 'generous and charitable disposition towards the poor of this house'. Mainwaring's governor-colleagues anyway had another question, and in reply he informed them 'in General of the Difference between Contracting with any One person for the Whole; and with Several different Workmen'.[25] The committee decided not to employ a general contractor, but itself to deal with the workmen and suppliers individually and directly in a procedure other hospitals had adopted. Such committees might include someone like Mainwaring, the professional co-opted by voluntarism, but also someone like Alexander Monro, the Professor of Anatomy who was glad (he later recalled) to correct William Adam's design for the Edinburgh Infirmary, its operating theatre *and* its proportions.[26]

This method of building was supposed to save money, and not just the contractor's percentage. Merchants and craftsmen directly enrolled might offer discounts, especially if they became governors too.[27] More fundamentally, the procedure enacted something upon which general stress was placed, the governors' mindfulness of their duty as trustees for every donor, and as such was amenable to useful glosses in publications. The Devon and Exeter Hospital announced in 1741 that its new building would be realized in as 'plain and frugal a Manner as possible, for which Purpose a Board of Works, composed of several Gentlemen' would direct the builders and examine their accounts. The surveyor John Richards (1690–1778) had donated the plan, but the gentlemen preferred to run construction themselves, as they informed Exeter and, via the *Gentleman's Magazine*, the English-speaking world. Edinburgh's building committee similarly promised that the fabric would be as frugal as its members' personal expenditure of 'Labour, Attention and Attendance' was lavish.[28] This work would, as at other hospitals, include putting off tradesmen desperate, and suing, for payment.[29]

As Peter Mills's (1598–1670) long governorship at St Bartholomew's suggests,[30] there was nothing new about architect-builders taking part in hospital management, which besides new construction often included the refurbishment of real property like the London's Whitechapel houses as well as the hospitals themselves. (Nor should we assume that their expertise, or activity, was confined to building and refurbishments.) The real difference was made by the great increase in the amount of construction planned after 1720, which involved many more architect-governors and the refinement of the associated etiquette. Gibbs was elected a governor of St Bartholomew's three months before a rebuilding committee was appointed in July 1723; Hawksmoor and the master mason John Townsend (1678–1742) also took their places on it.[31] Lord Burlington was probably influential in obtaining for Isaac Ware the job of converting Lanesborough House to St George's Hospital and a collaboration perhaps ensued between the two architect-governors, though another, Thomas Archer (c.1668–1743), was also involved in the work.[32] Its governor John Wood (1704–54) gave to the Bath General Hospital (opened 1742) in a 'free gift and benefaction' his plans and his 'care, labour and expenses for surveying and directing' construction, as its minutes record. The gift was implicit in Wood's own claim that 'every person concerned in bringing this Charity into Execution, performed his Part at his own Expence';[33] the care for the construction was, as we have seen, the larger gift. James Paine (1717–89), who began subscribing to the Middlesex in 1759, four years after his design for it was accepted, seems to have taken no fee thereafter and was eventually made an Honorary Perpetual Governor.[34] Several permutations of arrangements for designing, supplying labour and materials, inspecting work and accounts, and acknowledging the charitable imperative were possible. The younger George Dance, the hospital's Surveyor, took no fee for designing the St Luke's building begun in 1782 but contracted for its construction, like the principal subcontractors returned donations to the hospital after it was finished, and with them was then voted a Life Governor.[35]

The London foundations in particular boasted noble and even royal patrons and presidents, and physicians and clergymen jostled to become connected to hospitals on terms that can appear unpromising.[36] The architect's part brought advantage too. Gibbs found commissions for monuments and buildings all over the country as well as subscribers to his *Book of architecture* (1728) among his fellow-governors; Jacobitism was another common cause.[37] If not as lucrative as a substantial country house, a hospital was (as Joan Lane has pointed out) seen by more potential clients,[38] and a little virtue and even glamour might be expected to rub off on its author. In 1742 a lawyer wrote to one of his, and William Adam's, clients to reassure him that Adam's local reputation,

> is certainly far from being [that of] a money catcher; . . . He is certainly a great genius in his way and hath given proofs of it in our Royal Infirmary which is now almost quite finished and one of the grandest buildings of the age in our parts and meets with the general approbation from the best judges.

On the other hand, three years later Adam was obliged to remind the Edinburgh managers that they had long owed him £600 for timber,[39] a nuisance exacerbated by the context. No one likes to have to demand £600, plus interest, from the maimed and diseased poor.

There remains one general point to make about the voluntary hospitals, which can be illustrated by a later publication. In 1832 a history of the Glasgow Infirmary quoted a story from its annual report of 1824, about William Smith, an inkle (linen-tape) weaver. Smith, then a subscriber for thirty-five years, had been

> regularly in the practice of waiting on one of the Managers, on the first day of each year, and giving a guinea as his annual subscription. He as regularly waited on the same gentlemen for his copy of the Infirmary Report, which seemed to more than compensate him for his subscription.

Smith had 'sometimes been asked whether he was not perhaps giving more than he could afford: "No," he replied, "I can save a little, and my saving cannot be better bestowed." '[40] This story was printed and then reprinted to show how the Infirmary was the place at which, twice a year, the artisan William Smith met with his betters. Whether or not the hospitals really provided this common ground and if so for whom, precisely, are good questions, but this is one of the things that they represented themselves as doing in the printed reports, histories, and sermons that confirmed the solidity and universal acceptability of the enterprise, and which helped to compensate subscribers.

In a sense, the hospitals were themselves representations, 'conspicuous monument[s] of prestigious charity, distinct from the tainting and compulsory housekeeping of the poor law system' (Roy Porter); 'ostentatious constituents of a new civic culture that sought to document and enact residents' aspirations to civility, refinement and patriotism' (Kathleen Wilson).[41] This model explains their figurative prominence, in the English and Scottish urban scene, compared to the numbers of sick poor they could actually help, and their generally (in the first instance) unprepossessing buildings. The Edinburgh Infirmary opened in 1729 in a two-storey house called the 'little House', five rooms and a kitchen 20 feet from front to back. With four, and soon six beds it admitted thirty-five patients in its first year, a number inviting comparison with 352 'Contributors' and twenty 'Extraordinary Managers'.[42] The numbers do not necessarily mean that the Infirmary's foundation was the product of mass action – Alexander Monro, Professor of Anatomy at the School of Medicine, and George Drummond (1687–1766), first elected Lord Provost in 1725, were, and remained, the prime movers – but they do reflect the importance of a representation of consensus, of free volition. The Infirmary provides striking illustrations of how the ideal worked on the common ground that was the construction site.

The charitable construction of the Edinburgh Royal Infirmary

Scotland's political union with England in 1707 stripped Edinburgh of a parliament, a privy council, and a treasury, and left landlords, merchants, and trade guilds actively mourning the loss of the fashionable world.[43] With it, too, the Scottish Office of Works that had built and enlarged the Stuart palaces effectively ceased to exist and the mastership of work became a sinecure for Hanoverian loyalists.[44] No civil architect benefited from government patronage in eighteenth-century Scotland.[45] But Scots unhappy about the union determined to make the best of it, and others were not unhappy at all. Adam's clients included not only

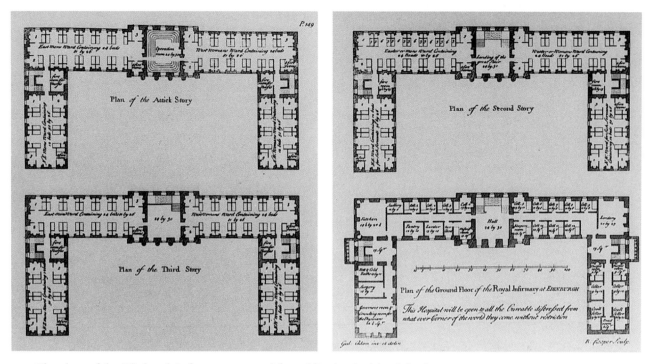

41. The plans of the Edinburgh Infirmary, engraved for publication in Adam's book.

42. Adam's elevation of the Edinburgh Infirmary; compare Figure 44, which shows the hospital more or less as it stood before its demolition in 1884.

zealous unionists like his friend (and relation by marriage) John Clerk of Penicuik, but some of the most active and powerful advocates of the Hanoverian succession.[46] And as the adjunct of the university Medical School whose formation in 1726 has been called the public inauguration of the Scottish Enlightenment, and which after 1750 became the 'pre-eminent centre of medical education in the English-speaking world', the Infirmary as an institution – and as a building – played an integral part in the 'process of reshaping and redirecting Edinburgh's intellectual life'.[47] No English equivalent springs to mind.

Led by Drummond, the Town Council backed the School's foundation.[48] This, Michael Barfoot has shown, also signified a pointed disqualification of the 200-year-old Incorporation of Surgeons. What was once the greatest and the wealthiest of the craft guilds had lost its position of authority on the Council, now generally unsympathetic to guild interests, and it would suffer a further blow when it was effectively excluded as a body from attendance at and the management of the Infirmary. Hence the opening, in 1736, of the Surgeons' Hospital in another adapted house. For two years, Edinburgh had two hospitals competing until the surgeons threw their lot in with the 'Physicians' Infirmary. The deal was struck, in part, on the basis of money they had accumulated for their new purpose-built hospital, a project now abandoned, for the Infirmary had committed itself to construction whose financing was by no means secure.

Like their English counterparts, the surgeons' and the physicians' hospitals presented themselves as mechanisms for getting poor folk back to work,

> for as the Riches of a Trading Nation chiefly consists [*sic*] in the Number of well employed Hands, so of consequence those who die through want of timely Help, are so many working Hands cut off from the Community.[49]

(The surgeons' metaphor is disconcerting.) What was distinctive was the proposition that these hospitals would generate wealth through teaching, too. The surgeons' *Memorial* of 1737 and 'Philanthropus', author of an Infirmary fund-raising pamphlet of the next year, even calculated what Scotland would reap when its medical sons came back for retirement laden with the 'Fortunes they have acquired abroad with Reputation': £100,000 annually, the former reckoned.[50] Philanthropus predicted (accurately) that, especially once augmented by the new Infirmary, the School would attract Dissenters and Catholics from England and Ireland, who could not matriculate at Oxford or Cambridge; they were all 'equally well lookt upon' in Edinburgh.[51] As the English hospitals discreetly offered themselves as bandages for the ruptures of faction (which is often to say, religious faction), the Infirmary trumpeted the profitability of tolerance. For Drummond and Monro, students could be imported, processed, and exported like any other manufacture.[52] Moreover, what was imported was a population of healthy young men who had nothing to do but study and spend money, the dream of every landlady and of every political arithmetician. Monro's son and successor Alexander *secundus* claimed in 1764 that 'since 1725 the town had received from anatomy students at least £300,000'.[53]

The 'Infirmary or Hospital for Sick Poor' became the Royal Infirmary by the charter of 1736,

> erecting the . . . Contributors and Donors . . . into a Corporation with perpetual Succession, and with Power to take Donations, to purchase Lands and Securities for Sums of Money lent; to erect Houses, to sue and be sued, and all other Things to do . . . , that may tend to promote the said charitable Design.[54]

Now incorporated or erected, the managers were anxious not to appear eager to build. When Adam presented his project (compare Figures 41 and 42 on p. 112) to them in April 1738, his estimate was only for 'that part of the house first proposed to be built'.[55] The idea was to strike a balance between fiscal prudence and the reduced income that fewer beds might mean; as more cures were effected, the managers predicted, so the reputation of the hospital would rise and more contributions would come in.[56] Medical teaching also entered the calculus: any 'Lover of his Country, who wishes its Prosperity', wrote Philanthropus, must want the larger building and with it more, and more varied, 'Cases' for the students to study. Potential students, contributors that they were, would also be encouraged by 'extraordinary Cures'.[57] The managers approved Adam's plans for 200 patients ('allowing each patient a bed'), but unwilling to 'act too forwardly' they decided to build for only sixty-six in the first instance. However, construction made its own demands:

> Upon considering Mr Adams plan of the whole Building, the Mannagers find, there is a necessity for Building Eighty foot at once Because there is not a midwall in ye Building nearer to the Gavel than at that distance.

One or the other half of the centre range as far as one of the partition walls, plus the stair adjoining at the top of the side wing had to go up together, and in the event its east side was built first.[58]

The large 'operation Room' planned for the top floor was also a priority. Big enough, Philanthropus claimed, for 'two or three hundred Students' (by now understood as comprising an increased number of surgical apprentices), it was an investment. Students paid to attend operations and because the existing room could not even accommodate twenty-four, the managers reckoned themselves deprived of £210 annually.[59] Less quantifiably, the operation room was a spectacular emblem of the Infirmary's pedagogic appeal, the clearest possible signal of the Edinburgh school's supersession of its most important model and, in the early years, rival the Leiden faculty and its famed anatomy theatre.[60] This appeal was essential, for the students were in effect the Infirmary's subscribers. In 1749 it described its income as constituted by student fees, plus the interest yielded on capital originating in gifts of money and commercial stocks, the Earl of Hopetoun's annual £150, and the hospital's one-third share in the profits of the Edinburgh Assembly Room. It was not, like 'most of the *English* Infirmaries . . . chiefly supported by annual Contributions'.[61]

Adam had to submit a number of estimates after 1738, as money and goods came in and the managers approved the construction of a bit more at a time. Although not finished for at least ten years,[62] the building was in use by the end of 1741 and the construction period was reasonable, especially given the disruptions of 1744–45: building was seasonal work, and the exigencies of financing (particularly in a cash-poor society), weather, and the availability of men and materials determined the schedule of any big project. As at Jacobsen's near-contemporary Foundling Hospital, the temporary necessity of housing both sexes on the same side of the building was explained as an incentive to keep going. The Edinburgh managers also announced that they wanted to be able to effect a different kind of 'Decency and Conveniency': the separation of 'different Ailings' and particularly that of 'acute Diseases' from the rest.[63]

Assuming that construction will be sporadic is a little different from making a plan that allows for partial occupancy and further construction simultaneously. According to Philanthropus' *Letter* of 1738, the managers 'thought it was their Duty to lay a Plan which might be executed piecemeal', as Adam's indeed might, once the minor problem of the first 80 feet was solved. The obligation was felt because 'none of them imagined that even the next Age would see it finished', and this needed careful explanation: perhaps the building was just too big, more than the 'Charity of this Part of the Kingdom is able to carry'? But, Philanthropus continued the next year,

> I cannot disa[p]prove of the Conduct of the Managers . . . ; it was not with them as with a Man building a House for himself, who is to consider his Funds and yearly Income, and adapt his Project to his Circumstances. No, the Undertaking was Great and Good, such as must be acceptable to all the valuable Part of Mankind.[64]

Universal acceptability justified a course too luxuriously wayward for a private man. We can assume that 'Philanthropus' was Monro, the Infirmary's most gifted propagandist, whose memoirs (written around 1760) explain that he and Drummond comprised the entire 'Building Committee'.[65]

Two years earlier, the governors of Edinburgh's Orphan Hospital (strictly, the Orphan-School, Hospital and Work-House), appealing for funds for another Adam design, simply explained that because they had too little money for all of it they would build the west side first.[66] This plan of action, and perhaps even this sort of plan, was perhaps not unusual for great houses and certainly not for great churches: Wren's 'Warrant' design (1675) for St Paul's was 'ordered so that it might be built and finished by parts' because of insufficient funds immediately available.[67] Ward blocks like Chelsea's and Greenwich's obviously lent themselves to building and filling by stages, and very long stages in Greenwich's case. What is striking is the regularity with which residential charities described their buildings as having been designed for phased construction, a practice tacitly encouraged by the medical desideratum of making ward blocks physically distinct from one another, and hence airier and even sometimes, like Edinburgh's, capable of separating 'different Ailings' (Chapter 6).

John Wood reported how in 1731 'Persons of Rank and Fortune, [had] desired' that his Bath Hospital 'might be so contrived, as that it might be increased from Time to Time as Benefactions should come in'. (How was that supposed to have worked? The Bath trustees had also elected to build on a *circular* plan.)[68] In London, St Bartholomew's, the Foundling, and the Middlesex hospitals were all recorded as designed so they could be built, as Philanthropus explained it,

> with Discretion as Funds came in, that is, to finish one Part of the Building, and bring it into Use, in Preference to . . . carrying on the building of the next Part, which could not have been of immediate Service.[69]

Demand, revenue, reputation, and construction were also balanced in distant Philadelphia. There one of the Pennsylvania Hospital managers, after showing to his colleagues the Edinburgh plans and 'consulting the several physicians in regard to the situation of the cells' for the insane and 'other conveniences', 'drew a design of the whole building . . . in such form, that one third part might alone be executed with tolerable symmetry; and containing, independent of the other parts, all accommodations requisite for the present purpose'.[70] The Pennsylvania's east wing opened in 1755, the west wing not until 1796, and they stood detached until the centre's completion in 1804. (Even then both sexes, very unusually, stayed on different floors in the east wing, because the other was reserved for the insane.)[71] At some hospitals the intermissions between campaigns were negligible. Both Glasgow's Infirmary – which in 1791 instructed William's son Robert Adam (1728–92) that his plan should be 'such that a part of it may be conveniently executed, and the other part, gradually carried on as the Demand may require, till the whole Plan be fully executed' – and twenty years later its Asylum gave up on phased construction, the latter explaining that its patients would not be helped by proximity to a building site.[72] The procedure however signified a due caution, even a due humility; no more splendidly sudden appearances of the Bethlem sort. Hospital buildings were expanding signs of charitable accumulation, and the print of Edinburgh's workhouse (begun 1739, Figure 43) shows how such signs looked while under way.[73] Accumulations themselves were nothing new: St Bartholomew's governors complained in 1729 that 'by being built at several Times' their fabric was 'so irregular that there is scarce any Communication between the several parts of it'. They had built as patients and funds presented themselves: a detached ward block costing £1,800 went up as recently as 1713–14. Just the same would happen henceforth, the governors were explaining, except that with Gibbs's plan they knew where the new accommodation would go and what it would look like. Incremental construction would be 'agreeable to one uniform Plan so that in process of the time the whole Fabrick may become Regular and more usefull' (St Bartholomew's, 1729); 'so that when the whole was completed, it would present one entire and perfect building' (William Barton, writing about American naval hospitals in 1814).[74]

As they regularly reminded the public, the Edinburgh managers might not draw upon their capital for building, and Philanthropus reported in 1738 that

43. 'A Perspective View of the Poor House of Edinburgh as it now stands unfinished'. The print shows the toothing on to which wings would be built; when they were, the workhouse looked remarkably like an unornamented Edinburgh Infirmary.

they expected a serious shortfall. Yet they 'don't seem to be under any Apprehensions for Want of Money; their Expectations have been so much outdone this Year, that they trust Providence for providing the needful Supplies for defraying the next Year's Charge'.[75] The next year he explained that when construction began there was not even £50 that could be used for it, but the hospital had managed to pay bills amounting to nearly that much every week thereafter. 'It is true, that their Funds have been often at so low a Pass, that when one week's Bill was cleared, they had not Money enough to pay the next', but Providence always interposed and enabled them to clear the accounts every Saturday night in time for an unspotted Sabbath. Maitland's *History of Edinburgh* (1753) alludes to Christ's feeding of the 5,000, but his source had a lighter touch.[76] Though in keeping with his attention to the Infirmary's architecture, Philanthropus' care in explaining the moral philosophy of the piecemeal is remarkable and we can suspect he was answering real objections that the Infirmary's construction was indeed more than charity could safely carry. He made effective use, too, of one kind of charity. This was the donation of goods and services by building tradesmen and merchants, gifts that, he was emphatic, would be recorded as carefully as those in cash.[77]

On 3 August 1738 the *Caledonian Mercury* described how the Infirmary's first stone was laid the day before. On that occasion, 'Several Societies and Persons of Condition' promised

large Contributions . . . for the Carrying on of the Work, Gentlemen Proprietors of Stone-Quarries having made presents of Stones, others of Lime, Merchants have given considerable Parcels of Timber, the Wrights and Masons have contributed largely, the Farmers in the Neighbourhood have agreed to carry all Materials gratis, the Journeymen Masons are to contribute their Labour in furnishing each a certain Quantity of hewn Stones. And as this Undertaking is for the Relief of the Diseased, lame and maimed Poor, even the Day-Labourers employed have agreed to work a Day in each Month gratis.[78]

When the farmers offered the transport, according to Philanthropus, their 'Language to the Managers . . . was, *It will be your own Fault if you pay a Farthing for Carriages*'. In short, he wrote,

> never was any Undertaking more universally approved, People of all Ranks speak of it with Pleasure, and seem to vye with one another who shall promote it most, and with what Earnestness to see it compleated.[79]

Mary's Chapel, the Edinburgh guild Incorporation of masons and other (mostly building) trades, which had always concerned itself with the relief of distressed members and their relicts,[80] was particularly active in this benign competition. 'Many of its Members have subscribed for Compliments of Work, such as, the Wrights to furnish Windows, the Glaziers to glaze them, the Slaters to lay on the Slates, all *gratis, &c*'; the Incorporation was donating the masters' share of the journeymen's wages, and the journeymen themselves offered eight days' work in season and two days a week during the winter to prepare materials for the next campaign.[81]

The Orphan Hospital in 1735 described its construction this way:

> some Journeymen Masons served as Volunteers, and only got their Meat. The Deacon of the Sclaters, and others of his Trade, bestowed Sclates; and he, with some of his Trade, caused cover the said Roof; and a Plumber did his Part, as to Work, all *gratis*: And some of the Timber merchants did very generously give largely to this work; and 'tis expected, that the Wrights and Glasiers will Contribute in their Way, towards this Undertaking.

And in 1737 the Surgeons' Hospital reported that 'Every Tradesman employed in fitting up' its first quarters had contributed something.[82]

All the voluntary hospitals presented themselves as enjoying broad support, as demanding universal approbation. Gifts in kind, which were not uncommon, were useful – a hospital's domestic requirements were not specialized – and their public welcome made them emblematically useful, too. Cutlery became the icon for the homily that charity may not be the prerogative of those with surplus cash:

> Would all others who have not money to give, yet give what they have to spare, as Broken Victualls, Old Cloaths, Linnen, Bedds, Bedding, Chairs, Stools, Pots, Dishes, Glasses &c. . . . what person is there who may not some way or other contribute to promote this charitable design . . . ?

So Patrick Cockburn in 1716, on behalf of what would become the Westminster Infirmary; thirty years later, Edinburgh's was still inviting donations of barley, blankets, coal, and 'Herbs and Roots'.[83] While acknowledging the usefulness of the gifts of labour and materials, therefore, we can understand the Edinburgh reports as mildly patronizing exhortation, and the *Mercury*'s account, the first quoted, may even have been commending the labourers' prudence in helping a charity to which they or their families, though not wealthier tradesmen, might have to apply. Kathleen Wilson, the only historian to have remarked upon this form of donation, more subtly argues that it illustrates how 'independent artisans and journeymen could underline their aspirations to respectability and citizenship through the scope of institutionalized charity'; the hospitals were, in general, offering 'mechanisms for setting off the middle sorts and respectable artisans from the laboring poor'.[84] Both the exhortative and mechanistic models are however insufficient to explain the donations of labour and materials to the Edinburgh charities (which were not Wilson's subject) first because they were on a unique scale, or at least the emphasis placed on them was. No English hospital presented itself as getting built this way,[85] though Philadelphia's did. There the managers claimed to have divided the contracts among as many suppliers and workers as possible. Though the 'trouble to the superintendents and assistants' was understandably much increased, this way 'scarce a tradesman, or even a labourer, was employed in any part of the work, or in providing the materials, without first engaging a reasonable part to be charitably applied in the premises'.[86] Secondly, the Edinburgh gifts (and Philadelphia's too)[87] formed part of a symbolic mechanism with a product more precise than the differentiation of rank, and this was Freemasonry. Finally, they marked the former capital's recovery; the making of classical Edinburgh (to borrow the title of A. J. Youngson's book [1966], which starts the story in mid-century) in fact began with the Orphan Hospital (begun 1734), George Watson's Hospital (1738), Infirmary (1738), and even the austere Charity Workhouse (1739).

Most analogous, in England, to the Edinburgh donations were Ralph Allen's gifts of Bath stone to St Bartholomew's rebuilding. Allen (1694–1764), a great entrepreneur as well as a model for charitable men, wanted his oolite, a fine freestone 'fit for the Walls of a Palace for the greatest Prince in Europe', taken up in the capital, to effect its 'Publique introduction'. In the singular absence of palace construction, and anyway anxious to marry commerce and philanthropy, he decided that the best way to do this would be to have it used at a great charitable building.[88] Greenwich Hospital was his first choice, but it declined to abandon Portland stone. Beginning in 1730, the value of the stone, transport, and labour Allen gave to St Bartholomew's amounted to £2,000, he finally estimated; some gifts were however inadvertent, as the changing body of governors was fairly consistently awkward.[89] The hospital was a worry for Allen until his death thirty-four years later, when it had also become apparent that Bath's stone was no match for London's air pollution. More satisfactory in these respects was his donation of 'all the Wall-Stone, Free-stone ready wrought, Paving-stone, and Lime used' at the Bath Hospital.[90] Though that was not quite so public a work as St Bartholomew's, in the capital, the hospital was a showpiece in a town generally extraordinary for its rate of improvements.

In Edinburgh on 2 August 1738 George Drummond, acting on behalf of his fellow managers, laid the new Infirmary's first stone together with the 'Grand Master of the Work': George Mackenzie, 3rd Earl of Cromarty, who was also Grand Master of the Grand Lodge of Scotland. Cromarty's brethren 'in their proper Cloathing and Jewels' entirely surrounded the 'Plan of the Foundation hand in hand'.[91] The first stone of the Infirmary's west block would be laid by the then Grand Master in May 1740 with near-equivalent ceremony and, as Grand Master in his turn Drummond laid that of the Royal Exchange in 1753.[92] The making of classical Edinburgh had a distinctly preclassical aspect, as the Scottish Grand Masters continued to lead re-enactments of Masonry's ultimate origins in the construction of the Temple of Solomon, and its direct inheritance of the wisdom of the men who had made buildings ever since. The making of Scottish hospitals did too.[93] In 1792, Glasgow's Lord Provost (and Master Mason) applied the Square and Plumb Rule to the Infirmary's first stone, then commanded the blessing of the Great Architect of the Universe upon it.[94]

In 1717 was formed, in London, a Grand Lodge of masons, the first in the world and the beginning of modern Freemasonry. Its third Grand Master (1719–20) was John Theophilus Desaguliers (1683–1744), clergyman, experimental philosopher, and inventor of a pioneering mechanical-ventilation system, among many other things. In 1721, Desaguliers travelled to Edinburgh on business connected with its water supply and there he visited the Lodge of Mary's Chapel. It shared a name, confusingly, with the Incorporation, but the Lodge and other Scottish lodges were smaller and more or less independent groups of masons whose relationship to the civic incorporations is uncertain. Certainly Mary's Chapel already included trade burgesses and professionals,[95] as well as men who earned their living cutting and building with stone. There Desaguliers attended (and may have conducted) the receptions of other men as 'accepted' apprentices and fellow-crafts, among them Drummond. His visit ultimately resulted in the formation in 1736 of the Grand Lodge of Scotland; and three months after Drummond helped lay the Infirmary's first stone he became Scotland's first 'master mason', in the then-highest third degree.[96] By then, most of the six lodges in the Edinburgh area were dominated by accepted masons[97] but Scottish Freemasonry long remained distinctive for the continuing involvement of 'operative', working masons.

Scottish masons and master masons of all sorts were, we can assume, ambitious for public construction to burnish civic pride and increase civic prosperity, not least through the maintenance of social order. In Dundee, local masons offered instrumental support for the construction of a new jail and workhouse in the 1730s; their lodge included significant numbers of non-operatives but, as Margaret Jacob has shown, the difference scarcely signified in this connection.[98] And if Dundee wanted public works so, certainly, did the former capital, whose workmen, tradesmen, and merchants understood that if they wanted to see Edinburgh start building again, they would have to prime the pump a little. They realized that they were promoting, not just noble charities and not just social order, but at least in the Infirmary's case a noble piece of masonry.

The accounts of the way in which the Edinburgh labourers and craftsmen donated their work are today still curiously reassuring, something that cannot be said of the reports, more usual in the hospital-promotion genre, of joyful 'Acclamations' from the poor faced with a new hospital, the bells they rang (Leeds, 1771) and the blessings they heaped upon 'their pious and generous Benefactors' (Exeter, 1741).[99] There is something pleasurable about the lists of plumbers, slaters, masons, and glaziers working with the timber, the stone, and the lime. The pleasures are simple ones, those we take from the confirmation that everyone has useful expertise, has something to offer; it is a fantasy of productivity, in the widest sense.

There were specifically architectural ways in which that charity could be presented as one of production, not of consumption, of 'loving relations between men actually working and producing what is ultimately . . . to be shared'.[100] These men included the English architects, master craftsmen, and committee men who supervised the construction of hospitals whose very forms embodied the ideal that they must be shared as soon as possible, while the work continued. At the Edinburgh Infirmary the production would extend to Scotland's balance of trade, as Philanthropus' *Letters* explain. Its method of construction, too, they skilfully represent as both rational and providential: hectic reckonings could be laid aside once a week, when God somehow ensured that the bills were paid again. The Infirmary could also be shown as built, in all senses, by the labouring poor themselves, on the one hand, and on the other by Freemasons, who saw in its real bricks and mortar a shadow of the Temple, and who found in the ritual of the stone-laying a direct manifestation of brotherhood. Edinburgh's was something of a special case, but all hospital construction was performance, or enactment, of a sort and so described, it sounds appealing. Why then did Smollett's Count Fathom have to abandon his hospital, his vision of raising himself into notice upon the carcases of the poor?

Protestant benevolence

In *The Idler*, in 1758, Samuel Johnson (1709–84) explained how hospitals perfectly exemplified the way in which the 'light of Revelation' had guided moderns to their place of superiority over classical antiquity. Britain however had two modernities, one Christian and the other Protestant Christian, and was the slightly embarrassed legatee of a number of pre-Reformation hospitals, some still functioning. Thomas Bowen's *Historical account* of Bethlem (1783) side-stepped the difficulty by having its career begin with Henry VIII's supposed seizure of the priory and its conversion to a hospital for the insane, which was neat if unconvincing, even then. The Reverend Bowen was however anxious to contrast the 'more enlarged spirit of PROTESTANT BENEVOLENCE' with the 'contracted views of monkish hospitality'.[101]

As we have seen, the spirit of benevolence was not afraid to acknowledge the occasional convergence of the public good and the public interest, and even private profit.[102] Much of the durability and even the glamour of modern charity as a species was understood as arising from this overlap with the commercial world. But commercialism inspired anxiety as well as self-congratulation. Johnson's *Idler* essay describes the 'open competition between different hospitals and the animosity with which their Patrons oppose one another', which not only encouraged public 'Inconstancy' but might in the end 'prejudice weak minds against them all'.[103] He doubtless had something more specific in mind, but even before the organization of the dispensaries, the new London hospitals seem to have been vulnerable to competition from charities that did not need bricks and mortar, and some were soon overbuilding anyway.[104] Construction remained a gamble which needed careful presentation before it paid off, particularly in this new climate of edgy consumerism and even Smollettian cynicism.

In 1739 William Adam gave the managers 100 copies of a 'full plan & Draught' (see Figures 41 and 42) of the Edinburgh Infirmary, which he had prepared for publication in *Vitruvius Scoticus*, his volume of engravings of Scottish buildings (most by William Adam), for which subscriptions were then also being collected. Such pictures might of course encourage donations: Philanthropus, remaining within the fiction that his pamphlet was a letter to a friend in the country, had already told his friend that he would send him a copy of the plate (which would moreover 'be sold in all the Booksellers shops in Town') rather than detain him any longer with a description of the hospital.[105]

Ten years later, the Infirmary obtained the services of a London agent, Adam Anderson (c.1692–1765), who was from the outset pessimistic about its chances,

> by reason of so many *new* Charity-*Projects* (if I may so speak) which are lately set up, & which, tho' merely *local* (& *some* of 'em not rational) do greatly interfere with much better calculated Designs, & often intercept what would have otherwise been bestow'd on such as yours![106]

His immediate aim was to hook a Colonel Sotheby, who had charitable funds at his disposal as the executor of an estate. Anderson showed Adam's prints to Sotheby and, encouraged by his response, asked for more copies from Edinburgh, 'together with any other papers that it may be proper to show to Gentlemen'. But, apparently on the basis of a manuscript history sent down for his benefit, Sotheby had 'got it strongly in his head' that the Infirmary had few or no patients in it because the poor were frightened of the place, and Anderson had to take a 'considerable Time' to persuade him otherwise.[107] Anderson's letter seems to have inspired the production, in 1749, of the Infirmary's first printed *History and statutes*,[108] which clarified the matter, perhaps all the more convincingly because it was printed. Meanwhile the topographical artist Paul Sandby, an Adam family friend then surveying the Highlands, donated a perspective view (Figure 44), which Anderson had engraved by the expert Paul Fourdrinier, along with new plans.[109] Three years later Anderson was still giving 'Gentlemen Books & plans' of the Infirmary, phrasing which suggests that he used the new book, an unillustrated small octavo, along with the loose and larger prints in his struggle against Londoners' 'frolicksome Disposition for new Charities'.[110] In 1764 Anderson would publish his life's work, the *Historic and chronological deduction of the origin of commerce*, to whose composition his experience of frolicksome dispositions and irrational schemes was probably useful.

Johnson warned that charity's commercial operations were, for better or for worse, now confirmed and he showed their connection with Protestant benevolence:

The equal distribution of wealth, which long commerce has produced, does not enable any single hand to raise edifices of piety like fortified cities, to appropriate Manors to religious uses, or to deal out such large and lasting beneficence as was scattered over the land in antient times, by those who possessed countries or provinces.[111]

The charities made by many-handed commercial wealth suffered from what he called fashion and Anderson called frolic, and their beneficence could not be as large or as lasting as the old forms. These had continued to offer a challenge. Daniel Defoe returned several times to the competing claims of Protestant and Papist charity in the course of his *Tour* of Britain, to the general benefit of the former. But the moderns had built nothing, he reported without editorializing, to compare with the hospital formerly annexed to the monastery at Ripon, Yorkshire; the Catholics' 'grand excitement of the health of their souls' had not been without issue. And this was the key: Protestants could seek no guarantee of immortality this way, for their gifts 'are merely acts of charity to the world'.[112] A 'Proposal to Augment the Foundling Hospital Fund' (1747) presents the difference without subtlety or qualification in an analysis embracing charitable ends, as well as means:

While the genius of this nation was depressed by a religion, which enslaves mankind, dishonours God, and destroys virtue, all our acts of publick liberality were vain, selfish and superstitious; to expiate our sins, we contributed to support in idleness and luxury great numbers, who having renounced society and all relative duties, were a growing burden upon the community.

44.   The Edinburgh Infirmary in Sandby's engraving (1749). The building is slightly different from that shown in Adam's older print (Figure 42) but the major changes are to the presentation. Sandby included some indications of lawn and passers-by, and the perspective permits the immediate understanding of the hospital's capacity.

> But since the reformation has banished ignorance, and restored Christianity, we have nobly distinguished ourselves by donations of another kind, such as are truly stiled *charities* . . .[113]

We could not, that is, freely give while enslaved by superstition, but we are all volunteers now. The trouble, as some charities saw it, was that freedom also meant the freedom to change one's mind.

Meanwhile, good men and women rushed to fill Defoe's 'merely' (which he meant neutrally, as 'only') with the myth of the entirely co-operative, interdependent society.[114] This myth is political and it was also theological, as hundreds of charity sermons sought to 'naturalize economic relations'.[115] Preaching on behalf of the Norfolk and Norwich Hospital around 1770, Philip Yonge, Bishop of Norwich took Proverbs 22:2 as his text: 'The Rich and Poor meet together: the Lord is the Maker of them All'. The rich must not despise the poor, and the poor must not envy the rich: 'Do you accuse them of luxury and vanity?' Yonge asked. 'You forget especially that the ordinary demands of the rich, create employment for the poor; and that their vanity, if you will have it so, is your bread.'[116] This is a society held together by both love and self-love, a paradox that the hospitals helped to reconcile. In this and other ways, they lent themselves to being understood as the corporate realizations of a charity which would restore the poor to healthy productivity, and which was completely voluntary, uncompelled by an old false religion or by modern Poor Law provision. In these performances hospital buildings had important and difficult roles.

Chapter 6

The appearances of the eighteenth-century civil hospital

Two men inspected English hospitals in the 1780s and recorded what they saw. John Howard's unexpected calls preparatory to his *Account of the principal lazarettos* (1789) instantly prompted a small mythology. The Leicester Infirmary unhappily had its windows closed on the day of his visit; in Bristol a fifteen-year-old surgical apprentice was the unwitting guide until Howard (1726–90) revealed himself and asked the boy to tell the Infirmary's managers that their (new) windows were too small.[1] Jacques Tenon's receptions at institutions in the summer of 1787 were on the other hand formal but often friendly, as befitted the 'high honour and compliment paid to the British nation and empire' which Sir Joseph Banks, President of the Royal Society, said that this tour on behalf of the French king and his Académie des Sciences represented.[2] Tenon's notes (not published until 1992) are more informative than Howard's about architecture, and he explained their presuppositions elsewhere. 'I have emphasized the windows', he wrote to George Dance about one of his earlier communications to the Académie, because they were not simply means of obtaining light and air but 'real therapeutic instruments' for the wards', and hence their occupants', requirements for 'air that is warm, cold, dry or humid, etc.'.[3] But if Tenon's journal singles out (for example) the windows of the Winchester Hospital (see Figure 53, p. 136), begun in 1755, can we assume that they were planned to face one another for the same reason that he praised the arrangement? 'Current utility may not be equated with historical origin', writes the evolutionary biologist Stephen Jay Gould,[4] and the Winchester's own records from the mid-1750s are silent about windows.

A new way of writing about hospitals in the English-speaking world had become apparent twenty years earlier, when Edward Foster published his *Essay*, subtitled *Succinct directions for the situation, construction, and administration of country hospitals* (1768). He was prescribing for the small infirmaries whose establishment had just been provided for by the Irish Parliament.[5] No equivalent legislation governed Britain; distinctive circumstances prompted the first (and, in English, for a long time the only) book dedicated to the subject. That comprised many things for Foster, including gardens, cleanliness, and gravelly soil, but his recommendations for construction underlined the need for simplicity. Hospitals, he wrote, must avoid over-large wings that render the 'Structure more complicated, and prevent the Access of free Air'.[6] Four years later, the translation of Pierre-Jean Grosley's travelogue described England's hospitals as having a

> variety of apartments for the reception of the different sorts of patients, built in solitary pavillions, as well as to prevent a communication, as to promote a circulation of air: this I took particular notice of at the hospital for sailors at Portsmouth[7]

– that is, Haslar. Grosley seems to have been making an important distinction. Air must circulate because stagnant air is always suspect and might have a dangerous stink. It must not however communicate, or be communicated, for it is the air and not the pavilions that ultimately ensures the isolation of different sorts of patient. They will then (we infer) benefit from regimens suited to their disorders without danger of further disordering by communications from other pavilions, that is, cross-infection or, as it was then called, mutual contagion.[8] If this difference, between circulation and communication, then meant something to hospital planners, civil-hospital promoters elided it. As Grosley implied, it need not make much difference to architecture, and contagion was perhaps best not mentioned anyway. In January 1771, the first annual report of the Norfolk and Norwich Hospital explained its proposed new building: the 'form of an H would be most convenient . . . as admitting the freest circulation of air – A provision for which had, by the Gentlemen of the Faculty of Physic, been most strongly recommended'.[9] That year, too, John Aikin published his *Thoughts on hospitals*, which include several, though vaguer, thoughts on freeing air. Some of his readers published amplifications. In 1773 Benjamin Gooch (?1707–76) reported the observation, made at a London hospital, of different mortality rates in wards of different heights but otherwise identical. Three years later John Jones described the principal wards of the brand new hospital in New York as 'well ventilated, not only from the opposite disposition of the windows' but by its central corridor, and in 1778 the *History and statutes* of the Edinburgh Royal Infirmary, designed forty years earlier, claimed that nothing had been more 'solicitously attended to, than ventilation' in that design.[10] These accounts credit specific built forms with actively encouraging the flow of air, the wind that is the *vent* in ventilation. An explicitly medicalized rhetoric or 'discourse' about hospital fabrics had been consolidated, and in Edinburgh it was even applied retrospectively. We can see how that happened with the help of the texts and images that accompanied the construction of the buildings themselves, while noting the temptations of retrospection.

Courtyard palaces

In 1729 its governors complained that St Bartholomew's' fabric, 'by being built at several Times[,] is so irregular that there is scarce any Communication between the several parts of it & the whole has hardly so much as the outward appear-

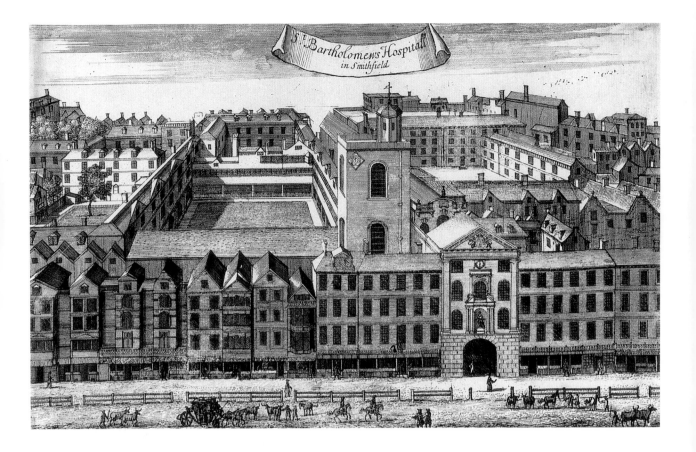

ance of an hospital'.[11] Today we might agree (Figure 45). Where did St Bartholomew's end and the rest of the world begin? The hospital was a cluster of courtyards surrounded by narrow buildings which in the picture gradually reveal themselves, by continuous rooflines and regular fenestration, to have been different from the houses and shops of Smithfields. But the text is best read (as we will see) with the stress on 'communication', in spite of that interesting reference to hospitals' appearances. London's other general hospitals, both in 1729 newly built, or rebuilt, were also series of quadrangles enclosed by ranges lined with open galleries, like that shown in one of the courts at old St Bartholomew's.

St Thomas' Hospital's rebuilding began in 1693 under the direction of Thomas Cartwright (d. 1702), perhaps in consultation with the governor Christopher Wren. New ranges defining three courts gradually replaced the old fabric, beginning with what came to be called Clayton Square, at the rear in the view (Figure 46); offices, a chapel, and a fine large hall filled the four wings surrounding the central court, which was named for Edward VI. The front square, for women, and the last to be ready (at the end of 1708), was open on one side. There, three wards were stacked in each flanking wing. Those on the ground floor had only twelve beds because they surrendered half their width to the galleries, open passageways behind Tuscan colonnades, which also lined the ground floors of the courts behind. Only one side of Clayton Square got a ground-floor ward, and a large 'Exact Plan' made of the hospital in 1718 shows its long upper wards as single piles reached by corner stairs.[12]

45. St Bartholomew's before its rebuilding, engraved for the 1720 edition of Stow's *Survey*.

46. This view of
St Thomas' Hospital,
which conveys very
clearly the way it was
hemmed in by its
neighbours, was
published in 1756.

The courts and their galleries – 'Piazzas' they are called on the plan – served,
Tenon reported, as *promenoirs* for the patients, and the arrangement might
seem cloister-like, conventual. But it is more precisely palatial, as the physician
Benjamin Golding called it in his *Historical account of St. Thomas's* (1819). By that
he meant, not just agreeably impressive, but in the form of great houses that had
comprised, as the hospital still did, a great variety of 'departments': offices,
accommodation, and places of display and collegiality. Francis Bacon's 'Of building', two centuries old, was Golding's authority for the usefulness of courts lined
by open galleries, 'by reason of the facilities of communication which can be
maintained with all its connections'. St Thomas' was therefore old-fashioned as
both a house and a hospital house, but one where 'convenience and comfort
appear to have been most particularly studied, which gives it an advantage not
to be found in others of later date'. Golding was defending St Thomas' against
the notion (on which, he wrote, there was no consensus) that 'squares behind

each other . . . prevent that free circulation of pure air, so essential to structures of this nature'. The defence was necessary because in an influential analysis Aikin had associated quadrangles' 'stagnating air' with the over-long wards that defined them, and the wards' length in turn with the misguidedly 'benevolent zeal' that stuffed them full (Chapter 10).[13]

According to Golding, palatialness lay not in a general appearance that might evoke wasteful and dangerous charitable zeal, but in a particular plan, one magnificently serviceable to the notably heterogeneous activities and populations of great houses and hospitals alike. He explained St Thomas' departments in detail, as if to remind his readers that there is more to hospitals than wards (for Aikin, at least, there was not) and as a functional explanation Golding's suffices. St Thomas' was a great household, brewing, for example, 81 gallons of beer for its 378 patients in the week of Tenon's visits. Newer and smaller foundations did not, on the whole, attempt such self-sufficiency any more than they did the courts; 'no slaughterhouse [or] brewhouse here', Tenon noted at the London Hospital.[14] But the typology – of expansive, operatively complex houses put together by simple means – is worth extending to them.

Thomas Guy was a St Thomas' governor. His own hospital began building across the road in 1722; it was intended for those excluded from St Thomas' because they suffered from insanity, or illnesses with doubtful prognoses. Guy's Hospital is also what his will calls 'Squares of Building' formed by ward wings lined at ground level by open galleries, here made by arcading.[15] The cross-wing separating the first two quadrangles, which were finished in 1725, was entirely raised on an open 'Colonnade', as it is still called. The intention was evidently always to build two wings perpendicular to the north front making a forecourt like St Thomas's; to build in stages, that is. (The east wing, with officers' residences and offices, was begun in 1738 and the other in 1774.) The wards were single-piled, and Guy's congratulated itself on their spaciousness and airiness, its physicians and surgeons in 1737 rejecting a proposal to install some kind of ventilator on the clean wards (as opposed to the 'foul' wards, for the venereally diseased) on these grounds.[16] The fact that the wards were at first all raised may have contributed to this pride; the arrangement would later be recommended for hospitals and something analogous for prisons.[17]

St Bartholomew's had always had tenant properties within its precinct, but after 1666 new shops were built, one ground-floor ward being converted for the purpose. This was to raise money: four other wards were closed because the hospital, which itself escaped, lost 190 houses in the Fire and its rental income was immediately reduced by £2,000 a year. The desperate shortage of properties by which City tradesmen could support their families justified these measures, and sixty years later the governors were still referring to the 'accommodation of the Cittizens who suffered in the great Calamity'. But the 'Erecting of buildings intermixed with those of the hospital' was then, in 1729, judged to have 'much obstructed' the 'free Course of the Air for the benefitt of the poor', that is the patients.[18] The tenants were anyway an increasing nuisance, particularly as the genteeler sort moved away; by 1754 'idle, loose, and disorderly persons, beggars and others' were 'crying and selling all manner of commodities very improper for the patients in and about the staircases and wards'.[19]

The construction of all three hospitals was effected in phases, each inaugurated by pushing back, one could say, more of the city (and in the case of Guy's Hospital, by the purchase of more land) and not until 1770, when the last of the wards was fitted out, was St Bartholomew's quadrangle cleared of the remaining shops and houses to 'Form the Square and area of the Hospital according to the plan & design'.[20]

In Gibbs's plan four detached rectangular blocks, nearly identical, together define a large square. The north block was mostly devoted to offices and a notably grand governors' court room, and the others each held twelve wards, four to a floor, in pairs each side of a spine wall. The print shown in Figure 47 is inaccurate, because the stairs and vestibules were actually in the centres of the blocks, with the wards pushed out to the ends,[21] but its lettering points out what we might overlook: the 'Private Room off of each Ward for the Nurse attending it'. Commodes, water tanks, and sinks for washing dressings were, Tenon noted,

47. Two of the new blocks for St Bartholomew's Hospital, as published (erroneously, in some respects) in 1754.

48. An engraving from 1812 showing one of the 'missing' corners of the St Bartholomew's quadrangle, and St Paul's Cathedral beyond.

fitted into the vestibules alongside the nurses' *cellules* and the stairs. Though St Thomas' had made comparable arrangements, according to the 1718 plan, St Bartholomew's ward blocks were unprecedented, as was the planning of the hospital as a whole. The blocks' insulation obviously permitted construction in stages, as the governors had wanted. It made the result a little awkward to describe, though not to understand. Another visiting investigator, the surgeon Johann Hunczovsky (1752–98), called the hospital 'quadrangular, but in such a way that in each corner one wing is separated from the next by a vacant space' (Figure 48). By then, the 1780s, the inference was that these vacancies permitted a hospital that was compact enough to be practical, but airy enough to be safe.[22]

Though Gibbs himself explained that detaching the blocks would reduce any fire risk,[23] the 1729 reference to the free course of the air is suggestive. Grace Goldin has pointed out that, when the St Bartholomew's rebuilding committee was appointed six years earlier, England had recently been terrified by what would turn out to be Western Europe's last great plague epidemic, the Marseilles outbreak of 1719–20.[24] Dr Richard Mead (1673–1754), the foremost expert on the plague, joined Gibbs, Hawksmoor, and the others on the committee. In his *Short discourse concerning pestilential contagion* (1720), Mead had concluded that the pestilence was indeed contagious, that is, transmitted by direct contact with infected persons or goods, but also that it found its full strength only in foul air. This compromise was the premise for his advice to take the stricken three or four miles out of town and to put them into '*clean* and *airy* Habitations', where the plague might not get its deadliest hold.[25] At least eight more, expanded editions of the *Discourse* and a number of commentaries were printed over the next quarter-century and Mead's prescriptions, though unspecific about construction, were quite sufficient to focus minds on the workings of cleanliness and fresh air with other diseases, too. The question is, whether the St Bartholomew's committee was anticipating a practice the hospital was adopting by mid-century: isolating cases of 'infectious' illnesses in their own wards, their own airs.[26] That is a slightly different use of air, but one perhaps best not advertised in the 1720s.

Conversions, single files, and square plans

Though the Navy maintained them at its hospitals because it was more anxious to make its patients stay put (Chapter 8), after Guy's virtually all new civil hospitals abandoned quadrangles.[27] Suburban sites did not, in any case, require the enclosure of spaces otherwise vulnerable to the mess of the city, to its loose and disorderly persons. The first voluntary hospital, the Westminster Public Infirmary, however opened in 1720 in the street called Petty France, in a house explained as at least preferable to the 'Closeness and Unwholesomeness' of many poor homes, 'which is too often one great Cause of their Sickness'.[28] It moved to nearby Chapel Street four years later. The new house became unsatisfactory and when the Westminster was offered three in Castle Lane and Petty France a treaty was agreed at a special general board meeting in early September 1733, which also decided that Lanesborough House at Hyde Park Corner, a property also proposed, was too remote. The ensuing row resulted in the formation six weeks later of a new medical-charitable society, which had already leased Lanesborough House for what would be called St George's Hospital, opened at the beginning of the new year. It and the Westminster were still the only two of their kind in England.

St George's publicists were anxious to absolve its founders of any imputation of deviousness in their negotiations for the house, acquired (during what was supposed to be a cooling-off period) in a coup that also carried off the Westminster's physicians and surgeons. With the latters' authority, they explained its preferability, as a building and as a site, to the 'old and ruinous' Chapel Street house, and to Castle Street's location in a 'low part of Westminster'.[29] As Westminster loyalists hinted that scandals about inferior-quality drugs had played a part in the secession,[30] St George's defenders wanted to show that it was an architectural affair. (In this they were perhaps encouraged by Mead, one of the founder-governors.) All the former Westminster physicians were reported as concurring that Lanesborough House was a 'larger, more substantial and more airy building', an airiness extending to its situation.

James, Viscount Lanesborough built his house in 1719 as a suburban alternative to his town house in Golden Square: the text 'It is my delight to be, / Both in the town and country' stood above its door. Like Lanesborough House, St George's was a villa, a handy retreat from the city and its unwholesomeness. An *Account* published early in 1734 explained that it was near enough to town to be convenient for physicians and governors, but far enough to provide the 'country air', which in the general Opinion of the Physicians, would be more effectual than Physick in the Cure of many Distempers, especially such as mostly affect the Poor who live in close and confin'd Places within the great Cities.

(Moreover, in that location the hospital 'could give no Offence to any one'.)[31] Even as it was, the house could accommodate sixty patients in rooms 'so contriv'd, as if they had been built' for their new use, and the ground would permit the addition of 'several spacious and airy Wards', airily envisaged as big enough to 'lodge some hundreds of Patients' more 'commodiously' than any other hospital in London.[32] By 1744, after alterations and extensions made in three major stages, St George's had assumed the form of a rough H: another, side wing is just visible on Isaac Ware's perspective (Figure 49).[33] Tenon saw six large (thirty-one-bed) wards stacked in each of the side wings, which they filled.[34]

'Rusticate' the diseases, wrote Mead's friend and colleague George Cheyne (1671–1743); let sweet country air drive them out of their noxious 'Habit'. Air in fact interested Cheyne less than diet, because the readers he wanted for *The English malady* (published the year of St George's foundation) could afford to remove themselves from the temptations and pressures of town, to rural 'Simplicity and Virtue'.[35] He was actually using the last phrase to put the English malady in a very broad historical context: it refers to the ancient customs of the Greeks, before they sank into the 'Effeminacy, Luxury, and Diseases' that are the inevitable adjuncts of progress. In this way Cheyne showed how civilization necessarily requires the study of physic – and, we could add, the construction of villas, equivocal signs of rural simplicity and virtue, because they acquire meaning only by contrast with the city's complexity and vice, and serve as retreats from its pestilences. Cheyne's English malady was anyway a distinctive syndrome of nervous disorders encouraged by slothful intemperance and refined sensibilities. It did not prevail among the poor, but their maladies still needed the charity of rustication.

Ware's perspective of St George's, which underlines suburbanism with the equestrians and the happy hound while demonstrating the excellent road connections for wheeled traffic, makes an instructive contrast with that of St Thomas' (Figure 46). It is a (slightly elevated) ground-level view because it does not need to show enclosure, the space gained from the city. Ward blocks might freely stretch out, and St George's could be admired (as the men in the carriage are doing) from the height of a human eye, not a bird's. William Bellers similarly painted, in 1752, the projected new London Hospital near the Whitechapel Road. The engraving (Figure 50) added more buildings to the skyline, perhaps because some subscribers had objected to the site as *too* remote: the painting shows only a couple of church spires.[36] (The print however increases the bucolic staffage, and the collision of a couple of herds seems imminent.) As shown in these prints, St George's and the London are, to borrow from Bacon, houses for looking on, and not for living in: the observers stand outside, we stand outside, and are not deposited into a courtyard. The sheer distance across which we can look was however a powerful illustration of salubrity and in the prints remained so, even as the city began to encroach on the hospitals themselves.[37] As a villa St George's

49. Ware's perspective (1733) of his St George's Hospital.

50. A later copy of the engraving (sold by subscription) of the London Hospital as it would look when rehoused.

ST GEORGE'S HOSPITAL.
Supported by Voluntary
Contributions &c.

View *of* ST GEORGE'S HOSPITAL, *at* Hyde Park Corner.

51. This 'View' of St George's, probably from a 1784 *History of London*, differs little from the pictures the hospital published at the top of its annual reports.

offered a way of life alternative to the city, and as such it differed from St Thomas', whose courts and galleries made a kind of house associated with the way of life that antedates the city.[38] Yet they shared a fundamental expansiveness, of wings around quadrangles and wings simply thrust out, that was antithetical to real villas or indeed to any but the grandest sort of modern house.

St George's attracted notably aristocratic, and architectural support. Lord Burlington drew an idiosyncratic hospital plan, perhaps for this one (whose venereal-disease ward for men he allowed to take his title).[39] Small, frontal pictures began to appear at the top of its annual reports in 1736 (Figure 51), and such representations became popular (see Figures 53 and 57), but unlike other early foundations St George's did not publish a plan of its building.

The Winchester Hospital's first home was very evidently a conversion (Figure 52). In 1736 this, the first of the provincial English voluntary hospitals, rented a very old courtyard house on a corner site. Extensions followed, of which the most substantial was the wing at the top ordered in 1737, which held a twelve-bed ward for women and, underneath, two small 'Private Wards' (marked as M and N).[40] The latter were the only wards on the ground floor, where offices entirely surrounded the courtyard. Hot and cold baths (E on the ground-floor plan) were available to the public (2 shillings hot, 1 shilling cold, payable to the matron or apothecary for deposit in the poor box), who ran no danger of encountering patients and might even peer into the apothecary's 'Elaboratory' (at D) *en route*; many British hospitals would offer public baths, often in raised basements that facilitated both water supplies and separate entrances.[41] The wing with the waiting room (T on the plan) was just one storey, so the six wards and nurses' accommodation on the upper floor took the shape of an F.

Almost immediately a neighbouring house was bought to create more room, and in 1753 the governors decided to rebuild the hospital on a new site occupied by a large seventeenth-century town house. Work began two years later. The old

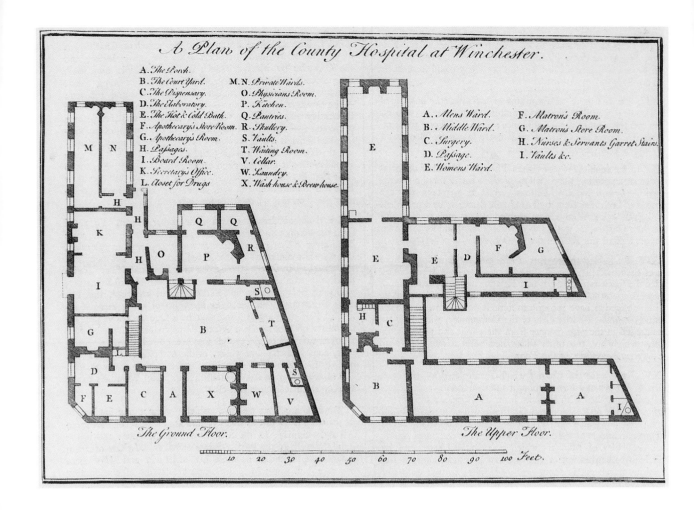

A Plan of the County Hospital at Winchester.

A. The Porch.
B. The Court Yard.
C. The Dispensary.
D. The Elaboratory.
E. The Hot & Cold Bath.
F. Apothecary's Store Room.
G. Apothecary's Room.
H. Passages.
I. Board Room.
K. Secretary's Office.
L. Closet for Drugs

M.N. Private Wards.
O. Physicians Room.
P. Kitchen.
Q. Pantries.
R. Skullery.
S. Vaults.
T. Waiting Room.
V. Cellar.
W. Laundry.
X. Wash house & Brew house.

A. Mens Ward.
B. Middle Ward.
C. Surgery.
D. Passage.
E. Womens Ward.

F. Matron's Room.
G. Matron's Store Room.
H. Nurses & Servants Garret Stairs.
I. Vaults &c.

The Ground Floor.

The Upper Floor.

10 20 30 40 50 60 70 80 90 100 Feet.

52. The plans published in the first annual reports of the Winchester Hospital.

53. The second Winchester Hospital, a conversion with extensions presenting a very regular front.

house got two new wings that permitted Tenon to characterize it, approvingly, as built on the *principes* of John Richards's Devon and Exeter Hospital (1741–43): that is, a main block laterally divided by a corridor, with single-pile ward wings extended to each side (Figure 53).[42] His approval was for the singleness of the wards ('Cette salle n'est point accouplée') with their opposed windows. No architect's name is associated with the Winchester rebuilding,[43] but Exeter was there to see, and they were siblings: Alured Clarke, in 1736 Prebendary (Canon) of Winchester Cathedral, and by 1741 Dean of Exeter, had effectively founded both hospitals.

The Bristol Infirmary opened in 1737 in a former brewery. At least two extensions, in line with and at right angles to the original rectangle, resulted in a U shape anticipated in William Halfpenny's huge and handsome plate (Figure 54) of 1742, but not realized until 1750.[44] All the wings were single piles; on the court side of the central block 'Piazzas', as Halfpenny called the colonnade, made an open corridor linking the central block's offices and wards with the side stairs and wings. The Liverpool Infirmary (Figure 55) boasted similar piazzas and they were also planned for the Devon and Exeter and Pennsylvania hospitals, which perhaps never got them. The Leicester Infirmary's were built (Figure 56), and Howard recommended them, 'to induce patients to take the air'.[45] Hawksmoor explained the Greenwich colonnades in terms of communication and air a decade before Bristol's foundation and their continuing value for communication we can infer from Golding's description of St Thomas'.

The conversions of the Winchester house and the Bristol brewery accompanied enlargements that took the simple form of ward-wing extensions that were, like the original buildings, single piles. Such wards were simple to add, and to extend, as funds permitted and demand justified, and that was how most hospitals were built, including entirely new ones: the Devon and Exeter saw at least two campaigns, which however followed each other closely.[46] Simple partitioning in such buildings could go a long way towards convenience, especially when new piazzas allowed a more flexible circulation: the matron's room at Bristol was described as 'well situated in the sphere of her business and in a point of view proper to inspect all parts of the Infirmary'.[47] The single piling that made houses too draughty and glaring (as Roger Pratt wrote)[48] made hospitals airy and light. Best not, however, to overstate the case for conversions: the first Winchester was not altogether convenient and it was the first hospital to get one of Stephen Hales's ventilators (Chapter 7). But the installation also reflects on its early public commitment to removing the poor from 'Closeness or Unwhol[e]som[e]ness' (it acknowledged the quotation from the Westminster) and into a 'free Air'. For some potential supporters the promise was perhaps reinforced by the many windows carefully marked on the plan.

Freedom was echoed in the Winchester's insistence that though the 'Poor are naturally averse to any thing that carries the Appearance of Constraint, or removing them from their own Families', they would thank the 'good Fortune [that] throws them into an Hospital, where they will be *more* taken Care of than many of their Betters'.[49] Picture fortune, then, plucking the poor out of their close, unwholesome dwellings and throwing them into the hospital, where they under-

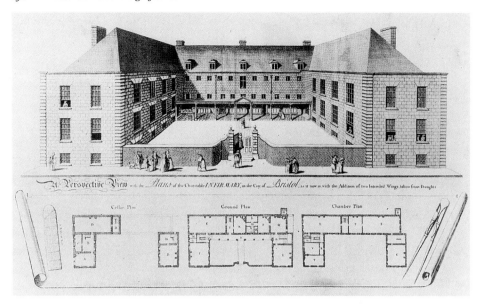

54. The first Bristol Infirmary.

stood that they had been delivered from constraint into expansiveness, and not the reverse.

Other early hospitals were compact, literally as well as figuratively villa-like.

John Wood the Elder finished his final design for the Bath General Hospital in early 1738, and its Trustees then asked Beau Nash to take it to London so that it 'might be first laid' before the royal family. This graceful gesture was immediately followed by the engraving of Wood's 'fair Plan and Elevation', and the opening of a very successful subscription. The print was, as Wood cheerfully admitted, 'for the Sake of Ornament . . . made different to that which was intended for Execution': the ornament lay in regularity, the squareness of the plan (the hospital was actually built askew, because of the site).[50] It resembles what was built (1738–42) in presenting wings surrounding three sides of a small rear court, of which one, Wood explained, could be extended. The plan shows five ground-floor wards lit by as few as two windows each. The actual building did better than that, but even so Tenon dismissed it with the brusquest sentence in his journal: 'We will certainly not give the dimensions of the wards because this is an old hospital that should not serve as a model.'[51] The Liverpool Infirmary (1745–47) also illustrated its plan (Figure 55), and with some justification. While maintaining compactness through the same general configuration of a U with a thick bottom, the Liverpool building managed to incorporate salivating (venereal-disease) wards and an operating theatre among a variety of other departments and six large wards, two running the building's entire depth on the first floor. A 'calm Retreat', its promoters called this hospital, in which the poor were 'provided with the neatest Accommodations'.[52] The accommodation was always purpose-built, which might have something to do with an interest in neatness. Like the General Hospital in Bath, but unlike other early voluntary hospitals, the Infirmary did not use an existing building in the first instance (although the

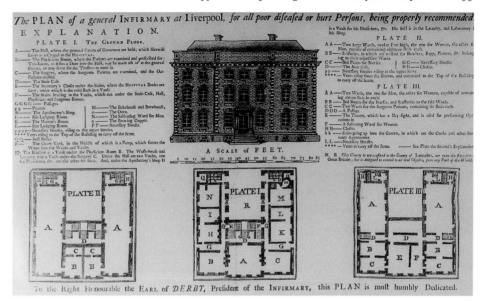

55. The Liverpool Infirmary held a variety of departments within a building whose compactness is here emphasized by its circumscription by the outlines.

slightly earlier York County Hospital, which had by 1745 moved into a new building resembling Liverpool's, did so).[53]

Another hospital of this type, and probably the second after Bath's, was Addenbrooke's in Cambridge, which Richard Hewlings has suggested was built in 1741 to the designs of the mathematician James Burrough (1691–1764), Cambridge's leading architect, only to be abandoned until its completion in 1763 and opening in 1766. (Like the Radcliffe Infirmary in Oxford, Addenbrooke's Hospital was founded by a single bequest, but this did nothing for the speed of either enterprise.) Addenbrooke's was, before its first enlargement in the early 1820s, a solid square in outline. Three vestibules together formed a passageway across its front. Behind them were, in the centre, a stairhall with rooms behind, and on each side, wards running the full depth of the building, flush with the centre pile.[54] An unrealized design for the Edinburgh Surgeons' Hospital dated 1738, and attributed to William Adam, similarly shows a solid triple pile with wards on each side of three floors.[55] There the stair was to be a splendid oval. Behind it, the operating theatre rises up through three floors, beginning on the first; the arrangement is that of the core of the Edinburgh Infirmary, begun a few months later, but a greater proportion of the Surgeons' Hospital was to be dedicated to surgical display.

These early purpose-buildings are not a different species from others: imagine Liverpool's wards semi-detached and turned out 90 degrees, and you have something very like the Devon and Exeter. Liverpool however presented itself as a tidy block in its print, and this conception of hospitals seems to have been discarded after the 1740s, with two exceptions. One is the Derby Infirmary (1804–9, Chapter 10), and the other is Salisbury's (begun 1767, opened 1771), designed by Wood's son John the Younger (1728–81), whose wards also ran across the building, though athwart and not from front to back. The ground-floor chapel and

56. The Leicester Infirmary, whose small pavilions held domestic offices and one 'infectious' ward. The building on the far left is the Asylum.

women's ward (the latter 20 feet high, Tenon noted) rose up through a mezzanine storey otherwise, like the basement and ground floor, given over to offices; the top floor held two large and two smaller wards. Around the central staircase, lit by a big skylight, everything was arranged with ingenuity.[56]

Salisbury also broke the stylistic mould. It was a kind of medieval tower house with side turrets (Figure 57), *petits pavillons* that Tenon described as supporting water tanks hidden behind the crenellations. These projections accommodated a variety of spaces on different sides of different floors: a scullery, small rooms for nurses, the chapel's chancel (neatly oriented east) – and the castle's garderobes. Those adjoining wards held their privies, each in this way pushed out of

57. The Salisbury Infirmary, an unprecedented stylistic excursion with a practical advantage

the body of the building and equipped with two windows. 'One cannot but be struck', *The Lancet* mused in 1880 about the then-new Edinburgh Infirmary, 'with the admirable manner in which the Scotch Baronial lends itself to sanitary purposes'.[57] The younger Wood's was the first, and for a long time the only, hospital to realize the potential of certain architectural styles to cope with human evacuation.

When the Salisbury Infirmary was begun, the hospitals conveniently addressed as H and U plans already formed the largest group among those built in eighteenth-century Britain. Edinburgh's was the most complex and, as we might expect, it got the fullest explanation.

A college in a hospital

The Edinburgh Infirmary's ground floor was devoted to offices and cells for lunatics (see Figure 41, p. 112). Above were three floors of wards on each side of the central block. Other wards filled the wings and in the corners between were lobbies with staircases on one side and nurses' rooms on the other. Women were to the west (right on the elevation) and men to the east on all floors. On the third floor, surgical wards flanked the operating theatre, which also came to serve as a lecture hall and chapel. In 1768, Edward Foster suggested that operating rooms could double as chapels; his *Essay on hospitals* was in several respects directed by his recent experience as a student in Edinburgh.[58]

Philanthropus' claims, in the *Letters* of 1738 and 1739, that the design was in every respect directed towards solidity, convenience, and cleanliness were buttressed with precision. For example,

> it is proposed to lay all the Floors of the Galleries between the Beams with Brick Arches resting on the Scantlings, to bring these to a Plain a-top with liquid Mortar, and to pave above this with unglaz'd Dutch Tile.[59]

The beds were the object of particular pride. Philanthropus described the 'little retiring Place' made by drawing the curtain at the foot of each, to form a 'kind of Room of the Space of two Beds, fronting one another, and the Area between them of 5 Foot by 8, with a large Window'. The projections flanking the windows, on the plans, are the closets for the patients' 'medicines, clothes, or other necessities'.[60]

The Infirmary would not have any 'Ornament, but in the Front of the 54 Foot in the Centre, as this is to be more properly a College than an Hospital'. This was the span of the stack made by the hall and, above it, the managers' room, offices for the treasurer, secretary, accountant, and apothecary, and on the top floor the 'convenient Operation-Room'. The large central stair joined these places of administration and display, the vertical 'College' externally distinguished by columns, pilasters, swags, scrolls, attic, and square dome, and internally separated by partition walls from the wards and lobbies that were the hospital:

> This [central] Part of the Building, . . . being all separate from the rest of the House by stone Walls, . . . also makes a proper Division betwixt the Men

and Womens Wards, and answering the same Ends as if they were distinct Buildings.

Adam's houses often had a service stair, as opposed to the 'State Stair' leading from a ground-floor vestibule to the beginning of the apartments' sequence above. His hospital had two, one for men and the other for women, at the junctions of the wards in the central range and those in 'that End of the Body of the House they are joined to'.[61]

The operation room was a 30-foot cube, 'to be put in the shape of a Theatre, so disposed, that two or three hundred Students and Apprentices may conveniently see any Operation performed, without disturbing those who perform it'.[62] This does not refer to an ill-timed cough. Rules published in 1749 enjoined the young men from standing on the benches and from pushing up close to the 'Operator' unless invited (and generally from causing 'Quarrels, Noise or Broils' in the house) and one former student recalled how his fellows had in the early 1770s bestowed 'very freely their marks of approbation or disapprobation on different operators'. (A physician, he seems to have thought that this kept the surgeons on their toes.)[63] Philanthropus reported that the partition walls would deafen any 'Noise that would be occasioned at the Performance of an Operation', which might certainly distress patients in the flanking wards, and

> To this Operation Room there is a very easy and convenient Access by the great stair, which goes the height of the Operation-Room, and by which no Disturbance can be given to the Patients of the House.[64]

Like the top floor itself, Edinburgh's central stair came to be defined as surgical territory. According to the *History and statutes* of 1778 it was wide and shallow enough to admit 'street-chairs, in which patients brought . . . with fractures, dislocations, or dangerous wounds' might safely ascend.[65]

Edward Foster thought that an operation room should be 'closely connected' to the hospital but detached from it, so that the patient's cries would not disturb others. Elevated to get the necessary skylights, it could be housed together with the (noisy) apothecary's shop, the (damp and noisy) wash-house, the (smelly) 'Necessary-house', and the 'Dead Room, as it is called', which was both smelly and noisy. (The mortuary produced not only 'contagious Miasmata', but the inevitable 'Noise of the Friends of the Defunct', and frequently 'bad Effects on weak Minds' among the living.)[66] Some English operating rooms may have been insulated in this way, either purposely or simply because they were afterthoughts. Even the huge naval hospital at Haslar lacked one for at least twenty years after its completion in 1761. At Exeter Tenon described a building beside the hospital in which the wash-house, laboratory, and pharmacy were accommodated underneath (presumably surgical) wards, and above them the operating theatre.[67]

From its inception Adam's building was understood as capable of effecting separations: between the college and the hospital, in a calm assignment of two building types under one roof, between the male and female patients who might as well be in 'distinct Buildings', between surgery and medicine, and between 'different Ailings', and particularly the segregation of 'acute Diseases' from the rest. The last phrase (from 1739) may be euphemistic. Certainly the Infirmary would, unlike many English hospitals, come to admit patients presenting a threat to pure air, 'infectious' cases of smallpox, fevers, and venereal disease. Until dedicated wards were set up, apparently in the 1780s, the small rooms in the ward corners may have been used for fever cases, as they were for smallpox.[68] All these separations were enabled by ward access via the side stairs and lobbies and were if necessary enforced by the occupants of the latter. (The door to the salivating ward for women, 'in a remote part of the house', was in 1778 said to be open only when a nurse was present.)[69] The Infirmary's plan also facilitated something that was not explained in its publications: the managers rented out empty wards, both for patients who were not supported by the hospital's charity, and for completely different uses altogether.[70] In some respects it did not much matter if a ward held parturient women or a bookseller's stock.

In 1750, a committee of managers visited the top ward of the Infirmary's west wing with Mr Hamilton, who proposed to rent it as a printing house, as well as a lower ward already occupied by 'James Scott Druggist'. It agreed that the high ward and garret could be let to Mr Hamilton for one year at £10.[71] This rent might be compared to the £5 per quarter, payable in advance, the managers proposed to charge her brother for the care of Mrs Graems 'disordered in her senses' in 1758, when they also, not coincidentally, decided to meet with William's eldest son John Adam to consider a 'house to be Built for Lunaticks'.[72] Adam became a tenant in turn: a managers' meeting in July 1774 resolved that he and a bookseller, then in possession of two 'garrets belonging to the House which is attended with inconveniency', would be given notice to leave.[73]

As the example of Mrs Graems suggests, the Infirmary's medical innovations may not always be distinguished from its commercial dealings. Other hospitals took the insane against payment,[74] but Edinburgh's regularly accepted other kinds of supernumerary patients. A self-financing servants' ward was an early, and disappointing, experiment but historical accident later strengthened the managers' conception of the hospital as, in part, a series of spaces for rental. The *History and statutes* of 1749 claimed, patriotically, that the Infirmary was taking soldiers as early as 1743, in the build-up to the Rebellion, and they like sailors came to comprise a big percentage of its admissions. Such patients needed particularly careful supervision but, as Guenter Risse suggests, this was not hard to manage in this building.[75] In 1755, the managers entered into a complicated agreement with the Professor of Midwifery Thomas Young, who proposed establishing a maternity ward. Though pregnant women had been barred from admission, as at most hospitals, it was agreed that Young could fit up and furnish a ward at his own expense and thereafter be responsible for its repair (at first in the east wing's attic, it later moved down a floor but was still 'sufficiently separated from the rest of the house').[76] In return he would be allowed four women 'to be maintained by the house' at a time, for six months in the year, and during the season he could also admit others, paying the house sixpence a day for each. Students holding tickets could attend Young's practice there, and the charity would bear the midwives' and nurses' wages. Five years later, Young asked the managers for two additional patients, to a total of six. They agreed, then turned their attention to the next item of business, authorizing the treasurer to lend £1,000 to the city of Edinburgh.[77]

In the 1980s, the municipality of Almere, in the Netherlands, funded research into the planning of local health centres. Eight models were designed, each generated by three choices between pairs of opposing desiderata. (One concerned construction techniques and would not have been available before the nineteenth century.) The model made by the stipulations that the building should be on one storey, and that 'as many rooms as possible should have an exterior wall, permitting daylight and natural ventilation through windows', is an H plan. Though more expensive than a rectangle, the H was judged to have additional benefits: easier adaptability, and a much greater potential for expansion, subdivision, and subletting[78] (U plans like Edinburgh's have the same properties). Most of the hospitals described in what follows have H plans. The type was explicitly privileged after 1770, when a new way of writing about hospital buildings underlined the importance of their air, but ventilation was not the only advantage it offered. Only in Edinburgh were the others so fully exploited.

Letter-plans

Wards like those in the side wings of the Exeter and Winchester hospitals, extended in a line with the main block, were attached to it only on one of their short sides, and their windows faced each other. Those on either side of Edinburgh's central 'College', as well as those perpendicular to them in the wings, can also be understood this way. At the Pennsylvania Hospital (begun 1755), planned in conscious imitation of Adam's, the central range was similar, with single-pile wards extending to each side. The Pennsylvania however became an H and not a U over its long construction period because its side wings straddled the centre line, and, though they came to include larger wards, the original intention was to fill them with additional cells for the insane, private apartments for certain (unspecified) classes of patient, and offices.[79] Foster's plan (see Figures 6 and 7, p. 36) of 1768, for a smaller hospital, which he did not imagine would be built in phases, proposed using the wings for small wards, stairs, and offices, while devoting the upper floors of the central block to large wards. A repertory of wards, offices, and piazzas and corridors in different arrangements was available, not forgetting those represented by St Thomas' and the so-far unique St Bartholomew's. With the exception of the compact type exemplified by the Bath and Liverpool hospitals, these configurations were all additive, both formally and literally put together by parts.

Perhaps because of its wide distribution (Figure 58), the plan of the London Hospital begun in 1752 has assumed a normative status among eighteenth-century purpose-buildings.[80] The double-piling of the central range on each side of a corridor would become common, and it was not the only hospital to put wards in the rear pile: the Devon and Exeter hospital already had small wards (including three for the venereally diseased) there. The handsome Leicester

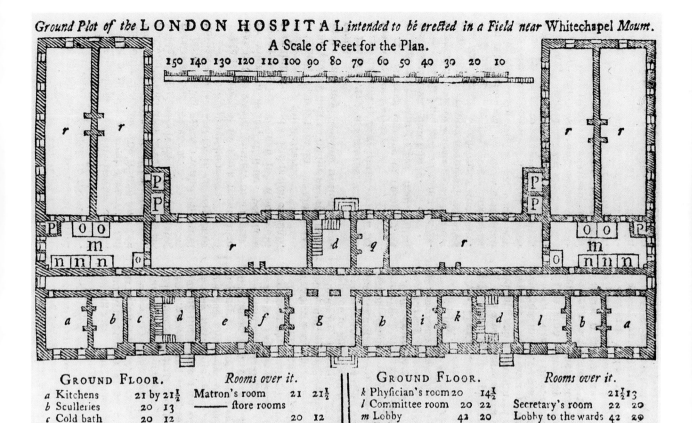

Ground Plot of the LONDON HOSPITAL intended to be erected in a Field near Whitechapel Mount.

A Scale of Feet for the Plan.

150 140 130 120 110 100 90 80 70 60 50 40 30 20 10

GROUND FLOOR.			Rooms over it.		
a Kitchens	21 by 21½		Matron's room	21	21½
b Sculleries	20	13	——— ſtore rooms		
c Cold bath	20	12		20	12
d Stair caſes	20	18½	Stair caſes		
e Surgery	20	22	Surgeon's priv. room		
f Bleeding room	20	14½	His man's room	20	14½
g Hall or lobby	21½	30	General court room		
h Apotheca. ſhop	21½	22	and chapel	68	30
i Apotheca. room	21½	13			

GROUND FLOOR.			Rooms over it.		
k Phyſician's room	20	14½		21½	13
l Committee room	20	22	Secretary's room	22	20
m Lobby	41	20	Lobby to the wards	41	20
n Sinks			Sinks to each ward		
o Nurſes rooms			Nurſes rooms		
p Privies			Privies		
q Steward's room	20	13	Wards		
r Wards					

Infirmary (Figure 56), built in 1767–71 under the direction of William Henderson (c.1737–1824), also filled the rear, south side of its main block with large wards. Henderson's plan shows how single-piled wards could be built, when funds permitted, on to and at right angles to the small pavilions linked by the piazzas to the main block. (At Leicester, unlike the London, the side wards were not added until the nineteenth century.)[81] The Devon and Exeter, the London, and the Leicester Infirmary were all built, or were intended to be built, in stages. Hence the centres that could stand alone with their offices and wards:

> The building must consist as usual, of a centre & wings; it will be a subject of your consideration, whether the centre shall be first erected, with rooms for the keeper, nurses, and a few sick, or whether the wings shall be first undertaken; the state of the funds must influence your determination.

The Massachusetts General Hospital's architect Charles Bulfinch (1763–1844) wrote (in 1817) as if this procedure were customary, and with it the form.[82]

58. The London's plan as published in the *Gentleman's Magazine* in 1752.

The London Hospital plan clearly shows how the joints between the wing- and central wards were filled by lobbies, each with nurses' rooms (o), sinks (N), and a privy (P). The arrangement, comparable to that shown on the St Bartholomew's, Edinburgh, and Liverpool plans (see Figures 47, 41, p. 112 and 55) permitted a measure of supervision,[83] and offered the conveniences of a coal bin, utensils cupboard, and sinks near each ward. Surveillance was a serious consideration at the naval hospitals, with generally unwilling patients often suffering from 'infectious' diseases, and both Haslar (begun 1746) and Plymouth (1758) made vigorous use of such lobbies. The latter's ward blocks (see Figure 70, p. 183) actually look very similar to the London's wings, in plan, if one imagines the latter isolated with their lobbies.

The London's pairing of the wing wards was however unique (as far as I know) for a hospital on an H or U plan. Tenon noted how its eighteen wards received 'daylight and air only on one side', but was intrigued by the air vents high in their walls though perhaps amused by their name: 'Voilà ce que l'on appelle ventilateur'.[84] The wards also had fireplaces – another simple way to ventilate: air is drawn through open windows when a fire burns[85] – and the London in any case had a situation so salubrious that it conducted more successful trepanations (an important criterion for Tenon) than any other hospital in the metropolis. Potted geraniums on the windowsills of the women's wards also flourished. At the London he inspected a ward with twenty-two beds; he saw another of the same capacity at the Middlesex Hospital, begun to James Paine's designs in 1755, and built in the same stages around the same time (centre range, and side wings completed c.1770 and c.1780). Though in straddling the centre line it lost three windows on one side, the Middlesex ward more nearly approached what Tenon considered the ideal.[86]

The explanation for the pairing perhaps lies in the hectic history of the London's planning, and certainly the building's real historical interest does. Of the eight schemes Mainwaring produced during the second half of 1751 (one differed from another simply in its external 'ornament'), the rebuilding committee chose number six to forward to the governors at large, who approved it in September. All we know about number six comes from the committee's report dated 13 December, which recommends that the Court of Governors now *reject* it, the committee having decided that it was after all 'capable of great Improvements'.[87] For 312 patients, this design would have had 'Three Detached or Separate Buildings', two with wards and one for the 'proper offices', all linked by colonnades. This sounds like a cross between Greenwich and St Bartholomew's. The latter had the paired wards also used, though now with shared lobbies, at the London as it was begun the next year, and at Plymouth, designed six years after that. If, as seems likely, they also featured in this project, we can imagine three-storey ward blocks with two wards of about twenty beds on each floor. The rebuilding committee was anyway by December arguing for a new plan, on four counts. In it, first,

Almost all the Wards will have a Southerly aspect (which in the Opinion of your Physicians & Surgeons is the most desireable for your Patients) and the

Rest will [by] the Continuity of the Building be Secured from Cold winds as well as from the dust of one of the most frequented Roads . . .

The medical men would also be secured from the winds and dust, for by the same 'Continuity',

> your Physicians and Surgeons and Apothecary, May at all times and in all Seasons attend your Patients in all the parts of it, Without the Danger and Inconvenience to which they might be exposed by their Attendance in different Detached parts as proposed by the former Plan.

The last two points concerned 'Durabl[en]ess' and economy: 'one Continued Building is in its Nature Stronger & More lasting, than the same Quantity Divided into Three Detached or Separate Buildings', and, although the new plan offered thirty-eight more beds, it 'will Consist of Two and a half Square of Solid Building less than the former Plan, Besides Saving the Expence of the Collonades'. The durability argument sounds flimsy, but the other is straightforward: flooring and roofing materials required for 250 square feet (the two-and-a-half square) of building would be saved if the London were built continuously, or rather (the wings were not finished until 1775 and 1778) contiguously. The Court of Governors unanimously approved the new plan.

In this way the rebuilding committee decided against building an anticipation of the naval hospital at Plymouth, whose detached ward blocks would become so celebrated. In doing so, however, they did not present the new plan as something radically different from the old. With the exception of that to the wards' orientation, all the improvements posit the new plan as once-separate parts pulled together into an advantageous 'Continuity', U-shaped as it turned out, that would not least obviate the necessity for those expensive colonnades. There was more to the change than that – for one thing, the London's centre acquired wards too – and the new plan was anyway best presented as a revision. Even the most docile court might wonder about a complete volte-face, over three months, on a matter that was supposed to have been under the committee's consideration for fifteen. None the less the report reveals a way of thinking about hospitals that is not dissimilar to that implied by the Edinburgh managers' willingness to rent wards out: as buildings they were buildings in parts.[88]

Tenon noted a family resemblance among a small group of provincial hospitals: the amateur Luke Singleton's Gloucester Infirmary (1757–61: Figure 59),[89] the Radcliffe Infirmary in Oxford (begun 1759, opened 1770), and Anthony Keck's rebuilding of the Worcester Infirmary (1767–70). These had H plans, with large wards filling the side wings and, in the central range, smaller wards and staff lodging-rooms above offices on the ground floor, all divided by a corridor running across. In a borrowing of a villa feature then fashionable, each had a canted bay projecting from the rear of the central block: at Gloucester this accommodated the governors' committee room, chapel, and operating theatre, one above the other.[90] Stiff Leadbetter, who built the Gloucester Infirmary, in fact designed the Radcliffe, and the Bristol philanthropist Edward Garlick, who gave

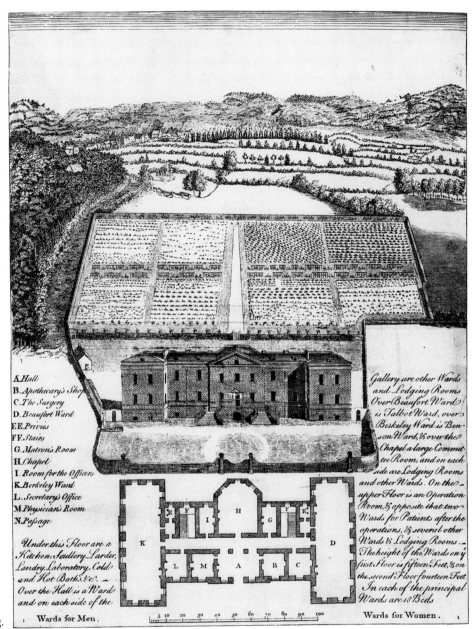

A.Hall
B.Apothecary's Shop
C.The Surgery
D.Beaufort Ward
E.E.Privies
F.F.Stairs
G.Matron's Room
H.Chapel
I.Room for the Officers
K.Berkeley Ward
L.Secretary's Office
M.Physician's Room
N.Passage

Under this Floor are a
Kitchen Scullery Larder,
Landry, Laboratory, Cold
and Hot Baths &c. —
Over the Hall is a Ward
and on each side of the

Gallery are other Wards
and Lodging Rooms
Over Beaufort Ward
is Talbot Ward, over
Berkeley Ward is Ben-
son Ward, & over the
Chapel a large Commit-
tee Room, and on each
side are Lodging Rooms
and other Wards. On the
upper Floor is an Operation
Room, & opposite that two
Wards for Patients after the
operations, & several other
Wards & Lodging Rooms.
The height of the Wards on
first Floor is fifteen Feet, & on
the second Floor fourteen Feet
In each of the principal
Wards are 18 Beds

Wards for Men.

Wards for Women.

59. A later copy of a print (first published in the annual report for 1763) of the Gloucester General Infirmary, with particularly informative lettering and landscaping.

£200 towards the purchase of Worcester's new site, had suggested to its governors that the Gloucester plan was the best in the country, 'being roomy, lofty, and dignified'.

Roominess and loftiness meant healthfulness, and were not irrelevant to dignity either. Historians have often remarked on the domestic appearance of eighteenth-century hospitals. The comparison works well with some, at least as they were presented on paper (John Wood's elevation of the Bath Hospital makes it look very much like a grand house, though for that matter so does his picture of his Bristol Exchange), and with hospitals' explicitly familial organization and recognized function as surrogate houses. Today, however, we are no longer capable of seeing distinctions once apparent. The Gloucester Infirmary, for example, would not have looked like a house to its first observers except analogously: what house so big and new would have been quite so plain? Important differences were also made by fenestration and the relative height of the storeys, as Adrian Forty has written: at hospitals the 'different floors often served the same functions; the upper floor plans often simply duplicated those below, unlike the mansion, where the different floors represented different degrees of social importance',[91] a relatively high *piano nobile*, for example, which also became larger and perhaps more elaborately surrounded windows. The letterpress with the Gloucester picture, which was used in the annual report for 1763, makes a point of the heights of the wards on two storeys, which were nearly equal and, at 15 and 14 feet, quite considerable; ward heights' implications for airiness were established. (In 1751 Mainwaring was instructed to make the London's no higher than the physicians and surgeons thought 'necessary for the health of the Patients'.)[92] In general, the print is efficiently demonstrating what Garlick also called 'real use and simplicity', domestic virtues that in this context produced something not altogether domestic-looking but which saved lives. In 1765 the Worcester governors invited ladies and gentlemen of the public to visit the hospital, still in the old house, and 'observe the distresses of their poor brethren panting for breath, incapable of receiving assistance from medicine for want of good and sufficient air'.[93] This drastic strategy assumed a public understanding of air's workings, in the body, alongside those of physic.

Depending on the width of the H plan's central block relative to the depth of the ward wings, the number of windows opposed across the wards varied. At Gloucester, the returns of the ward projections were only one window-bay deep.[94] At the Norfolk and Norwich Hospital (built 1770–76, opened 1772) designed by William Ivory (c.1738–1801) the wings could project much further, in part because the central range was whittled down to hold, on the ground floor, a single row of offices with a rear passageway. The result was singularly spindly, but the governors had wanted (as they explained publicly) a 'mode of building' directed towards something 'remarkably airy', as well as, inevitably, a mode that could be finished and occupied in parts. They had already defined the H form as 'admitting the freest circulation of air', a pioneering statement informed by the surgeon Benjamin Gooch's investigations, perhaps begun as early as 1759, of other hospitals. These also suggested the device of pushing the latrines out into side projections (they paid particular attention to the privies, Gooch explained privately, so effluvia were not a problem), as Wood had done more gracefully at the Salisbury Infirmary, begun three years earlier.[95] At the Lincoln County Hospital (1776–77) designed by John Carr of York (1723–1807), and Samuel Saxon's (1757–1831) Northampton Infirmary (1792–93), which both replaced house conversions (and the former a malthouse conversion, too) the central ranges were similarly reduced to single piles. Their wings were not built as long as the Norfolk and Norwich's but, as was simple enough, they were later extended by an extra couple of bays.[96] In inviting plans in 1790, the Northampton governors stipulated that the main wards should have opposite windows, offering northerly and southerly aspects, with no passage from one to another. They also specified the square and cubic footages (90 and 1,300–1,400 respectively) to be allowed each patient.[97] A considerable discursive shift had taken place in the fifty-four years since the Winchester Hospital had promised 'free Air' to the poor, and it would be lasting.

An accumulating weight of architectural precedent was one thing that permitted new precision in the correlation between architectural means and medical ends, and reference to precedent was itself part of the change. In 1794, subscribers to the Glasgow Infirmary congratulated themselves that 'in its internal disposition and arrangement, [the building] has been formed upon the most approved plans of the houses of that kind which have been hitherto erected'.[98] They were not specific, and the smaller hospital designed by Robert Adam (built 1792–94) was fundamentally similar to his father's in Edinburgh. Above a double-piled ground floor with its cells for the insane and rooms for domestic services (Figure 61), wards filled the width of the building beside the central stairs and their adjoining rooms for medical and administrative officers. The stairs led up to the operating theatre, a fine, aisled rotunda with an internal column-screen a few feet from the wall (Figure 60).[99] The major difference was that at Glasgow the 'Back stairs', water closets, and nurses' rooms, which at Edinburgh started the side wings that made its U, here extended in line with the wards to terminate the hospital's single file. A report taking the form of a letter sent to Thomas Beddoes in 1797 also suggests that the older hospital had set a standard. Even Glasgow's high wards had water closets, boasted Robert Cleghorn, one of the Infirmary's first two physicians, so 'we are seldom troubled with such smells as you may remember on the side stairs of the Edinburgh Infirmary' (Beddoes had been an Edinburgh student). 'Our wards too are more convenient. There are no [cupboard] projections from the walls, and the bed-posts are of iron.'[100]

There were also more particular inspirations for the new way of talking about hospitals. The enormous naval establishments at Haslar and Plymouth (Chapter 8), both completed in the early 1760s, could not and did not try to refuse patients on account of what was wrong with them, and their architecture was soon being described as an active hindrance to cross-infection, as Grosley (quoted at the beginning of this chapter) noted of Haslar. Now, at the end of the century, English general hospitals were beginning to accept cases of illnesses, and in particular the fevers, which they had formerly admitted only accidentally (Chapter 10); the example of the naval hospitals showed, not only that buildings could help to manage contagion, but also how that management could be explained.

The second impetus behind the new rhetoric was Tenon's tour, in 1787, of the residential institutions in the south and west Midlands of England, undertaken as part of the Paris Académie des Sciences' investigations into hospital design. It is not surprising that some of his hosts and others followed up on Tenon's own *Mémoires* and the Académie's reports, all published between 1786 and 1788. What is surprising is the specific use to which Cleghorn put the last of these, in writing that 'every part' of the Glasgow Infirmary had been designed

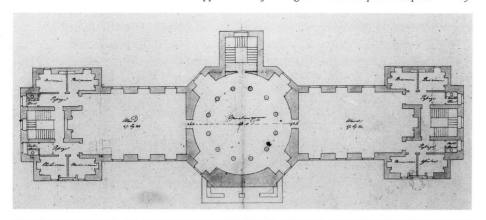

60. The top-floor plan of the Glasgow Infirmary, showing the operating theatre flanked by surgical wards.

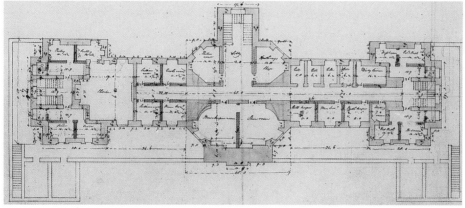

61. The ground-floor plan of the Glasgow Infirmary.

as much as possible, according to a report made to the late king of France, by a Committee of the Academy, who were desired to point out the faults of the Parisian hospitals, and to specify the best mode of correcting them. Happening to get their report and plans, I gave them to Mr Adams, who studied them carefully, and with much profit.[101]

In the final year of his life (1791–92), in attempting to secure the commission for the Edinburgh Bridewell, Adam assimilated the panoptical principle with confidence and skill enough to disarm Jeremy Bentham himself.[102] In Glasgow the Académie's recommendations (see Figure 75, p. 191) may simultaneously have been serving him the same way. Whatever the relative merits of Paris's and Edinburgh's claims to the Glasgow Infirmary, the architectural models were now potentially international, although it would be decades before British hospitals again publicly claimed to be following the French example.

In 1802 the Newcastle physician John Clark classed the Glasgow Infirmary, along with Northampton's, Leeds's, and others, among the 'improved Infirmaries', as opposed to 'older hospitals'. At 'old' Northampton, in the converted house, one in fourteen patients died, but at new Northampton, one in thirty-one. Glasgow, whose rate was one in twenty-one, however took 'infectious' cases; Clark was aware that admission patterns present a big problem to using general mortality rates as an index of the 'utility of ventilation, the advantages of different-sized wards, and the pernicious effects of vitiated air' in hospitals.[103] Nor did plans alone make the difference. Among the improved infirmaries, Leeds's was begun in 1768 to Carr of York's designs; though subsequently enlarged, it had managed to adhere to a clean U shape made by a double-piled centre and single ward wings.[104] New Northampton formed a more attenuated H, and Glasgow had no wings at all. It was to 'cleanliness, ventilation, and proper accommodations', Clark wrote, that the improved rates might unhesitatingly be attributed, and even the last was not purely an architectural affair: among the accommodations he admired at Leeds was the 'dark' ward for those who had had cataracts removed. As they convalesced the curtains were opened by degrees, and it became a lighter ward.[105] None the less, a new way of writing about hospital buildings was well and truly launched. Its reliability as a guide to earlier construction is less certain.

Appraisal

That the 'Order' at Edinburgh of which Philanthropus boasted in 1739 included the airiness claimed a few years earlier for St George's might be assumed from his itemization of ceiling heights and the widths of the 'galleries' between the rows of beds, and from his attention to those beds' placement beside 'large' windows and the ward chimneys (fireplaces).[106] Writing too early for 'ventilation', he did not however offer airiness as a general concept. Forty years later, the Infirmary's *History and statutes* cited the 'opposite windows', the chimneys, and the stair-doors in the wards, through which the 'current of air' to the fire might 'contribute to divert the infectious vapour from the other patients' when small-pox cases could not, for lack of space, be moved to one of the small rooms. 'In the construction of this fabric, nothing hath been more solicitously attended to, than ventilation.'[107] Maybe so, but we must recognize not only the danger of anachronistic inference, but the point at which built form starts to fail as a guide to practice. Edinburgh's large windows admitted light as well as air, and need not have been opened very often.

'Ill air . . . maketh an ill seat', wrote Bacon: it was an ancient commonplace.[108] Bad air was soon conventionally associated in England with heat, and in particular with urban crowding and stench. Coolness was purity, in a popular classification that was essentially humoral but worked no less well with late seventeenth- and eighteenth-century investigations of animal physiology.[109] Its application at hospitals was certainly tempered by common sense, the knowledge that some of their clientele had suffered in the cold of their own wretched homes: in 1693 the St Thomas' governors' decision to rebuild was recorded with a note that their largest wards were 'in a lofty old building' whose ruinous condition made it very cold.[110] That sweat expelled toxins was an ancient understanding too, one revived when the more 'insensible perspiration' that might be fatally discouraged by cold, damp air became a medical vogue in the mid-eighteenth century.[111] An 'Order for keeping the windows shut' was confirmed at an early meeting of Bristol's subscribers, and in 1749 the Edinburgh *History and statutes* innocently boasted of its little 'close warm Rooms' (that is, the four 'fire-rooms' in the corners of each ward)[112] even as 'close' was becoming more or less equivalent to 'lethal'.

Practice remains elusive; what did hospitals do with their windows? At the Norfolk and Norwich, Gooch explained, the upper parts of the sashes were let down daily 'for a due time', weather permitting; the Leicester Infirmary had its sashes shut on the day of Howard's surprise visit in 1787 and its governors rued the day, the 'closest and dampest that has been known this year'.[113] Hospitals had always had to contend with the changing state of the weather, the wards, and the patients alike, and continued to do so with equally contingent adjustments: opening the windows and lighting the fires, drawing the bed-curtains across to make little retiring places, as Philanthropus had explained. Curtains remained acceptable, but wooden bed-enclosures were increasingly suspect as invitations to bugs, and potentially suffocating.[114] The box beds, or bunks, that lined Guy's Hospital's wards were replaced by open iron bedsteads in the late 1780s, more or less in advance of Tenon's and Howard's incursions. The point is not that Guy's bunks somehow betrayed the promise of its wards' single-piling, just that bugs and reform dislodged them from their place in this economy of heat and air.[115]

At the same time, the windows began to be presented as the site of life-and-death struggles. Rehearsing a theme that remained vibrant for at least a century, Benjamin Franklin and his countryman John Jones quoted John Pringle's revelation (in his *Observations on the diseases of the army*, 1752) of hospitals' resident irony, that the doctor could only with difficulty convince patients and nurses of the grim 'necessity of opening the windows and doors at any time for a supply of fresh air'.[116] Hence the beneficence, which might have surprised the St Thomas' governors of the 1690s, of the makeshifts, the 'churches, barns, or ruinous houses ... where neither [the sick] nor their nurses can confine the air'.[117] Franklin adduced the healthiness of Burlington's dormitory at Westminster School, whose inhabitants regularly freed the air by breaking the windows, and of the Pennsylvania Hospital (in whose foundation he had played a leading role), where ward windows in the 'upper row', out of unaided reach, were generally kept open.[118] At Haslar Hospital, James Lind had the sashes nailed open every spring.[119] The educated were not free from the prejudice, but it was the ignorant who misapprehended, or maybe mis-felt; they 'feel the coldness of fresh air', wrote Jeremy Bentham, and not its necessity to 'health and life'. The Panopticon would ensure that sashes stayed open.[120]

A purposeful traveller could in 1750 have visited several civil hospitals – the London and the Middlesex, and those in Winchester, Northampton, Shrewsbury, and Worcester – still in adapted houses. Seven modern purpose-buildings were however then complete: the royal hospitals Bethlem and St Thomas's, and the voluntary foundations in Bath, Edinburgh, Exeter, York, and Liverpool.[121] St Thomas' was inward-turning, with its display towards its courtyards; even Cartwright's frontispiece (1682) with its statues of Edward VI and four charitable objects was moved inside, re-erected over the entrance to Edward Square in 1724 (see Figure 46).[122] As such it was different from, and viewed differently from the others mentioned, viewed more like the great house of the old style that it was (in 1819) explained as being. The other large London hospitals, St Bartholomew's and Guy's, formed quadrangles too. St Bartholomew's quadrangle was notable for its missing corners (two of its new blocks were in use and one building in 1750), and Guy's courts were behind the front range which, it was already apparent (one wing remained to be built), would present a U like Edinburgh's. Bath and Liverpool were compact, with relatively narrow rear courts and looked, broadly speaking, like newer kinds of houses. In a model that would prove to be far more durable, Bethlem, Edinburgh, and Exeter had the expansiveness made by single-piled ward wings, as if St Thomas's similarly constructed wards had been flung out. Edinburgh's arrangement seems to have been understood as permitting both ward rentals and, in a more or less related practice, the admission of military, maternity, and 'infectious' cases, instances of the flexibility more compact hospitals lost and whose full advantages English hospitals were not pursuing. Bethlem was magnificently built as a piece; newer hospitals' construction, and form of construction, were explained in terms of the prudent management of accumulating charitable funds. Such accumulation dictated the growth of the conversions, the Bristol Infirmary and St George's Hospital, which had also taken their final (for the moment) and more or less irregular forms by 1750.

References to a free air accompanied enough constructions to suggest that the unreformed hospital had its own history of reform,[123] but there was no purposeful traveller in 1750, and the buildings went mostly unexplained. Perhaps, however, there was not much to explain: airiness was self-evidently achieved by expansive, additive plans that could also be realized in stages. But by the end of the century there was quite a lot to say about hospital architecture. The following chapter describes the medical presuppositions underlying this new way of writing, and incidentally why its inauguration might be dated to 1750, the year of the Black Assizes.

Chapter 7
The breath of life

'One of the most striking proofs' of the value of pure air, wrote the physician Gilbert Blane in 1799, 'is the great difference in the success of the treatment of compound fractures, and other violent injuries, in private houses, from what it is at an hospital'.[1] After a chapter about the genial myths of production that surrounded the hospitals, and another about their increasingly explicit assumption of responsibility for healthy construction, it is time to remind ourselves that by the end of the century they were faced with hard truisms like these. Blane's pessimism is fundamentally a protest against the unnaturalness of hospitals, as opposed to houses, and specifically against their unnatural airs, which breed infection in bodies and buildings alike. It had however still seemed possible, forty years earlier, that they might be redeemed by a mechanical ventilator invented by Stephen Hales (1677–1761), whose workings he conceived as directly analogous to the body's own respiration. Hales's and related devices and analogies are the subject of the present chapter, which begins with the ways in which airs were believed to infect.

As how to keep entire populations large and healthy became the subject of attention all over eighteenth-century Europe, the hospital could appear to be an 'obsolete structure',

> A fragment of space closed in on itself, a place of internment of men and diseases, its ceremonious but inept architecture multiplying the ills in its interior without preventing their outward diffusion, the hospital is more a centre of death (*foyer de mort*) for the cities where it is sited, than a therapeutic agent for the population as a whole.[2]

Foucault is here describing a contemporary perception of metropolitan French hospitals, and in particular the Hôtel-Dieu in Paris, which was, and was known to be, the 'area of darkness' (*tache sombre*) that he called it. Historians have contested the generalization because the Hôtel-Dieu's mortality rate (almost one in four, according to Tenon) was exceptional, but they cannot contest the perception, for this rate directed discussions about hospitals from Vienna to Philadelphia.[3] And there were other, economic respects in which the hospital seemed obsolete, the institution no one wanted. The critiques were rehearsed with vigour in France, whose hospitals were distinctive in northern Europe for their central role in poor relief. Hospitals (in particular the *hôpitaux généraux*) supposedly kept potential workers in slothful vice; hospitals' own wealth, the patrimonial property that included their buildings, was just as unproductive and stagnant.[4] Comparable objections were raised in England, where charities were examined for signs of flexibility and efficiency. Buildings seemed to weigh down this quasi-commercial agility, implying as they did the provision of regular or guaranteed relief that would only exacerbate dependency. The idea that hospital buildings actually *killed* those entering them in hopes of cure was only an interesting extension of this general argument about waste and inutility.

Medical objections to the hospital centred on the enclosure that the building necessarily formed, and its rigidity. Only some kinds of illness could be treated there, and even with the help of bed-curtains and shutters – the latter increasingly suspect – it might not be possible to adjust the ward environment adequately to individual requirements.[5] James Gregory's teaching on hysteria, for example, made it clear that the tedium, and lack of fresh air or of opportunities for exercise within the Edinburgh Infirmary aggravated a complaint already aggravating for other patients – sometimes, he suspected, to the point of contagion. An Infirmary directive acknowledged that patients with consumption would similarly 'suffer from the air of the hospital': windows could be opened for them, but that would not help their ward-mates with feverish catarrh, who needed an even, warm temperature.[6] Nor, some thought, did diseases behave naturally in hospitals, and even therapeutics was uncertain: remedies working there might not work elsewhere.[7] All these arguments and more were advanced by proponents of the dispensaries, hospitals without beds. In 1802, John Reid, physician to the Finsbury Dispensary, compared hospital medicine to hothouse botany: interesting work, but scarcely revealing of plants, or diseases, in their natural state.[8]

The hospital's unnaturalness was potentially deadly. The eighteenth century came to see that artificiality as embracing the 'continued' or 'putrid' fevers apparently engendered in close spaces. What was called the ship, camp, hospital or jail fever, whose first symptoms were 'gentle horrors and little feverish heats', has been identified with typhus,[9] transmitted by the body louse and spread in dense populations. The *morbus castrensis* had been a fact of siege warfare, which confined people for long periods on both sides of the wall; its new prevalence, new names, and (for some) new nature accompanied new forms of warfare, bigger towns, and the new urban institutions.[10] Concern for the fever thus formed part of the eighteenth century's wider attention to the diseases of civilization, a distinctive application of the critique of luxury. 'When I have met with gaol fever in country prisons,' wrote John Howard, 'I have been almost constantly told that it was derived from those in London; as the corruption of manners, also flowing from that great fountain, spreads far and wide its malignant streams.'[11]

The 1771 annual report for the Liverpool Infirmary explained that its surgical apprentices had always 'been so ill lodged in close Rooms and unwholesome Air' that all were in danger and one had died from the fever.[12] How often it struck hospitals and prisons is not certain. Margaret DeLacy suggests that the latter suffered when they became overcrowded, but that overcrowding was by no means their usual state until the 1780s, and the same seems to hold for hospitals.[13] However, the fear it inspired cannot be doubted, particularly after the publication of two books by a former Physician-General of the Army, John Pringle. They were as widely read as Richard Mead's thirty-year-old *Discourse concerning pestilential contagion*, whose plague narrative they continued.

In May 1750 more than fifty Londoners died of the jail fever after attending an Old Bailey courtroom; 'putrid streams from the bail dock', in which stood two prisoners from Newgate, where the disease was then epidemic, had evidently reached the court and spectators to horrific effect.[14] (Why introduce the needless complication of a louse vector? Lice were always there; the fever was not.) Pringle's *Observations on the nature and cure of hospital and jayl-fevers*, price one shilling, was rushed out thirteen days after the beginning of these, the Black Assizes. In it Pringle emphasized that, just as a prisoner at trial might appear to be well, but still carry the poison, so an outbreak even a little less severe than the recent one might not have alarmed the public, so insidious was the fever – which was of the same genus as the 'true plague'. (The letter's ostensible aim was to reduce public alarm.)[15] Pringle identified it with the malignant fever he had observed among military populations, of which he published an account the same year in the Royal Society's *Philosophical Transactions*, the next year in the *Gentleman's Magazine*, and in 1752 in the first of seven editions of his *Observations of the diseases of the army*. The public was led to understand that the jail, hospital, ship, and camp fevers were the same disease, and over the next two decades the Navy was inspired to some remarkably robust hospital design (Chapter 8), military physicans were encouraged to build and demolish their huts, and civilians began to explain the forms of their hospitals with explicit reference to air circulation.

Sick people emanate poisons, wrote Pringle, and in sufficient concentration the tainted atmosphere of the overcrowded ward generates the 'pestilential ferment'. It is as if he were writing about a chemical retort, and this vision of the hospital enclosure did coincide with improvements in techniques and glassware allowing the gaseous products of chemical reactions to be collected, weighed, and given to animals to breathe, but Pringle had his own kind of laboratory. He made his observations among military and naval populations whose movements and occasional isolations are relatively easy to trace and thus clarify patterns of transmission: a good example is his seemingly hour-by-hour account of what happened after Brigadier Houghton's regiment, which had sailed with some infected prisoners, joined the army at Inverness in 1746.[16] Ships, prisons, workhouses, and hospitals – closed institutions we might call them, places 'where a multitude of people are closely and nastily kept', Stephen Hales called them – presented identical challenges to good management, which would help to avert the threat.[17]

The age of the enclosure mattered. Jails and 'dungeons', which were mostly older buildings, in Pringle's England, than general hospitals, were inherently more dangerous because the 'putrefaction' had been there longest, but hospitals offered the sharpest and most volatile threat, he explained, in their variety and quantity of 'poisonous effluvia of sores, mortifications, dysenteric and other putrid excrements'. Pringle's admirer Richard Brocklesby soon explained that their very fabrics could become infected too. At one of the 'close hovels, or miserable hospitals' he had been forced to use when an army physician on the Isle of Wight in 1758, four men put into the same corner died in succession. Only scraping away at the floors and walls, 'thereby substituting an intire new layer of the whole inside of the house' had extinguished the 'seeds of infection'.[18] By the early nineteenth century it was understood, too, that in such atmospheres wounds and sores could become 'Hospital sores' and then 'Hospital-gangrene', and the incidence of such accelerating decays was moreover 'in exact proportion to the size of an Hospital'.[19]

'Among the great causes of sickness and death in an army, the reader will little expect that I should mention . . . the hospitals' (Pringle, 1752); 'It is a melancholy consideration that these charitable institutions . . . may too often be ranked among the causes of sickness and mortality' (Thomas Percival, 1771); 'There cannot surely be a greater contradiction in the nature of things than a disease produced by a hospital' (Aikin, 1771). Pringle, who claimed that he had found other books of no help, invented a rhetoric given its definitive form by Florence Nightingale, the best writer of them all: the 'very first requirement of a hospital is that it should do the sick no harm'.[20]

Since Vitruvius, architecture had been framed as a figurative art, and the concept and fear of 'hospital' diseases applied the last and most durable shading to an anthropomorphic picture of buildings as bodies, here bodies afflicted with chronic 'inbred disease' or acute, 'traumatic' infections.[21] The first phrase is Aikin's, in 1771; the second from a report prepared in Swansea after an 1876 outbreak of erysipelas, a contagious skin infection. The intervening years saw medical changes that made possible Robert Koch's first important contribution to bacteriology, also dating from 1876, but the idea of diseases contracted in and even peculiar to hospitals would survive germ theory, for of course the infections – in the modern sense – have too.

Miasmata and other airs

Today 'infectious' diseases are caused by parasites like bacteria and fungi. 'Contagious' diseases, which may also be infectious, are passed directly from one person to another without an intermediary like the flea, louse, or mosquito. Bubonic plague is therefore infectious, but not contagious because it requires the flea vector, but pneumonic plague, the result of plague victims developing secondary pneumonia, is both contagious and infectious.[22] Personally, I have great trouble remembering the difference. A much older aetiology seems more satisfactory, and this supposes that, while immediate or close contact (contagion) can certainly transmit disease, contact does not account for the victim isolated from others by miles on the ground or by locked doors and shutters, or who has had no contact with suspect goods like foreign cargoes. One also needed the concept which was, confusingly, called 'infection' before that word acquired its modern meaning.

The 'miasma' (plural, 'miasmata'), the polluted air, has been invoked since antiquity in attempts to understand epidemics among persons so widely separated that it was difficult to believe that any direct transmission had taken place. One of the most obvious things that they shared was the air they breathed, already a consideration central to an environmental medicine for which air, soil, water, the season, diet – all the characteristics of a locality – were of determining importance.[23] The air breathed by people who became ill was evidently corrupted: 'infected'. In two millennia of miasmatism there would never be consensus on how, precisely, this happened. One could only think analogically:

> procedures of dyeing cloth, the tainting of substances, the effects of poisons, and the growth of a fire from an initial spark – that is, the spread of change in a medium and the affecting of a whole after an initial disruption – were called upon to answer the vexed question of what happened to the air to make it pathological.[24]

Such visible, or at least more perceptible, phenomena could also be used to explain what happened to the human body as it fell ill; Girolamo Fracastoro (c.1478–1553) invoked the actions of poisons, and the readiness with which lime and sponges soak up water.[25] For our purposes it will suffice to derive a definition of miasmata, as they signified to hospital planning, from what James Riley has in this context called the long list of things proposed by someone.[26]

The source of the corruption could be vaporous exhalations from stagnant water, urban filth, or the infected and putrefying animal or human body itself. Corruption *of* the air could alternatively be corruption *in* the air, pathogenic particles carried in suspension; or both, if these particles were the product of the degeneration of air already tainted. They were thought to be more or less poisonous, and more or less sticky, infecting by inhalation or by the handling of objects to which they had stuck. Many sixteenth-century students of miasma and contagion had been interested in the problem of receptivity. Why did some people become ill, and others not; why are some of us sponges, and others iron? The eighteenth century could however conceive of air as itself a primary agent and sufficient cause of disease, not a factor to be associated with some personal predisposition or susceptibility like a humoral imbalance. Miasmata, in other words, were no longer *like* poisons, they *were* poisons, and the sick were poisonous too.[27] Once infected, a person could infect another, and there was often no sense in hard distinctions between the external causes of disease: 'contagious Miasmata', Edward Foster's phrase, was not self-contradictory.[28]

Air and its corruptions were mostly invisible: the nose was a much surer guide than the eye. A bad smell was a certain sign of corrupted air; the worse the smell, the greater the danger. The degree to which one identified the smell with the miasma – did stench itself cause disease? – was becoming problematic but not, in practice, important given its certain value as a warning. Samuel Sutton wrote about the epidemic among the expeditionary force to Cartagena assembling in the autumn of 1740 that the ships stank 'to such a degree' that they 'infected one another'. On the other hand, the American Noah Webster reported in 1799 that his research on the air within privies, less noxious than one might expect, suggested that the relationship was more complex.[29]

Hospitals were by definition enclosed spaces with a large number of sick people, many emitting pocket-miasmata ('contagions') and in turn breathing 'nothing but a noisome atmosphere of the morbid streams exhaling from their own excrements and diseased bodies', as Smollett memorably described it.[30] Foul smells abounded in them. Domiciliary care (which the rich had been getting all along) was obviously preferable to the evils of the enclosure where the 'sick, the dying, and the dead are crammed together, in the same rooms, and often in the same beds': Thomas Jefferson was, in 1787, hoping that general hospitals would never be built in Virginia. There, in a kind of democratic reordering of the antique, natural medicine that Pliny the Elder had described, friendless paupers were boarded with good farmers, and neighbours cared for them in sickness.[31] Meanwhile air, which opened up the enclosure and dispelled the toxic stenches, was the prophylactic and the cure for the diseases of hospitals or, at least, the one which might be effected by architectural means. Largely for this reason, I suspect, ventilation achieved an imaginative prominence in the eighteenth century that scrubbing and chemical prophylaxis, also generally recommended, did not.[32]

What is air? '*Air*', wrote the physician William Oliver in 1704, 'is the Cause of all our Distempers, as well as of our Life.'[33] What air is and what it does for the bodies of plants and animals (besides conveying sudden death that is), were questions that had been asked with increasing precision since the early seventeenth century. Robert Boyle and his circle in Oxford and at the Royal Society in London, including Wren and Hooke, were particularly interested in the relations between respiration and action. They reached a consensus that some kind of vital constituent of the inhaled air is carried by the blood to the muscles, where it enters into a chemical reaction, enabling animal motion. Work with the air pump (and birds and mice) led Boyle to conclude that air then transports impurities back out of the lungs, and the body.[34] Wren liked the idea of devising a machine that could in turn remove these exhaled impurities, making it possible to rebreathe one's own exhalations: 'It would be no unpleasing spectacle to see a man live without new air, as long as you please.'[35] This was in 1663, a decade after the end of the first Dutch War and a couple of years before the beginning of the second; a 'Strainer of the Breath, to make the same Air serve in Respiration' is listed in *Parentalia* among fifty-three lively 'Theories, Inventions, Experiments, and Mechanick Improvements' devised by Wren, along with ways of 'submarine Navigation' and staying 'long under Water'. The Royal Society was a patriotic society and technology to enable North Sea *sub*marine warfare was distinctly promising.[36]

Like Boyle and Hooke, Wren adhered to a 'Mechanical Philosophy', most famously encapsulated in the Cartesian theory of the body-machine. As he wrote in 1662, 'in the Body of a Man, if we consider it only mechanically' – the 'only' is because this understanding is partial – 'we may indeed learn the Fabrick and

Action of the organical Parts'.[37] The analogy worked both ways. If the body is like a machine, operating in response to local and particular causes (René Descartes used the example of the way we 'involuntarily' withdraw our foot from a flame) then machines could be devised to work like bodies, to extend their capacities. Microscopes and telescopes, 'by which', Wren wrote, 'our sense is so infinitely advanc'd', are machines like this – in an ecstatic hymn to the heavens, he described men able to 'stretch out their Eyes, as Snails do, and extend them to *fifty* Feet in length'[38] – and the breathing machine was to be another.

Wren was also a proponent of what as early as 1657 he neatly called a 'true Astrology', the most broadly useful of all studies of air. This was the natural 'History of Things depending upon Alteration of the Air and Seasons', among them crops, cattle, insects, and

> epidemical Diseases of the Year; Histories of any new Disease that shall Happen; Changes of the old [diseases]; Difference of Operations in Medicine according to Weather and Seasons, both inwardly, and in Wounds: and . . . a due Consideration of the weekly and annual Bills of Mortality in London.[39]

This was, in his words, a 'Part of Physiology, which concerns us as near as the Breath of our Nostrils, and I know not any Thing wherein we may more oblige Posterity, than that which I now propose'.[40] Wren's scientific posterity came to regard medical meteorology as an investigation far more important than any technology inspired by a mechanistic model of the body, a model seen as irredeemably quaint by the end of the next century.[41] In the meantime however came such vigorous popularizations as Cheyne's – the 'Human Body is a Machin of an infinite Number . . . of different Channels and Pipes, filled with various and different Liquors and Fluids, perpetually running, glideing, or creeping' (1733)[42] – and the most interesting and influential example of that technology, the 'lungs', as he called them, with which the Revd Stephen Hales extended the model, and the metaphor, to architecture.

In the later years of his long life, Hales (that 'poor good primitive creature', Horace Walpole called him)[43] became an object of affectionate interest among the great men and women of England, who enjoyed the idea that the perpetual curate of Teddington, Middlesex (pop. 500) could become one of the most renowned scientists and inventors of his day. It was at Teddington that he conducted an enormous number of bloody experiments in order to understand the arithmetical and causal relations between animal weight and cardiac output, blood pressure, the anatomy of the cardiovascular system, and the constriction of the small blood vessels; and, more peaceably, comparable phenomena in plants. Hales invented a ventilator that was used in prisons, hospitals, and ships, and the word 'ventilator' itself.[44] His device was not prompted by his understanding that air can kill, which everyone knew anyway,[45] but by his habit of thinking about life's workings in terms of the flow of liquids in pipes: stems and roots; arteries, veins, and capillaries.

Taking his cue from the Royal Society men of the previous generation, Hales showed in *Vegetable staticks* (1727) that air could be not only 'elastic' or free but 'fixed', *part* of other things and essential to vegetable and animal metabolism. 'It is by this amphibious property of air', he wrote, 'that the main and principal operations of nature are carried out.' He conducted a rebreathing experiment upon himself as part of his investigation into how animals absorbed air: 'at the end of the minute, the suffocating uneasiness was so great, that I was forced to take away the bladder from my mouth'. This sensation was, he thought, a consequence of the air charging with 'gross' and 'dense' vapours and thereby losing its elasticity.[46] He may have understood comparable transformations as operating in closed institutions; each one, in effect, a bladder into which many people were breathing. Hales's recognition of the reactivity of air marked the effective beginning of pneumatic chemistry and the 'chemical revolution' of a later generation was to a great extent concerned with gases.[47] By 1772, Antoine Laurent Lavoisier (1743–94) was clear that matter comes in three states, including that 'of expansion or of vapours'.[48] From this realization – that solids and liquids are just cold gases – all our understandings of matter itself have followed.

That air expands and rises as it becomes warm, to be replaced by colder and heavier air, was understood, as was the apparent propensity of 'Vapours and Exhalations', as Foster called them, to grow more concentrated as they ascended. Hence both Foster and, twenty years later, the Paris Académie des Sciences' Hôtel-Dieu rebuilding committee, on which Tenon and Lavoisier sat, advised that hospitals should never be more than three storeys high; hence, too, the accommodation of Haslar Hospital's most 'contagious' patients in upper wards – no one, that is, could safely lie above them.[49] In 1785 Lavoisier identified another danger in crowded hospitals (and in the Comédie française): what Tenon called the degradation of the air as it passes through the animal body (Hales's 'gross' vapours). We do not return all the oxygen, as Lavoisier named it, we inhale, but substitute carbon dioxide, as it would be called, for part of it. Tenon explained that this deterioration is quite different from that due to disease.[50] However, because the feverish (for example), breathe faster than other patients, the natural physiological event has implications for the desirable volumes and therefore, Tenon showed, the heights of certain wards (heights, because he fixed ward widths at 25 feet). Wards' heights had long been related to their salubrity, but Tenon's enthusiasm for comparative tables of air volumes per patient encouraged this kind of cubic reckoning.[51] Though the nineteenth century saw some ingenious new hypotheses about miasmal dynamics, and carbon dioxide anyway presented no difficulties for Tenon's recommendations for construction, this closer identification of the nature of human exhalations was the last understanding of the nature of air, strictly speaking, to impinge upon recommendations for hospital design.

What is air, then? Even granted the sketchiness of the history just given, the answer remains incomplete. To understand what air was we have to understand more about Wren's reference to the 'Part of Physiology, which concerns us as near as the Breath of our Nostrils'.

It is an elegant simile, in the context of a natural history of the air and the seasons. It is also a little joke, because the breath in our nostrils is God, who breathed into Adam's the 'breath of life; and man became a living soul' (Gen. 2: 7). Wren's figure moreover constituted a graceful allusion, intentional or not, to one man in particular. As Mark Jenner explains, the Judaeo-Christian pneumatic tradition had in 1662 just been thoroughly rehearsed in sermons and other celebrations of King Charles's restoration, and the topos was by no means divorced from what we would now think were more practical inquiries into air.[52] John Evelyn's *Fumifugium* (1661) is at once an argument for legislation to control London's air pollution and an elaborate meditation on the city's 'new Spirit'. Air is the 'Vehicle of the Soul . . . and [of] this frail Vessell of ours which contains it' and Charles, 'who is the very Breath of our Nostrills', fills our sails. In England in the 1660s and 1670s the Galenic, and Genetic, associations among airs, health, and the soul were briefly expanded into a symbolic realm embracing God, king, public health, and submarines alike.

The metaphysics survived this occasion, as Barbara Stafford has shown in her account of the eighteenth century's 'mental meteorology': Samuel Johnson could define 'Pneumatick' and its cognates as relating both to the wind, and the spirit.[53] 'Pneumatics', a word derived from that for the breath, or spirit which God breathes into us, had come to signify the part of metaphysics which treats of 'spiritual substances, God, angels, and the souls of men' (Johnson) and by the end of the century it was approaching what we would call psychology. Pringle himself resigned as Edinburgh University's joint Professor of Ethic(s) and Pneumatic Philosophy in 1744 in order to embark upon his military career. In that career a peculiarly urgent application of the other pneumatics, 'which considers the doctrine of the air' would feature prominently. Though we do not need the figure of the philosopher-physician to appreciate air's continuing symbolic potency, Pringle's prose brought him international fame in his day, and he left a large legacy. The sick soldiers in the Crimea 'lay looking up at the open sky', wrote Nightingale in 1858, 'thro' the chinks – & slits' of their wretched huts and tents, and there twice as many survived than in the truly wretched enclosure that was the massive Scutari Hospital back in Constantinople.[54] The old ardour survived, and in phrasing that reminds us that air is, after all, the desirable, God-given, and, in the context of hospital construction, more or less unrealizable antithesis to man's works.[55] Compromise might, however, be achieved, if only because it had to be. For all the danger presented by the hospital's 'impure atmosphere, so contaminated with the effluvia of morbid bodies', wrote the Norfolk and Norwich Hospital's surgeon Benjamin Gooch in 1773, 'From the inevitable distresses of the poor, owing to a combination of causes, Institutions of this nature become more and more necessary.'[56]

Ships and Stephen Hales

Among what Alain Corbin has called the 'laboratories' of eighteenth-century hygienic improvement, which included prisons and hospitals,[57] ships had a special imaginative power. This was for two reasons. First, and most broadly, ships and their sailors were vastly more important than prisons and hospitals to European civilization and its attendant trade, colonies, war, and diplomacy: we must applaud Howard's efforts on behalf of the health of prisoners, wrote the former naval surgeon Charles Fletcher in 1786, but what about sailors, 'without whose assistance we might become, as a nation, even extinct'?[58] Secondly, surrounded as they were by moving air and running water, far from urban contagions, ships should have been the healthiest places on earth. But they were not, in a paradox recognized at the time. In 1758 Hales defended his ventilators' installation at suburban hospitals like St George's: it had, he wrote, been argued that they stood

> in so open and airy a Situation, that they have no Occasion for Ventilators, yet it is well known, that notwithstanding Ships at Sea are in so airy a Situation, that Millions of People have lost their Lives there by the Foulness and Putridness of the Air in Ships . . .[59]

Ships were filled, sometimes overfilled, with persons and animals from widely separated places forced into close proximity. Slave and hospital ships were obviously problematic; so, too, were men-of-war, as the impressment on which the Navy depended to man them gave rise to particular worries. Fletcher explained that the relation between the health of the Navy and that of prisoners was more than analogous, the 'former, in war-time, especially, necessarily deriving part of its strength from the latter'.[60] In July 1739 Admiral Philip Cavendish, Commander-in-Chief at Portsmouth, wrote to the Admiralty Board that, of 390 men just brought from London, he believed that more than 100,

> must be Turned away, being Bursten, full of the Pox, Itch, Lame, King's Evil, and all other Distempers, from the Hospitals at London, and will serve only to breed an Infection in the Ships . . .[61]

('Hospitals' here includes prisons.) Ships also sailed to parts of the earth, notably the West Indies, so unhealthy that captains kept destinations secret to prevent mass desertion and, once arrived, avoided landfall and even 'land air'.[62] They carried with them fixed platforms of putrescence in the form of sand or gravel in the hold, the ballast which accumulated filth, and the bilge-water, foul and 'stagnating in the bottom'. So wrote Richard Mead, who also invoked sea salt, 'some of which may have probably proceeded from the putrefied animals in that element', a display of delicacy comparable to Hales's suspicion of the 'sappy vapour' from green ships' timbers.[63]

Naval architecture and shipboard procedures had to reconcile conflicting demands. Livestock provided fresh meat, but did nothing for the air between decks. Even James Lind, a forceful advocate of cleanliness, worried that air dampened by washing would predispose men to scurvy.[64] Above all, a 'tight' ship was a ship difficult to ventilate. The fresh air traditionally introduced by windsails (cones of sailcloth attached to the masts whose ends, stiffened by hoops, were let down into hatches), as well as simply by opening ports and hatches, was as much for the ship's sake as for its company's because dry rot, fungi that thrive in moist air, could destroy a hull.[65] But the air in ships, especially below the lowest deck, immediately lethal at worst, was firmly linked with the two scourges of the

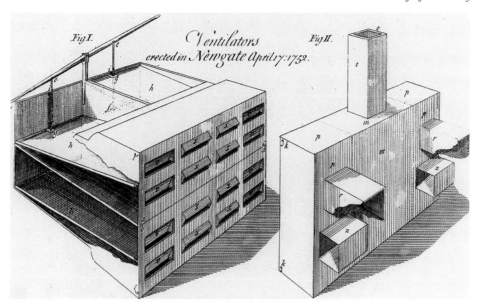

62. Hales's ventilators at Newgate, as illustrated in the *Gentleman's Magazine*. Each of the 'midriffs' marked as 'h', on the left, was nine feet long, which gives some idea of the installation's size.

Georgian Navy: scurvy and the fever.[66] The most informed opinion of the day considered them distinct, but related in the sense that both resulted from some combination of the peculiarities of life at sea: a limited and salty diet, moist and vitiated air,[67] and the difficulties of keeping clean.[68]

Recall Admiral Cavendish's report of the men brought to Portsmouth in 1739. Mass mobilization, of the sort that followed the outbreak of hostilities with Spain that year, always increased the risk of disease, and from 1739 to 1741 England and the home fleet suffered an epidemic (today invariably identified as typhus) that overloaded the Navy's medical facilities and reduced the number of mustered men as fast as new recruits could be added. One of the most notorious episodes in the history of the wars of 1739–48 began on 14 September 1740, as ships anchored off Spithead to prepare for a combined military and naval expedition to Cartagena in Colombia, then the Spanish Main. The force was delayed by the usual problem of manning, now exacerbated by the raging 'Malignant Distemper', and in later weeks by the difficulties of provisioning when captains hesitated to send out boats whose crews might never return. The squadron sailed on 26 October, but not before disease and desertion had cost it hundreds of men, whose predicament aroused much popular concern.[69] The deaths of the soldiers and sailors virtually within sight of Portsmouth was, like the Black Assizes ten years later and the incarceration of 146 Britons in an 18-square-foot room in Calcutta in 1756, famous not only as a mythopoeic event, but one to which advocates of ventilation and other prophylaxes returned again and again.[70]

In his *Description of ventilators* (1743), Stephen Hales told how, having heard of the illness among General Lord Cathcart's marines, he immediately wrote to the General's physician, suggesting various means of augmenting the standard 'antiseptic' procedures for cleansing ships with sickness aboard: hanging vinegar-soaked cloths between decks, burning brimstone. But then six months later, by his account, it occurred to Hales that 'large Ventilators' would also be 'very serviceable' in purifying the air and in May 1741 he read a paper to the Royal Society to that effect, 'as appears by the Minutes of that Society'.[71] Hales's first trial was conducted at a granary in Teddington, for which he constructed two pairs of large wooden bellows turning on a pivot. At any time, one bellows in each pair would be sucking air and the other expelling it.[72] The ventilator would often feature in the *Gentleman's Magazine*, with whose help it became probably the most widely publicized invention of the century and Figure 62, taken from it, illustrates two pairs of ventilators stacked, as they were installed at Newgate in 1752.[73] Their 'midriffs' (another anatomical borrowing, though not one original to Hales) were simultaneously moved up and down by the vertical iron rods, powered by a windmill on the roof. This is to simplify considerably: the detail of the accompanying explanation must have tested the curiosity of even the *Magazine*'s public-minded readership.

Hales's reference to the Royal Society minutes, which extended to the title of his book, was not casual; he wanted to establish his primacy. Artificial ventilation, that is, the forced and continuous substitution of fresh for stale air in a confined space, had been discussed for decades and it particularly interested landowners who wanted to sink mineshafts deeper.[74] Hales went so far as to refute at length any notion that his ventilator had anything to do with a 'foolish proposal' published eighty years earlier for a domestic 'air chamber', where air might be regulated and altered as a prophylaxis.[75] In 1741, at least three other men were at work on ventilating devices. One, the Swedish military architect Martin Triewald, Hales could discount after establishing that he had reported to the Academy in Stockholm eleven months after Hales went to the Royal Society.[76] The 'centrifugal blowing wheel' devised by Hales's friend the Freemason J. T. Desaguliers was already at work in the Palace of Westminster and Desaguliers had proposed its installation in ships' holds at least as early as 1735. He was however discouraged when the Navy, after asking for his help, failed to give him a proper trial; Sir Jacob Ackworth was notably obstinate.[77] Ackworth, a former shipwright who had been the Surveyor to the Navy Board since 1715 and through sheer force of personality became the most powerful man on the Board, has always been the villain in ventilation histories: 'Sir, I suppose you intend to throw air into the wells of ships', he sneered at the other hopeful, Samuel Sutton, as the latter reported it.[78] Sutton presented more of a problem, for until his death in 1749 he was prepared to meet Hales on his own grounds of Royal Society meetings, illustrated publications with testimonial apparatus, and the decks of warships in experimental trials. Hales never directly acknowledged his rival in print, and remarking this Sutton felt free to call Hales's ventilators 'absurd and ridiculous': 'His ventilators, he tells us, will keep a prison sweet, but my pipes will sweeten even a bog-house'.[79] Both men complained of naval obstruction and hinted at vested interest and even corruption at work.

Hales's ventilators were expensive, bulky, and labour-intensive, and answering these objections prompted his clearest presentation of the body-machine. The 'great Author of Nature has allotted', he wrote, near one half of the Trunk of our Body for the Office of Respiration, or Breathing[,] only: can any one therefore be so unreasonable, as to grudge the little Space, these will take up in a Ship, or the small Labour that they will require, to furnish great Plenty of fresh Air? Were an Animal to be formed of the Size of a large Ship, we are well assured by what we see in other Animals, that there would be ample Provision made to furnish that Animal with a constant Supply of fresh Air, by means of large Lungs, which are formed to inspire and breathe out Air in the same manner as these Ventilators do.[80]

Imagine a whale the size of a ship, and then the size of its lungs, Hales was asking; then imagine a hospital without the lungs. The building is like the swaddled infant whose bindings do not let its 'Breast nor Belly' rise to breathe.[81]

Can it therefore be an unreasonable or an improbable Proposal, to attempt to furnish Ships, Goals [*sic*], Hospitals, &c. in the same manner with the wholesome Breath of Life, in exchange for the noxious Air of confined Places . . . ?

Hospitals were as unnatural, in the long view, as the civilization that required them, but civilization could return them to some simulacrum of nature.

Hales's and Sutton's attempts to gain the ear of the Navy have been exhaustively described, not least by them. According to Sutton's *Historical account of a new method for extracting the foul air out of ships*, first published in 1745, he, too, had been touched by the plight of the soldiers and sailors off Spithead in the autumn of 1740. After the customary rebuff from Ackworth, Sutton secured the Admiralty Board's agreement to a trial, in September 1741; his was heat-aided, gravity ventilation, which relied on the suction effect of the cookhouse fire to draw foul air up through pipes let down into the ship's hold and thence up the galley chimney.[82] In November, by which time he had obtained the patronage of Dr Mead, Sutton installed his 'Air-Pump' on the *Norwich*, bound for the Guinea coast and the West Indies. The next year, Hales managed to get his ventilators put on the *Captain*, in ordinary near London:

And being each ten Feet long, four Feet three Inches wide, and thirteen Inches deep, [they] throw out at the Rate of a Tun of Air at each stroke, sixty Tuns in a Minute; three thousand six hundred in an Hour; which passing off thro' a Trunk a Foot square, the Air rushes out with a Velocity of twenty five Miles in an Hour.[83]

His system was mechanical, unlike Sutton's, and this example needed two men, working a 12-foot lever. The *Norwich* then arrived back home. Though her captain claimed to be unconvinced by the air pump, in 1744 Sutton was granted a patent and the pump was ordered to be fitted on to several ships.[84]

Neither Sutton nor Hales neglected to advertise ventilation's benefits to cargoes, and cargoes included convicts and Africans. As a trustee of the Georgia Colony and of another, associated, trust dedicated to converting slaves in America, Hales was interested in what happened to men and women on transatlantic voyages.[85] On a

Liverpool ship equipped with ventilators, wrote the old clergyman, 'not one of 800 Slaves died, except only a child, born in the Voyage'.[86] Hales's 'very ingenious Ventilator Maker', as he called him, the engineer Thomas Yeoman, became busy around 1749 fitting them to slave and transport ships,[87] and in 1756 the Navy Board ordered ventilators to be installed on all its ships. Those on foreign service were given preferential treatment, but the records do not reveal how many or what kinds of ventilator were actually installed, or how much they were used.[88]

Ventilators were also put into a number of institutions. According to Hales – the updating of his 1743 *Description of ventilators* to the 1758 *Treatise on ventilators* mostly comprises accounts of their 'happy effects' – the first was at the Winchester Hospital, that is, the very old house. There followed installations at St George's (1744), the Middlesex Smallpox Hospital (1747), the Northampton Infirmary (1748) and Gaol (1749), and the Savoy (1749), then serving as a holding place for naval deserters and pressed and foreign recruits. The Bristol Infirmary also acquired one around this time.[89] All the general hospitals Hales mentioned were in converted buildings, which may be significant, but purpose-built hospitals seem to have taken them too. (The question is complicated by the way 'venti-lator' came to embrace other devices.) Grosley explained, in the early 1770s, that those English 'hospitals whose apartments are under the same roof' (and not in the 'solitary pavillions') 'have the conveniency of ventilators, to introduce fresh air'.[90] The most famous installation was however in 1752, at Newgate, where earlier ventilators had been allowed to fall into disuse until the Black Assizes reminded the City of their benefits.

The rivals each found formidable medical backing: James Mead wrote on Sutton's behalf, and John Pringle for Hales. The description of the Newgate ventilators in Hales's *Treatise* of 1758 is supplemented by Pringle's 'Account of several persons seized with the gaol fever, by working in Newgate', which recounts the fate of the workmen who installed the machines. Pringle's chronicle of how the fever stalked, and sometimes caught men – Clayton Hand, Thomas Wilmot, Michael Sewel, Adam Chaddocks, John Dobie, and William Thompson – who thought themselves safe once back at their own hearths, is a true horror story, chilling by the very prosiness of the corroborative detail as well as by its account of the advance of inexorable, invisible death.[91] Publication itself was, of course, a way of making the invisible visible.

The invisibility of air and its attendant toxins presented difficulties to those seeking to demonstrate to their peers how air moved, and how they could 'throw' it. At one of his shipboard trials, Sutton made air extinguish candles 20 yards away. Henri Louis Duhamel du Monceau, author of the *Moyens de conserver la santé aux équipages des vaisseaux; avec la manière de purifier l'air des salles des hôpitaux* (1759), which publicized the Hales ventilator, set fire to a pile of straw in a ward of the Invalides. Smoke so thick that one could not see was completely dissipated by fifteen minutes of pumping. Benjamin Franklin, a keen student of ventilation in the 1760s and 1770s, cut cardboard into a spiral and suspended it by a thread to show air moving beside a warm fireplace, and let smoke from a just-extinguished candle do the same by a cold windowpane.[92]

Hales had the problem of making air visible to simpler folk, too. The Newgate ventilators, like that at St George's, were powered by a windmill (and even so required constant supervision), but others, for example at the Winchester and Northampton hospitals, were pumped by the patients themselves. Though like the inhabitants of jails, workhouses, and barracks they had 'full Leisure to work the Bellows', as miners for example did not, sometimes they did not work. Lacking the statistics – air 'tun' capacities, temperatures, before-and-after mortality rates – which Hales offered to his readers in 1758, the patients were apt to look upon the ventilator as 'working to no Purpose, since they can see no visible Effect that it has on the invisible Air'. Hales accordingly devised bells and miniature windmills to tinkle and twirl at the mouths of the ducts through which the stale air was drawn out. These were supposed to give the operators something to see, and to reassure others that 'they have their due Proportion of ventilation'.[93] The formulation would be elaborated by later authors, schooled in the recognition that the 'Exchange for . . . noxious air', as Hales's 1743 title had it, was by definition egalitarian, its distribution measured as volume per bed-unit.

In more extreme environments the ventilators' benefits were more 'sensible', that is perceptible, and men were willing to work to invisible effect. In 1749 Captain Thompson of the *Success* reported his sailors 'so sensible of the Benefit of them, that they required *no driving*' (his, or Hales's, emphasis) and on *The Earl of Halifax*, '340 Negroes were very sensible of the Benefits of constant Ventilation, and were always displeased when it was omitted', reported Captain Ellis four years later.[94] Brocklesby, the military physician, would however be less enthusiastic. He called the ventilator a magnificent invention, but it was not a portable one: he worked with regiments on the move. Moreover, the

> negligence, and laziness of the people in working them, and their diffidence of the utility of measures, which seem so simple and so trifling . . . made them fall very short of our expectations, whenever I attempted to enforce their use.[95]

Better the 'occasional huts' of wattle and straw, wrote Brocklesby in 1764, precisely the year in which Pringle began to wonder if the best thing to do with the sick (at least during the 'dysenteric season') was not just to put them in the churches, barns or ruinous houses where neither they nor their nurses could 'confine' the air.[96] The poor and illiterate, the nurses, the slaves, and the sailors had to be made to understand that buildings are just a substitute, and a dangerous one at that, for the desirable openness whose benefits however, and perversely, required their validation as sensible. In these accounts of the men – the real ventilators – at work, as in those of the related struggle to keep the ward windows open, we can trace the germ of a much bigger movement to make the poor understand the benefits of broader improvements, to cure ignorance and dirt.

By 1758, Hales claimed, there were 'Ventilators in *Durham* Gaol, and in an Hospital at *Naples* . . . in *Saxony*, *Silesia*, *Petersburg*, and *Lapland*, for divers uses'.[97] Though they continued to be built, especially for dry storage (corn, gunpowder), a shift in attitude is traceable from the 1760s, most neatly in the successive editions of Pringle's *Diseases of the army*. The first (1752) and second (1753) editions explain that doctors can never hope to cure in a full hospital, 'unless every ward is kept sweet by a ventilator', the word still being confined to Hales's device. In 1761 this became 'unless every ward be well ventilated', by whatever method. In the fourth (1764) and later editions the wards must instead be 'uncommonly well aired'.[98] Airiness had become ventilation, and then became airiness again.

The contingencies of military medicine were one problem. Donald Monro described, in 1764, the means he had devised for ensuring air circulation in extemporized wards: sliding panels in doors and 'casements' inserted into the corners of fixed windows. Hales himself offered to the Admiralty in 1756 a new method of 'conveying fresh Air into Sick Rooms', which turned on an open door and a screen between it and the bed to divert currents from the sufferer.[99] But the shift was bigger than the military sphere: Foster simply wrote that ventilators were an imperfect though necessary aid in hospital wards that could not be well aired because they did not have windows facing one another. The decline of the ventilator thus accompanied the new way of writing about hospital buildings, which in turn transferred the word to a simpler device: unlike mechanical ventilators or indeed windows, air vents ('ventilating holes') in walls and ceilings did not require anyone's co-operation to function.[100] In that sense, buildings could begin to ventilate themselves, or rather themselves transpire, in a way more like the skin's slow and insensible but vital 'perspiration' than the lungs' rougher work.[101]

Hales's *ventilateur* and Sutton's *machine* remained more topical in France, but there the latter was increasingly regarded as prophylaxis, the former as a weapon against mephitic emergency. In 1787 Jean-Noël Hallé called the ventilator a fire extinguisher, an emergency measure; obviously preferable was building for the sick in a way that prevents 'corruption . . . that is, to get a continuously circulating and pure body of air'.[102] The next year Paris saw the publication of two pavilion-ward plans, by Tenon and by his colleagues on the Académie des Sciences' committee, which were dedicated to getting that kind of air. Tenon's prescription is notable, too, for a fundamental anthropomorphism all the more radical for eschewing metaphor:

> The human being was at stake here, the sick human being, his height determines the length of the bed and the width of the wards; his step, shorter and less free than that of a healthy man, dictates the height of the stairs, just as the length of the stretcher that transports him regulates the width of the . . . staircases.

Tenon ignored symbolic correspondences between the building and the body aside from the most overarching one of all: 'The dimensions of wards are not arbitrary; they derive from nature as does all that relates to hospitals.'[103] Nature did not embrace the ventilator after all. In 1800 John Carter made 'air-engines' take their place among the sordid rubbish he discovered above the ceiling Wren had (to the antiquarian's disgust) fitted beneath the original, medieval vault of St

Stephen's Chapel in the Palace of Westminster. These 'dishonoured scenes I wish were but . . . the workings of a mind disturbed, the idle images of a dream of air, or any thing but what I see'.[104] The assonance of the air-engines and the dream of air is fortuitous, but striking. It was then, at the turn of the century, that assisted ventilation for hospital wards again became the subject of active inquiry; it was encouraged by new factory technologies and by fears about the diseases, in particular, the malignant fever, now associated with factories (Chapter 10).

In one respect, ventilators on ships were more surprising than those in general hospitals. Hales's machine was notably demanding of the manpower that was, after all, the Navy's scarcest commodity. Yet war and its financing was always the most pressing and visible issue for eighteenth-century ministries, the one on which they stood or fell. The manning of the British Navy, then 'by a large margin the largest industrial organization in the western world', was critical to any war effort, and the health of sailors was critical to the manning of the Navy.[105] That disease disabled more sailors than the enemy ever did was a commonplace. Hales, referring to prisoners-of-war, wrote that it was 'highly probable, that three in four of those who die in War, lose their Lives by the Stench of Jails, and Hospitals', and Sutton, that more men had 'died in America, for want of good air, than by the Spaniards'.[106] Cost-effectiveness has a specific meaning in the military context, and in the mid-eighteenth century the Navy devoted the funds to discovering a cure for scurvy and (in related efforts) to determining the best method of pickling beef and evaluating the usefulness of shipboard ventilators that it had, for example, dedicated to the search for a remedy for all manner of 'looseness' half a century earlier; no wonder that Sutton's was the first of 100 ventilator patents.[107] Compared to the investment Britain had then been making for a decade in naval hospital construction, however, it was nothing.

Chapter 8

Island hospitals

Some hospitals *were* ships, 'Hospitals at Sea'. In England, elderly men-of-war and hired merchantmen were regularly used this way after 1660.[1] Though by definition unprepossessing (it was proposed in 1757 to use the *Ipswich*, 'unfit for any other Service'),[2] they did not require much refurbishment: scuttles for ventilation could be cut into their sides, and gun decks were not hard to divide into small wards running athwart and therefore getting some light and air on two sides. After its reconditioning with 255 'cradles' in 1740 the *Blenheim* was able to partition, with canvas, cases of fever, ague, the flux, and the itch (Figure 63).[3] As ships they afforded only 'very indifferent conveniences for the Sick' (according to the Commissioners for Sick and Wounded Seamen, in 1759),[4] and one tremendous advantage. 'Water was the prison wall';[5] and they not only isolated sufferers during epidemics, they kept every patient away from land and its opportunities for drinking, gambling, and desertion. In July 1745 the Commissioners sent to the Admiralty their report of the numbers who had 'Run from the Hospitals in England' during the previous quarter: Plymouth's lost 167 men and Gosport's fifty-nine, but just three managed to get off the *Solebay*.[6] A decade later, more than a quarter of all the hospitalized seamen in Britain were on a hospital ship. Convalescent ships were a refinement introduced around then.[7]

The hospitals itemized in 1745 included ships, but also beds contracted for by the Commissioners, and supervised by agents also under contract. Some were in sick-quarters, that is, lodging- or public houses, and some in what were indeed hospitals, and substantial ones: Gosport's could then hold 332 men.[8] The contract system had, however, long been considered inefficient, open to peculation, and even cruel. As the list shows, it made desertion relatively easy and in 1744 the Admiralty was complaining about captains sending ashore sick 'Men they do not like' in the expectation of never seeing them again. At Gosport, it informed the Commissioners at the same time, a single adolescent surgeon's apprentice was available at night to assist hundreds of men who were moreover being systematically defrauded and robbed, 'especially the Dead'.[9] Both naval boards also knew that per capita payments did not encourage roomy and well-maintained accommodation; the quarters could be even worse than the ships. At one of Gosport's sick-quarters, Admiral Cavendish reported in the spring of 1740, the men were 'two or three in a Bed of different Diseases . . . and such a Stanch there is amongst them, that it is not unlikely it may breed the Plague', the stench despite the broken windows, during the severest winter of the century.[10]

Staffed by sailors, and women, the hospital ships were however the Crown's, as would be the new hospitals at Haslar and Plymouth, whose sites permitted them to share the ships' great advantage. Surrounded by sea and estuary mud, the Haslar peninsula, for example, was close to Gosport and Portsmouth but cut off from them, and until the end of the century its only access was by boat, directly from ships or across from Gosport with the hospital ferryman.[11] When space grew tight, Haslar sent patients back out to sea: one of its convalescent ships could hold 400 men.[12] The sailors' ideal progress through sickness and recovery was from their ships to boats and to the Royal Hospital on its peninsula, and then back again, perhaps via a convalescent ship. They would never touch land, at least not the land of taverns, and of recruiters like John Newman, in 1744 spotted trying 'to entice, and even to force' patients at Gosport into the service of the privateer *Winchilsea*, which would pay them twice what the king did. Like the ships, Haslar and Plymouth were insular, close to but detached from the world – or this was the idea, at least. (In 1780 inspectors of an over-crowded Haslar reported that its officers enjoyed no 'dignity or respect' from 'ungovernible' patients, fuelled by liquor smuggled in by their friends and relations.)[13] Insularity extended to their very wards, whose planning was not unprecedented but received an unprecedented kind of attention, in part because of the hospitals' singularity in admitting cases of all the different diseases to which Cavendish referred.

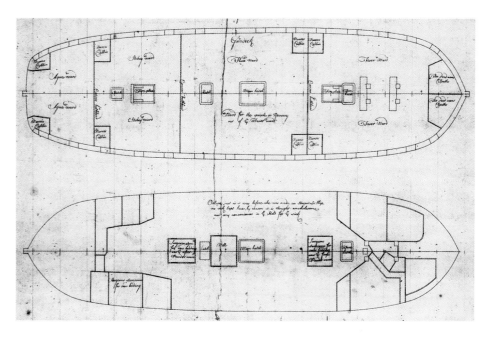

63. The gun and orlop decks of the hospital ship *Blenheim*, in 1743. The orlop deck was used only for storage, because 'it is thought unwholesome'.

The early naval hospitals

Smaller hospital ships sailed with seagoing squadrons, and hospitals or sick-quarters were set up on Jamaica in 1704, and soon in Lisbon (1706) and Port Mahon, Minorca (1708). The construction of a new building for the last began in 1711 on a small island in the harbour, again convenient for ships, but not for drinkers and deserters.[14] For thirty years Minorca's was the only purpose-built British naval hospital, but detailed proposals for another on Gibraltar were prepared in 1734, and in 1740 the Admiralty informed the Commissioners that it was about to take into consideration

> whether it would be more for the Publick good to continue the present method of Town Quarters and subsisting Seamen by contract, or to erect hospitals at the Publick expense with a proper establishment of officers and servants to take care of the sick and supply them with Physic, Diet, and necessaries from his Majesties Stores as their several cases shall require.[15]

In 1741 was authorized the construction of a permanent hospital (for 632 men) near Port Royal, Jamaica, another (for 1,000) on Gibraltar; and, with the Commissioners' enthusiastic support, the Admiralty proposed to the king in Council new hospitals at three domestic ports, including Portsmouth and Plymouth, an application renewed three years later and then successful.

The immediate cause of this unprecedented construction programme was the epidemic of 1739–41, which was understood to have started in the London prisons and to be spreading with impressment and mobilization.[16] Ships carrying the 'violent and malignant fever' arrived at Gibraltar and Plymouth in late 1739 and early 1740.[17] At home, the epidemic underlined the deficiencies of contracting, and chaos at the Gosport hospital features in the Admiralty's memorandum of 1744, to the king, which argues for containment under stricter discipline and in better conditions than the system was providing – in effect, that £38,000 worth of building was needed to keep 1,500 sick men sober at any one time in Portsmouth.[18] If confined, sober; if sober, quicker cured and back in the service.

The foreign hospitals comprised the 'large Quadrangle[s], with a spacious Piazza within' that the Admiralty in June 1745 specified for Portsmouth:[19] the colonnades lining the courts were to permit the men's airing and exercise. The thirteen wards of the Jamaica hospital, which was partly surrounded by a lagoon, made a square 390 feet wide, and the Gibraltar hospital designed by the engineer James Montresor is a two-storey quadrangle around a court 150 by 75 feet.[20] Though the latter's ranges were single-piled and all but two wards had opposite windows, those on the outside were not opened, at least not by the 1770s.[21]

Robin Evans has described the reconciliation which prison builders began attempting in the 1780s: 'security required enclosure; salubrity required exposure and fragmentation'.[22] Forty years earlier, naval hospitals presented the same challenge. As alternatives to contract establishments but analogues to hospital ships, they were to maintain the ships' security while avoiding their environmental defects, the bad air and confinement which together engendered, one way or another, the diseases of sailors. Courts and galleries were to reconcile security and salubrity at hospitals whose quadrangles were also bastions against local mess and disorder. The Commissioners' Lisbon agent Roderick Forbes begged them, in 1745, to buy the house he was using and let him rebuild it 'as an Hospital ought to be'.[23] He needed a fence, he explained, to stop his charges from getting 'up in the Country' to drink 'bad Wine and relapse', but he also wanted to keep out the local health officers, a 'parcel of Villains' demanding bribes. (They had just burned the cradles at his former hospital-house, 'and had there been a Contagion, as they pretended, they ought to have shut us up, instead of turning us in the street'.) Forbes thought that he might be 'freed from the Jurisdiction of these People' if the Navy bought the house. The Commissioners themselves would run Haslar and Plymouth, which were autonomous jurisdictions.

Security and salubrity were of course managerial as well as architectural concerns. In 1757 the Commissioners proposed issuing Haslar's patients with a 'Hospital Dress (which would greatly tend to the Peoples recovery)', because it would be cleaner than the men's own clothes (sailors were not yet equipped with uniforms); they were perhaps even anticipating the diagnostic labels that would be attached to some dresses. Dividing their efforts between prisoners-of-war and sick and wounded sailors, the Commissioners regularly linked the latters' recovery with their confinement: since the dresses, for example, which instantly revealed a Haslar inmate in daytime, were 'to be taken into the Nurses Cabbins when the men are in Bed, and delivered to them in the Morning, they could not then escape but in their Shirts'.[24] 'Lamps', they reported two years later,

> are placed on the outside Wall of the Hospital, and Centinels fixed round the same, by which means if the latter do their Duty the Patients may be as effectually secured as on board an Hospital Ship, and their Cure sooner Compleated.[25]

With the help of topography, hospital dresses, lamps, and sentinels this vast brick construction might aspire to the security of an elderly wooden vessel. What made the naval hospitals distinctive was this emphasis on containment, which was not a concern even at hospitals for the insane, where security comprised more localized measures: locked cell doors and strait-waistcoats. The naval hospitals also differed in being unable to refuse anyone on account of the nature of his sickness, something which presented additional difficulties for security and salubrity. In the short term, new construction required new assignments. When the Admiralty informed the Commissioners, in June 1745, of the acquisition of the Haslar site, and of the organizational arrangements for planning the hospital, it handed over to them its 'Inner Parts' and instructed them

> to consider attentively to the disposition, Situation, & Dimension of the Wards for sick Men, the Convenience of Light and Air; To avoid narrowness, as also crowding the Beds too close together.[26]

Charging the Commissioners for Sick and Wounded Seamen with responsibility for light and air may seem obvious, but the Commissioners and the Admiralty and Navy boards were all feeling their way in this new enterprise.

The royal hospitals at Haslar and Plymouth

In delegating Haslar's inner parts to the Commissioners, the Admiralty also informed them that it had instructed Jacob Ackworth, the Navy Board's Surveyor (and assisted-ventilation sceptic) to consult with Theodore Jacobsen about the plan Ackworth had prepared. Jacobson had been 'Voluntary concerned in projecting the Plan for Building the Hospital for Foundlings' (whose new accommodation opened three months later) and the Admiralty was in general becoming increasingly irritated with Ackworth, that 'brute of a Shipwright'.[27] Real shipwrights then designed the Navy's dock buildings, subject to the Surveyor's approval, so in this respect its hospitals differed.[28] Anyway, 'not entirely approving' of Ackworth's project, Jacobsen had promised to devise another 'which he believes may be better for the Purpose'. So the Commissioners, coordinating the various parties, reported back to the Admiralty.[29] The latter had already let the Commissioners know that the hospital was to be a

> Strong, durable, plain Building, consisting of Three Stories; The same to form a large Quadrangle, with a spacious Piazza within, the out Fronts to be decent, but not expensive, and to resemble as much as may be the enclosed Plan, which being plain, is for that reason agreeable to their Lordships.[30]

The Admiralty's plan, and/or Ackworth's, may have resembled one which survives from 1741, when the scheme for building a Portsmouth hospital first got as far as the king in Council.[31] This drawing shows an uninspiring and certainly plain arrangement of sixty-five wards for 1,500 men, arranged in double piles around a vast square. Jacobsen would design something different, and to understand what that was we should begin with the Foundling Hospital, with which the Admiralty introduced him to the Commissioners.[32] Demolished in 1928, it was a building whose interest has been overshadowed by that of the institution it housed, dedicated to the survival of the hard-working classes and Britain's first public space for art exhibition.

Among the projects considered in June 1742 for the Foundling's new building in Bloomsbury Fields, London was the elder George Dance's 'Square of 300 Feet within the Walls, with a Collonade all round; and an Area of 277 Feet between the Columns, and to contain 24 Wards'.[33] This sounds like a naval hospital, and the rationales would not have been dissimilar, though the Foundling's governors wanted to control admissions more than departures.[34] Dance's project was however judged too big and expensive, and Jacobsen's was chosen. The hospital's first stone was laid in September 1742. The west wing that opened three years later at first stood alone and was perforce for both boys and girls.

Charles Dickens would describe the Foundling's 'long dining-rooms, long bedroom galleries, long lavatories, long schoolrooms and lecture halls'.[35] Early

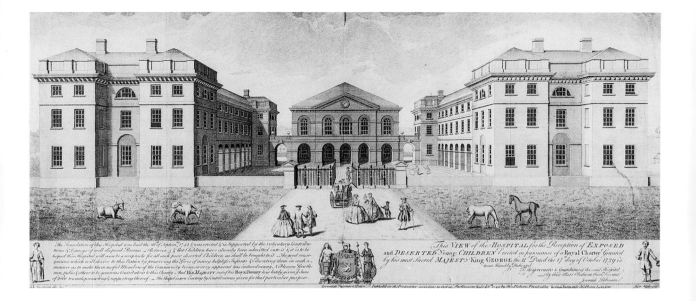

64. The Foundling Hospital. Two sashes are shown opened, perhaps to reinforce the idea of salubrity.

prints (Figure 64) show a great U enclosing the forecourt opening south to the city, but the U is not solid. The wings were linked to the central chapel by arcades that, with the chapel, constituted a separate undertaking for which Jacobsen's design was ready in 1746.[36] Children and staff were accommodated in effectively free-standing blocks, each 187 feet long and proportionately narrow, making Dickens's long rooms. More arcades, forming galleries open to the court, took up half their ground-floor widths. Parts of St Thomas' and Guy's hospitals had precisely this arrangement and Haslar would too, though with the difference that its ranges were split longitudinally, one could say, the arcades divided from the wards by narrow courts.[37] Jacobsen finished the ends of the Foundling's wings with pavilions broader than the ward ranges behind them, which were enlivened by side projections in turn.[38] The projections had no correlation with anything happening, architecturally speaking, behind the pavilions; the Foundling's first- and second-floor wards were double-piled and their partition walls mapped those on the ground floor, between the arcades and the slightly wider rooms beside them. But Haslar's equivalent projections always corresponded, during its planning, to the paired but distinct ward ranges behind. They were, in effect, the ends of the long naval wards.

Haslar, begun in 1746, was handsomely and enterprisingly (in axonometric projection) pictured by Fourdrinier in 1750.[39] His engraving, adapted for publication in the *Gentleman's Magazine* the next year (Figure 65), does not show the hospital as it would be when completed in 1762. The intention was always to build it and fill it in parts and the *Magazine* reported the first wing as nearly ready. (It officially opened in 1754, though pressure for beds was such that some patients were already being accommodated.)[40] A plan annotated in early 1756 shows the two side wings then authorized to be added, though still not as they were actually built, but it substitutes a wall with a gate for the fourth wing. This would have held the chapel, in the event built outside the enclosure around 1758.[41] A quadrangular hospital approximating what was, after Gibraltar's and Jamaica's,

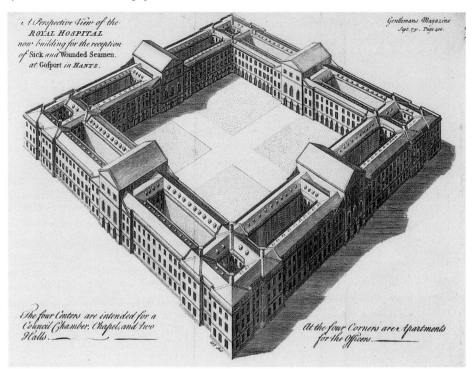

A Perspective View of the
ROYAL HOSPITAL
now building for the reception
of Sick and Wounded Seamen.
at Gosport in HANTS.

Gentlemans Magazine
Sept. 751. Page 400.

The four Centers are intended for a
Council Chamber, Chapel, and two
Halls.

At the four Corners are Apartments
for the Officers.

65. Fourdrinier's splendid projection of the Royal Hospital at Haslar appeared in the *Gentleman's Magazine*, whose readers were steadily informed about naval-medical advances in the 1750s.

becoming the standard naval type thus took the form of a U. The reason always proposed is budgetary: what was immediately recognized as England's biggest brick construction would when finished with just three ranges cost around £100,000, Haslar's physician James Lind (1716–94) thought in 1758, two and a half times the original estimate.[42]

Haslar's first management was under a quasi-contractual system which, with insufficient staff, did not work well, and desertions were frequent.[43] In 1755 it was taken fully into the 'Hands of the Crown', in fact of the Commissioners, who vested daily management in the hospital's Physician and Council. This was an administration closer, as was understood, to Greenwich than to Gosport Hospital,[44] and the resemblance can be extended. Haslar's paired ward blocks resemble not only the Foundling's, but Wren's arrangement of the King Charles building, the fragment of Webb's palace, with its base block (and that of the Queen Anne building, which matched: see Figure 24, p. 74).[45] None the less Haslar is, as Timothy Holmes noted in 1863, 'rather peculiar', meaning unlike anything else and difficult to describe.[46]

My description depends on those of two foreign emissaries. Johann Hunczovsky began his investigations of English and French hospitals at the behest of Joseph II of Austria in the late 1770s and his *Beobachtungen* (*Observations*) of 1783 include the first sustained account to be published of Haslar. Tenon's notes, made on behalf of his king in 1787, indicate the medical hopes by then entertained for that complicated architecture. What follows is further complicated by the changes made during the construction period, but we need to understand why Britain's biggest hospital briefly enjoyed a reputation as the healthiest.

Tenon described Haslar as a *corps de logis* (his usual term for an entrance range, whether it accommodated patients or not), with a pair of wings behind it on each side. The centre might itself be read as two thin wings held together by the entrance pavilion with its ground-floor vestibule running across.[47] (The small squares shown between the ranges, two on one side and one on the other, are kitchens.) Fourdrinier's print (Figure 65) shows similar pavilions in the centres of the other wings and the 1756 plan has these holding wards. In construction, these side pavilions were dissolved into pairs of free-standing blocks, for storage, facing one another across the narrow inner courts. Two storeys high, they are a floor lower than the stacks of wards on either side and hence, Hunczovsky wrote, did not interfere with air circulation.[48] Between them and the ward blocks run terraces resting on the arcades, a floor lower still (Figure 66). At ground level, therefore, one could walk through the outer arches and across the inner court (Figure 67) between the ward and storage blocks, then out under the arcade on the main court side. Tenon's fast sketch of the ground plan accordingly shows each side wing as made by pairs of isolated buildings – the end wards and the storage blocks – plus the wards attached to the central range.[49] The courts between them run clear down their lengths aside from the projections of the 'Bogg-houses', so-called on the 1756 plan. It also shows kitchens, dining rooms, and stairs inserted into these inner courts, as well as the centre cross-wards, but these were all omitted in execution, which meant that the wards could have more windows.[50] The wings' intersections with the ends of the main block always took the logically satisfying form of squares with central light-wells, as if pairs of narrow ranges had interwoven.

The 'Arcades' (c on Figure 68) formed galleries filling the widths of the wards above them. Hunczovsky described them as providing sheltered walks for convalescents, and convenient access to every part of the hospital for the staff.[51] Stairwells with adjoining 'Nurses' & Attendants' Rooms' (at L) interrupted the galleries, which allowed defined stretches to be allocated to different kinds of patient.

Of Haslar's 114 wards, Tenon wrote, all but fourteen had nineteen or twenty beds, the sort of rooms marked as B on Figure 68. Each had a stair landing and nurses' room at one narrow end and a door leading into its partner ward at the other, beside the latrines.[52] Hunczovsky reported that Lind had decided that ventilators were unnecessary if the ward windows were opened as often as possible, especially since they were opposite.[53] Two exceptionally large wards, with fifty-two beds each, stretched across the main front on the first and third floors (between was a mezzanine floor, for storage). Used only for patient overspill by the time Tenon visited, they represented a particularly explicit triumph for true magnificence. In August 1749 a distinguished group of site inspectors, including the First Sea Lord, had ordered that the great room intended for a council chamber, which then rose through two storeys across the width of the wing, be converted to make the extra wards.[54] Haslar was the 'noble, strong, and beautiful fabric' that the *Gentleman's Magazine* described, but nobility (as it explained) was also to be apprehended in the 'health and sweetness' comprised by deep and extensive sewers, a gravelly site, and delightful prospects.[55] Governors' Court

66. One of the side ranges at Haslar Royal Naval Hospital.

67. A view into one of the narrow courts between Haslar's ward ranges.

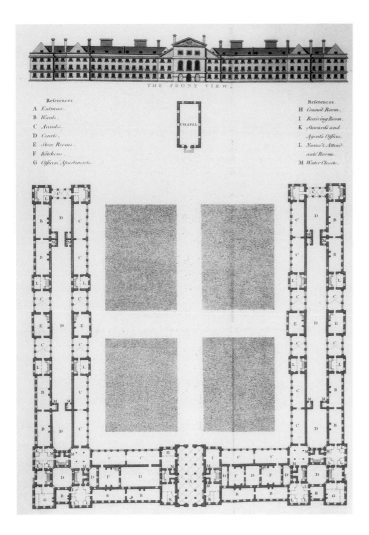

68. Haslar, as illustrated in John Howard's *Account of the principal lazarettos in Europe* (1789).

rooms featured splendidly in the old royal hospitals and at some of the new voluntary institutions, not least the Foundling, but the First Sea Lord and company showed that the Navy's hospitals were different.

The naval hospitals *were* different, accommodating as they did a single sex. Their clientele also had a propensity for 'running' – the expert Thomas Trotter (1760–1832) would decide, not entirely foolishly, that the experience of impressment brought on a mental disorder peculiar to seamen[56] – something additionally worrying because the hospitals could not try, as most of their civil counterparts did, to refuse sufferers from what were understood as infectious disorders, notably the malignant fevers. Lind, by then retired, told Tenon that 'certain types of contagion automatically dissipate when patients are well separated: their range of infection is limited'.[57] Contagion, here, is what emanates from the diseased, contagiousness their more or less potent attribute, while the danger they present to others is a measure of infectiousness. Navy-run hospitals in the home ports, long proposed (for example by Evelyn in 1665), were finally constructed after the epidemic of 1739–41 and, though scurvy accounted for huge numbers, more than half the patients admitted to Haslar in its first five years were fever cases.[58] The diagnosis is now medically uninformative, but the fever's implications for Haslar's planning can be inferred, and its effects on the way the building was used are clear: as Tenon described it the hospital was remarkable for the care with which it separated different kinds of patient and the dresses and bedding that they touched.

By the time Tenon visited, Haslar's patients were being organized both horizontally and vertically, something best explained by beginning with the convalescents. Patients recovering from measles, scabies, venereal disease, and smallpox had their own galleries for walking; SMALL POX was lettered on the front and rear of the latter's dress, in case they thought about running instead. (Measles was similarly identified.) Scurvy cases were also set apart, not because scurvy was contagious, Tenon was told, but because they all got the same therapy, consisting of vegetables, citrus fruit, wine, malt, and 'land air'.[59] No enthusiast for assisted ventilation, Lind (whose son John had succeeded him as the hospital's physician) was none the less convinced that scurvy cases required relief from sea air, as well as from sea rations.[60] Regulations that he drew up in 1777 specified the removal of 'Fevers and Fluxes of peculiar malignancy' from the 'common' sort, and the confinement of the fever wards to the far ends of the wings, 'to cut off all communications with other patients'.[61] A decade later Tenon described how the most 'contagious' were assigned to the top wards, abutted, we should recall, by nothing aside from their partners, on one short side. (Although it is not clear whether he was referring to fever and flux cases or to the generality of contagious patients, the latter seems more likely.) The less contagious went to the middle wards, whose floor levels corresponded to those of the terraces separating them from the storage blocks.[62] Convalescents went down to the ground floor, close to their *promenades*.[63]

Great expense might, as mentioned above, be one reason for the decision to abandon the fourth range, which was taken some time between 1750 and 1756, but Hunczovsky wrote that the omission allowed air to course freely, as part of his general insistence on Haslar's dedication to the circulation of air. This was its *Hauptzweck* (chief object),[64] a dedication that might explain the other decision, between 1756 and 1762, to keep the narrow courts between the side wings clear. Nor was the wall shown on the 1756 plan ever built to replace the fourth range. Though Haslar's 32 acres were themselves walled and remote, and a favourite escape route was down the latrines and through the noble sewers, the gap remained a worry. It was not filled until 1796, and then with iron railings 12 feet high; the ground-floor windows were fitted with heavy iron grilles. Not coincidentally, that year also saw the building of a bridge to Gosport, for both transport wagons and fire engines, should the latter be needed.[65] Insularity is not altogether suitable for hospitals, but in its organization and in particular its vertical organization Haslar represents some ingenious applications of the principle. Its downfall lay in the horizontal plane: the parallel wards, understood as pavilion wards by the late 1780s, were also by then too close together.

In July 1757, during the years of Haslar's construction, and changes to its planned construction, the Admiralty minuted its approval of the plans put forward by the Navy Board for a new hospital near Plymouth. Tenon described

VUE SUD-OUEST.

1.2.3.4.5.6.7.8.9.10. Quartiers séparés. 11. Quartier de la petite Vérole. 12. Chambres des Gardes Malades. 13. Cuisine et Refectoire.
14. Chambre des provisions. 15. Chapelle 16. Loges des Domestiques et des Portiers. 17. Concierges et Offices.
On a suprimé l'Elevation des quartiers 9. et 10.

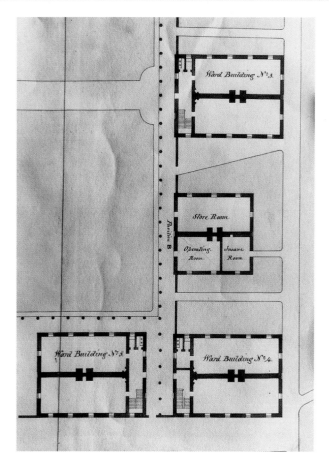

69.   The Royal Hospital at Plymouth as it was
illustrated in the French edition (1788) of John
Howard's *The state of the prisons*. The two front pavilions
are only outlines on the ground, because Howard
objected to their position.

70.   A detail of an early nineteenth-century plan of the
Royal Hospital at Plymouth.

the site of this 'beautiful' hospital as perfectly isolated and having a good air.[66] The first patients were admitted to the new royal hospital in early 1760, and it was finished just over two years later, about the same time as Haslar.

Describing a hospital, wrote Tenon, is like explaining an art or an industry.[67] Though his descriptions cover more than architecture, the analogy is useful: Plymouth is wood-chopping compared to Haslar's marquetry. It is much easier to describe, being fifteen buildings arranged around a square and linked by a colonnade lining it (Figure 69). The chapel faces the gate to the enclosure; both are flanked by pairs of ward blocks. On each side are two more ward blocks between lower, single-storey buildings, which were mostly used for offices, including a dining hall and kitchen. One also held wards for men suffering, and recovering, from smallpox, and another cells for the insane, who would, like those at Haslar, be moved on to Bethlem.[68] Other patients were assigned to buildings by diagnosis and we can speculate that they too went to higher, middle, or lower wards depending on how far their disease had carried them. Each floor of the ward blocks consisted of two wards side by side, sharing a central chimney-stack and in most cases a front vestibule with the stairs, washtubs, and latrines (Figure 70).[69] Plymouth's architect was Alexander Rovehead, whom Tenon called famous, but who was not and is not.[70] We know even less about Plymouth's genesis than we do about Haslar's, but the arrangement of the ward blocks is that of the London Hospital's side wings, which were planned and published but not yet built when Plymouth opened (see Figure 58, p. 145).[71] The latter's construction also coincided with that of the east block at St Bartholomew's (1758–62), whose ward planning was similar too. St Bartholomew's was of course another hospital in parts, as the London might have been had its building committee not in 1751 rejected the arrangement as inconvenient and extravagant.

Haslar and Plymouth look very different, but both formed great courts lined with galleries, though the latter's were uninterrupted,[72] and to that extent followed the naval pattern. Three storeys of doubled wards – end to end at Haslar, side by side at Plymouth – alternate with lower storage blocks, and the galleries between them were open on both sides, or were intended to be. At Plymouth, to cut the wind, a wall was built along the line made by the outer edges of the side pavilions, so the buildings were no longer 'entirely detached, [nor] the gallery open on both sides of the ward-blocks' (Tenon).[73]

Distinguishing storage and ward blocks, Tenon referred to the 'pavillons ou corps de logis séparés' at Plymouth. *Corps de logis* served him three weeks earlier at St Bartholomew's, whose buildings are bigger and grander-looking. As his tour continued, he also used *pavillons* for the small blocks interrupting Haslar's side wings, and for the projections running up two sides of the Salisbury Infirmary. At Plymouth, anyway, he quickly settled on calling all the blocks *pavillons*.[74] These applications are correct for *pavillon*/pavilion, which can refer to a detached structure or to a projecting part of something larger.

Tenon's journey formed part of what is probably the best-studied episode in the history of hospital architecture, comprising the deliberations that began with the fire at the Hôtel-Dieu in Paris at the end of 1772. The story will be recapitulated here because the new English naval hospitals came to be active players in these discussions, which identified them with the pavilions that ever since have defined a particular hospital type. In this way *l'affaire de l'Hôtel-Dieu* sheds a light on Haslar and Plymouth which clarifies some of their features while obscuring others.

Remaking the Hôtel-Dieu

Founded around 660, the Hôtel-Dieu in Paris is almost as old as Notre-Dame cathedral, beside which the hospital still sits (as rebuilt, finally, between 1864 and 1877) on the Ile de la Cité. The present cathedral, and the oldest of the wards existing in the eighteenth century, were begun at the end of the twelfth century.[75] In writing that the 'first hospitals in our country were the bishop's house',[76] Tenon acknowledged the ancient logic of the contiguity, but that had long since broken down. In 1548, the Hôtel-Dieu's governors requested the use of municipally owned houses on the Petit Pont, for victims of the plague. The city refused, explaining that the hospital was in the middle of Paris, 'like a heart in the middle of a man, such that bad air within it can infect the rest of the body, and all the parts and places of this city'; the expansion would be 'adding wood to fire, poison to poison'.[77] The metaphor had lost no urgency 200 years later, when the body, the hospital, and the city itself were increasingly entwined in France's preoccupation with the salubrity of the urban environment, its water and its air.[78]

There was no more fitting urban-hospital type than the island in a river running through a city, a situation both proximate to the city and isolated from it by moving water and air.[79] For some the archetype was the Tiber Island in Rome, in antiquity the cult site of the healing god Æsculapius: in the *Recueil et Parallèle des édifices de tout genre anciens et modernes* (1800–1), Jean-Nicolas-Louis Durand inserted a reconstruction of the classical island into his arrangement of lazaretto plans drawn to scale. He envisaged something like Milan's renowned Lazzaretto, begun in the late fifteenth century, a vast rectangular plain (the plan dwarfs every other on that page of the *Recueil*) surrounded by arcading and cells. The Tiber Island was lazaretto-like in the isolation afforded by the river; a moat and a stream separated the Milan hospital from the city, and later pesthouses sometimes had canals around them.[80] Supposed to be leaking its poisons into the city with the help of the Seine, into which it dumped its waste,[81] the Hôtel-Dieu was the bad island-hospital.

A hospital holding 5,000 was a city, and a city bigger than three-quarters of those in France, a committee of the Académie des Sciences pointed out in 1786.[82] By then the Hôtel-Dieu had spread to straddle the Seine on two bridges, one itself supporting wards, and ran down the south bank to make a shape like a giant, squared-off A (Figure 71). A decade earlier, a commission of inquiry found there 2,377 patients in 1,005 beds including, notoriously, 677 that might sleep up to eight. Christian welcome had no limits at the Hôtel-Dieu, wrote Tenon: that it was the most dangerous hospital in Europe was a commonplace and he suggested that the south building was, simply, the most dangerous place in the world.[83]

If intermittent construction directed by charity's expanding requirements was the more or less explicit rule at British hospitals, at the Hôtel-Dieu (as Tenon

71. The Hôtel-Dieu in Paris, copied from a 1739 map for Casimir Tollet's *Les Édifices hospitaliers* (1892), one of the first histories of its type.

and others explained it) it had been taken to a lunatic extreme. On both river-banks wards had been canted out over the water on piers through which boats bringing supplies navigated (Figure 72). Over time floors and vaults were hung between the piers, turning them into the corners of 'intricate, irregular, extemporized cellars' for laundries, storerooms, and workshops.[84] The fire that began in a candle shop on the island on 29 December 1772 was the hospital's most destructive of the century, but not the first. Tenon called attention to the 12,000 square metres of wood stored underneath the twenty wards on the south bank, which, beside the river and irredeemably damp, yet had no adequate water supply.[85] This was in his *Mémoires sur les hôpitaux de Paris* (1788), in some ways an awkward book, he admitted, put together in a hurry. Passages are however elegant in their way:

Uncleanliness is inevitable with large beds that cannot be moved and beneath which one cannot clean properly. It is inevitable in wards with four rows of beds, . . . with narrow, dark passages, where the walls are dirtied with spittle, the floor soiled with filth oozing from the mattresses and from the commodes when they are emptied, with pus and blood from wounds or venesections.

This is Saint-Jerôme, one of the surgical wards:

Since it communicates with the Saint-Paul ward, it receives that vitiated air, and the morgue beneath it fills the air with more stinking vapours. Further, near the morgue, there is a drain that emits a foul odour, and next to it is a terrace above the cellars on which urine, blood and other human refuse keep falling down from the mezzanines and, especially, from the labour ward.

Beside the labour ward was another for pregnant women, which was filled with terrible airs, via the staircases, from the two wards underneath. 'Those from the morgue also reach it, and those from the terrace [which is] filled with the discharges from the labour ward.'[86] One began to make sense of the labyrinth by following the stenches and the discarded tissues.

'Between 1772 and 1788 more than two hundred propositions were made for the re-establishment of the Hôtel Dieu, more than fifty architectural proposals set forth.'[87] The discussions formed part of ambitious investigations into poverty itself.[88] But can a prevailing and even intense interest in public health, along with vile sights and smells, really account for that astonishing number of projects? Interventions by the *directeur général des Finances* (until 1781) Jacques Necker, and then by the baron de Breteuil, *ministre de la Maison du Roi* with responsibility for Paris, did much for the glamour of the endeavour. Louis XVI and his

72.   'Vue de l'Hôtel-Dieu prise du pont St Michel', a nineteenth-century etching.

brother-in-law the Emperor Joseph allowed their personal interest to become known, too.[89]

What emerged was the pavilion-ward plan whose most immediate quality is its legibility, something that itself makes it another species from the 'shapeless heap'[90] that was the old hospital. Three pavilion plans were published in Paris in 1788 and 1789, by a committee of the Académie des Sciences and by two individuals, the surgeon Jacques Tenon and the physicist Jean-Baptiste Le Roy. Their differences do not much signify for our purposes. 'The first principle of hospital construction is to divide the sick among separate pavilions', wrote Florence Nightingale, detached ward blocks each with

> suitable nurses' rooms, ward sculleries, lavatories, baths, water-closets, all complete . . . and quite unconnected with any other pavilions . . . except by light airy passages or corridors. A pavilion is indeed a separate detached hospital, which has, or ought to have, as little connexion in its ventilation with any other part of the hospital, as if it were really a separate establishment miles away.[91]

All three plans more or less meet this definition, in which is implicit ventilation through opposite rows of windows, and to which the idea that every ward forms an 'individual and isolated hospital' (as the Académie committee put it) is central.[92] Tenon's text and the committee's design remained definitive in nineteenth-century France.[93] As presented to Britain in the late 1850s by Nightingale and others on the basis of French examples by then erected, the pavilion-ward hospital was similarly understood to have originated in Paris seventy years earlier. Though expensive, the type guided the conception and construction of large hospitals until well into the twentieth century. Who invented it?[94] Largely thanks to Le Roy, the question itself formed part of the pavilion ward's earliest conceptualizations.

In December 1785 a committee of the Académie des Sciences was instituted under the chairmanship of the astronomer Jean-Sylvain Bailly (1736–93). Other members included Lavoisier, Tenon, and (briefly) Le Roy.[95] Its initial assignment was to inspect a proposal published that year in a *Mémoire* by C.-P. Coquéau and the architect Bernard Poyet.[96] Magnificent illustrations (Figures 73, 74) underline the startling exoticism of a building which would have been shaped like a wheel with a hub-chapel surrounded by a circle of wards mirrored, in turn, by the larger circle forming the rim; between the concentric ward rings are sixteen ward spokes. Intended to be on the Ile des Cygnes, the hospital was its own island, made by a new canal around the top 'to isolate the site' and divided, underground, by an aqueduct 'continually bathed by running water' which would serve as a sewer. Isolation would be achieved by another fluid too. As they wrote,

> On this island the mobile atmosphere into which the Hôtel-Dieu will be plunged will envelop it on every side, and its continual movement, penetrating all the openings facing in every direction, which Poyet has multiplied to the greatest possible degree, will be propagated throughout the extent of the building.[97]

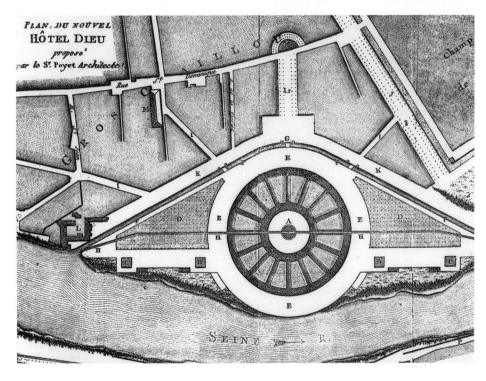

73. Coquéau and Poyet's 'Colosseum' project for a new Hôtel-Dieu, published in 1785. From Tollet's *Les Édifices hospitaliers.*

74. The plan of Coquéau and Poyet's project. From Tollet's *Les Édifices hospitaliers.*

There was nothing new about Coquéau and Poyet's medical presuppositions, and the Ile des Cygnes (where the Eiffel Tower stands now) had often been proposed for a relocated Hôtel-Dieu. Their imaginative use of the island was innovative, though the metaphor had already (or so he would claim) been developed even more strikingly by Le Roy.

Bailly began the public reading of his committee's first report in November 1786. (He is generally believed to have written all three reports.) It is unenthusiastic about Coquéau and Poyet's project and explains that the committee was recommending four smaller hospitals, together to constitute the Hôtel-Dieu, with detached buildings in ranges. The following June, Louis XVI authorized the construction of the new hospitals, each accommodating 1,200 patients in six pairs of parallel ward blocks arranged on each side of a garden and linked by covered walkways, with a chapel at their head. This was in accordance with the committee's preliminary recommendations and its third report, of March 1788, would include the plan drawn up for it by Poyet (Figure 75).

The first report concludes with the odd acknowledgement that, had the committee members only known it, the idea for a hospital of this type was Le Roy's[98] whose short 'Précis d'un ouvrage sur les hôpitaux' was published the next year. Marginal notes and footnotes explain that the essay had been read at the Academy's public meeting of 9 April 1777 (and subsequently), exactly as it was now being printed; and moreover that a memoir outlining the same principles and the same hospital (*mon Hôpital*) would have been read in 1773, too, had an unnamed minister of state not more or less forbidden Le Roy to do so, for fear of generating public alarm.[99] The unwavering reiteration of this story of recognition denied might seem like too much protest, but Louis Greenbaum has shown the strength of Le Roy's claim for primacy: Benjamin Franklin, his friend for nearly forty years – their shared interests included electricity, too – did, for example, write to him in June 1773, pleased to hear that he was working on hospitals. Franklin's wide acquaintance also included John Pringle and Alexander Small, whose writings on ventilation Le Roy then began translating for French publication.[100] Though it was perhaps the Hôtel-Dieu fire that prompted his interest in hospital design, he was soon well placed to undertake it.

To imagine his hospital, Le Roy wrote, think of the wards entirely isolated from one another, like tents in an army encampment, or the pavilions of Marly.[101] Marly, destroyed during the Revolution, was built between 1679 and 1684 as a private palace for Louis XIV, to the designs of Jules Hardouin-Mansart. It mysteriously (the idea's origins are not known) and splendidly comprised the King's Pavilion and twelve for his guests,[102] all linked by iron trellises covered by climbing plants and seemingly integral to the garden across which they faced one another. An Edenic place, therefore, whose innocence extended to the boisterous games that noblemen played amid the renowned water-works. As a palace it provided a traditional comparison for a hospital, one here useful for explaining how hospitals could be deconstructed, made fragmentary.[103] More fundamental, however, to Le Roy's conception were the tents in the encampment. The sick are demonstrably better cured under tents and in wooden huts than in a hospital – in Pringle's wake the observation had become a commonplace. As real structures the tents were healthy and as primordial structures they evoked the absence of cities, which were only hospitals writ large: the 'Franks our ancestors truly called cities the tombs of men'.[104] The twenty-two wards of Le Roy's hospital would however be elevated, raised on piers 'like a kind of island in the air', with their ceilings and floors perforated by chimneys and adjustable openings.[105] His similes spill over; the hospital is the palace fragmented, the tents in line, the constellation of islands.

The third pavilion plan, Tenon's, was, like the committee's, published in 1788. Their pavilions (Figure 75) would be served by a pair of corridors on each side of a long rectangular court, his by a central, two-storey corridor. (He calculated that someone visiting every first-floor ward would thereby be saved from climbing 1,344 steps.)[106] Mutual amity governed the differences between Tenon

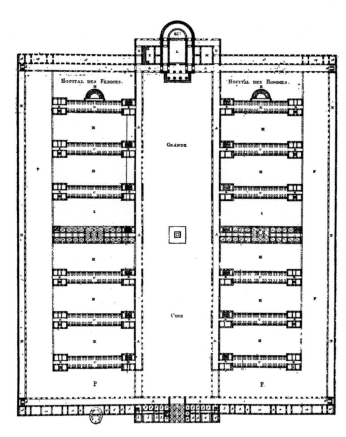

75. Poyet's rendering of the Paris Académie des Sciences' pavilion-ward plan for the Hôtel-Dieu. From Tollet's *Les Édifices hospitaliers.*

and his colleagues, which really centred on the question of whether every kind of hospital could or should be built this way: he countenanced other forms too.

Le Roy was however still unhappy, and at his insistence the Academy agreed to send to the *Journal de Paris* a letter over Bailly's signature, dated 4 May 1788. This mentions essential differences between its and Le Roy's hospitals, without elaborating, but acknowledges that Le Roy's came first and that both plans showed pavilions ranged in two rows on each side of a great court, with a chapel at one end. So far so good, but the letter also reminded the public that the 'honour of invention' was not after all the point of the exercise, and then introduced, obliquely, another candidate for that honour, at least when it came to the important end (*objet important*) of isolating the wards. The committee members sent to study the English hospitals had to their pleasure seen the idea put into execution at the Plymouth hospital, already a quarter-century old.[107] The implication was that Le Roy's essay could and should have mentioned Plymouth. That stung, and his notes to the 'Précis' as published vigorously deny any knowledge of the hospital at Plymouth (or Haslar) back in 1773.[108] In this way Bailly's committee, and Le Roy, identified Plymouth with the pavilion plan. The former's third report had already done so, as we will see, but it is the May letter, prompted by Le Roy's importunities, that contains the clearest statement that the English had anticipated all of them. As Plymouth is still seen as a pavilion hospital *avant la lettre*, it is worth pursuing the French a little longer.[109]

The committee's investigations included the English tour conducted in the summer of 1787 by Tenon and the engineer-physicist Charles de Coulomb, which it would hail as an instance of 'enlightened' international collaboration, showing the way in which countries might discard national jealousies to unite under the banner of medical-charitable improvement.[110] (The *Gentleman's Magazine* meanwhile described it as a unilateral tribute to British humanity and generosity.)[111] Tenon explained its genesis in his *Mémoires*. After helping to translate a copy of Hunczovsky's *Beobachtungen*, he circulated all over Europe a questionnaire about civilian hospitals, but no data came from England. The committee decided, he wrote, to go and get them, particularly since Hunczovsky had not entered into 'certain details' and his English observations were primarily of London hospitals. 'We went to England to seek enlightenment and found it there. It was Plymouth hospital that interested us most.'[112] But Tenon already knew from Hunczovsky's book that England's naval hospitals had been built on the scale required for Paris. French military hospitals had moreover developed medical and administrative procedures that were already influencing their civil counterparts, and their innovations were also architectural: the naval hospital at Rochefort, completed in 1788, effectively detached its ward blocks within its vast walled enclosure.[113] In other words, Tenon and his colleagues would have expected Haslar and Plymouth to be worth visiting even had Hunczovsky not devoted twenty pages to the former and its dedication to the free movement of air. The Plymouth hospital received a single paragraph:

> In Plymouth there is also a considerable sailors' hospital, where more than 1000 sick will be able to be cared for. On an extensive site a number of small buildings stand isolated, for men suffering from different ailments. As the internal arrangements, and the actual care of the sick, are the same as at Portsmouth, . . . a closer description is unnecessary.[114]

Given Haslar's description, however, this would have been interesting enough.

Tenon's failure to acknowledge the clear signposts put up by Hunczovsky, and others,[115] can be attributed to two things. First was an unwillingness to further complicate the dispute with Le Roy. More fundamental was his adherence to an inaugural statement in the *Mémoires*: 'There is no existing work on the structure and layout of hospitals and we have no principles for judging their perfection or their flaws. We had, therefore, to begin by assembling these principles.'[116] One would not learn from this admirable and modest book that anyone had ever written anything about the salubrity of hospital buildings before.[117] His colleagues shared the commitment to principle, which was manifested in a characteristic way of writing about English hospitals. On 7 July 1787, two weeks after the royal order for the four new hospitals but a week before Tenon actually visited Plymouth, Bailly wrote to him: 'It is very curious, and very useful, to find our great plan already executed. . . . an experiment already completed'.[118] Bailly associated Plymouth with no active agent, no experimenter, and the third report, published eight months later, sustains the rhetoric:

Although reason alone, without any experience whatever, provides sufficient
assurance that parallel buildings, isolated pavilions, will form healthful and
salubrious accommodation, it was still very satisfactory to find this experiment already carried out, and on a grand scale. The hospitals of Portsmouth
and Plymouth . . . are laid out in parallel lines, and in isolated pavilions,
with the difference, that the Portsmouth hospital offers parallel buildings
which are separated from one another by streets only 18 [*sic*] feet wide,
where the air cannot circulate freely enough; while that at Plymouth, also
made up of isolated pavilions, arranged around a vast court, has a layout
very similar (*presque semblable*) to that for which we had already expressed
a preference.[119]

Expérience means both an experiment, or test, and its English cognate, 'experience'; Bailly used the word both ways.

The formula fits national stereotypes then nascent: the French are subtle and
intellectual, while the English unreflectingly get down to business.[120] It was
publicly maintained in the *Journal de Paris* letter published six weeks later, in
which Plymouth is the 'idée executée'. An unpublished draft of the letter goes
into more detail, explaining that Bailly's committee had actually sought a middle
way between Le Roy's pavilions and Plymouth's. The former were too long and,
by implication, too complex in their provisions for ventilation. The latter were
double-piled, and 'We have published our reasons' – which indeed they had –
'for considering this configuration unsatisfactory'. The committee had therefore
single-piled the wards that at the naval hospital were coupled, to let them 'take
in the passing air'.[121] In truth Plymouth's are not pavilion wards, for precisely
this reason. It was however desirable to show, in the third report, that the
expensive experiment had already been conducted with positive results, and, in
the May letter as published, that while Le Roy's claims were justified in the
narrow context they were meaningless in the larger, and not quite in the spirit
of enlightened universalism anyway.

We could call the naval hospitals experimental, inasmuch as each in its
own way amounted to something entirely new; the relative success of naval-
architectural experimentation could anyway be tested more rigorously than at
civil hospitals, whose procedures varied so much. In 1799, Gilbert Blane compared their mortality rates during recent wars. Between 1793 and 1797, for
example, Haslar's was one in 14.3, significantly higher than Plymouth's one in
24.7. Blane pointed out his controls: the hospitals were 'equally well supplied
with accommodations, diet and attendance' and their patients enjoyed equal
cubic volumes of air. The Plymouth hospital was warmer in winter, and had a
site drier than Haslar's, but the difference must turn on architecture:

Haslar hospital consists of one great center building, and four pavilions
running backwards from each corner of it. These are placed in pairs, standing
parallel and very close to each other lengthwise, so as to intercept the free
course of air. . . . Plymouth hospital consists of twelve separate similar and

equal buildings, ranged in a large square, with wide intervals between each. Of these twelve, however, ten only are occupied by the sick.

In short, Haslar's inferiority derived from structures 'screening each other from the free current of the external air'. Blane's medical authority was John Pringle, who had so strongly and instructively, he wrote, argued for the value of pure air, but Tenon was his witness for Plymouth's superiority over every other hospital in Europe when it came to 'judicious construction and distribution'.[122]

The 'experience of the English has confirmed our principle' of restricting each ward to about thirty beds; 'theory teaches' that a detached building for about one hundred patients, containing three wards superimposed, would be sufficiently healthy, 'and if one wishes to consult experience, we would say that the English hospitals, all generally healthy enough, have three ward-ranges in three storeys':[123] in the French texts of the late 1780s English hospitals appear as the almost accidental manifestation or realization of a principle extrinsic to them, which had not consciously formed part of their genesis. (This was not chauvinism: the texts elide earlier, native principles too.) In England itself, principle was first influentially linked to hospital construction in 1720, by Richard Mead, anticipating the plague's return. Thirty years later, John Pringle identified the malignant jail fever with the plague, and the jail fever, in turn, with those of ships, camps, and hospitals. The first three editions of his *Observations of the diseases of the army* were published between 1752 and 1761, precisely the years during which the plan of Haslar Hospital, which was admitting those fevers, was altered in a way soon suggesting a dedication to the freeing of air. In these editions and their successors we can also trace Pringle's retreat from mechanically assisted ventilation, which became the 'imperfect Aid' that Foster called it in 1768. The latter's attention to the principles of civil-hospital construction was now explicitly corrective of earlier practice, in a way of writing about hospitals that had come to stay. The distinction between principle and experience, idea and manifestation, bears further investigation in this, the new light of reform. The following chapter will also set it in the older and wider context of luxury and its detection.

Chapter 9

Ornament and the architect

In April 1738 the managers of the Edinburgh Infirmary resolved that their new building would 'be Solid and Erected of the most durable Materialls, not slovenly, and yet that very little or no expence should be Laid out in useless ornament'.[1] The last phrase seems odd, just because the antithesis was proverbial. 'Nature, in her Contrivances, has made every part of a living Creature either for Ornament or Use': Charles Davenant was, in 1699, explaining that the useful parts of the body politic are, or ought to be, the poor.[2] His metaphor however leaves room for ornamental contributions (maybe by the rich) just as, in practice, the Edinburgh managers did; and Christians might anyway imagine ornament of a higher kind. St Peter instructed wives to put on only the 'ornament of a meek and quiet spirit, which is in the sight of God of great price', and Andrew Marvell described Appleton House, where 'A stately frontispiece of poor / Adorns without the open door'.[3] The meek ornament, the stately paupers, are oxymorons in one way, not at all in another: God sees no contradiction.

Institutional reformers similarly showed the grandeur in, for example, water closets. Some were even moved to explain that architects were incapable of grasping the paradox, that they recognized only the worldly kind of ornament, and that this accounted for hospitals' failure. The complaints are intermittent, unspecific, and bear little relation to the actual business of planning. Like the paradox itself, however, the complaints drew upon older ways of considering the relationships between the architect, the proprietor, and the building, relationships that may in turn be understood in terms of ornament and its antitheses. The latter certainly include the plain, the essential, and the natural, but also the immaterial and the imperceptible. This chapter concludes with asylums built in the early nineteenth century. They were also liable to accusations of useless ornament, but there the issue was both complicated by the mixed clientele (the poor man's ornament might be the rich man's necessity), and deepened, by nature's powerful and specific connotations in this new context.

Ornamental parts

The Edinburgh managers (or rather their publicist, 'Philanthropus') distinguished useless ornament from 'necessary useful Expence', like the unglazed Dutch tiles on the ward floors. More expensive than wooden boards, they guarded against 'Fire, Vermin and Stench', and muffled the noise of students trundling around the ward overhead.[4] Philanthropus also offered a more implicit antithesis to useless ornament, and this is the kind he explained as decent, or fitting. Most ornamental at the Infirmary was the masonry of the centre front, with its order. But without 'decently Dressing that Part which first attracts the Eye' the Infirmary would have a 'poor' appearance, one particularly inappropriate to that part's function as the 'College'.[5] Otherwise it had no 'hewn Work but what was thought absolutely necessary for Strength as well as Decency', that is, the quoins, rusticated basement, door- and window-surrounds, and the band of stone between the ground and first floors ('Belting', 'absolutely necessary in Order to make a proper Intake upon the Wall' which at this point stepped back). This structural justification was perhaps convincing, though the contemporary Charity Work-House (see Figure 43, p. 117) managed to stay up without quoins, belting or window surrounds.[6]

But what was 'ornament', precisely? At the end of the century, Humphry Repton explained: it 'should include every enrichment bearing the semblance of utility', which seems to turn on another interesting oxymoron. Repton was however distinguishing ornament from 'decoration' like statues and urns: the first includes the columns, pilasters, and entablatures without which buildings work perfectly well, but which represent ancient structural parts.[7] Though we cannot assume that his definition always governed architects' and hospital governors' uses of 'ornament' over the previous seventy years, for the former it connoted rustication, window- and door-surrounds, and the classical orders and, for the latter, was something that might or might not offer the semblance of a broader utility.

Ornament stood in, synecdochically, for the building that always needed at least ritual justification, as when the Edinburgh managers assured their public that the immediate relief of the sick poor did not suffer for the sake of the new construction.[8] Hospital promoters were responsible not only for utility but for the appearance of utility, rather like Dance the Younger's self-narrating windows at St Luke's. We can recall the Devon and Exeter's promise, made in 1741, that the hospital would be built plainly and frugally under the supervision of 'several Gentlemen'. The London Hospital's building committee reported ten years later that because designs submitted by Mainwaring represented more than the hospital could 'Engage in with Prudence', it had asked for another, 'without Ornaments, not so large', but 'Capable of further Extention and Enlargement, if . . . there should be Occasion for it'.[9] Prudence should govern the process of building, as well as its product, a process including the choice of project, the supervision of construction, and the near-inevitable expansion.

We do not know what Mainwaring's ornaments would have been, but those offered to and rejected by the Glasgow Infirmary's subscribers forty years later

seem to have been recorded. Robert Adam's project for the hospital was presented to the Glasgow Committee of Management in October 1791, when its cost
was given as £8,725 19 s. A sub-committee was then asked to inquire about the
cost of a 'plain Building of the same Extent and same conveniencies' and in particular 'whether the middle part of the Buildings . . . may not be rendered equally
convenient and suitable at much less Expence'. Within the month Adam was personally presenting the committee with a plainer alternative, also with four storeys
of wards and 112 beds, to cost £7,185 10 s., and he offered to contract for its construction, after adding 2.5 per cent to cover unforeseen expenses: £7,365.[10] The
committee expressed a unanimous preference for the £7,365 infirmary over the
£8,725 19s. (plus 2.5 per cent) infirmary and when, a week later, a general
meeting of subscribers was invited to choose between 'the one an Ornamented
Design, and the other a plain and less ornamented one' it, not surprisingly, did
the same. A further choice was offered, for,

> there being two Elevations or Fronts of the second or plain Design produced
> to the Meeting, the one having a rusticated Basement and the other a plain
> Basement, the Meeting made choice of the Design which has the rusticated
> Basement

– which would cost no more.[11]

If the alternative elevations presented in November 1791 are those recorded on
drawings now in Sir John Soane's Museum (Figures 76 and 77),[12] then there was
not much difference between the ornamented and the plain. Omitting
the six pairs of colonnettes in the central pavilion's attic, the larger column-pairs
flanking each side pavilion, and the rather Soanian, two-storey arch reveals
on the lower ward-ranges between may have made a difference of more than
£1,400, though one wonders if Adam's estimates were not allowing for some
kind of ritual of rejection, of choosing plainness. In any case the ritual was not
trivial, though the difference between the two designs was: to paraphrase Clifford Geertz, the alternative façades embodied in a form that men could address
with their eyes, and not just with their minds,[13] the problem of finding the limits
of charitable expenditure.

In 1660, Roger Pratt explained how to make an architectural model in a way
that allows us to see ornamentation acted out. Determine your scale, prepare your
wood, draw on it and give it to a joiner to cut and put together. Then 'are all the
ornaments to be made, and fastened . . . in their proper places'.[14] Ornaments
have to be fastened to something. Theoretically speaking they are 'attached or
additional', as Alberti explained,[15] and practically speaking they are subordinate
or consequent to the other part of architecture, the Dutch-tiled-flooring part. This
does not mean that ornament was some kind of optional extra, that it could
be discarded at buildings of even the slightest pretension: denying it to the
Edinburgh Infirmary's centre would have made the centre indecent, unseemly.
The relation is rather that of the idea and the phenomenon, which is what
Alberti was describing; of the essential and the ornamental, as Wren put it;[16] of
principle and accessory, as Jean-Baptiste Le Roy had it almost a century later,

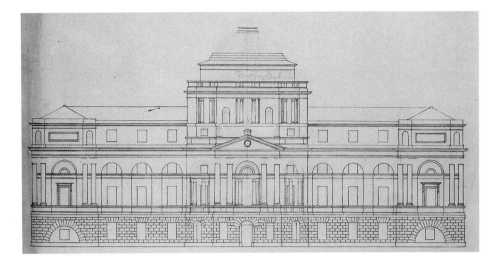

76. The rejected elevation of the Glasgow Infirmary.

now writing about hospital design. The architects would have had no quarrel with Le Roy's wording, but it acquires a distinct shading taken together with his other dichotomies: utility and frivolousness, usefulness and deadliness. An 'extreme cleanliness, as pure an air as possible – one cannot say it too often; this is the true, the only magnificence that one seeks in these buildings'.[17] The physicist will instruct the architect about meek ornament, the beauty made by usefulness.

For Alberti and Wren, ornament is that which gives architecture intelligible, appreciable beauty. It could however be recast as an optional extra if architects had to fall back on something like essence, or principle. In 1709 Vanbrugh (who was genuinely interested in the distinctions) called it 'form' when the Duchess of Marlborough expressed suspicions about Blenheim's kitchen court, and in particular its arcading, which looked too handsome for propriety, or budget. He used a variety of arguments to translate the arcades to decorous utility: they were not 'made out of respect to the Offices they lead to, but for the Shelter of the people', they had antique sanction (and the Duke's), and were cheaper than covered passageways would be. And, if the court looked finer than those at other houses, 'tis only owing to its Forme, not to its Workmanship or Ornaments'.[18] Eighty years later, comparable claims were made on behalf of three projects presented for the rebuilding of the Hôtel-Dieu in Paris. Coquéau and Poyet's vast cylinder (1785; see Figure 73, p. 189), Chirol's even vaster rectangle formed by stepped ward blocks (1787), and the Académie des Sciences' paired pavilions (1788; see Figure 75, p. 191) look very different from one another, but their authors explained each as forms and arrangements of forms so inherently and sufficiently *imposantes* (or *élégantes*) as to require no further ornament.[19]

Significantly few among the many Hôtel-Dieu projectors offered elevations along with their plans. The omission is symptomatic of what Bruno Fortier has described as a distinctive disqualification of architectural knowledge, as that was conventionally understood, in favour of another, more quantitative *savoir*

77. The contract elevation for the Glasgow Infirmary.

advanced by the physicians, anatomists, physicists and others along with their projects.[20] Paris in the 1770s and 1780s indeed heard some frank assessments of architects' inadequacy in the face of a building type where (Tenon explained) bad examples have tragic consequences:[21] professional lines were being drawn. Other lines were too. All concerned in hospital construction – physicians, architects, governors – not only aspired to but sometimes got the proprietorial, gentlemanly role.[22] This sometimes required defining the other role as ornamental, which is not necessarily useless but can be that of realizing the idea, or manifesting the principle.

Complaining and reforming

Most of the English gentry, wrote John Webb in 1660, 'have some knowledge of the Theory of Architecture'.[23] He was, politely, remonstrating with Charles II about the appointment of a notable royalist, and poet, as Surveyor of the King's Works. The gentry, he continued, may know the theory, but 'nothing of ye practique'; that is, the designing, ordering, and directing (as he described it) that Webb knew all about. Many gentlefolk would have disagreed. Just as some took to pharmacy and prescribed for their family and neighbours, others were happy to share their 'Opinion of Machines, conveying of Water, building or repairing Houses, improving their Lands &c.': so Alexander Monro *primus* described some of the fruits of his ceaseless quest for 'Universal Knowledge'.[24] 'All the gentry of this Country are Architects, they know, or think they know much more than any Professional man', Robert Adam reported in a letter sent from Scotland in 1791. The delusion was not just British. 'Proprietors' with a passion for building 'have pretensions to being architects', J.-F. Blondel warned in his *Cours d'architecture civile* (1771–77).[25]

Adam's correspondent was Jeremy Bentham (1748–1832), who had just sent his Panopticon plan to the economist James Anderson, so that he might,

Bentham told Adam, 'send me such hints as might occurr to him'. Bentham's explanation of Anderson's qualifications was not guaranteed to soften a professional man's eye (Anderson had 'written a little book on smoaky chimnies', he wrote, and had edited 'some elucidations relative to the origin and advantages of the Gothic stile, which to me who know nothing about the matter were new and seemed ingenious') and Adam was not anxious to see the Panopticon become the subject of what he called the usual sort of 'paper war'.[26] For, 'no sooner would your friend take up this affair, than others would combat all his notions, [and] form a million of Panopticons fraught with every sort of absurdity'. And in the end they would manage to build

> perhaps the worst design of the Cluster, only because the designer was a Lord, or Gentleman reckoned famous for taste, and the corrector of all plans, publick and private, by which correction this Town [Edinburgh] and Country is crowded with bad taste bad designs and wretched proportions.[27]

The vision of ghastly, genteel correction may have been a pre-emptive strike. Adam, approached by Bentham via a mutual acquaintance, quickly saw that a panoptical submission might get him the commission for the Edinburgh Bridewell. But he may also have understood the potential difficulties of his relationship with the proprietor, Bentham.

Records of complaints in the other direction, about architects, are in the nature of things commoner and older. They figure architects as at best wayward and irresponsible, at worst sinister in their essential incompleteness, their parasitic need for a client before they can fulfil their art, and not infrequently such complaints came from gentlemen and ladies reckoned famous for taste. In 1698 the amateur architect Roger North fervently characterized 'surveyors',[28] the professionals, as men who love

> To practise their own whims, at your cost. They having viewed many fabrics, in life, and in draught, with the ornaments of the antique and modern invention, have a world of crotchets of their own, occasioned or built upon them; all [of] which they have an itch to put in execution, and it is miraculous if they do it not [at] the first opportunity of building they are employed in. And let a man arm himself what he can, they will argue and persuade him beyond his intentions.[29]

Ten years later the Duchess of Marlborough jocularly forgave Vanbrugh for having 'vext me extreamly, in forcing me to things against my Inclination' at Blenheim, but by 1732 she knew no architect who was not 'mad or ridiculous':

> I know two gentlemen of this country [Yorkshire] who have great estates and who have built their houses without an architect, by able workmen that would do as they directed which no architect will, though you pay for it. . . . I intend to take this method myself, in building a hospital for distressed people of several sorts.

(In the meantime, Vanbrugh wondered why 'her Family don't agree to Lock her up'.)[30] The architect does not do what he is told because he is mad to try out his inventions. 'If you give up the reins, he will be so fond of new compositions and ornaments of his own framing and invention, that for the lechery of putting them in execution your purse shall be martyrized' (North).[31] This is the architect greedy, even lecherous, for novelty's gratification, like a spoiled child, perhaps even like a woman. 'Novelty', signifying a creativity completely untethered by principle, arbitrary and solipsistic,[32] remained a conventional attribute of architectural luxury.

All this novelty, oddly, produces nothing new. North's 'Of building' also explains that ancients like Vitruvius wrote 'in a positive style', that is explicitly, or prescriptively. They do not explain the reasoning behind the classical orders as 'philosophers' might, who 'would have learners understand as well as remember'.[33] Nevertheless, he continued, architects unreflectingly accept this positivism as a shield against carping envy:

> because all new inventions are exposed to caption, whereas ancient patterns are far from envy, and the artist is screened by [the] authority they bear. There-fore as a safety against erring, and indemnity against spite and petulant cap-tiousness, they walk upon old authenticated experience, and err (if at all) *cum patribus* [along with the fathers].

In architecture, the very centrality of the classical orders, however thoughtfully applied, signalled this deference to paternal authority, the architect's reluctance to reason for himself.

Madly inventive, architects were none the less fearfully hidebound by precedent. Here is one clue to the later critiques of hospitals designed (as the formula had it) according to aesthetic and not hygienic criteria. Another is in a note that Mandeville appended to some lines in his *The grumbling hive*, which explain that in the *post*-luxurious hive 'The Building Trade is quite destroy'd' ('Artificers are not employ'd'). In it he, like Alberti and a hundred others, retold Plutarch's story about the elder Leotychidas of Sparta, who, on catching sight of the ceiling in Corinth, asked if the tree trunks there grew square.[34] In this unpromising joke we have the kernel of every objection to architecture itself: that it was not natural. Hospitals were distinctively vulnerable to this accusation, which began to be regularly levelled in the 1770s. The literature of institutional reform has been well studied, but it does need to be put into the context of the complaints just outlined.

Historians have shown eighteenth-century Europe's determination to master the 'laws of the organism–environment relationship' through an exhaustive amassing of meteorological, topographical, epidemiological, and social data.[35] The research began to extend to buildings with John Howard's *The state of the prisons* (1777), the result of his visits to every prison in England and Wales, at each of which he noted physical dimensions, tables of fees and diets, the weights of the chains used, and so forth.[36] But as Bentham pointed out, with an appropriate metaphor, such records are not enough for new architecture: 'They afford a rich fund of materials; but a quarry is not a house.'[37] In this way he identified a prevailing mood, or technique, that was sometimes explicitly justified. As the physician John Aikin wrote, 'It does not belong to my profession to lay down an architectural plan for ... [hospitals], nor do I conceive it necessary. By pointing out what to avoid, we in effect give rules [of] what to aim at.' 'The danger of corrupted air in crowded close apartments', for example, 'will suggest the necessity of having them lofty, well ventilated, and thinly peopled.'[38] Indeed. Tenon did lay down plans for hospitals, but he wrote to Dance the Younger that his intentions in so doing were

> certainly not to set myself up as an architect, nor to discuss the construction of the building, or its ornament (*décoration*). These are subjects for distinguished gentlemen who, like yourself, are dedicated to an art comprising a number of areas of expertise, as well as many other arts; I have to consider hospitals only in relation to the sick person, ... to seek ... in the healing art, principles applicable to the form (*formation*) and planning (*distribution*) of buildings raised for [his] assistance.[39]

Eighteenth-century French architectural theorists availed themselves of the conventional distinctions: decoration, distribution, and construction.[40] Tenon was drawing upon conceptual categories that Dance (whom he held in affection and respect) understood.[41] He was also groping for a formulation clarifying the distinction between architecture-as-art and architecture as the satisfaction of a need lying outside art. The latter, by which buildings are objects and not art objects, was then beginning to present their fundamental problem for philosophers, too.[42] Others saw no problem. 'Magnificence and solidity are not enough for ... [a hospital]; essentially it requires salubrity. This last concern can be treated properly only by a doctor.' This was a doctor, Antoine Petit, in 1774.[43] Architectural writing had since the Renaissance addressed houses' siting, orientation, forms, and services in relation to their healthfulness, which was subsumed under distribution and construction.[44] Now salubrity had been translated outside the art, at least in the context of hospital reform: insalubrity might however take its place and become the architect's responsibility, his fault.

At hospitals, wrote Denis Diderot (for the eighth volume of the *Encyclopédie*, published 1765), the 'architect must subordinate his art to the opinions of the physician: to mingle the sick in the same place is to use them to kill each other'.[45] This is noteworthy, and not just for the instruction to subordinate. Whether intentionally or not, Diderot's punctuation, the intermediary colon, implicates the art in those deaths. Six years later, Aikin set a related theme rolling on a long course through the English- and soon French-speaking worlds. This was, that a dangerously misguided but 'benevolent zeal' ushered the sick poor into hospitals and stuffed them full. (Murderous help, Tenon would call it.)[46] The choice of a hospital's site and orientation was, Aikin added, up to the physician and therefore no problem. It was rather

> in the laying out of the building, and the internal conduct of the house that we are to look for the source of those errors which may prove so fatal. In

planning the building, two quite opposite and incompatible views are found to interfere.

With Aikin, like Diderot, the line between institutional and architectural practice begins to blur. The source of the first error was the architect, who

> considers it his business to manage his room and materials in such a manner, as to accommodate the greatest number of people in the least possible space. The physician on the contrary would leave as much vacant space, occupied by the fresh air alone circulating freely, as was in any degree compatible with use and convenience. It is to the prevalence of the former above the latter that all our complaints are owing.[47]

The American John Jones repeated the passage about the incompatible views nearly verbatim in his essay published in 1776, and prefaced it with the additional accusation that those superintending both the architecture and the management of the London and Paris hospitals 'have confined their views entirely to objects of conveniency, cheapness, or ornament'. The last subsumed an 'elegant' chapel recently built at a London lying-in hospital, which cost the equivalent of four wards.[48] The architect is miserly where he should be magnificent, and lavish when he should be frugal.

Aikin's central argument about crowding the sick would be made again and again. Thomas Percival immediately condemned this 'false oeconomy'; 'Economy in space is a sad extravagance' (W. A. F. Browne, 1837).[49] Tenon presented the case more positively and more comprehensively. If 'one were to impart a kind of splendour' to hospitals, he wrote, that would not take the form of 'useless decorations', but rather the 'methodical classification of disorders', the effective planning of wards and other buildings, and the proper distribution of 'water, sewers, staircases, vaults, promenades, roads, baths, toilets, sculleries'. Economy in these sorts of decoration would be false, and fatal. Tenon sought a 'rational and beneficent' splendour of sculleries, not unlike Marvell's frontispiece of poor.[50]

Reading Diderot, Aikin, and Jones, one might suspect that the hospital was then a point of tension, at the confluence of rival competences, but this reading risks simply recapitulating theirs.[51] It also ignores the antiquity of the complaints, in which the architect is child (or woman), the proprietor adult (or man). We might instead imagine medical men, architects, and gentlemen of the sort that comprised the Exeter 'board of works' all seeking the recognition of their adulthood, of their status as proprietors. Two episodes can serve by way of amplification: Jeremy Bentham's first efforts to get the Panopticon modelled and built, and Charles-François Viel's attempt to claim authorship of the pavilion plan. They also help us to understand what architects might do for reformers.

In August 1790, with *Panopticon* the book still a manuscript, Bentham was anxious to get a model made of Panopticon the building, 'to enable me to settle a number of details'; for this he needed a 'variety of information not to be obtained but from persons conversant in building'.[52] Bentham in fact wanted two architects, one to make the model and the other to contract for building. The division of responsibility would, he thought, prevent peculation, additions, and alterations during construction, when the 'proprietor' was so often at the architect-builder's mercy. It then occurred to him that Willey Reveley, whom he had met in Turkey five years earlier, might do to construct the model, prepare the estimates, and help him make the final adjustments.[33] (He would publicly and carefully acknowledge Reveley's contributions to the Panopticon.)[54] There was another use for the model, too. Anxiously and repeatedly, Bentham complained to his many correspondents about the difficulty of 'expressing the parts of a cylindrical building on a flat surface'; he feared the unintelligibility of these pictorial surfaces, 'notwithstanding the pains taken with the explanation'.[55] 'A Model any man may understand: few would understand the subject readily and *thoroughly* from a Draught; easy as it is, even without a Draught, to comprehend the general principle.'[56] In the cylindrical Panopticon, the occupants of the rim-cells must always assume they are being watched from a central core, and hence dare not transgress. (Bentham envisaged many applications for the type, but prisons then dominated his thinking.) The pretty, complicated, and flimsily built Panopticon would in this way, he wrote, be stronger than the 'massy piles of Newgate':[57] the principle of central inspection compensated for the frailty of its realization, as if architecture itself were approaching pure superfluity, or ornamentality.

Once published, a copy of *Panopticon* was, in May 1791, dispatched to Robert Adam.[58] Bentham hoped that Adam would make a model to show to the Edinburgh magistrates.[59] Adam agreed to do so, and while warning him about the million panopticons that the Edinburgh gentry might spawn, reassured Bentham about proprietorship: 'I always disclaim all merit' in 'talking of this plan, and the great Ingenuity of the Inventor and the Invention'. His only compromises would be in surrender to the site and other local requirements.[60] After Robert's sudden death in March 1792, James Adam took over the Bridewell project, as he did the Glasgow Infirmary. In July, Bentham demanded a meeting with James. He had by then been informed that the Edinburgh Bridewell was not, after all, a true panopticon, for the sleeping cells behind the work-rooms were not available to central surveillance.[61] Moreover the 'Panopticon plan is spoken of as a thing of his', that is, James Adam's, 'executing at Edinburgh and by him'.[62] During this translation from principle to realization, both the principle and the property were, disastrously, lost.

Three years before this – Bentham's first great disappointment – Le Roy's essay on hospitals was published. This mentions designs prepared for him by the architect Charles-François Viel (1745–1819) without naming him. According to Viel himself, Le Roy first approached him in 1776 with specifications against which he prepared drawings exhibited when Le Roy first read the essay to the Academy, the next year. Engravings were also prepared, around 1780, but some carry the unusual inscription 'Imaginée en 1773': the year was critical for 'our expert' ('notre savant'), as Viel would sardonically call him, and his quest to have himself acknowledged as the inventor of the pavilion-ward plan.[63] The prints had been shown to the Academy (Le Roy explained) several times since 1777. In these exhibitions accompanying the reading of the text – as now, in the publication of the text – they also made further explanation of the project's 'details' unnecessary.[64] Like Reveley's model, the prints made after Viel's drawings were ornamental, but in the important sense of supplementary to and also a manifestation of the principle that is panoptical in one case, ventilative in the other. Like it, too, they would be intelligible, imparting a ready and thorough (as Bentham explained the model) understanding that included all the details. The fact that Le Roy's details extended to entire buildings not mentioned in his essay presents no difficulties to this rather rarefied understanding of ornament. Nor, apparently, did it bother Le Roy.[65]

Angry, ironically enough, about his years of anonymity in connection with the development of a plan type that had remained the ideal in France, though one still unrealized, Viel published his own assignment of relative responsibilities in 1812. Le Roy, he wrote, had in 1776 given him a *programme* for a particular site on the river and 'comprising every desideratum for the salubrity of a hospital for 4,000 patients'.[66] Single-storey wards arranged in parallel blocks, the numbers to inhabit each, eight wards for contagious and surgical patients, and the method by which all was to be ventilated: these were specified, too. 'So much for the scientist's part' ('Voilà ce que appartient au savant').[67] The wards, and their mutual isolation, comprised Le Roy's sole interest, wrote Viel, at the expense of every single service on which a hospital depends. More fundamentally,

> This explanation became necessary in order to clarify what constitutes a work of architecture, which never belongs, as a composition, to the programme's author, because the arts of design do not express themselves in any way by *words*. Certainly, the art-school professors who dictate the painting, sculpture, and building programmes to be composed by their students exercise no claims over the works submitted to them. How, then, to explain the pretensions of the experts who have written on hospitals, who dare to call the creation of plans, of elevations and sections: their projects![68]

Viel was by then the most active hospital architect in Paris, and one of France's principal theoreticians of architecture. He had acquired a violent distaste for its descent into the purview of 'des ingénieurs, des calculateurs, des mécaniciens': 'architecture is an art and not a subsidiary of the exact sciences.'[69] The protest was fuelled, not just by a notable conservatism watchful for any sign that French architecture was running off the classical rails, but by a peculiar professional frustration. This was an intelligent attempt to turn the tables, to make the architects the proprietors, and to restore architectural manifestation to that which is irreducible to words. Viel was in effect redefining the words as the ornament, which, however serious, remains essentially supplementary.

Natural architecture

In 1817 the phrenologist J. G. Spurzheim exploded,

> Who shall make the plan? Who shall decide on its adoption? The architect, who is fond of his art, and likes to display architectural beauties, fine columns,

and external decorations? Or he who is ignorant of the human mind in its state of health and disease? Or medical men, who have paid particular attention to insanity?

Five rhetorical questions, with more or less venerable rhetorics behind them; that of the architect's narcissistic display was older than that of his authority over medical architecture, and here asylums. A few pages later, Spurzheim began to answer them:

> I declare not beautiful architecture, not fine columns, superb staircases, lofty domes, external decorations, magnificent committee rooms, to which my attention has often been called when I visited public establishments, but quite other requisites of a madhouse, seem to me the most essential.[70]

What was he talking about? James Lewis's new Bethlem (Figure 78) had opened in Southwark two years earlier with a dome and a giant Ionic portico whose indecorum, and worse, raised some eyebrows. The French specialist J.-E.-D. Esquirol told a Scottish visitor in 1818 that (as the latter reported it), Lewis's building had a 'sunk floor & too much sacrificed to outward show'; Esquirol may even have believed the defects connected, that classical proportioning had dictated a basement storey, to which Bethlem's incontinent patients were consigned. The architect James Bevans had reported to the parliamentary committee investigating asylums that the shade of that 'immense' portico thrust some rooms into gloom, in a diagrammatic opposition of ornament and use.[71] One of Spurzheim's targets was certainly the Edinburgh Asylum (Figure 79) designed by Robert Reid (1776–1856) and opened in 1813, to which he obliquely referred as the £8,000 building for thirty rich patients, which could not yet afford to admit the poor. (Nor could it for a long time after.)[72] Similar concerns were expressed about Glasgow's, another domed asylum (Figure 80), designed by William Stark (1770–1813) and which had opened after four years of construction in 1814.[73] So Spurzheim's target was at least one egregious failure of charity. More generally, his vehemence was fuelled by the ways in which hospitals for the mad had been construed over the previous thirty years. Their distinctiveness, which had quite a lot to do with rich patients, had specific implications for the understanding of ornament's, and architects', functions at asylums.

Tenon's *Mémoires* (1788) on the Parisian hospitals includes three designs of his own. Those for general hospitals on the La Roquette and central Paris sites were 'shelters', 'mere auxiliary means that help the prescribed regimen and promote the effects of medications',[74] at least by implication: however carefully he directed their planning towards the rational splendours of salubrity and convenience, they could be no different from the existing hospitals that he characterized in this way. But asylums must be inherently different, *in themselves* remedies, with the internal galleries and external promenades that his plan shows. For the first and paramount therapy for the madman is to offer him a 'certain amount of freedom and ensure that he may give vent to his natural impulses in moderation'; 'he should be able to leave his cell, walk around the

78. Thomas H. Shepherd's perspective of 'New Bethlem' in Southwark.

gallery, go to the promenade and take exercise that relaxes him and that nature requires'. For this reason, Bethlem and St Luke's (the 'two best designed mental hospitals that we know of') were his models.

The distinction is illogical. Galleries and promenades are no different from (say) rooms for fumigating the clothes of patients newly admitted to a general hospital; both promote cure. But one may be understood as positively doing so, and the other negatively, in thwarting the contagions carried by dirty garments. In imaginative terms, the difference between the shelter and the remedy, the passive and the active, is striking, and the prestige of the *Mémoires* helped to ensure the durability of this understanding of the asylum. There were other, broader-based pressures to encourage it: the asylum's centrality to the practice of what would eventually be called psychiatry, and in that practice an increasingly explicit faith in psychological management, and in particular that of the patient's emotions.

'Hospitals were not central to the professional lives of most medical practitioners, and they were certainly peripheral to the great Enlightenment project of keeping entire populations healthy and reproducing.'[75] They could also be understood as unnatural and even deadly. Psychiatry's very rise as a profession, roughly in the century from 1750 to 1850, was however indissoluble from the asylums which, Roy Porter has written, 'were not instituted for the practice of psychiatry; rather psychiatry was the practice which developed once the problem of managing asylum inmates arose'.[76] However else they were construed (as arenas for callous curiosity, for example) the asylums, unlike general hospitals, were

79. Reid's 'Sketch shewing the range of buildings which form one side of the square' of the Edinburgh Asylum. In the ground-floor 'arcading' Reid used the kind of lunettes thought so characteristic at, and of, the younger Dance's St Luke's.

never figured as buildings battling their own ostensible function, and lively hopes were entertained of them. Esquirol wrote in 1817 that, although the conversion of existing buildings was often proposed, asylums must be built entirely new, for a combination of new and old buildings would 'lack symmetry, the necessary sub-divisions'. The planning 'is not at all a trivial thing, to be left up to the architects'.[77] Least trivial of all were the subdivisions, the binary classifications: male, female; incurable, curable; violent, peaceable; dirty, clean.[78] Whatever the strengths of the physician's prognostic or 'taxonomic impulse',[79] architecture was of central importance to management, and hence to cure.

Encouraged by civic and maybe personal rivalry, two Scottish architects took precocious advantage of subdivisions. The first stone of the Royal Edinburgh Asylum for the Insane was laid in 1809. That year saw the publication of an *Address to the public* of the usual sort, but also of Robert Reid's *Observations on the structure of hospitals for the treatment of lunatics*, an explanation of his asylum given a universal title.[80] His inspiration was William Stark's similarly titled *Remarks on the construction of public hospitals for the cure of mental derangement*, first published in 1807, which incorporated an oblique criticism of Reid's project. Both architects were attentive to surveillance as well as classification, though with very different results. Reid envisaged a quadrangle around a court with, on each face, a three-storey central block linked by lower wings to two-storey corner pavilions (Figure 79), along with three detached garden blocks.[81] Stark sought to effect the isolation of patients of different sex, social class, and clinical state – sixteen subdivisions – in four ward blocks radiating from a domed hub (Figure 80).

Stark's book was unprecedented, and is remarkable for its graphic presentation of the patient categories, in a ground plan and in the 'General View of the Plan of Classification, and of the Distribution of Classes', a table showing each category's distance from the centre of the Asylum, and from the ground, its direct mapping 'into space and form'.[82] The table was also displayed in Glasgow's Tontine Rooms along with Stark's designs for the building, which was in this way made both intelligible and imaginatively captivating. The Asylum's annual

80. A detail of the frontispiece from Stark's book about the Glasgow Asylum. The dome rises above the flat roofs of the ward-arms; mostly glass, it represented a considerable technical feat.

reports pay unusually close attention to its architecture, too: that of 1814 describes the inspection to which Stark's project had been subjected by the public, by gentlemen 'skilled in different departments of business', and by doctors. It permitted a 'very minute classification of patients, according to their different characters, and the degrees of disease . . . as completely as if they lived at the greatest distance'.[83] The 1817 report mentions the 'frequent applications' made by 'Gentlemen engaged in erecting other asylums' for information about Glasgow's, but also the need for an entirely separate building for 'Incurables, Idiots, and Patients habitually noisy'.[84] More facilities joined the list, including a chapel, billiard room, and work-rooms, the latter for patients of the lower ranks. Above all the Asylum required more places for patients of higher ranks. Stark had imagined enlargements made simply by lengthening the wings, but this would not quite do.[85]

That mad persons of standing, or their family or friends, were prepared to pay for a higher standard of accommodation than charity allotted had long been evident, in Glasgow and everywhere else, and in arguing that madness requires the asylum, medical men encouraged them to do so. James Currie, physician at the Liverpool Infirmary, whose associated asylum would open three years later, explained in 1789 that normally the 'rich may have every assistance in their own homes, but under insanity, relief can seldom be obtained but from an establishment for the treatment of this particular disease'.[86] All species of accommodation for the insane – in general hospitals, private madhouses, and the new charitable foundations – were susceptible to fee-specific gradations. In contrast to most other kinds of patient, the insane often paid, and often at different rates.

Fee scales were therapeutically justifiable, particularly as an associationalist psychology began to permeate theories of asylum management: given lunatics' propensity to draw faulty conclusions on the basis of external stimuli, their environment had to be unambiguously soothing, and other patients formed part of the environment.[87] The Glasgow Asylum's report of 1816 boasts of 'no fewer than six keepers for seventy-three Patients': keepers could doubtless be spared if the patients were sometimes locked up or chained, 'but, instead of being a dwelling of comparative comfort, the Asylum would then put on the appearance of a Jail; Patients would become sullen or vindictive, and the chance of recovery reduced almost to nothing'.[88] Sullenness contributed as much to the appearance of a jail as the iron bars which John Bevans and William Tuke disguised within wooden sashes at the York Retreat.[89] The most important aspect of the cure, wrote E. P. Charlesworth of the Lincoln Asylum, is the 'absence of excitement, or of terrifying, loathsome, and degrading association'.[90] The Edinburgh Asylum provided large rooms with fireplaces in the corner pavilions of the main building as well as the garden blocks for patients of the highest class; there '*persons* whose friends object to their associating with the *patients*' (Reid made this interesting distinction) might keep 'servants' from the institution, carriages, and other conveniences.[91]

The presence of the affluent came to be susceptible to philosophical glosses too. Asylum fees had for half a century been presented as helping to subsidize the care of the poor, in an economic order whose naturalness was suggested by the asylum's very singularity in receiving the rich,[92] when W. A. F. Browne's well-received *What asylums were, are, and ought to be* (1837) explained that the pauper cannot desire, nor benefit from, the

> refinement and delicacies essential to the comfort, and instrumental in the recovery of the affluent. Most fortunately this arrangement, which is called for by the usages of society, is found to correspond with those higher and less artificial distinctions which are dictated by philosophy.[93]

In institutions run on more or less explicitly familial lines, what was also represented was the family of man. There the 'lower orders of society could coexist in harmony and tranquillity with their betters'[94] though not in proximity: for Browne (1805–85), the old ideal of the extended rural household offered the closest model for this society, which was both integrated and stratified.

Asylum appearances mattered in the same way that their plans did; actively, instrumentally, in themselves therapies. Hospital reformers' redefinition of apparent luxury as useful ornament (spaciousness, for example) was extended at this, the first institutional type intended to attract a middle-class clientele. Yet asylums remained liable to the powerful conviction that ornament is always purchased at the expense of utility, exteriors at the cost of interiors. Appearance is there to be distrusted, or at least appearance making no concession to this prejudice: Dance's characterful lunette windows at St Luke's were admired, but new Bethlem's giant portico was not. Even for a sympathetic audience, it was important to make the usual disclaimers. 'The Building though striking is plain. It was the wish of the Committee to avoid, on the one hand, unnecessary expense, and on the other, a mean and sordid appearance': this is the last we hear of sordidness in this, the Glasgow Asylum's annual report of 1814, but there is plenty to explain the expenditure. It goes on to acknowledge that the 'dome alone, on the head of ornament, can be supposed by any person liable to objection'.[95] But, it is to be considered, that . . . [the] dome contributes to render the whole more airy and open; that some little expense should be allowed to the architecture of a building, which is to last for ages; that a good moral effect is produced on the public mind by the combination of pleasure with utility; and lastly, that as the expense of the Institution was chiefly to be defrayed by the board of wealthy patients, the external appearance should be such as would attract the attention and correspond with the habits and feelings of persons of this description.[96]

The dome is doing a lot here: promoting airiness, confirming the Asylum's status as a public work that will 'last for ages', even effecting general public improvement. It will, finally, attract the wealthy patients whose fees will support the whole, and correspond to their habits and feelings. In the event, they and their friends remained unconvinced. The report of 1820 explains that it was the lack of 'two or more apartments, connected together, and detached from the common wards' that had prevented several 'Patients of high rank from being placed in the Asylum. To accommodate such Patients, cottages, with small gardens attached to them, would, probably, be most suitable',[97] on the Edinburgh model.

It was cottages, sometimes for the lower classes of patient, and not domes that held their place in a literature that increasingly figured the asylum as a rural village, or estate. Why rural? For so many reasons that one scarcely needed to adduce (as one French medical reference work did) the ancients' prescription for nervous disorders: frequent walks in gardens whose aromas and emanations soothe the senses, and which provide delightful views 'without offering the picture of physical and moral misery' associated with animal existence.[98] The old conviction that madness was a disease of civilization remained durable in the nineteenth century; Browne was among those who thought that the rural poor were largely immune.[99] The afflicted must be removed from the city's curious eyes – Bethlem had a lot to answer for – and, equally, from the painful associations of home and family.[100] Rural sites were cheap, and for the lower ranks enabled the kind of work on which great therapeutic, and sometimes economic, hopes were placed. It was non-industrial, even natural work, domestic for the women, agricultural or horticultural for the men; everyone had something to do in these great households.[101] The asylums represented a retreat to the past, as well as a retreat to the country.[102] The land, finally, offered the kind of apparent freedom of which Tenon had written, the views through grilles, or over the sunken or otherwise obscured fences on which asylum planners laid such stress.[103] 'This degree of harmless freedom', wrote Browne, referring in part to the freedom to view, 'tranquillises them amazingly'.[104] Like the Glasgow dome and the York Retreat's windows, the vistas would obviate the sensation of confinement, though now by omitting the architecture entirely. Depending on one's social class, the asylum was to be pastoral (easy) or georgic (productive); more radically, it was Edenic, the 'garden without a building', and a garden that would heal.[105]

Alberti had famously distinguished beauty and ornament in a way that underlined the superfluity (though by no means the worthlessness) of the latter.

> Beauty is that reasoned harmony of all the parts within a body, so that nothing may be added, taken away, or altered, but for the worse. . . . ornament, rather than being inherent, has the character of something attached or additional.[106]

Tenon's distinction, in his letter to Dance, between the arrangement governed by 'principle' and the construction and decoration determined by the art of the architect, is analogous, but he moved principle out of the architect's province, and into the physician's. Spurzheim's contrast of 'display' and essence (as in 'essential') went even further, pushing essence right outside architecture itself. He wanted something for asylums that was not architecture; in fact, it was nature.

> A building which costs a hundred thousand pounds is of less use than another might be which would cost half the sum, if the other half was expended in the purchase of fields surrounding it. To what purpose does ostentation with respect to walls, columns, and other architectural beauties, lead![107]

Nature was useful, and architecture was ornamental. Spurzheim reached the final terms of an analysis that had more or less explicitly directed rhetoric about hospital construction over the previous century.

Chapter 10
First principles

In a song written around 1785, William Blake satirized the mythology of hospitality, in one of its urban species. Mayor and aldermen sit down to a great feast and 'The hungry poor enter'd the hall, to eat good beef & ale.' The refrain is, 'Good English hospitality, O then it did not fail!'[1] Though not ironic, the words sung (to the tune of 'The Roast Beef of Old England') at Richard Arkwright's annual workers' feast in 1778 are equally knowing, equally conscious of a threadbare rhetoric:

> Ye Hungry and Naked, all hither repair,
> No longer in Want don't remain in Despair
> You'll meet with Employment, and each get a Share . . .

The song ends,

> To our noble Master, a Bumper then fill,
> The matchless Inventor of this Cotton Mill,
> Each toss off his Glass with a hearty Good-will,
> With a Huzza for the Mills now at Cromford
> All join with a jovial Huzza.[2]

The intensity of the song's story of want and rescue is notable, as is the straightforward relocation of hospitality from the hall to the mill. Upon his death in 1792 Arkwright left 'manufactories the income of which is greater than that of most German principalities' and real and personal property worth half a million pounds. The great man's own house, Willersley Castle at Cromford, was predictably called pretentious; no hospitable charity there, in other words.[3]

The very old critique of misappropriated or 'idle' (as Isaac Ware called it) domestic ornament had acquired some urgency in England in the 1730s, as Chapter 4 here describes. 'Mr Alderman *Pantile* . . . for these 30 Years past has been building himself a Palace in the Country': so witty 'Jenny Downcastle', in the *Universal Spectator* (1732). With the help of 'Mr *Afterthought* his Undertaker', Pantile has muddled away more Money under-ground in Aqueducts, &c. than would set an Hospital for *Incurables* upon it. There's not a Gate-Post near the House, nor a Broomstick in it, which is not turn'd or carv'd, according to some of the *Five Orders*: But his only Daughter is denied every Accomplishment, because her Shape, forsooth, inclines to the *Tuscan*.[4]

Pantile loves dead 'Stones and Dirt' at the expense of 'rational and breathing Edifices', that is, podgy daughters and the sick poor. But it was arguably hospitals, not houses, which then began to prompt the most pointed and interesting varieties of this anxiety about architectural luxury, because there it seemed the antithesis of life itself, and not just of love. Unlike the stereotypical citizens, the hospitals moreover forestalled objections, even answered back, but within the same frame of reference: were they to deny the poor the God-given 'luxuries' of air, light, cleanliness? This is not to say that houses disappeared as targets. One meets more aldermen, proud to decorate their suburban 'boxes' with pictures of London's public buildings (now we know where all the prints went),[5] and James Raven has shown how by the end of the century they were joined by manufacturers like Arkwright, Wedgwood, the Strutts, and the Whitbreads, and by the returned India men, the nabobs. These were the '*new men*', the horde (it was explained in 1789) ejecting the 'ancient families' and demolishing their 'venerable mansions of antiquity' to replace them with 'what seemeth good in their own eyes of glaring brick and ponderous stone'.[6] Despite the interest of its implications, the rhetoric itself, the denunciation of ignorant extravagance, again seems less vital than that produced by the new barbarians' institutions, notably William Strutt's Derby Infirmary.[7]

The Infirmary incorporated a pioneering system of heating and ventilation whose gradual but ultimately spectacular breakdown took the entire fabric with it. Not for Derby the qualified approval occasionally bestowed on old hospitals by late nineteenth-century memorialists who found, in the building about to be replaced, something congruent with the new one they were celebrating.[8] In 1891, a booklet marking the commencement of Young and Hall's great new pavilion hospital at Derby described how Strutt's 'complicated system of ventilation and warming . . . ceased to be understood, the key to it being lost as the years progressed and the personnel of the establishment altered':[9] a *fin-de-siècle* vision of a building in regression. Jeremy Taylor used the story of the Infirmary, its decline and its rebirth in the pavilions, to begin his book (1991) about nineteenth-century English hospital and asylum architecture; it is a kind of parable about modernity's evanescence. For all the Infirmary's innovations and idiosyncrasies, however, we can trace in its planning themes that have been our concern, though now with some ironic reversals.

Radical charity

Blake's song about good old English hospitality is prefaced by another whose subject was not so well defined by custom (both appear in his fragmentary novel now called *An island in the Moon*). This charity's recipients are vaguely indicated, but the nicely named Obtuse Angle describes their new house with precision:

'For he did build a house
'For aged men & youth
   'With walls of brick & stone.
'He furnish'd it within
'With whatever he could win
   'And all his own.

'He drew out of the Stocks
'His money in a box,
   'And sent his servant
'To Green the Bricklayer
'And to the Carpenter:
   'He was so fervent.

'The chimneys were three score,
'The windows many more,
   'And for convenience
'He sinks & gutters made,
'And all the way he pav'd
   'To hinder pestilence.

'Was this not a good man,
'Whose life was but a span,
   'Whose name was Sutton, –
'As Locke, or Doctor South,
'Or Sherlock upon Death,
   'Or Sir Isaac Newton?'

Here charity is 'simply a building programme', as Heather Glen has explained, and even that activity is displaced on to the servant, and to the bricklayer and carpenter in turn.[10] The programme can hinder pestilence with the chimneys, windows, and gutters that it reckons so carefully, but like Mr Pantile's villa, Sutton's house is seemingly the necessity, its inhabitants merely contingent.

Blake alluded to an old philanthropy: Sutton is Thomas Sutton, founder of London's Charterhouse. The song however chooses modern hygienic prophylaxes for its mockery of materialism – Sutton might not have got the joke, that is, even if he were so inclined – and Blake was not alone in his antipathy to institutional, and especially residential, charity. In later eighteenth-century England, 'legal charity', that extended by the Anglican-dominated parochial system under the terms of the Poor Law, was the biggest target for 'radical rethinking about appropriate ways of dealing with poverty'.[11] But charities with chimneys made more visible and satisfying targets.

At the simplest level, an institution's real charitable object was arguably not the poor boy (say), but the established Church. Mandeville called the charity schools a 'Party' phenomenon – 'Educating Children in the Principles of Religion, mean[s], inspiring them with a Superlative Veneration for the Clergy of the Church of England'. In them children are 'taught to serve a party', wrote the 'Rational Dissenter' or Unitarian George Dyer seventy years later, in 1793.[12] One did not need to be unorthodox to see a party at work in residential charities, among which London's 'royal' hospitals and schools were natural exemplars, but criticism might be dismissed on the grounds that one did: the notion that patients were beaten in Bethlem, explained its chronicler Thomas Bowen in 1783, had been 'adopted, chiefly indeed by that class of people, who are most prone to form prejudices against eleemosynary institutions',[13] that is by political or religious dissenters, or both. If we believe Bowen, a general distaste for institutions might be cloaked by objections to specific institutional practices, and architecture. The Unitarian John Aikin's condemnation of quadrangles made by long wards of twenty to fifty beds ('Stagnating air' collects in the quadrangles only to return, less stagnantly, to the wards) is perhaps a condemnation of the royal hospital St Thomas'.[14] His exaggeration, by implication, of the dominance of the quadrangular hospital type is certainly an aspect of his more general summation of hospitals as 'dismal prison[s], where the sick are shut up from the rest of mankind to perish by mutual contagion'.[15] The quadrangles stand in for the deadly enclosure of the hospital as a whole.

'What they saw everywhere they looked was *fever*':[16] Robert Kilpatrick has described Dissent's fascination with the epidemic fever sometimes named for closed institutions (the jail fever) but increasingly understood as not confined to them. Textile mills saw some notable outbreaks in the 1780s, though the isolation of many early factories may have made them seem more institutional than not: some workers, and physicians, believed that these large, hot buildings generated the disease. As their numbers grew they, like fever itself, came to be viewed as an integral part of an urban civilization that many, including mill-owners, believed demanded a medical-policing response more thoroughgoing than a visit from a parish officer, or a letter from an infirmary subscriber.[17] Housing had been an identifiable problem at least since 1719, when the Westminster Infirmary explained that the closeness and unwholesomeness of their homes was often a great cause of sickness among the urban working poor, but now the sickness was specified and so were the closeness and unwholesomeness. Dr John Ferriar (1761–1815) graphically described the two-room basement lodgings with their rear 'cell' in which entire Manchester families slept.[18]

Many Dissenting medical students trained in Edinburgh, whose Professor of Chemistry and later of Physic William Cullen (1710–90) stressed the way that confined spaces refracted fever's manifestations, and multiplied its victims.[19] But there the students also saw fevers hospitalized without catastrophe and, by the 1780s at least, in special wards.[20] In 1803 these were described as 'cleaner and better ventilated than most bed-chambers in Edinburgh'; patients even recovered without medicines. So little did the public fear them, moreover, that a plot of land only big enough for five houses, which adjoined the Infirmary's fever ward for women, fetched the 'amazing sum' of £11,000 at auction.[21] English voluntary hospitals' practices varied, even from year to year, but until the new century most tried hard to refuse cases of what were called the slow, malignant, or contagious fevers.[22] The dispensaries did not. The 'fever that prevails among our poor is remarkably uniform; it is pure typhus', explained the Liverpool Dispensary, which had seen 48,367 cases between 1780 and 1796.[23] Such statistical demonstrations seemed incontrovertible to what was virtually a national network of medical and lay intelligentsia who besides a concern with fever often shared Nonconformity, an interest in technology, and membership of provincial literary and natural-philosophical societies.[24]

At the end of the century some English hospitals began to set up fever wards, if only because cases might unknowingly ('accidentally') be admitted and present a danger to other patients. At the Chester Infirmary (1758–63) they were instituted as early as 1783 by John Haygarth (1740–1827) who, if not himself a Dissenter, was intimate with many. John Howard praised the sweetness of the Chester wards, which did accept patients directly, and quoted the rules ensuring their isolation: 'No fever patients, nor their nurses, are suffered to go into other parts of the house. No other patient is allowed to visit the fever wards'.[25] A notably radical and Unitarian interest at the Manchester Infirmary set up a dispensary there (very unusually) in 1792. A new wing with wards for patients who had contracted fever once inside the Infirmary was opened the next year, and in 1796 a detached 'House of Recovery' – in fact, four small houses – for direct fever admissions. (The euphemism, which became popular, was supposed to reassure those poor who might refuse to enter a fever hospital.)[26] The difference was important for a hospital's potential function as a fire wall against wider contagion. As the Derby subscribers' committee explained in 1805, 'whole families, and on some occasions even a large proportion of Districts, hav[e] by the timely removal of a few Patients, been in all probability removed from destruction'.[27]

John Clark (1744–1805), physician to the Newcastle Infirmary (and co-founder of the Dispensary there, in 1777), however failed to get the wards for 'infectious fevers of accidental occurrence' that he proposed in 1801. The phrase caused him a lot of trouble for a start. Some governors understandably thought that Clark was proposing to admit a few 'accidental' fever cases from among patients already in the Infirmary, not directly and potentially *en masse* from the town. He had used it, he protested the next year, with no intention of deceiving the governors, 'but merely to prevent the agitation of the question of contagion',[28] an explanation that probably just confused them further. With plenty of helpful testimony from the hospital-medical network, including Scottish colleagues, Clark was however arguing that while the disease arose (as some London physicians explained the year before) 'principally from neglect of cleanliness and ventilation', it then often spread by 'contagion introduced by a single person': we see that contagionism and miasmatism had become quite blurred when it came to the fever.[29] And, because this secondary contagion could not travel far through air alone, it followed that distance was not required for its safe containment. The fever cannot, Clark wrote,

> subsist at a few feet from the patients; for, by completely washing them before they are admitted, contagion is either destroyed, or rendered inert; and by ventilation and cleanliness afterwards constantly observed, the effluvia arising from the bodies of the patients are so diluted as to become innocent.[30]

Given this understanding, the Newcastle fever wards could be integral to the hospital's fabric, with their own kitchen and wash-house at the far end of a new extension (Figure 81: so safe was it that it could also have rooms for post-operative patients for whom 'perfect *quiet* and pure air are so essential to recovery').[31] Complete isolation would be effected by walling off the extension's yard and by locking the door between it and the rest of the hospital except when patients were transferred from other wards (access would normally be external). The new wards 'would be possessed of all the advantages of a *distinct* and *separate* house'.[32] But this integration seemed highly undesirable to the Newcastle governors, who instead built a house of recovery which was unambiguously located outside the town wall. The Derby Infirmary, completed in 1809 and opened the next year, however did incorporate its fever house entirely within its tidy frame, though so effectively 'distinct', its planning sub-committee boasted, from the rest of the hospital that it might as well be 'in the next field'.[33]

The Derby Infirmary was the conception of an exact contemporary of Blake's, an inventor and mill-owner like Arkwright. This was William Strutt (1756–1830), a Unitarian as capable as Obtuse Angle of rhyming 'convenience' with the hindering of 'pestilence'. Blake might have despised Strutt and his modest self-identification with Isaac Newton,[34] whose name ends Obtuse's song in order to evoke the foolishness of materialist optimism. However, Strutt did approach hospital architecture with his own species of rational dissent.

The dream of air

Arkwright's sometime partner and William's father Jedediah Strutt also invented, notably the 'Derby rib machine', for ribbed stockings.[35] Such machines were housed in mills of traditional construction, with masonry load-bearing walls and wooden floors on joists and beams. William Strutt's own inventions included nothing less than a new kind of architecture. 'He was the first person', his son explained, 'who attempted the construction of fire-proof buildings on a large scale in this country, and with the most perfect success.'[36] At the Derby Cotton Mill (1792–93) the floors were paved brick arches supported by the walls, cast-iron columns, and plastered wooden beams: no timber was exposed. In 1797, evidently with Strutt's encouragement, his friend Charles Bage also used metal for the beams at his Shrewsbury flax mill, the first iron-framed building. Strutt built the next, the North Mill (1803–4) at Belper near Derby, and continued to work on the technology. But of all his buildings, William Strutt loved the Infirmary best and his wide and knowledgeable acquaintance considered it his masterpiece.[37]

During a stay with the William Strutts in the spring of 1813, Maria Edgeworth (1767–1849), by then a renowned author, was given a comprehensive tour of the Belper mills and the Infirmary along with her father (an old friend of William's) and stepmother. Edgeworth admired good housekeeping, loved machines,[38] and explained what is important to know about the hospital:

> He [Strutt] built it. It is a noble building – as airy and clean as any private house much more so than most private houses – hot air from a *cockle* below

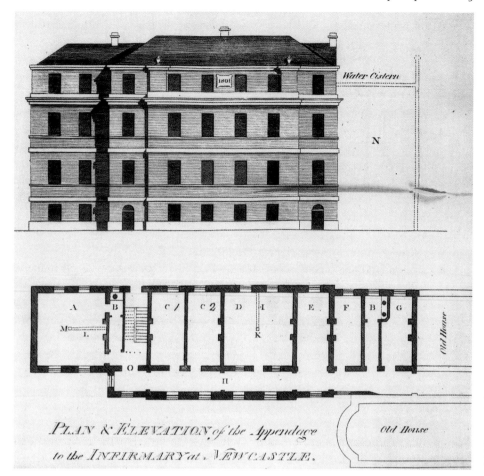

81. The Newcastle Infirmary extension for fever patients, illustrated in Clark's book of 1802. The wards' isolation would be aided by the 'Ventilating cross-gallery', also a dining-room, marked at E on the plan.

conveyed all over the house to produce a healthful and regulated warmth for the whole and any temperature that may be required for patients – the apartments so arranged that by shutting certain doors perfect quiet can be secured for the rest – the fever apartments safe from the rest – many contrivances for cleanliness . . . the effect of which is to make the whole Hospital fresh and free from every disagreeable smell. There are but two or three beds in most of the rooms – several small rooms with one only – Convalescent rooms &c – the kitchen so neat and beautifully useful as that in Mr. Strutts own house –

A domestic comparison was both appropriate and conventional, but this one acquires some resonance from Edgeworth's account, in the same letter, of the magnate's deep embarrassment at the suggestion that he show the guests his own house – in which, she was anxious to explain to her sister, the 'ostentation of wealth' nowhere appeared.[39]

The whole institution is altogether a most noble and touching sight. Such a *great* thing planned and carried into successful execution in a few years by one man! . . . My father declared that if he could have his family with him when ill he would rather be in this infirmary than in his own house.

We can begin with the cockle, which managed to make the Infirmary both warm and airy.

Heat is transmitted in three ways: by conduction, radiation, and convection, that is, by the movement of a heated medium like water or air. Strutt neatly explained the first two – 'Heat is communicated either by contact, or by radiation upon opake substances'[40] – and developed a system based on convection heating, which had been neglected. In this his first consideration was the prevention of fire, that terror of factory-masters especially after 1791, when the giant timber-framed Albion flour mill in London was gutted after a steam engine overheated; the problem also inspired Strutt's innovative construction techniques. A cockle is an iron stove, or furnace. Strutt surrounded his with brick casings with a honeycomb pattern of holes, which reduced the fire risk and allowed the air to be better controlled. At the Derby Infirmary this casing was a cube about four feet high (Figure 82), in turn surrounded by an apparatus of ducts, grates, flaps, and flues to deal with smoke and ashes, and to keep the air's velocity constant as it circulated through the 'hot air chamber' in which the casing stood. The air was drawn from a tower some distance away, whose cowl kept the inlet facing the wind, and thence conducted to the chamber by a long underground 'cold air flue' (seen at the top of the basement plan: Figure 83). Heated by the furnace if necessary (its temperature was already moderated by its passage through the ground), the air rose through great ducts into the hospital. Exhaust air did not recirculate but was carried off through openings in the walls to shafts that ran up to the roof, where another cowl perpetually turned itself away from the wind. This was not mechanical ventilation like Hales's because the air, thus encouraged and tempered, strictly speaking moved of its own accord.

Comparable but simpler systems were being tried at other hospitals and at least one was, like Derby's, directly inspired by innovations at the factories. In 1807, James Clarke of the Nottingham General Hospital boasted that its wards' central heating was 'upon the most improved plan, as used in some of the largest manufactories in Nottinghamshire and Derbyshire', and Robert Bruegmann believes that the system, installed in 1792, was specifically modelled on one in a Belper mill built the same year. Nottingham's wards were 'kept at nearly an equal temperature' (60 degrees F) by means of tubes whose mouths were 'closed by a door of cast iron gradated so as to increase or diminish the aperture at pleasure'. (The need for such traditional warming measures as tobacco, tea, and warm ale was in this way quite avoided, we read.)[41] Clark of Newcastle described the Royal (general military) Hospital at Woolwich, seemingly opened in 1796, and thereafter enjoying spectacularly low mortality rates: one reason was the introduction of 'warm atmospheric air . . . by means of earthen tubes placed perpendicularly', especially helpful for men with chest complaints.[42] Clark himself proposed similar tubes for the Newcastle extension, the plan of which (see Figure 81) carefully indicates (at I and L) those for conveying fresh air into the wards and foul air out, via the chimneys; again, valves allowed them to be opened and shut 'at

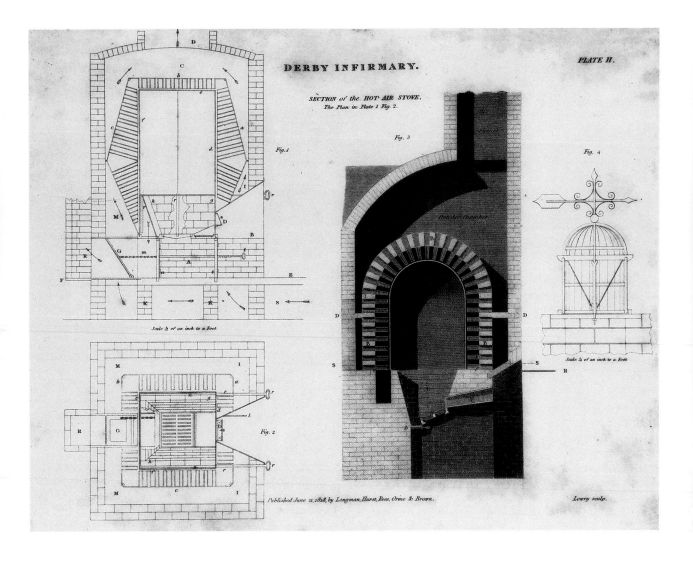

Published June 21, 1818, by Longman, Hurst, Rees, Orme & Brown.

pleasure'. We might ask, whose pleasure? – surely not that of the patients, some of whom might be suffering from 'inflammatory' conditions that required cooling.[43] Though their physicians would understand this, they might not. Ventilation at the Woolwich and Newcastle hospitals was to be encouraged by other means, too: at the latter, opposed windows or at least openings in the walls between the wards and galleries in line with their windows, and ward doors that could be locked back to stop the patients from shutting them.[44] Strutt's combined system did not, astonishingly, require open windows, which would in fact have disrupted the air flow.[45] I guess that patients were not to be tempted to, and in any case could not, disrupt it either.

Knowledge of the air, wrote Edward Foster in 1768, is the paramount qualification for siting and designing hospitals.[46] From an anonymous poet's jocular suggestion, in 1676, that the pure air of Moorfields was itself sufficient to cure the lunacy in Hooke's Bethlem, through Aikin and Le Roy's insistence a century later that free air's antitheses were architects' parsimony with space and fondness for decoration, respectively, we have seen air work hard in rhetoric

82. Charles Sylvester's diagram of the Derby Infirmary's 'Hot Air Stove'. F. D. Klingender described such pictures, made when the 'machines illustrated were still sufficiently simple to enable their construction to be explained with a measure of realism. Hence these old engines appear before us as solid bodies in a vacuum, clean-cut and precise, yet imbued with a strange inner life.'

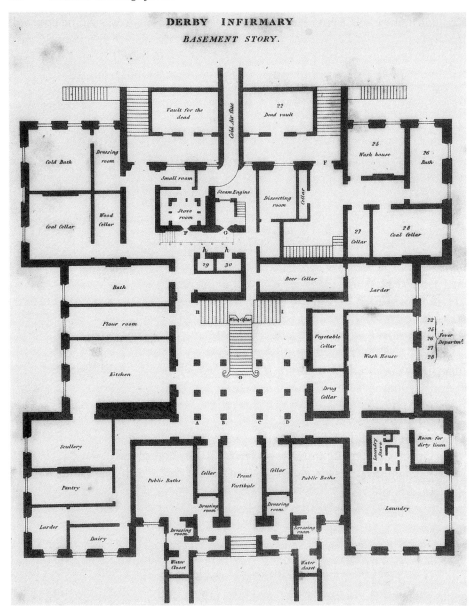

DERBY INFIRMARY
BASEMENT STORY.

83. The basement storey of the Derby Infirmary, showing (bottom centre) the public baths, almost as isolated from the rest of the hospital as the fever department at top right.

about hospitals, too. It had two incarnations: one was rank and stagnant, though capable of devilishly sly and rapid moves, the other sweet and free. This is not to deny that hospitals can stink (nor that there are other good reasons to air them), just to affirm the potency of a theme. Air had as much to do with order – the separation of that which must be kept separate – as with hygiene, and as much to do with the fundamental distinction between God's gifts and man's works as with attempts to order the latter.[47] 'Air, air in motion, air constantly renewed, air moderately heated, is the one central life-giving influence around which all hospital arrangements cluster themselves, and to which all are subservient', wrote one of the five physicians invited, in 1875, to assist in the planning of Baltimore's Johns Hopkins Hospital.[48] By then air was a true cult, with schismatic ritual differences: the relative merits of 'artificial' and 'natural' ventilation was the subject of keen dispute in the second half of the nineteenth century, and it was by proponents of the latter that the Derby Infirmary was condemned.[49]

Back in 1813, Edgeworth saw nobility, and touchingness, in the machines assisting Strutt's flow of air and the others in the Infirmary, which cooked, washed, and rotated lavatory doors.[50] Many were first developed for the textile mills. Strutt's friend Charles Sylvester – they met during the Infirmary's construction – installed the stove in turn at town houses (including Strutt's own), the Maidstone (Kent) Gaol and Leek (Staffordshire) Church, Watson and Pritchett's Wakefield (West Yorkshire) Pauper Lunatic Asylum of 1816–18, where the system was designed together with the architecture, and several ships involved in Admiral Parry's search for the North West Passage.[51] Through Sylvester's *Philosophy of domestic economy* (1819) and its handsome and evocative illustrations (Figure 82, for example),[52] these applications became internationally known. In Boston, Charles Bulfinch underlined passages about the Wakefield system in his copy, and coloured a diagram of flues.[53]

The architect Karl Friedrich Schinkel in 1826 was given almost the same tour as Edgeworth, though George Strutt, the middle brother, politely denied him permission to visit one of his mills. (Prussians had something of a reputation for industrial espionage.)[54] The same day Schinkel's

> request to Mr Strutt's brother [William], also a factory-owner, was, however, kindly received. He showed us his house and his pictures. . . .
>
> Visited the famous Infirmary with Mr Strutt, fine, pleasant building in every way. Magnificent staircase. The steps faced with lead plates. The famous hot-air heating, water-closet with shutters, movement of air in and out of the rooms, the stale air is drawn off by a rotating ventilator on the roof.

Thanks to Sylvester, the Infirmary was by then 'famous', with hot-air heating that was famous too. Under 'Derby', in an itinerary prepared in advance of his English journey, Schinkel listed '*Hospital, Infirmary, Warmluftheizung* [hot-air heating], *Abtritte* [exhaust]'.[55] For him the very town was associated with the Infirmary's air, and not surprisingly. If Hales sought to equip buildings with lungs and a midriff, Strutt made his entire hospital breathe.

The planning of the Derby Infirmary

The Infirmary began with a legacy, as a letter written to the Duke of Devonshire in early 1803 explains: £5,000 had become available for the purpose provided that satisfactory general interest was demonstrated by other donations.[56] Devonshire (he of the almshouse looking too magnificent for charity, described in Chapter 1) headed a long list of benefactors two months later with £2,000; the Duke of Rutland and the Corporation of Derby town followed with £500 each. A general meeting of subscribers in October decided that anyone giving £50 or more was entitled to membership of a committee of subscribers, which would undertake construction, and the brothers William and Joseph Strutt qualified, as donors of a carefully un-ducal £300 each. By February 1804, a site had been acquired; and the subscribers' committee had resolved that at least eighty beds would be provided, with additional accommodation in fever wards (totalling twelve beds) with a separate entrance, as well as two day rooms for convalescents.

Someone present at this last meeting was asked to convey these specifications to John Carr of York, who had already informed the committee that although he was (at the age of eighty) retired from active practice, he would be 'happy to afford . . . the best information in his power as to the most eligible plan for the proposed Building'.[57] Carr had exceptionally wide if not recent experience, having designed the Leeds Infirmary (begun 1768, opened 1771), which both John Howard and Clark of Newcastle had called, as some on the committee surely knew, one of the best hospitals in the kingdom,[58] the York County Lunatic Asylum (1774–77), the Lincoln County Hospital (1776–77) and, exotically, the Hospital of Santo Antonio in Oporto, Portugal (begun 1770). Carr claimed to have toured the principal English hospitals before making the design for Oporto,[59] but its ranges were to line four sides of a huge courtyard, with a grand domed chapel in the centre.

Carr's was a gentlemanly offer (and Lord Vernon of Sudbury Hall was his spokesman). Some of the disillusionment with architects later evident at Derby may already have arisen, as news of a potential commission circulated the previous year. Only a fortnight after the first public meeting George Rawlinson, a local architect, wrote to F. N. C. Mundy, who chaired the subscribers' committee:

> If the Gentlemen will adhere closely to the instruction, that is in my power, to give, and will not be led away with too much advice, which is often the case especially in Building, I will Venture to say, in a Building of that Magnitude, I will save them more than one Thous.ᵈ pound from the Com[mo]ⁿ Mode of Building. I have no other motive whatever, I want but a little, and not that little long. – I wish to be a friend to the Cause . . . [60]

In May 1803 John Rawstorne of York wrote to Mundy introducing himself as a former pupil of James Wyatt's in London and someone experienced in 'several similar Buildings'. Rawstorne's General Infirmary in Sheffield had opened in 1797.[61] A few months later John Simpson of East Retford wrote in response to an advertisement in the Derby papers announcing the committee's intention of taking a plan under consideration, though it was not calling for submissions. Simpson offered 'myself and services' to the committee, explaining that he had been consulted from the inception of the Nottingham General Hospital (1781–82) 'in giving of opinions drawing Plans, and in making Estimates . . . I flatter myself to a general satisfaction of the County at Large, which I refer you to the Several Copys of Letters which were granted me as a Recommendation to similar works.' He also sent a box of 'my manuscripts [and drawings] of what is required in constructing a General Infirmary which I depend on your goodness not to make them Public to an Artificier but for the Perusal of the Committee appointed, only'.[62] Simpson's caution was not unreasonable, but the committee wanted nothing to do with anyone's manuscripts at that stage.

Among the new eighteenth-century hospitals, those in Bath and Liverpool were long unique in having always had purpose-built accommodation. It says something for the general success of the species, however, that later foundations increasingly followed the example set by the Newcastle Infirmary, which upon its establishment in 1751 found a house for the interim but immediately started looking for plans and a site: Carr's Leeds Infirmary building, for example, was begun only a year after the hospital opened. The growing correlation of built form with medical desiderata thereafter seems to have encouraged purpose-building from the outset: the Leicester Infirmary, founded 1766, first opened its doors in Henderson's building five years later, and the Norfolk and Norwich (1770) managed the same within two years. The latter's surgeon Benjamin Gooch boasted of this speed, and in the same breath of the loftiness and airiness of the wards, and their different sizes.[63] By the end of the century this was standard procedure, and between Rawstorne and Simpson (whose Nottingham Hospital was then serving Derbyshire) the Derby committee had available to it direct experience of two new and comparable buildings. (For that matter, through his membership of the Derby Philosophical Society, which subscribed to an impressive range of periodicals, Strutt had the Académie des Sciences' and Le Roy's pavilion plans available to him too.)[64] The sub-committee charged with the actual construction later explained that it had also sought out models, ordering for example a plan of Rawstorne's Sheffield Infirmary on its governors' strong recommendation. This was also standard procedure. What was radical was the sub-committee's accompanying claim, that in the end the Infirmary had to be designed without reference to other hospitals because their architecture made no sense.

As Simpson pointed out, no architect can make a useful plan without clear specifications and a look at the site. However, the subscribers' committee wanted to see what would emerge out of more general directions, to 'leave the candidates to offer what their genius and experience might suggest, rather than fetter them by too minute instructions'.[65] In early 1804 it approved the draft of an advertisement to be placed in the Midlands newspapers:

Derbyshire intended Infirmary

Wanted

Plans of the Building

Any person willing and desirous to furnish such Plans shall receive, for that which may be approved or adopted by the Committee, a premium of 10 Guineas; and for that which may not be fully approved any other remuneration at the discretion of the Committee. The Building is to be of stone – to stand on level ground and to contain Fever Wards having a sep[a]rate Entrance as remote as may be from the principal one (there being convenient access to every side of the building). – The Fever Wards to contain 12 Beds and the whole Building 80 at least. Besides the usual accom[m]odation of an Hospital it is also intended to have two day rooms for the use of convalescent patients, viz., one for those of each sex.

No elevations sections or estimates of the intended Building are at present wanted as they will be expected only from the Candidate whose plan may be most approved or adopted.

The day rooms and the fever wards constituted accommodation not then usual to a general hospital. Competitors were expected to know what was usual, but also to apply their genius, as well as their experience.

Joseph and William Strutt attended every committee meeting; in April 1804 George came to his first, and it was William and George, along with a Dr Forestor (or Forester) and another who constituted the sub-committee reviewing the submissions, which met four days after the deadline. Four months later, in August, it reported that after examining fifteen entries it had been 'sorry to find'

that some of them are drawn without any knowledge of the subject – some without the requisites pointed out by the advertisement – others very inconvenient extended and expensive, and none of them designed as they conceived on a principle which is consistent with the greatest oeconomy in the construction, with the greatest convenience to the persons officially employed nor with the greatest advantage to the patients.[66]

The committee men were therefore 'under the painful necessity' of rejecting them all, and 'having no hope of better success by the same means, and unwilling to adopt an ineligible plan; they have no alternative but to propose a better'. Publicly, they would take collective responsibility for the Infirmary, but everyone knew that William Strutt was its author.[67] Nine years later he told Maria Edgeworth how some of his fellow-townsmen, well acquainted with his interests, had happily anticipated technical disasters.[68]

The sub-committee described the incompetence of the competition entries in a way suggesting that we might take the Infirmary's construction as a staging of the rhetoric described in the last chapter: that is, as a triumph of medically invested principle over dangerous inconvenience and vain expense. This interpretation is not affected by the Infirmary's idiosyncrasy, which was the result of the real depth of Strutt's radicalism in trying to give built form to his principles of economy and convenience. In the course of that pursuit, architects showed themselves to be over-anxious and over-anxiously bound to precedent: not quite luxury's wayward familiars, then, but none the less incapable of assuming the adult, proprietorial role, at least as far as the committee men were concerned. (One wonders what Robert Adam could have done with them.) The dismissal of precedent in favour of principle made an unusual hospital. The great central stairhall ('magnificent', Schinkel called it) running its full height was abutted by corner pavilions filled with suites of staff rooms and wards. The arrangement is reminiscent of some great house of two centuries earlier, though one more of the prodigal than the proverbially hospitable kind; this was no 'rambling foundation'.[69] The entrance portico however adopted a strikingly up-to-date Greek

Doric order, in consonance with the 15-foot terracotta statue of Æsculapius standing on the roof ridge (Figure 84. Æsculapius presented a technical challenge of his own to Derby manufacture: the first version exploded during firing.) When it 'resign'ed' the building into the hands of the subscribers, in June 1809, the committee explained that there had been 'very little expended in what is *ornamental*, and nothing spared to render it substantial and *useful*'.[70]

The 'leading principle' of the Derby sub-committee's work had been 'speedy and effectual relief' for the sick, and five means were applied to achieve this end, according to its manuscript report of August 1804.[71] These were the suites of small wards, and the provision of day rooms, the ventilation and heating system, an improved type of water closet, and a 'distinct', though not detached, fever house: Edgeworth would remark upon them all. Mundy, on behalf of the larger subscribers' committee, summarized the five desiderata in a printed *Report* of the following March, which reiterates that 'buildings of this kind are far from having arrived at that degree of perfection, which might be wished or expected'. Hence, even the best of the competition plans 'very much resembled, and had no advantage over similar Institutions'.

The first of the means was explained this way in 1804: it consisted in

providing a suite of small wards for each sex containing one, two three and four Beds in each Ward together with a lodging Room and scullery for the Nurse and also a Water-Closet all sep[a]rate from each other but very near together and contrived to be shut off from the general Noise of the House so as to be perfectly quiet and retired.[72]

84. The Derby Infirmary, in the frontispiece to Sylvester's *The philosophy of domestic economy* (1819). Figures 85 and 86 show that some windows were false. They were not needed for ventilation, but appearances had to be maintained.

The arrangement is apparent on the plans Sylvester published in 1818 (Figures 83, 85 and 86). Such small wards would permit the separation of 'acute from chronic diseases and the former from each other as may suit the nature of their complaints':

> The advantage of such a disposition, over that of assembling the acute and chronic diseases, the sickening, the dying and the convalescent, all in one large room day and night, as is the general practice, is too obvious to require further notice.

The *Report* published the next year added surgical and medical to the mix, but omitted the dying and the convalescent; it had already described the latter's accommodation, and the former are seldom mentioned by hospital promoters.

The passage just quoted is not precisely misleading, but its phrasing is a little hectic. The image of the large but over-populated room went back to Aikin. In its new displays it joined an increasing interest in the distribution of patients 'according to similarity of disease and wants' (the Newcastle reformers, surely the Derby builders' major inspiration, in 1801) or 'according to their different characters and the degrees of disease' (the General Committee of the Glasgow Asylum, in 1814),[73] and the concern about fever, whether accidentally occurring or not, in hospitals. Margaret DeLacy has shown how theories of disease transmission might suggest ward arrangements: if one understood the atmosphere as the leading agent, then easy cleaning and ventilation were of paramount importance; but if personal contact, contagion, was assigned an important part too, small wards were desirable and single-bed wards best of all.[74] These requirements were however reconcilable, particularly if ventilation were assisted, and this was just as well given that both miasmata and contagion were known to be at work in many disorders. The solution was for a while obvious, and not unprecedented. Though most kept quieter about such provision than the Edinburgh Infirmary did, Tenon saw a number of small wards used for 'contagious', including venereally diseased, patients at English hospitals. He admired, too, the sixty-four four-bedded wards in James Stuart's Infirmary building (1763–64) at Greenwich, which was thoroughly described in John Cooke and John Maule's *Historical account* of the hospital (1789).[75] Stuart's infirmary owes much to that projected by Hawksmoor decades earlier, but both adhere, in general terms, to the planning of Greenwich's residential blocks, whose small rooms Aikin had praised.[76]

'It would be a real improvement', wrote Dr Walker of Leeds to John Clark, if his two eleven-bed wards could be

> divided, not only for the sake of more free ventilation, but because the particular distress of individuals must render more disagreeable the situation of the other patients; and in case of accidental infection, such large wards are extremely inconvenient.[77]

In addressing the President and directors of the as yet unbuilt Massachusetts General Hospital in 1817, Bulfinch recommended small wards, as 'much more agreeable to the domestic habits of our people, to the feelings of the sick and their friends'. Small wards had many advantages, therefore, and, as Bulfinch also explained, a significant disadvantage: one needed more nurses.[78] Clark was not allowed his fever wards, but the Newcastle extension's wards were small, and those in the old building were converted to other uses or subdivided to take no more than seven beds each. In 1852 the Newcastle governors, however, enlarged their turn-of-the-century wards, joining a trend under way well before Nightingale's first interventions in hospital design at the end of the 1850s, but confirmed by her championship of the thirty-bed ward. Long, thin wards permitted nurses' efficient management of patients, something that for her was bound up with the direct benefits of rows of large, opposed windows.[79] Nightingale was a root-and-branch miasmatist.

In Derby, back in 1804, the second means of speedy and effectual relief was the insertion of day rooms where convalescents might dine and sit, a proposal that (the sub-committee remarked) had already attracted favourable notice from the 'best judges in these matters'; Howard had also recommended them and the Newcastle extension (Figure 81) included them.[80]

> The third improvement proposed, and which has long been a desideratum in buildings of this nature, consists in a [*simple* is here added, in another hand] means of compleatly & perpetually ventilating every ward with fresh unvitiated air, at the same time increasing the temperature [added, *by a small expence*] to any given degree [here deleted, *and at the expence of one small fire only for the whole building*]. The effecting of this object it is believed by the physicians would generally expedite the recovery and sometimes preserve the lives of the patients.

This is the ventilation and heating system.

The next improvement was to the water-closets which admittedly, the sub-committee explained, did not affect 'health and life' like the previous one, but were quite capable of nuisance. The modesty of the proviso is undermined a little by the gusto with which the improvement is presented. By a 'simple construction', the committee had rendered the closets

> so perfectly unobjectionable that if one of them was purposely filled with a suffocating vapour, that vapour, so far from entering the House, would not [*soon* is deleted] be perceived [added, *even in the Closet*] by a person entering immediately afterwards.

The Derby water-closets had doors with two leaves at a 45-degree angle within a curved alcove (seen in Figures 85 and 86). Both entry and exit forced fresh air into the cubicle, and departure also triggered the flushing of the cistern. The improvement was probably inspired by Howard. An automatically flushing Bramah toilet, which he commended, had been installed at Guy's Hospital around 1770; flushing, like keeping a window open, was considered to be beyond the ken of some patients.[81] Perfectly unobjectionable closets might be entirely

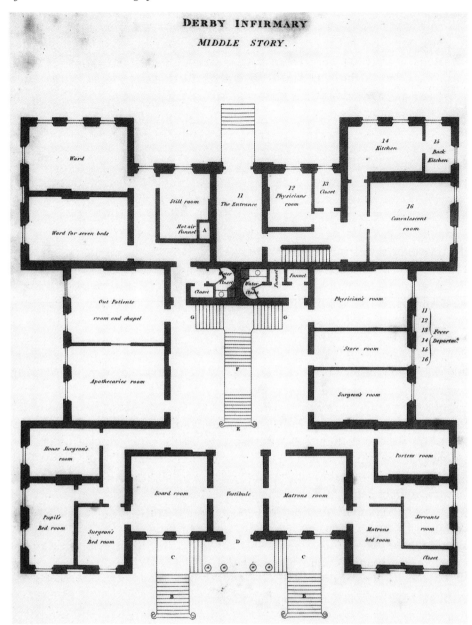

85. The ground ('middle') floor of the Derby Infirmary.

enfolded by the building, a distinct departure from what was becoming approved practice,[82] with implications for the hospital's appearance and (in the sub-committee's terms) convenience. Derby's published explanation was, that if water-closets are 'ventilated externally' – that is, by windows cut into the external projections they make – they are often too cold in winter, and anyway the 'draft which should be from the house outwards, is the reverse, especially if the house is warm'. Not since Philanthropus described the Edinburgh Infirmary seventy years earlier had the British public received such a close-grained explanation of a hospital's form.

Finally,

> The fever house, tho' under the same roof, . . . is as distinct from the Infirmary as if it were in the next field – This part of the plan was very awkwardly managed in the designs delivered for want perhaps of a procedure in other Infirmarys.

Organizational precedents were available, but those for fever's management by architecture, strictly speaking, were rarer. Henderson's designs for the Leicester Infirmary (1767–71) show an 'infectious' ward above the kitchen in its small west pavilion (that on the left on Figure 56, p. 140) and in 1803 the corresponding rooms above the east wing brewhouse were prepared for 'accidental' fever cases.[83] These patients could not harm what lay *below* them, or this was the understanding, and these wards were otherwise surrounded by open air; Haslar used at least some of its high wards, similarly isolated, the same way. The proposed Newcastle fever house was illustrated in print and in purely spatial terms Derby's was not dissimilar (though as we will see its sub-committee would have viewed the extravagant length of the Newcastle extension with disfavour). Both involved rooms contiguous with the rest of the hospital but internally accessible to it through only one door, generally kept locked. At Derby, however, the fever house (top right on Sylvester's plans) rose through three storeys and incorporated many services additional to Newcastle's wash-house and kitchens. Truly self-contained, what was by 1818 the fever 'department' has its own keys on the plans, the better for Sylvester's readers to appreciate the ingenuity of its isolation. At its entrance (at '11', at the top of Figure 85) was its physician's room, beyond which was another for convalescents and a kitchen. Stairs led up to four wards on the first floor (Figure 86), and down to the coal cellar, wash-house, bath, and mortuary ('dead vault'), reached by its own flight of steps at the rear of the building (at the top of Figure 83). The internal door was on the upper floor, which held most of the hospital's wards, so transferred patients need not be taken outside.[84] Derby's fever department really did have its own building, though externally it was indistinguishable from the other.

Derby's most radical improvement was however generated by the 'principle' to which Strutt's sub-committee alluded when describing the inconvenience, extent, and expense of some of the plans submitted to it: one 'consistent with the greatest oeconomy in the construction, with the greatest convenience to the persons officially employed [and] with the greatest advantage to the patients'.[85] The next year, the subscribers' committee published its determination that the

> Building is to be of Stone, of a Cubical form, with an elevation handsome, yet simple, and unornamented, and to contain a light central Hall with a double Staircase; this form was preferred from its having more contiguity, and being more convenient and agreeable than the long, and sometimes gloomy passages, which have been so generally adopted. It is worthy of remark that not one of the numerous plans delivered in, [was] designed on the former principle.

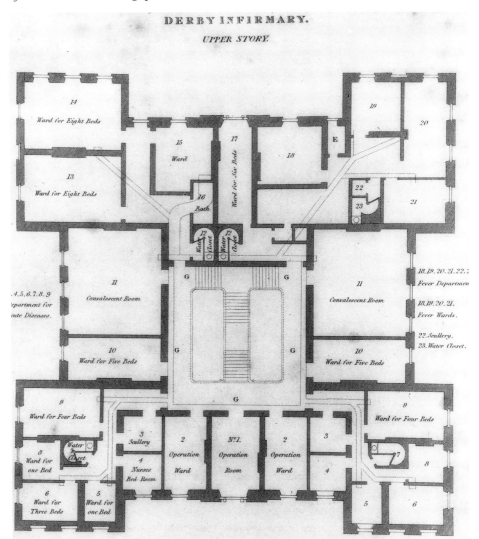

86. The upper floor of the Derby Infirmary, which held most of the wards and, in the centre front, the 'Operation Room'.

The principle is that the nearer a building approaches a square outline, the less masonry and tiling are needed to make it, and the fewer steps needed to get around it. The 'inconveniences of too much spreading are the great charge of wall, and roof', wrote Roger North more than a century earlier; the 'square figure hath most room for least walls'. But as he also wrote, the square 'brings all inconveniences together, as want of light in the mid[d]le'; it will work for small houses, but not for larger, 'which must be spread for air and light'.[86] Strutt made his own air, and the light in the Infirmary's middle would be provided by windows in the roof over the galleried stairhall which was, in human circulation terms, the precise equivalent of other hospitals' long gloomy passages, but more efficient because the distances were much shorter. The Infirmary had 'contiguity'. The logic is hard to fault, and it is unsurprising that the architects failed to hit upon the principle; of all the English hospitals built in the previous half-century, only Salisbury's had a plan remotely like Derby's. To John Syer Bristowe and Timothy Holmes, whose 280-page *Report* on British (and Irish, and Parisian) hospitals was published in 1864, the Infirmary's interior had 'been most ingeniously frittered away in the formation of narrow, ill-ventilated, intricate passages and lobbies'. One man's contiguity became another man's frittering, a quality the Victorians associated only with false economies of space.[87]

Economy, Strutt wrote to his son Edward in 1819, is 'under every circumstance of fortune a virtue, because it leaves more to be applied to better purposes than extravagance'.[88] He was not alone in this particular application of it. In 1812, another 'able engineer', Benjamin Henry Latrobe (1764–1820), wrote in connection with the proposed American naval hospitals that 'with the limited fund of the hospital . . . the first consideration in forming the design was to cover as little ground as possible', something he explicitly linked to ward size: Latrobe would not, he wrote, enter into the medical debate, but he was personally convinced that small wards were healthier, as well as more economical of ground and materials.[89] The intricacy of the Derby plan demanded intricacy in the heating and ventilation system, or perhaps it was the other way around. Nor can we readily assign priority, a determinative score, to the medically approved small wards on the one hand, or to economical snugness on the other.

In presenting more surfaces to external light and air, the extended, even fragmented hospital building was, for its eighteenth- and nineteenth-century students, self-evidently healthier. The type was also easier to construct in stages as funds permitted and demand encouraged, a procedure more common than not in the period. The possibility of undertaking construction in this way was ignored at the Derby Infirmary, which anyway had plenty of funds,[90] and we can see why from Sylvester's plans. Instead, the 1805 *Report* explained, it would simply be built too big, with wards left unfinished and unfurnished until they were needed. The *Report* also showed that a building of the expansive, additive type could itself be construed as wasteful, of building materials in the first instance. Utility, in hospital architecture, was not after all monolithic, except as luxury's adversary.

'Architectural rotondities'

When in 1804 the Derby sub-committee described its refusal to adopt an 'ineligible plan', it explained that this was on account of the 'vast importance of this step in the business, a step which, as it cannot but considerably influence the success of the undertaking in all future time, is worthy of the most deliberate investigation'.[91] The phrasing effectively conflates a plan, a diagram on paper, with the future distribution of actual, built rooms and other spaces, a distribution in turn identified as decisive for the hospital's success in its declared aim of speedy and effectual relief. The conflation was convenient, and the committee's insistence upon the gravity of the plan was not by then remarkable, though it got

very literal illustration when it dissuaded the Derby competitors from sub-
mitting sections and elevations. It is the combination of the stress on the plan
and the identification of a building with a diagram which in retrospect appears
noteworthy, because Nightingale did it to brilliant effect in her *Notes on hospitals*
(1859), a strikingly illustrated paean to simplicity. About a new and unnamed
London hospital, she wrote that 'All is complicated, and there is a want of that
simplicity of plan which is essential to the free circulation of air without as well
as within the sick wards'. She could have been describing the hospital itself, or
her illustration of its 'Plan with closed Courts and double Wards' (as the plate is
captioned); complication was created by lines on paper as much as by masonry
barriers to air on the ground. In the third (1863) edition of the *Notes*, a plan of
the Hôtel-Dieu in Paris as it stood before the 1772 fire provides the 'most remarkable illustration of the effects produced on the sick and maimed by agglomera-
tion'.[92] The ground plan cannot possibly illustrate those effects, but looking at it
with Nightingale, we might think that it does.

Nightingale's stress on architecture's power for good and evil was extreme,
and inseparable from her belief in 'infection' and its transmission: 'Infection acts
through the air. Poison the air breathed by individuals and there is infection.'
Both the emphasis and the belief formed part of her profound need to be useful,
to 'realize all that is right and good . . . by taking God's appointed means'.[93]
Nightingale was an unconventional Christian (as Lytton Strachey remarked, she
sometimes hardly distinguished 'between the Deity and the Drains')[94] but in her
writing we often find something of the biblical cadences and messianic fervour
of a Pringle or a Tilton, the military physicians of the previous century.

Charles Rosenberg has explained the *Notes on hospitals*, that 'sacred text' as
it became, as the shrewd application of an established consensus on hospital
planning, one 'underwritten' by personal witness and the 'new-style plausibility
of statistical analysis'[95] – and, we could add, that of architectural plans. Consensus had already departed from the view of the progressivists of William Strutt's
day, in directing a return to larger wards and in its wariness about reliance on
artificially assisted ventilation at hospitals.[96] Nightingale's precepts about hospital planning, which included the occasional meditation on the humble glories of
tents and huts, were thus closer to Pringle's than to Strutt's, but both men would
have understood the antitheses that structured them. Referring to 'beautiful but
unhealthy buildings', for example, Nightingale described how to cure them:
remove the 'warming and ventilating apparatus' and trust to 'their magnificent
supply of windows for fresh air'. Put open fireplaces into the wards, and forget
the cost of the fuel.[97] Windows and coal make the true magnificence, in opposition to the artifice that will only promote disease. Had Nightingale's principles
not been so firmly embedded in wider moral certainties, Rosenberg suggests,
she would surely not have been able to exert such a singular sway.

Contagion, which 'implies the communication of disease from person to
person by *contact*', was for Nightingale an hypothesis that was absurd, unproven,
and even wicked in its embrace of chance, the denial of the possibility of improvement through conformity to divine (and drainage) law. ' "Contagion" would . . .

shew God a Devil', she wrote; Nightingale variously rejected the contagiousness of syphilis, tuberculosis, and smallpox, let alone the hospital diseases.[98] Time was against her in this respect and at first, it might have seemed, in other respects too. Against her firm advocacy of the pavilion plan and her general conviction that hospitals were, or should be, as difficult to build as pocket-watches (though at the same time *un*complicated in their plans), a powerful alternative began to range itself in the 1860s and this was, simply, to disregard the finer points of hospital planning, or even to ignore planning entirely, on the grounds that it did not in itself make a significant difference to patients' chances of survival.[99] The story is as complex politically as it is medically (and I do not want to end this book by beginning another), but it seems appropriate, now, to sketch the ways in which the moral, as well as medical, anxieties that have occupied so much space here continued to pervade discussions of hospital architecture.

Hospital planning might not matter, first, because all hospitals were pest-houses anyway. Edinburgh's Sir James Simpson (1812–70) used 'hospitalism' to denote the morbidity inescapably generated by congregations of the sick. He acknowledged that the risk was lessened in the best-ventilated hospitals, but maintained that many lives would be saved if hospitals were changed 'from stone and marble palaces into wooden, or brick, or iron villages' of cottages or huts that could be destroyed when necessary. At the end of the 1860s, Simpson's very public call for a return to the hut seemed to pose a real threat to urban-hospital practice, education, and funding: *The Lancet* complained that he was frightening potential donors.[100] In a reaction to it, but also to Nightingale's insistence upon planning's critical importance, the surgeon Timothy Holmes (1825–1907) formally deprecated 'exaggerated' hopes for the number of lives that would be saved by attention to 'details of hospital construction, such as size, cubic space, arrangement of pavilions, ventilation, &c.'[101] Meanwhile Joseph Lister (1827–1912) was claiming that his antiseptic procedures made *all* these details completely irrelevant, in two ways. By treating the wounds whose emanations made the ward airs deadly, he would treat the ward airs themselves, and his carbolic was effective anywhere. 'From first to last he worked in old-fashioned hospitals', as an admirer wrote. What Lister called 'aesthetic' cleanliness, as opposed to the 'surgical' cleanliness he achieved, mattered little too; to the hospital's extreme annoyance he boasted, in 1869, of the (aesthetic) dirt on his wards at the Glasgow Infirmary.[102]

But the attention paid to hospitals' details and aesthetic cleanliness, especially inside operating theatres, became more intense, not less, in a development at first mourned by loyal Listerians. Scholars have shown the alchemy by which his followers and biographers managed to transform Lister's antisepsis, the destruction of infective agents by chemicals, into 'asepsis', their exclusion from the site of the wound, or operating field.[103] The two are antithetical in many respects, not least in their theoretical presuppositions and implications for hospital architecture, but Lister's achievement began to be presented as the first great triumph of asepsis, not its opposite, when after 1900 aseptic procedures were increasingly adopted for surgery. In the early biographies, however, we can still read about the ludicrousness and expense of the paraphernalia they demand: 'sterilizers, autoclaves, mosaic floors, tiled walls, sterilized water, air-filterers', and tennis shoes for surgeons.[104] This 'state of luxurious refinement' extended to 'architectural rotondities' – that is, grandiloquence – and 'mechanical specialities' (G. T. Wrench, in 1913); 'Never before have the architects been more indispensable. The least defect in the condition of an operation-room manifests itself by disasters' (Just Lucas-Champonnière, 1902).[105] The hostility was forgotten when sterilizers and architectural rotundities became facts of hospital life, but in the meantime, during the first two decades of the twentieth century, a debate about surgical procedures prompted the accusation that an architecture so ostentatiously utilitarian was no longer comfortable or natural. The hospital had entered the realm of the Corinthians' square trees and the gilt ceilings they make; it was after all Sutton's house, even Mr Pantile's villa.

Notes

The list of 'Manuscript Sources' contains the full references for the location abbreviations given in the notes. With a few exceptions (some periodical references appear in the notes in full) the full references for all other sources appear in the list of 'Works Cited'. Where translations are mine, the original texts are given in the notes.

Introduction

1. Boswell [1906], 2: 442.
2. Goldin's earlier work has been supplemented by the excellent photographs in her 1994 book; Robert Bruegmann's doctoral dissertation of 1976 (1980) is extremely valuable; Dieter Jetter's survey histories (1973, 1981) are very wide-ranging. Important shorter studies include Nikolaus Pevsner's chapter (1979), the essays by Barbara Duncum (1964) and Adrian Forty (1980), and Jacques Carré (1989), the latter's introduction to his edition of Tenon's *Journal* (1992), and the section called 'The sad' in Thomas Markus's book of 1993.
3. Sometime mistress of Rochester and of his master Charles II, Jane Roberts died the next year. Rochester 1980, pp. 197–98, 202; for Leather Lane, Pelling 1986, pp. 86, 87.
4. On this treatment, Bynum 1986; Brandt 1993, pp. 565–66; and (in an important context) Davenport-Hines 1991, pp. 40–42, 48. The symptoms of syphilis were not readily distinguishable from those of gonorrhoea (and from the mercury's side-effects) until well into the nineteenth century.
5. For 'hot-house', Pelling 1986, p. 103 and Keevil 1958, p. 167. Barton, at least, was evidently a real venereal-disease specialist: Rochester 1980, pp. 201, 182. Hunter and Macalpine 1963, p. 317 quote the surgeon Daniel Turner (1724): a poor soul obsessively convinced that he had syphilis, who, 'unknown to his Family, . . . got into some Quack's House, where he was laid down in a Salivation'. On the hospital wards, McInnes 1990, pp. 40–41, 61, 66; Pelling 1986, pp. 97–98, who notes that St Bartholomew's regularly 'overflowed into its own property, allowing rebates to tenants who accommodated the sick', including those with the pox; and Bettley 1984, who describes the hos-

pital's more formally constituted 'outhouses' increasingly used for the purpose.
6. Hunter and Macalpine reprint much English material useful for seventeenth- and eighteenth-century mad-houses; the mad-doctor's (or 'Nurse's') residence seems to be specified in a couple of instances (1963, pp. 105, 157); see also Porter, 'Madness' 1992, p. 279.
7. Hasegawa 1989, p. 157.
8. Lynaugh 1989, pp. 43–44. A visiting physician (quoted Risse 1999, p. 344) was impressed in 1846 by Boston's Massachusetts General Hospital, 'by no means exclusively a charity hospital, but . . . designed also as a resort for all such as are either absent from their homes, or who cannot be well attended to at home'.
9. Risse 1986, p. 139.
10. Hart 1980, p. 453: the regulation was still in force in the 1930s.
11. 'Physical hospital', which emerged in 1720 during the passage of Sir John Addenbrooke's estate to his trustees, is quoted by Hewlings n.d. The nomenclature has not been studied (though see Owen 1964, p. 37 and Porter 1989, p. 150); among the new hospitals, Gloucester's (founded 1754) wavered between 'County Hospital' and 'Infirmary' before settling on the latter (Frith 1961, p. 5), but Norfolk's (1771) did the reverse (Eade 1900, p. 36).
12. For the royal hospitals' politics, Rose 1989. The London Infirmary's switch was apparently prompted by its President, the Duke of Richmond, who was in 1748 'pleased to declare that from the great encouragement now given it, and the extensiveness of its benefits to the poor, it deserved' the appellation, 'Hospital': Morris 1926, p. 73.
13. See Jones 1989, pp. 9–10 (in relation to *hôpitaux généraux*), Spierenburg 1990, pp. 35, 52 (Amsterdam's and Hamburg's prison-workhouses), Houston 1994, p. 25 (Edinburgh's alms- and workhouse), and

Rothman 1990, pp. 42, 53 (colonial American institutions).

14. Defoe 1971, p. 197.

15. Among hospital historians, Charles Rosenberg is distinctive for his interest in the domestic or familial model's government of the physical, as well as fiscal and social, arrangements of older (in his case, American) hospitals: 'Inward vision' 1979, pp. 381–82; idem 1989, pp. 6–8; idem 1995, especially pp. 42, 118–19. Evans (1982, especially pp. 49–53) has similarly shown the architectural implications of the 'literal reinstatement' of the extended, patriarchal household in institutions like Bridewell.

16. Appendix to Foster 1768, pp. 22–23.

17. Quoted Clark, *Report* 1802, p. 211.

18. Aikin 1771, p. 20.

19. Prior has commented on the way that the same architectural form can be 'woven into entirely different [scientific] discourses': 1988, p. 101. More specifically, see Richardson 1998, p. 76 for Chelsea and Greenwich's importance to later military-hospital planning.

20. Quoted Davies 1988, pp. 63–64. For Nightingale's expertise as then perceived and the reasons for the perception, Rosenberg 1995, pp. 128–35; see also Taylor 1997, pp. 12–13, 41 and Brown 1990, pp. 26–27. Strachey wrote that her *Notes on hospitals* 'revolutionized the theory of hospital construction' (1918, p. 162); King 1966, p. 361 comments on this historiographical myth.

21. Godlee 1924, p. 121; compare Granshaw, ' "Upon this principle" ' 1992, p. 18. In 1913 Wrench blamed both anaesthesia and 'industrialism' for the old epidemics (pp. 78, 133–34); Lawrence and Dixey 1992, pp. 174, 183 sketch the historiography of the 'great fevers' in the Listerian context. On what Taylor (1991, pp. 11–15) calls the pressures for architectural change see also Woodward 1974, 'Hospital diseases', pp. 97–122; Cherry 1980, pp. 255–62; and Bynum's excellent survey, 'Science, disease, and practice', 1994, pp. 118–41.

22. *Builder* 14, no. 711 (20 September 1856): 509–11, here p. 509; see also King 1966, p. 364 and Taylor 1997, p. 61. St André was the first full-scale application of the pavilion type: Bruegmann 1976, pp. 72–73, and Foucart 1981, pp. 43, 46–47.

23. 'A chaque époque le programme de l'hôpital c'est l'état de la science médicale': a turn-of-the-century summation that must then have seemed reasonable, as Bruegmann (1976, p. 121, quoting Julian Guadet's *Élements et théorie de l'architecture*, 1901–4) points out in his account of late nineteenth- and early twentieth-century hospital historiography.

24. See Eribon 1993, p. 257 for the genesis of *Machines à guérir*. Foucault et al. 1979, p. 103: 'Certains programmes modernes, certains grands équipements sont apparus presque silencieusement; sans qu'on puisse leur prêter une origine précise . . . c'est le cas

des habitations collectives, de l'école ou encore des bureaux, et c'est le cas le plus fréquent.

'L'affaire des hôpitaux et plus exceptionelle: à partir de 1788, la distribution architecturale qu'adoptera le XIXe siècle est en effet produite et définitivement consacrée. . .'.

25. Bruegmann 1979, p. 211; Forty 1980, p. 61. See also idem 1983 on the fallacy that ideas generate buildings.

26. See Cavallo 1991, especially pp. 50–52 on the problems with analyses that interpret charity as essentially responsive.

27. I am thinking of Ballon (1991), Markus (1993), Stevenson (1993; idem '*Æsculapius Scoticus*' and 'Robert Hooke's Bethlem', both 1996), Richardson and her colleagues (1998), and John Henderson (*The Renaissance hospital*, forthcoming from Yale University Press). Cherry (1980) credits later eighteenth-century English hospital buildings with doing what they were intended to, that is, providing environments healthier than the houses of many sick poor. Carré (1989) draws attention to the importance of Mead's *Discourse* (1720) and Hales's *Description of ventilators* (1743) for contemporary hospital planners, and Risse considers that ventilation was a conscious desideratum at the Edinburgh Infirmary, and generally (1986, p. 30, idem 1999, pp. 242, 429).

28. Laugier 1972, pp. 169–70: 'Les Hôpitaux doivent être bâtis solidement, mais simplement. Il n'y a point d'édifice où la somptuosité soit plus contraire aux bienséances. Des maisons destinées à loger les pauvres, doivent tenir quelque chose de la pauvreté. . . . Tant de magnificence annonce ou beaucoup de superflu dans la fondation, ou peu d'économie dans l'administration; . . . c'est trop de beautés réunies dans une maison qui cesse d'intéresser la charité. . . . Il faut que les pauvres soient logés en pauvres. Beaucoup de propreté & de commodité, point de faste.'

29. Rosen 1968, pp. 166–67 describes *bienséance* as 'not only a significant esthetic criterion but also an important social value' in a culture greatly concerned with disorder.

30. Sekora 1977, pp. 1–2.

31. Examples I've used include McKendrick's essays of 1982, Baker 1995, and Paulson 1995; more generally, Brewer 1995 and idem 1997.

32. In addition to McClung's work (1977, 1981, 1983), see Cast 1984, Howard 1990, Thomson 1993, Saumarez Smith 1990, Gent 1995, Lubbock 1995, and Cooper 1999, the last two notably accentuating what Cooper (pp. 13–18) calls the (positive) 'sanctions for display'.

33. Quoted Slack 1985, p. 223, from the Privy Council's *Rules and orders* published May 1666; he suggests (p. 277) that these together held fewer than 600 persons.

34. Quoted Brings 1986, pp. 259–60.

35. Spurzheim 1817, p. 217.
36. McClung 1981, p. 279; see idem 1983, p. 51 and Freeman 1975, p. 265 for more general and earlier Christian attacks on architectural luxury.
37. North 1981, p. 24n.
38. Ibid., p. 5.
39. *Hospitale* is medieval Latin for a 'place of reception for guests', or a place where hospitality is extended, and in England it was the commonest Latin word for independent hospitals: Orme and Webster 1995, p. 39.
40. The 'Itchy Room', for men with the itch (a diagnosis embracing everything from poor personal hygiene to scabies: see Risse 1986, pp. 98, 161) is marked on NMM ART/2/35, a contemporary plan of James Stuart's Greenwich Infirmary (1763–64).
41. Jones 1971, p. 101.
42. Vidler (1987, p. 52) argues for the precocity of the type in France. Frank 1976, p. 415; Le Roy 1789, p. 599: 'une grande, une extrême propreté, un air aussi pur qu'il est possible, c'est, on ne peut trop le redire, la vraie & la seule magnificence qu'il faille rechercher dans ces édifices' (see also Vidler 1987, p. 61).
43. '...les hommes préfèrent toujours les choses d'éclat, & même frivole, à celles qui n'offrent qu'un triste object d'utilité'; 'En effet, sacrifiant, comme c'est assez la coutume parmi nous, le principal à l'accessoire, les auteurs de ces projets sembloient avoir oublié que la décoration n'est que la plus petite partie d'un pareil édifice': Le Roy 1789, p. 586.
44. Foucault 1980, p. 177 ('solonnelle mais maladroite'); Vidler 1987, p. 70 translates Mallet du Pin, writing about Poyet and Coquéau's *Mémoire*.
45. Saisselin 1992, p. 65.
46. Brocklesby 1764, pp. 70–81; Tilton 1813, p. 49.
47. McClung 1981, p. 280.
48. Used in William Mason's (undated) *Animadversions* on the York Asylum, quoted Langford 1991, p. 130.
49. Quoted Digby, *Madness* 1985, p. 54.
50. McClung 1981, p. 280, writing about country-house poetry. 'The notion of the purpose-built asylum acquires a thoroughly novel meaning' in the context of the Retreat: Scull 1993, p. 98 n. 173, and compare Digby, *Madness* 1985, p. 38.
51. For Hallé in 1787 (p. 575) Greenwich (which had a really impressive standard of housekeeping) was one of three older hospitals *dignes de servir d'exemple* for healthy hospital construction (the others were the Hôpital Saint-Louis and the Hôtel-Dieu in Lyons); see also Grosley 1772, 2: 42; and Tenon 1992, pp. 65–71.

Chapter 1: Hospitality, monuments, and patriarchal medicine

1. For medieval hospitals I have depended on Carlin 1989; Prescott 1992; Orme and Webster 1995, especially pp. 40–41 and Chapter 3; and Gilchrist 1995, Chapter 2. Risse 1999 offers excellent accounts of developments mentioned in the first part of this chapter: for summaries, see pp. 154–56, 216–19. At points in the following I have also borrowed from Stevenson 1993.
2. Carlin 1989, pp. 22–25; Rubin 1989; Gilchrist 1995, p. 11.
3. Prescott 1992, pp. 1–2, 51; Orme and Webster 1995, pp. 49–56. Rawcliffe 1995, pp. 1, 9, 19, 210 is more inclined to stress prayer's instrumentality for sufferers' own souls.
4. Orme and Webster 1995, p. 37; Rubin 1989, p. 56; Carlin 1989, p. 35; Andrews et al. 1997, pp. 111–12.
5. Prescott 1992, pp. 46–48. Orme and Webster (1995, pp. 127, 138–39) are anxious to qualify this and other received ideas about medieval hospitals, but acknowledge that significant changes did occur after the Black Death (1348–49).
6. Park and Henderson (1991, p. 175) suggest that this passage (from a 1684 translation of More's *Utopia*, quoted Chaney 1981, p. 183) is a 'distant echo' of Florence's S. Maria Nuova.
7. Orme and Webster 1995, p. 151.
8. See Woodward 1974, pp. 6–11, who quotes Petty p. 7. Webster (1975, pp. 295–300) argues that Petty's earlier proposal for a 'Nosocomium' is relevant to the Interregnum use of Ely House and the Savoy, and McMenemey (1964, p. 46; see also Cawson and Orde 1969, pp. 217, 219–20), that John Bellers inspired Thomas Guy's hospital, the first English institution devoted from its inception to the care of the sick.
9. Spencer 1965, 1: 140. Filarete's treatise was not published until the nineteenth century. Welch (1995) discusses the differences between Sforzinda's and Milan's hospitals.
10. Alberti 5.8, 1988, p. 129.
11. Ibid. (compare the editors' Introduction, p. x); for prisons, ibid. 5.13, p. 139.
12. Welch comments (1995, pp. 149–50) on the historiographical problems presented by the cruciform plan and in particular its diffusion (or not) from Tuscany to northern Italy; see also Henderson 1989, p. 75.
13. Giordano 1988, pp. 120–22; Welch 1995, pp. 137, 165–66.
14. Park and Henderson 1991; for the building, Colvin et al. 1975, pp. 196–206. It was for one hundred inmates; poor men stayed one night, the sick could stay longer.
15. Evelyn 1955, 2: 311. For Sto Spirito see Heydenreich 1995, pp. 66–67, with a plan; on English travellers' particular admiration for it, in part because of national connections, Chaney 1981, pp. 196, 200, 210, 214 n. 50.
16. Diez del Corral and Checa 1986, p. 122. The two dormitory chapels at the Savoy were at the top of the 'nave'

beyond the crossing, and at the end of one transept. The latter was certainly screened off as was, most likely, the former: Colvin et al. 1975, pp. 198, 204.

17. Evelyn 1955, 2: 46.

18. See Rosen 1974 for how sixteenth-century hospitals began to work with state perceptions of poor relief as a mechanism for maintaining social order; also Jones 1989, pp. 2–3, 35 and (for English hospitals) Orme and Webster 1995, pp. 150–55. Heal 1990, pp. 122–39 describes contemporary English tension between calls for the maintenance of Christian charity, broadly understood and with close links to domestic hospitality, and the well-established distinction between the deserving and undeserving poor.

19. Presumably in Florence: Chaney 1981, p. 192 and note.

20. Evelyn 1955, 2: 45 (Amsterdam), 101 (Paris).

21. Ballon 1991, Chapter 4; see ibid. p. 192 and Markus 1993, pp. 108–9 on Saint-Louis's spatial organization.

22. Quoted Ballon 1991, p. 193.

23. Ibid., pp. 197–98 and Bruegmann 1976, pp. 9, 14–15, 48, 80, 197 describe eighteenth- and nineteenth-century appreciation for Saint-Louis. The Paris Académie des Sciences' second report (1787) is quoted ibid., p. 11 ('très bel hôpital, bien bati, bien conservé et d'une construction part-tout dirigée avec intelligence, à la salubrité, et à la commodité des malades'); see also Tenon 1996, pp. 47–48, 83–93, 308 and Hallé 1787, p. 575 for informative analyses of what the latter called a 'modèle de tous les hôpitaux de l'Europe, pour la construction'.

24. Slack 1980, pp. 8–9, 11; idem 1985, pp. 217–19, 277.

25. Aston 1973, pp. 247–48, quoting John Aubrey p. 251.

26. Stow 1912, pp. 381–82.

27. Pugin 1969, pp. iii, 28. Hill 1999, p. 33 describes Pugin's debt to Stow and more generally to an antiquarian tradition that more or less explicitly mourned the Reformation.

28. Airs 1995, pp. 27–29, 133–35: a generation often passed before the old buildings were quarried, but this may reflect a surplus, as well as religious qualms.

29. See Fowler 1994, p. 61 for the topos. Herrick's 'A Panegyric to Sir Lewis Pemberton' (ibid., no. 18, ll. 119–20), published 1648, goes on to note that no religious house was stripped to provide building materials.

30. Spencer 1965, 1: 144.

31. *Odes* II.xviii: Horace 1967, p. 127. Compare *Odes* II.xvi (p. 121) on 'the worries / Circling the beams / Of fretted ceilings' and see Freeman 1975 for a witty history of this 'subgenre of diatribe against empty ostentation'.

32. Plutarch 1988, p. 23.

33. Sekora 1977, p. 115 and Berry 1994, p. 41 quote and comment.

34. McClung 1981, p. 286.

35. Sekora 1977, p. 48.

36. For examples, Thomson 1993, pp. 24–25 (who comments, pp. 38, 160, 195, on the generally scattered nature of 'criticisms . . . of wealth devoted to non-practical architectural glory' in sixteenth-century Europe); Diez del Corral and Checa 1986, pp. 122–23; Juan Luis Vivès in Salter 1926, pp. 15–17.

37. Quoted Rosenau 1970, p. 75 n.3: 'Pleust à Dieu . . . que les riches bourgeois . . . s'adonassent aussi tost à faire et fonder quelques hostels-dieu, ou colleges pour le soulagement des pauvres, et utilité du bien publique, que édifier un tas de superbes et magnifiques maisons qui ne leur servent que d'ennuie et malheur.'

38. Quoted Woodward 1974, p. 7.

39. Alberti, Prologue, 1988, p. 4; 9.1, p. 292; and the editors' notes to the former, p. 367. See Jenkins 1970 for the argument that the idea of architectural magnificence evolved as a defence of private patronage, and compare Filarete's, in Spencer 1965, 1: 106.

40. Heal 1990, pp. 24–25.

41. Ibid., pp. 10–11, 91–92, 179, 216. This is the fundamental study of the topic; see pp. 112–13 for the 'definition of customary hospitality as "other"'. It was being limited even before the sixteenth century, a period which saw some urgent calls for the maintenance of hospitable charity broadly understood (pp. 126–27, 168). For hospitality in relation to (real) domestic planning, Thompson 1995, especially pp. 99–101, 133–35; Platt 1994, pp. 34–37, 169–70; and Cooper 1999, pp. 264–72.

42. Quoted Downes 1968, p. 35. Evelyn like North was a well-informed student of 'modern' classicism, but as Lubbock shows (1995, pp. 156–78) this did not preclude the patriarchal impulse. Compare McClung 1977, p. 61, summarizing his argument that the houses built for prospect were, at least in the poetic genre's early days, not compact and classicized boxes.

43. North 1981, p. 63. Williams 1985 is the point of departure for any consideration of the values attached to rural life, to which Heal (1990, especially pp. 113–22) provides valuable amplification; see Cooper 1999, pp. 128–54 for the general influence of suburban and urban house-types.

44. North 1981, p. 69; Platt 1994, pp. 184–85; again, Cooper 1999 shows how houses started changing earlier than one might suppose from reading North (on this point of houses developing 'by a process of addition and subtraction' see especially pp. 3, 55, 61). McClung 1977, pp. 46, 52–54, 61 examines the iconography of the piecemeal.

45. 'Of building' (1625), in Bacon 1906, p. 133.

46. McClung 1981, p. 282. Among studies of country-house poetry, the last is (with Hibbard 1956, McClung 1977, and Gent 1995) the most interesting for architectural history; more recent works (Lubbock 1995, pp. 149–55; Cooper 1999, pp. 269–70) underline its

specifically political cast too. Fowler's collection (1994) is now indispensable, and I have found Kenny's summary of the 'country-house ethos' (1984, pp. 1–4) useful.

47. 'On Welbeck' by Richard Flecknoe (fl.1610–78?), ll. 15–16, no. 33 in Fowler 1994.

48. Hibbard 1956, p. 159. 'As emblem of the condition of fallen or degenerated human nature, architecture is evidence that compatibility with nature – the natural world, and human nature properly understood – has been lost': McClung 1983, p. 48.

49. Ward 1993, pp. 161–62.

50. In 'To Penshurst', Jonson opposed art and ' "use" (utility), which here as in other estate-poems is expressed in hospitality, the sustaining of a community of dependants and guests': McClung 1981, p. 282.

51. Mandeville 1924, p. 70.

52. Monro 1995, p. 113. Compare Rawcliffe 1995, p. 183, quoting a Parisian domestic instruction manual written from the early 1390s, and Pelling 1998, p. 30. Vivès wrote (1526) that 'there shall not in future be rich men saving their own money and demanding, from the funds of the poor, gifts [alms] for their servants, the members of their household, kindred, and their own intimate friends, . . . as we see to have happened in the hospitals' (Salter 1926, pp. 17–18), and Ned Ward satirically imagined (around 1700) a 'couple of old fellows who looked as if they were the superannuated servants of some great man, who to exempt himself from the charge of keeping 'em when past their labour, and to reward the faithful service of their youth, had got 'em into an hospital' (Ward 1993, p. 204).

53. Risse 1986, pp. 98–101, 132. Woodward 1974, pp. 40–43, Cherry 1980, p. 251, and Porter and Porter 1989, pp. 41–42 are fairly certain about servants' exclusion from English hospitals, but Langford 1991, pp. 498–99 is not: one of his examples is however London's Smallpox Hospital which obviously, like the Edinburgh Infirmary but unlike many others, took 'contagious' cases. Clark-Kennedy 1962, pp. 31–32, 94, 225 remarks on the way that London Hospital governors got their employees admitted; see also Risse 1999, p. 340 (regarding the Massachusetts General) and the *Abstract of some of the Statutes and Rules of the [Kent and Canterbury] Hospital* (1811), of which a copy is in the NMR file no. 101139, which explains that while the rules did not exclude domestic servants, they did prohibit the relief of anyone, or his family or apprentices, who could afford to pay: such 'misapplications' of subscription money disadvantaged both needier objects and physicians and surgeons who donated their services at hospitals, but not elsewhere.

54. R. Williams 1976, s.v. 'charity'; Heal 1990, pp. 14–17, 393–94.

55. 'Essay on Charity' (1723), in Mandeville 1989, p. 263.

56. 'The idea of *caritas*, as a Christian virtue to be practised in all kinds of neighbourly behaviour and in acts of social integration, gradually transmuted itself into a philanthropic concern for poverty which was distanced from the individual social act, and hence more readily expressed through monetary giving of an impersonal kind': Heal 1990, p. 124.

57. Houston 1994, p. 382 summarizes his analysis: the 'practice of providing in- rather than out-relief for the bulk of ordinary poor from the 1740s' was 'clearly a departure'. Maitland's (1753) Book VII describes the Edinburgh charities then existing. No architect's name is associated with the Charity Workhouse, but Adam was the specialist.

58. By Alured Clarke (quoted Goldberg 1991, p. 184), whose voice may also be heard in the quotation referenced at n. 60.

59. Forty 1980, p. 68.

60. 'A view of the many peculiar advantages of publick hospitals', *Gentleman's Magazine* 11 (1741): 476–77, on p. 476; compare Matt. 25: 35–36.

61. Ward 1993, p. 96.

62. *Brief account* 1735, p. 6; my emphasis.

63. Philasthenes 1739, p. 11; for Monro's missing two pounds, Erlam 1954, p. 103.

64. *The World* 1756, p. 1020; the author of this untitled essay is identified as the 'Hon. Mr. Boyle' in a contemporary printed list pasted into the flyleaf of one British Library copy (shelfmark 629.l.5) of this journal: John Boyle (1707–62), however, Earl of Cork and Orrery since 1753, was an active hammer of luxury. Andrews et al. 1997, p. 170 connect the developing cult of anonymity among Bethlem's benefactors with this essay, but if it had a specific target it was, I suspect, the Foundling Hospital.

65. *The World* 1756, pp. 1023–24: 'The raising a church, or endowing a hospital, are the two main objects of an elderly sinner's piety. . . . I shall venture to lay it down as a maxim, that there is no such thing as posthumous charity.' See Solkin 1996, pp. 469–70 on the oxymoron of posthumous charity, and the succinct demonstration in Langford 1991, pp. 491–92 of the eighteenth century's changing 'sense of what was appropriate in the charitable manners adopted by polite people'.

66. 'The very name' of one donor's family was 'obliterated every where, except where it pointed out the disposal of a very considerable fortune': *The World* 1756, p. 1022. Owen 1964, p. 77 quotes a newspaper report of 1748 about a bequest to relations, 'notwithstanding the current vanity . . . to leave a fortune to some public body which might give him [the testator] a name'.

67. Saunders 1993, p. 144 quotes K. D. Moritz and William Hutton, and illustrates the hospital (demolished 1894) on p. 145.

68. Mandeville 1989, p. 72. The emphasis on calculation, measuring, is important: see Williams 1985, pp. 48, 60, 63, 65.

69. According to Moritz: Saunders 1993, p. 144. 'To Bathurst', in Pope 1968, pp. 570–86, ll. 283–84, 265–66.

70. Erskine-Hill 1975, p. 32: this was Matthew Gibson, married to Kyrle's niece, in 1734. But Gibson was (his interlocutor wrote) a 'crazed man, and withall stingy'.

71. Mandeville 1989, pp. 272, 269; for his apparent feud with Radcliffe see Monro 1975, pp. 252–54.

72. The following is from Mandeville 1720, pp. 31–32. On Emilia see also Monro 1975, pp. 44–45; and compare *Part II* of the *Fable* (Mandeville 1924, p. 120) and *A letter to Dion* (1732): 'A Miser may go directly to Hell, . . . at the same Time, that the great Wealth he leaves, and the Hospital he builds, are a considerable Relief to the Poor, and Consequently a Publick Benefit' (idem 1954, p. 39).

73. I am paraphrasing Herrick (see n. 29, above) – 'Where laden spits, warped with large ribs of beef, / Not represent, but give relief' (ll. 9–10) – as well as Howarth's quotation (1997, p. 292) of Richard Brathwaite (1641): 'why do many sumptuous and goodly Buildings, whose faire Frontispice, promise much comfort . . . want their Masters' – gadding about at court – 'so their Store-House being made so strait, and their Gates so broad, I much feare me, that Provision . . . hath run out at their gates'.

74. Solkin 1996, p. 483, illustrated p. 482: this article demonstrates Guy's conflicting posthumous reputations, and their wider significance and artistic manifestations.

75. Quoted ibid., p. 475. For the Act, see also Owen 1964, pp. 87–88 and Andrew 1989, p. 47.

76. Quoted Borsay 1991, p. 226; for the announcements, Wood 1969, pp. 286, 289.

77. Owen (1964, p. 74) comments on the 'formidable' number of residential institutions founded by charitable trusts between 1696 and 1745 and a search on Michael Good's CD-Rom *Compendium* to Pevsner's *Buildings of England* yields records of 242 almshouses, not including those now destroyed or any in the Greater London area, with substantial construction from the period 1701–1830; see also Borsay 1989, pp. 109–10.

78. Davenant 1699, p. 52 (*Gentleman's Magazine* 6 [1736]: 26 misquotes him); for Davenant in relation to luxury, Sekora 1977, pp. 78–80, 116.

79. Coats 1976, pp. 104–5. See also Wilson 1969 and Foucault 1971, p. 55.

80. Quoted in *Gentleman's Magazine* 6 (1736): 26.

81. Bellers 1714, p. 3; on him and other political arithmeticians see Andrew 1989, pp. 9, 23, 26, and Woodward 1974, pp. 6–11.

82. See Foucault 1971, p. 229 on poverty's freeing, later in the century, 'from the old moral confusions. Men had seen unemployment assume, during crises, an aspect that could no longer be identified with that of sloth'. For an elegant summary of what political arithmetic represented see Brewer 1989, pp. 223–25.

83. And that only incidentally; the pamphlet comprises a rather convincing argument against the parish textile workhouses (not all penal) then being touted as a solution to unemployment.

84. Bellers's *Proposals for raising a college of industry* (1696) is quoted in Scull 1980, p. 41 (thanks to Roy Porter for identifying Paul's voice [2 Thess. 3: 10]); see Foucault 1971, p. 56 for the theology of employment.

85. Bellers 1714, p. 49.

86. Quoted Foster 1986, p. 637.

87. The London Hospital, for example, was dedicated to the 'relief of all sick and diseased persons, especially manufacturers, and seamen in merchant-service &c.' Taylor (1986, p. 644) and Andrew (1989, p. 54) suggest that medical and related charities were more likely to succeed if they eschewed humanitarian arguments in favour of broadly commercial but specific programmes in their appeals for funds.

88. Quoted in Spalding 1977, p. 6; see also Coleman 1976, pp. 20, 22. The Colony, mostly financed by Parliament, was surrendered to the Crown in 1752. Kenny 1984 is the starting-point on patriarchal myths in the imperial context.

89. *Gentleman's Magazine* 6 (1736): 25–26.

90. From a contemporary account, quoted in Spalding 1977, p. 15, with reference to the ban on legal 'plead[ing] for Hire'; see also pp. 50, 62–66 on the slaves. The Colony was however to support itself by the export of silk, wine, and olive oil to Britain! Ibid., pp. 58–59, 161.

91. Jones 1966, pp. 519–20; see Spalding 1977, p. 84.

92. Spalding 1977, pp. 23–24. Georgia's iconographies (broadly speaking) have prompted no analyses aside from Dabydeen's (1987, pp. 114–19); I think, however, he is wrong to find Africans in the picture reproduced here as Figure 2.

93. See Wear 1992 for a discussion very pertinent to mine; on these points, pp. 131, 139.

94. As Wear has pointed out (ibid., p. 127), the 'enterprise of colonizing America forced people to articulate their ideas of how to judge whether a place was healthy or not', and air is probably the most important single criterion in late sixteenth- and seventeenth-century accounts that hoped to invite further settlers.

95. Berkeley 1901, *Querist* pp. 422, 456. I'm struck by the contrast with Berkeley's notes (1717) on the architecture of Lecce, Italy (quoted Chaney 1991, pp. 87–89). He remarked a 'superfluity of ornaments' but his generous enjoyment of the 'general good *gout*, which descends down to the poorest houses' (which included 'ornamented doors and windows' etc.), is palpable.

96. Luce 1949, pp. 82–83; Chaney 1991. McParland 1995,

pp. 157–58, reckons Berkeley (who in 1750 wrote wistfully of being 'haunted with a taste for good company and the fine arts that I got at Burlington House') as among the most knowledgeable about architecture then in Ireland.

97. Berkeley 1901, *Querist* pp. 457–58.

98. Compare Swift's 'Proposal for the universal use of Irish manufacture' (1720): 'some ministers' in the previous two reigns had been 'apt, from their high elevation, to look down upon this kingdom as if it had been one of their colonies of outcasts in America': 1905, pp. 24–25. Although Berkeley 'had not been able to achieve the spiritual, moral and bodily cleansing of the New World, by the 1740s he became aware of the need to institute such a purifying project at home': Benjamin 1990, p. 169, referring to the tar-water.

99. The colonies were commonly seen as the repositories of wild, and wildly efficacious medicines and 'druggs' were among the first Georgian exports, in 1733 (Spalding 1977, pp. 14–15). On Berkeley's tar-water, Luce 1949, pp. 189 (the quotation), and 200–4; a potable tar preparation was in British pharmacopoeias until the twentieth century. Benjamin 1990 links it to Berkeley's metaphysics, and Berman 1994, pp. 171–79 extends the associations to the Rhode Island project.

100. Sekora 1977, pp. xi–xii.

101. See Vidler 1987, p. 54 for the relationships between colonial reveries and French calls for a ' "natural" form of poor relief, that would dismantle the castles of poverty and sickness'.

102. Jones 1966, p. 520; Coleman 1976, pp. 29–30 quotes the merchant (March 1733).

103. Pliny the Elder 29:8, 1962, p. 25: 'Non rem antiqui damnabant, sed artem'. Even medicine-the-thing was arguably superfluous in a true state of nature: see Porter 1991, pp. 164, 167 on eighteenth-century accounts of the rise of physic.

104. 'To Bathurst', in Pope 1968, pp. 570–86, ll. 269–70.

105. Quoted Woodward 1974, p. 37.

106. *Plan* 1777, pp. 8–9; compare Andrew 1989, p. 134.

107. Owen 1964, pp. 44, 48–50; Clark-Kennedy 1962, pp. 169–73, 181–82. Both hospitals built their side wings in the 1770s. The London, with a capacity of 400, held 130 patients on the day of Tenon's visit in 1787: Tenon 1992, p. 51.

108. *Plan* 1777, p. 7; compare George Armstrong, quoted Tröhler 1989, p. 27.

109. *Plan* 1777, pp. 8–9.

110. Jones 1971, p. 101. On him see Brings 1986, p. 268, who also quotes the American naval officer Edward Cutbush (1808): 'The wards of an hospital should never be crowded; two, three, or more patients should not be placed in the same bunk; there would be more humanity in placing them in an open field, where they would have some chance to recover.'

111. Tilton 1813, p. 49.

112. Ibid., p. 15.

113. Pringle 1752, p. 252; Brocklesby 1764, pp. 70, 80; Monro 1764, p. 361. 'Flying hospitals' were normally in tents, as they followed the troops; 'fixed hospitals' (or just 'hospitals') were in nearby towns, 'to receive such of the Sick as can be moved from the Flying Hospital': ibid., pp. 357–58. See Western 1965, pp. 388, 396 for some indication from War Office records of how English militia camps were run by the late 1770s. Turf huts were used for wives and families, and a fever outbreak at Coxheath camp in 1779 prompted the recommendation from Monro, Physician to the Army, that isolation hospitals should be set up, in barns if necessary, and to 'disinfect the camp' the commandant 'moved it for a few days, burned the straw and turned over the earth'.

114. Franklin 1882, pp. 311, 314–15. The paper, undated as far as I know, was translated by Le Roy and read to the Société Royale de Médecine in 1781; then as now, it was understood to incorporate Franklin's ideas. See ibid., p. 437 (letter of 23 August 1781 from Félix Vicq d'Azyr) and Greenbaum 1974, p. 125.

115. Tilton (1813, p. 49) called his hut an experiment, but it was one forced by the hard winter.

116. A good civil parallel is Thomas Beddoes's advocacy of the cow-house for consumptives, discussed by Porter 1991, pp. 172–73 and idem, *Doctor of society* 1992, pp. 105–6. Bruegmann 1976 is useful on this theme in nineteenth-century French writing; see pp. 74–75 on the reaction to the low mortality rates in unfinished, and unglazed, Parisian slaughterhouses used during the 1814–15 invasions.

117. Bell's *Principles of surgery* (1801–1808) is quoted in Wrench [1913], p. 78.

118. Vidler 1987, p. 8; this chapter, 'Rebuilding the primitive hut', also discusses eighteenth-century Europe's interest in native American architecture. On the hut, see also Picon 1992, pp. 41–42, 259, 266, 288, and McClung 1981, pp. 285–86 and idem 1983, pp. 114–16: it 'may claim to be the only necessary architecture' as one 'of very limited compromise . . . [with] the nature that craft generally profanes' (p. 114).

119. Picon 1992, p. 259: among J.-F. Blondel's pupils in France, 'The truth [of architecture] would sometimes be sought in a primitive knowledge on the basis of which everything might be reconstructed'.

120. This story is well told, in relation to Mead, Pringle, and Tilton, in Thompson and Goldin 1975, pp. 149–56, 170–79.

121. Pringle 1752, pp. iv–v: 'as war was their chief study, it is scarce to be doubted, but that the orders relating to the care of the sick, were no less perfect than the other branches of their military science'.

122. Brocklesby 1764, pp. 59–60. I haven't been able to find

the discussion to which Brocklesby refers (at least nine editions of the increasingly not-*Short discourse concerning pestilential contagion* were published) but it is entirely in keeping with Mead's antiquarian interests. Temkin has shown (1977, pp. 468–69) how eighteenth-century domestic advice literature comparably explained biblical strictures as 'wise sanitary prescriptions'; for him this signals the final 'secularization' of ancient notions of ritual pollution.

123. Tilton 1813, pp. 32–33.
124. Coleman 1976, pp. 13–17; Porter, 'Howard's beginning' 1995, p. 15.
125. Herbert 1978, pp. 5–6; Robinson 1979, pp. 36–37.
126. La Roche 1933, p. 176.
127. For example, the third report (1788) of the Paris Académie des Sciences' committee (in Lavoisier 1865, here p. 683) explains why patients must be bathed upon admission: 'On les guérit déjà en partie la rétablissement la propreté, une des sources de la santé des riches, et dont la privation est inséparable de la pauvreté.'
128. The paradox is well explained in relation to the French architect Claude-Nicolas Ledoux's *De l'Architecture* (1804) by Ozouf 1966, especially pp. 1283–84, and 1301: 'Il y a ... un luxe positif: c'est celui qui donne à chacun ce que la nature elle-même prodigue: l'air, l'eau, l'espace, la lumière, l'abri.' Directly comparable are the calls for enlightened, natural self-medication discussed by Porter 1991, who quotes (p. 161) William Buchan (1796): 'Air, water, and light, are taken without the advice of a physician'.

Chapter 2: Palaces and hospitals

1. Berkeley 1901, *Essay*, p. 333; Defoe 1704: the 'profuse extravagant humour of our poor people in eating and drinking, keeps them low'.
2. Remark L (1714) and *Grumbling hive* (1705): Mandeville 1989, pp. 144, 68. See Sekora 1977 and Berry 1994 for luxury's economic re-evaluations.
3. Goldsmith 1985, pp. 64–65.
4. Quoted ibid., p. 45, from *The Female Tatler* (1709). See Berry 1994, pp. 34, 130 for the luxury 'learning curve'.
5. Remark P (1714), Mandeville 1989, p. 190. As he often did, Mandeville was turning an older anti-luxury rhetoric on its head: compare William Harrison (1577), quoted in Howard 1987, p. 17: the 'basest home of a baron doth often match in our days with some honours of princes in old time'.
6. Quoted Jestaz 1990, p. 27: 'Entre les différents établissements que nous avons faits dans le cours de notre règne, il n'y en a point qui soit plus utile à l'État'. For later foundations for veterans, Sevestre 1974 and Pelser 1976.
7. Smith 1815, p. 32: Carlton House was a lodging-house

by contrast and St James's a 'place of confinement'. Lubbock 1995, pp. 6–7 describes how the old city-panegyric formula was adapted for London.
8. 'Great Brittains Beauty; or, Londons Delight' (1671), in Aubin 1943, pp. 185–88, ll. 17–20. London's new houses were 'even superior in Design, and Architecture, to the Palaces of Princes elsewhere': John Woodward in 1707, quoted Reddaway 1940, p. 285n.
9. Swift 1965, p. 424. John Raymond (1648) is quoted in Chaney 1981, p. 199; see other examples quoted ibid., pp. 204–5 and in Alsop 1981.
10. Franklin 1954, p. xxvi (quoted by the editor with no source cited).
11. 'Bethlehems beauty', ll. 35–36, 37–40, in Aubin 1943, pp. 245–48.
12. *The Tatler* 127 (31 January 1710): Bond 1987, 2: 243. Jacob 1723, p. 5.
13. Brown 1730, p. 30; his phrasing ('As the Buildings took their Magnificence from a Palace at *Paris*, ... and if we have been witty upon the *French* in giving *Bedlam* the Resemblance of the *Louvre*') suggests that the story needed no explanation, but I haven't found an earlier version. The palaces' names were interchangeable, even to the French; what Bethlem did resemble, as Whinney (Whinney and Millar 1957, p. 206) suggested, was Louis Le Vau's short-lived Louvre river front (completed 1661).
14. Bowen 1783, p. 5n.; see Defoe 1971, p. 329 (from the second volume [1725] of the *Tour*) and Stevenson, 'Robert Hooke's Bethlem' 1996, p. 256 for further references.
15. Bowen 1783, p. 8; Swift 1965, p. 448, a 1735 letter from Alexander Pope commending Swift's future hospital ('of all charities, this is the most disinterested, and least vainglorious').
16. Newell 1984, p. 18.
17. Faulkner 1805, p. 46.
18. Von Uffenbach 1934, pp. 20–21. The costs are taken from NMM ART/1/67, an abstract of expenses to the end of September 1727 including Thornhill's work, and ART/1/63–64, a large plan dated 1728, with estimates, among them the 'The Colonade & Porticoes on the West 430 fo.ᵗ long ... [£]14,288.4.11'; 'The East Colonade ... When finished may cost ... [£]12,500.0.0.'
19. North 1981, pp. 58, 57n., the last from the British Library draft.
20. Ibid., p. 61 (British Library draft): he continued, 'The like is done at Chelsey College where both the middle and 2 wings are adorned by like distinctions; so that you see a sort of portall in the middle with its frontoon above, and pavillions at each corner.' Chelsea's end pavilions are not in fact much distinguished, visually, from the rest of the ward wings (Wren disliked prominent 'Pavilions in the Corners': Wren Society 1942,

19: 62) and it is interesting that North picked up on the generic resemblance to Bethlem, on which see Whinney and Millar 1957, pp. 216–17 and Downes 1988, p. 84.

21. BCGM, for 11 July 1674, pp. 15–16; Hooke 1935, p. 112, for 10 and 11 July 1674. Few drawings for the building have survived: see the references in Colvin, *Biographical dictionary* 1995, s.v. 'Hooke, Robert'.

22. For contemporary uses, Stevenson, 'Robert Hooke's Bethlem' 1996, p. 259, and Cooper 1999, p. 337 n.88.

23. For Montagu House, Downes 1966, pp. 57–58 and pl. 133; and Keller 1986, pp. 732–34. Ramsbury Manor, Wiltshire (begun *c.*1680) was also a double pile (Colvin 1975; plan in Hill and Cornforth 1966, p. 180), as was Lord Conway's house at Ragley, Warwickshire (begun 1679), though of a complicated sort (Batten 1936–37, pp. 97–103 and Girouard 1978, pp. 135–36, with a plan).

24. Andrews et al. 1997, pp. 242–43; I've since realized that Rocque's 1746 map of London (Hyde 1982) shows the enlarged building as at least 710 feet long, with the original, as far as I can tell, about 600 feet.

25. Andrews et al. 1997, pp. 220, 273, 275; Tenon 1992, p. 73 on the new wings' double-piling.

26. North 1981, pp. 64, 71, 32; compare Pratt (1928, p. 25), writing around 1660, and Cooper 1999, pp. 141–42: 'In characterising the old-fashioned layout as cell-like – as a series of units – North put his finger on the essentially additive nature of the traditional, linear plan.' Useful in this connection are Thompson 1987, pp. 43, 46–47, 54–55, 63–64, 126; Howard 1987, especially pp. 59–68; Bold 1983 and idem 1993, pp. 112–13; and Thompson 1995, p. 156, who explains how the 'idea of one long structure of parallel walls, two storeyed and subdivided into compartments entered by separate doors' perhaps first arose at castles, became generally attractive in the fourteenth century, and the norm for domestic and institutional types ('colleges, schools, hospitals, almshouses and even inns') in the fifteenth and sixteenth centuries: courtyards were easy to make out of such ranges, and buildings in turn easy to expand, by adding more courts.

27. North 1981, p. 65. This type (which in 1803 Humphry Repton called objectionable, 'because it is a mere single house in the centre' [Loudon 1840, p. 270]) should be distinguished from newer, deeper houses with side wings, on which see Cooper 1999, p. 242.

28. Particularly when used with the internal corridor by which 'communication is at once facilitated and, paradoxically, impeded: the chance encounter . . . is no longer encouraged': Bold 1993, p. 114. On economy with building materials, North 1981, pp. 9, 69 and Pratt 1928, p. 24.

29. North 1981, pp. 69, 9; Bold 1993, p. 114.

30. Pratt 1928, p. 24; North 1981, p. 69: the 'rooms are single so as the lights are thro, and you cannot retire from heat and cold'.

31. Foster 1768, pp. 26–27.

32. Clay 1909, p. 120. For almshouse architecture, Godfrey 1955 and Prescott 1992, pp. 55–65; brief but to the point are Girouard 1990, pp. 60–63 and Markus 1993, p. 97. On the durable infirmary-hall type and its variants, Prescott 1992, pp. 4–5, 7–15, 41–47, Gilchrist 1995, pp. 17–24, and Orme and Webster 1995, pp. 85–92.

33. Prescott 1992, p. 64.

34. Though English medieval 'hospitals of all types seem to have employed a close, cloister, quadrangle or courtyard as their means of central planning': Gilchrist 1992, p. 103. Downes identifies collegiate architecture, as well as a 1660s Webb project for Whitehall, as possible antecedents for Chelsea's hall–chapel alignment (1988, pp. 84–85); Whinney (1971, p. 148) remarks on Chelsea's influence on *later* university colleges in this respect.

35. For Aske's Hospital, Batten 1936–37, pp. 103–4: her illustration shows only the ground-floor plan and I had thought that an enclosed gallery might have stood over the open loggia (Stevenson, 'Robert Hooke's Bethlem' 1996, p. 259) but Hatton's description (1708, 2: 747) is unambiguous: the twenty houses each had one room behind an open loggia on the ground floor and stairs up to two rooms above. At Bishop Seth Ward's Hospital in Buntingford, Herts (*c.*1689), attributed to Hooke, houses for four almsmen and four women were built on three sides of a quadrangle, each with a ground-floor living room with front and back entrances, a bedroom above, and another small room on both floors. For Morden, Defoe 1971, p. 115.

36. The only example I know is Trinity Hospital, Greenwich, begun in 1614 for twenty men: Godfrey 1955, p. 58. Girouard 1990, p. 62 suggests that almshouse rooms on 'two or more floors approached by enclosed corridors' became commoner in the eighteenth century.

37. Hillier and Hanson 1984, p. 146: every building 'identifies at least one "inhabitant" in this sense'. I should say that I am using only a small part of their work, and that simplified.

38. Heal 1990, p. 30.

39. Andrews et al. 1997, p. 182 and in general Chapter 13, 'Visiting'.

40. Ibid., pp. 132–33.

41. Ward 1993, pp. 55–58 (quotation p. 58); Brown 1730, pp. 29–32.

42. Hallett 1999, p. 102.

43. Stow 1720, 1: 193 quotes an order of 11 August 1699, that the hospital servants must refuse entry to anyone that 'they in the least Suspect to be lewd or disorderly Persons, nor any Boys or Girls, that they think are Apprentices, and come there to idle away their Time'.

44. The regulations, including the table of diet, drawn up in 1677 were on display by 1681 (Andrews et al. 1997, p. 211) and the new edition of Stow's *Survey* reprinted an 'Abstract' of them in 1720 (1: 193).

45. For Bethlem's interior see also Stevenson, 'Robert Hooke's Bethlem' 1996, pp. 261–62, and Andrews et al. 1997, pp. 204–9, 242–46.

46. [Hatton] 1708, 2: 732; Smith 1815, pp. 34–35 describes in detail the governors' room, in which were also hung an elevation and a plan of Hooke's building.

47. [Hatton] 1708, 2: 732.

48. Or so I assume: in 1720 Stow (1: 136) gave a total of 136 cells, noting that more had been 'lately finished' to bring the total to 150.

49. Stevenson, 'Robert Hooke's Bethlem' 1996, pp. 266–67; Andrews et al. 1997, pp. 220, 247.

50. BCGM, for 20 April 1676, p. 243.

51. Which is what the Bethlem governors always called them. The phrase is suggestive but Coope (1984, pp. 449, 450) concludes that 'long gallery' remained a fluid term for another century in England; see Andrews et al. 1997, pp. 244–48, for further references. Pratt defined a gallery simply as a room more than twice as long as its breadth: 1928, p. 65.

52. Andrews et al. 1997, pp. 219–20, 303.

53. Bacon used 'gallery' at least three different ways in 'Of Building' (1625) though twice together with 'stately': Bacon 1906, pp. 133–36. Celia Fiennes used the word for the attic corridor at Pratt's Coleshill House (completed 1662): Morris 1995, p. 47. Henderson (1995, pp. 111, 133) is sensitive to the ambiguities inherent in the closely related 'loggia', and see Tucker in Andrews et al. 1997, p. 45 on 'room' itself.

54. See the references in Stevenson, 'Robert Hooke's Bethlem' 1996, p. 274 n.96, and Cooper 1999, pp. 301–5.

55. First printed 1681: Kermode and Walker 1990, pp. 27–29.

56. Quoted in Coope 1986, p. 59; and see p. 45 for evidence for fifteenth- and sixteenth-century 'corridor galleries' used as similarly 'useful "socially neutral" ground'.

57. Fabricant 1987, pp. 264–65: 'In this way the moral authority of tradition is combined with the emotional power of nostalgia and put to the service of promoting a very new commercial enterprise'. Heal (1990, pp. 208–9) explains that country-house tourism, apparent by the late sixteenth century, was no cause for surprise in the 1630s, but the relationship between owner (or his or her surrogate) and visitor remained 'essentially one of host and guest': Tinniswood 1989, p. 65.

58. Wren Society 1942, 19: 73; Dean 1950, pp. 143, 150, 53. Faulkner advertised his book about the hospital (1805, p. i) as the first guide dedicated to one of the 'splendid buildings round the metropolis, which attract the attention of foreigners and visitors'.

59. Newell 1984, p. 43.

60. Andrews et al. 1997, pp. 189–91, 297.

61. Quoted Dean 1950, p. 145.

62. Faulkner remarked in 1805 (p. 63) that the men never sat down in hall to dine, preferring to take meals back to their berths, and communal dining was officially abandoned in 1858: Dean 1950, pp. 145–47.

63. Hillier and Hanson 1984, p. 184.

64. 'Keys even seem . . . to have been entrusted to [Bethlem's] patients on occasion, and as late as the 1760s patients were still being permitted by staff to "Walk Idle up and down the House Shewing it to Strangers and begging Money"': Andrews et al. 1997, p. 194. Foucault discusses (1971, pp. 68–69) contemporary significances attached to the practice of allowing the mad to show the mad to asylum visitors. Geoffrey Hudson tells me that what little there is in the Chelsea records about the practice indicates that pensioners showed visitors around for tips. The Greenwich records are more informative because the institution's anxiety to preserve its own dignity led to the placing of all kinds of formal, petty restrictions on the work the men could undertake, including this kind (though they did it anyway). At Greenwich, whose Porter held the monopoly on visitors' tips, Hudson believes that the 'pensioners were not so much inhabitants as barely tolerated guests'.

65. Brewer 1989, pp. 55, 59–60. For what follows, ibid., pp. 155–57; Solkin 1992, pp. 22–23; and Berry 1994, p. 133, all with references to Pocock's analysis.

66. Pocock 1987, p. 51: 'If man was by nature a citizen, and if the citizen was by nature or necessity an arms-bearer, what became of the nature of man when arms-bearer and citizen became irrevocably specialized as two distinct social types?'

67. 'Where once service was owed, now it was bought, and all essential elements of life were measured by monetary value': Sekora 1977, p. 78; compare p. 81, on eighteenth-century historiography.

68. Foucault, *Discipline* 1979, p. 136.

69. Ibid., p. 137.

70. Foucault 1975, p. 138; idem, *Discipline* 1979, p. 136.

71. Dean 1950, pp. 37, 22.

72. As pointed out to me by Geoffrey Hudson, whose research (in press) on the county-based pensions scheme (in effect from 1593 to 1679) suggests that the military hospitals were unlikely to have been founded in the hope of obviating embezzlement in this particular sphere, for there was little; compare, for example, Dean 1950, p. 38.

73. Brocklesby 1764, pp. 25, 52, 54 provides vivid accounts of the system, on which see Baugh 1965, p. 49 and Kempthorne 1937, p. 373.

74. McInnes 1990, p. 54.

75. In 1679 most of the Savoy was taken over for barracks, and it was formally dissolved as an institution in 1700: Somerville 1960, pp. 73–93; Keevil 1958, p. 104.

76. Keevil 1958, pp. 24, 75, 80, 129, 195.

77. Evelyn 1955, 3: 430–31 (8 and 20 February 1666). See Keevil 1958, p. 105.

78. Evelyn 1955, 3: 447–48 (17 August 1666); Dean 1950, p. 19.

79. Quoted Dean 1950, p. 172.

80. Kempthorne 1937, pp. 376–77 (quoting orders of April 1691); see also Cook 1990, pp. 10–11.

81. Brocklesby (1764, pp. 79–80) advised that officers would anyway wander along to the infirmaries 'for want of something else to do': camp life was that boring.

82. Jones 1989, p. 213 quotes an early seventeenth-century French report: 'A body of troops which camps cannot remain for long in the same place, without an extreme infection occurring as a consequence of the dirtiness of the soldiers, the horses which are there and the entrails of the beasts slaughtered.'

83. '*Grand renfermement*': Foucault 1972, Chapter 2, abridged in Foucault 1971.

84. Jones emphasizes the authoritarian-pietistic and mercantilist impulses fuelling these hospitals' foundations: 1989, pp. 39–43, 112, 174–76.

85. Order of the Bureau de l'Hôpital Général, 9 February 1658: 'Pour éviter de tomber dans l'inconvénient de faire des bâtiments irreguliers à la maison', quoted Sainte Fare Garnot 1986, p. 64. This article gives a useful history of the early Hôpital Général and especially the Salpêtrière; see also Saint-Geours et al. 1987, pp. 61–81, with good illustrations.

86. Fanshawe 1907, pp. 156–58; see also Fowler 1994, p. 135. On the Invalides' resemblance to the Escorial, Hautecoeur 1974, p. 21 and Jestaz 1990, pp. 63–64, who doubts whether Bruant was making a conscious reference.

87. Sainte Fare Garnot 1986, pp. 68–71; Saint-Geours et al. 1987, p. 64.

88. Jestaz 1990, p. 69.

89. *Pattern* 1695, p. 26.

90. After the Hôtel-Dieu and the Hôpital Saint-Louis, at least in 1787: Tenon 1996, p. 106. Brockliss and Jones (1997, pp. 689–90) draw attention to the acknowledged procedural and architectural excellences of the infirmaries, for which Jules Hardouin-Mansart signed the contract in 1676; see too the description in *Pattern* 1695, p. 51.

91. *Pattern* 1695, p. 18; compare Le Jeune 1683, p. 8.

92. Jones 1989, pp. 214, 217–19; Jestaz 1990, pp. 27–30.

93. 'üne milice au service du ciel': Hautecoeur 1974, p. 21, quoting an unspecified source, and see Berger 1994, p. 91. The Invalides was to some extent superseding the religious houses that had taken veterans in an older form of pensioning.

94. *Pattern* 1695, p. 26. An explanatory addition? I have been unable to find the matching phrase in Le Jeune's *Description*.

95. Jestaz 1990, p. 33. The church at the Hôpital Saint-Louis worked comparably: Ballon 1991, pp. 186, 193.

96. Alberti 5.7, 1988, p. 127.

97. Dean 1950, pp. 131, 140.

98. Ibid., pp. 75–80 is interesting on the architectural implications of their entry.

99. Evelyn 1955, 4: 269–70 (27 January 1682). On Chelsea College, [Hatton] 1708, 2: 737 and [Faulkner] 1805.

100. Hallé 1787, p. 575: 'aussi propre & aussi salubre q'un monastère de femmes'; Grosley 1772, 2: 42. Bibles were put in the Chelsea galleries in 1739 (Dean 1950, p. 211) and at Greenwich they may similarly have been an eighteenth-century introduction.

101. 'Greenwich' 1865, p. 632, citing Abel Boyer (probably *The history of King William the Third*, 1702–3).

102. For Kilmainham's foundation, Dean 1950, pp. 23–24. McParland (n.d.) compares its planning and detailing with the Invalides' and Loeber suggests (1981, p. 89) that Robinson, sent abroad in the king's service in 1677, may then have inspected the hospital in Paris. Craig 1982, pp. 153–55 extends the comparison to the entablature's semicircular leap over Kilmainham's chapel window – the equivalent frames the Invalides' entrance's carved tympanum – but believes that this is the only suggestive resemblance between the two hospitals.

103. Jestaz 1990, pp. 66–67; Berger 1994, p. 94. See Hautecoeur 1974, p. 24, for the specifications mentioned in the caption to Figure 17.

104. McParland n.d.: the pedestals of the clock tower also supported gilded carvings of exploding grenades, now gone.

105. Mulvany 1969, p. 262.

106. See Wren Society 1942, 19: pl. XL. Dean (1950, p. 49) refers to the removal of carved stonework from the pediment field in 1762, as unsafe.

107. *Pattern* 1695, p. 52.

108. Evans 1982, pp. 34–40 describes Newgate prison as rebuilt after the Great Fire with forty-two chambers, or wards, grouped around shared stairs. The cell's introduction into the prison is one of his major topics.

109. Wren Society 1928, 5: 33.

110. [Hatton] 1708, 2: 732.

111. Stow 1720, 1: 196.

112. Passages from the 1683 translation of Willis's book are excerpted in Hunter and Macalpine 1963, pp. 191–92.

113. Aikin 1771, p. 71.

114. Andrews et al. 1997, p. 45.

115. See Hooke 1961, pp. 107–14 for the fascinating way the application of 'cell' develops, with the help of a fossil shell like a chambered nautilis, and the already-established usage for the 'sexangular cells' of

a honeycomb. Harwood draws attention (1989, pp. 138–39) to *Micrographia*'s metaphors and puns.

116. From Henry VII's will, dated 21 April 1509 (spelling modernized), in Loftie 1878, pp. 87–88.

117. Colvin et al. 1975, p. 204; Somerville 1960, pp. 14–15.

118. Box-beds can be studied in the illustrations in Thompson and Goldin 1975, pp. 28–30, 41–44, 86.

119. Poynter 1963, p. 98; see Woodward 1974, pp. 8–9 on contemporary English admiration for Dutch hospitals.

120. Nigel Barker found two contracts relating to this hospital (1985, 1: 288–91), the only one built by the Ordnance between 1660 and 1750, though the king earlier had a garrison hospital built at Tangier. Charles's inspection of the Portsmouth fortifications in August 1679 coincided with a fever epidemic: Dean 1947, pp. 280–81. The latter describes the hospital, then (and now?) still extant in altered form: its 'projecting central bay . . . was probably pedimented, and as late as 1828 bore the royal coat of arms in bold relief, but these features have since been removed'.

121. Quoted Barker 1985, 1: 289. Compare Dean 1947, p. 283, who did not know the contract: in 'each ward the ceiling is supported by four massive oaken posts spaced evenly down the middle of the room. These posts measure 21 by 12 inches, are reeded, and have a nine-inch deeply moulded cap. Wainscotted berths may have been fitted between the posts, similar to those [at Chelsea]. . . . If so each ward would have accommodated ten patients, and the whole building forty.'

122. Colvin, *Biographical dictionary* 1995, s.v. 'Fitch, Thomas'; Dean 1947, p. 282. Hooke's *Diary* (1935) often refers to the brothers, especially John; see 'Espinasse 1956, pp. 93–94 for his high regard for them.

123. Charles inspected it in 1683: Dean 1947, pp. 280, 282, 283.

124. Ibid., p. 282.

125. Hawksmoor 1728, p. 11.

126. Bold 1989, pp. 122–34.

127. Because he 'wished the old men to have as much light and air as possible', Wren 'rejected the plan of the Invalides, with its small and dark side courts': Whinney 1971, p. 147, who similarly describes Wren's six ward-block plan for Greenwich as giving the 'interiors the maximum of light and air' (p. 188). Compare the reference to Wren's 'practical humanity' in Whinney and Millar 1957, p. 325, where she also cited Bethlem's example as influential for Wren's use of brick and stone at Chelsea (p. 216). Kerry Downes has told me that Dr Whinney related Wren's ward plans to Hooke's example more specifically in her teaching; and compare Downes 1988, p. 84: at Chelsea, 'Wren also had the close example of Hooke's Bedlam Hospital (1674–6) whose single long line of two-storey blocks

punctuated by taller pavilions set new standards for the admission of light and air into institutional buildings'.

128. Wren Society 1942, 19: 79; Dean 1950, pp. 63, 78, 80.

129. Dean 1950, pp. 125, 159, 178; he quotes *Parentalia*, p. 123.

130. See Loeber 1981 (s.v. 'Robinson, William'; 'Jones, Richard') and Colvin, *Biographical dictionary* 1995 (s.v. 'Jones'). Robinson's peculations were not specifically connected to Kilmainham; for Ranelagh's, Ascoli 1975; Wren Society 1942, 19: 81, 84; and Dean 1950, pp. 121–22. Chelsea's executive was small in comparison to Greenwich's and its management was peculiarly and dangerously informal for a while. Dean suggests (pp. 159–61) that Fox and Wren tried, with some success, to reduce Ranelagh's discretionary access to hospital funds, but even so, the in-pensioners' pay was cut at the end of the century and some in- and out-pensioners were still owed money by Ranelagh on their deaths.

131. Wren Society 1942, 19: 80; Dean 1950, pp. 83–90, 284–85.

132. In 1805 Faulkner (p. 55) called it 'plain, yet not inelegant'; Wren seemed to have 'carefully avoided all superfluous ornaments, . . . wishing to save expense'.

133. Wren Society 1942, 19: 65; Dean 1950, p. 56.

134. Godfrey 1927, p. 20.

135. Von Uffenbach 1934, pp. 13–14; he was however surprised at the number of visitors walking in the grounds.

136. Dean 1950, p. 61; Binney 1982 describes the enlargement of the pensioners' bunks in the 1960s.

137. Wren Society 1942, 19: 76.

138. Foucault, *Discipline* 1979, pp. 141, 143.

139. According to Dean (1950, p. 131) the decision to organize the 416 infantrymen in the sixteen galleries into eight companies was made as late as 1688; Evelyn had however envisaged a regimental organization much earlier (1955, 4: 269 [27 January 1682]).

140. Quoted Dean 1950, p. 46.

141. Wren Society 1942, 19: 67–68; Dean 1950, pp. 46, 99. The 1685 show was for Charles, just before his death.

142. Newell 1984, p. 18; Wren Society 1929, 6: 39.

143. Wren Society 1929, 6: 36 (the meeting on 3 September 1697), 38; compare the drawing (All Souls College, Oxford), Wren vol. IV: 68, reproduced ibid., p. 94.

144. Newell 1984, p. 18.

145. La Roche 1933, p. 167.

146. Describing Sir John Morden's almshouses: Defoe 1971, p. 115.

147. Rawcliffe 1984, p. 12, in connection with Richard Whittington's almshouse (founded 1424); the statutes of William Elsyng's (1331), also in London, similarly arranged for the 'equipment of private cells'. See also Clay 1909, p. 120 and Orme and Webster 1995, pp. 91–92.

148. Evelyn 1955, 4: 270, for 27 January 1682.
149. La Roche 1933, p. 251.
150. Clay 1909, p. 120: 'Formerly, inmates gathered round an open hearth or in a capacious ingle-nook. . . . The chimney . . . is a new feature indicating a change of life.' Later dining practice perhaps depended on the sex and status of the almshouses' occupants. At the relatively grand Bromley College, Kent (1670–72), which had no hall, the clergymen's widows each lived with a servant and a spinster relation and had their own kitchen. At Morden however, whose plan was very similar, rules drawn up in 1700 enjoined the men from taking food away from the hall: Collins 1996, p. 25.
151. According to *Pattern* 1695, p. 26, the Invalides' officers' rooms were at the ends of the galleries, the 'better to observe the Soldiers', but I have been unable to find the matching passage in Le Jeune's *Description*. Could it have been the supervisory implications, as well as Oxonian conservatism, that led to the rejection of Hawksmoor's design of 1708–9 for Queen's College, which broke with collegiate tradition by arranging rooms in each lodging-block on either side of a central corridor? See Downes 1970, pp. 74–75 (and pp. 76–77 for comparable, contemporary projects for All Souls) and idem 1966, p. 119: 'This arrangement, which is a commonplace of modern life, probably derived from the plan of ward blocks at Chelsea and Greenwich which had set new standards of convenience in communal accommodation'.

Chapter 3: Publicity and public buildings

1. Rochester 1980, pp. 197, 201–2. This chapter's title, and the kinds of associations it makes, are indebted to Peter Borsay's example: 'Publications and public works', in 1989, pp. 250–52.
2. 'He, *Weaves* Straw-Bracelets, which he calls her *Hair*, / And She, o'th' *Wall* writes Letters to her *Dear*, / Th'only *True Lovers* now adays are here': 'Bethlehems beauty' (1676) in Aubin 1943, pp. 245–48, ll. 69–71.
3. For the etymology of 'pageant' see Backscheider 1993, p. 14, and Peacock 1995, p. 1. Cavallo (1991, pp. 55, 60) has shown the way that 'Hospitals, rebuilt . . . in sumptuously baroque style, became the backdrop of civic prestige, and offered symbolic confirmation of the intense processes of social ascent and formation of new wealth' then taking place.
4. Zevi 1974, p. 300; see also pp. 30, 50.
5. Following from BCGM for 23 October 1674, beginning p. 48: the committee's reports for 13, 16, and 20 October 1674.
6. Following the account in Stow 1720, 1: 192.
7. Smith 1815, p. 32.
8. In 1660: Pratt 1928, pp. 25–26. The concern was then evident at houses, too: Cooper 1999, p. 98 quotes Aubrey on Wilton, where around 1683 the court's high wall was replaced by an 'Enclosure with Piles, and Iron-barres' permitting a 'delightful visto' for passers-by.
9. Stevenson, 'Robert Hooke's Bethlem' 1996, pp. 260–61.
10. BCGM for 23 July 1675, p. 153; 10 September 1675, p. 173; 24 September 1675, p. 177.
11. The experience can still be appreciated at the National Trust's Ashdown House (*c.*1664), Oxfordshire, which is 'tall and square like the Bedlam pavilions': Downes 1966, p. 5. See Cooper 1999, pp. 240–44, who also quotes (p. 328) a late seventeenth-century reference to a cupola 'for pleasure only' and reproduces (p. 5) an anonymous painting (*c.*1658) of Wisbech Castle, Cambs., showing every possible vantage-point in use, including a cupola and a balcony.
12. Hooke's building was illustrated in at least thirty-six books published in 1681 and after: see Adams 1983, which does not list prints sold singly. Edward Haytley's 1746 painting of Bethlem (Thomas Coram Foundation, London) does offer an oblique view, as does another of Smith's etchings (Adams 1983, 115/17).
13. BCGM for 8 and 16 May 1674, pp. 638, 642. Hunter and Macalpine 1963, pp. 198–99 quote John Archer's *Every man his own doctor* (1673) , in which he announced that he could place those who had lost 'the use of Reason' in an 'excellent Air nere the City, fit for that purpose; and with the greatest security and delight to patients; there being no better way for their Recovery' and (p. 281) David Irish's similar boast (1700) for his Surrey madhouse.
14. Evelyn 1955, 4: 133–34 (18 April 1678). For what follows, I have borrowed from my chapter ('The architecture of Bethlem at Moorfields') in Andrews et al. 1997.
15. [Hatton] 1708, 2: 731; Stow 1720, 1: 192.
16. 'Bethlehems beauty', ll. 45, 47–53, in Aubin 1943, pp. 245–48. The transcription errs at l. 53: Aubin has '[as]sisted' for 'stifled', which reverses the sense.
17. Andrews et al. 1997, p. 338 comment on the ambiguity of the phrase.
18. See Wear 1993, pp. 1287–88 for a summary discussion on which I have depended here. 'Non-naturals' affect the strength of the organs and the bodily system as a whole: the others are food and drink, sleep and waking, movement and rest, retention and evacuation, and emotions or passions.
19. Palmer 1993, pp. 62–63.
20. In general, as Pelling points out (1998, p. 19), the relationship, as perceived, between people and their environment has not been much studied for the early modern period, but see the instances ibid., pp. 23–24; Gilchrist 1992, p. 112; Rawcliffe 1995, pp. 41–43 (who quotes Erasmus citing Galen on the importance of cross-draughts in houses); Henderson 1992, pp. 138,

145; Palmer 1993, pp. 65–66; and Tittler 1991, quoting Francis Bacon: the 'most pernicious infection next the plague is the smell of the jail'.

21. Lubbock 1995, pp. 30–33.

22. Wear 1992, pp. 141, 145–47, idem 1993, p. 1292.

23. In Aubin 1943, pp. 136–50, ll. 517–24.

24. See Jenner 1995 for the general point; on Bethlem specifically, Andrews et al. 1997, pp. 248–49.

25. See Jose 1984, especially pp. 1, 57, 36–37: 'The age was all too ready to contemplate itself in terms of grand unchanging monuments, and political issues were quickly linked with art-works – the religious settlement with the rebuilding of St Paul's, for example.'

26. Erskine-Hill 1979, p. 150, tells the story of how Lord Burlington 'is said, when he saw the completed St. Paul's . . . , to have remarked that when the Jews saw the second temple they remembered the first temple and wept'.

27. Aubin 1936 provides a chronological list of 'building' (as opposed to country-house) poems; town- and building-poetry was not well cultivated in England before 1660 but the Fire and the new availability of printed images encouraged it (p. 147).

28. Dean 1950, pp. 23–24.

29. At least after James II doubled the size of the Army: Wren Society 1942, 19: 65–66 (the Treasurer's accounts for 1682–1702 are summarized p. 81) and Dean 1950, pp. 25–27, 35–36.

30. Supplemented by court-martial fines (after 1698) and unclaimed prize money (1707): Keevil 1958, p. 201; Lloyd and Coulter 1961, p. 197. See the statement of income from 1696 to August 1703 transcribed in Wren Society 1929, 6: 45.

31. Dean 1950, p. 36 quoting Fox's undated memorandum (spelling modernized).

32. The letter is transcribed in Hutt 1872, p. 14; Dean (1950, p. 41) suggests that Fox drafted it.

33. Dean 1950, p. 35, and p. 43 for Fox's 'Memoriall' of 1712, recalling Charles's visit to the hospital in February 1685. The king 'was glad to see it & said . . . That Fox and Hee had done that great worke without the help of the Trea[su]ry, who indeed never gave the least countenance towards it'.

34. Hutt 1872, p. 14, from Charles's letter to Sancroft, in which he explained that a standing army would be necessary.

35. Dean 1950, pp. 24, 38–42. Hutt comments (1872, pp. 14–15) that 'frequent insertions in the *London Gazette* of paragraphs such as "Since his Majesty hath been pleased to lay [Chelsea's] first stone, the nobility have contributed largely"' did not have the desired effect. Admittedly, the Navy did not suffer the way the Army did (being, among other things, useless for civil policing) and Greenwich's subscription income was not wonderful either.

36. Quoted Hutt 1872, p. 14 (spelling modernized); see Dean 1950, p. 22 on how the Army that now (in the early 1680s) needed pensioning had arisen out of a revolutionary outbreak in 1661.

37. Wilson 1713, pp. 3–4.

38. Le Jeune 1683, preface ('Au Lecteur'): 'Ce qu'ils en ont publié, a fait naistre de la curiosité dans les autres Nations, & obligé un grand Roy voisin & quelques autres Princes étrangers de souhaiter d'en avoir les plans & un fid[è]le description.' I don't know enough about illustrated publications of single buildings to be able to assess hospitals' importance to the genre. See Rowan 1990, p. 13 for William Adam's interest in it: Adam owned Le Jeune's *Description* and borrowed (and kept) Jacob van Campen's volume (1664) on the Amsterdam town hall, which was probably Le Jeune's model, if he needed or wanted one.

39. 'Vous voulez bien que je vous prie encore de me faire avoir le plan de l'hostel des Invalides tiré sur le modèle avec toutes les faces, car le Roy sera bien aise de le voir'; quoted Dean 1950, p. 23, who suggests that no drawings were then sent.

40. Whinney and Millar 1957, p. 217; Wren Society 1942, 19: 66; Dean 1950, pp. 75, 96.

41. A 'Large Port Folio of finished drawings of the Hôtel des Invalides' (no longer to be found) was sold at an auction of his drawings in 1749: Jeffery 1996, pp. 70, 72, who speculates (p. 366) that these drawings were either those Louvois sent in 1678, or among the 'Military Ordonances and some other things that relate to the Hôpital des Invalides' that Sir William Turnbull, the Envoy Extraordinary to the French Court, procured for Blathwayt in March 1686. See also Dean 1950, p. 75.

42. Le Jeune 1683, pp. 11–12: '[C]'est celuy sur lequel on voit naistre & s'élever hors de terre un Edifice'; 'On distingue par le noir & le blanc de cette Planche, ce qui est fermé de murailles, comme les Eglises & les appartemens, d'avec ce qui est exposé à l'air, comme les Courts & les Jardins: le noir marque ce qui est massif de maçonnerie, comme les pilastres, les murs de face & de ref[e]nd, dont quelques-uns sont pleins, comme dans les quatre Refectoirs, où les jours ne sont que d'un coté; presque tous les autres sont percez de croisées, dont les appuis sont marquez par deux lignes.'

43. Ibid., facing p. 1 ('Quel miracle soudain fait dans ce prez charmans / Naistre ce grand Palais, ces long Apparte-mens? / D'un regard étonné la Seine les découvre, / Et doute quelque temps, si c'est un nouveau Louvre') and preface.

44. BCGM for 25 September 1674, p. 37.

45. Though the 'Structure be so large and magnificent, yet by the great Application that was made in hastning the Building, 'twas finished the next Year': Stow 1720, 1: 192. A lot of work, including the digging for the

foundations, preceded the official starting date and much remained after the summer of 1676: Stevenson, 'Robert Hooke's Bethlem' 1996, p. 259.

46. Spencer 1965, 1: 143.

47. Printed with an instructive introduction in Aubin 1943, pp. 136–40, see ll. 336–44. The inscription on Hooke and Wren's Monument partly reads, in translation, 'London rises again, whether with greater speed or greater magnificence is doubtful; three short years completed that which was considered the work of an age': Reddaway 1940, p. 244.

48. Or so I interpret the entry: 'noe person be p'mitted to ingrave a platt or print of the said Hospitall in respect care is taken by the Governo^rs of this Hospitall that a print thereof shall be made in the most exacte manner': BCGM for 30 March 1677, p. 364.

49. Ibid., p. 367: 'to make the severall Additons to the said plott to be engraven would create noe greater worke or Charge than is required to make the said Vacancyes or ffeilds [?] compleate.'

50. The Bethlem plan might even have represented an advance on the *Micrographia* plates as Harwood (1989, p. 145) analyses them; he quotes (p. 119) Hooke on the 'Judgment and Caution' to be exercised in illustration.

51. This map, first advertised for sale on 26 January 1677 (i.e. 1676–7) was first published by William Morgan; more satisfactory in this respect was Morgan's 1682 map. Hyde has published both maps in facsimile (Ogilby and Morgan 1992; Morgan 1977). For Hooke's cartography see Taylor 1937, who quotes 'draughts and prospects' p. 533.

52. BCGM for 30 March 1677, p. 367; Hooke 1935, p. 284 (6 April 1677).

53. Dean (1950, p. 23), who did not know the 1713 publication, cites this as a manuscript of *c*.1702, published 1760.

54. Hawksmoor 1728, pp. 6, 9. The abridgement of the *Remarks* in Wren Society 1929, 6: 17–27 excludes much of the political material.

55. Hawksmoor 1728, pp. 5, 6.

56. Bold 1989, pp. 141, 144, 146; compare pp. 121–27 on Whitehall.

57. Keevil 1958, pp. 199–201: the hospital was commissioned 2 March 1695. Now definitive is John Bold's *Greenwich: an architectural history of the Royal Hospital for Seamen and the Queen's House* (Yale University Pres, 2000), alas published too late for the purposes of this book.

58. Hawksmoor 1728, p. 14. Some London craftsman called in to advise had moreover suggested that from the demolition might be salvaged 'Ornaments for slighter Buildings, such as the private Hotels, or the Houses commonly built by the London Workmen, often burning, and frequently tumbling down': another antithesis, there (ibid., p. 13).

59. Ibid., pp. 8–9. The widows were accommodated inasmuch as the nurses were recruited from among them: Tenon 1992, p. 70.

60. Webb 1930–31, p. 124 (26 October 1729). See Davies 1956, pp. 133–34 for the state of the hospital by 1728.

61. Hawksmoor 1728, p. 9 and, for the quotations following, pp. 6, 8.

62. Spencer 1965, 1: 106; Filarete was not writing about any work in particular. As Gandon would explain in his 'On the progress of architecture in Ireland', 'public works of art form the leading features, which must invariably attract the attention and notice of strangers', and posterity: Mulvany 1969, pp. 261–62.

63. Quoted Hawksmoor 1728, p. 9.

64. Ibid., pp. 13–14.

65. Ibid., pp. 9, 12. Whinney and Millar's juxtaposition of illustrations (1957, pls 61a and 61b) of a 1694 design for Greenwich and a view of Chelsea from the river makes the resemblance very clear. The grant is reprinted in Cooke and Maule 1789, pp. 1–7.

66. Now in the National Maritime Museum (ART/4; with no key surviving, except on the 'dissection'); Wren Society 1929, 6: pls II–IX.

67. Compare the redrawn plans in Bold 1989, p. 135.

68. One of these in fact (or later) became a ward, according to the drawing (National Maritime Museum) reproduced as Wren Society 1929, 6: pl. XIX top left. This shows the King Charles and its base block as the end of the latter was rebuilt according to the General Court's resolution of 15 November 1711; see Davies 1956, p. 133 and Newell 1984, pp. 26, 26. Compare also the first-floor Warrant plan and that of *c*.1711, Wren Society 1929, 6: pl. XIX top right.

69. Reproduced as Wren Society 1929, 6: pl. VIII.

70. According to Tenon (1992, p. 66), the King Charles building was distinctive for its Chelsea-like cabins: 'chaque matelot a sa cellule qui d'une grande propreté'.

71. Communication from John Bold; Richardson 1998, p. 79.

72. Grosley 1772, 2: 42; compare Tenon 1992, p. 66. For illustrations see Wren Society 1929, 6: pl. XXX bottom and pl. XLV bottom, respectively reproducing the National Maritime Museum's drawings ART/1/45 (the first [ground]-floor plan of the Queen Mary building) and ART/1/7 (a plan initialled 'N.H.' by a draftsman, showing all the buildings, including Hawksmoor's proposed infirmary).

73. Aikin 1771, p. 20.

74. Downes 1988, pp. 108–9; Wren Society 1929, 6: pls XXIV, XXV show the elevations, in Soane's Museum.

75. Downes 1988, p. 109; Wren Society 1929, 6: pl. XXVI (showing All Souls IV: 21, 22).

76. Downes 1979, pp. 83–85; idem 1988, p. 109.

77. Thompson and Goldin 1975, p. 149, following Dieter Jetter (1973, p. 50); compare Markus 1993, pp. 117–18.

78. Wren Society 1929, 6: 97. The relevant plans are in All Souls College, Oxford, Wren vols IV: 21–22 (six ward blocks) and V: 29 (twelve ward blocks; Figure 25 here) and were like the other Wren drawings in the College acquired in 1751, two years after the Wren sale.

79. Newell 1984, pp. 17–18; Wren Society 1929, 6: 39.

80. Downes 1994, p. 41. The only earlier example I know is the engraving (or engravings) of Wren's proposed Trinity College, Library, prepared by David Loggan in 1675, which was used to support a printed appeal for funds: McKitterick 1995, pp. 7–8; Colvin, 'The building' 1995, p. 38, Fig. 35.

81. Vanbrugh 1928, pp. 43–44. For the history of such prints, Clayton 1997, pp. 52, 57, 75–77, who speculates on patrons' motives, and Bryant 1996, p. 17, who speculates on buyers'.

82. Wren Society 1929, 6: 40.

83. See Downes 1979, p. 85 and idem 1994, p. 64 n. 31 for these prints.

84. Wren Society 1929, 6: 40, 41.

85. Wren may or may not have already discarded it when he went to the king because he also took with him a wooden model, for which Hawksmoor was paid early in 1699, that *does* show the block arrangement as it was built: Downes 1979, pp. 86–87.

86. Wren Society 1929, 6: 60.

87. Quoted in Downes 1994, p. 40.

88. *Pattern* 1695, p. 21; compare Le Jeune 1683, p. 9.

89. [Hatton] 1708, 2: 738.

90. Compare the definitions in the 1734 *Builder's dictionary*, ed. Russell 1997, s.v. 'Colonnade', 'Gallery', 'Piazza'.

91. Hawksmoor 1728, p. 16.

92. The figure is from Hawksmoor's large plan of 1728: NMM ART/1/63–64; Downes 1979, cat. 361.

93. Whinney 1971, p. 188.

94. With mouldings at impost level and around the arch, as Bruand had used at the Invalides and Robinson at Kilmainham. The resemblance is even clearer in an elevation for the Hall: Wren Society 1931, 8: pl. XXV (All Souls V:34).

95. Soo 1998, p. 159; on the dating, see her introduction to the tracts, and Bolton in Wren Society 1942, 19: 122–24.

96. Von Uffenbach's admiration is quoted in Chapter 2, at n. 18; La Roche described (1933, p. 250) how her walk through the 'great peristyle' was spoiled by rain.

97. Soo 1998, p. 156.

98. Wren's understanding of porticoes' significance for urban planning in classical antiquity would have been reinforced by his reading of Palladio (*The four books of architecture*, 3.17, 18) and Vitruvius' description of the Greek forum (*The ten books on architecture*, 5.1.1).

99. Soo 1998, pp. 156–57.

100. Quoted in Casey 1994, p. 89.

101. NMM ADM Y/G/52.

102. Soo 1998, pp. 158–59, 167–68.

103. Hawksmoor 1728, p. 16.

104. Giles Worsley (1995, p. 54) makes the point about Hawksmoor's Latin. He also identifies (p. 77) the 'monumentality of the colonnade' as central to one strain of Baroque architecture around 1700 and notes its use in unexecuted projects by Hawksmoor (pp. 58, 88), Wren (78–79), and Henry Aldrich (88–89) as well as their realization at Greenwich and at Edward Lovett Pearce's Parliament Buildings, Dublin, begun 1729 (166).

105. On the basis of Wren's tracts, Shaftesbury's strictures on modern cities (on which see Ogborn 1998, pp. 83–84) and, possibly, Berkeley's 1721 *Essay* (the passage quoted by Chaney 1991, p. 85, mentions Greek cities' discouragement of private luxury, and encouragement of porticoes, among other public works) I am inclined to identify colonnades with a contemporary understanding of 'Greek' architecture, as well as with admiration for such modern realizations as Bernini's at St Peter's in Rome (Worsley 1995, p. 77, and again compare Berkeley, in Chaney 1991, pp. 79, 85). See also Colvin, 'The building' 1995, p. 36 on Wren's use of columns underneath the Trinity College Library, which he explained with reference to the 'forum'.

106. Hawksmoor 1728, p. 13. Though it was well placed for the naval yards at Deptford and Woolwich: see Keevil 1958, p. 201.

107. Defoe 1971, pp. 176, 181.

108. Soo 1998, p. 153.

109. Klein 1996 re-examines our habit of favouring binary oppositions, and in particular their unsatisfactoriness regarding public–private distinctions in eighteenth-century England.

110. Webb 1930–31, p. 153 (17 August 1734).

111. See Colvin, *Biographical dictionary* 1995, s.v. 'Ripley, Thomas' for his service to the wit of Pope, among others; John Bold has written to me that 'Ripley's contribution was much more significant than has been allowed – he finished the [Queen Mary] building in circumstances which although financially easier than before, were still difficult, and he got more pensioners in, by narrowing the corridors and increasing the size of cabins'.

112. Vanbrugh 1928, p. 138 (26 August 1721).

113. Compare the essay reprinted in the *Gentleman's Magazine* in 1739 (9: 640–42): in it a proud house owner shows his visitors round improvements each named for the public office, or bribe, that enabled its construction.

Chapter 4: Looking at asylums

1. [Hatton] 1708, 2: 737, 740.

2. Quoted in Gifford 1989, p. 84.

3. Hewett (1725) is quoted in McParland 1994, p. 22. For the mutual animus, idem 1995, p. 161 and Colvin, *Biographical dictionary* 1995, s.v. 'Hewett, Sir Thomas'. See Downes 1968, pls 98–99 for examples of the keystones, and Beaufort 1995, pp. 27–28 for Hawksmoor's defence of the flag tower.

4. Colley 1994, p. 197 (the others were Somerset House, Hampton Court Palace, and Windsor Castle); Brewer 1997, pp. 8–13.

5. Saisselin 1992, p. 56: French Physiocrats' model for the arts was 'not that of the Roman aesthetes, as with Winckelmann and the antiquarians. Rather, it was the practical antiquity of public works, aqueducts, city squares, public markets, roads, and amphitheaters that was felt worthy of true emulation.' See Brewer 1995, pp. 342–43 for the 'cultural vacuum' left by the failure to 'use the arts as an adjunct of kingship' (however, he notes the general lack of enthusiasm for any 'cult of monarchy') and Ayres 1990 for the politics of 'imperial works' as they impinged upon Pope via his virtuoso friends.

6. Harris and Savage 1990, p. 322 mention that Robert Morris (who admired Wren) believed that Inigo Jones had designed Chelsea – did many think so? In 1763 Samuel Johnson 'remarked that the structure of Greenwich hospital was too magnificent for a place of charity' but also, interestingly, 'that its parts were too much detached to make one great whole': Boswell [1906], 1: 284.

7. Borsay 1989, p. 305: 'Baroque's individualistic nature . . . made it difficult to establish the social value of architecture, since criticisms derived from objective external standards could be deflected by stressing the originality of a design.'

8. Harris and Savage 1990, s.v. 'Morris, Robert'; his books do not seem to have been very widely read.

9. Morris 1971, pp. 20–21, xii–xiii.

10. Ibid.: the phrases are from pp. 33, 70, 88, 21, 49, 50.

11. Sekora (1977, pp. 44–48) describes how luxury, for Augustine and Shakespeare a carnal lust, was almost entirely desexualized in eighteenth-century England.

12. Borsay 1989, pp. 305–7, extending arguments advanced by Neil McKendrick (1982, especially pp. 11, 54–57, 95, 113). Borsay's own discussion has in turn been very usefully directed to early eighteenth-century studies of the mind by Suzuki (1995).

13. Reprinted in the *Gentleman's Magazine* 9 (1739): 640–42, on p. 641. Lubbock (1995, pp. 44–46) draws some fascinating connections between opposition to Walpole in this period, a new theory of conspicuous consumption (Mandeville was enormously influential, in this reading), and an attempt to revive old understandings of appropriate private magnificence.

14. Pope 1968, p. 587, from the 'Argument' to *Epistle IV. To Richard Boyle, Earl of Burlington* (1731); Borsay 1989, p. 291 quotes Ware.

15. Erskine-Hill's book (1983) is central to any understanding of the 'Augustan idea' and literary and architectural practice in relation to it. For the theme, and the 'Epistle' to Burlington in relation to it, see also idem 1975 (Chapter 10, 'Imperial works', pp. 318–26), idem 1979, and Ayres 1990.

16. Pope 1968, p. 595: ll. 195–98 and Pope's note. See Erskine-Hill 1995, pp. 226–27 on the political implications of the substitution of '*Till* Kings call forth' for the Chatsworth Draft's '*While* Kings Call forth'.

17. In adding the Oglethorpe material to the 1737 version of the poem, Savage was taking advantage of contemporary infanticide scares and public interest in Oglethorpe's visit to England early that year. 'It was always Mr. Savage's Desire to be distinguished', wrote his biographer Samuel Johnson (1971, p. 83), 'and when any Controversy became popular, he never wanted some Reason for engaging in it with Ardour'.

18. Kenny 1984, pp. 195–96: Public Spirit's 'economy would be based on the frugality of bold schemes of public utilities to make life easier and more prosperous'.

19. Wilson 1713, pp. 2–3; my emphasis.

20. Lettsom is quoted in Loudon 1981, p. 341; Voltaire 1785, p. 241; Johnson 1761, pp. 19, 17–18. See Goldberg 1991, pp. 181, 184 for explanations from sermons (1729, 1771) of 'anything passing for benevolence and charity before the age of Christianity as mere defect'.

21. The 'Common Enemy': Pope was describing (April 1731) to Burlington these new lines, which he had added to the first draft: Erskine-Hill 1995, p. 223.

22. 'To Burlington', in Pope 1968, pp. 586–95, ll. 31–36. See Wittkower 1974, pp. 155–68 for a renowned analysis of the Venetian window in eighteenth-century England, where its rather casual uses differed from more monumental applications in sixteenth-century Italy, in ways easily related to ornament on the one hand and necessity on the other.

23. For these wings' construction see O'Donoghue 1914, pp. 244, 406, and Andrews et al. 1997, p. 220. This east wing was for men; the women's wing was built 1733–36. J. T. Smith's 1814 etching *South-west view of Bethlem Hospital and London Wall* (Adams 1983, no. 115/17) shows another Venetian window on the latter's rear corner.

24. Rutter 1717, pp. 3, 4. Aubin 1936, pp. 158–59 remarks that the poem's successful evocation of terror marks a new stage within the 'building' genre.

25. Ward 1993, pp. 50–51, 54–55 (for the Orphans' Fund, from which the City had been borrowing even before the Fire, see Reddaway 1940, pp. 68, 177, 308); Brown 1730, p. 29.

26. Harris and Savage 1990, s.v. 'Ralph, James'. See also Rogers 1972, p. 362 and Paulson 1992, pp. 78–79, 81.

27. [Ralph] 1734, pp. 7–8. He added that Bethlem looks so

much like Moorgate itself (rebuilt 1672; the resemblance was real) that the spectator is confused.

28. *Gentleman's Magazine* 9 (1739): 640–42, on p. 642: 'The Front of the House I observ'd was very irregular, one Part on't very low and old, but lately vamp'd and stucco'd, the other new and lofty, and both agreeing very ill together.'

29. Kunzle 1966, p. 343.

30. Though no one has adduced the print, this has been understood: O'Donoghue 1914, pp. 244–47. Hogarth's architecture is a compositional device, not a record of Bethlem: see Kromm 1985, p. 239, and Kunzle 1966, pp. 343–44.

31. [Dodsley] 1761, 1: 297. The six volumes' seventy-six engravings do not, perhaps significantly, include one of the building, though Dodsley did illustrate Cibber's invariably admired sculptures (compare Figure 10, p. 41).

32. For this building see French 1951, pp. 9–13 and Stroud 1971, pp. 49–50. According to the former, it was a conversion of the so-called Foundry (a former cannon manufactory), but Stroud is more reliable in this connection.

33. [Dodsley] 1761, 4: 205. The description was copied in later topographies; compare Noorthonck's *History of London* (1773), quoted in French 1951, p. 11 and the pseudonymous 'Harrison' 1776, pp. 543–44. The print *Enthusiasm displayed* (c.1755, Robert Pranker after John Griffiths) includes a more informative perspective view of the hospital (Bindman 1997, p. 123, cat. 65), in which the fenestration differs a little from that shown in other prints.

34. Maitland 1756, 2: 1315.

35. A bald summary of one of the central episodes in the history of the nascent specialism. See Andrews et al. 1997, especially pp. 276–78 ('The plain façade of St Luke's just across the way at Moorfields was in stark contrast to the classical opulence and old notion of spectacle enshrined at Bethlem') and pp. 266, 268, 274, and notes on pp. 285–86 for other challenges presented by the new foundation.

36. Brown 1730, p. 32.

37. 'The Lady's Dressing Room' (perhaps written 1730, published 1732): Swift 1983, pp. 448–52, l. 144.

38. Rogers 1972, pp. 143–44.

39. 'The Lady's Dressing Room', ll. 97–98.

40. Paulson 1989, p. 26.

41. Pelling 1986, p. 99. The 'frightening possibility that nothing stood behind decorum . . . the total disagreement between seeming and being' forms a theme in Stafford 1991, writing of the eighteenth century: see especially pp. 86, 288–90. The metaphors come full circle with St John Chrysostom (d. 407, quoted Rawcliffe 1995, p. 171): women are 'nothing more than "phlegm, blood, bile, rheum and the fluid of digested food . . . behind . . . a whitened sepulchre"'.

42. Lines 29–30, no. 13 in Fowler 1994.

43. Tryon 1973, pp. 289–91; Ibbot 1719, p. 29.

44. [Ralph] 1734, p. 17; [Morris] 1970, pp. 8, 13, from 'The art of architecture', published anonymously in 1742 (for the authorship, see Harris and Savage 1990, s.v. 'Morris, Robert').

45. As Anthony Vidler has summarized Colin Rowe: see the former's essay 'Losing face' in Vidler 1992, pp. 85–99, quotation p. 85. Gent 1995, p. 390 offers Matisse and others as her examples.

46. Another bald summary of a complex development: see Andrews et al. 1997, Chapter 13, 'Visiting'.

47. Scull 1993, p. 52; Stevenson 2000; pp. 26–27.

48. Trusler [1768], p. 38.

49. Lichtenberg 1966, p. 266.

50. Kunzle (1966, p. 343) and Paulson (1992, p. 30) comment.

51. See Wilson 1988, a suggestive reading of Pope's *Essay on criticism* (1711), and Schor 1987, especially pp. 16–19 for a demonstration of the eighteenth-century associations of particularity, the feminine, and the ornamental. This is not to deny that the distinctions were pinned on those of class too: Shaftesbury (as summarized by Paulson 1989, p. 2) defined taste as an 'aristocratic faculty, dominated by judgment, which made distinctions' as opposed to the 'plebian fancy [which] made random connections and unwarranted leaps'.

52. Laugier 1972, p. 170: '. . . c'est trop de beautés réunies dans une maison qui cesse d'intéresser la charité, dès que la curiosité trouve trop à s'y satisfaire. Il faut que les pauvres soient logés en pauvres.'

53. Saisselin 1975, pp. 239, 248.

54. Tenon 1996, pp. 28 (Plymouth), 334 (the asylums).

55. With the exception of the Friends' Retreat these buildings have not had much analysis, and the first St Luke's remains mysterious. Their study should begin with the references in Colvin's *Biographical dictionary* (1995), the National Monuments Record files, and Smith 1999, pp. 15–16. These are the asylums in Newcastle (built 1765–67 and demolished c.1766: Colvin, s.v. 'Newton, William'); Manchester (opened 1766; some illustrations in Brockbank 1952, and see Aikin 1771, p. 71); York (opened 1777, and the first 'lunatic asylum' as opposed to 'lunatic hospital': Colvin, s.v. 'Carr, John'; RCHM(E) 1975, pp. 47–49; and Digby 1986); Leicester (mostly built 1781 but not completed and opened, for ten patients, until 1794: Colvin, s.v. 'Harrison, William' and 'Firmadge, William', and Frizelle and Martin 1971, pp. 84–86, who reproduce a site plan by Firmadge); Liverpool (projected 1789, opened 1792 adjacent to the Infirmary); the Friends' Retreat, York (built 1794–96: Colvin, s.v. 'Bevans, John', and Digby, 'Moral treatment' and *Madness*, both 1985); and Hereford (opened 1799 in the Infirmary grounds, according to Smith a 'prestigious building' designed by John Nash).

56. Smith 1999, p. 37.
57. Markus 1993, p. 131 credits Bethlem with the introduction of the recreational gallery, a 'unique space which is locally free but securely bounded' that 'was almost exclusive to English-speaking countries'. Little is known about the houses apparently purpose-built (in 1728, and replaced in 1744) for the twenty insane patients at Guy's Hospital but the 'new Lunatick House', built 1790–97, splayed two small wings at an angle of approximately 90 degrees: Cameron 1954, p. 71, and see the illustration reproduced by Richardson 1998, p. 161. For Irish asylums, Reuber, 'Architecture' and '"Moral management"' (both 1996); for England, Smith 1999, pp. 163–64 and the section 'Buildings for the mentally ill' in Taylor 1991, especially pp. 133–48; for construction with emphasis on Scotland, Markus 1982, pp. 90–103 and idem 1993, pp. 135–41. Jetter 1981 includes redrawn plans that are extremely useful for comparative purposes.
58. Philo 1989, p. 278 quotes an anonymous contributor (1861) to the *Journal of Mental Science*, and Taylor 1991, p. 135 quotes Hine. Rothman 1990, pp. 135–36 mentions nineteenth-century American observations of Central European monasteries converted to asylums. For criticisms of 'corridor' asylums and the appearance of the pavilion type, Scull 1980, pp. 52–54 and Philo 1989, pp. 276–78.
59. The line (484) from the 'Verses on the Death of Dr Swift' (composed 1731) is quoted in Malcolm 1989, p. 18. On the purpose-built Bethel Hospital, Norwich (completed 1713; its core survives), see Winston 1994, pp. 29, 36–37, and the photograph in Richardson 1998, p. 156. There, incidentally, casual visiting was permitted though after 1725 under restrictions (Winston, p. 40); it was not permitted at St Patrick's (Malcolm, pp. 30, 65).
60. Swift 1965, pp. 67, 70, 68: Fownes's letter of 9 September 1732. See Malcolm 1989, pp. 19–20: to take priority would be the construction of 'six or eight strong Cells, for outrageous Lunaticks . . . after the form of those made at the Infirmary of the Royal hospitall', Kilmainham.
61. Swift 1965, p. 67: at this point Fownes was referring to other parts of the asylum.
62. Malcolm 1989, pp. 40–46 describes Semple's selection and quotes the unsigned, undated memorandum. For the building, see also Markus 1993, pp. 131–33 and Reuber 1995.
63. Moorfields's delights are splendidly evoked by Rogers 1972, pp. 45–52.
64. Sharpe 1815, pp. 64, 155, 163. See Becher's appearances (indexed) in Smith 1999.
65. Boswell [1906], 2: 459–60, and see Rogers 1972, p. 45. Mrs Burney had wondered that anyone could live in Moorfields, 'in so shocking a situation as between Bedlam and St. Luke's Hospital'.
66. Tenon 1992, p. 73 ('*vitrées à demeure*'); I'm grateful to Kerry Downes for his help with the windows.
67. Malcolm 1989 reproduces Semple's 1750 elevation drawing after p. 52. It does not explain the front windows but there seems no reason to doubt that they were sashes like today's.
68. Richardson 1998, p. 155. Though it began with a house conversion, St George's had expanded substantially since, while the Westminster, London, and Middlesex hospitals were all still occupying one or several houses.
69. 'The window-type obviously formed part of the now-lost program for the new hospital': du Prey 1982, p. 43. It is shown on the section attributed to Gandon (see n. 76, below), on Soane's two designs (reproduced ibid., pp. 47, 49), and, according to du Prey, on William Newton's section (though this is not clear in his reproduction, p. 44), which he links with this competition (Evans 1982, p. 128 identifies it as a prison design). 'Lunette' and 'lunacy' both derive from the Latin *luna*, moon.
70. The cell drawings are Soane's Museum, Dance Cabinet (henceforth, 'SM Dance') 4/1/20 and 4/1/21; a later drawing (4/1/22) has annotations.
71. The NMR file (no. 101994) on Bethlem at Southwark contains a typewritten transcription of what is headed, 'Bethlem Building Ctte / 18 April 1811 / Report of Surveyor', i.e. James Lewis. It explains that in the projected new building, 'all the patients' sleeping rooms will be arched or groined, which will prevent accidents from fire and the noises of the turbulent affecting those above and below them' (spelling modernized).
72. James Wyatt's design (1784) for the Petworth, Sussex, House of Correction (reproduced Evans 1982, p. 138) is a good example, as is the Moulsham County Jail in Chelmsford, Essex, built to William Hillyer's designs 1773–77, though perhaps only after alterations (which according to Colvin, *Biographical dictionary* 1995, s.v. 'Johnson, John', took place 1782–91: see the illustration from 1810 in Evans, p. 43). Compare also Soane's entries for the national penitentiary competition announced in 1781, reproduced in du Prey 1982, pp. 210–15, and the high rounded windows, though not lunettes, seen in William Blackburn's drawing (reproduced Evans, p. 135) for the Dorchester County Gaol, built 1785–89. Evans (pp. 354, 357) evocatively describes the cell windows at the Model Prison, Pentonville, London (Joshua Jebb, 1840–42), which were 'just high enough to be difficult to see out of': 'The cell was blind: the form and content of the exterior world were obliterated. . . . The window was simply to let in a formless smudge of daylight.'
73. See Smith 1999, pp. 161–62 and Malcolm 1989, p. 90, who quotes William Saunders Hallaran (1810): small, high cell windows were 'necessary both "to guard against glare" and "to avoid all intercourse from

without". Conversely, the convalescent insane needed to be re-introduced to bright light and to the bustle of the outside world, though in a gradual and controlled manner.'

74. 'Harrison' 1776, p. 543.

75. Stroud 1971, p. 141 and du Prey 1982, pp. 38–39 describe the site (with a frontage of 550 feet along Old Street) and the lease's acquisition from the St Bartholomew's governors.

76. French 1951, p. 28. McParland 1985, p. 26 (reluctantly) attributes the Soane's Museum elevation (SM Dance 4/1/3; the corresponding section is 4/1/4) to Gandon. See du Prey 1982, pp. 38–54 for the competition; he reproduces the newspaper advertisement p. 40, and these drawings p. 42.

77. Rawes 1919, p. 28.

78. Soane's drawings (SM 13/1/7 and 13/1/9) comprising this entry were labelled with a '7' and those showing the looser curve (13/1/4 and 13/1/5) a '3'. Du Prey (1982, p. 51, who reproduces the plans on pp. 48–49, with a useful analysis) believes that '7' is the later; it also shows a cheaper building.

79. The newspaper advertisement states that entrants might get 'further Information . . . relative to the Number of Patients' at the hospital.

80. Rawes 1919, p. 28; Tenon 1992, pp. 43–48. The next year, Tenon published his plan of a general hospital for the La Roquette site in Paris, which includes an 'iron gate' in the central gallery linking the pavilions. This would separate the men's and women's sections but could be 'opened as the service requires': idem 1996, p. 318, plan reproduced facing p. 326.

81. The contract plans (SM Dance 4/2/1–3) show the wings, to be built when funds permitted, but there was no delay: Tenon (1992, p. 43) described them as under construction in June 1787. An article headed 'Lost for 137 years' (publication date presumably 1919) in the Soane Museum's volume of cuttings, etc. about St Luke's describes the foundation stone's discovery in a then-internal wall between the central range and the west wing. The wings 'simply butt against the older wall', which was carefully pointed, 'with a straight joint right from top to bottom'. The author correctly assumed that the additions were planned from the beginning, but points out the oddness of placing the stone where it would turn up only if the building were demolished. Confidence may have grown between 1782 and 1787, perhaps as a result of the successful open house at the end of 1786. The building was sold in 1916 to the Bank of England and became its St Luke's Printing Works; it was reported as under demolition in 1964. The quotation in the caption to Figure 38 is from Summerson 1947, p. 19.

82. They may have been altered, or so a *Builder* article (21 January 1860, pp. 43–44, copy in the NMR file

no. 101117) suggests: when the then-resident medical officer first arrived, a 'large portion of what is now the principal light of the ward, was blocked up'. What with the frequent cleaning demanded by bare wooden floors and 'imperfectly whitewashed' brick walls, this impediment to ventilation was thought to have caused the erysipelas formerly common in the hospital.

83. Tenon 1992, p. 44. Stroud (1971, p. 141) calls the windows 'bricked in except for their semi-circular heads'; and Stillman (1988, 2: 401), 'arcades with all of the arch but the lunette at the top filled with blank panels'.

84. The lunettes are explained more clearly by Soane's other project's section (SM 13/1/4), reproduced by du Prey 1982, p. 47. Soane's arches are also very reminiscent of the early fourth-century Roman basilica at Trier, Germany. Hugh May used something similar at Windsor Castle, and Hawksmoor liked the effect: Downes 1966, p. 17 and pls 5, 6, 544, 545.

85. Du Prey 1982, p. 52. A better comparison is the way Robert Mylne gave the ward fronts lunettes set into reveals which continue down to the ground in his (unexecuted) design of 1770 for 'an Hospital & Infirmary for Belfast', but I have no idea how widely that circulated (Richardson redrew it for reproduction in his book of 1955 [p. 43]; see Stillman 1988, 2: 399).

86. See the illustrations in Evans 1982, pp. 159, 160, 190; he quotes William Blackburn on the 'piazzas' p. 157.

87. Quoted Cashman 1992, p. 74. The distinctively mounted lunette was used at Guy's (see n. 57, above) and the so-called criminal blocks opened in 1816 at James Lewis's new Bethlem at Southwark (that for women is illustrated in O'Donoghue 1914, facing p. 340) and, earlier, by Wing in Bedford and by Francis Stone at the Norfolk Lunatic Asylum, Norwich (1811–14): see pls 2 and 4 in Smith 1999.

88. Emphasis in the original: Sharpe 1815, pp. 8 (the first Report), 148 (Upton's testimony), 119–20, 127–28 (the disclaimers of the Physician, Thomas Monro, and the Apothecary, John Haslam). Smith 1999, p. 160 describes the problems county asylums had well into the nineteenth century with idlers standing in public roads, and even on asylum walls, calling to and insulting inmates.

89. Quoted Kalman 1971, p. 108.

90. Louden 1840, p. 303, from Repton's *Observations on the theory and practice of landscape gardening* (1803); see Kalman 1971, p. 109. Useful on character are Saisselin 1975 and Archer 1979.

91. Archer 1979, p. 365 quotes Archibald Alison (1790) and Repton (as in Louden 1840, p. 303).

92. Elmes 1847, p. 379; I am indebted to David Watkin's interpretation (1993, p. 52) of this passage. 'Icon of functionality' is taken from Schor's exegesis (1987, p. 57) of Baudrillard's 'naturalizing' detail.

93. Both Pelling and Stafford show these reversals (see the references at n. 41 above). See also Wigley 1992, pp. 352–60: the surface layers of plaster (skin, cosmetics) which Alberti advocated for private houses comprise a 'mechanism for purification' that 'screens off the bodily condition of the body and yet reveals its formal order'.

94. Kaufman 1987, p. 33.

95. Andrews et al. 1997, pp. 189, 191: there was a 'squeamishness at the heart of such reactions that threatened to shut madness more firmly away'.

Chapter 5: Raising the hospital, each performing his part

1. Smollett 1990, pp. 328–29; he gave up on the idea 'insomuch that almost every street is furnished with one of these charitable receptacles'. See Turner 1958, pp. 68–69.

2. Owen 1964, pp. 69–71. Lindsay Granshaw has summarized the balance of lay and medical interests in eighteenth-century foundations ('Rise of the modern hospital', 1992, pp. 204–5, idem 1993, pp. 1185–86) on which see also Bynum 1985.

3. The case with, for example, the Salisbury Infirmary (Haskins 1922, p. 2), the Nottingham General Hospital (Iliffe and Baguley 1974, p. 79), and the Derby Infirmary (Chapter 10 here).

4. The corporate giving self-evident in Scotland has not been much studied in connection with the English hospitals (compare Macdonald 1999, especially p. 103), but see Owen 1964, p. 48 (town corporations effectively donating the site in Liverpool and Newcastle) and Money 1977, p. 9 (regarding the Birmingham General Hospital).

5. Hart 1980 summarizes the various 'gift relations', as Porter (1989) has it in an essay that remains the point of departure for the new hospitals' study. Langford 1991, pp. 496–500 notes their increasing tendency to equate gubernatorial and sponsorship privileges, but reminds us that they weren't necessarily the same thing and that variety was, again, the rule. At the General Hospital at Bath (in several ways distinctive) only medical men could recommend patients: Borsay 1991, pp. 211, 213.

6. Borsay 1989, p. 221.

7. *Reasons* 1760, p. 5; Langford 1991, p. 498 uses the same example.

8. Foster 1768, p. 40.

9. Wilson 1990, pp. 10–24.

10. Woodward 1974, pp. 147–48, lists twenty-eight provincial foundations to 1800; Bynum 1985, pp. 124–27, all the London medical charities to 1800.

11. Or four: see below for Edinburgh's Surgeons' Hospital, which did not survive. Glasgow's Town's Hospital, a workhouse from 1733, acquired a detached infirmary seven years later: Macdonald 1999 argues for its voluntary status, and for an enlarged view of what voluntarism constitutes in this context. The original hospital was on an H plan but with the infirmary and other additions its buildings eventually surrounded a quadrangle: see ibid. and Markus 1982, pp. 38–39 for the evidence. The Aberdeen Infirmary opened with six beds in 1742: Levack and Dudley 1992.

12. The Lock Hospital, founded 1746, on which see Bettley 1984 and Andrew 1991; the future Queen Charlotte's Lying-in Hospital (c.1739), the Lying-in Hospital for Married Women (1749), and the City (of London) Lying-in Hospital (1750), on which see ibid., Versluysen 1981, and Kennedy 1995.

13. Owen 1964, p. 69.

14. See Hart 1980, pp. 449–50; 'donors of expertise' is Janet Foster's phrase (1986, p. 641).

15. 'Charity and the liberal arts were intimately associated, precisely because both were seen to promote the moral improvement of their devotees': Borsay 1989, p. 266. For the Foundling, McClure 1981, pp. 66–67, 70–71, and Nicolson 1972, pp. 20–21. Its significance as the provider of London's first public-institutional exhibition space has been well demonstrated: Allen 1986; Paulson 1992, pp. 78–97, 323–41; Solkin 1992, Chapter 5, 'Exhibitions of sympathy'.

16. Suggestive as much of their rhetoric is, and particularly when it comes to what Jürgen Habermas calls 'bracketing', that is, the temporary elision of social differences 'to create a theoretically inclusive public sphere that readdresses the state' (the summary is Ogborn's: 1998, p. 77), the hospitals were not part of the public sphere in Habermas's sense. 'Bracketing' remains highly useful in this context, and in seeking models for the eighteenth-century rhetoric of collaboration at hospitals we might apply it to earlier practice, including at hospitals like St Bartholomew's. Very little work has been done on seventeenth-century corporate, secular building, but see Chapter 3 in Tittler 1991, on the financing of English town halls; Chalklin 1998, on county magistrates' construction; and Woodward 1995, pp. 98–99 on labour conscription in northern towns.

17. '... qu'il ait du talent dont l'hôpital puisse tirer avantage': Tenon 1992, p. 100.

18. Jacobsen is so described in Jacob Ackworth's letter of 28 June 1745 to the Admiralty (NMM ADM/B/129). The other designs were (according to Nicolson 1972, p. 11) from George Dance the Elder, George Sampson (d. ?1759), Surveyor to Guy's and St Thomas' among other institutions, and (John?) James.

19. Churchill was writing in 1732, about Lord Burlington: Thomson 1943, p. 58. See Colvin 1994 for a valuable summary of the relations between design, execution, and gentlemen: amateurs might design, but they did not contract to build.

20. Nichols and Wray 1935, p. 43; McClure 1981, pp. 63, 65–66; Colvin, *Biographical dictionary* 1995, s.v. 'Horne, James'.

21. LH/A/5/2, pp. 244 (14 July 1747), 300 (12 January 1748). Though Isaac Ware designed its first extension, into Chamber Street (Clark-Kennedy 1962, p. 56) Mainwaring is listed as the London's Surveyor in the annual sermon of 1750 (Mawson) though not in that of 1747 (Herring); I have not checked previous arrangements for recompensing him. For the hospital's various leaks, Clark-Kennedy, pp. 69, 127.

22. LH/A/5/2, pp. 307–8 (2 February 1748).

23. LH/A/5/4, pp. 27, 39, 48, 53 (17 July, 11 September, 16 October, and 6 November 1751). See also Clark-Kennedy 1962, pp. 112–21.

24. Jenkins 1961, pp. 145–46; they might also sell materials, as William Adam did (see the source cited in n. 39).

25. LH/A/5/4, p. 66 (18 December 1751); Foster 1986, p. 641 quotes the St Bartholomew's Court's thanks to Gibbs of 1749. Architects' services as county magistrates are directly comparable, and Mainwaring would later try to obtain 5 per cent from Middlesex for his surveying work: Colvin, *Biographical dictionary* 1995, s.v. 'Mainwaring, Boulton'.

26. Erlam 1954, p. 98.

27. When the Middlesex's side wings were constructed, 'individual agreements were made directly with the craftsmen, many of whom were governors of the hospital and did their work at "prime cost"': Leach 1988, p. 195.

28. 'Account' 1741, p. 652; Philasthenes 1739, p. 10. The managers' minutes refer to Adam, who as far as I know never became a manager, having 'generously assisted them with a plan': LHB 1/1/1, p. 142 (20 April 1738).

29. Michael Barfoot has told me that the Edinburgh Infirmary was eventually sued by every tradesman involved in its construction; see Clark-Kennedy 1962, p. 126 for the London's embarrassment in late 1753.

30. Colvin, *Biographical dictionary* 1995, s.v. 'Mills, Peter'.

31. Power 1926, pp. 11–12; Friedman 1984, pp. 14, 29, 213–14; Foster 1986, p. 636.

32. Carré 1982, p. 66; Friedman 1984, p. 309; Kingsbury 1995, pp. 39–42. According to Peachey (1910–14, pt 2: 99, 101), while Ware may have enlisted Burlington's support for the commission, he worked with Archer on the design.

33. Wood 1969, p. 293; the minutes are quoted by Borsay (1991, p. 217) as part of a discussion of how the new 'social dimension of philanthropy steered altruism towards the achievement of status'.

34. Though the bricklayer Edward Gray contracted for the Middlesex's first, central range: Leach 1988, p. 195.

35. French 1951, p. 32.

36. Langford (1991, pp. 256–64, 562–63) argues that all the new charities had a powerful advantage in this respect over the parish vestries administering Poor Law relief.

37. Friedman 1984, p. 220; Foster 1986, p. 641.

38. Lane (1992, pp. 7–8) shows how patronage networks worked around infirmaries, using James Paine (Middlesex) and Henry Keene (Worcester) as examples.

39. LHB 1/1/2, p. 105; Fleming 1962, p. 58 quotes James Naysmith.

40. Buchanan 1832, p. 14.

41. Porter 1989, p. 152; Wilson 1995, p. 73.

42. Risse 1986, pp. 27–29 points out the disproportion; Stevenson, '*Æsculapius Scoticus*', 1996, p. 53 (at points in what follows I borrow from this article). Compare Wilson 1990, p. 13, on London hospitals, and Clark-Kennedy 1962, p. 81, who contrasts the London's massed ranks of distinguished governors with the dirty little houses that physically comprised it at first.

43. Morrell 1976, p. 52, Christie 1974, p. 126. The problems for construction were longer-term. Edinburgh saw a 'notable growth in building activity in the first decades after 1660' but this had stopped with the national economic and human disasters of the 1680s and 1690s: Stevenson, *First Freemasons* 1988, p. 43.

44. Stevenson, *Origins of Freemasonry* 1988, pp. 75–76; Colvin 1986, pp. 169–70.

45. The Adams, notably, prospered as the builders of Fort George after 1745.

46. Simpson 1990, pp. 76, 78 explains the idealism of unionism and its importance to Adam's career.

47. Cunningham 1990, p. 57; Lawrence 1985, p. 153; Barfoot (n.d.).

48. The following is entirely indebted to Barfoot's 'Pedagogy, practice and politics', which clarifies the difference 1707 made to the relative fortunes of the Incorporation of Surgeons on the one hand and the Royal College of Physicians of Edinburgh, the Infirmary, and the Medical School on the other. See also Morrell 1976; Eaves Walton 1979, p. 9; and Lawrence 1985, p. 154.

49. *Memorial* 1737, p. 7.

50. Ibid., p. 4, noting that surgeons were an important 'branch of Trade to our indigent Country'; Philanthropus 1738, p. 6. John Bellers's proposal for hospitals 'for every particular Capital Distemper' to be built around London he partly justified as preventing physicians 'from Travelling to Foreign Hospitals to Learn' (1714, p. 7).

51. Philasthenes 1739, p. 3. Nor did the University impose residency restrictions, or require entrance examinations or qualifications, unlike Oxbridge (which anyway offered no clinical teaching): Morrell 1983, pp. 40, 43.

52. As Morrell puts it: 1976, p. 53. See also Christie 1974, pp. 127–28, Risse 1986, p. 26, idem 1989, p. 5, and Lawrence 1985, pp. 157–62.

53. Morrell 1976, p. 56. That year Monro had 436 pupils, a number greater than the total matriculating at Oxford and Cambridge each session: idem 1983, pp. 39–40.

54. Quoted in Maitland 1753, p. 454.

55. LHB 1/1/1, p. 140 (10 April 1738).

56. Ibid., p. 147 (20 April 1738): 'it is very reasonable to hope, That as the Reputation of the house will rise in proportion as the number of patients Cured in it Increases, So the Charitable Contributions towards its Support & Increase of its Capital will keep pace therewith.'

57. Philanthropus 1738, pp. 9, 6; compare Philasthenes 1739, pp. 3–4. The 1739 *Letter* is signed with the last pseudonym ('friend to the weak') but there is no reason to doubt that the authors were the same, and I use the first pen-name to stand for both in my text.

58. LHB 1/1/1, pp. 144, 147 (20 April 1738). Adam's plans (and Philanthropus in 1738) reckoned 24 beds on each of the ward floors, which would offer 72 beds. The minutes for 7 April 1740 refer to the commencement of the 'west part': LHB 1/1/1, p. 210.

59. Philanthropus 1738, p. 3. The managers recorded themselves as wanting to accommodate at least 100 'pupils': LHB 1/1/1, p. 147 (20 April 1738). The second stage of construction, approved 5 March 1739, was identified as that of the central block 'in which the opperation Roume is designed to be' (p. 187).

60. Illustrated in Markus 1993, p. 230. See Goslings 1976 and Cunningham 1990 for the Leiden faculty's general attractiveness as a model, and Stevenson, *'Æsculapius Scoticus'* 1996, p. 54. Maitland boasted in 1753 (p. 459) that Edinburgh's theatre was the 'best adapted to the purpose of any one in Europe', apparently on the basis of a claim in Philasthenes 1739 (which I haven't checked for this passage).

61. *History and statutes* 1749, pp. 17–18, which made a rather feeble attempt to attract a 'handsome Revenue' this way. Risse 1986, pp. 34–36 summarizes the Infirmary's finances.

62. The year 1748 is the usual completion date given but Monro recalled it as 1751 (Erlam 1954, p. 85). More to the point, as Thin (1927, p. 155) pointed out, it was then a long time before the building was used to capacity.

63. Philasthenes 1739, p. 10; compare Maitland 1753, p. 459. On the Foundling, Nichols and Wray 1935, p. 44.

64. Philanthropus 1738, p. 6; Philasthenes 1739, pp. 4–5. 'The mannagers were and still are of oppinion, That in this Building . . . they ought in forming the plan to have a regard not only to ye Capital Stock at present But to what it may be Encreased to in future ages': LHB 1/1/1, pp. 141–42 (20 April 1738).

65. Erlam 1954, p. 85. The memoirs do not mention the *Letters* of 1738 and 1739, but they do claim (p. 84) Munro's authorship of the 1725 *Proposals for employing the remaining stocks of the fishery* (i.e. on the hospital).

Michael Barfoot has told me that Monro co-wrote the *Account* of c.1730 and wrote the *Vindication of the Managers . . . from aspersions* (1737; the aspersions were being cast by the Incorporation of Surgeons).

66. *Brief account* 1735, p. 6. The hospital (demolished 1845) was built, west to east, in 1734–35, 1736, and 1791: Simpson, notes to Adam 1980, p. 32.

67. Quoted Whinney 1971, p. 92. Saumarez Smith has suggested that Castle Howard's plan (1699) was devised for construction by stages (1990, pp. 61, 84); for Scottish domestic examples see Macaulay 1987, pp. 16, 36.

68. Wood 1969, pp. 284–85.

69. Friedman 1984, pp. 213–14 (St Bartholomew's); Leach 1988, p. 195 (Middlesex); Nicolson 1972, pp. 11–12 (Foundling).

70. [Franklin] 1817, p. 76: this addendum to Franklin's *Account* of 1754 was produced by a committee under the professional builder and hospital manager Samuel Rhoads (see Cohen's Introduction to Franklin 1954, p. xxiv), whom W. H. Williams (1976, pp. 21–22), names as its architect.

71. Thompson and Goldin 1975, pp. 76, 97–99, with useful illustrations; Morton and Woodbury 1897, p. 38; and Tomes 1994, pp. 29, 335 n. 26.

72. The instructions to Adam are from HB 14/1/1, p. 24 (19 July 1791). The committee soon decided that the temporary saving of about £600 was not worth the nuisance: ibid., p. 58 (12 January 1792). For the Asylum, *Report* 1814, p. 9: its directors however explained three years later that they were attempting to buy more land 'for all the [detached] buildings that can be required for several centuries': *Report* 1817, p. 19.

73. Maitland 1753, pp. 430–31 includes Fourdrinier's engraving (reproduced in Markus 1982, p. 37) of the completed workhouse, which Gifford et al. 1988, p. 733, date to 1739–43. Its north wing survives, converted into tenements.

74. Barton 1814, p. 3. Foster 1986, p. 638 quotes the explanation drawn up in 1729, upon the approval of Gibbs's plan, with the intention of sending a printed copy to each governor; for the 1713–14 building, Power 1926, pp. 10–11.

75. Philanthropus 1738, p. 8. The Philadelphia managers would decide to build, 'confiding in the same Divine Providence, which had hitherto blessed their pious endeavours beyond their most sanguine hopes': [Franklin] 1817, p. 75.

76. Philasthenes 1739, p. 9; Maitland 1753, pp. 458, 460. The Orphan Hospital's *Brief account* (1735) also stresses its governors' trust in Providence. Compare Monro's memoirs (Erlam 1954, p. 85): 'It would require almost as much Faith, as some of the Managers had who undertook this House, to believe that in such a poor Country as Scotland a House which cost £12,000

Sterl. was finished, tho' begun when the Treasurer had not £5 that cou'd be applyed for such a Purpose. Yet so has it been.' Paying builders on Saturdays was the English custom, largely to avoid hangover-absenteeism: Woodward 1995, p. 38.

77. Philasthenes 1739, pp. 9, 10.

78. Quoted Thin 1927, p. 153; Maitland (1753, p. 460) added that 'many Joiners gave Sashes for the Windows'. Some journeymen masons had in late 1712 seceded from Mary's Chapel (the Lodge) to form their own Lodge of Journeymen Masons (Lyon 1900, pp. 143–44; Stevenson, *First Freemasons* 1988, pp. 42–51) to which this quotation (and that referenced at n. 82, below) might be referring. Maitland however used 'Journeymen' to mean the trade rank, not the Lodge.

79. Philanthropus 1738, p. 8. There 'appears such a Spirit in Persons of all Ranks to encourage it, that 'tis not doubted but the Building may be finished without the least Encroachment upon the Capital Stock': the *Caledonian Mercury* in 1738 (quoted Thin 1927, p. 153).

80. Stevenson, *First Freemasons* 1988, p. 17. Early in the eighteenth century various Edinburgh incorporations founded the nicely named Trades Maiden Hospital, for the 'Entertainment and Education of the Daughters of their own poor Members': Maitland 1753, p. 463, with an illustration.

81. Philanthropus 1738, pp. 7–8.

82. *Brief account* 1735, p. 6 (see Gifford 1989, pp. 167–68); *Memorial* 1737, p. 6.

83. Cockburn's 'Charitable Proposall' is transcribed in Rose 1989, here p. 174; the Edinburgh *History and statutes* 1749, p. 17. For such gifts, which were at least commonly solicited, Porter 1989, p. 158.

84. Wilson 1995, pp. 76, 80, discussing the Newcastle Infirmary, where glass was donated in 1751 (see also Hume 1906, p. 7, for the Company of Bricklayers' gift of 47,000 bricks, apparently the same year). But the 'Proprietors of the Plate Glass-houses' in Newcastle had donated enough to glaze the central block of the Edinburgh Infirmary too (Philasthenes 1739, p. 11) and Newcastle was possibly a special, Edinburgh-influenced case: according to Thin (1927, p. 155) George's sister May Drummond, a Quaker preacher who indefatigably collected donations on her travels, had already persuaded the Newcastle 'company of glass-workers, in which some of her own persuasion were interested' to send the glass to Edinburgh.

85. The Newcastle *Statutes* of 1752 (see the previous note) mentions nothing about gifts in kind in its history of the Infirmary. A Mr Drayton of Kingsthorpe donated £1,000 worth of stone for Samuel Saxon's North-ampton Infirmary, begun 1791 (Waddy 1974, p. 29); Ralph Allen's gifts are described below. Other donations seem to have been in a lower key: see the reference to the Middlesex's craftsmen-governors at n. 27, above. The bricklayer worked gratis during the West-minster's minor expansion at the end of the 1720s: Humble and Hansell 1966, pp. 27–28.

86. [Franklin] 1817, p. 78; see W. H. Williams 1976, p. 23. As Michael Barfoot has pointed out to me, too, the stress placed on Mary's Chapel's generosity was also a direct response to local political differences recently negotiated when its brethren in the surgeons' Incor-poration dropped their plans to build a rival hospital.

87. Masonic rites attended the laying of the Pennsylvania Hospital's first stone: Morton and Woodbury 1897, p. 39. Physicians prominent at the hospital were lodge members, and Benjamin Franklin himself was a former Grand Master of Pennsylvania: Bullock 1996, p. 62. Both hospitals also received considerable Quaker support (for the former, see n. 84 above, and the collections described in LHB 1/1/1, *passim*) and Quakers and Freemasons might seem odd bedfellows, but Bullock (ibid., p. 59) and Stevenson (*First Free-masons* 1988, pp. 138–40) illuminate the problem.

88. Boyce 1967, quoting (p. 31) John Wood and (p. 42) Allen's letter of 18 July 1730 to the St Bartholomew's governors.

89. Ibid., p. 41.

90. Varey 1990, p. 75 quotes the third edition (1742) of Defoe's *Tour*, which identifies Allen as the Bath hos-pital's 'chief Benefactor'. Allen's gifts featured in the Hospital's annual reports (Borsay 1991, p. 217), and Erskine-Hill 1975, p. 209 quotes the claim (*c.*1776) by Richard Jones, Allen's former Clerk of Works, that they amounted to at least £960 worth.

91. Quoted Thin 1927, p. 152, from the *Caledonian Mercury*.

92. Ibid., p. 155. As Acting Grand Master Drummond laid the stone for the North Bridge ten years later, and the Grand Master that for Robert Adam's Bridewell, in 1791: Lyon 1900, pp. 236–37, 460–64.

93. Brewer 1982, p. 225 notes English lodges' interest in almshouses and hospitals, but I've found no references to Masonic ritual at English hospitals where, if the first stone were laid with ceremony, this was done by a grandee of one sort or another acting in a non-Masonic capacity. For example, at Bath (whose architect John Wood was almost certainly a Freemason, as Mowl and Earnshaw 1988 have shown) in 1738 this was William Pulteney, Earl of Bath, and at Exeter, in 1741, Alured Clarke.

94. HB 14/1/1, pp. 72–73, a report of the occasion pre-sented to the Committee of Subscribers on 7 June 1792.

95. Among them John Clerk of Penicuik, admitted in 1710: Lyon 1900, p. 157; Stevenson, *First Freemasons* 1988, p. 33.

96. Lyon 1900, pp. 160–63, 231–32; Stevenson, *Origins of Freemasonry* 1988, p. 35.

97. Lyon 1900, pp. 190–91.

98. Jacob 1991, pp. 35–43: she is distinctive among modern historians for attending to the significance of actual building for Freemasons.

99. Anning 1963, p. 10 quotes the *Leeds Intelligencer*; 'Account' 1741, p. 497. See Goldberg 1991, p. 196 on the conventional economy of compassion and gratitude.

100. Williams 1985, pp. 30–31: Christian charity, a charity of consumption, tends to elide the possibility of a charity of production.

101. Bowen 1783, p. 2: for his historiography, O'Donoghue 1914, p. 278 and Andrews et al. 1997, p. 367.

102. Barfoot (n.d.) has remarked the distaste with which a later generation regarded the '"coarse"' eighteenth century and specifically the Edinburgh surgeons' 'frankly Mandevillian' arguments of the late 1730s.

103. Johnson 1761, p. 22.

104. See Chapter 1, at n. 107. Andrew 1989, pp. 127–29, 133, 140, 155–56 suggests that in the 1760s charities like Jonas Hanway's Marine Society (founded 1756), which sent boys to sea, increasingly attracted support precisely because they required no construction. Johnson's essay coincided with a very public debate about mortality rates at the Foundling, which had incidentally threatened him with legal action the year before: McClure 1981, pp. 106–7.

105. Philanthropus 1738, p. 5; the British Library copy is unillustrated but the elevation prefaces the Lambeth Palace Library copy of Philasthenes 1739. *Vitruvius Scoticus* had to wait until 1811 for publication, by his grandson; see James Simpson's Introduction to Adam 1980, pp. 3, 6–11. Adam's gift was reported on 1 January 1739: LHB 1/1/1, p. 174.

106. Emphases in the original: LHB 1/72/2 (8.), Anderson to George Drummond (5 November 1748).

107. LHB 1/72/2 (8.) and (10.), Anderson to Drummond (5 November and 17 November 1748). The *DNB* lists the father of the poet William Sotheby as William (d. 1766), FSA and colonel in the Coldstream Guards.

108. LHB 1/72/3 (5.) (taken from the summary).

109. The managers told Anderson to order as many copies of the plans as he needed, plus 200 for their use: LHB 1/1/3, pp. 18–19 (7 August 1749). The Lothian Health Services Archive holds printed plans (LHB 1/68: 11.–14.) that are probably those of 1749 because they show the 'apothecaries shop' opened in 1747 (Risse 1986, p. 71) at the front of the east wing. On Fourdrinier, Clayton 1997, p. 113.

110. LHB 1/72/8 (2.), Anderson to Hamilton (21 March 1752). Maitland's *History of Edinburgh* (1753) used the Sandby perspective but the 1778 *History and statutes* reverted to the Adam plans and elevations, perhaps because copies of them were still in Edinburgh waiting for *Vitruvius Scoticus*' publication; see Chapter 6, at n. 73.

111. Johnson 1761, pp. 19–20.

112. Defoe 1971, pp. 619, 509, 334, 354. He was probably referring to Ripon's St Mary Magdalene, on which see Prescott 1992, pp. 147–48.

113. '. . . for it is surely an exercise of that most Christian virtue, to heal the sick, feed the hungry, cloath the naked, and inform the ignorant': reprinted in the *Gentleman's Magazine* 17 (1747): 163–64 (see Andrew 1991, p. 94).

114. A phrase borrowed from Hibbard 1956, p. 172: the myth also fuelled, among other things, the country-house poem.

115. Goldberg 1991, p. 194; the discussion in Raven 1992, pp. 103–9 is also very pertinent.

116. The sermon is transcribed by Eade 1900, pp. 21–30, quotation p. 23.

Chapter 6: The appearances of the eighteenth-century civil hospital

1. For Leicester, Frizelle and Martin 1971, pp. 71–72 and Cherry 1980, p. 73 (whose note should read Leicester, not Leeds), quoting the report of a committee afterwards set up: it 'had the satisfaction to find that no disease from infection had taken place in the House, and that Mr. Howard would probably not have entertained an opinion to its discredit, if he had visited it on a day when the weather would have allowed the windows to be opened; the day of his enquiry being the closest and dampest that has been known this year'. On the Bristol visit, Munro Smith 1917, pp. 141–42.

2. 'Commercial treaty of humanity', *Gentleman's Magazine* 57 (1787): 530.

3. Part of the letter (not dated, but it might in 1788 have accompanied a gift-copy of Tenon's *Mémoires*) is transcribed in Foucault et al. 1979, p. 146: 'J'avais insisté dans un autre ouvrage [published 1780] sur les croisées; elles ne sont pas simplement des moyens d'éclairer les salles, d'en renouveler l'air, ce sont de véritables instruments de physique qui selon qu'ils sont appropriés aux salles, servent en même temps, suivant les circonstances: à les sécher, à y introduire l'air froid, chaud, sec ou humide, etc.'

4. Gould 1991, p. 114.

5. See the Preface to Foster 1768, and Luce 1949, p. 197. Foster's book was published in Dublin and not widely circulated, or so I assume from its rarity in English public collections now.

6. Foster 1768, p. 28.

7. Grosley 1772, 2: 43, a precise translation from the 1770 edition, which the British Library identifies as the second, subtitled *Ouvrage d'un françois. Augmenté dans cette édition des notes d'un anglois*. If there was in fact an Englishman and the observation about the hospitals is his, that does not affect its significance.

8. A formulation prompted by Worboys's (1992, p. 52): 'The [tuberculosis] sanatorium was not . . . an isolation hospital where pure air was the therapeutic agent; rather pure air provided the isolation and the hospital regime the therapy.' 'Mutual contagion' is Aikin's phrase: 1771, p. 9.

9. Quoted Eade 1900, p. 40.

10. Gooch [1773], pp. v–vi. Jones 1971, p. 103n; for the New York Hospital (begun 1773, burned 1775, and reopened 1791), Thompson and Goldin 1975, p. 100, which reproduces an 1811 plan. *History and statutes* 1778, p. 12.

11. Quoted Foster 1986, p. 638.

12. This informative plan is in the London Metropolitan Archives, and recorded in the NMR file on St Thomas', no. 101158. Descriptions of St Thomas' before its removal from Southwark in 1862 depend on Golding's (1819), of which Thompson and Goldin (1975, pp. 84–86) make good use. For the rebuilding see also Parsons 1934 and McInnes 1990, pp. 62–69.

13. Golding 1819, p. 120. Compare Bacon 1906, pp. 133–36 and Aikin 1771, pp. 11–13. Repton described old courtyard houses in 1803: 'Perhaps there is no form better calculated for convenience of habitation, . . . provided the dimensions are such as to admit free circulation of air': Loudon 1840, p. 269.

14. 'Il n'y a point ici de boucherie, de brasserie, de buanderie': 1992, p. 55 (the last is a slip: the London had a laundry); for St Thomas's beer, ibid., pp. 60–61. Bought-in provisioning was attractive to Tenon and his colleagues: Lavoisier 1865, pp. 684–85; Greenbaum 1971, p. 330.

15. Hunter and Macalpine 1963, p. 330 transcribe part of the will. In 1788 the arcades were filled in and windows inserted, to make new wards: Cawson and Orde 1969, pp. 232–33.

16. Cameron 1954, p. 43 n.35, who also quotes (p. 73) a medical-staff recommendation of 22 October 1788, 'That the system of ventilation, successful in the Foul Wards, be used in attic Wards.' What were the machines? 1737 is too early for that of Hales. Tenon (1992, p. 81) describes the ventilators in use when he visited.

17. See the caption to Figure 6 here. The illustrations in the first part (1777) of John Howard's *The state of the prisons* include his model plan for a county jail, 'half a dozen irregularly spaced pavilions . . . each raised wholly off the ground on arcades "that it may be more airy, and leave under it a dry walk in wet weather"'. Evans 1982, pp. 114–15 describes the scheme, with a reproduction, and quotes Howard.

18. Quoted in Foster 1986, p. 638.

19. Quoted in Power and Waring 1923, p. 18; see also Whitteridge and Stokes 1961, p. 31.

20. Foster 1986, p. 640, quoting the governors' 1766 declaration of intent to give the tenants notice.

21. Though Figure 47 is confusing on the orientation, and mixes up the fenestration (the 'south' block matched the 'north' in being fifteen bays wide; the other two were thirteen bays) it has generally been accepted as evidence for the ward blocks' planning. Richardson 1998, p. 19 however reproduces an 1848 plan identified as showing the original internal arrangements, and which does accord better with Tenon's account (1992, pp. 94–95), though he did not mention the windows the plan shows on the narrow ends of the wards.

22. Hunczovsky 1783, p. 4: 'veierechigt, doch so, daß in jedem Winkel ein Flügel von dem andern durch einen leeren Raum . . . getrennt wird'. Frank (1976, pp. 419, 421) associated St Bartholomew's with the Paris Academie's pavilion plan for this reason. Friedman (1984, p. 308) quotes Gibbs himself: 'four large buildings . . . [that] only appear to be joyned by iron gates'.

23. Friedman 1984, pp. 214, 345 n.4, and compare p. 237.

24. Thompson and Goldin 1975, pp. 147, 149, including a summary of Mead's aetiology (on which see also DeLacy 1986, pp. 85–86); Goldin unfortunately wasn't aware of his connection with the hospital.

25. Emphasis Mead's: 1720, pp. 38–39. In 1721 government sought advice from Mead and his senior colleagues, who recommended the housing of the infected in six 'barracks' around the city, away from other pesthouses for the still-healthy: Slack 1985, pp. 332–35.

26. See Power 1927, p. 7 for the 1752 order that men and women 'who shall be taken ill with the Small pox after their admission into the Hospital' be removed to two attic wards of the 'second Pile'. Richardson and her colleagues write (1998, pp. 18–20) that 'Gibbs's layout was praised by later hospital reformers for its innovative use of detached blocks to reduce the spread of cross-infection . . . However it is unlikely that this was Gibbs's intention'.

27. For a fascinating exception, the Chester Infirmary built 1758–63 to the designs of William Yoxall (1705–70), see the NMR file no. 102132, with copies of published sources and nineteenth-century plans.

28. The preamble to the 1719 subscription roll (as reprinted in the 1723 annual report) is quoted in Woodward 1974, p. 11. For the Westminster's early housing and the dispute and secession see Peachey 1910–14, Humble and Hansell 1966, and Gould and Uttley 1997.

29. *Account* 1734; see also Peachey 1910–14, pt I: 24.

30. *Defence* 1733; see also the 1734 *Remarks upon the foregoing account* (i.e., upon the *Account* of the same year). Peachey transcribes the three pamphlets: 1910–14, pt I: 26–27, 32–37, 41–46.

31. Seven years later the Devon and Exeter promised that its building presented no civic danger ('Account' 1741, p. 474), but thereafter civil hospitals seemingly felt little need to give such assurances.

32. *Account* 1734; for Lanesborough House, Peachey 1910–14, pt 2: 83–88.

33. For Ware's print and its dating, Peachey 1910–14, pt 2: 90, 94–95.

34. Tenon's account of St George's is 1992, pp. 31–36; four small (nine-bed) wards were in the centre. Gould and Uttley 1997, pp. 5–19, list fifteen wards by 1744, acquired in stages to 1736, 1738, and 1744.

35. Cheyne 1991, pp. 55, 56. See Porter's introduction to this edition, and idem 1991, especially pp. 163–65.

36. The painting (London Hospital) is reproduced in colour in Collins 1995, p. 3; for the engraving, Daunton 1990, p. 37.

37. Tenon and Coulomb were reported as observing that hospitals like St George's and St Luke's 'had most wisely been built in detached situations, free from buildings . . . but that at present they were totally, or nearly, surrounded with habitations': 'Further particulars of the visit of the French commissioners', *Gentleman's Magazine* **57** (1787): 688. Compare Tenon's note on the London's (then still open) site (1992, p. 51) and Risse 1986, p. 37 and idem 1999, p. 366 for the managers' attempts to control construction near the Edinburgh Infirmary.

38. I borrow the formulation from McClung 1977, p. 104.

39. Kingsbury 1995, pp. 40–42 reproduces and explains Burlington's hospital design in the context of St George's; for Burlington Ward, Peachey 1910–14, pt 2: 126.

40. HRO 5M63/1, p. 40. Turner 1986, pp. 6–9 notes that the mysterious private wards were not, at least, for paying patients.

41. HRO 5M63/8, p. 86 (8 February 1737). For baths, compare e.g. the Exeter plan reproduced in Richardson 1988, p. 22 and Figure 83 here.

42. Tenon 1992, p. 175 (Winchester), 165–67 (Devon and Exeter), and see Carré's introduction (ibid., p. 7). Bristowe and Holmes illustrated the Winchester plan (1864, p. 678) and described arrangements on its three floors. The nine- (window-) bay wings shown in a view of the Devon and Exeter from 1744 (reproduced in Harris 1922; compare Richardson 1998, p. 22) were reduced to five bays in construction. Richardson and her colleagues point out its foreshadowing of pavilion plans, aside from its small (six- to twelve-bed) wards in the centre block.

43. Turner 1986, p. 31. The Committee of Management reported to the Court of Governors that it had taken several plans into consideration (HRO 5M63/2, p. 109 [2 October 1753]) and later that the surveyor Mr Russell had proposed useful alterations to that chosen (p. 119 [14 January 1755]).

44. Compare the 1781 elevation, reproduced Munro Smith 1917, facing p. 140, and see pp. 44, 48–49, 63, 138–43 on the extensions and the replacement, designed by

Thomas Paty and Daniel Hague, which was under construction during Tenon's visit (1992, pp. 146–48). Bristol's overcrowding had already led to outbreaks of hospital fever: see Cherry 1980, pp. 72–74.

45. Duncum 1964, p. 210 quotes the 1791 edition of the *Account of the principal lazarettos*. For the Devon and Exeter's colonnade, Richardson 1988, p. 22, where it is noted as having been omitted, and for the Pennsylvania Hospital's, [Franklin] 1817, p. 76 (none is shown on the plan in Thompson and Goldin 1975, p. 98, which however dates from 1897). See below on the Leicester Infirmary.

46. Harris 1922, p. 24.

47. Quoted Munro Smith 1917, p. 48 from an unspecified source apparently dating from c.1740.

48. Pratt 1928, p. 24.

49. 'Some farther considerations in behalf of a proposal for erecting a publick hospital, &c.' (dated 1736), p. 10 (free air and good fortune), and 'Introduction', p. 7, the preamble to the first 'Subscription-paper (according to the manner of the Infirmary at Westminster)': both in Clarke 1737, which also explains that the Winchester's rules were based on St George's.

50. Wood 1969, p. 290. See Rolls 1988, p. 21, where the print is reproduced p. 16.

51. 'Nous ne donnerons point les dimensions de ces salles parce que c'est un vieil hôpital qui ne saurait servir de modèle.' Tenon 1992, p. 141. Wood 1969, pp. 291–92 and Rolls 1988, pp. 21–23 describe the hospital as built (it survives, but the original arrangements can only be conjectured), and see the NMR file no. 101073, with copies of plans (Bath City Record Office) there identified as post-1842.

52. Quoted Woodward 1974, p. 14 from a 1749 *Address*. The hospital was replaced in the 1820s, to make way for St George's Hall.

53. Tillott 1961, pp. 467–68 reproduces a print of the purpose-built York hospital (demolished 1851), seven bays wide and seven deep.

54. Hewlings, n.d. This passageway was, after 1823, effectively doubled by a colonnade giving access to two new wards then built on each side of the original building. Rook et al. 1991 reproduce Charles Humfrey's 1823 design for the alterations and Bristowe and Holmes's plan (pp. 94, 152). The report (by Robert Taylor) in the NMR file no. 88551 however proposes that Humfrey 'cut a corridor out of the west end of the two ground-floor wards in order to give access to his new wings' as well as adding the colonnade.

55. The plan is reproduced in Markus 1982, p. 29.

56. [RCHM(E)] 1980, p. 53, with excellent plans; see also Haskins 1922, p. 8 and Tenon 1992, pp. 171–73.

57. Quoted Bruegmann 1976, p. 233. Goldin has remarked on neo-medieval styles' usefulness in this respect: like the 'architecture of which it was the derivative, it freed

[the hospital's] component parts': Thompson and Goldin 1975, p. 168.

58. Foster 1768, p. 31; see the Preface and p. 52 for his studies (1764–65) in Edinburgh, which culminated in the presentation of the dissertation forming, he explained, the basis of his book. For the theatre's functions, Stevenson, '*Æsculapius Scoticus*' 1996, pp. 56–57; at points in what follows I have borrowed from this article.

59. Philasthenes 1739, p. 9. Again, I will be using 'Philanthropus' to stand for both pen-names in the text.

60. Philanthropus 1738, p. 4 (compare Maitland 1753, pp. 456–57); *History and statutes* 1778, p. 10.

61. Philanthropus 1738, pp. 4, 3; Philasthenes 1739, p. 7; for Adam's domestic stairs, Simpson 1990, p. 80.

62. Philasthenes 1739, p. 7.

63. *History and statutes* 1749, p. 59; James Gregory's *Memorial* (1800) is quoted Risse 1986, pp. 268–69; ibid., pp. 246–47 on student disorder.

64. Philasthenes 1739, p. 7; compare Maitland 1753, p. 457.

65. *History and statutes* 1778, p. 10. Philasthenes 1739, pp. 6, 7 however implies that all patients used the side stairs (compare Maitland 1753, p. 457) and the difference could be related to the fortunes, over time, of the surgeons and their pupils within the Infirmary. What seems certain, as Michael Barfoot has pointed out to me, is that their activity was restricted to the top floor.

66. Foster 1768, pp. 30–31. The key to his ground-floor plan (see Figure 6, p. 36) however explains that on the third floor (which he did not illustrate), the operation room would be where the hall was (at '7') and the mortuary, where porch and porters' rooms were (at '8' and '9').

67. Tenon 1992, p. 167. It was proposed to build operating rooms at the Bristol Infirmary in the early 1750s (Munro Smith 1917, p. 63), at the Westminster in 1767 (Humble and Hansell 1966, p. 43) and at Haslar in 1780 (WL MS 5992, fol. 5v; Lloyd and Coulter 1961, p. 213). Addenbrooke's apparently did not get one until its enlargement in the 1820s (Rook et al. 1991, p. 93). The surgical amphitheatre ordered for St Bartholomew's in 1766 (Power 1927, pp. 18–19) was accessed, Tenon reported (1992, p. 94) by stairs that led students to their seats, but not to the operating area itself.

68. See the description from the 1778 *History and statutes* referenced at n. 107 below; and compare the Glasgow arrangements described in n. 101. On the fever wards, Risse 1986, pp. 107, 108, 133 and idem 1999, p. 236. His main interest is the period 1770–1800, and I am not clear how earlier admissions worked, but 'accidental' admissions were always possible and the incidence of smallpox and the fevers would have varied.

69. *History and statutes* 1778, p. 11; Risse 1986, pp. 105–6 describes the 'high' (attic) venereal wards. Did these patients pay? As references in this chapter to venereal

disease wards suggest, not all English general hospitals refused these cases: see also Woodward 1974, pp. 48–49, 51.

70. The Bristol Infirmary let one of its cellars in 1740 (Munro Smith 1917, p. 48) and after a financial crisis enforced the closure of two wards at the Bath Hospital in the 1750s, its governors considered letting them, but decided against it (Rolls 1988, p. 25).

71. LHB 1/1/3, pp. 44, 48 (5 and 7 March 1750); see also Risse 1986, p. 37.

72. LHB 1/1/3, p. 322 (13 November 1758); ibid., p. 323 (4 December 1758).

73. In the garrets were probably the printed sheets, and possibly the copper plates, for *Vitruvius Scoticus* itself: Stevenson, '*Æsculapius Scoticus*' 1996, p. 62 n.21.

74. Woodward 1974, pp. 40–43. Rosenberg 1977, p. 20 points out how the early American hospitals in Philadelphia, New York, and Boston differed from English hospitals, but not Edinburgh's, in this respect.

75. In 1758 the Infirmary entered the Navy's contracting system. *History and statutes* 1749, p. 12; Thin 1927, p. 156; Risse 1986, pp. 92–97, 101–5. Idem 1999, p. 242 relates the building's form as a kind of 'large house with separate rooms' to its ability to admit the soldiers and sailors 'who could be placed under guard in separate wards to prevent desertion'.

76. *History and statutes* 1778, p. 10. The negotiations are recorded in LHB 1/1/3, pp. 211, 218 (7 July and 6 October 1755). For the ward and its closure in 1793, Risse 1986, pp. 86, 106–7, 269–71, who judges that the 'managers barely tolerated' it for the sake of the revenue, but even that was not worth the disruption of 'having students, nurses, and at times the parturient women themselves seeking admission at all hours'.

77. LHB 1/1/3, p. 365 (4 November 1760). 'The early Treasurer's accounts of the Infirmary showed it functioned as something of a cross between a bank, a building society and a property developer, lending its capital at interest to favoured customers who were almost always donors and often men closely associated with its foundation and subsequent management': Barfoot 1991, p. 4.

78. Hoogdalem 1990, pp. 181–87.

79. [Franklin] 1817, p. 77. Compare the plan reproduced by Thompson and Goldin 1975, p. 98.

80. Thompson and Goldin 1975, pp. 91–92; Forty 1980, pp. 70–72; Markus 1993, pp. 109–10. The *Gentleman's Magazine* plan accords with that published by Bristowe and Holmes (1864, facing p. 583), which shows how the side wings were in 1830 and 1840 extended by lobbies and additional wards, and the spine walls between the wards each perforated by two openings.

81. Henderson's designs were selected from among those submitted, by invitation, by four architects; Benjamin

Wyatt, who was acting as an independent assessor, modified them to some uncertain extent. See Frizelle and Martin 1971, p. 36, who reproduce (p. 39) Henderson's drawing (1768) of the ground plan, and the very useful report (by Kathryn Morrison) in the NMR file no. 100289, which also includes copies of the upper-floor plans (all Leicestershire Record Office). The central range survives. Wyatt's son William would soon design the rather differently planned Stafford Infirmary, on which see Robinson 1979, pp. 21–22, with an illustration.

82. Quoted Eaton 1950, p. 11: Bulfinch was writing to the hospital's directors.

83. Forty comments on the 'close surveillance intended over the patients by the [London's] ward lobby arrangement' (1980, pp. 70–71), and Summerson on the way its 'ward wings and tiers of privies in the angles . . . foreshadow the arrangement of the typical Victorian hospital' (1978, p. 119).

84. The wards 'ne reçoivent le jour et l'air que d'un côté': his account of the London is Tenon 1992, pp. 51–54.

85. Foster (1768, p. 28) prescribed a chimney on every ward, in large ones two, for heating and 'pumping out, as it were, the foul Air of the Rooms, and so inducing a Supply of fresh Air'. See also Bruegmann 1978, pp. 148–49.

86. Tenon described (1992, p. 201) six windows on one long side and three on the other, with another on the short end of the wing; compare Paine's perspective print (reproduced Leach 1988, p. 101), the Rowlandson and Pugin view of the ward interior (reproduced Thompson and Goldin 1975, p. 92), and the ground-floor plan in Sir John Soane's Museum (62/10/3).

87. LH/A/4/2, pp. 146–47 (the committee's report to the Court, 25 September 1751, recommending the first design) and ibid., pp. 154–56 (the report of 13 December, recommending the design that was used); the quotations that follow are taken from the latter. Clark–Kennedy 1962, pp. 118–21 describes this episode.

88. Is it pertinent that St Bartholomew's called Gibbs's blocks both 'wings' and 'piles' during their construction period (1730–32, 1736–40, 1743–52, 1757–69)? See the quotations in Power 1926, pp. 19, 20, 24, and idem 1927, pp. 7, 9, 11, 18.

89. Singleton took advice from Wood the Younger: Colvin, *Biographical dictionary* 1995, s.v. 'Singleton, Luke'. For the building (demolished 1984), Tenon 1992, pp. 171–73; Frith 1961; Richardson 1998, pp. 23–24.

90. Tenon 1992, pp. 133–34. The committee room and chapel swapped places in 1783: Whitcombe 1903, p. 19. Markus 1993, pp. 110–11, undertakes a spatial analysis of the Gloucester plan. See Binney 1984, p. 17 and the captions to pls 35 and 40 for Robert Taylor's use of such bays at villas built from the mid-1750s on. The Leicester Infirmary used a semi-elliptical bow in the same position (figure 56), as did the contemporary Leeds Infirmary (see the photograph in Anning 1963, facing p. 20).

91. Forty 1980, p. 70.

92. LH/A/5/4, p. 34 (14 August 1751); John Howard would recommend 15 feet (Duncum 1964, p. 210).

93. McMenemey 1947, pp. 103–4 quotes a report of 1765 recording the governors' dissatisfaction with the house's bad air, for 'want of room and ventilation' and the *Worcester Journal* advertisement of the same year; see also Cherry 1980, p. 73n.

94. Compare Bristowe and Holmes 1864, p. 661 on the Radcliffe: 'The hospital is built in a block, the ends projecting from the centre, but so little that the wards at the end do not obtain through ventilation by means of opposite windows, though they have windows on more than one side.'

95. The hospital's inspiration came from Thomas Hayter (Bishop of Norwich 1749–61), at whose behest Gooch 'visited all the great Hospitals in London with the utmost attention': Gooch [1773], p. iii. The first annual report (January 1771) and the 'Report to the auditors' (October 1772) are quoted by Eade (1900, pp. 33–34, 40), who reproduces a plan of the hospital on p. 41. Its east wing survives: see the NMR file no. 100523. James Alsop has kindly sent to me transcriptions of relevant passages from Gooch's letters (in the British Library) to Dr Messenger Monsey. Two from 1770 mention the latrines, and that Gooch was seeking information about the ward sizes, etc., at St George's, Guy's and St Bartholomew's, as well as at another, unspecified London hospital. In 1771, Gooch expressed his disgust that his plan for the Norwich and Norfolk had *not* been adopted, but he evidently became reconciled to the building.

96. The Lincoln hospital was also extended, some time before its replacement in 1878, by lengthening the central block and running another ward wing off it: Sympson 1878, plan facing p. 51. For Northampton, see the NMR file no. 100411, which includes the Royal Commission's reconstruction of the original first-floor plan, showing wards running, as Foster had recommended, the full depth of the centre range, and the plan in Waddy 1974, p. 41. There it was specified in 1790 that 'No patients [were] to be lodged on the ground floor': ibid., pp. 27–28.

97. Waddy 1974, pp. 27–28.

98. HB 14/1/1, for 5 May 1794, p. 107. The search for models went back to the Infirmary's inception: ibid., pp. 4, 5 (7 June and 12 December 1787). Jenkinson 1994, pp. 18–21 describes the early deliberations about the Infirmary.

99. Inspired, King (1991, p. 63) suggests, by the fourth-century Sta Costanza in Rome, which Adam had studied.

100. Beddoes 1799, p. 17.
101. Ibid.; Duveen and Klickstein (1955, p. 177) were the first to spot the reference. John Clark would repeat the claim (*Report* 1802, pp. 212–13), adding that the small rooms reserved for contagious cases, attached to each ward, 'range along the passage to the water-closets, – and opposite to their doors is the door of the stair-case, forming a complete ventilation'; 'For the purpose of ventilation, the windows are placed directly opposite to each other; the door of each ward opens opposite the chimney, by which a current of air sweeps along the middle, without annoying the patients.' This description works with the plan drawings (Figures 60, 61), which label some small rooms adjoining the 'Passage' to the water closets at each end of the building as 'Bedroom[s]'.
102. MacInnes 1993, pp. 16–18.
103. Rates for 'compound fractures, fractures of the skull, and after amputation' were better markers: Clark, *Report* 1802, pp. 209–10, 215–16.
104. Anning 1963 reproduces a number of illustrations of the Infirmary, for whose construction and enlargements see pp. 7–13; Bristowe and Holmes 1864 give a plan p. 608. Cherry 1980, p. 73 and Richardson 1998, pp. 23, 27 comment on its success.
105. Clark, *Report* 1802, pp. 217, 211.
106. Philanthropus 1738, pp. 3, 4; Philasthenes 1739, p. 12.
107. *History and statutes* 1778, pp. 10–13, 84–85, which also draws attention to the 'constantly fresh air' in the surgical wards and notes that ventilators had been installed where necessary.
108. Bacon 1906, p. 135.
109. Smith 1984; Porter 1985, p. 162 for cold (and sweat) in humoral medicine.
110. Note taken from the minute book of the General Court of Governors, for ?20 April 1693, in NMR file for St Thomas' (no. 101158). About a decade earlier, however, a committee had recommended 'That no consumptive patients be admitted except in extraordinary circumstances and then they shall be placed in the most airy wards': quoted (with modernized spelling) Parsons 1934, p. 114.
111. Insensible perspiration is central to the first (1753) edition of James Lind's *Treatise of the scurvy*, for example, and Carpenter 1986, pp. 57–61 shows its general theoretical importance, which lasted until about 1770. Patients might however also be bathed to encourage this evacuation through the skin's pores, 'cette transpiration, qui est le premier des remèdes', as the third report of the Académie des Sciences' Hôtel-Dieu committee explains: Lavoisier 1865, p. 683.
112. *History and statutes* 1749, p. 7; a few years later was recommended at Bristol 'to the consideration of the Physicians and Surgeons . . . the opening of the Windows for the benefit of the House', and investi-

gating ventilators was also mentioned: quoted, without references, by Munro Smith 1917, pp. 49–50.
113. Gooch [1773], p. vi; n.1, above, for Leicester. Woodward quotes (1974, p. 101) Howard on the London hospitals' 'injurious prejudices against washing floors, and admitting fresh air'. Both prejudices perhaps originated in a fear of dampness.
114. Waddy 1974, pl. 3 reproduces a print (first published 1744, with the anniversary-day sermon) purporting to show a Northampton ward interior with rows of beds with testers and curtains. Foster recommended linen curtains: 'Wainscot folding doors, though often used' are to be avoided since they can 'stifle' the patient when closed, and may direct a 'Current of Air' upon him or her 'when kept, even the least open' (1768, p. 25).
115. Richardson 1998, p. 16: Guy's 'wards were lit by opposed windows . . . but box beds lined the walls with no regard to the fenestration, impairing the ventilation'. In 1787 Tenon saw only (or was shown only) iron bedsteads (1992, p. 80); Cameron (1954, pp. 72–73) describes John Howard's visit a year later and its repercussions for beds, among other things.
116. Jones 1971, p. 111; Franklin 1906, p. 309 (from Small's paper about ventilation, which cites the fourth edition [1764] of Pringle's book). Taylor (1997, p. 61) quotes John Roberton (1858) on the problem of patients' and nurses' control of the air.
117. Pringle 1752, p. 252.
118. Franklin 1882, pp. 312, 316, from the Small paper. I can make no sense of its description of the Pennsylvania Hospital: the 'wards are two stories high, with two rows of windows in each'.
119. Buchanan 1996, p. 26.
120. Bentham, *Panopticon* (*Postscript*) 1843, p. 96. Franklin and/or Small commended the Adam brothers' 'manner of ventilating' the (Royal) Society of Arts's meeting room, 'by leaving spaces between the panes of glass in the sky-lights, the panes overlaying each other. These spaces being concealed from the eye, do not alarm those fearful of cold air'. Franklin 1882, pp. 315–16.
121. And again, if we count it, the infirmary at Glasgow's Town's Hospital. The Bethel Hospital for the insane in Norwich opened in 1724 in purpose-built accommodation.
122. McInnes 1990, pp. 56–57.
123. The phrase is Margaret DeLacy's (1986, p. 53), writing about prisons, whose 'reform' followed a few years later.

Chapter 7: The breath of life

1. Blane 1799, p. 177.
2. Foucault, 'La Politique' 1979, p. 14; the translation (with a change) is from idem 1980, p. 177. Compare

the vivid evocation of the 'strange chemistry that seethed behind the walls of confinement' in idem 1971, pp. 202–7. See Osborne 1994, pp. 36–38 on Foucault's demonstration that the 'critique of the hospital was midwife at the birth of the clinic', in a dialectic elided here.

3. Jones 1989, pp. 11, 48–50. Vienna is Hunczovsky and Philadelphia is John Jones: 1971, pp. 102–3. Sigsworth 1972, pp. 101–2 shows how Tenon's analysis of the Hôtel-Dieu influenced 1950s historiography of *British* hospitals; see also Risse 1986, pp. 85, 289–90, 293.

4. Greenbaum 1976, especially pp. 899–900; idem 1992, pp. 309–10. For what Foucault (1971, pp. 233–34) called that 'dangerous financing' see also Mortier 1979, p. 176, Jones 1989, pp. 5, 20, 51, 83, and Brockliss and Jones 1997, pp. 717–19. The idea that French hospitals enjoyed enormous wealth was 'extremely wide of the mark' (ibid., p. 719).

5. Pelling 1993, p. 315; Rosenberg, 'Therapeutic revolution' 1979, especially pp. 5–15.

6. Risse 1988, pp. 7, 19, 20–21, for hysteria, and idem 1986, pp. 142–43 for consumption; he quotes the 1778 *History and statutes*. Hart 1980, p. 453 quotes a regulation at the Middlesex Hospital referring to those whose 'complaints are likely to be aggravated rather than relieved by confinement within the walls of a Hospital'.

7. Foucault 1976, pp. 16–18, 39; Greenbaum 1976, p. 930; and (regarding therapeutic innovation) Warner 1989, pp. 198–99.

8. Loudon 1981, p. 336. See also Risse 1986, pp. 110, 118; Tröhler 1989, especially pp. 26–30; and Kilpatrick 1990.

9. Though it is not always possible to identify every outbreak in retrospect *as* typhus. For the symptoms, Pringle 1750, p. 3.

10. Wilson 1993, p. 399: it was a 'continued' as opposed to an 'intermittent' fever like malaria (or that *of* malaria, as we would now say). Its connection with poverty, and the concentration of the poor in courtrooms, workhouses, factories, and towns generally was clearly understood: ibid., pp. 398–401; Smith 1981; Pickstone 1984, pp. 403–4; Risse 1985; Bynum 1979, pp. 97–98; idem 1994, pp. 21–22, 66–67. For siege disease, Duffy 1979, pp. 253–54. By 1770, many believed that a 'significant shift in fever type had indeed occurred in Great Britain': Woodward 1974, p. 98. Evans's chapter 'Gaol fever' (1982, pp. 94–117) is an excellent critical analysis; see also DeLacy's 'The decision to reform' (1986, pp. 70–94), which argues that *fear* of the fever was the prime mover in the prison reforms of the 1780s, prompting architectural devices (cells, for example) soon attached to moral improvement.

11. Kilpatrick 1990, p. 264 quotes Howard (1777). For

'diseases of civilization' see Porter's essay (1993) of that name, especially pp. 589–92.

12. Quoted McLoughlin 1978, p. 99.

13. DeLacy 1986, pp. 28–29, 54, 91. Risse (1986, p. 289) notes that hospital-acquired diseases rarely come up in the records, but see the instances cited by Woodward in his chapter 'Hospital disease' (1974, pp. 97–122), and Cherry (1980, pp. 72–75).

14. Ignatieff 1978, pp. 44–45. It was alternatively proposed that the putridity had entered the courtroom via an open window facing Newgate: Clark-Kennedy 1929, pp. 193–94.

15. Pringle 1750, pp. 2–3; he 'thought it his duty, to offer these few sheets to the public'.

16. Ibid., p. 5.

17. Hales, in the *Gentleman's Magazine* **23** (1753): 71. For management, which this model of disease suggested might well be a medical business, see Jordanova 1979, pp. 133–35; Lawrence 1985, pp. 171–72; and Porter, 'Howard's beginning' 1995.

18. Pringle 1750, p. 10, and as quoted by Woodward 1974, p. 98; Brocklesby 1764, pp. 62–65, who wrote that this substitution was generally impracticable or impossible.

19. Woodward 1974, pp. 105–6 quotes John Bell (1803).

20. Pringle 1752, p. viii; Dr Percival (1740–1804) from his 'Letter' in Aikin 1771, pp. 85–86; Aikin himself p. 19; Nightingale 1863, p. iii. Her immediate inspiration may have been the second of the three *Builder* articles (which King [1966, p. 371] showed to be by John Roberton) she reprinted in the first two editions of the *Notes*. The second article begins,

'Hospitals,' wrote an eminent French physician of the last century, 'are a curse to civilization.'
'Hospitals,' said Sir John Pringle, 'are among the chief causes of mortality in armies.' (Nightingale 1859, p. 93)

21. The quotations are from Risse 1986, p. 23 and Davies 1988, p. 80. For the metaphor, Peacock 1990, pp. 160–65, and Sawday 1995, p. 28 (on the 'machine-body') and Chapter 5, 'Sacred anatomy and the order of representation'.

22. Cipolla 1992, p. ix.

23. See Riley 1987, pp. ix–xi for a summary account of environmental medicine.

24. Hannaway 1993, p. 295.

25. Nutton 1990, p. 199.

26. Riley 1987, p. 91. Understandings of miasmata differed from writer to writer and changed emphasis over the course of the century: see, for example, Allan and Schofield 1980, pp. 87–88 on how Samuel Sutton's two experts, William Watson and Richard Mead, differed in accounts published in the same book (Sutton 1749) and to the same end.

27. Cipolla 1992, pp. 4–5; Riley 1987, pp. 15–16; Corbin 1986, pp. 46–47.

28. Foster 1768, p. 31. Nutton's essay shows the problems of distinguishing between contagion and 'infection' in the Renaissance, which Henderson 1992 and Risse's useful summary (1999, p. 197) also underline: both 'remained ambivalent and complementary concepts that expressed both environmental and human agency in the spread of pestilence', the latter writes. DeLacy 1986, pp. 89–90 is however inclined to draw a sharper distinction for the eighteenth century: see Chapter 10, n. 74.

29. Sutton (1749, p. 1), misdating the event to 1739. Riley 1987, pp. 97–98 quotes Webster; see also Corbin on faeces (1986, pp. 28–29, 212) and Temkin on stink (1977, pp. 461–63). In modern French the adjective *infect* still refers to something that stinks.

30. Describing a shipboard 'sick berth or hospital' in *The adventures of Roderick Random* of 1748 (1981, p. 149), which incorporates lightly fictionalized versions of his experiences as a naval surgeon on the Cartagena expedition.

31. Jefferson 1972, pp. 133–34: some scepticism about physic can be inferred because he thought surgical hospitals might be useful. See Greenbaum 1992 for Jefferson and the French reformers, and Rothman 1990, pp. 32–33 for colonial Virginia's boarding of the poor. Jefferson's French friends applauded the sentiment, and themselves worked a theme that culminated with 'Barère's law' (11 May 1794), which called for the erasure of the 'words "alms" and "hospital" . . . from the republican vocabulary': Rosen 1956, p. 147 as part of an excellent guide to Revolutionary deliberations. Most generally, see Illich 1976, pp. 163–64 for the primitivist dream of sickness in its 'wild' state, 'which is self-limiting and can be borne with virtue and style and cared for in the homes of the poor'.

32. Percival, for example, wrote that 'supplies of the purest air are insufficient to destroy contagion', which must also be combated with sprinkling and washing with vinegar and so forth: in Aikin 1771, p. 89.

33. Quoted Keevil 1958, p. 297.

34. Bennett 1982, pp. 79–82; Hunter 1991, p. 110; Brock 1992, p. 71 (I have depended on this excellent history for the chemistry in what follows). Compare Evelyn's understanding, explained Jenner 1995, pp. 538, 545, 546–47.

35. From a letter of July 1663, quoted Bennett 1982, p. 81.

36. Bennett (ibid., p. 82) makes the connection.

37. It is *chemistry* that explains the motion of these parts, 'as of the Spring in the Barrel Wheel': Wren 1965, p. 221, from an address to the Royal Society. See Hunter 1991, pp. 109–10 and, generally, Roger Smith's and Christopher Lawrence's entries 'Man-machine' and 'Iatromathematics' in Bynum et al. 1981.

38. From a lecture of 1657: Wren 1965, p. 205. 'The power of the new scientific instruments . . . resided in their capacity to enhance perception and to constitute new perceptual objects': Shapin and Schaffer 1985, p. 36. For Hooke's fascination with the idea, see also Bennett 1980, p. 37 and idem 1982, pp. 38–42.

39. From his 1662 address to the Royal Society: Wren 1965, p. 223 (p. 203 for 'true Astrology'). See Bennett 1982, pp. 82–83; and, for medical meteorology, Hannaway 1993, pp. 296–300 and Riley 1987.

40. Wren 1965, p. 222; see Bennett 1982, p. 83.

41. Lawrence 1996, p. 81, who quotes Thomas Beddoes (1795): formerly, 'investigations relative to medicine, had been carried on just as rationally as if to discover the qualities of the horse, the naturalist were to direct his attention to the movements of a windmill'.

42. Cheyne 1991, p. 4; compare the editor's introduction, pp. xx–xi.

43. In 1752: quoted in Clark-Kennedy 1929, p. 222.

44. Johnson defined 'ventilator' as an 'instrument contrived by Dr Hales to supply close places with fresh air'; the *OED* grants Hales with the first printed use of 'ventilate' and 'ventilator'.

45. It is 'tempting to seek the origin of the technology of ventilation [as] . . . an advance in practice stemming from an advance in knowledge. But this was not the case.' Evans 1982, p. 97, with reference to Hales.

46. Quoted in Clark-Kennedy 1929, pp. 98, 102, 105; for 'elasticity', Zuckerman 1976–77, pp. 225, 227; Allan and Schofield 1980, pp. 87–88. Hales's own youngest brother William had died in prison, probably from jail fever: ibid., p. 85.

47. Brock 1992, pp. 77–78, 89–90, 113; and see pp. 98, 103 for Joseph Black's demonstration (in 1756) that 'fixed air' (carbon dioxide) differs from ordinary air.

48. Quoted in Brock 1992, p. 98; see also Corbin 1986, pp. 8–31 for this understanding of air.

49. Foster 1768, p. 7; Duveen and Klickstein 1955, p. 171 summarize the Académie des Sciences' 1780 report on the prisons of Paris, which makes the point about air warming and rising, and the committee's recommendation; Tenon 1992, p. 183 for the high wards at Haslar.

50. Tenon 1996, p. 179. Duveen and Klickstein 1955 is a comprehensive account of Lavoisier's many applications of his research; on vitiated air (also understood as lighter than ordinary air, and therefore itself a rising danger too, if charged with disease) pp. 168–69, 176. See also Greenbaum 1972, pp. 654–66 for Lavoisier's work on the air in buildings and mines, and Middleton 1992, p. 19.

51. Tenon's tables are reproduced as pp. 172–77 in his 1996 edition. They did not originate such calculations: see Monro 1764, p. 364 and Richardson 1998, p. 82 for the Navy's Commissioners for Sick and Wounded's specifications of 1781 and 1785.

52. In his afflictions Job protests (Job 27: 3) that 'All the

while my breath is in me, and the spirit of God is in my nostrils'. 'Breath of our nostrils' refers to the 'anointed of the Lord' in Lam. 4: 20; compare Jenner 1995, pp. 543–44 on this point, and generally for *Fumifugium*. 'Judeo-Christian pneumatic tradition' is Stafford's phrase: see the next note.

53. Johnson's definition is quoted by Stafford at the beginning of an analysis (1991, pp. 417–36) ultimately directed at aesthetics. Rawcliffe 1995, p. 45 explains the spirit-*pneuma* and its relationships to air, the heart, and animal spirits as these were understood in medieval medicine.

54. Nightingale, writing to Edwin Chadwick in 1858, actually about the less metaphysical issue of whether patients in satisfactorily ventilated hospitals caught cold or not: Vicinus and Nergaard 1990, p. 210.

55. An 'elevation of pastoral plainness at the expense of sophisticated contrivance is as much part of [Milton's] *Paradise Lost* as of [Lucretius'] *De Rerum Natura*. In addition, both works treat buildings, even highly wrought ones, as limited substitutes for a more desirable openness': Freeman 1975, p. 258.

56. Gooch [1773], pp. x, xi.

57. Corbin 1986, p. 105.

58. Fletcher 1786, p. x.

59. Hales 1758, pt 2, p. 21; a similar point is made p. 28.

60. Fletcher 1786, p. vii.

61. Quoted Baugh 1965, p. 165 (see also p. 179). On the health of sailors Zuckerman 1987, pp. 77–79; Gradish 1980, p. 173; and Rosen 1939. Lind, Blane, and Trotter would all emphasize the danger of impressment in regard to typhus (ibid., p. 736).

62. Baugh 1965, p. 148n.; Gradish 1980, pp. 178–79; Rodger 1986, pp. 98–99. Once home again, the ships' companies might not be released: Keevil 1958, p. 188.

63. Mead, 'A discourse on scurvy', in Sutton 1749, p. 102; Hales 1758, pt 2, p. 82.

64. See Lawrence 1996, pp. 93 and 102 n.75 for the relation between naval diet and architecture, and Rodger 1986, p. 106 and Carpenter 1986, pp. 57–61 for Lind, who considered the moisture that discourages insensible perspiration to be the 'principal and main predisposing cause' of scurvy, or at least did until the early 1770s.

65. See Clark-Kennedy 1929, pp. 165–68 and Baugh 1965, pp. 241–44, for ventilators in this context. For windsails, Zuckerman 1987, p. 80 and on their disadvantages, especially on hospital ships, William Watson's 'Some observations upon Mr Sutton's invention', in Sutton 1749, pp. 58–60.

66. Rodger 1986, p. 54, and Zuckerman 1987, p. 78 repeat eighteenth-century accounts of suffocations in ships' holds and Keevil 1958, pp. 296–98 summarizes the conclusions drawn from such incidents. Scurvy results from a deficiency of ascorbic acid, vitamin C. In the

eighteenth century, the assignment of a single cause to (and the prescription of a specific against) such a disease would have seemed like naïve quackery. See Lawrence 1996 for a critical examination of scurvy's history, and historiography.

67. Zuckerman 1976–77, pp. 225–27. Lawrence 1996, p. 86 quotes Pringle: the 'corruption of the bilge water, is not only a main cause of sea scurvy, but often concurs in crowded ships, to raise a fever of the hospital or jayl kind'. Experienced sailors, wrote Hales (1758, pt 2, p. 81), knew that scurvy is 'occasioned more by the noxious putrid Air in Ships . . . than by the salt Flesh' that comprised so much of the diet. See Carpenter 1986, pp. 84–91 on the pneumatic therapeutics developed in the wake of Hales's research.

68. Lawrence 1996, pp. 84–86, 90, 95–96: to this list Lawrence adds 'moral laxity'. See Longfield-Jones 1995, p. 75 for indications that all these factors, including the laxity, were being cited at least as early as 1617: I am grateful to Dr Longfield-Jones for her help on this.

69. Baugh 1965, pp. 192, 197–201. Historians do not agree on what was killing the men: scurvy, typhus, or both.

70. The 'Black Hole of Calcutta' was not named as often as the other two incidents, perhaps because most of the deaths were evidently the result of simple suffocation. Hallé (1787, p. 572), who dated the event to 1745, however reported that several of the twenty-three survivors later succumbed to the *fièvre maligne des prisons*. Mead (1720, p. 42) and Pringle (1752, p. 346) cited another 'Black Assizes', killing 300, in Oxford in July 1577. Evans (1982, pp. 94–95) discusses such assizes' 'nasty reminders of the fever's power to break the boundaries of its proper location'.

71. Hales 1743, pp. ix–x. On 'antiseptics' (Pringle's later coinage), Allan and Schofield 1980, p. 89; Riley 1987; Lawrence 1996, p. 86.

72. For fuller descriptions of his ventilators see Hales's own accounts; Clark-Kennedy 1929, pp. 153–54; Allan and Schofield 1980, pp. 86–87.

73. The 'Description of Dr. Hales's ventilators fixed in Newgate', *Gentleman's Magazine* 22 (1752): 179–82. Edward Cave, the *Magazine*'s editor, was a proprietor of the Northampton cotton-mill where Thomas Yeoman became manager in 1742, and Yeoman soon became Hales's 'Ventilator Maker': Robinson 1962, p. 208.

74. See Chapter 7, centring on Desaguliers, in Stewart 1992.

75. Hales 1743, pp. xv–xix; for Nathaniel Henshaw, a friend of Evelyn's, see Jenner 1995, p. 546 and Allan and Schofield 1980, pp. 85–86. Bruegmann 1976, pp. 197–99; idem 1978, pp. 149–50; and Corbin 1986, pp. 95–98 recount the history of assisted ventilation.

76. Hales 1743, pp. xi–xii, xiv. This machine, very similar to Hales's (an 'extraordinary circumstance', wrote

Hales), was successfully used in warships in the summer of 1742 and thereafter (Clark-Kennedy 1929, pp. 152–53); Triewald also suggested its application to 'Hospitals and Barracks for the Sick'.

77. Stewart 1992, pp. 225, 233; Zuckerman 1987, pp. 81–82. Desaguliers's wheel is now identified as a landmark in the history of building systems, and its installation at Britain's political heart then had symbolic resonance: Riley 1987, p. 107.

78. Sutton 1749, p. 8; Hales got a comparable response (Clark-Kennedy 1929, p. 154). See, however, Baugh 1965, pp. 40, 48, 89–92.

79. Sutton 1749, pp. 13, 37–38; Clark-Kennedy 1929, pp. 152–53; Zuckerman 1987, p. 85.

80. Hales 1743, p. 39. His letter of 10 June 1752 to Alderman Janssen about the Newgate ventilators is quoted in Clark-Kennedy 1929, pp. 203–4: 'It is a great Pleasure to me . . . to see the Ventilators worked by a Windmill, drawing, like large heavy Lungs, . . . out of several Wards at the same time'. See Evans 1982, pp. 100–2 for this inspired 'organic analogy'.

81. Hales's observations on swaddling (and the practice of bandaging healthy infants' skulls) were published the same year: *Gentleman's Magazine* 13 (1743): 430.

82. See Zuckerman 1976–77, p. 231 (where Sutton's diagram is reproduced) and idem 1987, pp. 84–85.

83. Hales 1743, p. 25; Clark-Kennedy 1929, p. 156.

84. Sutton 1749, p. 25; Clark-Kennedy 1929, pp. 156–60; Zuckerman 1987, p. 85.

85. Probably using his influence as a Georgia Colony trustee, he saw his ventilators installed as early as 1742 on merchant ships, where their success was such that they were adopted by the Board of Trade and Plantations long before the Navy took them up: Clark-Kennedy 1929, pp. 131–54, 161–62, 170–87.

86. Hales 1758, pt 2, p. 86.

87. Hales is taken from NMM ADM/F/13 (24.), a copy of an extract from a letter dated 17 April 1752; Robinson 1962, p. 209.

88. PRO Adm 106/2189, p. 177 is a letter of April 1757 explaining why one ship had not been fitted at Plymouth: the carpenters were too busy. All modern sources grapple with this problem, best analysed by Riley 1987, p. 108; we can add that La Roche implied in 1788 that their use was general on English men-of-war: 1933, p. 252.

89. See Clark-Kennedy 1929, pp. 189–91 for the Savoy, whose prevailing conditions are described by Somerville 1960, pp. 85–93. I take the installation dates from Robinson 1962, p. 207 and Allan and Schofield 1980, pp. 84–85; Hales did not usually give them in his *Treatise*. The Winchester ventilator is described Hales 1758, pt 2, p. 14; St George's, p. 18 (see also Clark-Kennedy 1929, p. 159 and Duncum 1964, p. 209); Northampton, p. 21; Bristol, p. 22 (see also

Munro Smith 1917, p. 50); the 'Hospital for the Small-Pox' at 'Sir John Oldcastles's, near London', p. 23; Newgate, p. 31. Hales also mentions or describes ventilators at jails at Winchester (p. 25), Northampton, Shrewsbury, Maidstone, Bedford, Aylesbury (62), and Durham (63).

90. Grosley 1772, 2: 42. The first large wards at the Pennsylvania Hospital, begun 1755, had 'fire places . . . , and vintulators to carry off the foul air' ([Franklin] 1817, p. 77). The 'bellows' ventilator that Rolls (1988, p. 24) mentions as installed at the Bath Hospital seems unambiguous. See also n. 100 below for the expanding meaning of 'ventilator'.

91. Riley 1987, pp. 99, 106; Pringle presented this account to the Royal Society in 1753 and Hales had it published in the *Gentleman's Magazine* 23 (1753): 71–74. Thomas Laqueur has productively analysed the 'humanitarian narrative', of which Pringle's is a prime example. In it, 'quantities of fact, of minute observations, about people who had before been beneath notice become the building blocks of the "reality effect," of the literary technique through which the experiences of others are represented as real' (1989, p. 177).

92. 'On ventilation', in Franklin 1906, pp. 308, 312–13. For Sutton, Clark-Kennedy 1929, pp. 152, 155; for Duhamel, see Hallé 1787, p. 573. Today the eddies of turbulence (a phenomenon of great pure-mathematical as well as engineering interest) are studied with the help of smoke wands in wind tunnels, and dye injectors in water tanks.

93. Hales 1743, p. 22; idem 1758, pt 2, pp. 14, 22, and pp. 17, 31 for the statistics.

94. The ships' captains are quoted in the *Treatise* of 1758 and by Clark-Kennedy 1929, pp. 163–65; Ellis's letter was published in the *Gentleman's Magazine* 24 (1754): 114–15.

95. Brocklesby 1764, p. 57. For portable ventilators, Robinson 1962, p. 208.

96. Pringle 1764, p. 293: this procedure is in earlier editions described as the 'next' expedient to well-ventilated wards, not the 'best', when dysentery threatened.

97. Hales 1758, pt 2, p. 63.

98. The page references in the successive editions of *Diseases of the army* are (1752), p. 252; (1753), p. 242; (1761), p. 249; (1764), p. 293. Aikin (1771, pp. 88–89) seems to have favoured something like Sutton's device; Evans (1982, pp. 102–3) notes that while Howard recommended ventilators for prison infirmaries in the first edition of *The state of the prisons*, he 'later declared them unnecessary in a well-designed institution'.

99. Monro 1764, pp. 369–70; for Hales's correspondence, NMM ADM/F/13 (24.) for 21 April 1756. He traced the path of the air with arrows in his accompanying diagram.

100. Foster 1768, p. 26. Anning 1963, p. 13 quotes John Howard on the 'six circular apertures or ventilators' in

the wards of the Leeds Infirmary, evidently inspired by Leicester's: Richardson 1998, p. 23. For ventilating holes (as Bristowe and Holmes called them: 1864, p. 661), see Bruegmann 1976, pp. 196–97. The Académie des Sciences committee wrote in its third report that in spite of the use of *ventouses* at Saint-Louis among other French hospitals, 'nous avons pensé que la chambre la plus aérée ne peut l'être qu'autant qu'en ouvre les fenêtres', but Tenon's English observations had shown that the vents offered the great advantages of inconveniencing neither patients nor staff, and of functioning on their own: Lavoisier 1865, p. 683.

101. My analogy was prompted by the Académie committee's juxtaposition of references to the patient's *transpiration* and to the hospital's *ventouses*: Lavoisier 1865, p. 683. The vents' significance has been overlooked; it was only with their aid that, as Béguin (1979, p. 40) puts it, hospitals were supposed to be able to abandon 'des appareils de ventilation, au profit d'effets "climatiques" produits par le corps même du batiment. . . . les seules ressources d'architecture'.

102. Hallé 1787, p. 574 ('la pompe pour l'incendie'); 'pour prévenir la corruption de l'air, c'est-à-dire, pour avoir une masse d'air toujours mobile & pure, parce qu'elle est sans cesse renouvelée, il faut avoir recours à des moyens plus doux, plus simples, & qui soient pris dans la construction & dans la disposition du lieu dont on veut écarter le méphitisme.' He discussed Sutton's machine in a section on hospital construction, though recommended that both be installed on hospital ships (pp. 574–75). See also Corbin 1986, pp. 98–100 and Riley 1987, p. 107.

103. Tenon 1996, pp. 11, 178; compare his amplifications regarding staircases (142–44), and the editor's comments (xii, xix).

104. [Carter] 1800, p. 837; Crook 1995, pp. 36–37 describes Carter's work at the chapel (whose upper part was destroyed in the 1834) in 1791. See Bruegmann 1978, p. 149 n. 22 for the legend that Wren installed pyramidal air tubes at the Palace.

105. Rodger 1986, p. 29; see also Baugh 1965, pp. 10–11 and Mathias 1975.

106. Hales's letter of 11 July 1751 is quoted Clark-Kennedy 1929, p. 200; Sutton 1749, p. 22, from a petition written some time after November 1741. Lloyd and Coulter (1961, pp. 41–42, 113) quote James Lind's *Essay on the . . . health of seamen* to the same effect.

107. According to John S. Billings's *Ventilation and heating* (1893), cited Zuckerman 1987, p. 86. The points about cost-effectiveness, and scurvy, are made by Mathias 1975, p. 76; for Cockburn's powder see Cook 1990, pp. 22–25. These articles usefully show the distinctiveness of military and naval medicine in the century or more after 1688, and their ultimate importance for wider practice. Baugh 1965, pp. 427–28 describes the pickling experiments.

Chapter 8: Island hospitals

1. On hospital ships, Shaw 1936; Keevil 1958, pp. 89–90, 125, 238–48 (p. 238 for the quotation from a royal order of 1710); Lloyd and Coulter 1961, pp. 67–69; and Gradish 1980, pp. 188–90, 194–95.
2. PRO Adm 98/6, pp. 248–49 (4 April 1757).
3. Lloyd and Coulter 1961, pp. 67–68; PRO Adm 3/65, for 16 December 1756.
4. PRO Adm 98/7, p. 374 (7 February 1759).
5. Baugh 1965, pp. 208–9.
6. NMM ADM/F/6 (17 July 1745).
7. Gradish 1980, p. 189.
8. NMM ADM/E/11 ([42.], 17 November 1744); see Baugh 1965, pp. 180–82 for this hospital, which was surely not under one roof.
9. NMM ADM/E/11 ([42.], 17 November 1744); the complaint about the captains is (43.), 20 November 1744. Baugh suggests that the latters' motives were often humane: 1965, pp. 209–10.
10. Quoted Baugh 1965, p. 181.
11. Buchanan 1996, p. 22; see the map in Coad 1983, p. 22.
12. Tenon 1992, p. 179; the other ship held 200.
13. During the 1739–48 war privateers and merchant ships were paying 50–60 shillings a month to able seamen, compared to the Navy's 24: Baugh 1965, p. 229. For Newman, NMM ADM/E/11 ([10.], 3 March 1744). For the report on Haslar, WL Ms 5992, quotations from fol. 6v.
14. It was (and in part still is) a single-storey central range, 310 feet long, divided by a central chapel opening on to a vestibule forming part of an arcaded 'piazza' linking it to the five wards (each 22 x 32 feet) on each side. Long (125-foot) wings extended from both ends, with three more wards each. Coad 1983, pp. 31, 143–45 and Buchanan 1996, pp. 12–15.
15. Quoted in Revell 1978, p. 6. Buchanan 1996, p. 16 describes James Wibault's two alternative plans for Gibraltar, in the National Maritime Museum; the estimates (dated 16 April 1734) are NMM ADM/Y/G/51.
16. Rodger 1986, p. 173 describes Lind's analysis of its progress in his *Essay on the . . . health of seamen* (1757).
17. Coad 1983, p. 146. The decision to build the Gibraltar hospital preceded the arrival of infected ships: it was becoming a major station, and 'two Sheds, or Hutts, capable of receiving about Thirty Men' were all that was available: Baugh 1965, pp. 221–22. 'Although it did not receive its first patients until the Seven Years' War, Haslar Hospital was . . . a monument to the disasters of 1740 and 1741': ibid., p. 51, and see pp. 179–86, 216–22 for the epidemic's implications for manning and hospital construction.
18. Lloyd and Coulter 1961, pp. 194–95: the Admiralty was still requesting funds for three hospitals, but

Portsmouth's was to take priority. This text was used more than once that year in the circuit made by the Admiralty, Navy, and Sick and Hurt boards, and modern accounts date it differently. Though not abandoned, the contract system became supplementary to the hospitals run by the Commissioners themselves: ibid., pp. 187, 192.

19. NMM ADM/E/11 (not numbered, filed after [20.], 18 June 1745).

20. On the Jamaica hospital and its disastrously malarial site, Lloyd and Coulter 1961, pp. 101–4 and Baugh 1965, pp. 217–18. It was ordered to be replaced by a new building elsewhere in 1756: Gradish 1980, p. 186. For the Gibraltar hospital, which survives, as completed in 1756 see Lawrance 1994 and Coad 1983, pp. 145–47 (the latter notes on p. 146 that the wards 'could be isolated if necessary by using [the] verandahs as corridors'); for the projects, Buchanan 1996, pp. 16–17.

21. As the Scottish army surgeon Alexander Small then noted in disgust. He also reported that at a Minorca hospital (seemingly not the Navy's) the windows and doors were 'necessarily shut every night, to prevent the irregularities soldiers might be guilty of', but because the chimneys were also blocked, by morning the air in the wards 'often brought on a vomiting'. He devised ventilation that did not require the windows and doors to be opened: Franklin 1882, pp. 316–17.

22. Evans 1982, pp. 142–43.

23. NMM ADM/F/6 (9 August 1745): Forbes enclosed a plan of his existing hospital-house with its large and small wards, surgery, parlours, and 'Walk before the House faceing the River'.

24. PRO Adm 98/6, p. 150 (19 January 1757).

25. PRO Adm 98/7, pp. 374–75 (7 February 1759: does the last mean that Haslar was providing better than indifferent conveniences for the sick, or simply effective confinement)? The Commissioners were arguing that the *Blenheim* could be taken out of service, 'We being of Opinion that all the purposes of that Ship will be fully answered' by the accommodation by then finished at Haslar. Moreover, the 'Expence of Contracting with the Pursers is greater than Victualling the Patients in Hospitals ashore'.

26. NMM ADM/E/11 (not numbered, filed after [20.], 18 June 1745).

27. Baugh 1965, pp. 48 (quoting a remark from 1747), 89, 251–52. Ackworth was blocking changes in ship design that the Admiralty wanted, and failing to improve efficiency at the dockyards. See Baugh, too, for how the Navy then worked. As Surveyor, in charge of the design, maintenance, and construction of ships and dockyards, Ackworth was a senior (in practice, the senior) member of the Navy Board (Commissioners of the Navy). This Board, to which the Sick and Hurt Board (Commissioners for Sick and Wounded Seamen) was subordinate, was responsible for the Navy's 'civil economy', i.e. everything except the deployment of ships and the recruitment and management of personnel. The Navy Commissioners were subordinate to the Admiralty Commissioners, but the latter were political appointees and the former professionals in offices with much longer histories, which made a difference.

28. Coad 1983, pp. 21, 23, 149. He attributes the procedure to the hospitals' 'size and specialized nature'; Jacobsen was the 'best qualified architect of the day'.

29. NMM ADM/F/6 (not numbered, 27 June 1745).

30. NMM ADM/E/11 (not numbered, filed after [20.], 18 June 1745).

31. Admiralty Library: discovered and reproduced by Pugh 1976, p. 104.

32. Buchanan (1996, pp. 24–25) draws attention to the Foundling's importance in understanding Haslar.

33. Quoted Nichols and Wray 1935, p. 28; see also Nicolson 1972, p. 11.

34. Nichols and Wray 1935, p. 30 quote the General Committee's report (1 October 1740) to the General Court of Governors, specifying a 'Court Yard before the Hospital walled in (at least) Six Feet high, with a Porter to attend' to admit persons arriving with children for deposit.

35. Quoted Nichols and Wray 1935, p. 286.

36. For this arrangement and the changes made to it, Godfrey and Marcham 1952, pp. 11–12, who reproduce twentieth-century plans complemented by the fine photographs in Nichols and Wray 1935.

37. At Guy's and the Foundling, the arcades were eventually filled in to make enclosed and not open rooms and the same happened at Haslar during the Second World War: Lloyd and Coulter 1961, p. 210.

38. The projections show up to advantage in Samuel Wales's two perspective engravings (1749), reproduced and well analysed in Solkin 1992, pp. 161–63.

39. Pugh 1976, p. 110 reproduces the 1750 version, dedicated to the First Lord by John Turner, the master carpenter who with James Horne supervised construction.

40. Lloyd and Coulter 1961, pp. 211–12.

41. The 1756 plan (Admiralty Library) is reproduced by Pugh 1976, p. 115. The chapel's relocation adhered to the spirit, though not the letter of the Admiralty's instructions of June 1745, that it 'would have no building of any kind in the Area of the Quadrangle; The Chappel and all other Conveniences are to be in the Body of the Building'. NMM ADM/E/11 (not numbered, filed after [20.], 18 June 1745).

42. Lind believed Haslar would be the largest hospital in Europe when finished: Lloyd and Coulter 1961, p. 216. Tenon 1992, pp. 179–80 called it England's biggest hospital; Hunczovsky 1783, p. 49, its biggest brick construction.

43. Gradish 1980, pp. 182–84, 190–94 describes the problems and the new establishment and procedures introduced at Haslar, which were copied at Plymouth, as well as the changes concurrently taking place at other naval hospitals. Lloyd and Coulter 1961, pp. 216–17 transcribe relevant documents.

44. NMM ADM/F/12 (filed after 21 April 1755), 'Propose that the Management of Haslar Hospital be taken into the Hands of the Crown'; ADM/F/13 (5 February 1756), 'Recommend Mr Stephen Stonestreet to be Steward of Haslar Hospital', 'As the original Plan of Haslar Hospital is founded upon That of Greenwich, . . . a Man who is well Acquainted with the Business of the Steward of this Last, must be a very fit One for the carrying on of the Other'. 'Plan' is sadly to be understood in the administrative, not architectural sense but this passage has led to some confusion, e.g. Revell 1978, p. 13.

45. Lloyd and Coulter 1961, p. 207; compare Tait 1905, p. 15, and Richardson 1998, p. 79. The Queen Anne building was still holding Greenwich's sick pensioners, though in side-by-side wards within each range.

46. Bristowe and Holmes 1864, p. 720; see Lambert 1963, pp. 344–45 for their survey of British hospital provision, undertaken on behalf of the Privy Council's medical officer John Simon. Kathryn Morrison's report, in the NMR file no. 100117, includes a close description of Haslar as it now stands after some destruction by bombing in the Second World War and more attending the construction of the 'cross link' across the court in 1983.

47. Tenon 1992, p. 179. Hunczovsky read the wings as single but consisting of two parallel but detached buildings: 1783, p. 49.

48. Hunczovsky 1783, p. 50.

49. Reproduced Tenon 1992, facing p. 181.

50. Fourdrinier's print shows *no* windows on the narrow courts. They could have been omitted for the sake of pictorial tidiness, but the Foundling's dormitories had windows on one side only (Tenon 1992, p. 206).

51. Hunczovsky 1783, p. 51.

52. Tenon 1992, p. 180.

53. Hunczovsky 1783, p. 52: 'Es waren vormals zu Lüftung der Zimmer Ventilators bestimmt; Dr. Lind fand aber, daß dieselben bey weiten der Bestimmung nicht so ein Genüge thun, als die, so viel möglich, offen gehaltenen Fenster, zumal da sie einander angebracht sind.'

54. Revell 1978, p. 16.

55. *Gentleman's Magazine* 21 (1751): 408, with the print facing.

56. Tait 1905, p. 142.

57. Tenon 1996, p. 375.

58. Gradish 1980, pp. 178–79: the British naval hospitals 'were built primarily to care for the victims of fever' of one kind or another. His Table 5 (p. 202) shows that 7,014 of the 13,099 men admitted to the end of 1757 had 'fever', as distinguished from 'ague' (presumably malaria), at 71 men far less significant. Lloyd and Coulter 1961, pp. 114–15 give Lind's tallies for his first two years at Haslar (1758–60): though the proportion was now less than half, 'fever' was much the biggest single category.

59. Hunczovsky 1783, p. 52; Tenon 1992, pp. 183–84. The scurvy remedies are listed among other notes derived (Tenon wrote) from his conversations with Lind senior: idem 1996, p. 375.

60. He had observed that ships' ventilators did not necessarily reduce scurvy's incidence at sea: Carpenter 1986, pp. 59–60, and see also Lawrence 1996, pp. 84–85.

61. The regulations 'Of receiving patients' are quoted in Lloyd and Coulter 1961, pp. 219–20; compare Lind's letter of 1758, quoted ibid., p. 216.

62. It is tempting to imagine these serving as open-air bridges, as Tenon's wording suggests: 'De chaque côté, entre le pavillon et les salles est une terrasse revêtue de plomb': Tenon 1992, p. 184. He would soon advocate a two-storey gallery and the elevation of patients' wards above service buildings for his plan for a hospital at La Roquette (idem 1996, p. 332, 326). Richardson 1998, p. 80 describes the roofs of Plymouth's equivalent colonnade as an ambulatory, probably in a misreading of Howard's awkward description (1784, p. 389); compare Tenon's (1992, p. 154).

63. Tenon 1992, p. 183.

64. Hunczovsky 1783, pp. 49, 50; compare Grosley (1772, 2: 43), quoted in Chapter 6.

65. Lloyd and Coulter 1961, pp. 210–11, 253; for the walls and drains, ibid., pp. 205, 216, 253. Tait 1905, pp. 17, 141–42, 182 also describes new security measures, including sentry boxes on wheels, undertaken at the end of the century. Tenon noted the hospital's dissatisfaction, in 1787, with the supply of water potentially available in case of fire: 1992, pp. 188–89.

66. PRO Adm 3/65 (7 July 1757). Tenon 1992, p. 150 ('parfaitement isolé, et en bon air'); 'bel hôpital' represents his notes' height of enthusiasm.

67. Tenon 1996, p. 15.

68. Lloyd and Coulter 1961, pp. 267–69 transcribe the description by Richard Creke, appointed governor in 1795; Tenon 1992, p. 182 mentions Bethlem and idem 1996, p. 28 the reasoning behind accommodating the smallpox victims in this way.

69. Tenon 1992, pp. 154–55, who explained that surgical patients were separated from medical, and the latter according to whether they suffered from fever, ship fever, dysentery, scurvy, smallpox, phthisis, scabies, or venereal disease.

70. Colvin, *Biographical dictionary* 1995, s.v. 'Rouchhead, Alexander' (d. 1776), a man who 'appears to have

been identical with the "Alexander Rovehead" of London, who apparently designed, and certainly superintended, the erection' of the hospital. Cherry and Pevsner (1991, pp. 654–55) suggest that William Robinson (*c.*1720–75), Clerk of Works at Greenwich, acted as consultant, which Carré (1989, p. 19) finds significant. A 'Williamson Robinson' was Clerk of Works at St Bartholomew's by 1757, and in or after December 1767 was paid for overseeing the construction of the fourth block there (see Power 1927, pp. 12, 15); could this be the same man?

71. Though their foundations were laid: the east wing was built 1770–75 and the west *c.*1770–78: Clark-Kennedy 1962, pp. 157–58, 160.

72. Tenon noted (1996, pp. 329–30) that the men were free to walk around, though supervised by sentries.

73. Tenon 1992, p. 154: 'Autrefois tous les pavillons étaient entièrement séparés et la galerie était ouverte des deux côtés entre chaque corps de logis. On l'a fermée d'un mur qui s'aligne sur les pavillons de côté, ce qui diminue le froid. On se loue dans l'hôpital de cette amélioration.'

74. Ibid., pp. 153–55 (Plymouth), 93–94 (St Bartholomew's), 184 (Haslar), 173 (Salisbury).

75. Thompson and Goldin 1975, p. 118; Goldin's account of the old Hôtel-Dieu (pp. 118–25) is well illustrated and forceful. See Jetter 1973, p. 14 for a helpful plan showing the age of its different parts by 1772.

76. Tenon 1996, p. 119.

77. Quoted and translated by Ballon 1991, p. 173.

78. Air's meanings in this context are shown by Ozouf 1966, especially pp. 1279–80, and Etlin 1977. See Duveen and Klickstein 1955, pp. 165–66 for Lavoisier and his colleagues' concern for the purity of Paris's drinking water. Water was both a potential generator of miasmata and, Lavoisier believed, a *direct* source of disease.

79. Béguin 1979, pp. 39–40 has remarked on the way that sanitary principles formerly invested in or entrusted to moats and islands were explicitly transferred to the architectural domain, in the 'conversion d'anciennes formules territoriales, parfois quasi-rituelles, d'anti-contagion en principes de composition architecturale'.

80. Thompson and Goldin 1975, pp. 49–52; Risse 1999, pp. 202–10. The Tiber Island acquired a hospital during the Middle Ages and, in an emergency measure whose symbolic resonance Risse has shown, a temporary lazaretto was also opened in 1656; see the illustration following p. 338.

81. At least a third of Paris took its drinking water from the river (Greenbaum 1976, p. 909), and Tenon's *Mémoires* carefully specify his proposed hospitals' location relative to the direction of the stream, and the contagiousness, or not, of their patients (1996, pp. 22, 308–9).

82. From Bailly's committee's first report, as transcribed by Foucault et al. 1979, here p. 94. (They give the nominal and not the actual publication dates for the three reports of 1786–88, published in the Académie's proceedings for 1785 and 1786. Lavoisier's editor included the committee's reports in the *Oeuvres* and I have also used that version below.) Tenon wrote that one (double) ward alone had more patients than any other hospital in France, bar Lyons': 1996, p. 169.

83. Tenon 1996, pp. 139, 169.

84. Thompson and Goldin 1975, p. 122.

85. Tenon 1996, p. 144.

86. Ibid., pp. 203, 213. Thalamy evokes the 'incohérence' of the Hôtel-Dieu, 'cet incroyable imbroglio spatial': 1979, p. 31.

87. Middleton 1992, p. 17 (from Foucault et al. 1979, p. 6). My generation was introduced to this subject by Rosenau's (1970) 'Hospital' chapter. Middleton (1992, 1993) summarizes the debates in the context of French institutional planning through to the late nineteenth century and Etlin (1997, pp. 131–33) in that of eighteenth-century France's preoccupation with healthy air. Bruegmann's dissertation (1976) is largely concerned with the Hôtel-Dieu, and with Vidler's 'Confinement and cure: reforming the hospital, 1770–1789' (in Vidler 1987) it is the best analysis of the episode's significance for the history of architecture.

88. Foucault et al. 1979 provides forceful analyses of and lengthy extracts from the contemporary texts. Gillispie's 'Sanitation, prisons, and hospitals' (1980, pp. 244–56) is succinct and lively. Greenbaum's articles together provide a comprehensive account of medical-social thinking in pre-Revolutionary France in relation to the rebuilding debates, of which Weiner's introduction to Tenon 1996 is a useful new summary.

89. For the prestige of, and public interest in, the Hôtel-Dieu discussions see Greenbaum 1971, especially pp. 322–23, and idem 1974, p. 140. Duveen and Klickstein 1955, p. 174 consider Joseph's 'horrified' reaction to the hospital, during a 1783 visit, to have been one instigator of reform.

90. Le Roy 1789, p. 593: 'amas informe'.

91. Nightingale 1863, p. 56.

92. 'Nous croyons que la disposition la plus salubre pour les hôpitaux serait celle où chaque salle, si cela était possible, formerait un hôpital particulier et isolé'; 'Ce pavillon sera donc réellement un petit hôpital.' From the Académie's first and third reports as transcribed by Foucault et al. 1979, pp. 133, 138.

93. Tenon's *Mémoires* were enormously influential (not superseded in France until the 1860s, according to Bruegmann 1976, p. 170) but it was the Académie's version that was mostly followed in construction (ibid., p. 159). See also Greenbaum 1975, p. 44 and idem 1976, p. 927; Middleton 1992, pp. 20–21 and idem 1993, p. 26.

94. Bruegmann 1976: 'The plan was not invented in the eighteenth century at all. It had probably been invented or reinvented dozens of times . . . as a similar solution to a similar problem of grouping a number of isolated, identical structures in a given area' at Marly, for example, or Plymouth (pp. 153–54). Taylor (1997) shows the variety achieved by hospital architects in later nineteenth-century England alone.

95. Greenbaum 1974, pp. 128–30: Le Roy asked the Academy to publish his memoir four days after the committee's inauguration. He was thereupon asked to leave it, though it is not clear why: when the committee studied Tenon's project he merely absented himself from the meetings.

96. For these men see Bruegmann 1976, pp. 58–59. The designs are usually attributed to Poyet, the verbal *Mémoire* to Coquéau, but Richmond 1961, pp. 346–47 credits Poyet with the passages describing the project.

97. Translated Vidler 1987, p. 65; the original is transcribed in Foucault et al. 1979, p. 104.

98. 'Nous devons dire que l'idée de cette forme d'hôpital appartient à M. Leroy . . . qui l'a exposée dans un Manuscrit lu en 1777, non encore imprimé, et dont nous regrettons de n'avoir pas eu connaissance': in Foucault et al. 1979, pp. 133–34. Greenbaum (1974, p. 131) shows that the claim for ignorance could not be true: I have depended upon his account of Le Roy and his struggles.

99. Le Roy again read the essay to the academy in May 1777 and December 1786: Greenbaum 1974, p. 131.

100. Franklin 1906, p. 60; see Greenbaum 1974, p. 127, who believes that Franklin's ideas 'are prominently discernible in Le Roy's own work, particularly the therapeutic necessity of fresh air, the correct spacing of windows, and the use of ventilating flues' (p. 125), but these were not distinctive. For the translations, ibid., pp. 124–25.

101. Le Roy 1789, pp. 588, 594.

102. Berger 1994, pp. 143–53; by the 1690s the story was current that the idea for Marly had been Louis XIV's (p. 179).

103. A year earlier Sophie von la Roche (1933, p. 250) described Greenwich in a simile capturing both fragmentation and magnificence: 'The six buildings of this hospital, which stand detached', share a 'grand and noble structure, creating the impression of summer palaces, which so many great lords had planned to build here'.

104. Le Roy 1789, pp. 591, 590: 'aussi les anciens Germains nos ancêtres, appeloient-ils avec raison les villes les tombeaux des hommes'.

105. '. . . comme une espèce d'île dans l'air'. Vidler reproduces Le Roy's ward section (1987, p. 61, pl. 55), which Greenbaum 1974, pp. 126, 128 also discusses.

106. Tenon 1996, p. 332. Bruegmann suggests (1976, p. 156) that the height of this corridor may have disqualified this solution in his colleagues' eyes, as reducing light and air.

107. The published letter is transcribed and discussed by Greenbaum 1974, pp. 133–34: 'On voit dans ce plan comme dans le nôtre une suite de pavillons rangés sur deux files, une vaste cour au milieu, la chapelle dans le fond, les bâtimens d'un côté pour les hommes & l'autre pour les femmes.' It repeats that the committee had earlier been ignorant of Le Roy's proposals.

108. Le Roy 1789, note to p. 600.

109. Compare Greenbaum 1974, p. 132 (the Academy's plan was 'based on English prototypes, particularly the naval hospital at Plymouth'); Thompson and Goldin 1975, p. 142; Forty 1980, p. 78; Middleton 1992, p. 18; and Weiner's introduction to Tenon 1996, p. xxv ('Had Tenon not discovered this model at Plymouth and made it known on the Continent, the world would have had to wait for another twenty years for the hospital plan that was to predominate throughout the nineteenth century.')

110. '. . . le grand ouvrage de nos hôpitaux sera le résultat des lumières générales, par lesquelles toutes les nations doivent commencer, sans prétention de la part de celle qui donne, commme sans jalousie de la part de celle qui reçoit': from the third report, which remarks the unstinting help the travellers received, including of course at the military establishments, and is generous in its praise for English hospital practice, embracing everything from latrines to subscription lists: Lavoisier 1865, pp. 691–92, and compare Tenon 1996, pp. 26–27. The latter privately thought that the English did not have much to teach the French about therapeutics: Carré's introduction to Tenon 1992, pp. 12–13.

111. 'The commercial treaty of humanity', *Gentleman's Magazine* 57 (1787): 530 (but see its paraphrase of Banks, quoted at the beginning of Chapter 6).

112. Tenon 1996, pp. 11, 25–26, 329. According to two *Gentleman's Magazine* correspondents in 1787 (57: 530, 688) Tenon and Coulomb declared that their plan of visiting 'all the Hospitals, of every sort, in Great Britain and Ireland' had to be abandoned for lack of time. Tenon seems already to have collected some Scottish material.

113. Rochefort, whose architect was Pierre Toufaire, is awkward within the standard narrative of these events, just because the Académie committee seems to have ignored it: it may have been too new to provide proof of healthiness or for whatever reason a less desirable 'experiment' than its English counterparts. Greenbaum (1974, p. 137) first drew attention to Rochefort in this context; see also Bruegmann 1976, pp. 27, 72, and the plans (both identified as from 1782) reproduced by Foucault et al. 1979, p. 132, and Voldman 1981, p. 31.

The drawings differ in the degree of detachment, the former showing four wards entirely insulated. The importance of the military hospitals to civil-hospital practice in France forms a theme in Brockliss and Jones 1997: see especially pp. 689–703.

114. Hunczovsky 1783, p. 72: 'Zu *Plymouth* ist ebenfalls ein ansehnliches Matrozenhospital, worin mehr als 1000 Kranke versorgt werden können. In einem beträchtlichen Umfange stehen mehrere kleine Gebäude einzeln, in welchen die Kranken von verschiedenen Gattungen liegen. Da die innere Einrichtung des Spitals, und die Behandlung der Kranken mit der Portsmouther übereinstimmung ist, und zu eben der Zeit keine Kranken da waren, so halte ich eine genauere Beschreibung davon für unnöthig.' Compare Howard's description: 1784, p. 389.

115. Duveen and Klickstein 1955, p. 177, Greenbaum 1971, p. 322, and idem 1974, pp. 136–37 describe the enthusiasm for and interest in English hospitals reflected in other French-language publications and manuscript accounts, to which we could add [Grosley] 1770.

116. Tenon 1996, p. 10, prefaced by an equivocal account of Le Roy's 'efforts'; they 'were fruitless, but they prepared the way for a change of mind'.

117. The Hôpital Saint-Louis, for example, had and long continued to enjoy a fine reputation (see the references in Chapter 1, n. 23) but Tenon presents it as untouched by earlier analysis. He explained (1996, p. 83) that he took his illustrations of Saint-Louis from Duhamel du Monceau's *Moyens de conserver la santé aux équipages des vaisseaux; avec la manière de purifier l'air des salles des hôpitaux* (1759), but not why it featured there; even the title of the book was abbreviated, to refer only to ships.

118. Quoted in Greenbaum 1971, pp. 340–41: 'Nous applaudissons à votre voyage à Plymouth. Il est en effet très curieux et très utile de voir notre grand Plan déjà exécuté. M. Tenon a raison, c'est une Expérience déjà faite qui nous mettra à même d'en voir et d'en connoître les avantages et les inconvéniens; ce voyage étoit essentiel.' Greenbaum suggests that Bailly was anxious for the data that would corroborate the committee's advocacy of the pavilion type, just confirmed by the second report: see also idem 1974, p. 132 and 1992, p. 308.

119. I have taken the translation, with a couple of changes, from Grace Goldin's, in Thompson and Goldin 1975, p. 142; compare Lavoisier 1865, p. 682. Tenon (1992, p. 186) measured the gaps between the wings, or wards, as five *toises* three *pieds*, i.e. 33 feet.

120. Colley 1994 (e.g. pp. 5, 34, 252) is useful on British self-definitions *vis-à-vis* the 'subtle, intellectually devious' French.

121. This longer draft is transcribed in Greenbaum 1974, pp. 134–35, with an interesting analysis: 'les Salles sont doubles, ... Nous avons exposé les raisons qui nous faisoient regarder cette disposition comme vicieuse: le renouvellement de l'air étant le premier principe de salubrité dans un hôpital, nous avons préféré des salles simples qui pussent recevoir un air passant'. Greenbaum reads *salles simples* incorrectly: the Academy's wards are not here 'simple' but 'single' (-piled). He suggests that this unpublished version (found among Lavoisier's papers, and with corrections in his hand) might have been thought to concede too much to Le Roy.

122. Blane 1799, pp. 175–76: Tenon, who 'had made a comparative review of most of the hospitals of Europe, ... and visited this one in 1787, gives the preference to it over all others'.

123. '... l'expérience des Anglais a confirmé notre principe ... Voilà ce qu'enseigne la théorie; et si l'on veut consulter l'expérience, nous dirons que les hôpitaux d'Angleterre, tous en général assez salubres, ont trois rangs de salles et trois étages': Foucault et al. 1979, pp. 137, 138.

Chapter 9: Ornament and the architect

1. LHB 1/1/1, p. 142 (20 April 1738).

2. Davenant 1699, p. 52.

3. 1 Peter 3: 4. Marvell, 'Upon Appleton House' (1667), ll. 65–66: Fowler 1994, no. 56.

4. Philasthenes 1739, p. 9; Stevenson, 'Æsculapius Scoticus' 1996, p. 58.

5. Philanthropus 1738, p. 4 and Philasthenes 1739, p. 7; compare Maitland 1753, p. 457.

6. One set of donations was specifically directed towards the ornamentation of the centre pavilion (Stevenson, 'Æsculapius Scoticus' 1996, p. 58) and Michael Barfoot has suggested to me that the stipulation might have been prompted by the strong resemblance, otherwise, between the hospital and the workhouse.

7. Loudon 1840, p. 259, from Repton's *Observations* (1803). Compare the relative incoherence of *The builder's dictionary* (1734): Russell 1997, s.v. 'Decoration' and 'Ornaments'.

8. Maitland 1753, p. 459: 'yea, I am even told, they *took a little from the Building Funds* for that Service, and many hundreds have thereby been relieved.' He was (he stated) quoting Philasthenes (1739), which I have not checked for this passage.

9. 'Account' 1741, p. 652; LH/A/4/2, p. 146 (25 September 1751).

10. HB 14/1/1, p. 49 (13 October and 10 November 1791).

11. Ibid., pp. 49–51 (16 November 1791). Both surviving elevations have a rusticated basement. Three sets of tenders and estimates, for which the Infirmary had advertised before Christmas, were considered on 12 January 1792. Among them was Adam's, now at

£7,768 'for the whole buildings' including extras and the 2.5 per cent: ibid., p. 58. After Robert's sudden death on 3 March the committee, 'informed that two Brothers of his [that is, James and William jun.] are connected with him in Business of that kind' decided to write to them, to see if they would take up the contract: ibid., p. 63 (8 March 1792). James (1732–94) at first declined, but then declared his willingness on 18 April 1792 to act as 'Inspector and Surveyor of the Buildings' contracted with Messrs Morison and Burns: ibid., pp. 65–66.

12. SM Adam vol. 48/8 (Figure 76) is labelled, 'Infirmary at Glasgow' and 48/9 (Figure 77) 'Another design for the Infirmary at Glasgow', both inscriptions top centre. 48/9 has additional, smaller writing bottom left and right: '[Th]is is the right Copy according to the Contract' and 'Edin.' 8. May', which must be May 1792, two months after Robert's death and ten days before the first stone was laid. As part of his helpful description of the Infirmary (demolished 1907) as it was built, King (1991, pp. 61–64) proposes that the executed design was James Adam's, but the hospital records suggest to me that it was Robert's, and the 'right copy' so inscribed after his death.

13. Geertz 1976, pp. 1499, 1478.

14. Pratt 1928, p. 23.

15. Alberti 6.2, 1988, p. 156; he unambiguously subsumed the orders under ornament. See Hedrick 1987, p. 125 on the ' "logic of the supplement" ' (he quotes Jacques Derrida), whereby 'that which is the "supplement" or dependent category' – ornament in this case – 'on the one hand appears *superfluous* and on the other appears *necessary for completion*' (emphases in the original).

16. Alberti 1988, editors' note on p. 420. Wren is from the second 'Tract': Soo 1998, p. 159.

17. Le Roy 1789, p. 586: 'Mais en réfléchissant davantage sur ce qui avoit pu empêcher ces architectes de diriger leurs vues essentiellement vers l'objet que je viens d'indiquer; je conçus, par la connoissance que j'avois des talens & de la capacité de plusiers d'entr'eux, que c'étoit uniquement faute d'avoir eu une connoissance suffisante des observations dont je viens de parler.' Compare pp. 585, 599.

18. Vanbrugh 1928, p. 31: from a letter to the Duchess, 11 June 1709.

19. For Coquéau and Poyet's *Mémoire*, Foucault et al. 1979, p. 105; for Chirol's project (reproduced ibid. p. 89; only Chirol's surname is known), Bruegmann 1976, p. 55, who also quotes (p. 228) the Academy's third report to this effect. Grosley had described Haslar hospital as 'composed of detached parts, all conspiring in one general plan, the grandeur of which is not so much in the ornaments as in the building itself': 1772, 2: 47.

20. Fortier 1976, p. 72; Bruegmann 1976, p. 56 points out the significance of the absent elevations.

21. Tenon 1996, p. 78: he did not disqualify architects.

22. Vidler 1987, p. 62 refers to 'surrogate' patronage in this context.

23. Quoted Colvin, *Biographical dictionary* 1995, s.v. 'Webb, John': the appointee was Sir John Denham.

24. Erlam 1954, p. 100.

25. Bentham 1981, p. 310: letter 792, Adam to Bentham, 7 June 1791; Picon 1992, p. 95 quotes Blondel. The 'gentry were almost always their own architects': James Gandon described Ireland. When he arrived there in 1781, 'skill in arrangement or good work was not [to] be expected'. Though Gandon allowed the usefulness of the 'true enlightened critic', 'intrusive interference', especially in public works, was commoner: Mulvany 1969, pp. 51n., 273.

26. Bentham 1981, p. 306: letter 789 to Robert Adam, 28 May 1791.

27. Ibid., p. 310: letter 792, Adam to Bentham, 7 June 1791.

28. For the purposes of this argument about the proprietor's perception of the professional's investment in inessentials I am conflating two jobs that the professional surveyor might be expected to do c.1698: design, and measuring/surveying the work under the supervision of the designer. See Colvin, *Biographical dictionary* 1995, p. 25 and Airs 1995, pp. 70, 207–8, who places more emphasis on the distinction.

29. North 1981, p. 23. See Brown 1994, pp. 49–50 for a pertinent account of how one builder, Clerk of Penicuik, worked with the 'tow'ring Fancy of an Architect', William Adam.

30. The Duchess's letter of 2 November 1709 is in Vanbrugh 1928, pp. 185–86; that of 21 July 1732 is Thomson 1943, p. 52. The notably large Marlborough Almshouses in St Albans (1735–36, on which see Bailey 1988, p. 150) were built with the help of William and Francis Smith, about whom (Andor Gomme has told me) the Duchess had no complaints. Vanbrugh's remark is in a letter of 2 February 1721 (Vanbrugh 1928, p. 127).

31. North 1981, p. 24n., from the British Library draft.

32. See Kindler 1974, especially p. 24, for a very helpful exposition of novelty's place in early nineteenth-century architectural criticism.

33. North 1981, pp. 18–19. North was probably thinking of his friend the natural philosopher Christopher Wren; they liked to discuss the discrimination of kinds of beauty, which was North's concern at this point in the treatise.

34. Mandeville, 'The grumbling hive' (1705), p. 74, and Remark 'S' (1714), p. 234, in Mandeville 1989; compare Alberti 9.1, 1988, p. 291 and Hedrick 1987, p. 124.

35. Jordanova 1979, p. 120.

36. Ignatieff 1978, p. 52.

37. Quoted in Semple 1993, p. 93: Bentham continued, 'No leading principles – no order – no connexion.'

Robin Evans has commented (1982, p. 75): 'Expectations regarding [prison] architecture were high, but were at first experienced in nebulous generalizations and enigmatic allusions'; it needed Blackburn and Bentham to 'forge the links between discipline and building'.

38. Aikin 1771, p. 20.
39. 'Mes vues dans ce travail, ne sont point de m'ériger en architecte, de parler de la construction de la bâtisse, de la décoration de ces maisons de charité, objets réservés aux hommes célèbres qui, comme vous Monsieur, se consacrent à votre Art, lequel embrasse une multitude de connaissances et renferme en même temps beaucoup d'autres Arts; j'ai dû seulement considérer les hôpitaux dans leur rapport avec l'homme malade, . . . rechercher . . . dans l'art de guérir des principes applicables à la formation et à la distribution des maisons élevées pour les secourir.' The undated letter is quoted in Foucault et al. 1979, p. 146.
40. Picon 1992, pp. 51, 72–85: *distribution* is the arrangement of rooms in a building, or of a building with its courts, outbuildings, and gardens. Compare Russell 1997, s.v. 'Distribution'.
41. In Tenon's travel journal Dance is that 'homme habile, obligeant', 'habile architecte . . . de qui nous avons reçu toutes sortes d'honnêtés': 1992, pp. 43, 58, and see also idem 1996, p. 27.
42. For Immanuel Kant (1724–1804), architecture was the 'most inferior of the arts because it is the most bound to the utilitarian realm the aesthetic supposedly transcends' (Wigley 1993, p. 13), and for G. W. F. Hegel (1770–1831) it was but the beginning of art because it presupposes a purpose external to it, a 'need lying indeed outside art, and its appropriate satisfaction has nothing to do with fine art and does not evoke any works of art': Hegel 1975, 2: 631–32; see also Vidler 1992, pp. 122–24.
43. Professor of Anatomy and Surgery, in fact; translated and quoted in Vidler 1987, p. 59, who comments p. 60.
44. See Howard 1988 for a discussion in regard to sixteenth-century England.
45. 'Un hôpital des malades est un édifice où l'architecte doit subordonner son art aux vûes du medecin: confondre les malades dans un même lieu, c'est les détruire les uns par les autres.' Diderot 1765, p. 264; see Mortier 1979 for Diderot's sources for this article.
46. Aikin 1771, p. 11 (*Thoughts on hospitals* was published in French translation in 1777); Tenon 1996, p. 315, and compare p. 186 on the 'sort of league' among 'persons of good will' dedicated to keeping the poor out of the Hôtel-Dieu.
47. Aikin 1771, pp. 12, 13. Compare Frank (1976, p. 419) on the architect's 'misplaced parsimony'.
48. Jones 1971, pp. 104–5, possibly referring to the City Lying-in Hospital, rebuilt to Robert Mylne's designs 1770–73.

49. Percival is from a 'Letter' appended to Aikin's book (1771, p. 85; see also the quotation from his *Medical ethics* [1803] in DeLacy 1986, p. 89); Browne is Scull 1991, p. 183. Compare Jones 1971, p. 105 on the 'same false maxims of oeconomy'.
50. Tenon 1996, pp. 303–4. What 'was being presented' in the Hôtel-Dieu discussions 'was not an "architecture without architects," but rather another kind of architecture, [finding] . . . its means for "embellishment" not in the classical repertory, but in the forms of need.' Vidler 1987, p. 56.
51. Vidler 1987, p. 55: 'what was to become of the traditional apparatus of classical precedent, proper characterization, and monumental aesthetics; where indeed might the expertise of the architect be required at all, save for the mundane task of translating doctors' diagrams into building specifications? This, at least, was how many architects and doctors posed the problem'.
52. Bentham 1981, p. 172: letter 711 to Sir John Parnell, c.26 August 1790.
53. Ibid., p. 199: letter 719 to Reveley, c.3 September 1790.
54. Bentham, *Panopticon (Postscript)* 1843, pp. 80–81.
55. Bentham 1981, p. 284: letter 772 to Robert Hobart, c.9 May 1791. Compare his disclaimers in the letter (no. 776, 11 May 1791) presenting the Panopticon to George III (p. 291); and in another (no. 789, 28 May 1791) to Robert Adam (p. 306).
56. Emphasis Bentham's: ibid., p. 174: letter 711, to Parnell.
57. Bentham, *Panopticon* 1843, p. 66.
58. Bentham 1981, p. 291: letter 777 to Carew, 11 May 1791.
59. Ibid., pp. 306–7: letter 789.
60. Ibid., p. 310: letter 792, Adam to Bentham, 7 June 1791.
61. Ibid., pp. 372–73: letter 848, Bentham to James Adam, 13 July 1792; the editor also quotes Samuel Bentham's correspondence with Lord Elgin on this matter. It is not clear which Adam the Bentham brothers blamed for what Samuel called the spoiling, or impairment, of the Panopticon idea, but the disenchantment with Robert was by then complete. See Markus 1982, pp. 69, 72–82 for a discussion using the correspondence and reproducing the surviving designs for the Bridewell; and MacInnes 1993, pp. 13–17, who also shows the significance of its style.
62. Bentham 1981, p. 375: letter 850, to George Rose, 16 July 1792. Compare Samuel Romilly's letter (no. 922) to Bentham, 2 September 1793: 'The plan is [James] Adam's and I am informed he admits that he took the idea of it from your brother'.
63. Greenbaum 1974, pp. 134, 136.
64. Le Roy 1789, notes to p. 600.
65. Bruegmann 1976, pp. 31 n.27, 154, 227. The text also suggests five or six ventilation cupolas in each ward, but Viel's section has many more; he also showed hundreds of columns surrounding the ward blocks.

What Bruegmann calls this 'curious duality' of text and image is not unique to Le Roy's projects: discrepancies between the Coquéau–Poyet description of their project and its illustrations were pointed out at the time (ibid., p. 37).

66. 'Ce savant me communiqua, en 1776, un programme qui réunissait toutes les conditions désirables pour la salubrité d'un hôpital des malades dont le nombre serait de quatre mille.' Foucault et al. 1979, p. 150.

67. Ibid., p. 152.

68. My emphasis. 'Cette explication devenait nécessaire pour fixer les idées sur ce qui constitue un morceau d'architecture qui n'appartient jamais comme composition à l'auteur du programme; parce que ce ne sont nullement par des mots que les arts de dessin s'expriment. Certainement, les professeurs dans les écoles des arts, qui donnent les programmes des tableaux, des sculptures, et des édifices à composer par les élèves, n'ont aucune prétention sur les ouvrages qui leur sont soumis. Comment expliquer les prétentions des savants qui ont écrit sur les hôpitaux, qui osent appeler l'invention de plans, d'élevations et de coupes: leurs projects!' Foucault et al. 1979, pp. 153–54. See Vidler 1987, p. 62, whose translation I have also adapted, on the disingenuousness of Le Roy's disclaimer of architecture, the 'eagerness to demonstrate freedom from convention'.

69. 'L'architecture est un art et non une suffrageante des sciences exactes.' For his career and writings, see Pérouse de Montclos 1966 (quotation p. 266), Braham 1980, pp. 242–43, and Pérez-Gómez 1983, pp. 315–21.

70. Spurzheim 1817, pp. 214–15, 217.

71. Bevans is quoted in Richardson 1998, p. 160 and Alexander Morison's diary entry in Hunter and Macalpine 1963, p. 738. Kindler 1974, p. 27 quotes a magazine correspondent (also 1818): 'there must be something radically wrong where the same sort of portico may be applied to the New Bedlam, Carlton House, Covent-garden Theatre, and Mary-Le-bonne church'.

72. According to a Lothian Health Services Archive typescript, 'Royal Edinburgh Hospital', pauper patients were not admitted until William Burn's West House opened in 1842. Spurzheim visited Edinburgh in 1816–17; its was the third Scottish public asylum, after Montrose's (opened 1781) and Aberdeen's (1800). Glasgow's would be the fourth.

73. Halliday 1816, pp. 16–17: unless a large proportion of its patients were 'in opulent circumstances, the benefit which it can afford to Paupers is very trifling'. The Asylum's annual report for that year however reported that some paupers were lodged in rooms intended for patients of a higher class (*Report* 1816, pp. 10–11).

74. The La Roquette hospital was to have the pavilion plan. The following is taken from Tenon 1996, pp. 17, 197,

334. On the historical importance of his understanding of asylums see Pinon 1989, pp. 37–39.

75. Stevenson 1993, pp. 1505–6.

76. Porter, 'Madness' 1992, p. 289; the argument is extended in Porter, 'Shaping psychiatric knowledge' 1995. See also Scull 1991, pp. viii–ix, and idem 1993, especially pp. 41–42.

77. '. . . ce qui est déjà fait est mauvais, et les anciens bâtimens nuiront a ceux qu'on projette; les uns et les autres manqueront de symétrie, de subdivisions nécessaires.' . . . 'Le plan d'un hospice d'aliénés n'est point une chose indifférent et qu'on doive abandonner aux seuls architectes'. From 'Des Établissements', according to Esquirol written in 1817 and first published in 1818: Esquirol 1838, pp. 414, 421.

78. See Porter, 'Madness' 1992, p. 297. Browne's summary analysis (1872) of classificatory desiderata is useful: Scull 1991, pp. 199–202.

79. Porter, 'Shaping psychiatric knowledge' 1995, pp. 267–68.

80. Both publications were intended, not just to promote interest in the charity, but to be money-making ventures in themselves: LHB 7/1/1, managers' minutes for 25 May 1809.

81. Markus 1982, pp. 90–91, 93–94 describes the building and reproduces more of Reid's illustrations from the *Observations*.

82. A 'spectacular prescription': idem 1993, pp. 20–21. For the building, ibid., pp. 135–36; idem 1982, pp. 94–96 (with reproductions of the plan and 'General View'); and Snedden 1993, especially pp. 28–30.

83. *Report* 1814, pp. 7–8.

84. *Report* 1817, pp. 17–18, which also mentions the favourable testimony presented about the asylum to the House of Commons Select Committee.

85. An appendix to the 1821 *Report* lists instructions to an architect planning additions; the chapel was completed in 1828. The Asylum was almost immediately overcrowded and plans for its enlargement were under way less than two years after it opened (*Report* 1817, p. 14; *Report* 1819, p. 14); Snedden 1993, pp. 28–29 describes the extensions undertaken between 1822 and 1838, and the accommodation available for persons of rank. In 1840 the building was sold to the Town's Hospital, which had furnished its first inmates only twenty-six years before, and a replacement was built on another, much larger site: ibid., pp. 30–31.

86. Quoted in Hunter and Macalpine 1963, p. 518.

87. Hoeldtke 1967.

88. *Report* 1816, p. 13.

89. Digby, 'Moral treatment' 1985, p. 55; this essay and the same author's *Madness* 1985, especially pp. 36–40 illustrate the demonstrable relationships between an asylum building, its form and siting, and conceptions of the nature and management of insanity.

90. Charlesworth 1828, p. 15.
91. [Reid] 1809, p. 77; emphases mine. See Markus 1982, pp. 90–91, 93 for what is now the Royal Edinburgh Hospital and Digby, *Madness* 1985, p. 248 for its debt to the Retreat.
92. Currie explained that 'It is the policy of an asylum to make these two classes connect with each other, so the increased payments made by the rich, may serve to diminish in some degree, the demands on the poor': quoted Hunter and Macalpine 1963, p. 519. Other statements along this line are quoted by Digby 1986, pp. 7 (regarding the York Asylum, in 1788) and 10 (an early attack on the Asylum as a 'palace for... the opulent lunatic'), and Bailey 1971, pp. 178–79 (the proposed Gloucester Asylum, 1793); see also the 1807 *Address* about the Edinburgh Asylum, p. 8. Smith 1999, pp. 16–17 summarizes the eighteenth-century provincial asylums.
93. Scull 1991, p. 199. Compare pp. 201–2: a poor but well-educated lunatic ought not be be denied the company of his (natural) peers.
94. Scull 1985, p. 124, mostly with reference to texts from the 1830s and after. For familial organization see idem 1983, especially pp. 245–47, and Digby, *Madness* 1985, p. 10 and the section ('The domestic milieu') beginning p. 49.
95. *Report* 1814, p. 8.
96. Ibid., pp. 8–9. For the technicalities of the dome, mentioned in the picture caption, see Gomme and Walker 1987, pp. 70–71.
97. *Report* 1820, p. 14; the most pressing need was however identified as additional wards for 'Boarders' at lower rates, and for the 'Paupers', who were greatly overcrowded.
98. *Dictionaire* 1812, p. 201, s.v. 'Agriculture'.
99. Scull 1991, p. xxxi, from his summary 'Madness and civilization', pp. xxx–xxxiv: for Browne, although madness was a disease of civilization, it was not a necessary adjunct to it.
100. See Hoeldtke 1967, p. 54 and Parry-Jones 1972, p. 233 for what the latter calls the 'strong belief in the therapeutic value of severing the patient's association with his home and the prevention of early or indiscriminate visiting by relatives and acquaintances'.
101. By the 1850s writers were associating the mills and factories with a new prevalence of mental disease among the urban poor: see Philo 1987, pp. 404–5, 407 (an article generally useful on this subject, though concerning the second half of the century) and idem 1989, p. 269. The index heading for 'work' in Leonard Smith's study of early nineteenth-century county asylums has no fewer than twenty-seven subheadings, from 'agricultural' to 'window cleaning'.
102. Compare Rothman 1990, pp. 127, 154: in Jacksonian America medical superintendents 'were trying to re-create in the asylum their own vision of the colonial community'.
103. At the York Retreat (initially on an 11-acre site) patients could see over low boundary walls to grounds 'made as varied and interesting as possible to manipulate the patients' emotions and so to cheer the melancholics': Digby, 'Moral treatment' 1985, pp. 55, 53, who also notes (p. 63) early patients' resistance to manual labour. See also Philo 1987, pp. 407–8 for the continuing stress placed on prospects.
104. Scull 1991, p. 221. Browne was describing Esquirol's private asylum at Ivry, where 'troublesome or excited patients' might look out of a 'plain, neat, high railing, like that of Tuilleries Garden'. Pinon 1989 is informative on French manipulations of walls and ditches to produce illusions of boundlessness; see especially pp. 117, 175–77.
105. The distinctions are from McClung 1983, pp. 14, 44. Nature's (especially *vegetable* nature's) prowess in the face of insanity was a large theme in the period, about which I have written in the context of Denmark (Stevenson 1988). The fundamental modern analysis remains Foucault's 'The return to the immediate' (1972, pp. 191–97).
106. Alberti 6.2, 1988, p. 156.
107. Spurzheim 1817, p. 217.

Chapter 10: First principles

1. Glen 1983, p. 117, part of her exploration of Blake's three songs about public charity; on this one see also Heal 1990, p. 403.
2. Quoted in Fitton and Wadsworth 1958, pp. 99–100. While the benevolence of the factory masters (and institutional reformers) 'is often interpreted as an effort to introduce an idealized version of rural paternalism into an industrial and institutional context', Ignatieff (1978, p. 76) is more cautious about characterizing it this way; but compare Langford 1991, p. 487, writing with reference to Arkwright and William Strutt.
3. Fitton and Wadsworth 1958, pp. 91 and 97–98, for the *Gentleman's Magazine* notice, quoted; Pevsner 1986, p. 160; Raven 1992, pp. 219–20.
4. 'Of extravagance in building' reprinted in the *Gentleman's Magazine* 2 (1732): 765–66; see Friedman 1990 on this essay.
5. Clayton 1997, pp. 139–40; compare Brewer's reproduction (1997, pl. 4) of a delightful picture (1771) of a 'Modern Built Villa near Clapham'.
6. Quoted in Raven 1992, p. 219.
7. The Whitbreads' contemporary Bedford Infirmary and Asylum, the subjects of Cashman 1988 and 1992, are the other obvious examples of institutions in whose foundation a manufacturing family took a dominant role.

8. Thomas Sympson (1878, p. 5), a senior surgeon at the Lincoln County Hospital, for example praised Carr's building for the volume of space it afforded each patient.

9. Quoted in Taylor 1991, p. 4. Dr Leveaux's book (1999) about the infirmary came to my attention too late to be able to make any use of it here, unfortunately.

10. Glen 1983, p. 116.

11. Cunningham 1998, p. 9; Pickstone 1984, p. 404 makes the point that voluntary schemes were a way for Manchester Dissenters to assert themselves independently of the parish machinery.

12. 'Essay on Charity' (1723), Mandeville 1989, p. 313; Ditchfield 1998, p. 201 quotes Dyer.

13. Bowen 1783, p. 12.

14. Aikin 1771, pp. 13–14, 16. This is a speculative reading, but five years later Aikin's admirer John Jones explicitly named St Thomas' and St Bartholomew's in this connection: 1971, pp. 102–3. The French would with more justification identify the *forme carré* as the dominant hospital type, and condemn it for the same reason: Bruegmann 1976 p. 167 n.3 and Vidler 1987 p. 57 quote Antoine Petit (1774); compare Le Roy 1789, p. 593. Bailly's committee's first report (1786) associated it with cross-infection, too: Foucault et al. 1979, p. 133.

15. Aiken 1771, p. 9. Kilpatrick argues (1990, p. 263) that Quaker philanthropy's characteristic emphasis on enabling the 'labouring poor to help themselves to become self-supporting' reflects a general ethos of 'freedom from constraint' also seen in its opposition to institutions 'such as prisons, madhouses and hospitals'.

16. Kilpatrick 1990, p. 265.

17. Good introductions to this large subject are Webster 1978 and Pickstone and Butler 1984: see especially pp. 232–33, 237 in the latter. The anonymous 'Putrid fever' 1958 describes measures taken to clean and fumigate one Lancashire cotton mill after an outbreak in 1782; medical debates on the mills' role in generating the disease; and how a *nouveau-riche* owner might be accused of having failed in his (patriarchal) duty of protecting workers: pp. 28, 30–31, 33.

18. Ferrir 1798, pp. 48–50; for the Westminster, Woodward 1974, p. 11.

19. Cullen taught that natural human 'effluvia . . . acquire a singular virulence' in confined spaces, 'and in that state . . . become the cause of a fever, which is highly contagious': quoted Kilpatrick 1990, pp. 266–67, with reference to Lettsom's training. See also Pickstone and Butler 1984, p. 321; Risse 1986, pp. 131–33, which describes Cullen's fever classifications; and Lobo 1990, especially pp. 220–22, for Cullen's continuing centrality to the English 'Dissenting intellectual network'.

20. Risse 1986, p. 107, and see ibid., pp. 7–9 for popular and medical perceptions of fever in relation to Edinburgh's culture, climate, and housing.

21. James Gregory is quoted ibid., p. 133; the land sale is from the *Report*, p. 57, in Clark 1802. In 'Manchester the main resistance to the House of Recovery came from property owners in the vicinity': Pickstone 1984, p. 414.

22. Woodward 1974, Chapter 7 'Fever cases', pp. 61–74, explains the complexities: accidentally or not, they were sometimes admitted. Cherry 1980, p. 252, is more emphatic about later eighteenth-century exclusions.

23. In 1805: Loudon 1981, p. 331n., and pp. 332–33 for material that follows, as well as Cherry 1980, pp. 68–70, 264, who argues that the view that epidemic diseases were the 'most extensive killers' in eighteenth- and early nineteenth-century English towns needs modification in view of the prominence of chronic and endemic, especially respiratory, illnesses.

24. Webster 1978, especially pp. 217, 221, 222 (with reference to Manchester and Newcastle); Pickstone and Butler 1984. Bruegmann 1976, pp. 187–89 and idem 1978, pp. 144–46 draws attention to the importance of technology like William Strutt's to such radical schemes as the Panopticon and, more generally, to the Midlands natural-philosophical milieu to which Strutt was instrumental; see also Hacker 1960, pp. 62–63.

25. Howard 1789, p. 209; compare Woodward 1974, p. 63. For the wards (which, Haygarth wrote, did 'ten times more real good in the prevention of misery, than all the other parts of the Infirmary': quoted Webster 1978, p. 219) see Richardson 1998, p. 133 and Hunter and Macalpine 1963, p. 445. On Haygarth, Lobo 1990.

26. Ferrir 1798, pp. 64, 70; Pickstone and Butler 1984, who show (pp. 232, 237) the Manchester–Haygarth connection as part of the social and political ramifications of Manchester's innovations; Webster 1978, pp. 218–20. Manchester's is sometimes called the first British fever hospital, but see Richardson 1998, pp. 132–33. The Infirmary itself, built 1754–55, was by 1797 publishing a very distinctive plan (reproduced Markus 1982, p. 37) with many small wards ranged off spine corridors; it was much altered in the meantime. See the NMR file no. 102063, whose report (by Ian Pattison) notes the contradictory nature of the eighteenth-century visual evidence, and also Brockbank 1952, which reproduces much of the latter.

27. A copy of the printed *Report of the Committee . . .* , 23 March 1805, is DRO D1190/1/2. As it is only three pages long, I will not reference it henceforth. All quotations from DRO material in what follows are by permission of the County and Diocesan Archivist, Derbyshire Record Office.

28. Clark, *Collection* 1802, p. 14. See Webster 1978, pp. 221–22.

29. Bynum 1979, p. 101 quotes the letter read at the London Fever Hospital's organizational meeting; Pelling 1978, pp. 18–19 describes the durability of this view of the 'mixed character of continued fevers'.

30. Clark, *Collection* 1802, pp. 29–30. Compare Bynum (1979, pp. 102–3), describing Haygarth's identical convictions, published as early as 1778; and Pickstone (1984, pp. 405–6), on those of Percival and his Manchester circle, in which he finds some interesting political ramifications too.

31. Duncum 1964, p. 212 quotes Clark's *Account* of 1801. The architect was John Stockoe (1756–1836).

32. Clark, *Collection* 1802, p. 14 and *Report* p. 230. For additional illustrations after those Clark published the previous year see Hume 1906 facing p. 35, which shows the walls, and Forty 1980, p. 76.

33. See below. In the meantime the London Fever Hospital ('Institution for the Cure and Prevention of Contagious Fever in the Metropolis') opened in 1802 and the Hull Infirmary instituted two 'Wards of Prevention' against what it identified as typhus in the next year. For the future of fever's (infectious-diseases') accommodation, Woodward 1974, pp. 65, 74; Taylor 1991, pp. 105–18; Richardson 1998, pp. 132–38.

34. See Strutt's charming letter to his son, in Fitton and Wadsworth 1958, p. 172.

35. Ibid. 1958, pp. 1, 38; Hacker 1960, p. 50.

36. Quoted in Johnson and Skempton 1956, p. 181; the Derby Cotton Mill was named the first ever 'fire-proof mill' in 1802 (ibid., p. 180). For Strutt's innovations in their technical (and imaginative) context, ibid., and Markus 1993, pp. 125 and 267–81 *passim*.

37. Fitton and Wadsworth 1958, p. 186.

38. 'Machinery so perfect appears to act with the happy certainty of instinct and the foresight of reason combined', she wrote about an invention of Marc Brunel's: quoted Rolt 1970, p. 33.

39. Edgeworth 1971, pp. 26–27: 'He laughed and colored and said "There was nothing to shew and that it seemed ridiculous to shew the house"', which she also described as 'quite a palace, yet there is more *comfort* than magnificence and it is plain that the convenience of the inhabitants and guests has been consulted in everything' (ibid., p. 25).

40. From a letter of January 1817 to Maria's father R. L. Edgeworth, quoted by Egerton (1968, here p. 74), on whom I depend for the following explanation.

41. Clarke 1807, p. 313; Bruegmann 1978, p. 146 and idem 1976 pp. 187, 189.

42. Clark, *Report* 1802, p. 208; he wrote with enormous approval of the Royal Hospital at Woolwich (where his informant was the Surgeon-General Dr John Rollo), to be replaced at mid-century by the great Herbert Hospital.

43. Cullen's influence did not necessarily extend to therapeutics, as Bynum (1979, pp. 103, 111) shows: differences turned on whether one considered fever a disease of general debility, as Cullen did, or an 'inflammation or other condition of hyperactivity, which dictated lowering the patient's system', in part through ventilation's cooling effects.

44. Duncum (1964, pp. 211–12) describes these techniques with quotations from Newcastle's publications. The proposed heating system was a 'useful invention . . . by which atmospheric air, passing through a square opening made in the wall on a level with the floor in the basement story, is heated by a sand-bath; and is conveyed by earthen tubes placed perpendicularly, into the galleries and thence into the wards'.

45. Egerton 1968, p. 82. For the system see also Taylor 1991, pp. 1–3; Bruegmann 1976, pp. 187–89; and idem 1978, pp. 144–46.

46. Foster 1768, pp. 4–5.

47. Mary Douglas has shown (1991, pp. 1, 32) that the conventional nineteenth-century view of 'primitive religion' as 'inextricably confused with defilement and hygiene' is too limited: 'pollution powers . . . inhere in the structure of ideas itself and . . . punish a symbolic breaking of that which should be joined or joining of that which should be separate' (p. 113). To impose order is to exercise power; Douglas makes the relation clear.

48. Brieger 1965, pp. 521–22 quotes Dr Caspar Morris.

49. Specifically, Bristowe and Holmes (1864), who loathed 'ducted or "artificial" air circulation' as opposed to 'natural' ventilation (Taylor 1991, pp. 12, 56) though they did not object to the Infirmary on this ground alone, as Taylor explains.

50. Schinkel (1993, pp. 134, 136) noted the rotating-cylinder washing machine and, for cooking, the steam-table and roaster ('very practical') designed by analogy with the cockle stove; see also Egerton 1968, p. 86 and Hacker 1960, pp. 57, 59.

51. Sylvester 1819, p. vii; Edgeworth (1971, p. 26) mentioned the cockle at Strutt's house as part of the method of 'warming the house, keeping it at an equal temperature and getting rid of all kitchen smells, and bad air'. Egerton 1968, pp. 83–86 and Bruegmann 1978, pp. 155–57 describe others' early applications.

52. Sylvester was a pioneer in his presentation of building services: Markus 1993, p. 114, and see also Egerton 1968, p. 83. Klingender (1947, pp. 61–65) describes the peculiar charm of mechanical drawings like Sylvester's, 'not yet reduced to an abstract system of lines and measurements. . . . The objects illustrated are carefully shaded to give the impression of solid bodies, but they are isolated from their normal setting and shown, partly in their natural appearance, partly in section, as required by the need for elucidation' (p. 64; see also the caption to Figure 82).

53. Eaton 1957, p. 85. For the book's circulation, Bruegmann 1978, p. 146 and idem 1976, p. 187.

54. Schinkel 1993, p. 134; see the editors' note to this page and David Bindman's introductory essay, p. 12. Genteel natives who thought that they should be receiving customary hospitality at the factories, as at great houses and hospitals, were also sometimes disappointed, and affronted: Raven 1992, pp. 233–34.

55. Schinkel 1993, pp. 135–36, 212; I'm grateful to Katya Robinson for help with the last translation. The itinerary includes places Schinkel did not manage to visit.

56. Hacker 1960, p. 55; Devonshire became the hospital's first President in 1810 (ibid., p. 59). The following is taken from DRO D1190/1/1.

57. DRO D1190/1/1 (1 November 1803).

58. Woodward 1974, pp. 102, 104. Stillman describes (1988, 2: 399) Carr's English hospitals, on which see also the relevant entries in the York Georgian Society's catalogue of his works (1973).

59. In a letter of 5 November 1769. The hospital, to have measured 540 x 520 feet overall, was never completed to Carr's design, though it remains impressive enough: see York Georgian Society (1973), Wragg and Wragg 1959, and Taylor 1961.

60. DRO D1190/1/4, 20 April 1803. For Rawlinson (whose spelling I have corrected) and the other architects mentioned, see Colvin, *Biographical dictionary* 1995.

61. DRO D1190/1/5; Stillman 1988, 2: 401 describes the Infirmary, with further references.

62. DRO D1190/1/6, 3 November 1803. A draft of a reply sounds nonplussed: if Simpson were happy to have the documents remain with the committee until it came to 'deliberate on a plan', no one else would see them: DRO D1190/1/7.

63. Gooch [1773], p. v.

64. Robinson 1953, pp. 362–63; the Society's library, as formed by its first President Erasmus Darwin (whom Strutt succeeded upon his death in 1802), also included a large collection of works on pneumatic chemistry.

65. The 1805 *Report* (DRO D1190/1/2), which explains that 'The two deviations from the general practice . . . were specified . . . ; but with respect to the other improvements which had suggested themselves, it was thought better not to mention them'.

66. DRO D1190/1/1 (4 August 1804); see Hacker 1960, p. 55. Little evidence remains of the entries in the Infirmary records. DRO D1190/89–92 includes elevations, both dated 1804, by Rawstorne and by George Moneypenny, Derby-born but by then based in London; see Saunders 1993, p. 159.

67. Hacker 1960, pp. 49–50, 56–57 summarizes the evidence for the attribution. As the sub-committee was required to award some premium, that would go to Rawstorne, whose plan was '*most* approved'. The *Report* of 1805 alludes to the subscribers' committee's embarrassment about this failed competition.

Sylvester (1819, p. 2) describes how the 'necessary drawings and working plans' were prepared by Samuel Brown, a drawing master.

68. Edgeworth 1971, pp. 27–28.

69. See Chapter 1, n. 44.

70. My emphasis. From a printed *Report of the Committee* (DRO D1190/1/3), signed by Mundy, dated 1 June 1809; for the statue, Taylor 1991, pp. 1, 246.

71. The following is taken from DRO D1190/1/1 (4 August 1804).

72. The 1805 *Report* (DRO D1190/1/2) amplified: each suite would be 'shut off from the body of the house', that is, from the central stairhall, by a single door, thus 'procuring silence and darkness, (which is essential in some cases) as well as every other convenience in a degree perhaps superior to most private houses'.

73. Duncum (1964, p. 213) quotes Clark's *Account* (1801); the Glasgow *Report* 1814, p. 8.

74. DeLacy 1986, pp. 89–90. The paradigm needs qualification for this period, when longer and bigger wards were generally unpopular, that is, before miasmatic aetiologies made them seem a necessity, as they did to Nightingale.

75. Tenon 1992, p. 69; Cooke and Maule 1789, pp. 117–20, with an elevation. It was a brick quadrangle around a central court whose rooms opened off a central corridor in each side range: subsequently the Dreadnought Seaman's Hospital, it survives in altered form. The NMR file (101280) contains a good brief typescript history, photographs, and copies of plans of this building, which has so far escaped much printed discussion.

76. See, for example, Hawksmoor's drawings reproduced as Wren Society 1929, 6: pl. XLVIII bottom (SM [old] vol. 1 ['Greenwich' album]:58) and pl. XLIX left (NMM ART/1/56).

77. Clark, *Report* 1802, p. 211 quotes the 'communication of Dr Walker'. Compare the 1785 recommendations for overseas naval hospitals by the Commissioners for Sick and Wounded Seamen, quoted in Richardson 1998, p. 82: the 'patient was not to be spared from the "dying looks of his companions" by cubicles, since they obstructed the circulation of air'.

78. Bulfinch's letter is transcribed in Eaton 1950, here p. 11. Bristowe and Holmes (quoted in Taylor 1991, p. 4) commented that the Derby nurses, 'each of whom has to take charge of several wards, are unable to keep a proper watch over the patients'.

79. Forty 1980, pp. 78–80; DeLacy 1986, p. 90.

80. Howard 1789, pp. 140–41, and as quoted (from the second edition of the *Account of the lazarettos*) by Duncum 1964, p. 210; a new ward (completed 1792) at Leeds was reserved for convalescents, apparently on his personal recommendation (Anning 1963, p. 12).

81. At least, Dr Caspar Morris recommended a similar system for Baltimore's Johns Hopkins Hospital in

1875 for exactly that reason: Brieger 1965, p. 523. For the Guy's closets, Cawson and Orde 1969, p. 227; Bruegmann 1976, p. 207; and Duncum 1964, p. 210, quoting Howard's general recommendations for hospitals. Schinkel would carefully diagram the Derby closet type (1993, p. 135), which had been introduced to the Leicester Infirmary in 1815, after an inspection and favourable report by its architect: Frizelle and Martin 1971, p. 73.

82. Testifying about St Luke's to the parliamentary Committee of Madhouses in 1815, Edward Wakefield described the privies which, 'from being in the interior of the house, are frequently offensive': Sharpe 1815, p. 163. Bristowe and Holmes (quoted in Taylor 1991, p. 4) described the Derby water-closets which 'seem, with curious infelicity, to have been squeezed into the most objectionable nooks, to have little ventilation, except what they get from the corridors, and . . . are certainly not sweet'.

83. See the report by Kathryn Morrison in the NMR file no. 100289, which includes copies of Henderson's plans.

84. The 1805 *Report* (DRO D1190/1/2) however claimed 'no internal connection whatever with the Infirmary'.

85. DRO D1190/1/1 (4 August 1804): the committee had 'endeavored to plan the construction with the least possible quantity of Walling and Roof and in all other respects with the greatest oeconomy'.

86. North 1981, pp. 9, 69.

87. Taylor 1991, p. 4 quotes Bristowe and Holmes. Compare 'The Lincoln County Hospital', *Lancet* (25 October 1873): 611–12 (copy in the NMR file no. 102430): the 'hospital should, as far as practicable, be simple in construction and limited by the requirements of the patients . . . instead of being massed together like the separate pieces of a puzzle, for the purpose of being packed into the smallest compass into any and every convenient vacant space'.

88. Quoted Hacker 1960, p. 68.

89. 'Mr Latrobe's Report on marine hospitals', in Barton 1814, p. 112.

90. With its land the Infirmary cost £17,870 3s.4d., considerably less than contributions with interest accumulated by 1809: Hacker 1960, p. 59.

91. DRO D1190/1/1 (4 August 1804).

92. Nightingale 1859, p. 22; idem 1863, p. 11.

93. Nightingale 1859, p. 7; idem 1863, p. 10; Smith 1982,

p. 184 quotes her *Suggestions for thought* (1860).

94. Strachey 1918, p. 171.

95. What follows in this paragraph is drawn from Rosenberg 1995, pp. 128–37; see also idem 'Florence Nightingale', 1979.

96. The most extreme instance of a failure from the first half of the nineteenth century, besides Derby's, mentioned by Taylor (1991, p. 55) is that of the new County Hospital, York (1851), whose system enforced its temporary closure by the end of the decade. See ibid., pp. 88–89, 100, 106–8 for other, more or less successful examples of systems (some supplemented by natural ventilation) from this period.

97. Nightingale 1863, pp. 77, 10.

98. Nightingale 1859, p. 6; idem 1863, pp. 8–9; Smith 1982, p. 100 quotes her letter to Benjamin Jowett of 1866 or 1867, and see ibid., pp. 97–100 for her resistance to contagionist aetiologies.

99. On the upheavals of what Bynum calls a 'period of heightened hospital accountability', see now Hayward 1998. Useful general guides are Bynum 1994, pp. 132–37, Risse 1999, pp. 373–78, and Rosenberg 1995, Chapter 5: a particularly spirited account centring on the United States but very useful for Britain.

100. Simpson 1868–69, p. 818, quoting his own (1867) address to the National Association for the Promotion of Social Science; Selwyn 1965, pp. 243, 244 suggests he was influenced by Pringle and Brocklesby in his advocacy of the cottages. 'Salubrity of hospitals', *Lancet* i (23 January 1869): 128–9; see Hayward 1998, p. 52 on this leader.

101. Woodward 1974, p. 121 quotes Holmes, from the St George's Hospital *Reports* of 1874–76; see also Wrench [1913], p. 133. For the mutual loathing of the Holmes–Sir John Simon and Nightingale camps, see the latter's appearances (indexed) in Lambert 1963, and Hayward 1998, pp. 39–40.

102. Wrench [1913], p. 335 quotes Hector Cameron on Lister; for the Glasgow wards, Godlee 1924, p. 247. On the difference between treating the wound and hence the hospital, or vice versa, see Lawrence and Dixey 1992, pp. 156, 184.

103. See Fox 1988; Granshaw, '"Upon this principle"' 1992; and Lawrence and Dixey 1992.

104. Wrench [1913], pp. 331, 466.

105. Ibid., pp. 332 and (quoting Lucas-Champonnière, a French Listerian pioneer) 326.

Manuscript sources and abbreviations

BCGM Archives, Bethlem Royal Hospital, Beckenham, Kent

Court of Governors Minutes

DRO Derbyshire Record Office, Matlock

D1190/1/1, Proceedings relative to the establishment of the Derbyshire General Infirmary, 1803–10

D1190/1/2, *Report of the Committee appointed at a General Meeting of Subscribers to the Fund for . . . the Intended Derbyshire Infirmary . . .* , dated 23 March 1805

D1190/1/3, *Report* of the Subscribers Committee, dated 1 June 1809

D1190/1/4–14, Correspondence regarding plans and site 1802–1831

D1190/89–92, Architects' drawings showing elevations submitted for competition 1804

HB Greater Glasgow Health Board Archive

14/1/1, Glasgow Royal Infirmary, Minute Books, 1787 to 1802

HRO Hampshire Record Office, Winchester

5M63/1, County Hospital, Winchester, Court of Governors Minute Book, 1736–41

5M63/2, Court of Governors' Minute Book, 1741–71

5M63/8, Committee of Management Minute Book, 1736–39

LH The Royal London Hospital Archives Centre and Museum

A/4/2, Court of Governors: Reports, 18 March 1748–26 Nov. 1753

A/5/2, House Committee: Minutes, 24 Sept. 1745–31 May 1748

A/5/4, House Committee: Minutes, 26 March 1751–18 June 1754

LHB Lothian Health Services Archive, Special Collections, Edinburgh University Library

1/1/1, Royal Infirmary of Edinburgh, Managers' Minutes, Feb. 1728–Dec. 1741

1/1/2, Managers' Minutes, Jan. 1742–Jan. 1749

1/1/3, Managers' Minutes, Feb. 1749–Dec. 1760

1/68, Plans

1/72/2, Correspondence 1747–48

1/72/3, Correspondence 1748–49

1/72/8, Correspondence Dec. 1751–July 1753

7/1/1, Royal Edinburgh Hospital, Minutes of the Association for Instituting a Lunatic Asylum, from 1807, the Minutes of the Managers of the Edinburgh Lunatic Asylum, Feb. 1792–Jan. 1816

NMM National Maritime Museum, London

ADM/B/129, Admiralty. In Letters from the Navy Board, May–July 1745

ADM/E/11, Commissioners for Sick & Hurt Seamen. In Letters from the Admiralty, 1744–45

ADM/F/6, Admiralty. In Letters from the Sick & Hurt Board, May–Aug. 1745

ADM/F/12, Admiralty. In Letters from the Sick & Hurt Board, Feb. 1755–Jan. 1756

ADM/F/13, Admiralty. In Letters from the Sick & Hurt Board, Feb.–Sept. 1756

ADM/Y/G/51. James Wibault's estimates, dated 16 April 1734, for two alternative projects for a hospital at Gibraltar

ADM/Y/G/52. Three designs (modern label as plans for a hospital at Gibraltar) drawn James Montresor, engineer, 1739

ART/1–3. Greenwich Hospital. Prints, plans, drawings collected by R. Mylne, 1793, including

ART/1, 'The Planns of the Royal Hospital of Greenwich as the Work is now carried on and Advancing Anno 1728', itself including ART/1/63–64, a large plan dated

1728, with estimates, and ART/1/67, an 'Abstract' of total expenses to the end of September 1727

ART/2/35, a ground-floor plan of the Infirmary

ART/4, the 1696 Warrant for the Royal Hospital at Greenwich, with plans and estimates

NMR National Monuments Record, London and Swindon

PRO Public Record Office, London

Adm 3/65, Admiralty Board minute book, 19 Nov. 1756–16 Jan. 1758

Adm 98/6, Sick and Wounded Board's Out-Letters to the Admiralty from 30 Oct./1 Nov. 1756–57 to 9 Oct. 1757

Adm 98/7, Sick and Wounded Board's Out-Letters to the Admiralty from 10 Oct. 1757 to 1759

Adm 106/2189, Navy Board's Out-Letters to the Admiralty, 1757

SM Sir John Soane's Museum, London

WL Wellcome Library for the History and Understanding of Medicine, London

Ms 5992, Observations by Charles Middleton, Comptroller of the Navy, on Reports of Conditions at Haslar Hospital, Gosport (1780)

Works cited

Account (c.1730): *An account of the rise and establishment of the Infirmary, or Hospital for Sick Poor, erected at Edinburgh.* Edinburgh, n.p.

——(1734): *An account of the occasion and manner of erecting an hospital at Lanesborough-House ... published ... February the 6th, 1733[/4].* [London], n.p.

'Account' (1741): 'An account of the Devon and Exeter Hospital ...'. *Gentleman's Magazine* 11, 474–75, 652–55.

Adam, William (1980): *'Vitruvius Scoticus', reproduced in facsimile from the copy in the University of Glasgow Library ...,* ed. James Simpson. Edinburgh, Paul Harris.

Adams, Bernard (1983): *London illustrated 1604–1851: a survey and index of topographical books and their plates.* London, Library Association.

Address (1807): *Address to the public, respecting the establishment of a lunatic asylum at Edinburgh.* Edinburgh, James Ballantyne.

Aikin, John (1771): *Thoughts on hospitals.* London, Joseph Johnson.

Airs, Malcolm (1995): *The Tudor and Jacobean country house: a building history.* Stroud, Gloucs, Alan Sutton.

Alberti, Leon Battista (1988): *On the art of building in ten books,* ed. and trans. Joseph Rykwert, Neil Leach, and Robert Tavernor. Cambridge, Mass. and London, MIT Press.

Allan, D. G. C. and Schofield, R. E. (1980): *Stephen Hales: scientist and philanthropist.* London, Scolar.

Allen, Brian (1986): 'Engravings for charity'. *Journal of the Royal Society of Arts* 134, 646–50.

Alsop, J. D. (1981): 'Some notes on seventeenth-century Continental hospitals'. *British Library Journal* 7, no. 1 (Spring), 70–74.

Andrew, Donna (1989): *Philanthropy and police: London charity in the eighteenth century.* Princeton, NJ, Princeton University Press.

——(1991): 'Two medical charities in eighteenth-century London: the Lock Hospital and the Lying-in Charity for Married Women', pp. 82–97 in *Medicine and charity before the welfare state,* ed. Jonathan Barry and Colin Jones. London, Routledge.

Andrews, Jonathan; Briggs, Asa; Porter, Roy; Tucker, Penny; and Waddington, Keir (1997): *The history of Bethlem.* London, Routledge.

Anning, S. T. (1963): *The General Infirmary at Leeds,* vol. 1, *The first hundred years.* Edinburgh, E. & S. Livingstone.

Archer, John (1979): 'Character in English architectural design'. *Eighteenth-century studies* 12, 348–71.

Ascoli, David (1975): 'Royal Hospital, Chelsea: a mystery'. *Country Life* 157, 1491–95.

Aston, Margaret (1973): 'English ruins and English history: the Dissolution and the sense of the past'. *Journal of the Warburg and Courtauld Institutes* 36, 231–55.

Aubin, Robert Arnold (1936): *Topographical poetry in XVIII-century England.* New York, Modern Language Association of America.

——, ed. (1943): *London in flames, London in glory: poems on the Fire and rebuilding of London 1666–1709.* New Brunswick, NJ, Rutgers University Press.

Ayres, Philip (1990): 'Pope's *Epistle to Burlington*: the Vitruvian analogies'. *Studies in English literature 1500–1900* 30, 429–44.

Backscheider, Paula R. (1993): *Spectacular politics: theatrical power and mass culture in early modern England.* Baltimore, Maryland, Johns Hopkins University Press.

Bacon, Francis (1906): *The essays or counsels civil and moral* (1625). London and New York, J. M. Dent & Sons and E. P. Dutton.

Bailey, Ann (1971): 'An account of the founding of the first Gloucestershire County Asylum, now Horton Road Hospital, Gloucester 1792–1823'. *Transactions of the Bristol and Gloucester Archaeological Society* 90, 178–91.

Bailey, Brian (1988): *Almshouses.* London, Robert Hale.

Baker, Malcolm (1995): 'Squabby Cupids and clumsy Graces: garden sculpture as luxury in eighteenth-century England'. *Oxford Art Journal* 18, 3–13.

Ballon, Hilary (1991): *The Paris of Henri IV: architecture and urbanism.* Cambridge, Mass., MIT Press.

Barfoot, Michael (1991): 'Reading records and writing

hospital history: the Royal Infirmary of Edinburgh in the 18th century'. *Disease and documents: Scottish Records Association Conference Report* **16**, 2–4.

——(n.d.): 'Pedagogy, practice and politics: the Gregory–Bell dispute and the nature of early 19th-century Edinburgh medicine' (typescript).

Barker, Nigel Patrick (1985): 'The architecture of the English Board of Ordnance 1660–1750', 3 vols. Ph.D. Dissertation, University of Reading.

Barton, William P. C. (1814): *A treatise containing a plan for the internal organization and government of marine hospitals, in the United States: together with observations on military and flying hospitals, and a scheme for amending and systematizing the Medical Department of the Navy.* Philadelphia, the author.

Batten, M. I. (1936–37): 'The architecture of Robert Hooke'. *Walpole Society* **25**, 83–113.

Baugh, Daniel (1965): *British naval administration in the Age of Walpole.* Princeton, NJ, Princeton University Press.

Beaufort, Dianna (1995): 'Hawksmoor and Gibbs: pleas in print and the authorship of a library', pp. 24–32 in *Architects, books and libraries*, ed. Pierre de la Ruffinière du Prey. Kingston, Ont., Agnes Etherington Art Centre, Queen's University.

Beddoes, Thomas, ed. (1799): *Contributions to physical and medical knowledge, principally from the West of England.* London, T. N. Longman & O. Rees.

Béguin, François (1979): 'La Machine à guérir', pp. 39–43 in *Les Machines à guérir: aux origines de l'hôpital moderne*, by Michel Foucault, Blandine Barret Kriegel, Anne Thalamy, François Béguin, and Bruno Fortier. Brussels, Pierre Mardaga.

Bellers, John (1714): *An essay towards the improvement of physick in twelve proposals, by which the lives of many thousands of the rich, as well as of the poor, may be saved yearly. With an essay for imploying the able poor; by which the riches of the Kingdom may be greatly increased.* London, J. Sowle.

Benjamin, Marina (1990): 'Medicine, morality and the politics of Berkeley's tar-water', pp. 165–93 in *The medical Enlightenment of the eighteenth century*, ed. Andrew Cunningham and Roger French. Cambridge, Cambridge University Press.

Bennett, J. A. (1980): 'Robert Hooke as mechanic and natural philosopher'. *Notes and Records of the Royal Society* **35**, 33–48.

——(1982): *The mathematical science of Christopher Wren.* Cambridge, Cambridge University Press.

Bentham, Jeremy (1843): *Panopticon; or, the inspection house: containing the idea of a new principle of construction applicable to any sort of establishment, in which persons . . . are to be kept under inspection . . . in a series of letters, written in the year 1787 . . .* (1791), pp. 37–172 in *Works*, ed. John Bowring, vol. 4. London, Simpkin, Marshall.

——(1981): *Correspondence*, ed. Alexander Taylor Milne, vol. 4, *October 1788 to December 1793.* London, Athlone.

Berger, Robert W. (1994): *A royal passion: Louis XIV as patron of architecture.* Cambridge, Cambridge University Press.

Berkeley, George (1901): *An essay towards preventing the ruin of Great Britain* (1721) and *The querist* (1735–37), pp. 319–38, 415–76 in *The works of George Berkeley D.D.; formerly Bishop of Cloyne. Including his posthumous works*, vol. 4, *Miscellaneous works 1707–50*, ed. Alexander Campbell Fraser. Oxford, Clarendon Press.

Berman, David (1994): *George Berkeley: idealism and the man.* Oxford, Clarendon Press.

Berry, Christopher J. (1994): *The idea of luxury: a conceptual and historical investigation.* Cambridge, Cambridge University Press.

Bettley, James (1984): '*Post voluptatem misericordia*: the rise and fall of the London lock hospitals'. *London Journal* **10**, 167–75.

Bindman, David (1997): *Hogarth and his times: serious comedy.* London, British Museum Press.

Binney, Marcus (1982): 'The Royal Hospital, Chelsea'. *Country Life* **177**, 1474–77, 1582–85.

——(1984): *Sir Robert Taylor: from rococo to neo-classicism.* London, George Allen & Unwin.

Blane, Gilbert (1799): *Observations on the diseases incident to seamen*, 3rd edn. London, Murray & Highley.

Bold, John (1983): 'Of building' [essay review]. *Oxford Art Journal* **5**, 60–62.

——(1989): *John Webb: architectural theory and practice in the seventeenth century.* Oxford, Clarendon Press.

——(1993): 'Privacy and the plan', pp. 107–19 in *English architecture public and private: essays for Kerry Downes*, ed. John Bold and Edward Chaney. London and Rio Grande, Ohio, Hambledon.

Bond, Donald, ed. (1987): *The Tatler*, 3 vols. Oxford, Clarendon Press.

Borsay, Anne (1991): 'Cash and conscience: financing the General Hospital at Bath c.1738–1750'. *Social History of Medicine* **4**, 207–29.

Borsay, Peter (1989): *The English urban renaissance: culture and society in the provincial town, 1660–1770.* Oxford, Clarendon Press.

Boswell, James [1906]: *The life of Samuel Johnson*, 2 vols. London, Robert Rivière.

Bowen, Thomas (1783): *An historical account of the rise, progress and present state of Bethlem Hospital, founded by Henry the Eighth, for the cure of lunatics. . . .* London, n.p.

Boyce, Benjamin (1967): *The benevolent man: a life of Ralph Allen of Bath.* Cambridge, Mass., Harvard University Press.

Braham, Allan (1980): *The architecture of the French Enlightenment.* London, Thames & Hudson.

Brandt, Alan M. (1993): 'Sexually transmitted diseases', pp. 562–84 in *Companion encyclopedia of the history of medicine*, ed. W. F. Bynum and Roy Porter. London and New York, Routledge.

Brewer, John (1982): 'Commercialization and politics', pp. 197–262 in *The birth of a consumer society: the commercialization of eighteenth-century England*, by Neil McKendrick, John Brewer, and J. H. Plumb. London, Europa.

——(1989): *The sinews of power: war, money and the English state, 1688–1783.* London, Unwin Hyman.

——(1995): '"The most polite age and the most vicious": attitudes towards culture as a commodity, 1660–1800', pp. 341–61 in *The consumption of culture, 1600–1800: image, object, text*, ed. Ann Bermingham and John Brewer. London, Routledge.

——(1997): *The pleasures of the imagination: English culture in the eighteenth century*. London, HarperCollins.

Brief account (1735): *A brief account of the rise, progress, management and state of the Orphan-School, Hospital and Work-House at Edinburgh, as on the 1st January 1735*. Edinburgh, printed by Thomas Lumsden and John Robertson.

Brieger, Gert H. (1965): 'The original plans for the Johns Hopkins Hospital and their historical significance'. *Bulletin of the History of Medicine* **29**, 518–28.

Brings, Hans (1986): 'New medicine comes ashore: establishing the first permanent US naval hospitals'. *Journal of the History of Medicine* **41**, 257–92.

Bristowe, John Syer and Holmes, Timothy (1864): *Report . . . on the hospitals of the United Kingdom*, Appendix 15 to the *Sixth Report* of the Medical Officer of the Privy Council, 1863, *Parliamentary Papers 1864, XXVIII*, pp. 467–753 [printed as pp. 463–743].

Brock, William H. (1992): *The Fontana history of chemistry*. London, Fontana.

Brockbank, William (1952): *Portrait of a hospital 1752–1848. To commemorate the bi-centenary of the Royal Infirmary, Manchester*. London, William Heinemann.

Brocklesby, Richard (1764): *Oeconomical and medical observations . . . tending to the improvement of military hospitals*. London, T. Becket & P. A. De Hondt.

Brockliss, Laurence and Jones, Colin (1997): *The medical world of early modern France*. Oxford, Clarendon Press.

Brown, Dale R. (1990): 'The expanding role of the physician in defining 19th century hospital architecture, as evidenced in Dr. John Shaw Billings' designs for Johns Hopkins Hospital (1876–1889)' (typescript).

——(1991): 'Medico-architectural determinism in nineteenth-century hospital designs' (typescript).

Brown, Iain Gordon (1994): 'Judges of architectory: the Clerks of Penicuik as amateurs', pp. 44–52 in *The role of the amateur architect* ed. Giles Worsley. London, Georgian Group.

Brown, Thomas (1730): *The third volume of the works of Mr. Thomas Brown; Being amusements serious and comical, calculated for the meridian of London*, 7th edn. London, Edward Midwinter.

Bruegmann, Robert (1976): 'Architecture of the hospital, 1770–1870: design and technology'. Ph.D. Dissertation, University of Pennsylvania [Ann Arbor: University Microfilms International, 1980].

——(1978): 'Central heating and forced ventilation: origins and effects on architectural design'. *Journal of the Society of Architectural Historians* **37**, 143–60.

——(1979): [Review of Foucault et al., *Les Machines à guérir*]. *Journal of the Society of Architectural Historians* **38**, 210–11.

Bryant, Julius (1996): 'Villa views and the uninvited audience', pp. 11–24 in *The Georgian villa*, ed. Dana Arnold. Stroud, Gloucs, Alan Sutton.

Buchanan, Emmakate (1996): 'Naval hospital architecture in the eighteenth century'. MA Dissertation, Courtauld Institute, University of London.

Buchanan, Moses Steven (1832): *History of the Glasgow Royal Infirmary*. Glasgow, James Lumsden.

Bullock, Steven C. (1996): *Revolutionary brotherhood: Freemasonry and the transformation of the American social order, 1730–1840*. Chapel Hill and London, University of North Carolina Press for the Institute of Early American History and Culture.

Bynum, W. F. (1979): 'Hospital, disease, and community: the London Fever Hospital, 1801–1850', pp. 97–115 in *Healing and history: essays for George Rosen*, ed. Charles E. Rosenberg. New York and Folkestone, Kent, Science History Publications and Dawson.

——(1985): 'Physicians, hospitals, and career structures in eighteenth-century London', pp. 105–28 in *William Hunter and the eighteenth-century medical world*, ed. W. F. Bynum and Roy Porter. Cambridge, Cambridge University Press.

——(1986): 'Treating the wages of sin: venereal disease and specialism in eighteenth-century Britain', pp. 5–28 in *Medical fringe and medical orthodoxy 1750–1850*, ed. W. F. Bynum and Roy Porter. London, Croom Helm.

——(1994): *Science and the practice of medicine in the nineteenth century*. Cambridge, Cambridge University Press.

Bynum, W. F.; Browne, E. J.; and Porter, Roy, eds (1981): *Dictionary of the history of science*. London, Macmillan.

Cameron, H. C. (1954): *Mr Guy's Hospital, 1726–1948*. London, Longmans, Green.

Carlin, Martha (1989): 'Medieval English hospitals', pp. 21–39 in *The hospital in history*, ed. Lindsay Granshaw and Roy Porter. London and New York, Routledge.

Carpenter, Kenneth J. (1986): *The history of scurvy and vitamin C*. Cambridge, Cambridge University Press.

Carré, Jacques (1982): 'Burlington's public buildings', pp. 60–71 in *Lord Burlington and his circle*. Papers given at a Georgian Group Symposium on 22 May 1982, ed. Roger White. London, Georgian Group.

——(1989): 'Les Nouveaux hôpitaux britanniques au dix-huitième siècle', pp. 15–25 in *Ville et santé en Grande-Bretagne, XVIIIe–XXe siècles. Actes du colloque du Clermont-Ferrand (1986)*, ed. Jacques Carré. Clermont-Ferrand, Association des publications de la Faculté des Lettres.

[Carter, John] (1800): 'The pursuits of architectural innovation. No. XXVI. The antient palace of the Kings of England at Westminster, continued'. *Gentleman's Magazine* **20**, 837–40.

Casey, Christine (1994): '"De Architectura": an Irish eighteenth-century gloss'. *Architectural History* **37**, 80–95.

Cashman, Bernard (1988): *Private charity and the public purse. The development of Bedford General Hospital: 1794–1988*. Bedford, North Bedfordshire Area Health Authority.

——(1992): *A proper house: Bedford Lunatic Asylum (1812–1860)*. Bedford, North Bedfordshire Health Authority.

Cast, David (1984): 'Seeing Vanbrugh and Hawksmoor'. *Journal of the Society of Architectural Historians* **43**, 310–27.

Cavallo, Sandra (1991): 'The motivations of benefactors: an overview of approaches to the study of charity', pp. 46–62 in *Medicine and charity before the welfare state*, ed. Jonathan Barry and Colin Jones. London, Routledge.

Cawson, R. A. and Orde, T. H. E. (1969): 'The design and building of Mr. Guy's Hospital'. *Guy's Hospital Reports* 118, 217–36.

Chalklin, Christopher (1998): *English counties and public building 1650–1830*. London and Rio Grande, Ohio, Hambledon.

Chaney, Edward (1981): ' "Philanthropy in Italy": English observations on Italian hospitals, 1545–1789', pp. 183–217 in *Aspects of poverty in early modern Europe*, ed. Thomas Riis. Aalphen aan den Rijn, Sijthoff.

——(1991): 'Architectural taste and the Grand Tour: George Berkeley's evolving canon'. *Journal of Anglo-Italian Studies* 1, 74–91.

Charlesworth, E. P. (1828): *Remarks on the treatment of the insane . . . being the substance of a return from the Lincoln Lunatic Asylum to the circular of His Majesty's Secretary of State*. London, Rivington.

Cherry, Bridget and Pevsner, Nikolaus (1991): *Devon*, 2nd edn. (*Buildings of England*). London, Penguin.

Cherry, S. (1980): 'The hospitals and population growth: the voluntary general hospitals, mortality and local populations in the English provinces in the eighteenth and nineteenth centuries'. *Population Studies* 34, 59–75, 251–65.

Cheyne, George (1991): *The English malady, or, a treatise of nervous diseases of all kinds* (1733), repr. ed. Roy Porter. London and New York, Tavistock/Routledge.

Christie, J. R. R. (1974): 'The origins and development of the Scottish scientific community'. *History of Science* 12, 122–41.

Cipolla, Carlo (1992): *Miasmas and disease: public health and the environment in the pre-industrial age*, trans. Elizabeth Potter. New Haven and London, Yale University Press.

Clark, John (1802): *A collection of papers, intended to promote an institution for the cure and prevention of infectious fevers in Newcastle and other populous towns. Together with the communications of the most eminent physicians relative to the safety and importance of annexing fever-wards to the Newcastle and other infirmaries* (including the *Collection* and the *Report of the Committee*, separately paginated). Newcastle, S. Hodgson.

Clarke, Alured (1737): *A sermon preached in the Cathedral Church of Winchester, before the Governors of the County-Hospital for sick and lame, etc., at the opening of the said Hospital, on St. Luke's Day, October 18, 1736. To which are added, a collection of papers relating to the Hospital, in which are Rules and Orders for the management . . . of the House.* London, J. & J. Pemberton.

Clarke, James (1807): 'Report from the General Hospital near Nottingham, from March 25th 1806, to March 25th 1807'. *Edinburgh Medical and Surgical Journal* 3, 309–22.

Clark-Kennedy, A. E. (1929): *Stephen Hales, D.D., F.R.S. An eighteenth century biography*. Cambridge, Cambridge University Press.

——(1962): *The London: a study in the voluntary hospital system*, vol. 1, *The first hundred years 1740–1840*. London, Pitman Medical.

Clay, Rotha Mary (1909): *The mediaeval hospitals of England*. London, Methuen.

Clayton, Timothy (1997): *The English print, 1688–1802*. New Haven and London, Yale University Press.

Coad, J. G. (1983): *Historic architecture of the Royal Navy: an introduction*. London, Gollancz.

Coats, A. W. (1976): 'The relief of poverty, attitudes to labour, and economic change in England, 1660–1782'. *International Review of Social History* 21, 98–115.

Coleman, Kenneth (1976): *Colonial Georgia: a history*. New York, Charles Scribner's Sons.

Colley, Linda (1994): *Britons: forging the nation 1707–1837*. London, Pimlico.

Collins, Helen (1996): 'The quadrangular almshouse, its development, form, patron and patronised, as exemplified by Trinity Hospital, Bromley College and Morden College'. MA thesis, Courtauld Institute of Art, London.

Collins, Sheila M. (1995): *The Royal London Hospital: a brief history*. London, The Royal London Hospital Archives and Museum.

Colvin, Howard (1975): 'Robert Hooke and Ramsbury Manor'. *Country Life* 157, 194–95.

——(1986): 'The beginnings of the architectural profession in Scotland'. *Architectural History* 29, 168–81.

——(1994): 'What we mean by amateur', pp. 4–6 in *The role of the amateur architect. Papers given at the Georgian Group Symposium, 1993*, ed. Giles Worsley. London, Georgian Group.

——(1995): *A biographical dictionary of British architects, 1600–1840*, 3rd edn. New Haven and London, Yale University Press.

——(1995): 'The building', pp. 28–49 in *The making of the Wren Library, Trinity College, Cambridge*, ed. David McKitterick. Cambridge, Cambridge University Press.

Colvin, H. M.; Ransome, D. R.; and Summerson, John (1975): *The history of the King's Works*, vol. 3, pt 1 (1485–1660). London, HMSO.

Cook, Harold J. (1990): 'Practical medicine and the British armed forces after the "Glorious Revolution" '. *Medical History* 34, 1–26.

Cooke, John and Maule, John (1789): *An historical account of the Royal Hospital for Seamen at Greenwich*. London, G. Nicol.

Coope, Rosalys (1984): 'The gallery in England: names and meanings'. *Design and practice in British architecture: studies in architectural history presented to Howard Colvin. Architectural History* 27, 446–55.

——(1986): 'The "long gallery": its origins, development, use and decoration'. *Architectural History* 29, 43–84.

Cooper, Nicholas (1999): *Houses of the gentry 1480–1680*. New Haven and London, Yale University Press.

Corbin, Alain (1986): *The foul and the fragrant: odor and the French social imagination*, trans. Miriam L. Kochan. Leamington Spa, Berg.

Craig, Maurice (1982): *The architecture of Ireland from the earliest times to 1880*. London and Dublin, B. T. Batsford and Eason.

Crook, J. Mordaunt (1995): *John Carter and the mind of the Gothic Revival*. Leeds, W. S. Maney in association with the Society of Antiquaries of London.

Cunningham, Andrew (1990): 'Medicine to calm the mind: Boerhaave's medical system, and why it was adopted in Edinburgh', pp. 40–66 in *The medical Enlightenment of the eighteenth century*, ed. Andrew Cunningham and Roger French. Cambridge, Cambridge University Press.

Cunningham, Hugh (1998): 'Introduction', pp. 1–14 in *Charity, philanthropy and reform from the 1690s to 1850*, ed. Hugh Cunningham and Joanna Innes. Basingstoke, Macmillan.

Dabydeen, David (1987): *Hogarth's Blacks: images of Blacks in eighteenth-century English art*. Manchester, Manchester University Press.

Daunton, Clare, ed. (1990): *The London Hospital illustrated: 250 years*. London, B. T. Batsford.

Davenant, Charles (1699): *An essay upon the probable methods of making a people gainers in the ballance of trade . . .* London, James Knapton.

Davenport-Hines, Richard (1991): *Sex, death and punishment: attitudes to sex and sexuality in Britain since the Renaissance*. London, Fontana.

Davies, J. H. (1956): 'The dating of the buildings of the Royal Hospital at Greenwich'. *Archaeological Journal* **113**, 126–36.

Davies, T. G. (1988): *Deeds not words: a history of the Swansea General and Eye Hospital 1817–1948*. Cardiff, University of Wales Press.

Dean, C. G. T. (1947): 'Charles II's garrison hospital, Portsmouth'. *Papers and Proceedings of the Hampshire Field Club and Archaeological Society* **16**, 280–83.

——(1950): *The Royal Hospital Chelsea*. London, Hutchinson.

Defence (1733): *A defence of the majority of the Infirmary at Westminster, against a small minority of it*. [London], n.p.

Defoe, Daniel (1704): *Giving alms no charity and employing the poor a grievance to the nation, being an essay upon this great question, whether work-houses, corporations, and houses of correction for employing the poor, as now practis'd in England; or parish-stocks, as propos'd in a late pamphlet, entituled, A Bill for the better relief, imployment and settlement of the poor, etc. are not mischievous to the nation, tending to the destruction of our trade, and to encrease the number and misery of the poor . . .*, accessed 17 Sept. 1997 at <http://www.socserv2.socsci.mcmaster.ca/~econ/ugcm/3113/defoe/alms>.

——(1971): *A tour through the whole Island of Great Britain* (1724–26), ed. Pat Rogers. Harmondsworth, Penguin.

DeLacy, Margaret (1986): *Prison reform in Lancashire, 1700–1850: a study in local administration* (Remains historical and literary connected with the Palatine Counties of Lancaster and Chester, Third Series, 33). Manchester, Manchester University Press for the Chetham Society.

Dictionaire (1812): *Dictionaire [sic] des sciences médicales*, ed. F. P. Chaumeton and F. V. Mérat de Vaumartoise, vol. 1. Paris.

Diderot, Denis (1765): 'Hôpital, Hôtel-Dieu', in *Encyclopédie, ou Dictionnaire raisonné des sciences, arts et métiers*, ed. Denis Diderot and Jean le Rond d'Alembert, vol. 8. [Paris].

Diez del Corral, Rosario and Checa, Fernando (1986): 'Typologie hospitalière et bienfaisance dans l'Espagne de la Renaissance: croix greque, panthéon, chambres des merveilles'. *Gazette des Beaux-Arts* **107**, 118–26.

Digby, Anne (1985): *Madness, morality and medicine: a study of the York Retreat, 1796–1914*. Cambridge, Cambridge University Press.

——(1985): 'Moral treatment at the Retreat, 1796–1846', pp. 52–72 in *The anatomy of madness: essays in the history of psychiatry*, vol. 2, *Institutions and society*, ed. W. F. Bynum, Roy Porter, and Michael Shepherd. London and New York, Tavistock.

——(1986): *From York Lunatic Asylum to Bootham Park Hospital* (Borthwick Papers 69). York, St Anthony's Press.

Ditchfield, G. M. (1998): 'English rational dissent and philanthropy, c.1760–c.1810', pp. 193–207 in *Charity, philanthropy and reform from the 1690s to 1850*, ed. Hugh Cunningham and Joanna Innes. Basingstoke, Macmillan.

[Dodsley, Robert] (1761): *London and its environs described containing an account of whatever is most remarkable for grandeur, elegance, curiosity or use . . .*, 6 vols. London, R. and J. Dodsley.

Douglas, Mary (1991): *Purity and danger: an analysis of the concepts of pollution and taboo*. London, Routledge.

Downes, Kerry (1966): *English Baroque architecture*. London, A. Zwemmer.

——(1968): 'John Evelyn and architecture: a first inquiry', pp. 28–39 in *Concerning architecture: essays on architectural writers and writing presented to Nikolaus Pevsner*, ed. John Summerson. London, Allen Lane.

——(1970): *Hawksmoor*. London, Thames & Hudson.

——(1979): *Hawksmoor*, 2nd edn. London, Zwemmer.

——(1988): *The architecture of Wren*, 2nd edn. [Reading], Redhedge.

——(1994): 'Sir Christopher Wren, Edward Woodroffe, J. H. Mansart, and architectural history'. *Architectural History* **37**, 37–67.

Duffy, Christoper (1979): *Siege warfare: the fortress in the early modern world, 1494–1660*. London, Routledge & Kegan Paul.

Duncum, Barbara (1964): 'The development of hospital design and planning', pp. 207–29 in *The evolution of hospitals in Britain*, ed. F. N. L. Poynter. London, Pitman Medical.

du Prey, Pierre de la Ruffinière (1982): *John Soane: the making of an architect*. Chicago and London, University of Chicago Press.

Duveen, Denis I. and Klickstein, Herbert S. (1955): 'Antoine Laurent Lavoisier's contributions to medicine and public health'. *Bulletin of the History of Medicine* **29**, 164–79.

Eade, Peter (1900): *The Norfolk & Norwich Hospital, 1770 to 1900*. London, Jarrold.

Eaton, Leonard K. (1950): 'Charles Bulfinch and the Massachusetts General Hospital'. *Isis* **41**, 8–10.

——(1957): *New England hospitals, 1790–1833*. Ann Arbor,
University of Michigan Press.

Eaves Walton, P. M. (1979): 'Foundation and development
of the Royal Infirmary and the Simpson Memorial
Pavilion', pp. 9–15 in *The Royal Infirmary of Edinburgh
1729–1879–1979; The Simpson Memorial Maternity Pavilion
1879–1979*. Edinburgh, Royal Infirmary.

Edgeworth, Maria (1971): *Letters from England, 1813–1844*, ed.
Christina Colvin. Oxford, Clarendon Press.

Egerton, M. C. (1968): 'William Strutt and the application of
convection to the heating of buildings'. *Annals of Science*
24, 73–87.

Elmes, James (1847): 'History of architecture in Great
Britain. A brief sketch of the rise and progress of architecture in Great Britain'. *Civil Engineer and Architect's
Journal* **10**, 166–70, 209–10, 234–38, 268–71, 300–2,
337–41, 378–83.

Eribon, Didier (1993): *Michel Foucault* (1989), trans. Betsy
Wing. London, Faber & Faber.

Erlam, H. D., ed. (1954): 'Alexander Monro *primus*; auto-
biography'. *University of Edinburgh Journal* **17**, 77–105.

Erskine-Hill, Howard (1975): *The social milieu of Alexander
Pope: lives, example and the poetic response*. New Haven and
London, Yale University Press.

——(1979): 'Heirs of Vitruvius: Pope and the idea of architecture', pp. 144–56 in *The art of Alexander Pope*, ed.
Howard Erskine-Hill and Anne Smith. London, Vision.

——(1983): *The Augustan idea in English literature*. London,
E. Arnold.

——(1995): '"Avowed Friend and Patron": the third Earl of
Burlington and Alexander Pope', pp. 217–29 in *Lord
Burlington: architecture, art and life*, ed. Toby Barnard and
Jane Clark. London, Hambledon.

'Espinasse, Margaret (1956): *Robert Hooke*. London, William
Heinemann.

Esquirol, Jean-Etienne-Dominique (1838): 'Des Établissements des aliénés en France et des moyens d'améliorer le
sort de ces unfortunés' (1818), pp. 399–431 in *Des Malades
mentales considerées sous les rapports médical, hygiénique, et
médico-légal*, vol. 2. Paris, J. B. Baillière.

Etlin, Richard (1977): 'L'Air dans l'urbanisme des Lumières'.
Dix-huitième siècle **9**, 123–34.

Evans, Robin (1982): *The fabrication of virtue: English prison
architecture 1750–1840*. Cambridge, Cambridge University
Press.

Evelyn, John (1955): *Diary*, ed. E. S. de Beer, 6 vols. Oxford,
Clarendon Press.

Evelyn, John (1661): *Fumifugium: or, the inconvenience of the aer
and smoak of London dissipated . . . published at His Majestie's
Command*, ed. Guy de la Bédoyère, accessed 27 Sept. 1997 at
<http://ftp.cac.psu.edu/pub/humanities/John_Evelyn/
fumifug.wp>.

Fabricant, Carole (1987): 'The literature of domestic tourism

and the public consumption of private property', pp.
254–75, 310–13 in *The new eighteenth century: theory, politics, English literature*, ed. Felicity Nussbaum and Laura
Brown. New York and London, Methuen.

Fanshawe, Ann (1907): *The memoirs of Ann Lady Fanshawe*.
London, John Lane/The Bodley Head.

[Faulkner, Thomas] (1805): *An historical and descriptive
account of the Royal Hospital . . . at Chelsea*. London, T.
Faulkner.

Ferriar, John (1798): 'Account of the establishment of fever-
wards in Manchester', pp. 41–92 in *Medical histories and
reflections, volume third*. London, Cadell & Davis.

Fitton, R. S. and Wadsworth, A. P. (1958): *The Strutts and the
Arkwrights 1758–1830: a study of the early factory system*.
Manchester, Manchester University Press.

Fleming, John (1962): *Robert Adam and his circle in Edinburgh and London*. London, John Murray.

Fletcher, Charles (1786): *A maritime state considered, as to
the health of seamen; with effectual means for rendering the
situation of that valuable class of people more comfortable
. . .* Dublin, M. Mills.

Fortier, Bruno (1976): 'Architecture de l'hôpital', pp. 71–86
in *Les Machines à guérir: aux origines de l'hôpital moderne*,
by Michel Foucault, Blandine Barret Kriegel, Anne
Thalamy, François Béguin, and Bruno Fortier. Paris,
Institut de l'Environnement.

Forty, Adrian (1980): 'The modern hospital in England and
France: the social and medical uses of architecture', pp.
61–93 in *Buildings and society: essays on the social development of the built environment*, ed. Anthony D. King.
London, Routledge & Kegan Paul.

——(1983): 'Architecture as punishment' [essay review]. *Art
History* **6**, 481–84.

Foster, Edward (1768): *An essay on hospitals. Or, succinct
directions for the situation, construction, and administration
of country hospitals*. Dublin, the author.

Foster, Janet (1986): 'The rebuilding of St Bartholomew's
Hospital, 1730–70'. *Journal of the Royal Society of Arts* **134**,
636–41.

Foucart, Bruno (1981): 'Au Paradis des hygiénistes: l'architecture hospitalière au XIXe siècle'. *L'Architecture des hôpitaux: Monuments historiques* **114**, 43–52.

Foucault, Michel (1971): *Madness and civilization: a history of
insanity in the Age of Reason*, trans. Richard Howard.
London, Tavistock.

——(1972): *Histoire de la folie à l'age classique*, 2nd edn.
Paris, Gallimard.

——(1975): *Surveillir et punir: naissance de la prison*. Paris,
Gallimard.

——(1976): *The birth of the clinic: an archaeology of medical perception*, 2nd edn, trans. A. M. Sheridan. London, Tavistock.

——(1979): *Discipline and punish: the birth of the prison*,
trans. Alan Sheridan. Harmondsworth, Penguin.

——(1979): 'La Politique de la santé au XVIIIe siècle', pp.
7–18 in *Les Machines à guérir: aux origines de l'hôpital*

moderne, by Michel Foucault, Blandine Barret Kriegel, Anne Thalamy, François Béguin, and Bruno Fortier. Brussels, Pierre Mardaga.

——(1980): 'The politics of health in the nineteenth century', pp. 166–82 in *Power/knowledge. Selected interviews and other writings, 1972–1977*, ed. Colin Gordon. Brighton, Harvester.

Foucault, Michel; Barret Kriegel, Blandine; Thalamy, Anne; Béguin, François; and Fortier, Bruno (1979): *Les Machines à guérir: aux origines de l'hôpital moderne* (first published 1976, in slightly different form). Brussels, Pierre Mardaga.

Fowler, Alastair, ed. (1994): *The country house poem: a cabinet of seventeenth-century estate poems and related items*. Edinburgh, Edinburgh University Press.

Fox, Nicholas J. (1988): 'Scientific theory choice and social structure: the case of Joseph Lister's antisepsis, humoral theory and asepsis'. *History of Science* **26**, 367–97.

Frank, Johann Peter (1976): 'Location, type of construction, and equipment of a public hospital' (1827), pp. 415–23 in *A system of complete medical police: selections*, ed. Erna Lesky. Baltimore, Johns Hopkins University Press.

[Franklin, Benjamin] (1817): *Some account of the Pennsylvania Hospital; from its first rise to the beginning of the fifth month, called May, 1754* [with] *Continuation of the account of the Pennsylvania Hospital; from the first of May, 1754, to the fifth of May 1761. With an alphabetical list of the contributors. . . .* Philadelphia, Printed at the Office of the United States' Gazette.

Franklin, Benjamin (1882): *Works*, 10 vols, ed. Jared Sparks, vol. 6, *Letters and papers on philosophical subjects*. London, Benjamin Franklin Stevens.

——(1906): *Writings*, 10 vols, ed. Albert Henry Smith, vol. 6, *1773–1776*. New York, Macmillan.

——(1954): *Some account of the Pennsylvania Hospital* (1754), facsimile edn with an Introduction by I. Bernard Cohen (Biblioteca Medica Americana 6). Baltimore, Johns Hopkins Press.

Freeman, James A. (1975): ' "The roof was fretted gold" '. *Comparative Literature* **27**, 254–66.

French, C. N. (1951): *The story of St Luke's Hospital*. London, William Heinemann.

Friedman, Terry (1984): *James Gibbs*. New Haven and London, Yale University Press.

——(1990): ' "Mr *Inigo Pilaster* and Sir *Christopher Cupolo*": on the advantages of an architectural farrago', pp. 34–48 in *William Adam*, ed. Deborah Howard. Edinburgh, Edinburgh University Press.

Frith, Brian (1961): *The story of Gloucester's Infirmary*. Gloucester, Stroud and the Forest Hospital Management Committee.

Frizelle, Ernest R. and Martin, Janet D. (1971): *The Leicester Royal Infirmary 1771–1971*. Leicester, Leicester No. 1 Hospital Management Committee.

Geertz, Clifford (1976): 'Art as a cultural system'. *MLN* **91**, 1473–501.

Gent, Lucy (1995): 'The "rash gazer": economies of vision in Britain, 1550–1660', pp. 377–93 in *Albion's classicism: the visual arts in Britain, 1550–1660*, ed. Lucy Gent. New Haven and London, Yale University Press.

Gifford, John (1989): *William Adam, 1689–1748: a life and times of Scotland's universal architect*. Edinburgh, Mainstream.

Gifford, John; McWilliam, Colin; and Walker, David (1988): *Edinburgh (Buildings of Scotland)*, revised edn. Harmondsworth, Penguin.

Gilchrist, Roberta (1992): 'Christian bodies and souls: the archaeology of life and death in later medieval hospitals', pp. 101–18 in *Death in towns: urban responses to the dying and the dead, 100–1600*, ed. Steven Bassett. Leicester, Leicester University Press.

——(1995): *Contemplation and action: the other monasticism*. Leicester, Leicester University Press.

Gillispie, Charles Coulston (1980): *Science and polity in France at the end of the Old Regime*. Princeton, NJ, Princeton University Press.

Giordano, Luisa (1988): 'Il trattato del Filarete e l'architettura Lombarda', pp. 115–28 in *Traités d'architecture. Actes du colloque tenu à Tours du 1er au 11 juillet 1981*, ed. Jean Guillaume. Paris, Picard.

Girouard, Mark (1978): *Life in the English country house*. New Haven and London, Yale University Press.

——(1990): *The English town*. New Haven and London, Yale University Press.

Glen, Heather (1983): *Vision and disenchantment: Blake's 'Songs' and Wordsworth's 'Lyrical Ballads'*. Cambridge, Cambridge University Press.

Godfrey, Walter H. (1927): *The Royal Hospital, Chelsea (Survey of London 11: The Parish of Chelsea, pt 4)*. London, London County Council.

——(1955): *The English almshouse, with some account of its predecessor, the medieval hospital*. London, Faber & Faber.

Godfrey, Walter H. and Marcham, W. McB. (1952): *King's Cross neighbourhood: the Parish of St Pancras*, part 4 (*Survey of London* 24). London, London County Council.

Godlee, Sir Rickman John (1924): *Lord Lister* (1917), 3rd edn. Oxford, Clarendon Press.

Goldberg, Rita (1991): 'Charity sermons and the poor: a rhetoric of compassion'. *The Age of Johnson* **4**, 171–216.

Goldin, Grace (1994): *Work of mercy: a picture history of hospitals*. Erin, Ont., AMS / Boston Mills Press.

Golding, Benjamin (1819): *Historical account of St. Thomas's Hospital, Southwark*. London, Longmans, etc.

Goldsmith, M. M. (1985): *Private vices, public benefits: Bernard Mandeville's social and political thought*. Cambridge, Cambridge University Press.

Gomme, Andor and Walker, David (1987): *Architecture of Glasgow*, revised edn. London, Lund Humphries.

Gooch, Benjamin [1773]: *Medical and chirurgical observations, as an Appendix to a former publication* [i.e. to *A practical treatise on wounds . . .*]. London and Norwich, G. Robinson and R. Beatniffe.

Goslings, W. R. O. (1976): 'Leiden and Edinburgh: the seed, the soil and the climate', pp. 1–18 in *The early years of the Edinburgh Medical School*, ed. R. G. Anderson and A. D. Simpson. Edinburgh, Royal Scottish Museum.

Gould, Stephen Jay (1991): *Bully for Brontosaurus: reflections in natural history*. New York and London, W. W. Norton.

Gould, Terry and Uttley, David (1997): *A short history of St George's Hospital and the history of its ward names*. London, Athlone.

Gradish, Stephen (1980): *The manning of the British Navy during the Seven Years' War*. London, Royal Historical Society.

Granshaw, Lindsay (1992): 'The rise of the modern hospital in Britain', pp. 197–218 in *Medicine and society: historical essays*, ed. Andrew Wear. Cambridge, Cambridge University Press.

——(1992): '"Upon this principle I have based a practice": the development and reception of antisepsis in Britain, 1867–90', pp. 17–46, 202–12 in *Medical innovations in historical perspective*, ed. John Pickstone. Basingstoke, Macmillan.

——(1993): 'The hospital', pp. 1180–203 in *Companion encyclopedia of the history of medicine*, ed. W. F. Bynum and Roy Porter. London and New York, Routledge.

Greenbaum, Louis S. (1971): '"The commercial treaty of humanity": la tournée des hôpitaux anglais par Jacques Tenon en 1787'. *Revue d'histoire des sciences* 24, 317–50.

——(1972): 'The humanitarianism of Antoine Laurent Lavoisier'. *Studies on Voltaire and the Eighteenth Century* 88, 651–75.

——(1974): 'Tempest in the Academy: Jean-Baptiste Le Roy, the Paris Academy of Sciences and the project of a new Hôtel-Dieu'. *Archives internationales d'histoire des sciences* 24, 122–40.

——(1975): '"Measure of civilization": the hospital thought of Jacques Tenon on the eve of the French Revolution'. *Bulletin of the History of Medicine* 49, 43–56.

——(1976): 'Health-care and hospital-building in eighteenth-century France: reform proposals of Du Pont de Nemours and Condorcet'. *Studies on Voltaire and the Eighteenth Century* 52, 895–930.

——(1992): 'Thomas Jefferson's University of Virginia and the Paris hospitals on the eve of the French Revolution'. *Medical History* 36, 306–19.

'Greenwich' (1865): 'Greenwich Hospital'. *Cornhill Magazine* 12, 631–40.

[Grosley, Pierre-Jean] (1770): *Londres. Ouvrage d'un françois. Augmenté dans cette édition des notes d'un anglois*, 2nd edn, 3 vols. Neuchatel, Aux dépens de la Société Typographique.

Grosley [Pierre-Jean] (1772): *A tour of London; or, new observations on England, and its inhabitants*, trans. Thomas Nugent, 2 vols. London, Lockyer Davis.

Hacker, C. L. (1960): 'William Strutt of Derby (1756–1830)'. *Journal of the Derbyshire Archaeological and Natural History Society* 80, 49–70.

Hales, Stephen (1743): *A description of ventilators: wherby great quantities of fresh air may . . . be conveyed into mines, goals [sic], hospitals, work-houses and ships, in exchange for their noxious air . . . Read before the Royal Society in May 1741*. London, W. Innys and others.

——(1758): *A treatise on ventilators. Wherein an account is given of the happy effects of many trials that have been made of them . . .* London, Richard Manby.

Hallé, Jean-Noël (1787): 'Air. Hygiène', pp. 492–590 in *Encyclopédie méthodique . . . Médecine*, ed. Félix Vicq d'Azyr. Paris, Panckoucke.

Hallett, Mark (1999): *The spectacle of difference: graphic satire in the age of Hogarth*. New Haven and London, Yale University Press.

Halliday, Sir Andrew (1816): *A letter to . . . Lord Binning . . . containing some remarks on the state of lunatic asylums, and on the number and condition of the insane poor in Scotland*. Edinburgh.

Hannaway, Caroline (1993): 'Environment and miasmata', pp. 292–308 in *Companion encyclopedia of the history of medicine*, ed. W. F. Bynum and Roy Porter. London and New York, Routledge.

Harris, Eileen and Savage, Nicholas (1990): *British architectural books and writers 1556–1785*. Cambridge, Cambridge University Press.

Harris, J. Delpratt (1922): *The Royal Devon and Exeter Hospital*. Exeter, for the Hospital Committee.

'Harrison, Walter' (1776): *A new and universal history, description and survey of the Cities of London and Westminster . . .* London, J. Cooke.

Hart, Harold W. (1980): 'Some notes on the sponsoring of patients for hospital treatment under the voluntary system'. *Medical History* 24, 447–60.

Harwood, John T. (1989): 'Rhetoric and graphics in *Micrographia*', pp. 119–47 in *Robert Hooke: new studies*, ed. Michael Hunter and Simon Schaffer. Woodbridge, Suffolk, Boydell.

Hasegawa, Toshihiko (1989): 'A comparative study of development of the modern hospital in Japan and the U.S.A', pp. 149–60 in *History of hospitals: the evolution of health care facilities*, ed. Yosio Kawakita, Shizu Sakai, and Yasuo Otsuka. Tokyo, Taniguchi Foundation.

Haskins, Charles (1922): *The history of Salisbury Infirmary*. Salisbury, Salisbury Times.

[Hatton, Edward] (1708): *A new view of London; or, an ample account of that City*, 2 vols. London, R. Chiswell and others.

Hautecoeur, Louis (1974): 'Avant-propos', pp. 9–40 in *Les Invalides: trois siècles d'histoire*, ed. René Baillargeat. Paris, Musée de l'Armée.

Hawksmoor, Nicholas (1728): *Remarks on the founding and carrying on the buildings of the Royal Hospital at Greenwich*. London, printed by N. Blandford.

Hayward, Richard A. (1998): 'The changing concept of infection and its influence on hospital design, 1850–1890'. Ph.D. Dissertation, University of Keele.

Heal, Felicity (1990): *Hospitality in early modern England*. Oxford, Clarendon Press.

Hedrick, Donald Keith (1987): 'The ideology of ornament: Alberti and the erotics of Renaissance urban design'. *Word and Image* 3, 111–37.

Hegel, G. W. F. (1975): *Aesthetics. Lectures on fine art*, trans. T. M. Knox, 2 vols. Oxford, Clarendon Press.

Henderson, John (1989): 'The hospitals of late-medieval and Renaissance Florence: a preliminary survey', pp. 63–92 in *The hospital in history*, ed. Lindsay Granshaw and Roy Porter. London and New York, Routledge.

——(1992): 'The Black Death in Florence: medical and communal responses', pp. 136–50 in *Death in towns: urban responses to the dying and the dead, 100–1600*, ed. Steven Bassett. Leicester, Leicester University Press.

Henderson, Paula (1995): 'The loggia in Tudor and early Stuart England: a preliminary survey', pp. 109–45 in *Albion's classicism: the visual arts in England, 1550–1660*, ed. Lucy Gent. New Haven and London, Yale University Press.

Herbert, Gilbert (1978): *Pioneers of prefabrication: the British contribution in the nineteenth century*. Baltimore and London, Johns Hopkins University Press.

[Herring,] Thomas, Lord Archbishop of York [1747]: *A sermon preached before His Grace Charles, Duke of Richmond, Lenox, and Aubigny, President; and the Governors of the London Infirmary, in Goodman's-Fields, for the relief of all sick and diseased persons, especially manufacturers, and seamen in merchant-service, &c. At the parish church of St. Lawrence-Jewry, on Tuesday, March 31, 1747*, 2nd edn. London, printed by H. Woodfall.

Hewlings, Richard (n.d.): 'The first Addenbrooke's Hospital' (typescript).

Heydenreich, Ludwig (1995): *Architecture in Italy, 1400–1500*, ed. Paul Davies. New Haven and London, Yale University Press.

Hibbard, G. R. (1956): 'The country house poem of the seventeenth century'. *Journal of the Warburg and Courtauld Institutes* 19, 159–74.

Hill, Oliver and Cornforth, John (1966): *English country houses: Caroline, 1625–85*. London, Country Life.

Hill, Rosemary (1999): 'Reformation to millennium: Pugin's *Contrasts* in the history of English thought'. *Journal of the Society of Architectural Historians* 58, 26–41.

Hillier, Bill and Hanson, Julienne (1984): *The social logic of space*. Cambridge, Cambridge University Press.

History and statutes (1749): *The history and statutes of the Royal Infirmary of Edinburgh*. Edinburgh, printed by Thomas and Walter Ruddiman.

——(1778): *The history and statutes of the Royal Infirmary of Edinburgh*. Edinburgh, Balfour & Smellie.

Hoeldtke, Robert (1967): 'The history of associationism and British medical psychology'. *Medical History* 11, 46–65.

Hoogdalem, Herbert van (1990): 'Design guidelines for architects and users', pp. 171–88 in *Building for people in hospitals: workers and consumers*, ed. Rosalyn Moran, Robert Anderson, and Pascal Paoli. Dublin, European Foundation for the Improvement of Living and Working Conditions.

Hooke, Robert (1935): *The diary of Robert Hooke, 1672–1680*, ed. H. W. Robinson and Walter Adams. London, Taylor & Francis.

——(1961): *Micrographia: or some physiological descriptions of minute bodies made by magnifying glasses. With observations and inquiries thereupon* (1665), facsimile edn, ed. R. T. Gunther. New York, Dover.

Horace (1967): *Odes*, trans. James Michie. Harmondsworth, Penguin.

Houston, R. A. (1994): *Social change in the Age of Enlightenment: Edinburgh, 1660–1760*. Oxford, Clarendon Press.

Howard, John (1784): *The state of the prisons in England and Wales, with preliminary observations, and an account of some foreign prisons and hospitals*, 3rd edn. Warrington, W. Eyres.

——(1789): *An account of the principal lazarettos in Europe; with various papers relative to the plague: together with further observations on some foreign prisons and hospitals: and additional remarks on the present state of those in Great Britain and Ireland*. London, T. Cadell and others.

Howard, Maurice (1987): *The early Tudor country house: architecture and politics 1490–1550*. London, George Phillip.

——(1988): 'The ideal house and the healthy life: the origins of architectural theory in England', pp. 425–33 in *Traités d'architecture. Actes du colloque tenu à Tours du 1er au 11 juillet 1981*, ed. Jean Guillaume. Paris, Picard.

——(1990): 'Self-fashioning and the classical moment in mid-sixteenth-century English architecture', pp. 198–217 in *Renaissance bodies: the human figure in English culture c.1540–1660*, ed. Lucy Gent and Nigel Llewellyn. London, Reaktion.

Howarth, David (1997): *Images of rule: art and politics in the English Renaissance, 1485–1649*. Basingstoke and London, Macmillan.

Hudson, Geoffrey (in press): 'The social dynamics of disability: ex-servicemen and the State, 1600–1800', in *War, medicine, and Britain 1600–1800*, ed. Geoffrey Hudson. Amsterdam, Rodopi.

Humble, J. G. and Hansell, Peter (1966): *Westminster Hospital 1716–1966*. London, Pitman Medical.

Hume, George Haliburton (1906): *The history of Newcastle Infirmary*. Newcastle upon Tyne, Andrew Reid.

Hunczovsky, Johann (1783): *Medicinisch-chirurgische Beobachtungen auf seinen Reisen durch England und Frankreich besonders über die Spitäler*. Vienna, Rudolph Graffer.

Hunter, Michael (1991): 'The making of Christopher Wren'. *London Journal* 16 (2), 101–16.

Hunter, Richard and Macalpine, Ida, eds (1963): *Three hundred years of psychiatry 1535–1860: a history presented in selected English texts*. London, Oxford University Press.

Hutt, George, ed. (1872): *Papers illustrative of the origin and early history of the Royal Hospital at Chelsea, London*. London, Eyre & Spottiswoode.

Hyde, Ralph, ed. (1982): *The A to Z of Georgian London* [John Rocque's *Plan of the Cities of London and Westminster and Borough of Southwark, 1746*]. London, Topographical Society.

Ibbot, Benjamin (1719): *The parable of the unjust steward, explain'd. A sermon. . . .* London, J. Wyat.

Ignatieff, Michael (1978): *A just measure of pain: the penitentiary in the Industrial Revolution 1750–1850.* London, Macmillan.

Iliffe, Richard and Baguley, Wilfred (1974): 'The General Hospital', pp. 79–100 in *Victorian Nottingham: a story in pictures,* vol. 13. Nottingham, Nottingham Historical Film Unit.

Illich, Ivan (1976): *Limits to medicine. Medical nemesis: the expropriation of health.* Harmondsworth, Penguin.

Jacob, Hildebrand (1723): *Bedlam, a poem.* London, W. Lewis & Tho. Edlin.

Jacob, Margaret C. (1991): *Living the Enlightenment: Freemasonry and politics in eighteenth-century Europe.* Oxford, Oxford University Press.

Jefferson, Thomas (1972): *Notes on the State of Virginia* (1787), ed. William Peden. New York, W. W. Norton.

Jeffery, Paul (1996): *The City churches of Sir Christopher Wren.* London and Rio Grande, Ohio, Hambledon.

Jenkins, A. D. Fraser (1970): 'Cosimo de' Medici's patronage of architecture and the theory of magnificence'. *Journal of the Warburg and Courtauld Institutes* 33, 162–70.

Jenkins, Frank (1961): *Architect and patron: a survey of professional relations and practice in England from the sixteenth century to the present day.* London, Oxford University Press.

Jenkinson, Jacqueline (1994): 'Blessing upon the foundation, 1794–1815', pp. 11–46 in Jacqueline Jenkinson, Michael Moss, and Iain Russell, *The Royal: the history of Glasgow Royal Infirmary, 1794–1994.* Glasgow, The Bicentenary Committee on behalf of the Glasgow Royal Infirmary NHS Trust.

Jenner, Mark (1995): 'The politics of London air: John Evelyn's *Fumifugium* and the Restoration'. *Historical Journal* 38, 535–51.

Jestaz, Bertrand (1990): *L'Hôtel et l'eglise des Invalides.* Paris, Picard.

Jetter, Dieter (1973): *Grundzüge der Hospitalgeschichte.* Darmstadt, Wissenschaftliche Buchgesellschaft.

——(1981): *Grundzüge der Geschichte des Irrenhauses.* Darmstadt, Wissenschaftliche Buchgesellschaft.

Johnson, H. R. and Skempton, A. W. (1956): 'William Strutt's cotton mills, 1793–1812'. *Transactions of the Newcomen Society,* 179–201.

Johnson, Samuel (1761): *The Idler,* vol. 1. London, J. Newbury.

——(1971): *Life of Savage* (1744), ed. Clarence Tracy. Oxford, Clarendon Press.

Jones, Colin (1989): *The charitable imperative: hospitals and nursing in ancien régime and Revolutionary France.* London and New York, Routledge.

Jones, George Fenwick, ed. (1966): *Henry Newman's Salzburger letterbooks.* Athens, University of Georgia Press.

Jones, John (1971): *Plain concise practical remarks, on the treatment of wounds and fractures; to which is added, an Appendix, on camp and military hospitals; principally designed, for the use of young military and naval surgeons, in North-America* (1776), reprint New York, Arno Press and The New York Times.

Jordanova, Ludmilla (1979): 'Earth science and environmental medicine: the synthesis of the late Enlightenment', pp. 119–46 in *Images of the earth: essays in the history of the environmental sciences,* ed. Ludmilla Jordanova and Roy Porter. Chalfont St Giles, British Society for the History of Science.

Jose, Nicholas (1984): *Ideas of the Restoration in English literature 1660–1671.* London, Macmillan.

Kalman, Harold D. (1971): 'The architecture of George Dance the Younger'. Ph.D. Dissertation, Princeton University [Ann Arbor, University Microfilms International, 1972].

Kaufman, Edward N. (1987): 'Architectural representation in Victorian England'. *Journal of the Society of Architectural Historians* 46, 30–38.

Keevil, J. J. (1958): *Medicine and the Navy, 1200–1900,* vol. 2, *1649–1714.* Edinburgh and London, E. & S. Livingstone.

Keller, Fritz-Eugen (1986): 'Christian Eltester's drawings of Roger Pratt's Clarendon House and Robert Hooke's Montague House'. *Burlington Magazine* 128, 732–37.

Kempthorne, G. A. (1937): 'The medical services of William the Third's army'. *Journal of the Royal Army Medical Corps* 68, 372–82.

Kennedy, Rachel M. H. (1995): ' "Gone to take the air": single women and the London lying-in hospital, 1800–1840'. MA Thesis, University of London, Royal Holloway and Bedford New College.

Kenny, Virginia C. (1984): *The country-house ethos in English literature 1688–1750: themes of pastoral retreat and national expansion.* [Brighton,] Sussex, Harvester.

Kermode, Frank and Walker, Keith, eds (1990): *Andrew Marvell* (The Oxford Authors). Oxford, Oxford University Press.

Kilpatrick, Robert (1990): ' "Living in the Light": dispensaries, philanthropy and medical reform in late-eighteenth-century London', pp. 254–80 in *The medical Enlightenment of the eighteenth century,* ed. Andrew Cunningham and Roger French. Cambridge, Cambridge University Press.

Kindler, Roger A. (1974): 'Periodical criticism 1815–40: originality in architecture'. *Architectural History* 17, 22–37.

King, Anthony (1966): 'Hospital planning: revised thoughts on the origin of the pavilion principle in England'. *Medical History* 10, 360–73.

King, David (1991): *The complete works of Robert and James Adam.* Oxford, Butterworth Architecture.

Kingsbury, Pamela D. (1995): *Lord Burlington's town architecture.* London, RIBA Heinz Gallery.

Klein, Lawrence E. (1996): 'Gender and the public/private distinction in the eighteenth century: some questions about evidence and analytic procedure'. *Eighteenth-century studies* 29, 97–109.

Klingender, F. D. (1947): *Art and the Industrial Revolution*. London, Noel Carrington.

Kromm, Jane E. (1985): 'Hogarth's madmen'. *Journal of the Warburg and Courtauld Institutes* **48**, 238–42.

Kunzle, David (1966): 'Plagiaries-by-memory of the *Rake's Progress* and the genesis of Hogarth's second picture story'. *Journal of the Warburg and Courtauld Institutes* **29**, 311–48.

Lambert, Royston (1963): *Sir John Simon 1816–1904 and English social administration*. London, Macgibbon & Kee.

Lane, Joan (1992): *Worcester Infirmary in the eighteenth century*. Worcester, Worcestershire Historical Society.

Langford, Paul (1991): *Public life and the propertied Englishman 1689–1798*. Oxford, Clarendon Press.

Laqueur, Thomas W. (1989): 'Bodies, details and the humanitarian narrative', pp. 176–204 in *The new cultural history*, ed. Lynn Hunt. Berkeley, University of California Press.

La Roche, Marie Sophie von (1933): *Sophie in London, 1786, being the diary of Sophie v. la Roche*, ed. and trans. Clare Williams. London, Jonathan Cape.

Laugier, Marc-Antoine (1972): *Essai sur l'architecture*, 2nd edn (1755), repr. Geneva, Minkoff.

Lavoisier, Antoine-Laurent (1865): 'Examen d'un Projet de translation de l'Hôtel-Dieu de Paris, et d'une nouvelle construction d'hôpitaux pour les malades', pp. 603–68 in *Oeuvres*, vol. 3. *Mémoires et rapports sur divers sujets de chimie et de physique pures . . .*, ed. J. B. A. Dumas. Paris, Imprimerie Impériale.

Lawrance, Christine (1994): *The history of the Old Naval Hospital Gibraltar 1741 to 1922*. Lymington, C. Lawrance.

Lawrence, Christopher (1985): 'Ornate physicians and learned artisans: Edinburgh medical men, 1726–1776', pp. 153–76 in *William Hunter and the eighteenth-century medical world*, ed. W. F. Bynum and Roy Porter. Cambridge, Cambridge University Press.

——(1996): 'Disciplining disease: scurvy, the Navy, and imperial expansion 1750–1825', pp. 80–106 in *Visions of empire: voyages, botany, and representations of nature*, ed. David Philip Miller and Peter Hanns Reill. Cambridge, Cambridge University Press.

Lawrence, Christopher and Dixey, Richard (1992): 'Practising on principle: Joseph Lister and the germ theories of disease', pp. 153–215 in *Medical theory, surgical practice: studies in the history of surgery*, ed. Christopher Lawrence. London, Routledge.

Leach, Peter (1988): *James Paine*. London, Zwemmer.

Le Jeune de Boulencourt (1683): *Description générale de l'Hôtel Royal des Invalides établi par Louis le Grand . . . avec les plans, profils & elevations de ses faces, coupes & appartemens*. Paris, n.p.

Le Roy, Jean-Baptiste (1789): 'Précis d'un ouvrage sur les hôpitaux, dans lequel on expose les principes résultant des observations de physique & de médecine qu'un doit avoir en vue dans la construction de ces édifices; avec un projet d'hôpital disposé d'après ces principes'. *Histoire de l' Académie royale des sciences. Année M.DCCLXXXVIII. Avec les mémoires de mathématique & de physique, pour la même année*, 585–601.

Levack, Iain D. and Dudley, Hugh A. F., eds (1992): *Aberdeen Royal Infirmary: the people's hospital of the North-East*. London, Baillière Tindall.

Leveaux, V. M. (1999): *The history of the Derbyshire General Infirmary 1810–1894*. Cromford, Scarthin.

Lichtenberg, Georg Christoph (1966): *Lichtenberg's commentaries on Hogarth's engravings*, ed. and trans. Innes and Gustav Herden. London, Cresset.

Lloyd, Christopher and Coulter, Jack L. S. (1961): *Medicine and the Navy, 1200–1900*, vol. 3, *1714–1815*. Edinburgh and London, E. & S. Livingstone.

Lobo, Francis M. (1990): 'John Haygarth, smallpox and religious Dissent in eighteenth-century England', pp. 217–53 in *The medical Enlightenment of the eighteenth century*, ed. Andrew Cunningham and Roger French. Cambridge, Cambridge University Press.

Loeber, Rolf (1981): *A biographical dictionary of architects in Ireland 1600–1720*. London, John Murray.

Loftie, William John (1878): *Memorials of the Savoy: the palace, the hospital, the chapel*. London, Macmillan.

Longfield-Jones, G. M. (1995): 'John Woodall, Surgeon General of the East India Company. Part II: A consideration of the provison made for treating injuries and diseases at sea'. *Journal of Medical Biography* **3**, 71–8.

Loudon, Irvine (1981): 'The origin and growth of the dispensary movement in England'. *Bulletin of the History of Medicine* **55**, 322–42.

Loudon, J. C., ed. (1840): *The landscape gardening and the landscape architecture of the late Humphry Repton, Esq. Being his entire works on these subjects . . .* London, the editor.

Lubbock, Jules (1995): *The tyranny of taste: the politics of architecture and design in Britain 1550–1960*. New Haven and London, Yale University Press.

Luce, A. A. (1949): *The life of George Berkeley, Bishop of Cloyne*. London, Thomas Nelson.

Lynaugh, Joan E. (1989): *The community hospitals of Kansas City, Missouri, 1870–1915*. New York, Garland.

Lyon, David Murray (1900): *History of the Lodge of Edinburgh (Mary's Chapel), No. 1. Embracing an account of the rise and progress of Freemasons in Scotland*, 2nd ('Tercentenary') edn. London, Gresham.

Macaulay, James (1987): *The classical country house in Scotland 1660–1800*. London, Faber & Faber.

Macdonald, Fiona A. (1999): 'The Infirmary of the Glasgow Town's Hospital, 1733–1800: a case for voluntarism?'. *Bulletin of the History of Medicine* **73**, 64–104.

MacInnes, Ranald (1993): 'Robert Adam's public buildings', pp. 10–22 in *Robert Adam*, ed. John Lowrey. Edinburgh, Architectural Heritage Society of Scotland.

Maitland, William (1753): *The history of Edinburgh. . . .* Edinburgh, the author.

——(1756): *The history [and survey] of London from its foundation to the present time*, 2 vols. London, T. Osborne and J. Skipton.

Malcolm, Elizabeth (1989): *Swift's hospital: a history of St Patrick's Hospital, Dublin, 1746–1989*. Dublin and New York, Gill and Macmillan.

Mandeville, Bernard (1720): *Free thoughts on religion, the church, and national happiness*. London, T. Jauncy and J. Roberts.

——(1924): *The fable of the bees: or, private vices, publick benefits*, ed. F. B. Kaye, vol. 2, *The fable of the bees part II* (1729). Oxford, Clarendon Press.

——(1954): *A letter to Dion* (1732), ed. Bonamy Dobrée. Liverpool, University Press of Liverpool.

——(1989): *The fable of the bees*, ed. Phillip Harth. London, Penguin.

Markus, Thomas A. (1982): 'Buildings for the sad, the bad and the mad in urban Scotland, 1780–1830', pp. 25–114 in *Order in space and society: architectural form and its context in the Scottish Enlightenment*. Edinburgh, Mainstream.

——(1993): *Buildings and power: freedom and control in the origin of modern building types*. London and New York, Routledge.

Mathias, Peter (1975): 'Swords and ploughshares: the armed forces, medicine and public health in the late eighteenth century', pp. 73–90 in *War and economic development*, ed. J. M. Winter. Cambridge, Cambridge University Press.

[Mawson,] Matthias, Lord Bishop of Chichester. [1750]: *A sermon preached before His Grace Charles, Duke of Richmond, Lenox, and Aubigny, President; and the Governors of the London Infirmary, in Goodman's-Fields, for the relief of all sick and diseased persons, especially manufacturers, and seamen in merchant-service, &c. At the parish church of St. Lawrence-Jewry, on Friday, April 6, 1750*. London, printed by H. Woodfall.

McClung, William Alexander (1977): *The country house in English Renaissance poetry*. Berkeley and Los Angeles, University of California Press.

——(1981): 'The matter of metaphor: literary myths of construction'. *Journal of the Society of Architectural Historians* **40**, 279–88.

——(1983): *The architecture of Paradise: survivals of Eden and Jerusalem*. Berkeley, University of California Press.

McClure, Ruth (1981): *Coram's children: the London Foundling Hospital in the eighteenth century*. New Haven and London, Yale University Press.

McInnes, E. M. (1990): *St Thomas' Hospital*, 2nd edn with new chapters by John M. T. Ford. London, Special Trustees for St Thomas' Hospital.

McKendrick, Neil (1982): 'The consumer revolution of eighteenth-century England', 'The commercialization of fashion', 'Josiah Wedgwood and the commercialization of the potteries', pp. 9–33, 34–99, 100–45 in *The birth of a consumer society: the commercialization of eighteenth-century England*, by Neil McKendrick, John Brewer, and J. H. Plumb. London, Europa.

McKitterick, David (1995): 'Introduction', pp. 1–27 in *The making of the Wren Library, Trinity College, Cambridge*, ed. David McKitterick. Cambridge, Cambridge University Press.

McLoughlin, George (1978): *A short history of the first Liverpool Infirmary 1749–1824*. Chichester, Phillimore.

McMenemey, W. H. (1947): *A history of the Worcester Royal Infirmary*. London, Press Alliance.

——(1964): 'The hospital movement of the eighteenth century and its development', pp. 43–71 in *The evolution of hospitals in Britain*, ed. F. N. L. Poynter. London, Pitman Medical.

McParland, Edward (1985): *James Gandon: Vitruvius Hibernicus*. London, Zwemmer.

——(1994): 'Sir Thomas Hewett and the New Junta for Architecture', pp. 21–26 in *The role of the amateur architect. Papers given at the Georgian Group Symposium, 1993*, ed. Giles Worsley. London, Georgian Group.

——(1995): 'Edward Lovett Pearce and the New Junta for Architecture', pp. 151–64 in *Lord Burlington: architecture, art and life*, ed. Toby Barnard and Jane Clark. London and Rio Grande, Ohio, Hambledon.

——(n.d.): *The Royal Hospital Kilmainham, Co. Dublin: a national centre for culture and the arts in Ireland*, reprinted from *Country Life*, 9 and 16 May 1985. Dublin, Irish Architectural Archive.

Mead, Richard (1720): *A short discourse concerning pestilential contagion, and the methods to be used to prevent it*. London, Sam. Buckley and Ralph Smith.

Memorial (1737): *Memorial concerning the Surgeons Hospital*. Edinburgh, 18 February.

Middleton, Robin (1992): 'Sickness, madness and crime as the grounds of form [part 1]'. *AA Files* **24**, 16–30.

——(1993): 'Sickness, madness and crime as the grounds of form [part 2]'. *AA Files* **25**, 14–29.

Money, John (1977): *Experience and identity: Birmingham and the West Midlands, 1760–1800*. Manchester, Manchester University Press.

Monro, Alexander (1995): *The professor's daughter: an essay on female conduct contained in letters from a father to his daughter* [written 1739], ed. P. A. G. Monro. Cambridge, P. A. G. Monro.

Monro, Donald (1764): *An account of the diseases which were most frequent in the British military hospitals in Germany, from January 1761 to . . . March 1763. To which is added, an essay on the means of preserving the health of soldiers, and conducting military hospitals*. London, A. Millar, D. Wilson & T. Durham.

Monro, Hector (1975): *The ambivalence of Bernard Mandeville*. Oxford, Clarendon Press.

Morgan, William (1977): *London &c. actually survey'd* (1682), facsimile edn with an introduction by Ralph Hyde. Lympne, Kent, Harry Margary and the Guildhall Library.

Morrell, J. B. (1976): 'The Edinburgh Town Council and its University, 1717–1766', pp. 46–65 in *The early years of the*

Edinburgh Medical School, ed. R. G. Anderson and A. D. Simpson. Edinburgh, Royal Scottish Museum.

——(1983): 'Medicine and science in the eighteenth century', pp. 38–52 in *Four centuries: Edinburgh University life 1583–1983*, ed. Gordon Donaldson. Edinburgh, Edinburgh University Press.

Morris, Christopher, ed. (1995): *The illustrated journeys of Celia Fiennes 1685–c.1712*. Stroud, Gloucs, Alan Sutton.

Morris, E. W. (1926): *A history of the London Hospital*, 3rd edn. London, Edward Arnold.

[Morris, Robert] (1970): *The art of architecture, a poem in imitation of Horace's Art of Poetry* (1742), ed. William A. Gibson (Augustan Reprint Society 144). Los Angeles, William Andrews Clark Memorial Library.

Morris, Robert (1971): *An essay in defence of ancient architecture* (1728), repr. Farnborough, Hants, Gregg.

Mortier, Roland (1979): 'Diderot et l'assistance publique, ou la source et les variations de l'article "Hôpital" de l'Encyclopédie', pp. 175–85 in *Enlightenment studies in honour of Lester G. Crocker*, ed. Alfred J. Bingham and Virgil W. Topazio. Oxford, Voltaire Foundation.

Morton, Thomas G. and Woodbury, Frank (1897): *The history of the Pennsylvania Hospital 1751–1895*, revised edn. Philadelphia, Times Printing House.

Mowl, Tim and Earnshaw, Brian (1988): *John Wood: architect of obsession*. Bath, Millstream.

Mulvany, Thomas J., ed. (1969): *The life of James Gandon . . . from materials collected and arranged by his son, James Gandon . . .* (1846), repr. ed. Maurice Craig. London, Cornmarket.

Munro Smith, G. (1917): *A history of the Bristol Royal Infirmary*. Bristol, J. W. Arrowsmith.

Newell, Philip (1984): *Greenwich Hospital: a royal foundation 1692–1983*. [Holbrook,] The Trustees of Greenwich Hospital.

Nichols, R. H. and Wray, F. A. (1935): *The history of the Foundling Hospital*. London, Oxford University Press, Humphrey Milford.

Nicolson, Benedict (1972): *The treasures of the Foundling Hospital*. Oxford, Clarendon Press.

Nightingale, Florence (1859): *Notes on hospitals. Being two papers read before the National Association for the Promotion of Social Science, at Liverpool, in October, 1858. With evidence given to the Royal Commission on the State of the Army in 1857*. London, John W. Parker.

——(1863): *Notes on hospitals*, 3rd edn, 'Enlarged and for the most part re-written'. London, Longman, Green.

North, Roger (1981): *Of building: Roger North's writings on architecture*, ed. Howard Colvin and John Newman. Oxford, Oxford University Press.

Nutton, Vivian (1990): 'The reception of Fracastoro's theory of contagion: the seed that fell among thorns'. *Osiris*, 2nd ser. **6**, 196–234.

O'Donoghue, Edward Geoffrey (1914): *The story of Bethlehem Hospital from its foundation in 1247*. London, T. Fisher Unwin.

Ogborn, Miles (1998): *Spaces of modernity: London's geographies, 1680–1780*. New York, Guilford Press.

Ogilby, John and Morgan, William (1992): *[A large and accurate map of the City of London] The A to Z of Restoration London (the City of London, 1676)*, facsimile edn, ed. Ralph Hyde. Lympne Castle, Kent, Harry Margary for the Guildhall Library.

Orme, Nicholas and Webster, Margaret (1995): *The English hospital, 1070–1570*. New Haven and London, Yale University Press.

Osborne, Thomas (1994): 'On anti-medicine and clinical reason', pp. 28–47 in *Reassessing Foucault: power, medicine and the body*, ed. Colin Jones and Roy Porter. London, Routledge.

Owen, David (1964): *English philanthropy, 1660–1960*. Cambridge, Mass., Harvard University Press.

Ozouf, Mona (1966): 'L'Image de la ville chez Claude-Nicolas Ledoux'. *Annales. Economies, sociétés, civilisation* **21**, 1273–304.

Palmer, Richard (1993): 'In bad odour: smell and its significance in medicine from antiquity to the seventeenth century', pp. 61–68, 285–87 in *Medicine and the five senses*, ed. W. F. Bynum and Roy Porter. Cambridge, Cambridge University Press.

Park, Katharine and Henderson, John (1991): '"The first hospital among Christians": the Ospedale di Santa Maria Nuova in early sixteenth-century Florence'. *Medical History* **35**, 164–88.

Parry-Jones, William Ll. (1972): *The trade in lunacy: a study of private madhouses in England in the eighteenth and nineteenth centuries*. London, Routledge & Kegan Paul.

Parsons, F. G. (1934): *The history of St Thomas's Hospital*, vol. 2, *From 1600 to 1800*. London, Methuen.

Pattern (1695): *A Pattern of a well-constituted and well-governed hospital . . . the Royal Hospital of the Invalides, near Paris*. London, Richard Baldwin.

Paulson, Ronald (1989): *Breaking and remaking: aesthetic practice in England, 1700–1820*. New Brunswick, NJ, Rutgers University Press.

——(1992): *Hogarth*, vol. 2, *High art and low, 1732–1750*. New Brunswick, NJ, Rutgers University Press.

——(1995): 'Emulative consumption and literacy: the Harlot, Moll Flanders, and Mrs. Slipslop', pp. 383–400 in *The consumption of culture, 1600–1800: image, object, text*, ed. Ann Bermingham and John Brewer. London, Routledge.

Peachey, George C. (1910–14): *The history of St George's Hospital*, 6 pts in 4 vols. London, John Bale, Sons, & Danielsson.

Peacock, John (1990): 'Inigo Jones as a figurative artist', pp. 154–79 in *Renaissance bodies: the human figure in English culture c. 1540–1660*, ed. Lucy Gent and Nigel Llewellyn. London, Reaktion.

——(1995): *The stage designs of Inigo Jones: the European context*. Cambridge, Cambridge University Press.

Pelling, Margaret (1978): *Cholera, fever and English medicine 1825–1865*. Oxford, Oxford University Press.

—— (1986): 'Appearance and reality: barber-surgeons, the body and disease', pp. 82–112 in *London 1500–1700: the making of the metropolis*, ed. A. L. Beier and Roger Finlay. London, Longman.

—— (1993): 'Contagion / germ theory / specificity', pp. 309–34 in *Companion encyclopedia of the history of medicine*, ed. W. F. Bynum and Roy Porter. London and New York, Routledge.

—— (1998): 'Medicine and the environment in Shakespeare's England', pp. 19–37 in *The common lot: sickness, medical occupations and the urban poor in early modern England*. London and New York, Longman.

Pelser, Hans Otto (1976): 'Die Invalidenhaus als Beitrag zur Entwicklung der Kriegsopferversorgung'. Inaugural dissertation, Albert-Ludwigs-Universität, Freiburg im Breisgau.

Pérez-Gómez, Alberto (1983): *Architecture and the crisis of modern science*. Cambridge, Mass. and London, MIT Press.

Pérouse de Montclos, Jean-Marie (1966): 'Charles-François Viel, architecte de l'Hôpital général et Jean-Louis Viel de Saint-Maux, architecte, peintre et avocat au Parlement de Paris'. *Bulletin de la Société de l'Histoire de l'Art français*, 257–67.

Pevsner, Nikolaus (1979): 'Hospitals', pp. 139–58 in *A history of building types*. London, Thames & Hudson.

—— (1986): *Derbyshire*, revised by Elizabeth Williamson (*Buildings of England*). Harmondsworth, Penguin.

'Philanthropus' (1738): *A letter from a gentleman in town, to his friend in the country, relating to the Royal Infirmary of Edinburgh*. n.p., n.p.

'Philasthenes' (1739): *A letter from a gentleman in town, to his friend in the country, relating to the Royal Infirmary of Edinburgh*. n.p., n.p.

Philo, Chris (1987): ' "Fit localities for an asylum": the historical geography of the "mad business" in England as viewed through the pages of the *Asylum Journal*'. *Journal of Historical Geography* 13, 398–415.

—— (1989): ' "Enough to drive one Mad": the organization of space in 19th-century lunatic asylums', pp. 258–90 in *The power of geography: how territory shapes social life*, ed. Jennifer Wolch and Michael Dear. London, Unwin Hyman.

Pickstone, John V. (1984): 'Ferriar's fever to Kay's cholera: disease and social structure in Cottonopolis'. *History of Science* 22, 401–19.

Pickstone, John V. and Butler, S. V. F. (1984): 'The politics of medicine in Manchester, 1788–1792: hospital reform and public health services in the early industrial city'. *Medical History* 28, 227–49.

Picon, Antoine (1992): *French architects and engineers in the Age of Enlightenment*, trans. Martin Thom. Cambridge, Cambridge University Press.

Pinon, Pierre (1989): *L'Hospice de Charenton: temple de la raison ou folie d'archéologie / The Charenton Hospital: temple of reason or archaeological folly*, trans. Murray Wylie (Archives de l'Institut Français d'Architecture). Brussels, Pierre Mardaga.

Plan (1777): *A plan of the Surr[e]y Dispensary . . . for the relief of the poor inhabitants of Southwark . . . at their own habitations. Instituted in . . . 1777*. London, James Phillips.

Platt, Colin (1994): *The great rebuildings of Tudor and Stuart England: revolutions in architectural taste*. London, UCL Press.

Pliny the Elder (1962): *Histoire naturelle. Livre XXIX*, trans. and ed. A. Ernout. Paris, Les Belles Lettres.

Plutarch (1988): *Plutarch on Sparta*, trans. and ed. Richard J. A. Talbert. London, Penguin.

Pocock, J. G. A. (1987): 'Modernity and anti-modernity in the anglophone political tradition', pp. 44–59 in *Patterns of modernity*, vol. 1, *The West*, ed. S. N. Eisenstadt. New York, New York University Press.

Pope, Alexander (1968): *Poems*, ed. John Butt. London, Methuen.

Porter, Dorothy and Porter, Roy (1989): *Patient's progress: doctors and doctoring in eighteenth-century England*. Cambridge, Polity.

Porter, Roy (1985): 'Lay medical knowledge in the eighteenth century: the case of the *Gentleman's Magazine*'. *Medical History* 29, 138–68.

—— (1989): 'The gift relation: philanthropy and provincial hospitals in eighteenth-century England', pp. 149–78 in *The hospital in history*, ed. Lindsay Granshaw and Roy Porter. London and New York, Routledge.

—— (1991): 'Civilisation and disease: medical ideology in the Enlightenment', pp. 154–83 in *Culture, politics and society in Britain, 1660–1800*, ed. Jeremy Black and Jeremy Gregory. Manchester, Manchester University Press.

—— (1992): *Doctor of society: Thomas Beddoes and the sick trade in late-Enlightenment England*. London and New York, Routledge.

—— (1992): 'Madness and its institutions', pp. 277–301 in *Medicine in society: historical essays*, ed. Andrew Wear. Cambridge, Cambridge University Press.

—— (1993): 'Diseases of civilization', pp. 585–600 in *Companion encyclopedia of the history of medicine*, ed. W. F. Bynum and Roy Porter. London and New York, Routledge.

—— (1995): 'Howard's beginning: prisons, disease, hygiene', pp. 5–26 in *The health of prisoners: historical essays*, ed. Richard Creese, W. F. Bynum, and J. Bearn. Amsterdam and Atlanta, Rodopi.

—— (1995): 'Shaping psychiatric knowledge: the role of the asylum', pp. 255–73 in *Medicine in the Enlightenment*, ed. Roy Porter. Amsterdam and Atlanta, Rodopi.

Power, D'Arcy (1926): 'The rebuilding of the Hospital in the eighteenth century, part I'. *St Bartholomew's Hospital Reports* 59, 9–34.

—— (1927): 'The rebuilding of the Hospital in the eighteenth century, part II'. *St Bartholomew's Hospital Reports* **60**, 7–24.

Power, D'Arcy and Waring, H. J. (1923): *A short history of St Bartholomew's Hospital 1123–1923.* London, for the Hospital.

Poynter, F. N. L., ed. (1963): *The journal of James Yonge (1647–1721), Plymouth surgeon.* London, Longmans.

Pratt, Roger (1928): *The architecture of Sir Roger Pratt: Charles II's commissioner for the rebuilding of London after the Great Fire, now printed for the first time from his note-books,* ed. R. T. Gunther. Oxford, Oxford University Press.

Prescott, Elizabeth (1992): *The English medieval hospital 1050–1640.* London, Seaby.

Pringle, John (1750): *Observations on the nature and cure of hospital and jayl-fevers. In a letter to Doctor Mead. . . .* London, A. Millar & D. Wilson.

——(1752): *Observations on the diseases of the army, in camp and garrison. In three parts. With an appendix, containing some papers of experiments, read at several meetings of the Royal Society.* London, A. Millar, D. Wilson, and T. Payne.

——(1764): *Observations on the diseases of the army,* 4th edn. London, A. Millar, D. Wilson, T. Durham, and T. Payne.

Prior, Lindsay (1988): 'The architecture of the hospital: a study of spatial organization and medical knowledge'. *British Journal of Sociology* **29**, 86–113.

Pugh, P. D. Gordon (1976): 'The planning of Haslar'. *Journal of the Royal Naval Medical Service* **62**, 103–20.

Pugin, A. Welby (1969): *Contrasts: or, A parallel between the noble edifices of the Middle Ages, and corresponding buildings of the present day; shewing the present decay of taste,* 2nd edn (1841), facsimile, ed. H. R. Hitchcock. Leicester, Leicester University Press.

'Putrid fever' (1958): 'The putrid fever at Robert Peel's Radcliffe Mill'. *Notes and Queries* **103**, 26–37.

[Ralph, James] (1734): *A critical review of the publick buildings, statues and ornaments. In, and about London and Westminster.* London, J. Wilford & J. Clarke.

Raven, James (1992): *Judging new wealth: popular publishing and responses to commerce in England, 1750–1800.* Oxford, Clarendon Press.

Rawcliffe, Carole (1984): 'The hospitals of later medieval London'. *Medical History* **28**, 1–21.

——(1995): *Medicine and society in later medieval England.* Stroud, Gloucs, Alan Sutton.

Rawes, William (1919): 'Extracts from "A short history of St. Luke's Hospital"'. *The Britannia Quarterly,* 25–29, 50–52.

[RCHM(E)] Royal Commission on Historical Monuments (England) (1975): *An inventory of the historical monuments in the City of York,* vol. 4, *Outside the city walls east of the Ouse.* London, HMSO.

——(1980): *Ancient and historical monuments in the City of Salisbury,* vol. 1. London, HMSO.

Reasons (1760): *Reasons for the establishing and further encouragement of St Luke's Hospital for Lunaticks. Together with rules and orders for the government thereof.* London, n.p.

Reddaway, Thomas F. (1940): *The rebuilding of London after the Great Fire.* London, Jonathan Cape.

[Reid, Robert] (1809): *Observations on the structure of hospitals for the treatment of lunatics, and on the general principles on which the cure of insanity may be most successfully conducted. To which is annexed, an account of the intended establishment of a lunatic asylum at Edinburgh.* Edinburgh, James Ballantyne for Archibald Constable.

Remarks (1734): *Remarks upon the foregoing account* [i.e. *An account of the occasion and manner of erecting an hospital at Lanesborough-House . . .*]. London.

Report (1814): *Report of the General Committee appointed to carry into effect the proposal for a lunatic asylum in Glasgow, with a minute of the first General Meeting of qualified subscribers. . . .* Glasgow, James Hedderwick.

——(1816): *Second Annual Report of the Directors of the Glasgow Asylum for Lunatics.* Glasgow, James Hedderwick.

——(1817): *Third Annual Report of the Directors of the Glasgow Asylum for Lunatics.* Glasgow, W. Lang.

——(1819): *Fifth Annual Report of the Directors of the Glasgow Asylum for Lunatics.* Glasgow, James Hedderwick.

——(1820): *Sixth Annual Report of the Directors of the Glasgow Asylum for Lunatics.* Glasgow, James Hedderwick.

——(1821): *Seventh Annual Report of the Directors of the Glasgow Asylum for Lunatics.* Glasgow, James Hedderwick.

Reuber, Markus (1995): 'Jonathan Swifts Irrenhaus in Dublin: Irlands Einstieg in die Anstaltspsychiatrie vor 250 Jahren'. *Fortschritte der Neurologie Psychiatrie* **63**, 373–79.

——(1996): 'The architecture of psychological management: the Irish asylums (1801–1922)'. *Psychological Medicine* **26**, 1179–89.

——(1996): '"Moral management" und Panoptizismus: öffentliche Irrenanstalten in Irland 1810–1845'. *Würzburger medizinhistorische Mitteilungen* **14**, 511–36.

Revell, A. L. (1978): *Haslar, the Royal Hospital.* Gosport, Hants, Gosport Society.

Richardson, Albert E., ed. (1955): *Robert Mylne, architect and engineer 1733 to 1811.* London, B. T. Batsford.

Richardson, Harriet, ed. (1998): *English hospitals 1660–1948: a survey of their architecture and design* (contributors Ian Goodall, Kathryn Morrison, Ian Pattison, Harriet Richardson, Robert Taylor, and Colin Thom). Swindon, Royal Commission on the Historical Monuments of England.

Richmond, Phyllis Allen (1961): 'The Hôtel-Dieu of Paris on the eve of the Revolution'. *Journal of the History of Medicine* **16**, 335–53.

Riley, James C. (1987): *The eighteenth-century campaign to avoid disease.* London, Macmillan.

Risse, Guenter B. (1985): '"Typhus" fever in eighteenth-century hospitals: new approaches to medical treatment'. *Bulletin of the History of Medicine* **59**, 176–95.

——(1986): *Hospital life in Enlightenment Scotland: care and teaching at the Royal Infirmary of Edinburgh.* Cambridge, Cambridge University Press.

——(1988): 'Hysteria at the Edinburgh Infirmary: the

construction and treatment of a disease'. *Medical History* **32**, 1–22.

—— (1989) [for 1987–88]): 'Clinical instruction in hospitals: the Boerhaavian tradition in Leyden, Edinburgh, Vienna and Pavia'. *Clio Medica* **21**, 1–20.

—— (1999): *Mending bodies, saving souls: a history of hospitals*. New York and Oxford, Oxford University Press.

Robinson, Eric (1953): 'The Derby Philosophical Society'. *Annals of Science* **9**, 359–67.

—— (1962): 'The profession of civil engineer in the eighteenth century: a portrait of Thomas Yeoman, F. R. S., 1704 (?)–1781'. *Annals of Science* **18**, 195–215.

Robinson, John Martin (1979): *The Wyatts: an architectural dynasty*. Oxford, Oxford University Press.

Rochester, John Wilmot Earl of (1980): *Letters*, ed. Jeremy Treglown. Oxford, Basil Blackwell.

Rodger, N. A. M. (1986): *The wooden world: an anatomy of the Georgian Navy*. London, Collins.

Rogers, Pat (1972): *Grub Street: studies in a subculture*. London, Methuen.

Rolls, Roger (1988): *The hospital of the nation: the story of spa medicine and the Mineral Water Hospital at Bath*. Bath, Bird.

Rolt, L. T. C. (1970): *Isambard Kingdom Brunel* (1957). Harmondsworth, Penguin.

Rook, Arthur; Carlton, Margaret; and Cannon, W. Graham (1991): *The history of Addenbrooke's Hospital, Cambridge*. Cambridge, Cambridge University Press.

Rose, Craig Mark (1989): 'Politics, religion and charity in Augustan London *c*.1680–*c*.1720'. Ph.D. Dissertation, University of Cambridge.

Rosen, George (1939): 'Occupational diseases of English seamen during the seventeenth and eighteenth centuries'. *Bulletin of the History of Medicine* **7**, 751–58.

—— (1956): 'Hospitals, medical care and social policy in the French Revolution'. *Bulletin of the History of Medicine* **30**, 124–49.

—— (1968): *Madness in society: chapters in the historical sociology of mental illness*. Chicago, University of Chicago Press.

—— (1974): 'The hospital: historical sociology of a community institution', pp. 274–303 in *From medical police to social medicine: essays in the history of health care*. New York, Science History Publications.

Rosenau, Helen (1970): *Social purpose in architecture: Paris and London compared 1760–1800*. London, Studio Vista.

Rosenberg, Charles E. (1977): 'And Heal the Sick: the hospital and the patient in 19th-century America'. *Journal of Social History* **10**, 428–47.

—— (1979): 'Florence Nightingale on contagion: the hospital as moral universe', pp. 116–36 in *Healing and history: essays for George Rosen*, ed. Charles E. Rosenberg. New York, Science History Publications.

—— (1979): 'Inward vision and outward glance: the shaping of the American hospital, 1880–1914'. *Bulletin of the History of Medicine* **53**, 346–91.

—— (1979): 'The therapeutic revolution: medicine, meaning, and social change in nineteenth-century America', pp. 3–25 in *The therapeutic revolution: essays in the social history of American medicine*, ed. Morris J. Vogel and Charles E. Rosenberg. Philadelphia, University of Pennsylvania Press.

—— (1989): 'Community and communities: the evolution of the American hospital', pp. 3–17 in *The American general hospital: communities and social contexts*, ed. Diana Elizabeth Long and Janet Golden. Ithaca, NY and London, Cornell University Press.

—— (1995): *The care of strangers: the rise of America's hospital system*, paperback edn. Baltimore, Maryland, Johns Hopkins University Press.

Rothman, David J. (1990): *The discovery of the asylum: social order and disorder in the new Republic*, 2nd edn. Boston, Little, Brown.

Rowan, Alistair (1990): 'William Adam's library', pp. 8–33 in *William Adam*, ed. Deborah Howard. Edinburgh, Edinburgh University Press.

Rubin, Miri (1989): 'Development and change in English hospitals', pp. 41–59 in *The hospital in history*, ed. Lindsay Granshaw and Roy Porter. London and New York, Routledge.

Russell, Terence M., ed. (1997): *The builder's dictionary* (1734) (The Encyclopaedic Dictionary in the Eighteenth Century: Architecture, Arts and Crafts 3). Aldershot, Hants, Ashgate.

Rutter, John (1717): *Bethlem Hospital. A poem in blank verse*. London, E. Smith.

Sainte Fare Garnot, Nicolas (1986 [for 1984]): 'Evolution du plan masse de la Salpêtrière: du petit Arsenal à l'Hôpital Général'. *Bulletin de la Société de l'Histoire de Paris et de l'Ile de France* **III**, 57–71.

Saint-Geours, Yvonne; Sainte Fare Garnot, P. Nicolas; and Simon-Dhouailly, Nadine (1987): *Musée de l'Assistance Publique de Paris*. Paris, Musée de l'Assistance Publique.

Saisselin, Rémy G. (1975): 'Architecture and language: the sensationalism of Le Camus de Mézières'. *British Journal of Aesthetics* **15**, 239–53.

—— (1992): *The Enlightenment against the Baroque: economics and aesthetics in the eighteenth century*. Berkeley, University of California Press.

Salter, F. R., ed. (1926): *Some early tracts on poor relief*. London, Methuen.

Saumarez Smith, Charles (1990): *The building of Castle Howard*. London, Faber & Faber.

Saunders, Edward (1993): *Joseph Pickford of Derby: a Georgian architect*. Stroud, Gloucs, Alan Sutton.

Savage, Richard (1737): *Of public spirit in regard to public works. An epistle to . . . Frederick, Prince of Wales*. London, R. Dodsley.

Sawday, Jonathan (1995): *The body emblazoned: dissection and the human body in Renaissance culture*. London and New York, Routledge.

Schinkel, Karl Friedrich (1993): *The 'English' journey: journal of a visit to France and Britain in 1826*, ed. David Bindman and Gottfried Riemann, trans. F. Gayna Wills. New Haven and London, Yale University Press.

Schor, Naomi (1987): *Reading in detail: aesthetics and the feminine.* New York and London, Methuen.

Scull, Andrew (1980): 'A convenient place to get rid of inconvenient people: the Victorian lunatic asylum', pp. 37–60 in *Buildings and society: essays on the social development of the built environment*, ed. Anthony D. King. London, Routledge & Kegan Paul.

——(1983): 'The domestication of madness'. *Medical History* 27, 233–48.

——(1985): 'A Victorian alienist: John Conolly, FRCP, DCL (1794–1866)', pp. 103–50 in *The anatomy of madness: essays in the history of psychiatry*, vol. 1, *People and ideas*, ed. W. F. Bynum, Roy Porter, and Michael Shepherd. London and New York, Tavistock.

——ed. (1991): [W. A. F. Browne, *What asylums were, are, and ought to be*, 1837] *The asylum as utopia: W. A. F. Browne and the mid-nineteenth century consolidation of psychiatry* (Tavistock Classics in the History of Psychiatry). London and New York, Tavistock/Routledge.

——(1993): *The most solitary of afflictions: madness and society in Britain 1700–1900.* New Haven and London, Yale University Press.

Sekora, John (1977): *Luxury: the concept in Western thought, Eden to Smollett.* Baltimore, Maryland and London, Johns Hopkins University Press.

Selwyn, Sydney (1965): 'Sir James Simpson and hospital cross-infection'. *Medical History* 9, 241–48.

Semple, Janet (1993): *Bentham's prison: a study of the panopticon penitentiary.* Oxford, Clarendon Press.

Sevestre, Bernard (1974): 'Un modèle pour l'Europe', pp. 337–50 in *Les Invalides: trois siècles d'histoire*, ed. René Baillargeat. Paris, Musée de l'Armée.

Shapin, Steven and Schaffer, Simon (1985): *Leviathan and the air pump: Hobbes, Boyle, and the experimental life.* Princeton, NJ, Princeton University Press.

Sharpe, James Birch, ed. (1815): *Report, together with the minutes of evidence, and an appendix of papers, from the committee appointed to consider provision made for the better regulation of madhouses in England. Each subject of evidence arranged under its distinct head . . .* London, Baldwin, Craddock, & Joy.

Shaw, J. J. Sutherland (1936): 'The hospital ship, 1608–1740'. *The Mariner's Mirror* 22, 422–26.

Sigsworth, E. M. (1972): 'Gateways to death? Medicine, hospitals and mortality 1700–1850', pp. 97–110 in *Science and society 1600–1800*, ed. Peter Mathias. Cambridge, Cambridge University Press.

Simpson, James (1990): 'The practical architect', pp. 74–83 in *William Adam*, ed. Deborah Howard. Edinburgh, Edinburgh University Press.

Simpson, J. Y. (1868–69): 'Our existing system of hospitalism and its effects'. *Edinburgh Medical Journal* 14, 816–30, 1084–115.

Slack, Paul (1980): 'Books of orders: the making of English social policy 1577–1631'. *Transactions of the Royal Historical Society*, 5th ser. 30, 1–22.

——(1985): *The impact of plague in Tudor and Stuart England.* London, Routledge & Kegan Paul.

Smith, Dale C. (1981): 'Medical science, medical practice, and the emerging concept of typhus in mid-eighteenth-century Britain', pp. 121–34 in *Theories of fever from Antiquity to the Enlightenment*, ed. W. F. Bynum and Vivian Nutton. London, Wellcome Institute for the History of Medicine.

Smith, F. B. (1982): *Florence Nightingale: reputation and power.* London and Canberra, Croom Helm.

Smith, Ginnie (1984): 'The physiology of air: eighteenth-century fever therapy in the advice literature'. *Bulletin of the Society for the Social History of Medicine* 35, 21–23.

Smith, John Thomas (1815): *Ancient topography of London; containing not only views of buildings, which in many cases no longer exist, and for the most part were never before published; but some account of places and customs either unknown, or overlooked by the London historians.* London, John Thomas Smith.

Smith, Leonard D. (1999): *'Cure, comfort, and safe custody': public lunatic asylums in early nineteenth-century England.* Leicester, Leicester University Press.

Smollett, Tobias (1981): *The adventures of Roderick Random* (1748), ed. Paul Gabriel Boucé. Oxford and New York, Oxford University Press.

——(1990): *The adventures of Ferdinand Count Fathom* (1753), ed. Paul-Gabriel Boucé. London, Penguin.

Snedden, Ann (1993): 'Environment and architecture', pp. 25–50 in *'Let there be light again': a history of Gartnavel Royal Hospital from its beginning to the present day*, ed. Jonathan Andrews and Iain Smith. Glasgow, Gartnavel Royal Hospital.

Solkin, David (1992): *Painting for money: the visual arts and the public sphere in eighteenth-century England.* New Haven and London, Yale University Press.

——(1996): 'Samaritan or Scrooge? The contested image of Thomas Guy in eighteenth-century England'. *Art Bulletin* 78, 467–84.

Somerville, Robert (1960): *The Savoy: manor, hospital, chapel.* London, Chancellor and Council of the Duchy of Lancaster.

Soo, Lydia M., ed. (1998): *Wren's 'Tracts' on architecture and other writings.* Cambridge, Cambridge University Press.

Spalding, Phinizy (1977): *Oglethorpe in America.* Chicago and London, University of Chicago Press.

Spencer, John R., ed. (1965): *Filarete's Treatise on architecture. Being the treatise by Antonio di Piero Averlino, known as Filarete*, 2 vols. New Haven and London, Yale University Press.

Spierenburg, Pieter (1990): 'Prisoners and beggars: quantitative data on imprisonment in Holland and Hamburg, 1597–1752'. *Historical Social Research* 15 (4), 33–56.

Spurzheim, J. G. (1817): *Observations on the deranged manifestations of the mind, or insanity*. London, Baldwin, Craddock, & Joy.

Stafford, Barbara Maria (1991): *Body criticism: imaging the unseen in Enlightenment art and medicine*. Cambridge, Mass. and London, MIT Press.

Statutes (1752): *Statutes, rules, and orders for the government of the Infirmary for the Sick and Lame Poor of the Counties of Durham, Newcastle upon Tyne, and Northumberland.... To which is prefixed, an account of the rise, progress, and state of this charity*. Newcastle upon Tyne, I. Thompson.

Stevenson, Christine (1988): 'Madness and the picturesque in the Kingdom of Denmark', pp. 13–47 in *Anatomy of Madness*, vol. 3, *The asylum and its psychiatry*, ed. W. F. Bynum and Roy Porter. London, Routledge.

—— (1993): 'Medicine and architecture', pp. 1495–519 in *Companion encyclopedia of the history of medicine*, ed. W. F. Bynum and Roy Porter. London and New York, Routledge.

—— (1996): '*Aesculapius Scoticus*'. *Georgian Group Journal* 6, 53–62.

—— (1996): 'Robert Hooke's Bethlem'. *Journal of the Society of Architectural Historians* 55, 252–75.

—— (2000): 'Hogarth's mad king and his audiences'. *History Workshop Journal* 49, 24–43.

Stevenson, David (1988): *The first Freemasons: Scotland's early lodges and their members*. Aberdeen, Aberdeen University Press.

—— (1988): *The origins of Freemasonry: Scotland's century, 1590–1710*. Cambridge, Cambridge University Press.

Stewart, Larry (1992): *The rise of public science: rhetoric, technology and natural philosophy in Newtonian Britain*. Cambridge, Cambridge University Press.

Stillman, Damie (1988): *English neo-classical architecture*, 2 vols. London, Zwemmer.

Stow, John (1720): *Survey of London*, ed. John Strype, 2 vols. London, A. Churchill et al.

—— (1912): *The survey of London* (1598, 'increased' 1603), with an introduction by Henry B. Wheatley (Everyman's Library). London and New York, J. M. Dent and E. P. Dutton.

Strachey, Lytton (1918): *Eminent Victorians*. London, Chatto & Windus.

Stroud, Dorothy (1971): *George Dance, architect: 1741–1825*. London, Faber & Faber.

Summerson, John (1947): *The microcosm of London by T. Rowlandson and A. C. Pugin* (1943), revised edn. London and New York, Penguin.

—— (1978): *Georgian London*. Harmondsworth, Penguin.

Sutton, Samuel (1749): *An historical account of a new method for extracting the foul air out of ships . . . second edition. To which are annexed two relations given thereof to the Royal Society, by Dr. Mead and Mr. Watson; and a discourse on the scurvy by Dr. Mead*. London, J. Brindley.

Suzuki, Akihito (1995): 'Anti-Lockean Enlightenment? Mind and body in early eighteenth-century English medicine', pp. 336–59 in *Medicine in the Enlightenment*, ed. Roy Porter. Amsterdam, Rodopi.

Swift, Jonathan (1905): *The prose works of Jonathan Swift, D.D.*, vol. 7, *Historical and political tracts – Irish*, ed. Temple Scott. London, George Bell.

—— (1965): *The correspondence*, ed. Harold Williams, vol. 4, *1732–1736*. Oxford, Clarendon Press.

—— (1983): *The complete poems*, ed. Pat Rogers. Harmondsworth, Penguin.

Sylvester, Charles (1819): *The philosophy of domestic economy, as exemplified in the mode of warming, ventilating, washing . . . adopted in the Derbyshire General Infirmary*. Nottingham, H. Barnett.

Sympson, Thomas (1878): *A short account of the old and of the new Lincoln County Hospitals*. Lincoln, James Williamson.

Tait, William (1905): *A history of Haslar Hospital*. Portsmouth, Griffin.

Taylor, E. G. R. (1937): 'Robert Hooke and the cartographical projects of the late seventeenth century (1666–1696)'. *Geographical Journal* 90, 529–40.

Taylor, James Stephen (1986): 'Jonas Hanway: Christian mercantilist'. *Journal of the Royal Society of Arts* 134, 641–45.

Taylor, Jeremy (1991): *Hospital and asylum architecture in England 1840–1914: building for health care*. London, Mansell.

—— (1997): *The architect and the pavilion hospital: dialogue and design creativity in England 1850–1914*. Leicester, Leicester University Press.

Taylor, René (1961): 'The architecture of port-wine'. *Architectural Review* 129, 388–99.

Temkin, Owsei (1977): 'An historical analysis of the concept of infection' (1953), pp. 456–71 in *The double face of Janus and other essays in the history of medicine*. Baltimore, Maryland, Johns Hopkins University Press.

Tenon, Jacques (1992): *Journal d'observations sur les principaux hôpitaux et sur quelques prisons d'Angleterre*, ed. Jacques Carré (Publications de la Faculté des Lettres et Sciences humaines, new ser. 37). Clermont-Ferrand, Université Blaise-Pascal.

—— (1996): *Memoirs on the Paris hospitals (Mémoires sur les hôpitaux de Paris, 1788)*, trans. anon., ed. Dora B. Weiner (Resources in Medical History). [Canton, MA,] Science History Publications.

Thalamy, Anne (1979): 'La Médicalisation de l'hôpital', pp. 31–38 in *Les Machines à guérir: aux origines de l'hôpital moderne*, by Michel Foucault, Blandine Barret Kriegel, Anne Thalamy, François Béguin, and Bruno Fortier. Brussels, Pierre Mardaga.

Thin, Robert (1927): 'The Old Infirmary and earlier hospitals'. *The Book of the Old Edinburgh Club* 15, 135–63.

Thompson, John D. and Goldin, Grace (1975): *The hospital: a social and architectural history*. New Haven and London, Yale University Press.

Thompson, M. W. (1987): *The decline of the castle*. Cambridge, Cambridge University Press.

—— (1995): *The medieval hall: the basis of secular domestic life, 600–1600 AD*. Aldershot, Hants, Scolar.

Thomson, David (1993): *Renaissance architecture: critics, patrons, luxury*. Manchester, Manchester University Press.

Thomson, Gladys Scott, ed. (1943): *Letters of a grandmother 1732–1735, being the correspondence of Sarah, Duchess of Marlborough with her granddaughter Diana, Duchess of Bedford*. London, Jonathan Cape.

Tillott, P. M., ed. (1961): *A history of Yorkshire: the city of York* (The Victoria History of the Counties of England). London, Oxford University Press for the Institute of Historical Research.

Tilton, James (1813): *Economical observations on military hospitals; and the prevention and cure of diseases incident to an army*. Wilmington, Del., J. Wilson.

Tinniswood, Adrian (1989): *A history of country house visiting: five centuries of tourism and taste*. Oxford, Basil Blackwell and the National Trust.

Tittler, Robert (1991): *Architecture and power: the town hall and the English urban community c.1500–1640*. Oxford, Clarendon Press.

Tomes, Nancy (1994): *The art of asylum-keeping: Thomas Story Kirkbride and the origins of American psychiatry*. Philadelphia, University of Pennsylvania Press.

Tröhler, Ulrich (1989 [for 1987–88]): 'The doctor as naturalist: the idea and practice of clinical teaching and research in British policlinics 1770–1850'. *Clio Medica* **21**, 21–34.

Trusler, John (1768): *The works of Mr. Hogarth moralized*. London, [S. Hopper and Jane Hogarth].

Tryon, Thomas (1973): 'A discourse of the causes, natures and cure of phrensie, madness or distraction', from *A treatise of dreams and visions* [1689], ed. Michael V. DePorte (Augustan Reprint Society 160). Los Angeles, William Andrews Clark Memorial Library.

Turner, Barbara Carpenter (1986): *A history of the Royal Hampshire Hospital*. Chichester, Sussex, Phillimore.

Turner, E. S. (1958): *Call the doctor: a social history of medical men*. London, Michael Joseph.

Vanbrugh, John (1928): *The complete works of Sir John Vanbrugh*, vol. 4, *The letters*, ed. Geoffrey Webb. London, Noncsuch.

Varey, Simon (1990): *Space and the eighteenth-century English novel*. Cambridge, Cambridge University Press.

Versluysen, Margaret Connor (1981): 'Midwives, medical men and "poor women labouring of child": lying-in hospitals in eighteenth-century London', pp. 18–49 in *Women, health and reproduction*, ed. Helen Roberts. London, Routledge & Kegan Paul.

Vicinus, Martha and Nergaard, Bea, eds (1990): *Ever yours, Florence Nightingale: selected letters*. Cambridge, Mass., Harvard University Press.

Vidler, Anthony (1987): *The writing of the walls: architectural theory in the late Enlightenment*. Princeton, NJ, Princeton University Press.

—— (1992): *The architectural uncanny: essays in the modern unhomely*. Cambridge, Mass. and London, MIT Press.

Voldman, Danièle (1981): 'Laboratoires précurseurs: les hôpitaux militaires au siècle des Lumières'. *L'Architecture des hôpitaux: Monuments historiques* **114**, 25–32.

Voltaire, François Marie Arouet, *dit* (1785): 'Charité, maisons de charité, de bienfesance, hôpitaux, hôtels-dieu, &c' (*Dictionnaire philosophique*, 1764), pp. 239–47 in *Oeuvres complètes*, vol. 49. n.p., Societé Littéraire-Typographique.

von Uffenbach, Zacharias Conrad (1934): *London in 1710. From the travels of Zacharias Conrad von Uffenbach*, ed. W. H. Quarrell and Margaret Mare. London, Faber and Faber.

Waddy, F. F. (1974): *A history of Northampton General Hospital 1743 to 1948: two hundred and five years as a voluntary hospital*. Northampton, for the Northampton and District Hospital Management Committee.

Ward, Ned (1993): *The London spy*, 4th edn (1709), ed. Paul Hyland. East Lansing, Mich., Colleagues Press.

Warner, John Harley (1989): 'From specificity to universalism in medical therapeutics: transformation in the nineteenth-century United States', pp. 193–224 in *History of hospitals: the evolution of health care facilities*, ed. Yosio Kawakita, Shizu Sakai, and Yasuo Otsuka. Tokyo, Taniguchi Foundation.

Watkin, David (1993): 'Adam, Dance and the expression of character in architecture', pp. 50–54 in *Adam in context: papers given at the Georgian Group Symposium 1992*, ed. Giles Worsley. London, Georgian Group.

Wear, Andrew (1992): 'Making sense of health and the environment in early modern England', pp. 119–47 in *Medicine in society: historical essays*, ed. Andrew Wear. Cambridge, Cambridge University Press.

—— (1993): 'The history of personal hygiene', pp. 1283–308 in *Companion encyclopedia of the history of medicine*, ed. W. F. Bynum and Roy Porter, vol. 2. London and New York, Routledge.

Webb, Geoffrey (1930–31): 'The letters and drawings of Nicholas Hawksmoor relating to the building of the Mausoleum at Castle Howard, 1726–42'. *Walpole Society* **19**, 111–64.

Webster, Charles (1975): *The Great Instauration: science, medicine and reform 1626–1660*. London, Duckworth.

—— (1978): 'The crisis of the hospitals during the Industrial Revolution', pp. 214–23 in *Human implications of scientific advance*, Proceedings of the XVth International Congress of the History of Science, ed. E. G. Forbes. Edinburgh, Edinburgh University Press.

Welch, Evelyn S. (1995): *Art and authority in Renaissance Milan*. New Haven and London, Yale University Press.

Western, J. R. (1965): *The English militia in the eighteenth century: the story of a political issue, 1660–1802*. London and Toronto, Routledge & Kegan Paul and University of Toronto Press.

Whinney, Margaret (1971): *Wren*. London, Thames & Hudson.

Whinney, Margaret and Millar, Oliver (1957): *English art 1625–1714* (Oxford History of English Art 8). Oxford, Clarendon Press.

Whitcombe, George (1903): *The General Infirmary at Gloucester and the Gloucestershire Eye Institution: its past and present*. Gloucester, John Bellows.

Whitteridge, Gweneth and Stokes, Veronica (1961): *A brief history of the Hospital of Saint Bartholomew*. London, the Governors.

Wigley, Mark (1992): 'Untitled: the housing of gender', pp. 326–89 in *Sexuality and space*, ed. Beatriz Colomina. Princeton, NJ, Princeton Architectural Press.

——(1993): *The architecture of deconstruction: Derrida's haunt*. Cambridge, Mass. and London, MIT Press.

Williams, Raymond (1976): *Keywords: a vocabulary of culture and society*. London, Fontana.

——(1985): *The country and the city*. London, Hogarth Press.

Williams, William H. (1976): *America's first hospital: the Pennsylvania Hospital, 1751–1841*. Wayne, Penn., Haverford House.

Wilson, Adrian (1990): 'The politics of medical improvement in early Hanoverian London', pp. 4–39 in *The medical Enlightenment of the eighteenth century*, ed. Andrew Cunningham and Roger French. Cambridge, Cambridge University Press.

Wilson, Charles (1969): 'The other face of mercantilism' (1959), pp. 118–39 in *Revisions in mercantilism*, ed. D. C. Coleman. London, Methuen.

Wilson, Kathleen (1995): *The sense of the people: politics, culture and imperialism in England 1715–1785*. Cambridge, Cambridge University Press.

Wilson, Leonard G. (1993): 'Fevers', pp. 382–411 in *Companion encyclopedia of the history of medicine*, ed. W. F. Bynum and Roy Porter. London and New York, Routledge.

Wilson, Penelope (1988): 'Feminism and the Augustans: some readings and problems', pp. 80–92 in *Futures for English*, ed. Colin MacCabe. Manchester, Manchester University Press.

Wilson, Thomas (1713): *An account of the foundation of the Royal Hospital of King Charles II. near Dublin, for the relief and maintenance of antient and infirm officers and soldiers serving in the army of Ireland. . . .* Dublin, printed by Edw. Sandys.

Winston, Mark (1994): 'The Bethel at Norwich: an eighteenth-century hospital for lunatics'. *Medical History* **38**, 27–51.

Wittkower, Rudolf (1974): *Palladio and English Palladianism*. London, Thames & Hudson.

Wood, John (1969): *A description of Bath . . .* (2nd edn, 1749), repr. Bath, Kingsmead.

Woodward, Donald (1995): *Men at work: labourers and building craftsmen in the towns of northern England, 1450–1750*. Cambridge, Cambridge University Press.

Woodward, John H. (1974): *To do the sick no harm: a study of the British voluntary hospital system to 1875*. London, Routledge & Kegan Paul.

Worboys, Michael (1992): 'The sanatorium treatment for consumption in Britain, 1890–1914', pp. 47–71, 212–22 in *Medical innovations in historical perspective*, ed. John Pickstone. Basingstoke, Macmillan.

Worsley, Giles (1995): *Classical architecture in Britain: the heroic age*. New Haven and London, Yale University Press for the Paul Mellon Centre for Studies in British Art.

Wragg, R. B. and Wragg, Mary (1959): 'Carr in Portugal'. *Architectural Review* **125**, 127–28.

Wren, Christopher, ed. (1965): *Parentalia; or, Memoirs of the family of the Wrens . . .* (1750), repr. Farnborough, Hants, Gregg.

Wrench, G. T. [1913]: *Lord Lister: his life and work*. London and Leipzig, T. Fisher Unwin.

Wren Society (1928) 5: *The fifth volume of the Wren Society. Designs of Sir Chr. Wren for Oxford, Cambridge, London, Windsor, etc. . . .*, ed. Arthur T. Bolton and H. Duncan Hendry. Oxford, University Press for the Wren Society.

Wren Society (1929) 6: *The sixth volume of the Wren Society . . . The Royal Hospital for Seamen at Greenwich 1694–1728*, ed. Arthur T. Bolton and H. Duncan Hendry. Oxford, University Press for the Wren Society.

Wren Society (1931) 8: *The eighth volume of the Wren Society . . . Being thirty-two large drawings for Whitehall, Windsor and Greenwich 1694–1698. Original Wren drawings, purchased by Dr. Stack, F.R.S., in 1749, being now volume V in the collection at All Souls*, ed. Arthur T. Bolton and H. Duncan Hendry. Oxford, University Press for the Wren Society.

Wren Society (1942) 19: *The nineteenth volume of the Wren Society . . . The Royal Hospital, Chelsea; . . . and the five tracts on architecture by Sir Chr. Wren*, ed. Arthur T. Bolton and H. Duncan Hendry. Oxford, University Press for the Wren Society.

York Georgian Society (1973): *The works in architecture of John Carr*. York, York Georgian Society.

Youngson, A. J. (1966): *The making of classical Edinburgh*. Edinburgh, Edinburgh University Press.

Zevi, Bruno (1974): *Architecture as space: how to look at architecture*, revised edn, trans. Milton Grendel. New York, Horizon.

Zuckerman, Arnold (1976–77): 'Scurvy and the ventilation of ships in the Royal Navy: Samuel Sutton's contribution'. *Eighteenth-century studies* **10**, 222–34.

——(1987): 'Disease and ventilation in the Royal Navy: the woodenship years'. *Eighteenth-century life*, new ser. **11**, 77–89.

Index

Notes are listed where they contain material aside from bibliographic information to which there is no obvious reference in the text.